Collins

Collins

Thesaurus
A–Z

LOVE

TANMAY

Collins

Collins
Thesaurus
A–Z

HarperCollins Publishers
Westerhill Road
Bishopbriggs
Glasgow
G64 2QT
Great Britain

This edition 2008

© HarperCollins Publishers 2008

ISBN 978-0-00-723698-5

Collins® is a registered trademark of
HarperCollins Publishers Limited

www.collinslanguage.com

A catalogue record for this book is
available from the British Library

Typeset by Wordcraft, Glasgow

Printed in Great Britain by
Clays Ltd, St Ives plc

Acknowledgements
We would like to thank those authors
and publishers who kindly gave
permission for copyright material
to be used in the Collins Word Web.
We would also like to thank Times
Newspapers Ltd for providing valuable
data.

HarperCollins do not accept
responsibility for the content or
reliability of the web addresses
featured in this dictionary.

When you buy a Collins dictionary
or thesaurus and register on
www.collinslanguage.com for the free
online and digital services, you will
not be charged by HarperCollins for
access to Collins free Online Dictionary
content or Collins free Online Thesaurus
content on that website. However,
your operator's charges for using the
internet on your computer will apply.
Costs vary from operator to operator.
HarperCollins is not responsible for
any charges levied by online service
providers for accessing Collins free
Online Dictionary or Collins free Online
Thesaurus on www.collinslanguage.com
using these services.

HarperCollins does not warrant
that the functions contained in
www.collinslanguage.com content
will be uninterrupted or error free,
that defects will be corrected, or that
www.collinslanguage.com or the
server that makes it available are free
of viruses or bugs. HarperCollins is not
responsible for any access difficulties
that may be experienced due to
problems with network, web, online
or mobile phone connections.

Contents

EDITORIAL STAFF

EDITORS
Lorna Gilmour

FOR THE PUBLISHERS
Morven Dooner
Elaine Higgleton
Lorna Knight

Preface

The purpose of Collins Dictionaries is simple: to take as sharp and as true a picture of language as possible. In order to stay at the forefront of language developments we have an extensive reading, listening and viewing programme, taking in broadcasts, websites and publications from around the globe – from the British Medical Journal to The Sun, from Channel Africa to CBC News. These are fed into our monitoring system, an unparalleled 2.5-billion-word analytical database: the Collins Word Web.

Every month the Collins Word Web grows by 35 million words, making it the largest resource of its type. When new words and phrases emerge, our active system is able to recognize the moment of their acceptance into the language, the precise context of their usage and even subtle changes in definition – and then alert us to them.

And since English is shaped by the people who use it every day, we've come up with a way for our readers to have more of a say in the content of our dictionaries. The Collins Word Exchange website (www.collins.co.uk/wordexchange or www.harpercollins.com.au/wordexchange) is a revolutionary concept in dictionary publishing. By visiting the site you can submit neologisms you have just heard, dialect words you have always used but never seen in print, or new definitions for existing terms which have taken on novel meanings. You can also stoke the fires of debate with comments on English usage, spelling, grammar – in fact any linguistic convention you care to espouse or explode. Every suggestion will be scrutinized by Collins lexicographers and considered whenever a new edition of one of our dictionaries is compiled. All of which ensures that when you use a Collins dictionary, you are one of the best-informed language users in the world.

USING THIS THESAURUS

Main entry words

Main entry words are
printed in bold type:

altogether

Parts of speech

Parts of speech are
shown (in italics)
when the entry has
more than one partof
speech. Where a word has
several senses for one part
of speech, the senses are
numbered:

abandon *verb* 1

Alternatives

Alternatives are
introduced by an equals
sign: =
The key synonym for
each sense is
underlined, with
other alternatives
given in roman:

altogether 1 =
<u>absolutely</u> quite,
completely, totally,
perfectly, fully,
thoroughly, wholly,
utterly, downright,
one hundred per cent
(*informal*), undisputedly,
lock, stock and barrel
2 = <u>completely</u>, all,
fully, entirely,
comprehensively,
thoroughly, wholly,
utterly, downright, o
ne hundred per
cent (*informal*), in every
respect

Opposites

Opposites are
introduced by an equals
sign with a line through it

= partially

ABBREVIATIONS USED IN THIS THESAURUS

AD	anno Domini
adj	adjective
adv	adverb
anat	anatomy
archit	architecture
astrol	astrology
Aust	Australia(n)
BC	before Christ
biol	biology
Brit	British
chem	chemistry
C of E	Church of England
conj	conjunction
E	East
eg	for example
esp	especially
etc	et cetera
fem	feminine
foll	followed
geom	geometry
hist	history
interj	interjection
lit	literary
masc	masculine
med	medicine

a

abandon VERB 1 = <u>leave</u>, strand, ditch, forsake, run out on, desert, dump 2 = <u>stop</u>, give up, halt, pack in (*Brit. informal*), discontinue, leave off ≠ continue 3 = <u>give up</u>, yield, surrender, relinquish ≠ keep
● NOUN = <u>recklessness</u>, wildness ≠ restraint
abandonment = <u>desertion</u>, leaving, forsaking
abbey = <u>monastery</u>, convent, priory, nunnery, friary
abduct = <u>kidnap</u>, seize, carry off, snatch (*slang*)
abide VERB = <u>tolerate</u>, suffer, accept, bear, endure, put up with, take, stand
● PHRASES **abide by something** = <u>obey</u>, follow, agree to, carry out, observe, fulfil, act on, comply with
abiding = <u>enduring</u>, lasting, continuing, permanent, persistent, everlasting ≠ brief
ability 1 = <u>capability</u>, potential, competence, proficiency ≠ inability 2 = <u>skill</u>, talent, expertise, competence, aptitude, proficiency, cleverness
able = <u>capable</u>, qualified, efficient, accomplished, competent, skilful, proficient ≠ incapable
abnormal = <u>unusual</u>, different, odd, strange, extraordinary, remarkable, exceptional, peculiar ≠ normal
abnormality 1 = <u>strangeness</u>, peculiarity, irregularity, singularity 2 = <u>anomaly</u>, oddity, exception, peculiarity, deformity, irregularity
abolish = <u>do away with</u>, end, destroy, eliminate, cancel, get rid of, ditch (*slang*), throw out ≠ establish
abolition = <u>eradication</u>, ending, end, destruction, wiping out, elimination, cancellation, termination
abort 1 = <u>terminate</u> (*a pregnancy*), miscarry 2 = <u>stop</u>, end, finish, check, arrest, halt, cease, axe (*informal*)
abortion = <u>termination</u>, miscarriage, deliberate miscarriage
abound = <u>be plentiful</u>, thrive, flourish, be numerous, proliferate, be abundant, be thick on the ground
about PREPOSITION 1 = <u>regarding</u>, on, concerning, dealing with, referring to, relating to, as regards 2 = <u>near</u>, around, close to, nearby, beside, adjacent to, in the neighbourhood of
● ADVERB = <u>approximately</u>, around, almost, nearly, approaching, close to, roughly, just about
above 1 = <u>over</u>, upon, beyond, on top of, exceeding, higher than ≠ under 2 = <u>senior to</u>, over, ahead of, in charge of, higher than, superior to, more powerful than
abroad = <u>overseas</u>, out of the country, in foreign lands
abrupt 1 = <u>sudden</u>, unexpected, rapid, surprising, quick, rash, precipitate ≠ slow 2 = <u>curt</u>, brief, short, rude, impatient, terse, gruff, succinct ≠ polite
absence 1 = <u>time off</u>, leave, break, vacation, recess, truancy, absenteeism, nonattendance 2 = <u>lack</u>, deficiency, omission, scarcity, want, need, shortage, dearth
absent ADJECTIVE 1 = <u>away</u>, missing, gone, elsewhere, unavailable, nonexistent ≠ present 2 = <u>absent-minded</u>, blank, vague, distracted, vacant, preoccupied, oblivious, inattentive ≠ alert
● PHRASES **absent yourself** = <u>stay away</u>, withdraw, keep away, play truant
absolute 1 = <u>complete</u>, total, perfect, pure, sheer, utter, outright, thorough 2 = <u>supreme</u>, sovereign, unlimited, ultimate, full, unconditional, unrestricted, pre-eminent 3 = <u>autocratic</u>, supreme, all-powerful, imperious, domineering, tyrannical
absolutely = <u>completely</u>, totally, perfectly, fully, entirely, altogether, wholly, utterly ≠ somewhat
absorb 1 = <u>soak up</u>, suck up, receive, digest, imbibe 2 = <u>engross</u>, involve, engage, fascinate, rivet, captivate
absorbed = <u>engrossed</u>, lost, involved, gripped, fascinated, caught up, wrapped up, preoccupied
absorbing = <u>fascinating</u>, interesting, engaging, gripping, compelling, intriguing, enticing, riveting ≠ boring
absorption 1 = <u>soaking up</u>, consumption, digestion, sucking up 2 = <u>immersion</u>, involvement, concentration, fascination,

preoccupation, intentness

abstract ADJECTIVE = <u>theoretical</u>, general, academic, speculative, indefinite, hypothetical, notional, abstruse ≠ actual
- NOUN = <u>summary</u>, résumé, outline, digest, epitome, rundown, synopsis, précis ≠ expansion
- VERB = <u>extract</u>, draw, pull, remove, separate, withdraw, isolate, pull out ≠ add

absurd = <u>ridiculous</u>, crazy (*informal*), silly, foolish, ludicrous, unreasonable, irrational, senseless ≠ sensible

abundance = <u>plenty</u>, bounty, exuberance, profusion, plethora, affluence, fullness, fruitfulness ≠ shortage

abundant = <u>plentiful</u>, full, rich, liberal, generous, ample, exuberant, teeming ≠ scarce

abuse NOUN 1 = <u>maltreatment</u>, damage, injury, hurt, harm, exploitation, manhandling, ill-treatment 2 = <u>insults</u>, blame, slights, put-downs, censure, reproach, scolding, defamation 3 = <u>misuse</u>, misapplication
- VERB 1 = <u>ill-treat</u>, damage, hurt, injure, harm, molest, maltreat, knock about *or* around ≠ care for 2 = <u>insult</u>, offend, curse, put down, malign, scold, disparage, castigate ≠ praise

abusive 1 = <u>violent</u>, rough, cruel, savage, brutal, vicious, destructive, harmful ≠ kind 2 = <u>insulting</u>, offensive, rude, degrading, scathing, contemptuous, disparaging, scurrilous ≠ complimentary

academic ADJECTIVE 1 = <u>scholastic</u>, educational 2 = <u>scholarly</u>, learned, intellectual, literary, erudite, highbrow, studious 3 = <u>theoretical</u>, abstract, speculative, hypothetical, impractical, notional, conjectural
- NOUN = <u>scholar</u>, intellectual, don, master, professor, fellow, lecturer, tutor, acca (*Austral. slang*)

accelerate 1 = <u>increase</u>, grow, advance, extend, expand, raise, swell, enlarge ≠ fall 2 = <u>expedite</u>, further, speed up, hasten ≠ delay 3 = <u>speed up</u>, advance, quicken, gather momentum ≠ slow down

acceleration = <u>hastening</u>, hurrying, stepping up (*informal*), speeding up, quickening

accent NOUN = <u>pronunciation</u>, tone, articulation, inflection, brogue, intonation, diction, modulation

- VERB = <u>emphasize</u>, stress, highlight, underline, underscore, accentuate

accept 1 = <u>receive</u>, take, gain, pick up, secure, collect, get, obtain 2 = <u>acknowledge</u>, believe, allow, admit, approve, recognize, yield, concede

acceptable = <u>satisfactory</u>, fair, all right, suitable, sufficient, good enough, adequate, tolerable ≠ unsatisfactory

acceptance 1 = <u>accepting</u>, taking, receiving, obtaining, acquiring, reception, receipt 2 = <u>acknowledgement</u>, agreement, approval, recognition, admission, consent, adoption, assent

accepted = <u>agreed</u>, common, established, traditional, approved, acknowledged, recognized, customary ≠ unconventional

access 1 = <u>admission</u>, entry, passage 2 = <u>entrance</u>, road, approach, entry, path, gate, opening, passage

accessible = <u>handy</u>, near, nearby, at hand, within reach, at your fingertips, reachable, achievable ≠ inaccessible

accessory 1 = <u>extra</u>, addition, supplement, attachment, adjunct, appendage 2 = <u>accomplice</u>, partner, ally, associate (*in crime*), assistant, helper, colleague, collaborator

accident 1 = <u>crash</u>, smash, wreck, collision 2 = <u>misfortune</u>, disaster, tragedy, setback, calamity, mishap, misadventure 3 = <u>chance</u>, fortune, luck, fate, hazard, coincidence, fluke, fortuity

accidental 1 = <u>unintentional</u>, unexpected, incidental, unforeseen, unplanned ≠ deliberate 2 = <u>chance</u>, random, casual, unplanned, fortuitous, inadvertent

accidentally = <u>unintentionally</u>, incidentally, by accident, by chance, inadvertently, unwittingly, randomly, haphazardly ≠ deliberately

acclaim VERB = <u>praise</u>, celebrate, honour, cheer, admire, hail, applaud, compliment
- NOUN = <u>praise</u>, honour, celebration, approval, tribute, applause, kudos, commendation ≠ criticism

accommodate 1 = <u>house</u>, put up, take in, lodge, shelter, entertain, cater for 2 = <u>help</u>, support, aid, assist, cooperate with, abet, lend a hand to 3 = <u>adapt</u>, fit, settle, alter, adjust, modify, comply, reconcile

accommodating = <u>obliging</u>, willing,

kind, friendly, helpful, polite, cooperative, agreeable ≠ unhelpful

accommodation = housing, homes, houses, board, quarters, digs (*Brit. informal*), shelter, lodging(s)

accompaniment 1 = backing music, backing, support, obbligato 2 = supplement, extra, addition, companion, accessory, complement, decoration, adjunct

accompany 1 = go with, lead, partner, guide, attend, conduct, escort, shepherd 2 = occur with, belong to, come with, supplement, go together with, follow

accompanying = additional, extra, related, associated, attached, attendant, complementary, supplementary

accomplish = realize, produce, effect, finish, complete, manage, achieve, perform ≠ fail

accomplished = skilled, able, professional, expert, masterly, talented, gifted, polished ≠ unskilled

accomplishment 1 = achievement, feat, act, stroke, triumph, coup, exploit, deed 2 = accomplishing, finishing, carrying out, conclusion, bringing about, execution, completion, fulfilment

accord NOUN 1 = treaty, contract, agreement, arrangement, settlement, pact, deal (*informal*) 2 = sympathy, agreement, harmony, unison, rapport, conformity ≠ conflict

● PHRASES **accord with something** = agree with, match, coincide with, fit with, correspond with, conform with, tally with, harmonize with

accordingly 1 = consequently, so, thus, therefore, hence, subsequently, in consequence, ergo 2 = appropriately, correspondingly, properly, suitably, fitly

account NOUN 1 = description, report, story, statement, version, tale, explanation, narrative 2 = importance, standing, concern, value, note, worth, weight, honour

● PLURAL NOUN (*Commerce*) = ledgers, books, charges, bills, statements, balances, tallies, invoices

● VERB = consider, rate, value, judge, estimate, think, count, reckon

accountability = responsibility, liability, culpability, answerability, chargeability

accountable = answerable, subject, responsible, obliged, liable, amenable, obligated, chargeable

accountant = auditor, book-keeper, bean counter (*informal*)

accumulate = build up, increase, be stored, collect, gather, pile up, amass, hoard ≠ disperse

accumulation 1 = collection, increase, stock, store, mass, build-up, pile, stack 2 = growth, collection, gathering, build-up

accuracy = exactness, precision, fidelity, authenticity, correctness, closeness, veracity, truthfulness ≠ inaccuracy

accurate 1 = precise, close, correct, careful, strict, exact, faithful, explicit ≠ inaccurate 2 = correct, true, exact, spot-on (*Brit. informal*)

accurately 1 = precisely, correctly, closely, truly, strictly, exactly, faithfully, to the letter 2 = exactly, closely, correctly, precisely, strictly, faithfully, explicitly, scrupulously

accusation = charge, complaint, allegation, indictment, recrimination, denunciation, incrimination

accuse 1 = point a *or* the finger at, blame for, denounce, hold responsible for, impute blame to ≠ exonerate 2 = charge with, indict for, impeach for, censure with, incriminate for ≠ absolve

accustom = familiarize, train, discipline, adapt, instruct, school, acquaint, acclimatize

accustomed 1 = used, trained, familiar, given to, adapted, acquainted, in the habit of, familiarized ≠ unaccustomed 2 = usual, established, expected, common, standard, traditional, normal, regular ≠ unusual

ace NOUN 1 (*Cards, dice*) = one, single point 2 (*Informal*) = expert, star, champion, authority, professional, master, specialist, guru

● ADJECTIVE (*Informal*) = great, brilliant, fine, wonderful, excellent, outstanding, superb, fantastic (*informal*), booshit (*Austral. slang*), exo (*Austral. slang*), sik (*Austral. slang*), ka pai (*N.Z.*)

ache VERB = hurt, suffer, burn, pain, smart, sting, pound, throb

● NOUN = pain, discomfort, suffering, hurt, throbbing, irritation, tenderness, pounding

achieve = accomplish, fulfil, complete, gain, perform, do, get, carry out

achievement = accomplishment, effort,

feat, deed, stroke, triumph, coup, exploit

acid 1 = <u>sour</u>, tart, pungent, acerbic, acrid, vinegary ≠ sweet 2 = <u>sharp</u>, cutting, biting, bitter, harsh, barbed, caustic, vitriolic ≠ kindly

acknowledge 1 = <u>admit</u>, own up, allow, accept, reveal, grant, declare, recognize ≠ deny 2 = <u>greet</u>, address, notice, recognize, salute, accost ≠ snub 3 = <u>reply to</u>, answer, notice, recognize, respond to, react to, retort to ≠ ignore

acquaintance 1 = <u>associate</u>, contact, ally, colleague, comrade ≠ intimate 2 = <u>relationship</u>, connection, fellowship, familiarity ≠ unfamiliarity

acquire = <u>get</u>, win, buy, receive, gain, earn, secure, collect ≠ lose

acquisition 1 = <u>acquiring</u>, gaining, procurement, attainment 2 = <u>purchase</u>, buy, investment, property, gain, prize, asset, possession

acquit VERB = <u>clear</u>, free, release, excuse, discharge, liberate, vindicate ≠ find guilty
● PHRASES **acquit yourself** = <u>behave</u>, bear yourself, conduct yourself, comport yourself

act VERB 1 = <u>do something</u>, perform, function 2 = <u>perform</u>, mimic
● NOUN 1 = <u>deed</u>, action, performance, achievement, undertaking, exploit, feat, accomplishment 2 = <u>pretence</u>, show, front, performance, display, attitude, pose, posture 3 = <u>law</u>, bill, measure, resolution, decree, statute, ordinance, enactment 4 = <u>performance</u>, show, turn, production, routine, presentation, gig (*informal*), sketch

acting NOUN = <u>performance</u>, playing, performing, theatre, portrayal, impersonation, characterization, stagecraft
● ADJECTIVE = <u>temporary</u>, substitute, interim, provisional, surrogate, stopgap, pro tem

action 1 = <u>deed</u>, act, performance, achievement, exploit, feat, accomplishment 2 = <u>measure</u>, act, manoeuvre 3 = <u>lawsuit</u>, case, trial, suit, proceeding, dispute, prosecution, litigation 4 = <u>energy</u>, activity, spirit, force, vitality, vigour, liveliness, vim 5 = <u>effect</u>, working, process, operation, activity, movement, functioning, motion 6 = <u>battle</u>, fight, conflict, clash, contest, encounter, combat, engagement

activate = <u>start</u>, move, initiate, rouse, mobilize, set in motion, galvanize ≠ stop

active 1 = <u>busy</u>, involved, occupied, lively, energetic, bustling, on the move, strenuous ≠ sluggish 2 = <u>energetic</u>, quick, alert, dynamic, lively, vigorous, animated, forceful ≠ inactive 3 = <u>in operation</u>, working, acting, at work, in action, operative, in force, effectual

activist = <u>militant</u>, partisan

activity 1 = <u>action</u>, labour, movement, energy, exercise, spirit, motion, bustle ≠ inaction 2 = <u>pursuit</u>, project, scheme, pleasure, interest, hobby, pastime

actor or **actress** = <u>performer</u>, player, Thespian, luvvie (*informal*)

actual = <u>real</u>, substantial, concrete, definite, tangible

actually = <u>really</u>, in fact, indeed, truly, literally, genuinely, in reality, in truth

acute 1 = <u>serious</u>, important, dangerous, critical, crucial, severe, grave, urgent 2 = <u>sharp</u>, shooting, powerful, violent, severe, intense, fierce, piercing 3 = <u>perceptive</u>, sharp, keen, smart, sensitive, clever, astute, insightful ≠ slow

adamant = <u>determined</u>, firm, fixed, stubborn, uncompromising, resolute, unbending, obdurate ≠ flexible

adapt 1 = <u>adjust</u>, change, alter, modify, accommodate, conform, acclimatize 2 = <u>convert</u>, change, transform, alter, modify, tailor, remodel

adaptation 1 = <u>acclimatization</u>, naturalization, familiarization 2 = <u>conversion</u>, change, variation, adjustment, transformation, modification, alteration

add 1 = <u>count up</u>, total, reckon, compute, add up, tot up ≠ take away 2 = <u>include</u>, attach, supplement, adjoin, augment, affix, append

addict 1 = <u>junkie</u> (*informal*), freak (*informal*), fiend (*informal*) 2 = <u>fan</u>, lover, nut (*slang*), follower, enthusiast, admirer, buff (*informal*), junkie (*informal*)

addicted
● PHRASES **addicted to** = <u>hooked on</u>, dependent on, accustomed to (*slang*), habituated to

addiction = <u>dependence</u>, habit, obsession, craving, enslavement *with to* = <u>love of</u>, passion for, attachment to

addition NOUN 1 = <u>extra</u>, supplement, increase, gain, bonus, extension, accessory, additive 2 = <u>inclusion</u>, adding, increasing, extension, attachment, insertion, incorporation, augmentation ≠ removal 3 = <u>counting up</u>, totalling, adding up, computation, totting up ≠ subtraction
● PHRASES **in addition to** = <u>as well as</u>, along with, on top of, besides, to boot, additionally, over and above, to say nothing of

additional = <u>extra</u>, new, other, added, further, fresh, spare, supplementary

address NOUN 1 = <u>location</u>, home, place, house, point, position, situation, site 2 = <u>speech</u>, talk, lecture, discourse, sermon, dissertation, homily, oration
● VERB = <u>speak to</u>, talk to, greet, hail, approach, converse with, korero (*N.Z.*)

adept ADJECTIVE = <u>skilful</u>, able, skilled, expert, practised, accomplished, versed, proficient ≠ unskilled
● NOUN = <u>expert</u>, master, genius, hotshot (*informal*), dab hand (*Brit. informal*)

adequate 1 = <u>passable</u>, acceptable, average, fair, satisfactory, competent, mediocre, so-so (*informal*) ≠ inadequate 2 = <u>sufficient</u>, enough ≠ insufficient

adhere to = <u>stick to</u>, attach to, cling to, glue to, fix to, fasten to, hold fast to, paste to

adjacent ADJECTIVE = <u>adjoining</u>, neighbouring, nearby ≠ far away
● PREPOSITION *with* **to** = <u>next to</u>, touching, close to, neighbouring, beside, near to, adjoining, bordering on

adjoin = <u>connect with</u> *or* to, join, link with, touch on, border on

adjoining = <u>connecting</u>, touching, bordering, neighbouring, next door, adjacent, abutting

adjourn = <u>postpone</u>, delay, suspend, interrupt, put off, defer, discontinue ≠ continue

adjust 1 = <u>adapt</u>, change, alter, accustom, conform 2 = <u>change</u>, reform, alter, adapt, revise, modify, amend, make conform 3 = <u>modify</u>, alter, adapt

adjustable = <u>alterable</u>, flexible, adaptable, malleable, movable, modifiable

adjustment 1 = <u>alteration</u>, change, tuning, repair, conversion, modifying, adaptation, modification 2 = <u>acclimatization</u>, orientation, change,

regulation, amendment, adaptation, revision, modification

administer 1 = <u>manage</u>, run, control, direct, handle, conduct, command, govern 2 = <u>dispense</u>, give, share, provide, apply, assign, allocate, allot 3 = <u>execute</u>, give, provide, apply, perform, carry out, impose, implement

administration 1 = <u>management</u>, government, running, control, handling, direction, conduct, application 2 = <u>directors</u>, board, executive(s), employers 3 = <u>government</u>, leadership, regime

administrative = <u>managerial</u>, executive, directing, regulatory, governmental, organizational, supervisory, directorial

administrator = <u>manager</u>, head, official, director, executive, boss (*informal*), governor, supervisor, baas (*S. African*)

admirable = <u>praiseworthy</u>, good, great, fine, wonderful, excellent, brilliant, outstanding, booshit (*Austral. slang*), exo (*Austral. slang*), sik (*Austral. slang*), ka pai (*N.Z.*) ≠ deplorable

admiration = <u>regard</u>, wonder, respect, praise, approval, recognition, esteem, appreciation

admire 1 = <u>respect</u>, value, prize, honour, praise, appreciate, esteem, approve of ≠ despise 2 = <u>adore</u>, like, love, take to, fancy (*Brit. informal*), treasure, cherish, glorify 3 = <u>marvel at</u>, look at, appreciate, delight in, wonder at, be amazed by, take pleasure in, gape at

admirer 1 = <u>fan</u>, supporter, follower, enthusiast, partisan, disciple, devotee 2 = <u>suitor</u>, lover, boyfriend, sweetheart, beau, wooer

admission 1 = <u>admittance</u>, access, entry, introduction, entrance, acceptance, initiation, entrée 2 = <u>confession</u>, declaration, revelation, allowance, disclosure, acknowledgement, unburdening, divulgence

admit 1 = <u>confess</u>, confide, own up, come clean (*informal*) 2 = <u>allow</u>, agree, accept, reveal, grant, declare, acknowledge, recognize ≠ deny 3 = <u>let in</u>, allow, receive, accept, introduce, take in, initiate, give access to ≠ keep out

adolescence = <u>teens</u>, youth, minority, boyhood, girlhood

adolescent ADJECTIVE 1 = <u>young</u>, junior,

teenage, juvenile, youthful, childish, immature, boyish **2** = <u>teenage</u>, young, teen (*informal*)

● NOUN = <u>teenager</u>, girl, boy, kid (*informal*), youth, lad, minor, young man

adopt 1 = <u>take on</u>, follow, choose, maintain, assume, take up, engage in, become involved in **2** = <u>take in</u>, raise, nurse, mother, rear, foster, bring up, take care of ≠ abandon

adoption 1 = <u>fostering</u>, adopting, taking in **2** = <u>embracing</u>, choice, taking up, selection, assumption, endorsement, appropriation, espousal

adore = <u>love</u>, honour, admire, worship, esteem, cherish, revere, dote on ≠ hate

adoring = <u>admiring</u>, loving, devoted, fond, affectionate, doting ≠ hating

adorn = <u>decorate</u>, array, embellish, festoon

adrift ADJECTIVE **1** = <u>drifting</u>, afloat, unmoored, unanchored **2** = <u>aimless</u>, goalless, directionless, purposeless

● ADVERB = <u>wrong</u>, astray, off course, amiss, off target, wide of the mark

adult NOUN = <u>grown-up</u>, mature person, person of mature age, grown or grown-up person, man or woman

● ADJECTIVE **1** = <u>fully grown</u>, mature, grown-up, of age, ripe, fully fledged, fully developed, full grown **2** = <u>pornographic</u>, blue, dirty, obscene, filthy, indecent, lewd, salacious

advance VERB **1** = <u>progress</u>, proceed, come forward, make inroads, make headway ≠ retreat **2** = <u>accelerate</u>, speed, promote, hasten, bring forward **3** = <u>improve</u>, rise, develop, pick up, progress, upgrade, prosper, make strides **4** = <u>suggest</u>, offer, present, propose, advocate, submit, prescribe, put forward ≠ withhold **5** = <u>lend</u>, loan, supply on credit ≠ withhold payment

● NOUN **1** = <u>down payment</u>, credit, loan, fee, deposit, retainer, prepayment **2** = <u>attack</u>, charge, strike, assault, raid, invasion, offensive, onslaught **3** = <u>improvement</u>, development, gain, growth, breakthrough, step, headway, inroads

● ADJECTIVE = <u>prior</u>, early, beforehand

● PHRASES **in advance** = <u>beforehand</u>, earlier, ahead, previously

advanced = <u>sophisticated</u>, foremost, modern, revolutionary, up-to-date, higher, leading, recent ≠ backward

advancement = <u>promotion</u>, rise, gain, progress, improvement, betterment, preferment

advantage 1 = <u>benefit</u>, help, profit, favour ≠ disadvantage **2** = <u>lead</u>, sway, dominance, precedence **3** = <u>superiority</u>, good

adventure 1 = <u>venture</u>, experience, incident, enterprise, undertaking, exploit, occurrence, caper **2** = <u>excitement</u>, action, passion, thrill, animation, commotion

adventurous = <u>daring</u>, enterprising, bold, reckless, intrepid, daredevil ≠ cautious

adversary = <u>opponent</u>, rival, enemy, competitor, foe, contestant, antagonist ≠ ally

adverse 1 = <u>harmful</u>, damaging, negative, destructive, detrimental, hurtful, injurious, inopportune ≠ beneficial **2** = <u>unfavourable</u>, hostile, unlucky **3** = <u>negative</u>, opposing, hostile, contrary, dissenting, unsympathetic, ill-disposed

advert (*Brit. informal*) = <u>advertisement</u>, notice, commercial, ad (*informal*), announcement, poster, plug (*informal*), blurb

advertise = <u>publicize</u>, promote, plug (*informal*), announce, inform, hype, notify, tout

advertisement = <u>advert</u> (*Brit. informal*), notice, commercial, ad (*informal*), announcement, poster, plug (*informal*), blurb

advice = <u>guidance</u>, help, opinion, direction, suggestion, instruction, counsel, counselling

advise 1 = <u>recommend</u>, suggest, urge, counsel, advocate, caution, prescribe, commend **2** = <u>notify</u>, tell, report, announce, warn, declare, inform, acquaint

adviser = <u>counsellor</u>, guide, consultant, aide, guru, mentor, helper, confidant

advisory = <u>advising</u>, helping, recommending, counselling, consultative

advocate VERB = <u>recommend</u>, support, champion, encourage, propose, promote, advise, endorse ≠ oppose

● NOUN **1** = <u>supporter</u>, spokesman, champion, defender, campaigner, promoter, counsellor, proponent **2** (*Law*) = <u>lawyer</u>, attorney, solicitor, counsel, barrister

affair 1 = <u>matter</u>, business, happening, event, activity, incident, episode, topic

2 = relationship, romance, intrigue, fling, liaison, flirtation, amour, dalliance

affect¹ 1 = influence, concern, alter, change, manipulate, act on, bear upon, impinge upon 2 = emotionally move, touch, upset, overcome, stir, disturb, perturb

affect² = put on, assume, adopt, pretend, imitate, simulate, contrive, aspire to

affected = pretended, artificial, contrived, put-on, mannered, unnatural, feigned, insincere ≠ genuine

affection = fondness, liking, feeling, love, care, warmth, attachment, goodwill, aroha (N.Z.)

affectionate = fond, loving, kind, caring, friendly, attached, devoted, tender ≠ cool

affiliate = associate, unite, join, link, ally, combine, incorporate, amalgamate

affinity 1 = attraction, liking, leaning, sympathy, inclination, rapport, fondness, partiality, aroha (N.Z.) ≠ hostility 2 = similarity, relationship, connection, correspondence, analogy, resemblance, closeness, likeness ≠ difference

affirm 1 = declare, state, maintain, swear, assert, testify, pronounce, certify ≠ deny 2 = confirm, prove, endorse, ratify, verify, validate, bear out, substantiate ≠ refute

affirmative = agreeing, confirming, positive, approving, consenting, favourable, concurring, assenting ≠ negative

afflict = torment, trouble, pain, hurt, distress, plague, grieve, harass

affluent = wealthy, rich, prosperous, loaded (slang), well-off, opulent, well-heeled (informal), well-to-do ≠ poor

afford 1 = have the money for, manage, bear, pay for, spare, stand, stretch to 2 = bear, stand, sustain, allow yourself 3 = give, offer, provide, produce, supply, yield, render

affordable = inexpensive, cheap, reasonable, moderate, modest, low-cost, economical ≠ expensive

afraid 1 = scared, frightened, nervous, terrified, shaken, startled, fearful, cowardly ≠ unafraid 2 = reluctant, frightened, scared, unwilling, hesitant, loath, disinclined, unenthusiastic 3 = sorry, apologetic, regretful, sad, distressed, unhappy ≠ pleased

after PREPOSITION = at the end of,

following, subsequent to ≠ before

● ADVERB = following, later, next, succeeding, afterwards, subsequently, thereafter

■■■ RELATED WORD

prefix: post-

aftermath = effects, results, wake, consequences, outcome, sequel, end result, upshot

again 1 = once more, another time, anew, afresh 2 = also, in addition, moreover, besides, furthermore

against 1 = beside, on, up against, in contact with, abutting 2 = opposed to, anti (informal), hostile to, in opposition to, averse to, opposite to 3 = in opposition to, resisting, versus, counter to, in the opposite direction of 4 = in preparation for, in case of, in anticipation of, in expectation of, in provision for

■■■ RELATED WORDS

prefixes: anti-, counter-

age NOUN 1 = years, days, generation, lifetime, length of existence 2 = old age, experience, maturity, seniority, majority, senility, decline (of life), advancing years ≠ youth 3 = time, day(s), period, generation, era, epoch

● VERB 1 = grow old, decline, weather, fade, deteriorate, wither 2 = mature, season, condition, soften, mellow, ripen

aged = old, getting on, grey, ancient, antique, elderly, antiquated ≠ young

agency 1 = business, company, office, firm, department, organization, enterprise, establishment 2 (Old-fashioned) = medium, means, activity, vehicle, instrument, mechanism

agenda = programme, list, plan, schedule, diary, calendar, timetable

agent 1 = representative, rep (informal), negotiator, envoy, surrogate, go-between 2 = author, worker, vehicle, instrument, operator, performer, catalyst, doer 3 = force, means, power, cause, instrument

aggravate 1 = make worse, exaggerate, intensify, worsen, exacerbate, magnify, inflame, increase ≠ improve 2 (Informal) = annoy, bother, provoke, irritate, nettle, get on your nerves (informal) ≠ please

aggregate NOUN = total, body, whole, amount, collection, mass, sum, combination

● ADJECTIVE = collective, mixed, combined,

collected, accumulated, composite, cumulative

● VERB = combine, mix, collect, assemble, heap, accumulate, pile, amass

aggression 1 = hostility, malice, antagonism, antipathy, ill will, belligerence, destructiveness, pugnacity 2 = attack, campaign, injury, assault, raid, invasion, offensive, onslaught

aggressive 1 = hostile, offensive, destructive, belligerent, unfriendly, contrary, antagonistic, pugnacious, aggers (*Austral. slang*), biffo (*Austral. slang*) ≠ friendly 2 = forceful, powerful, convincing, effective, enterprising, dynamic, bold, militant ≠ submissive

agitate 1 = stir, beat, shake, disturb, toss, rouse 2 = upset, worry, trouble, excite, distract, unnerve, disconcert, fluster ≠ calm

agony = suffering, pain, distress, misery, torture, discomfort, torment, hardship

agree 1 = concur, be as one, sympathize, assent, see eye to eye, be of the same opinion ≠ disagree 2 = correspond, match, coincide, tally, conform 3 = suit, get on, befit

agreement 1 = treaty, contract, arrangement, alliance, deal (*informal*), understanding, settlement, bargain 2 = concurrence, harmony, compliance, union, agreeing, consent, unison, assent ≠ disagreement 3 = correspondence, similarity, consistency, correlation, conformity, compatibility, congruity ≠ difference

agricultural = farming, country, rural, rustic, agrarian

agriculture = farming, culture, cultivation, husbandry, tillage

ahead 1 = in front, in advance, towards the front, frontwards 2 = at an advantage, in advance, in the lead 3 = in the lead, winning, leading, at the head, to the fore, at an advantage 4 = in front, before, in advance, in the lead

aid NOUN = help, backing, support, benefit, favour, relief, promotion, assistance ≠ hindrance

● VERB 1 = help, support, serve, sustain, assist, avail, subsidize, be of service to ≠ hinder 2 = promote, help, further, forward, encourage, favour, facilitate, pave the way for

aide = assistant, supporter, attendant, helper, right-hand man, second

ailing 1 = weak, failing, poor, flawed, unstable, unsatisfactory, deficient 2 = ill, poorly, sick, weak, crook (*Austral. & N.Z. informal*), unwell, infirm, under the weather (*informal*), indisposed

ailment = illness, disease, complaint, disorder, sickness, affliction, malady, infirmity

aim VERB 1 = try for, seek, work for, plan for, strive, set your sights on 2 = point

● NOUN = intention, point, plan, goal, design, target, purpose, desire

air NOUN 1 = wind, breeze, draught, gust, zephyr 2 = atmosphere, sky, heavens, aerosphere 3 = tune, song, theme, melody, strain, lay, aria 4 = manner, appearance, look, aspect, atmosphere, mood, impression, aura

● PLURAL NOUN = affectation, arrogance, pretensions, pomposity, swank (*informal*), hauteur, haughtiness, superciliousness

● VERB 1 = publicize, reveal, exhibit, voice, express, display, circulate, make public 2 = ventilate, expose, freshen, aerate

■ RELATED WORD

adjective: aerial

airborne = flying, floating, in the air, hovering, gliding, in flight, on the wing

airing 1 = ventilation, drying, freshening, aeration 2 = exposure, display, expression, publicity, vent, utterance, dissemination

airplane (*U.S. & Canad.*) = plane, aircraft, jet, aeroplane, airliner

aisle = passageway, path, lane, passage, corridor, alley, gangway

alarm NOUN 1 = fear, panic, anxiety, fright, apprehension, nervousness, consternation, trepidation ≠ calmness 2 = danger signal, warning, bell, alert, siren, alarm bell, hooter, distress signal

● VERB = frighten, scare, panic, distress, startle, dismay, daunt, unnerve ≠ calm

alarming = frightening, shocking, scaring, disturbing, distressing, startling, horrifying, menacing

alcoholic NOUN = drunkard, drinker, drunk, toper, lush (*slang*), tippler, wino (*informal*), inebriate, alko *or* alco (*Austral. slang*)

● ADJECTIVE = intoxicating, hard, strong, stiff, brewed, fermented, distilled

alert ADJECTIVE 1 = attentive, awake,

vigilant, watchful, on the lookout, circumspect, observant, on guard ≠ careless **2** = quick-witted, bright, sharp
● NOUN = warning, signal, alarm, siren ≠ all clear
● VERB = warn, signal, inform, alarm, notify, tip off, forewarn ≠ lull

alien ADJECTIVE **1** = foreign, strange, imported, unknown, exotic, unfamiliar **2** = strange, new, foreign, novel, unknown, exotic, unfamiliar, untried ≠ similar
● NOUN = foreigner, incomer, immigrant, stranger, outsider, newcomer, asylum seeker ≠ citizen

alienate = antagonize, anger, annoy, offend, irritate, hassle (*informal*), estrange

alienation = estrangement, setting against, separation, turning away, disaffection, remoteness

alight¹ 1 = get off, descend, get down, disembark, dismount **2** = land, light, settle, come down, descend, perch, touch down, come to rest ≠ take off

alight² = lit up, bright, brilliant, shining, illuminated, fiery

align 1 = ally, side, join, associate, affiliate, cooperate, sympathize **2** = line up, order, range, regulate, straighten, even up

alike ADJECTIVE = similar, close, the same, parallel, resembling, identical, corresponding, akin ≠ different
● ADVERB = similarly, identically, equally, uniformly, correspondingly, analogously ≠ differently

alive 1 = living, breathing, animate, subsisting, existing, functioning, in the land of the living (*informal*) ≠ dead **2** = in existence, existing, functioning, active, operative, in force, on-going, prevalent ≠ inoperative **3** = lively, active, vital, alert, energetic, animated, agile, perky ≠ dull

all PRONOUN **1** = the whole amount, everything, the total, the aggregate, the totality, the sum total, the entirety, the entire amount **2** = every, each, every single, every one of, each and every
● ADJECTIVE = complete, greatest, full, total, perfect, entire, utter
● ADVERB = completely, totally, fully, entirely, absolutely, altogether, wholly, utterly

allegation = claim, charge, statement, declaration, accusation, assertion, affirmation

allege = claim, charge, challenge, state, maintain, declare, assert, uphold ≠ deny

alleged = claimed, supposed, declared, assumed, so-called, apparent, stated, described

allegiance = loyalty, devotion, fidelity, obedience, constancy, faithfulness ≠ disloyalty

allergic = sensitive, affected by, susceptible, hypersensitive

allergy = sensitivity, reaction, susceptibility, antipathy, hypersensitivity, sensitiveness

alleviate = ease, reduce, relieve, moderate, soothe, lessen, lighten, allay

alley = passage, walk, lane, pathway, alleyway, passageway, backstreet

alliance = union, league, association, agreement, marriage, connection, combination, coalition ≠ division

allied 1 = united, linked, related, combined, integrated, affiliated, cooperating, in league **2** = connected, linked, associated

allocate = assign, grant, distribute, designate, set aside, earmark, give out, consign

allocation 1 = allowance, share, portion, quota, lot, ration **2** = assignment, allowance, allotment

allow VERB **1** = permit, approve, enable, sanction, endure, license, tolerate, authorize ≠ prohibit **2** = let, permit, sanction, authorize, license, tolerate, consent to, assent to ≠ forbid **3** = give, provide, grant, spare, devote, assign, allocate, set aside **4** = acknowledge, accept, admit, grant, recognize, yield, concede, confess
● PHRASES **allow for something** = take something into account, consider, plan for, accommodate, provide for, make provision for, make allowances for, make concessions for

allowance 1 = portion, lot, share, amount, grant, quota, allocation, stint **2** = pocket money, grant, fee, payment, ration, handout, remittance **3** = concession, discount, reduction, repayment, deduction, rebate

all right 1 = satisfactory, O.K. *or* okay (*informal*), average, fair, sufficient, standard, acceptable, good enough ≠ unsatisfactory **2** = well, O.K. *or* okay (*informal*), whole, sound, fit, safe, healthy, unharmed ≠ ill

ally NOUN = partner, friend, colleague, associate, mate, comrade, helper, collaborator, cobber (*Austral. & N.Z. old-fashioned informal*), E hoa (*N.Z.*) ≠ opponent

● PHRASES **ally yourself with something** *or* **someone** = unite with, associate with, unify, collaborate with, join forces with, band together with

almost = nearly, about, close to, virtually, practically, roughly, just about, not quite

alone ADJECTIVE 1 = solitary, isolated, separate, apart, by yourself, unaccompanied, on your tod (*slang*) ≠ accompanied 2 = lonely, abandoned, isolated, solitary, desolate, forsaken, forlorn, destitute

● ADVERB 1 = solely, only, individually, singly, exclusively, uniquely 2 = by yourself, independently, unaccompanied, without help, on your own, without assistance ≠ with help

aloud = out loud, clearly, plainly, distinctly, audibly, intelligibly

already = before now, before, previously, at present, by now, by then, even now, just now

also = and, too, further, in addition, as well, moreover, besides, furthermore

alter 1 = modify, change, reform, vary, transform, adjust, adapt, revise 2 = change, turn, vary, transform, adjust, adapt

alternate VERB 1 = interchange, change, fluctuate, take turns, oscillate, chop and change 2 = intersperse, interchange, exchange, swap, stagger, rotate

● ADJECTIVE = alternating, interchanging, every other, rotating, every second, sequential

alternative NOUN = substitute, choice, other (*of two*), option, preference, recourse

● ADJECTIVE = different, other, substitute, alternate

alternatively = or, instead, otherwise, on the other hand, if not, then again, as an alternative, as another option

although = though, while, even if, even though, whilst, albeit, despite the fact that, notwithstanding

altogether 1 = absolutely, quite, completely, totally, perfectly, fully,

thoroughly, wholly 2 = completely, fully, entirely, thoroughly, wholly, in every respect ≠ partially 3 = on the whole, generally, mostly, in general, collectively, all things considered, on average, for the most part 4 = in total, in all, all told, taken together, in sum, everything included

always 1 = habitually, regularly, every time, consistently, invariably, perpetually, without exception, customarily ≠ seldom 2 = forever, for keeps, eternally, for all time, evermore, till the cows come home (*informal*), till Doomsday 3 = continually, constantly, all the time, forever, repeatedly, persistently, perpetually, incessantly

amass = collect, gather, assemble, compile, accumulate, pile up, hoard

amateur = nonprofessional, outsider, layman, dilettante, layperson, non-specialist, dabbler

amaze = astonish, surprise, shock, stun, alarm, stagger, startle, bewilder

amazement = astonishment, surprise, wonder, shock, confusion, admiration, awe, bewilderment

amazing = astonishing, surprising, brilliant, stunning, overwhelming, staggering, sensational (*informal*), bewildering

ambassador = representative, minister, agent, deputy, diplomat, envoy, consul, attaché

ambiguity = vagueness, doubt, uncertainty, obscurity, equivocation, dubiousness

ambiguous = unclear, obscure, vague, dubious, enigmatic, indefinite, inconclusive, indeterminate ≠ clear

ambition 1 = goal, hope, dream, target, aim, wish, purpose, desire 2 = enterprise, longing, drive, spirit, desire, passion, enthusiasm, striving

ambitious = enterprising, spirited, daring, eager, intent, enthusiastic, hopeful, striving ≠ unambitious

ambush VERB = trap, attack, surprise, deceive, dupe, ensnare, waylay, bushwhack (*U.S.*)

● NOUN = trap, snare, lure, waylaying

amend VERB = change, improve, reform, fix, correct, repair, edit, alter

● PLURAL NOUN (usually in *make amends*) = compensation, redress, reparation, restitution, atonement, recompense

amendment 1 = addition, change, adjustment, attachment, adaptation, revision, modification, alteration 2 = change, improvement, repair, edit, remedy, correction, revision, modification

amenity = facility, service, advantage, comfort, convenience

amid or **amidst** 1 = during, among, at a time of, in an atmosphere of 2 = in the middle of, among, surrounded by, amongst, in the midst of, in the thick of

ammunition = munitions, rounds, shot, shells, powder, explosives, armaments

amnesty = general pardon, mercy, pardoning, immunity, forgiveness, reprieve, remission (of penalty), clemency

among or **amongst** 1 = in the midst of, with, together with, in the middle of, amid, surrounded by, amidst, in the thick of 2 = in the group of, one of, part of, included in, in the company of, in the class of, in the number of 3 = between, to

amount NOUN = quantity, measure, size, supply, mass, volume, capacity, extent
● PHRASES **amount to something** 1 = add up to, mean, total, equal, constitute, comprise, be equivalent to 2 = come to, become, develop into, advance to, progress to, mature into

ample 1 = plenty of, generous, lavish, abundant, plentiful, expansive, copious, profuse ≠ insufficient 2 = large, full, extensive, generous, abundant, bountiful

amply = fully, completely, richly, generously, abundantly, profusely, copiously ≠ insufficiently

amuse 1 = entertain, please, delight, charm, cheer, tickle ≠ bore 2 = occupy, interest, involve, engage, entertain, absorb, engross

amusement 1 = enjoyment, entertainment, cheer, mirth, merriment ≠ boredom 2 = diversion, fun, pleasure, entertainment 3 = pastime, game, sport, joke, entertainment, hobby, recreation, diversion

amusing = funny, humorous, comical, droll, interesting, entertaining, comic, enjoyable ≠ boring

anaesthetic NOUN = painkiller, narcotic, sedative, opiate, anodyne, analgesic, soporific
● ADJECTIVE = pain-killing, dulling, numbing, sedative, deadening, anodyne, analgesic, soporific

analogy = similarity, relation, comparison, parallel, correspondence, resemblance, correlation, likeness

analyse 1 = examine, test, study, research, survey, investigate, evaluate, inspect 2 = break down, separate, divide, resolve, dissect, think through

analysis = examination, test, inquiry, investigation, interpretation, breakdown, scanning, evaluation

analytical or **analytic** = rational, organized, exact, precise, logical, systematic, inquiring, investigative

anarchy = lawlessness, revolution, riot, disorder, confusion, chaos, disorganization ≠ order

anatomy 1 = structure, build, make-up, frame, framework, composition 2 = examination, study, division, inquiry, investigation, analysis, dissection

ancestor = forefather, predecessor, precursor, forerunner, forebear, antecedent, tupuna or tipuna (N.Z.) ≠ descendant

ancient 1 = classical, old, former, past, bygone, primordial, primeval, olden 2 = very old, aged, antique, archaic, timeworn 3 = old-fashioned, dated, outdated, obsolete, out of date, unfashionable, outmoded, passé ≠ up-to-date

and 1 = also, including, along with, together with, in addition to, as well as 2 = moreover, plus, furthermore

anecdote = story, tale, sketch, short story, yarn, reminiscence, urban myth, urban legend

angel 1 = divine messenger, cherub, archangel, seraph 2 (Informal) = dear, beauty, saint, treasure, darling, jewel, gem, paragon

anger NOUN = rage, outrage, temper, fury, resentment, wrath, annoyance, ire ≠ calmness
● VERB = enrage, outrage, annoy, infuriate, incense, gall, madden, exasperate ≠ soothe

angle 1 = gradient, bank, slope, incline, inclination 2 = intersection, point, edge, corner, bend, elbow, crook, nook 3 = point of view, position, approach, direction, aspect, perspective, outlook, viewpoint

angry = furious, cross, mad (informal),

outraged, annoyed, infuriated, incensed, enraged, tooshie (*Austral. slang*), off the air (*Austral. slang*) ≠ calm

angst = anxiety, worry, unease, apprehension ≠ peace of mind

anguish = suffering, pain, distress, grief, misery, agony, torment, sorrow

animal NOUN 1 = creature, beast, brute 2 = brute, devil, monster, savage, beast, bastard (*informal, offensive*), villain, barbarian
● ADJECTIVE = physical, gross, bodily, sensual, carnal, brutish, bestial

animate ADJECTIVE = living, live, moving, alive, breathing, alive and kicking
● VERB = enliven, excite, inspire, move, fire, stimulate, energize, kindle ≠ inhibit

animated = lively, spirited, excited, enthusiastic, passionate, energetic, ebullient, vivacious ≠ listless

animation = liveliness, energy, spirit, passion, enthusiasm, excitement, verve, zest

announce = make known, tell, report, reveal, declare, advertise, broadcast, disclose ≠ keep secret

announcement 1 = statement, communication, broadcast, declaration, advertisement, bulletin, communiqué, proclamation 2 = declaration, report, reporting, revelation, proclamation

annoy = irritate, trouble, anger, bother, disturb, plague, hassle (*informal*), madden ≠ soothe

annoying = irritating, disturbing, troublesome, maddening, exasperating ≠ delightful

annual 1 = once a year, yearly 2 = yearlong, yearly

annually 1 = once a year, yearly, every year, per year, by the year, every twelve months, per annum 2 = per year, yearly, every year, by the year, per annum

anomaly = irregularity, exception, abnormality, inconsistency, eccentricity, oddity, peculiarity, incongruity

anonymous 1 = unnamed, unknown, unidentified, nameless, unacknowledged, incognito ≠ identified 2 = unsigned, uncredited, unattributed ≠ signed

answer VERB = reply, explain, respond, resolve, react, return, retort ≠ ask
● NOUN 1 = reply, response, reaction, explanation, comeback, retort, return,

defence ≠ question 2 = solution, resolution, explanation 3 = remedy, solution

anthem = song of praise, carol, chant, hymn, psalm, paean, chorale, canticle

anthology = collection, selection, treasury, compilation, compendium, miscellany

anticipate 1 = expect, predict, prepare for, hope for, envisage, foresee, bank on, foretell 2 = await, look forward to, count the hours until

anticipation = expectancy, expectation, foresight, premonition, prescience, forethought

antics = clowning, tricks, mischief, pranks, escapades, playfulness, horseplay, tomfoolery

antique NOUN = period piece, relic, bygone, heirloom, collector's item, museum piece
● ADJECTIVE = vintage, classic, antiquarian, olden

anxiety = uneasiness, concern, worry, doubt, tension, angst, apprehension, misgiving ≠ confidence

anxious 1 = eager, keen, intent, yearning, impatient, itching, desirous ≠ reluctant 2 = uneasy, concerned, worried, troubled, nervous, uncomfortable, tense, fearful ≠ confident

apart 1 = to pieces, to bits, asunder 2 = away from each other, distant from each other 3 = aside, away, alone, isolated, to one side, by yourself 4 *with from* = except for, excepting, other than, excluding, besides, not including, aside from, but

apartment 1 (*U.S.*) = flat, room, suite, penthouse, crib 2 = rooms, quarters, accommodation, living quarters

apathy = lack of interest, indifference, inertia, coolness, passivity, nonchalance, torpor, unconcern ≠ interest

apiece = each, individually, separately, for each, to each, respectively, from each ≠ all together

apologize = say sorry, express regret, ask forgiveness, make an apology, beg pardon

apology NOUN = regret, explanation, excuse, confession
● PHRASES **apology for something** *or* **someone** = mockery of, excuse for, imitation of, caricature of, travesty of, poor

substitute for

appal = horrify, shock, alarm, frighten, outrage, disgust, dishearten, revolt

appalling 1 = horrifying, shocking, alarming, awful, terrifying, horrible, dreadful, fearful ≠ reassuring 2 = awful, dreadful, horrendous

apparatus 1 = organization, system, network, structure, bureaucracy, hierarchy, setup (*informal*), chain of command 2 = equipment, tackle, gear, device, tools, mechanism, machinery, appliance

apparent 1 = seeming, outward, superficial, ostensible ≠ actual 2 = obvious, marked, visible, evident, distinct, manifest, noticeable, unmistakable ≠ unclear

apparently = seemingly, outwardly, ostensibly

appeal VERB 1 = plead, ask, request, pray, beg, entreat ≠ refuse
● NOUN 1 = plea, call, application, request, prayer, petition, overture, entreaty ≠ refusal 2 = attraction, charm, fascination, beauty, allure ≠ repulsiveness
● PHRASES **appeal to someone** = attract, interest, draw, please, charm, fascinate, tempt, lure

appealing = attractive, engaging, charming, desirable, alluring, winsome ≠ repellent

appear 1 = look (like *or* as if), seem, occur, look to be, come across as, strike you as 2 = come into view, emerge, occur, surface, come out, turn up, be present, show up (*informal*) ≠ disappear

appearance 1 = look, form, figure, looks, manner, expression, demeanour, mien (*literary*) 2 = arrival, presence, introduction, emergence 3 = impression, air, front, image, illusion, guise, façade, pretence

appease 1 = pacify, satisfy, calm, soothe, quiet, placate, mollify, conciliate ≠ anger 2 = ease, calm, relieve, soothe, alleviate, allay

appendix = supplement, postscript, adjunct, manifest, appendage, addendum, addition

appetite 1 = hunger 2 = desire, liking, longing, demand, taste, passion, stomach, hunger ≠ distaste

applaud 1 = clap, encourage, praise, cheer, acclaim ≠ boo 2 = praise, celebrate, approve, acclaim, compliment, salute,

commend, extol ≠ criticize

applause = ovation, praise, cheers, approval, clapping, accolade, big hand

appliance = device, machine, tool, instrument, implement, mechanism, apparatus, gadget

applicable = appropriate, fitting, useful, suitable, relevant, apt, pertinent ≠ inappropriate

applicant = candidate, claimant, inquirer

application 1 = request, claim, appeal, inquiry, petition, requisition 2 = effort, work, industry, trouble, struggle, pains, commitment, hard work

apply VERB 1 = request, appeal, put in, petition, inquire, claim, requisition 2 = be relevant, relate, refer, be fitting, be appropriate, fit, pertain, be applicable 3 = use, exercise, carry out, employ, implement, practise, exert, enact 4 = put on, work in, cover with, lay on, paint on, spread on, rub in, smear on
● PHRASES **apply yourself to something** = work hard at, concentrate on, try at, commit yourself to, buckle down to (*informal*), devote yourself to, be diligent in, dedicate yourself to

appoint 1 = assign, name, choose, commission, select, elect, delegate, nominate ≠ fire 2 = decide, set, choose, establish, fix, arrange, assign, designate ≠ cancel

appointed 1 = decided, set, chosen, established, fixed, arranged, assigned, designated 2 = assigned, named, chosen, selected, elected, delegated, nominated 3 = equipped, provided, supplied, furnished, fitted out

appointment 1 = selection, naming, election, choice, nomination, assignment 2 = job, office, position, post, situation, place, employment, assignment 3 = meeting, interview, date, arrangement, engagement, fixture, rendezvous, assignation

appraisal = assessment, opinion, estimate, judgment, evaluation, estimation

appreciate 1 = enjoy, like, value, respect, prize, admire, treasure, rate highly ≠ scorn 2 = be aware of, understand, realize, recognize, perceive, take account of, be sensitive to, sympathize with ≠ be unaware of 3 = be grateful, be obliged,

be thankful, give thanks, be indebted, be
in debt, be appreciative ≠ be ungrateful
for **4** = <u>increase</u>, rise, grow, gain, improve,
enhance, soar ≠ fall

appreciation 1 = <u>admiration</u>, enjoyment
2 = <u>gratitude</u>, thanks, recognition,
obligation, acknowledgment,
indebtedness, thankfulness, gratefulness
≠ ingratitude **3** = <u>awareness</u>,
understanding, recognition, perception,
sympathy, consciousness, sensitivity,
realization ≠ ignorance **4** = <u>increase</u>, rise,
gain, growth, improvement, escalation,
enhancement ≠ fall

apprehension 1 = <u>anxiety</u>, concern, fear,
worry, alarm, suspicion, dread, trepidation
≠ confidence **2** = <u>arrest</u>, catching, capture,
taking, seizure ≠ release **3** = <u>awareness</u>,
understanding, perception, grasp,
comprehension ≠ incomprehension

apprentice = <u>trainee</u>, student, pupil,
novice, beginner, learner, probationer
≠ master

approach VERB **1** = <u>move towards</u>, reach,
near, come close, come near, draw near
2 = <u>make a proposal to</u>, speak to, apply to,
appeal to, proposition, solicit, sound out,
make overtures to **3** = <u>set about</u>, tackle,
undertake, embark on, get down to,
launch into, begin work on, commence on
● NOUN **1** = <u>advance</u>, coming, nearing,
appearance, arrival, drawing near
2 = <u>access</u>, way, drive, road, passage,
entrance, avenue, passageway **3** *often
plural* = <u>proposal</u>, offer, appeal, advance,
application, invitation, proposition,
overture **4** = <u>way</u>, means, style, method,
technique, manner

appropriate ADJECTIVE = <u>suitable</u>, fitting,
relevant, to the point, apt, pertinent,
befitting, well-suited ≠ unsuitable
● VERB **1** = <u>seize</u>, claim, acquire, confiscate,
usurp, impound, commandeer, take
possession of ≠ relinquish **2** = <u>allocate</u>,
allow, budget, devote, assign, designate,
set aside, earmark ≠ withhold **3** = <u>steal</u>,
take, nick (*slang, chiefly Brit.*), pocket,
pinch (*informal*), lift (*informal*), embezzle,
pilfer

approval 1 = <u>consent</u>, agreement,
sanction, blessing, permission,
recommendation, endorsement, assent
2 = <u>favour</u>, respect, praise, esteem, acclaim,
appreciation, admiration, applause

≠ disapproval

approve VERB = <u>agree to</u>, allow, pass,
recommend, permit, sanction, endorse,
authorize ≠ veto
● PHRASES **approve of something** *or*
someone = <u>favour</u>, like, respect, praise,
admire, commend, have a good opinion
of, regard highly

apt 1 = <u>appropriate</u>, fitting, suitable,
relevant, to the point, pertinent
≠ inappropriate **2** = <u>inclined</u>, likely, ready,
disposed, prone, liable, given, predisposed
3 = <u>gifted</u>, skilled, quick, talented, sharp,
capable, smart, clever ≠ slow

arbitrary = <u>random</u>, chance, subjective,
inconsistent, erratic, personal, whimsical,
capricious ≠ logical

arbitration = <u>decision</u>, settlement,
judgment, determination, adjudication

arc = <u>curve</u>, bend, bow, arch, crescent,
half-moon

arcade = <u>gallery</u>, cloister, portico,
colonnade

arch¹ NOUN **1** = <u>archway</u>, curve, dome,
span, vault **2** = <u>curve</u>, bend, bow, crook,
arc, hunch, sweep, hump
● VERB = <u>curve</u>, bridge, bend, bow, span,
arc

arch² = <u>playful</u>, sly, mischievous, saucy,
pert, roguish, frolicsome, waggish

archetypal = <u>typical</u>, standard, model,
original, classic, ideal, prototypic *or*
prototypical

architect = <u>designer</u>, planner,
draughtsman, master builder

architecture 1 = <u>design</u>, planning,
building, construction **2** = <u>construction</u>,
design, style **3** = <u>structure</u>, design, shape,
make-up, construction, framework, layout,
anatomy

archive NOUN = <u>record office</u>, museum,
registry, repository
● PLURAL NOUN = <u>records</u>, papers, accounts,
rolls, documents, files, deeds, chronicles

arctic (*Informal*) = <u>freezing</u>, cold, frozen,
icy, chilly, glacial, frigid

Arctic = <u>polar</u>, far-northern, hyperborean

ardent 1 = <u>enthusiastic</u>, keen, eager, avid,
zealous ≠ indifferent **2** = <u>passionate</u>,
intense, impassioned, lusty, amorous, hot-
blooded ≠ cold

area 1 = <u>region</u>, quarter, district, zone,
neighbourhood, locality **2** = <u>part</u>,
section, sector, portion **3** = <u>realm</u>, part,

department, field, province, sphere, domain

arena 1 = ring, ground, field, theatre, bowl, pitch, stadium, enclosure 2 = scene, world, area, stage, field, sector, territory, province

argue 1 = quarrel, fight, row, clash, dispute, disagree, squabble, bicker 2 = discuss, debate, dispute 3 = claim, reason, challenge, insist, maintain, allege, assert, uphold

argument 1 = reason, case, reasoning, ground(s), defence, logic, polemic, dialectic 2 = debate, questioning, claim, discussion, dispute, controversy, plea, assertion 3 = quarrel, fight, row, clash, dispute, controversy, disagreement, feud ≠ agreement

arise 1 = happen, start, begin, follow, result, develop, emerge, occur 2 (Old-fashioned) = get to your feet, get up, rise, stand up, spring up, leap up 3 = get up, wake up, awaken, get out of bed

aristocrat = noble, lord, lady, peer, patrician, grandee, aristo (informal), peeress

aristocratic = upper-class, lordly, titled, elite, gentlemanly, noble, patrician, blue-blooded ≠ common

arm[1] = upper limb, limb, appendage

arm[2] VERB = equip, provide, supply, array, furnish, issue with, deck out, accoutre
● PLURAL NOUN = weapons, guns, firearms, weaponry, armaments, ordnance, munitions, instruments of war

armed = carrying weapons, protected, equipped, primed, fitted out

armour = protection, covering, shield, sheathing, armour plate, chain mail, protective covering

armoured = protected, mailed, reinforced, toughened, bulletproof, armour-plated, steel-plated, ironclad

army 1 = soldiers, military, troops, armed force, legions, infantry, military force, land force 2 = vast number, host, gang, mob, flock, array, legion, swarm

aroma = scent, smell, perfume, fragrance, bouquet, savour, odour, redolence

around PREPOSITION 1 = surrounding, about, enclosing, encompassing, framing, encircling, on all sides of, on every side of 2 = approximately, about, in, nearly, close to, roughly, just about, in the region of, circa (used with dates)

● ADVERB 1 = everywhere, about, throughout, all over, here and there, on all sides, in all directions, to and fro 2 = near, close, nearby, at hand, close at hand

arouse 1 = stimulate, encourage, inspire, prompt, spur, provoke, rouse, stir up ≠ quell 2 = inflame, move, excite, spur, provoke, stir up, agitate 3 = awaken, wake up, rouse, waken

arrange 1 = plan, agree, prepare, determine, organize, construct, devise, contrive, jack up (N.Z. informal) 2 = put in order, group, order, sort, position, line up, organize, classify, jack up (N.Z. informal) ≠ disorganize 3 = adapt, score, orchestrate, harmonize, instrument

arrangement 1 often plural = plan, planning, provision, preparation 2 = agreement, contract, settlement, appointment, compromise, deal (informal), pact, compact 3 = display, system, structure, organization, exhibition, presentation, classification, alignment 4 = adaptation, score, version, interpretation, instrumentation, orchestration, harmonization

array NOUN 1 = arrangement, show, supply, display, collection, exhibition, line up, mixture 2 (Poetic) = clothing, dress, clothes, garments, apparel, attire, finery, regalia
● VERB 1 = arrange, show, group, present, range, display, parade, exhibit 2 = dress, clothe, deck, decorate, adorn, festoon, attire

arrest VERB 1 = capture, catch, nick (slang, chiefly Brit.), seize, detain, apprehend, take prisoner ≠ release 2 = stop, end, limit, block, slow, delay, interrupt, suppress ≠ speed up 3 = fascinate, hold, occupy, engage, grip, absorb, entrance, intrigue
● NOUN 1 = capture, bust (informal), detention, seizure ≠ release 2 = stoppage, suppression, obstruction, blockage, hindrance ≠ acceleration

arresting = striking, surprising, engaging, stunning, impressive, outstanding, remarkable, noticeable ≠ unremarkable

arrival 1 = appearance, coming, arriving, entrance, advent, materialization 2 = coming, happening, taking place, emergence, occurrence, materialization 3 = newcomer, incomer, visitor, caller, entrant

arrive 1 = come, appear, turn up, show up (*informal*), draw near ≠ depart 2 = occur, happen, take place 3 (*Informal*) = succeed, make it (*informal*), triumph, do well, thrive, flourish, be successful, make good

arrogance = conceit, pride, swagger, insolence, high-handedness, haughtiness, superciliousness, disdainfulness ≠ modesty

arrogant = conceited, proud, cocky, overbearing, haughty, scornful, egotistical, disdainful ≠ modest

arrow 1 = dart, flight, bolt, shaft (*archaic*), quarrel 2 = pointer, indicator, marker

arsenal = armoury, supply, store, stockpile, storehouse, ammunition dump, arms depot, ordnance depot

art 1 = artwork, style of art, fine art, creativity 2 = skill, craft, expertise, competence, mastery, ingenuity, virtuosity, cleverness

article 1 = feature, story, paper, piece, item, creation, essay, composition 2 = thing, piece, unit, item, object, device, tool, implement 3 = clause, point, part, section, item, passage, portion, paragraph

articulate ADJECTIVE = expressive, clear, coherent, fluent, eloquent, lucid ≠ incoherent
● VERB 1 = express, say, state, word, declare, phrase, communicate, utter 2 = pronounce, say, talk, speak, voice, utter, enunciate

artificial 1 = synthetic, manufactured, plastic, man-made, non-natural 2 = insincere, forced, affected, phoney or phony (*informal*), false, contrived, unnatural, feigned ≠ genuine 3 = fake, mock, imitation, bogus, simulated, sham, counterfeit ≠ authentic

artillery = big guns, battery, cannon, ordnance, gunnery

artistic 1 = creative, cultured, original, sophisticated, refined, aesthetic, discerning, eloquent ≠ untalented 2 = beautiful, creative, elegant, stylish, aesthetic, tasteful ≠ unattractive

as CONJUNCTION = when, while, just as, at the time that
● PREPOSITION 1 = in the role of, being, under the name of, in the character of 2 = in the way that, like, in the manner that 3 = since, because, seeing that, considering that, on account of the fact that

ashamed 1 = embarrassed, sorry, guilty, distressed, humiliated, self-conscious, red-faced, mortified ≠ proud 2 = reluctant, embarrassed

ashore = on land, on the beach, on the shore, aground, to the shore, on dry land, shorewards, landwards

aside ADVERB = to one side, separately, apart, beside, out of the way, on one side, to the side
● NOUN = interpolation, parenthesis

ask 1 = inquire, question, quiz, query, interrogate ≠ answer 2 = request, appeal to, plead with, demand, beg 3 = invite, bid, summon

asleep = sleeping, napping, dormant, dozing, slumbering, snoozing (*informal*), fast asleep, sound asleep

aspect 1 = feature, side, factor, angle, characteristic, facet 2 = position, view, situation, scene, prospect, point of view, outlook 3 = appearance, look, air, condition, quality, bearing, attitude, cast

aspiration = aim, plan, hope, goal, dream, wish, desire, objective

aspire to = aim for, desire, hope for, long for, seek out, wish for, dream about, set your heart on

ass 1 = donkey, moke (*slang*) 2 = fool, idiot, twit (*informal*, *chiefly Brit.*), oaf, jackass, blockhead, halfwit, numbskull or numskull, dorba or dorb (*Austral. slang*), bogan (*Austral. slang*)

assassin = murderer, killer, slayer, liquidator, executioner, hit man (*slang*), hatchet man (*slang*)

assassinate = murder, kill, eliminate (*slang*), take out (*slang*), terminate, hit (*slang*), slay, liquidate

assault NOUN = attack, raid, invasion, charge, offensive, onslaught, foray ≠ defence
● VERB = strike, attack, beat, knock, bang, slap, smack, thump

assemble 1 = gather, meet, collect, rally, come together, muster, congregate ≠ scatter 2 = bring together, collect, gather, rally, come together, muster, amass, congregate 3 = put together, join, set up, build up, connect, construct, piece together, fabricate ≠ take apart

assembly 1 = gathering, group, meeting, council, conference, crowd, congress, collection, hui (*N.Z.*), runanga (*N.Z.*) 2 = putting together, setting up, construction, building up, connecting, piecing together

assert VERB 1 = state, argue, maintain, declare, swear, pronounce, affirm, profess ≠ deny 2 = insist upon, stress, defend, uphold, put forward, press, stand up for ≠ retract
● PHRASES **assert yourself** = be forceful, put your foot down (*informal*), put yourself forward, make your presence felt, exert your influence

assertion 1 = statement, claim, declaration, pronouncement 2 = insistence, stressing, maintenance

assertive = confident, positive, aggressive, forceful, emphatic, insistent, feisty (*informal, chiefly U.S. & Canad.*), pushy (*informal*) ≠ meek

assess 1 = judge, estimate, analyse, evaluate, rate, value, check out, weigh up 2 = evaluate, rate, tax, value, estimate, fix, impose, levy

assessment 1 = judgment, analysis, evaluation, valuation, appraisal, rating, opinion, estimate 2 = evaluation, rating, charge, fee, toll, levy, valuation

asset NOUN = benefit, help, service, aid, advantage, strength, resource, attraction ≠ disadvantage
● PLURAL NOUN = property, goods, money, funds, effects, capital, riches, finance

assign 1 = give, set, grant, allocate, give out, consign, allot, apportion 2 = select for, post, commission, elect, appoint, delegate, nominate, name 3 = attribute, credit, put down, set down, ascribe, accredit

assignment = task, job, position, post, commission, exercise, responsibility, duty

assist 1 = help, support, aid, cooperate with, abet, lend a helping hand to 2 = facilitate, help, further, serve, aid, forward, promote, speed up ≠ hinder

assistance = help, backing, support, aid, cooperation, helping hand ≠ hindrance

assistant = helper, ally, colleague, supporter, aide, second, attendant, accomplice

associate VERB 1 = connect, link, ally, identify, join, combine, attach, fasten ≠ separate 2 = socialize, mix, accompany, mingle, consort, hobnob ≠ avoid
● NOUN = partner, friend, ally, colleague,

mate (*informal*), companion, comrade, affiliate, cobber (*Austral. & N.Z. old-fashioned informal*), E hoa (*N.Z.*)

association 1 = group, club, society, league, band, set, pack, collection 2 = connection, union, joining, pairing, combination, mixture, blend, juxtaposition

assorted = various, different, mixed, varied, diverse, miscellaneous, sundry, motley ≠ similar

assume 1 = presume, think, believe, expect, suppose, imagine, fancy, take for granted ≠ know 2 = take on, accept, shoulder, take over, put on, enter upon 3 = simulate, affect, adopt, put on, imitate, mimic, feign, impersonate 4 = take over, take, appropriate, seize, commandeer ≠ give up

assumed = false, made-up, fake, bogus, counterfeit, fictitious, make-believe ≠ real

assumption 1 = presumption, belief, guess, hypothesis, inference, conjecture, surmise, supposition 2 = taking on, managing, handling, shouldering, putting on, taking up, takeover, acquisition 3 = seizure, taking, takeover, acquisition, appropriation, wresting, confiscation, commandeering

assurance 1 = promise, statement, guarantee, commitment, pledge, vow, declaration, assertion ≠ lie 2 = confidence, conviction, certainty, self-confidence, poise, faith, nerve, aplomb ≠ self-doubt

assure 1 = convince, encourage, persuade, satisfy, comfort, reassure, hearten, embolden 2 = make certain, ensure, confirm, guarantee, secure, make sure, complete, seal 3 = promise to, pledge to, vow to, guarantee to, swear to, confirm to, certify to, give your word to

assured 1 = confident, certain, positive, poised, fearless, self-confident, self-assured, dauntless ≠ self-conscious 2 = certain, sure, ensured, confirmed, settled, guaranteed, fixed, secure ≠ doubtful

astonish = amaze, surprise, stun, stagger, bewilder, astound, daze, confound

astounding = amazing, surprising, brilliant, impressive, astonishing, staggering, sensational (*informal*), bewildering

astute = intelligent, sharp, clever, subtle, shrewd, cunning, canny, perceptive

≠ stupid

asylum 1 (*Old-fashioned*) = mental hospital, hospital, institution, psychiatric hospital, madhouse (*informal*) 2 = refuge, haven, safety, protection, preserve, shelter, retreat, harbour

athlete = sportsperson, player, runner, competitor, sportsman, contestant, gymnast, sportswoman

athletic ADJECTIVE = fit, strong, powerful, healthy, active, trim, strapping, energetic ≠ feeble
● PLURAL NOUN = sports, games, races, exercises, contests, sporting events, gymnastics, track and field events

atmosphere 1 = air, sky, heavens, aerosphere 2 = feeling, character, environment, spirit, surroundings, tone, mood, climate

atom = particle, bit, spot, trace, molecule, dot, speck

atrocity 1 = act of cruelty, crime, horror, evil, outrage, abomination 2 = cruelty, horror, brutality, savagery, wickedness, barbarity, viciousness, fiendishness

attach 1 = affix, stick, secure, add, join, couple, link, tie ≠ detach 2 = ascribe, connect, attribute, assign, associate

attached ADJECTIVE = spoken for, married, partnered, engaged, accompanied
● PHRASES **attached to** = fond of, devoted to, affectionate towards, full of regard for

attachment 1 = fondness, liking, feeling, relationship, regard, attraction, affection, affinity, aroha (*N.Z.*) ≠ aversion 2 = accessory, fitting, extra, component, extension, supplement, fixture, accoutrement

attack VERB 1 = assault, strike (at), mug, ambush, tear into, set upon, lay into (*informal*) ≠ defend 2 = invade, occupy, raid, infringe, storm, encroach 3 = criticize, blame, abuse, condemn, knock (*informal*), put down, slate (*informal*), have a go (at) (*informal*)
● NOUN 1 = assault, charge, campaign, strike, raid, invasion, offensive, blitz ≠ defence 2 = criticism, censure, disapproval, abuse, bad press, vilification, denigration, disparagement 3 = bout, fit, stroke, seizure, spasm, convulsion, paroxysm

attacker = assailant, assaulter, raider, intruder, invader, aggressor, mugger

attain 1 = obtain, get, reach, complete, gain, achieve, acquire, fulfil 2 = reach, achieve, acquire, accomplish

attempt VERB = try, seek, aim, struggle, venture, undertake, strive, endeavour
● NOUN 1 = try, go (*informal*), shot (*informal*), effort, trial, bid, crack (*informal*), stab (*informal*) 2 = attack

attend VERB 1 = be present, go to, visit, frequent, haunt, appear at, turn up at, patronize ≠ be absent 2 = pay attention, listen, hear, mark, note, observe, heed, pay heed ≠ ignore
● PHRASES **attend to something** = apply yourself to, concentrate on, look after, take care of, see to, get to work on, devote yourself to, occupy yourself with

attendance 1 = presence, being there, attending, appearance 2 = turnout, audience, gate, congregation, house, crowd, throng, number present

attendant NOUN = assistant, guard, servant, companion, aide, escort, follower, helper
● ADJECTIVE = accompanying, related, associated, accessory, consequent, resultant, concomitant

attention 1 = thinking, thought, mind, consideration, scrutiny, heed, deliberation, intentness 2 = care, support, concern, treatment, looking after, succour, ministration 3 = awareness, regard, notice, recognition, consideration, observation, consciousness ≠ inattention

attic = loft, garret, roof space

attitude 1 = opinion, view, position, approach, mood, perspective, point of view, stance 2 = position, bearing, pose, stance, carriage, posture

attract 1 = allure, draw, persuade, charm, appeal to, win over, tempt, lure (*informal*) ≠ repel 2 = pull, draw, magnetize

attraction 1 = appeal, pull (*informal*), charm, lure, temptation, fascination, allure, magnetism 2 = pull, magnetism

attractive 1 = seductive, charming, tempting, pretty, fair, inviting, lovely, pleasant ≠ unattractive 2 = appealing, pleasing, inviting, tempting, irresistable ≠ unappealing

attribute VERB = ascribe, credit, refer, trace, assign, charge, allocate, put down
● NOUN = quality, feature, property,

character, element, aspect, characteristic, distinction

audience 1 = <u>spectators</u>, company, crowd, gathering, gallery, assembly, viewers, listeners 2 = <u>interview</u>, meeting, hearing, exchange, reception, consultation

aura = <u>air</u>, feeling, quality, atmosphere, tone, mood, ambience

austerity 1 = <u>plainness</u>, simplicity, starkness 2 = <u>asceticism</u>, self-discipline, sobriety, puritanism, self-denial

authentic 1 = <u>real</u>, pure, genuine, valid, undisputed, lawful, bona fide, dinkum (*Austral. & N.Z. informal*), true-to-life ≠ fake 2 = <u>accurate</u>, legitimate, authoritative

authenticity 1 = <u>genuineness</u>, purity 2 = <u>accuracy</u>, certainty, validity, legitimacy, faithfulness, truthfulness

author 1 = <u>writer</u>, composer, novelist, hack, creator, scribbler, scribe, wordsmith 2 = <u>creator</u>, father, producer, designer, founder, architect, inventor, originator

authoritarian ADJECTIVE = <u>strict</u>, severe, autocratic, dictatorial, dogmatic, tyrannical, doctrinaire ≠ lenient
● NOUN = <u>disciplinarian</u>, dictator, tyrant, despot, autocrat, absolutist

authoritative 1 = <u>commanding</u>, masterly, imposing, assertive, imperious, self-assured ≠ timid 2 = <u>reliable</u>, accurate, valid, authentic, definitive, dependable, trustworthy ≠ unreliable

authority 1 *usually plural* = <u>powers that be</u>, government, police, officials, the state, management, administration, the system 2 = <u>prerogative</u>, influence, power, control, weight, direction, command, licence, mana (*N.Z.*) 3 = <u>expert</u>, specialist, professional, master, guru, virtuoso, connoisseur, fundi (*S. African*) 4 = <u>command</u>, power, control, rule, management, direction, mastery

authorize 1 = <u>empower</u>, commission, enable, entitle, mandate, accredit, give authority to 2 = <u>permit</u>, allow, grant, approve, sanction, license, warrant, consent to ≠ forbid

automatic 1 = <u>mechanical</u>, automated, mechanized, push-button, self-propelling ≠ done by hand 2 = <u>involuntary</u>, natural, unconscious, mechanical, spontaneous, reflex, instinctive, unwilled ≠ conscious

autonomous = <u>self-ruling</u>, free, independent, sovereign, self-sufficient, self-governing, self-determining

autonomy = <u>independence</u>, freedom, sovereignty, self-determination, self-government, self-rule, self-sufficiency, home rule, rangatiratanga (*N.Z.*) ≠ dependency

availability = <u>accessibility</u>, readiness, handiness, attainability

available = <u>accessible</u>, ready, to hand, handy, at hand, free, to be had, achievable ≠ in use

avalanche 1 = <u>snow-slide</u>, landslide, landslip 2 = <u>large amount</u>, barrage, torrent, deluge, inundation

avant-garde = <u>progressive</u>, pioneering, experimental, innovative, unconventional, ground-breaking ≠ conservative

avenue = <u>street</u>, way, course, drive, road, approach, route, path

average NOUN = <u>standard</u>, normal, usual, par, mode, mean, medium, norm
● ADJECTIVE 1 = <u>usual</u>, standard, general, normal, regular, ordinary, typical, commonplace ≠ unusual 2 = <u>mean</u>, middle, medium, intermediate, median ≠ minimum
● VERB = <u>make on average</u>, be on average, even out to, do on average, balance out to
● PHRASES **on average** = usually, generally, normally, typically, for the most part, as a rule

avert 1 = <u>ward off</u>, avoid, prevent, frustrate, fend off, preclude, stave off, forestall 2 = <u>turn away</u>, turn aside

avoid 1 = <u>prevent</u>, stop, frustrate, hamper, foil, inhibit, avert, thwart 2 = <u>refrain from</u>, bypass, dodge, eschew, escape, duck (out of) (*informal*), fight shy of, shirk from 3 = <u>keep away from</u>, dodge, shun, evade, steer clear of, bypass

await 1 = <u>wait for</u>, expect, look for, look forward to, anticipate, stay for 2 = <u>be in store for</u>, wait for, be ready for, lie in wait for, be in readiness for

awake ADJECTIVE = <u>not sleeping</u>, sleepless, wide-awake, aware, conscious, aroused, awakened, restless ≠ asleep
● VERB 1 = <u>wake up</u>, come to, wake, stir, awaken, rouse 2 = <u>alert</u>, stimulate, provoke, revive, arouse, stir up, kindle

awaken 1 = <u>stimulate</u>, provoke, alert, stir up, kindle 2 = <u>awake</u>, wake, revive, arouse, rouse

award NOUN = <u>prize</u>, gift, trophy, decoration, grant, bonsela (*S. African*), koha (*N.Z.*)
● VERB 1 = <u>present with</u>, give, grant, hand out, confer, endow, bestow 2 = <u>grant</u>, give, confer

aware = <u>informed</u>, enlightened, knowledgeable, learned, expert, versed, up to date, in the picture ≠ ignorant

awareness
● PHRASES **awareness of** = <u>knowledge of</u>, understanding of, recognition of, perception of, consciousness of, realization of, familiarity with

away ADJECTIVE = <u>absent</u>, out, gone, elsewhere, abroad, not here, not present, on vacation
● ADVERB 1 = <u>off</u>, elsewhere, abroad, hence, from here 2 = <u>aside</u>, out of the way, to one side 3 = <u>at a distance</u>, far, apart, remote, isolated 4 = <u>continuously</u>, repeatedly, relentlessly, incessantly, interminably, unremittingly, uninterruptedly

awe NOUN = <u>wonder</u>, fear, respect, reverence, horror, terror, dread, admiration ≠ contempt
● VERB = <u>impress</u>, amaze, stun, frighten, terrify, astonish, horrify, intimidate

awesome = <u>awe-inspiring</u>, amazing, stunning, impressive, astonishing, formidable, intimidating, breathtaking

awful 1 = <u>disgusting</u>, offensive, gross, foul, dreadful, revolting, sickening, frightful, festy (*Austral. slang*), yucko (*Austral. slang*) 2 = <u>bad</u>, poor, terrible, appalling, foul, rubbish (*slang*), dreadful, horrendous ≠ wonderful, ka pai (*N.Z.*) 3 = <u>shocking</u>, dreadful 4 = <u>unwell</u>, poorly (*informal*), ill, terrible, sick, crook (*Austral. & N.Z. informal*), unhealthy, off-colour, under the weather (*informal*)

awfully 1 (*Informal*) = <u>very</u>, extremely, terribly, exceptionally, greatly, immensely, exceedingly, dreadfully 2 = <u>badly</u>, woefully, dreadfully, disgracefully, wretchedly, unforgivably, reprehensibly

awkward 1 = <u>embarrassing</u>, difficult, sensitive, delicate, uncomfortable, humiliating, disconcerting, inconvenient, barro (*Austral. slang*) ≠ comfortable 2 = <u>inconvenient</u>, difficult, troublesome, cumbersome, unwieldy, unmanageable, clunky (*informal*) ≠ convenient 3 = <u>clumsy</u>, lumbering, bumbling, unwieldy,

ponderous, ungainly, gauche, gawky, unco (*Austral. slang*) ≠ graceful

axe NOUN = <u>hatchet</u>, chopper, tomahawk, cleaver, adze
● VERB 1 (*Informal*) = <u>abandon</u>, end, eliminate, cancel, scrap, cut back, terminate, dispense with 2 (*Informal*) = <u>dismiss</u>, fire (*informal*), sack (*informal*), remove, get rid of
● PHRASES **the axe** (*Informal*) = <u>the sack</u> (*informal*), dismissal, the boot (*slang*), termination, the chop (*slang*)

axis = <u>pivot</u>, shaft, axle, spindle, centre line

b

baas (*S. African*) = <u>master</u>, bo (*informal*), chief, ruler, commander, head, overlord, overseer

baby NOUN = <u>child</u>, infant, babe, bairn (*Scot.*), newborn child, babe in arms, ankle-biter (*Austral. slang*), tacker (*Austral. slang*)
● ADJECTIVE = <u>small</u>, little, minute, tiny, mini, wee, miniature, petite

back NOUN 1 = <u>spine</u>, backbone, vertebrae, spinal column, vertebral column 2 = <u>rear</u> ≠ front 3 = <u>reverse</u>, rear, other side, wrong side, underside, flip side
● ADJECTIVE 1 = <u>rear</u> ≠ front 2 = <u>rearmost</u>, hind, hindmost 3 = <u>previous</u>, earlier, former, past, elapsed ≠ future 4 = <u>tail</u>, end, rear, posterior
● VERB 1 = <u>support</u>, help, aid, champion, defend, promote, assist, advocate ≠ oppose 2 = <u>subsidize</u>, help, support, sponsor, assist

backbone 1 = <u>spinal column</u>, spine, vertebrae, vertebral column 2 = <u>strength of character</u>, character, resolution, nerve, daring, courage, determination, pluck

backer 1 = <u>supporter</u>, second, angel (*informal*), patron, promoter, subscriber, helper, benefactor 2 = <u>advocate</u>, supporter, patron, sponsor, promoter

backfire = fail, founder, flop (*informal*), rebound, boomerang, miscarry, misfire

background 1 = upbringing, history, culture, environment, tradition, circumstances 2 = experience, grounding, education 3 = circumstances, history, conditions, situation, atmosphere, environment, framework, ambience

backing 1 = support, encouragement, endorsement, moral support 2 = assistance, support, help, aid, sponsorship, patronage

backlash = reaction, response, resistance, retaliation, repercussion, counterblast, counteraction

backward 1 = underdeveloped, undeveloped 2 = slow, behind, retarded, underdeveloped, subnormal, half-witted, slow-witted

backwards *or* **backward** = towards the rear, behind you, in reverse, rearwards

bacteria = microorganisms, viruses, bugs (*slang*), germs, microbes, pathogens, bacilli

bad 1 = harmful, damaging, dangerous, destructive, unhealthy, detrimental, hurtful, ruinous ≠ beneficial 2 = poor 3 = unfavourable, distressing, unfortunate, grim, unpleasant, gloomy, adverse 4 = inferior, poor, inadequate, faulty, unsatisfactory, defective, imperfect, substandard, bush-league (*Austral. & N.Z. informal*), half-pie (*N.Z. informal*), bodger *or* bodgie (*Austral. slang*) ≠ satisfactory 5 = incompetent, poor, useless, incapable, unfit, inexpert 6 = grim, severe, hard, tough 7 = wicked, criminal, evil, corrupt, immoral, sinful, depraved ≠ virtuous 8 = naughty, defiant, wayward, mischievous, wicked, unruly, impish, undisciplined ≠ well-behaved 9 = rotten, off, rank, sour, rancid, mouldy, putrid, festy (*Austral. slang*)

badge 1 = image, brand, stamp, identification, crest, emblem, insignia 2 = mark, sign, token

badger = pester, harry, bother, bug (*informal*), bully, plague, hound, harass

badly 1 = poorly, incorrectly, carelessly, inadequately, imperfectly, ineptly ≠ well 2 = severely, greatly, deeply, seriously, desperately, intensely, exceedingly 3 = unfavourably, unsuccessfully

baffle = puzzle, confuse, stump, bewilder, confound, perplex, mystify, flummox ≠ explain

bag NOUN = sack, container, sac, receptacle ● VERB 1 = get, land, score (*slang*), capture, acquire, procure 2 = catch, kill, shoot, capture, acquire, trap

baggage = luggage, things, cases, bags, equipment, gear, suitcases, belongings

baggy = loose, slack, bulging, sagging, sloppy, floppy, roomy, ill-fitting ≠ tight

bail NOUN (*Law*) = security, bond, guarantee, pledge, warranty, surety ● PHRASES **bail out** = escape, withdraw, get away, retreat, make your getaway, break free *or* out ◆ **bail something** *or* **someone out** (*Informal*) = save, help, release, aid, deliver, recover, rescue, get out

bait NOUN = lure, attraction, incentive, carrot (*informal*), temptation, snare, inducement, decoy ● VERB = tease, annoy, irritate, bother, mock, wind up (*Brit. slang*), hound, torment

baked = dry, desert, seared, scorched, barren, sterile, arid, torrid

bakkie (*S. African*) = truck, pick-up, van, lorry, pick-up truck

balance VERB 1 = stabilize, level, steady ≠ overbalance 2 = weigh, consider, compare, estimate, contrast, assess, evaluate, set against 3 (*Accounting*) = calculate, total, determine, estimate, settle, count, square, reckon ● NOUN 1 = equilibrium, stability, steadiness, evenness ≠ instability 2 = stability, equanimity, steadiness 3 = parity, equity, fairness, impartiality, equality, correspondence, equivalence 4 = remainder, rest, difference, surplus, residue 5 = composure, stability, restraint, self-control, poise, self-discipline, equanimity, self-restraint

balcony 1 = terrace, veranda 2 = upper circle, gods, gallery

bald 1 = hairless, depilated, baldheaded 2 = plain, direct, frank, straightforward, blunt, rude, forthright, unadorned

ball = sphere, drop, globe, pellet, orb, globule, spheroid

balloon = expand, rise, increase, swell, blow up, inflate, bulge, billow

ballot = vote, election, voting, poll, polling, referendum, show of hands

ban VERB 1 = <u>prohibit</u>, bar, block, veto, forbid, boycott, outlaw, banish ≠ permit 2 = <u>bar</u>, prohibit, exclude, forbid, disqualify, preclude, debar, declare ineligible
● NOUN = <u>prohibition</u>, restriction, veto, boycott, embargo, injunction, taboo, disqualification, rahui (*N.Z.*) ≠ permission

band[1] 1 = <u>ensemble</u>, group, orchestra, combo 2 = <u>gang</u>, company, group, party, team, body, crowd, pack

band[2] = <u>headband</u>, strip, ribbon

bandage NOUN = <u>dressing</u>, plaster, compress, gauze
● VERB = <u>dress</u>, cover, bind, swathe

bandit = <u>robber</u>, outlaw, raider, plunderer, mugger (*informal*), looter, highwayman, desperado

bang NOUN 1 = <u>explosion</u>, pop, clash, crack, blast, slam, discharge, thump 2 = <u>blow</u>, knock, stroke, punch, bump, sock (*slang*), smack, thump
● VERB 1 = <u>resound</u>, boom, explode, thunder, thump, clang 2 = <u>bump</u>, knock, elbow, jostle 3 *often with on* = <u>hit</u>, strike, knock, belt (*informal*), slam, thump, clatter
● ADVERB = <u>exactly</u>, straight, square, squarely, precisely, slap, smack, plumb (*informal*)

banish 1 = <u>exclude</u>, ban, dismiss, expel, throw out, eject, evict 2 = <u>expel</u>, exile, outlaw, deport ≠ admit 3 = <u>get rid of</u>, remove

bank[1] NOUN 1 = <u>financial institution</u>, repository, depository 2 = <u>store</u>, fund, stock, source, supply, reserve, pool, reservoir
● VERB = <u>deposit</u>, keep, save

bank[2] NOUN 1 = <u>side</u>, edge, margin, shore, brink 2 = <u>mound</u>, banking, rise, hill, mass, pile, heap, ridge, kopje *or* koppie (*S. African*) 3 = <u>mass</u>
● VERB = <u>tilt</u>, tip, pitch, heel, slope, incline, slant, cant

bank[3] = <u>row</u>, group, line, range, series, file, rank, sequence

bankrupt = <u>insolvent</u>, broke (*informal*), ruined, wiped out (*informal*), impoverished, in the red, destitute, gone bust (*informal*) ≠ solvent

bankruptcy = <u>insolvency</u>, failure, disaster, ruin, liquidation

banner = <u>flag</u>, standard, colours, placard, pennant, ensign, streamer

banquet = <u>feast</u>, spread (*informal*), dinner, meal, revel, repast, hakari (*N.Z.*)

bar NOUN 1 = <u>public house</u>, pub (*informal*, *chiefly Brit.*), counter, inn, saloon, tavern, canteen, watering hole (*facetious slang*) 2 = <u>rod</u>, staff, stick, stake, rail, pole, paling, shaft 3 = <u>obstacle</u>, block, barrier, hitch, barricade, snag, deterrent ≠ aid
● VERB 1 = <u>lock</u>, block, secure, attach, bolt, blockade, barricade, fortify 2 = <u>block</u>, restrict, restrain, hamper, thwart, hinder, obstruct, impede 3 = <u>exclude</u>, ban, forbid, prohibit, keep out of, disallow, shut out of, blackball ≠ admit

barbarian 1 = <u>savage</u>, monster, beast, brute, yahoo, swine, sadist 2 = <u>lout</u>, yahoo, bigot, philistine, hoon (*Austral. & N.Z.*), cougan (*Austral. slang*), scozza (*Austral. slang*), bogan (*Austral. slang*), boor, vulgarian

bare 1 = <u>naked</u>, nude, stripped, uncovered, undressed, unclothed, unclad, without a stitch on (*informal*) ≠ dressed 2 = <u>simple</u>, spare, stark, austere, spartan, unadorned, unembellished, unornamented ≠ adorned 3 = <u>plain</u>, simple, basic, obvious, sheer, patent, evident, stark

barely = <u>only just</u>, just, hardly, scarcely, at a push ≠ completely

bargain NOUN 1 = <u>good buy</u>, discount purchase, good deal, steal (*informal*), snip (*informal*), giveaway, cheap purchase 2 = <u>agreement</u>, deal (*informal*), promise, contract, arrangement, settlement, pledge, pact
● VERB = <u>negotiate</u>, deal, contract, mediate, covenant, stipulate, transact, cut a deal

barge = <u>canal boat</u>, lighter, narrow boat, flatboat

bark[1] VERB = <u>yap</u>, bay, howl, snarl, growl, yelp, woof
● NOUN = <u>yap</u>, bay, howl, snarl, growl, yelp, woof

bark[2] = <u>covering</u>, casing, cover, skin, layer, crust, cortex (*Anatomy*, *botany*), rind

barracks = <u>camp</u>, quarters, garrison, encampment, billet

barrage 1 = <u>bombardment</u>, attack, bombing, assault, shelling, battery, volley, blitz 2 = <u>torrent</u>, mass, burst, stream, hail, spate, onslaught, deluge

barren 1 = <u>desolate</u>, empty, desert, waste ≠ fertile 2 (*Old-fashioned*) = <u>infertile</u>, sterile, childless, unproductive

barricade NOUN = <u>barrier</u>, wall, fence,

blockade, obstruction, rampart, bulwark, palisade

● **VERB** = <u>bar</u>, block, defend, secure, lock, bolt, blockade, fortify

barrier = <u>barricade</u>, wall, bar, fence, boundary, obstacle, blockade, obstruction

base¹ NOUN 1 = <u>bottom</u>, floor, lowest part ≠ top 2 = <u>support</u>, stand, foot, rest, bed, bottom, foundation, pedestal 3 = <u>foundation</u>, institution, organization, establishment 4 = <u>centre</u>, post, station, camp, settlement, headquarters, starting point 5 = <u>home</u>, house, pad (*slang*), residence 6 = <u>essence</u>, source, basis, root, core

● **VERB** 1 = <u>ground</u>, found, build, establish, depend, construct, derive, hinge 2 = <u>place</u>, set, post, station, establish, locate, install

base² = <u>dishonourable</u>, evil, disgraceful, shameful, immoral, wicked, sordid, despicable, scungy (*Austral. & N.Z.*) ≠ honourable

bash NOUN (*Informal*) = <u>attempt</u>, go (*informal*), try, shot (*informal*), bid, crack (*informal*), stab (*informal*)

● **VERB** (*Informal*) = <u>hit</u>, beat, strike, knock, smash, belt (*informal*), slap, sock (*slang*)

basic ADJECTIVE 1 = <u>fundamental</u>, main, essential, primary, vital, principal, cardinal, elementary 2 = <u>vital</u>, needed, important, key, necessary, essential, primary, crucial 3 = <u>essential</u>, key, vital, fundamental ≠ secondary 4 = <u>main</u>, key, essential, primary 5 = <u>plain</u>, simple, classic, unfussy, unembellished

● **PLURAL NOUN** = <u>essentials</u>, principles, fundamentals, nuts and bolts (*informal*), nitty-gritty (*informal*), rudiments, brass tacks (*informal*)

basically = <u>essentially</u>, mainly, mostly, principally, fundamentally, primarily, at heart, inherently

basis 1 = <u>arrangement</u>, way, system, footing, agreement 2 = <u>foundation</u>, support, base, ground, footing, bottom, groundwork

bask = <u>lie</u>, relax, lounge, sprawl, loaf, lie about, swim in, sunbathe, outspan (*S. African*)

bass = <u>deep</u>, low, resonant, sonorous, low-pitched, deep-toned

batch = <u>group</u>, set, lot, crowd, pack, collection, quantity, bunch

bath NOUN = <u>wash</u>, cleaning, shower, soak, cleansing, scrub, scrubbing, douche

● **VERB** = <u>clean</u>, wash, shower, soak, cleanse, scrub, bathe, rinse

bathe 1 = <u>swim</u> 2 = <u>wash</u>, clean, bath, shower, soak, cleanse, scrub, rinse 3 = <u>cleanse</u>, clean, wash, soak, rinse 4 = <u>cover</u>, flood, steep, engulf, immerse, overrun, suffuse, wash over

baton = <u>stick</u>, club, staff, pole, rod, crook, cane, mace, mere (*N.Z.*), patu (*N.Z.*)

batter = <u>beat</u>, hit, strike, knock, bang, thrash, pound, buffet

battery = <u>artillery</u>, ordnance, gunnery, gun emplacement, cannonry

battle NOUN 1 = <u>fight</u>, attack, action, struggle, conflict, clash, encounter, combat, biffo (*Austral. slang*) ≠ peace 2 = <u>conflict</u>, campaign, struggle, dispute, contest, crusade 3 = <u>campaign</u>, drive, movement, push, struggle

● **VERB** 1 = <u>wrestle</u>, war, fight, argue, dispute, grapple, clamour, lock horns 2 = <u>struggle</u>, work, labour, strain, strive, toil, go all out (*informal*), give it your best shot (*informal*)

battlefield = <u>battleground</u>, front, field, combat zone, field of battle

batty = <u>crazy</u>, odd, mad, eccentric, peculiar, daft (*informal*), touched, potty (*Brit. informal*), off the air (*Austral. slang*), porangi (*N.Z.*)

bay¹ = <u>inlet</u>, sound, gulf, creek, cove, fjord, bight, natural harbour

bay² = <u>recess</u>, opening, corner, niche, compartment, nook, alcove

bay³ VERB = <u>howl</u>, cry, roar (*used of hounds*), bark, wail, growl, bellow, clamour

● **NOUN** = <u>cry</u>, roar (*used of hounds*), bark, howl, wail, growl, bellow, clamour

bazaar 1 = <u>market</u>, exchange, fair, marketplace 2 = <u>fair</u>, fête, gala, bring-and-buy

be = <u>be alive</u>, live, exist, survive, breathe, be present, endure

beach = <u>shore</u>, coast, sands, seaside, water's edge, seashore

beached = <u>stranded</u>, grounded, abandoned, deserted, wrecked, ashore, marooned, aground

beacon = <u>signal</u>, sign, beam, flare, lighthouse, bonfire, watchtower

bead = <u>drop</u>, tear, bubble, pearl, dot, drip, blob, droplet

beam VERB 1 = <u>smile</u>, grin 2 = <u>transmit</u>,

show, air, broadcast, cable, send out, relay, televise **3** = <u>radiate</u>, flash, shine, glow, glitter, glare, gleam

● NOUN **1** = <u>ray</u>, flash, stream, glow, streak, shaft, gleam, glint **2** = <u>rafter</u>, support, timber, spar, plank, girder, joist **3** = <u>smile</u>, grin

bear VERB **1** = <u>carry</u>, take, move, bring, transfer, conduct, transport, haul ≠ put down **2** = <u>support</u>, shoulder, sustain, endure, uphold, withstand ≠ give up **3** = <u>display</u>, have, show, hold, carry, possess **4** = <u>suffer</u>, experience, go through, sustain, stomach, endure, brook, abide **5** = <u>bring yourself to</u>, allow, accept, permit, endure, tolerate **6** = <u>produce</u>, generate, yield, bring forth **7** = <u>give birth to</u>, produce, deliver, breed, bring forth, beget **8** = <u>exhibit</u>, hold, maintain **9** = <u>conduct</u>, carry, move, deport

● PHRASES **bear something out** = <u>support</u>, prove, confirm, justify, endorse, uphold, substantiate, corroborate

bearer 1 = <u>agent</u>, carrier, courier, herald, envoy, messenger, conveyor, emissary **2** = <u>carrier</u>, runner, servant, porter

bearing NOUN **1** *usually with* **on** *or* **upon** = <u>relevance</u>, relation, application, connection, import, reference, significance, pertinence ≠ irrelevance **2** = <u>manner</u>, attitude, conduct, aspect, behaviour, posture, demeanour, deportment

● PLURAL NOUN = <u>way</u>, course, position, situation, track, aim, direction, location

beast 1 = <u>animal</u>, creature, brute **2** = <u>brute</u>, monster, savage, barbarian, fiend, swine, ogre, sadist

beastly = <u>unpleasant</u>, mean, awful, nasty, rotten, horrid, disagreeable ≠ pleasant

beat VERB **1** = <u>batter</u>, hit, strike, knock, pound, smack, thrash, thump **2** = <u>pound</u>, strike, hammer, batter, thrash **3** = <u>throb</u>, thump, pound, quake, vibrate, pulsate, palpitate **4** = <u>hit</u>, strike, bang **5** = <u>flap</u>, thrash, flutter, wag **6** = <u>defeat</u>, outdo, trounce, overcome, crush, overwhelm, conquer, surpass

● NOUN **1** = <u>throb</u>, pounding, pulse, thumping, vibration, pulsating, palpitation, pulsation **2** = <u>route</u>, way, course, rounds, path, circuit

●PHRASES **beat someone up** (*Informal*) = <u>assault</u>, attack, batter, thrash, set about, set upon, lay into (*informal*), beat the living daylights out of (*informal*)

beaten 1 = <u>stirred</u>, mixed, whipped, blended, whisked, frothy, foamy **2** = <u>defeated</u>, overcome, overwhelmed, cowed, thwarted, vanquished

beautiful = <u>attractive</u>, pretty, lovely, charming, tempting, pleasant, handsome, fetching ≠ ugly

beauty 1 = <u>attractiveness</u>, charm, grace, glamour, elegance, loveliness, handsomeness, comeliness ≠ ugliness **2** = <u>good-looker</u>, lovely (*slang*), belle, stunner (*informal*)

because CONJUNCTION = <u>since</u>, as, in that

● PHRASES **because of** = <u>as a result of</u>, on account of, by reason of, thanks to, owing to

beckon = <u>gesture</u>, sign, wave, indicate, signal, nod, motion, summon

become 1 = <u>come to be</u>, develop into, be transformed into, grow into, change into, alter to, mature into, ripen into **2** = <u>suit</u>, fit, enhance, flatter, embellish, set off

becoming 1 = <u>flattering</u>, pretty, attractive, enhancing, neat, graceful, tasteful, well-chosen ≠ unflattering **2** = <u>appropriate</u>, seemly, fitting, suitable, proper, worthy, in keeping, compatible ≠ inappropriate

bed 1 = <u>bedstead</u>, couch, berth, cot, bunk, divan **2** = <u>plot</u>, area, row, strip, patch, ground, land, garden **3** = <u>bottom</u>, ground, floor **4** = <u>base</u>, footing, basis, bottom, foundation, underpinning, groundwork, bedrock

before PREPOSITION **1** = <u>earlier than</u>, ahead of, prior to, in advance of ≠ after **2** = <u>in front of</u>, ahead of, in advance of **3** = <u>in the presence of</u>, in front of **4** = <u>ahead of</u>, in front of, in advance of

● ADVERB **1** = <u>previously</u>, earlier, sooner, in advance, formerly ≠ after **2** = <u>in the past</u>, earlier, once, previously, formerly, hitherto, beforehand

■ RELATED WORDS
prefixes: ante-, fore-, pre-

beforehand = <u>in advance</u>, before, earlier, already, sooner, ahead, previously, in anticipation

beg 1 = <u>implore</u>, plead with, beseech, request, petition, solicit, entreat **2** = <u>scrounge</u>, bum (*informal*), touch (someone) for (*slang*), cadge, sponge on (someone) for, freeload (*slang*), seek charity, solicit charity ≠ give

beggar = tramp, bum (*informal*), derelict, drifter, down-and-out, pauper, vagrant, bag lady (*chiefly U.S.*), derro (*Austral. slang*)

begin 1 = start, commence, proceed ≠ stop 2 = commence, start, initiate, embark on, set about, instigate, institute, make a beginning 3 = start talking, start, initiate, commence 4 = come into existence, start, appear, emerge, arise, originate, come into being 5 = emerge, start, spring, stem, derive, originate ≠ end

beginner = novice, pupil, amateur, newcomer, starter, trainee, apprentice, learner ≠ expert

beginning 1 = start, opening, birth, origin, outset, onset, initiation, inauguration ≠ end 2 = outset, start, opening, birth, onset, commencement 3 = origins

behave 1 = act 2 *often reflexive* = be well-behaved, mind your manners, keep your nose clean, act correctly, conduct yourself properly ≠ misbehave

behaviour 1 = conduct, ways, actions, bearing, attitude, manner, manners, demeanour 2 = action, performance, operation, functioning

behind PREPOSITION 1 = at the rear of, at the back of, at the heels of 2 = after, following 3 = supporting, for, backing, on the side of, in agreement with 4 = causing, responsible for, initiating, at the bottom of, instigating 5 = later than, after

● ADVERB 1 = after, next, following, afterwards, subsequently, in the wake (of) ≠ in advance of 2 = behind schedule, delayed, running late, behind time ≠ ahead 3 = overdue, in debt, in arrears, behindhand

● NOUN (*Informal*) = bottom, butt (*U.S. & Canad. informal*), buttocks, posterior

being 1 = individual, creature, human being, living thing 2 = life, reality ≠ nonexistence 3 = soul, spirit, substance, creature, essence, organism, entity

beleaguered 1 = harassed, troubled, plagued, hassled (*informal*), badgered, persecuted, pestered, vexed 2 = besieged, surrounded, blockaded, beset, encircled, assailed, hemmed in

belief 1 = trust, confidence, conviction ≠ disbelief 2 = faith, principles, doctrine, ideology, creed, dogma, tenet, credo 3 = opinion, feeling, idea, impression,

assessment, notion, judgment, point of view

believe 1 = think, judge, suppose, estimate, imagine, assume, gather, reckon 2 = accept, trust, credit, depend on, rely on, have faith in, swear by, be certain of ≠ disbelieve

believer = follower, supporter, convert, disciple, devotee, apostle, adherent, zealot ≠ sceptic

bellow VERB = shout, cry (out), scream, roar, yell, howl, shriek, bawl

● NOUN = shout, cry, scream, roar, yell, howl, shriek, bawl

belly = stomach, insides (*informal*), gut, abdomen, tummy, paunch, potbelly, corporation (*informal*), puku (*N.Z.*)

belong = go with, fit into, be part of, relate to, be connected with, pertain to

belonging = fellowship, relationship, association, loyalty, acceptance, attachment, inclusion, affinity

belongings = possessions, goods, things, effects, property, stuff, gear, paraphernalia

beloved = dear, loved, valued, prized, admired, treasured, precious, darling

below PREPOSITION 1 = under, underneath, lower than 2 = less than, lower than 3 = subordinate to, subject to, inferior to, lesser than

● ADVERB 1 = lower, down, under, beneath, underneath 2 = beneath, following, at the end, underneath, at the bottom, further on

belt 1 = waistband, band, sash, girdle, girth, cummerbund 2 = conveyor belt, band, loop, fan belt, drive belt 3 (*Geography*) = zone, area, region, section, district, stretch, strip, layer

bemused = puzzled, confused, baffled, at sea, bewildered, muddled, perplexed, mystified

bench NOUN 1 = seat, stall, pew 2 = worktable, stand, table, counter, trestle table, workbench

● PHRASES **the bench** = court, judges, magistrates, tribunal, judiciary, courtroom

benchmark = reference point, gauge, yardstick, measure, level, standard, model, par

bend VERB = twist, turn, wind, lean, hook, bow, curve, arch

● NOUN = curve, turn, corner, twist, angle, bow, loop, arc

beneath PREPOSITION 1 = <u>under</u>, below, underneath, lower than ≠ over 2 = <u>inferior to</u>, below 3 = <u>unworthy of</u>, unfitting for, unsuitable for, inappropriate for, unbefitting

● ADVERB = <u>underneath</u>, below, in a lower place

◼︎ RELATED WORD
prefix: sub-

beneficial = <u>favourable</u>, useful, valuable, helpful, profitable, benign, wholesome, advantageous ≠ harmful

beneficiary 1 = <u>recipient</u>, receiver, payee 2 = <u>heir</u>, inheritor

benefit NOUN 1 = <u>good</u>, help, profit, favour ≠ harm 2 = <u>advantage</u>, aid, favour, assistance

● VERB 1 = <u>profit from</u>, make the most of, gain from, do well out of, reap benefits from, turn to your advantage 2 = <u>help</u>, aid, profit, improve, enhance, assist, avail ≠ harm

benign 1 = <u>benevolent</u>, kind, kindly, warm, friendly, obliging, sympathetic, compassionate ≠ unkind 2 (*Medical*) = <u>harmless</u>, innocent, innocuous, curable, inoffensive, remediable ≠ malignant

bent ADJECTIVE 1 = <u>misshapen</u>, twisted, angled, bowed, curved, arched, crooked, distorted ≠ straight 2 = <u>stooped</u>, bowed, arched, hunched

● NOUN = <u>inclination</u>, ability, leaning, tendency, preference, penchant, propensity, aptitude

● PHRASES **bent on** = <u>intent on</u>, set on, fixed on, predisposed to, resolved on, insistent on

bequeath 1 = <u>leave</u>, will, give, grant, hand down, endow, bestow, entrust 2 = <u>give</u>, accord, grant, afford, yield, lend, pass on, confer

berth NOUN 1 = <u>bunk</u>, bed, hammock, billet 2 (*Nautical*) = <u>anchorage</u>, haven, port, harbour, dock, pier, wharf, quay

● VERB (*Nautical*) = <u>anchor</u>, land, dock, moor, tie up, drop anchor

beside PREPOSITION = <u>next to</u>, near, close to, neighbouring, alongside, adjacent to, at the side of, abreast of

● PHRASES **beside yourself** = <u>distraught</u>, desperate, distressed, frantic, frenzied, demented, unhinged, overwrought

besides PREPOSITION = <u>apart from</u>, barring, excepting, other than, excluding, as well (as), in addition to, over and above

● ADVERB = <u>also</u>, too, further, otherwise, in addition, as well, moreover, furthermore

besiege 1 = <u>harass</u>, harry, plague, hound, hassle (*informal*), badger, pester 2 = <u>surround</u>, enclose, blockade, encircle, hem in, shut in, lay siege to

best ADJECTIVE = <u>finest</u>, leading, supreme, principal, foremost, pre-eminent, unsurpassed, most accomplished

● NOUN = <u>finest</u>, top, prime, pick, flower, cream, elite, crème de la crème (*French*)

● ADVERB = <u>most highly</u>, most fully, most deeply

bestow = <u>present</u>, give, award, grant, commit, hand out, lavish, impart ≠ obtain

bet VERB = <u>gamble</u>, chance, stake, venture, hazard, speculate, wager, risk money

● NOUN = <u>gamble</u>, risk, stake, venture, speculation, flutter (*informal*), punt, wager

betray 1 = <u>be disloyal to</u>, dob in (*Austral. slang*), double-cross (*informal*), stab in the back, be unfaithful to, inform on or against 2 = <u>give away</u>, reveal, expose, disclose, uncover, divulge, unmask, let slip

betrayal = <u>disloyalty</u>, sell-out (*informal*), deception, treason, treachery, trickery, double-cross (*informal*), breach of trust ≠ loyalty

better ADVERB 1 = <u>to a greater degree</u>, more completely, more thoroughly 2 = <u>in a more excellent manner</u>, more effectively, more attractively, more advantageously, more competently, in a superior way ≠ worse

● ADJECTIVE 1 = <u>well</u>, stronger, recovering, cured, fully recovered, on the mend (*informal*) ≠ worse 2 = <u>superior</u>, finer, higher-quality, surpassing, preferable, more desirable ≠ inferior

between = <u>amidst</u>, among, mid, in the middle of, betwixt

◼︎ RELATED WORD
prefix: inter-

beverage = <u>drink</u>, liquid, liquor, refreshment

beware 1 = <u>be careful</u>, look out, watch out, be wary, be cautious, take heed, guard against something 2 = <u>avoid</u>, mind

bewilder = <u>confound</u>, confuse, puzzle, baffle, perplex, mystify, flummox, bemuse

bewildered = <u>confused</u>, puzzled, baffled, at sea, muddled, perplexed, at a loss, mystified

beyond 1 = <u>on the other side of</u>
2 = <u>after</u>, over, past, above 3 = <u>past</u>
4 = <u>except for</u>, but, save, apart from, other
than, excluding, besides, aside from
5 = <u>exceeding</u>, surpassing, superior to, out
of reach of 6 = <u>outside</u>, over, above

bias NOUN = <u>prejudice</u>, leaning, tendency,
inclination, favouritism, partiality
≠ impartiality
● VERB = <u>influence</u>, colour, weight,
prejudice, distort, sway, warp, slant

biased = <u>prejudiced</u>, weighted, one-sided,
partial, distorted, slanted

bid NOUN 1 = <u>attempt</u>, try, effort, go
(*informal*), shot (*informal*), stab (*informal*),
crack (*informal*) 2 = <u>offer</u>, price, amount,
advance, proposal, sum, tender
● VERB 1 = <u>make an offer</u>, offer, propose,
submit, tender, proffer 2 = <u>wish</u>, say, call,
tell, greet 3 = <u>tell</u>, ask, order, require, direct,
command, instruct

bidding = <u>order</u>, request, command,
instruction, summons, beck and call

big 1 = <u>large</u>, great, huge, massive, vast,
enormous, substantial, extensive ≠ small
2 = <u>important</u>, significant, urgent, far-
reaching ≠ unimportant 3 = <u>powerful</u>,
important, prominent, dominant,
influential, eminent 4 = <u>grown-up</u>,
adult, grown, mature, elder, full-grown
≠ young 5 = <u>generous</u>, good, noble,
gracious, benevolent, altruistic, unselfish,
magnanimous

bill¹ NOUN 1 = <u>charges</u>, rate, costs,
score, account, statement, reckoning,
expense 2 = <u>act of parliament</u>, measure,
proposal, piece of legislation, projected
law 3 = <u>list</u>, listing, programme, card,
schedule, agenda, catalogue, inventory
4 = <u>advertisement</u>, notice, poster, leaflet,
bulletin, circular, handout, placard
● VERB 1 = <u>charge</u>, debit, invoice, send
a statement to, send an invoice to
2 = <u>advertise</u>, post, announce, promote,
plug (*informal*), tout, publicize, give
advance notice of

bill² = <u>beak</u>, nib, neb (*archaic, dialect*),
mandible

bind VERB 1 = <u>oblige</u>, make, force, require,
engage, compel, constrain, necessitate
2 = <u>tie</u>, join, stick, secure, wrap, knot, strap,
lash ≠ untie
● NOUN (*Informal*) = <u>nuisance</u>,
inconvenience, hassle (*informal*), drag

(*informal*), spot (*informal*), difficulty, bore,
dilemma, uphill (*S. African*)

binding = <u>compulsory</u>, necessary,
mandatory, obligatory, irrevocable,
unalterable, indissoluble ≠ optional

binge (*Informal*) = <u>bout</u>, spell, fling, feast,
stint, spree, orgy, bender (*informal*)

biography = <u>life story</u>, life, record,
account, profile, memoir, CV, curriculum
vitae

bird = <u>feathered friend</u>, fowl, songbird
■ RELATED WORDS
adjective: avian
male: cock
female: hen
young: chick, fledg(e)ling, nestling
collective nouns: flock, flight
habitation: nest

birth 1 = <u>childbirth</u>, delivery, nativity,
parturition ≠ death 2 = <u>ancestry</u>, stock,
blood, background, breeding, pedigree,
lineage, parentage
■ RELATED WORD
adjective: natal

bit¹ 1 = <u>slice</u>, fragment, crumb, morsel
2 = <u>piece</u>, scrap 3 = <u>jot</u>, iota 4 = <u>part</u>

bit² = <u>curb</u>, check, brake, restraint, snaffle

bite VERB = <u>nip</u>, cut, tear, wound, snap,
pierce, pinch, chew
● NOUN 1 = <u>snack</u>, food, piece, taste,
refreshment, mouthful, morsel, titbit
2 = <u>wound</u>, sting, pinch, nip, prick

biting 1 = <u>piercing</u>, cutting, sharp, frozen,
harsh, penetrating, arctic, icy 2 = <u>sarcastic</u>,
cutting, stinging, scathing, acrimonious,
incisive, virulent, caustic

bitter 1 = <u>resentful</u>, angry, offended, sour,
sore, acrimonious, sullen, miffed (*informal*)
≠ happy 2 = <u>freezing</u>, biting, severe,
intense, raw, fierce, chill, stinging ≠ mild
3 = <u>sour</u>, sharp, acid, harsh, tart, astringent,
acrid, unsweetened ≠ sweet

bitterness 1 = <u>resentment</u>, hostility,
indignation, animosity, acrimony, rancour,
ill feeling, bad blood 2 = <u>sourness</u>, acidity,
sharpness, tartness, acerbity

bizarre = <u>strange</u>, unusual, extraordinary,
fantastic, weird, peculiar, eccentric,
ludicrous ≠ normal

black 1 = <u>dark</u>, raven, ebony, sable,
jet, dusky, pitch-black, swarthy ≠ light
2 = <u>gloomy</u>, sad, depressing, grim, bleak,
hopeless, dismal, ominous ≠ happy
3 = <u>terrible</u>, bad, devastating, tragic,

fatal, catastrophic, ruinous, calamitous
4 = <u>wicked</u>, bad, evil, corrupt, vicious, immoral, depraved, villainous ≠ good
5 = <u>angry</u>, cross, furious, hostile, sour, menacing, moody, resentful ≠ happy

blackmail NOUN = <u>threat</u>, intimidation, ransom, extortion, hush money (*slang*)
● VERB = <u>threaten</u>, squeeze, compel, intimidate, coerce, dragoon, extort, hold to ransom

blame VERB **1** = <u>hold responsible</u>, accuse, denounce, indict, impeach, incriminate, impute ≠ absolve **2** = <u>attribute to</u>, credit to, assign to, put down to, impute to **3** (used in negative constructions) = <u>criticize</u>, condemn, censure, reproach, chide, find fault with ≠ praise
● NOUN = <u>responsibility</u>, liability, accountability, onus, culpability, answerability ≠ praise

bland 1 = <u>dull</u>, boring, plain, flat, dreary, run-of-the-mill, uninspiring, humdrum ≠ exciting **2** = <u>tasteless</u>, insipid, flavourless, thin

blank ADJECTIVE **1** = <u>unmarked</u>, white, clear, clean, empty, plain, bare, void ≠ marked **2** = <u>expressionless</u>, empty, vague, vacant, deadpan, impassive, poker-faced (*informal*) ≠ expressive
● NOUN **1** = <u>empty space</u>, space, gap **2** = <u>void</u>, vacuum, vacancy, emptiness, nothingness

blanket NOUN **1** = <u>cover</u>, rug, coverlet **2** = <u>covering</u>, sheet, coat, layer, carpet, cloak, mantle, thickness
● VERB = <u>coat</u>, cover, hide, mask, conceal, obscure, cloak

blast NOUN **1** = <u>explosion</u>, crash, burst, discharge, eruption, detonation **2** = <u>gust</u>, rush, storm, breeze, puff, gale, tempest, squall **3** = <u>blare</u>, blow, scream, trumpet, wail, resound, clamour, toot
● VERB = <u>blow up</u>, bomb, destroy, burst, ruin, break up, explode, shatter

blatant = <u>obvious</u>, clear, plain, evident, glaring, manifest, noticeable, conspicuous ≠ subtle

blaze VERB **1** = <u>burn</u>, glow, flare, be on fire, go up in flames, be ablaze, fire, flame **2** = <u>shine</u>, flash, beam, glow, flare, glare, gleam, radiate
● NOUN **1** = <u>inferno</u>, fire, flames, bonfire, combustion, conflagration **2** = <u>flash</u>, glow, glitter, flare, glare, gleam, brilliance,

radiance

bleach = <u>lighten</u>, wash out, blanch, whiten

bleak 1 = <u>dismal</u>, dark, depressing, grim, discouraging, gloomy, hopeless, dreary ≠ cheerful **2** = <u>exposed</u>, empty, bare, barren, desolate, windswept, weather-beaten, unsheltered ≠ sheltered **3** = <u>stormy</u>, severe, rough, harsh, tempestuous, intemperate

bleed 1 = <u>lose blood</u>, flow, gush, spurt, shed blood **2** = <u>blend</u>, run, meet, unite, mix, combine, flow, fuse **3** (*Informal*) = <u>extort</u>, milk, squeeze, drain, exhaust, fleece

blend VERB **1** = <u>mix</u>, join, combine, compound, merge, unite, mingle, amalgamate **2** = <u>go well</u>, match, fit, suit, go with, correspond, complement, coordinate **3** = <u>combine</u>, mix, link, integrate, merge, unite, amalgamate
● NOUN = <u>mixture</u>, mix, combination, compound, brew, union, synthesis, alloy

bless 1 = <u>sanctify</u>, dedicate, ordain, exalt, anoint, consecrate, hallow ≠ curse **2** = <u>endow</u>, give to, provide for, grant for, favour, grace, bestow to ≠ afflict

blessed = <u>holy</u>, sacred, divine, adored, revered, hallowed, sanctified, beatified

blessing 1 = <u>benefit</u>, help, service, favour, gift, windfall, kindness, good fortune ≠ disadvantage **2** = <u>approval</u>, backing, support, agreement, favour, sanction, permission, leave ≠ disapproval **3** = <u>benediction</u>, grace, dedication, thanksgiving, invocation, commendation, consecration, benison ≠ curse

blight NOUN **1** = <u>curse</u>, suffering, evil, corruption, pollution, plague, hardship, woe ≠ blessing **2** = <u>disease</u>, pest, fungus, mildew, infestation, pestilence, canker
● VERB = <u>frustrate</u>, destroy, ruin, crush, mar, dash, wreck, spoil, crool or cruel (*Austral. slang*)

blind 1 = <u>sightless</u>, unsighted, unseeing, eyeless, visionless ≠ sighted **2** *often with* *to* = <u>unaware of</u>, unconscious of, ignorant of, indifferent to, insensitive to, oblivious of, unconcerned about, inconsiderate of ≠ aware **3** = <u>unquestioning</u>, prejudiced, wholesale, indiscriminate, uncritical, unreasoning, undiscriminating

blindly 1 = <u>thoughtlessly</u>, carelessly, recklessly, indiscriminately, senselessly, heedlessly 2 = <u>wildly</u>, aimlessly

blink VERB 1 = <u>flutter</u>, wink, bat 2 = <u>flash</u>, flicker, wink, shimmer, twinkle, glimmer

● PHRASES **on the blink** (*Slang*) = <u>not working (properly)</u>, faulty, defective, playing up, out of action, malfunctioning, out of order

bliss 1 = <u>joy</u>, ecstasy, euphoria, rapture, nirvana, felicity, gladness, blissfulness ≠ misery 2 = <u>beatitude</u>, blessedness

blister = <u>sore</u>, boil, swelling, cyst, pimple, carbuncle, pustule

blitz = <u>attack</u>, strike, assault, raid, offensive, onslaught, bombardment, bombing campaign

bloc = <u>group</u>, union, league, alliance, coalition, axis

block NOUN 1 = <u>piece</u>, bar, mass, brick, lump, chunk, hunk, ingot 2 = <u>obstruction</u>, bar, barrier, obstacle, impediment, hindrance

● VERB 1 = <u>obstruct</u>, close, stop, plug, choke, clog, stop up, bung up (*informal*) ≠ clear 2 = <u>obscure</u>, bar, obstruct 3 = <u>shut off</u>, stop, bar, hamper, obstruct

blockade = <u>stoppage</u>, block, barrier, restriction, obstacle, barricade, obstruction, impediment

bloke (*Informal*) = <u>man</u>, person, individual, character (*informal*), guy (*informal*), fellow, chap

blonde *or* **blond** 1 = <u>fair</u>, light, flaxen 2 = <u>fair-haired</u>, golden-haired, tow-headed

blood 1 = <u>lifeblood</u>, gore, vital fluid 2 = <u>family</u>, relations, birth, descent, extraction, ancestry, lineage, kinship

bloodshed = <u>killing</u>, murder, massacre, slaughter, slaying, carnage, butchery, blood-letting

bloody 1 = <u>cruel</u>, fierce, savage, brutal, vicious, ferocious, cut-throat, warlike 2 = <u>bloodstained</u>, raw, bleeding, blood-soaked, blood-spattered

bloom NOUN 1 = <u>flower</u>, bud, blossom 2 = <u>prime</u>, flower, beauty, height, peak, flourishing, heyday, zenith 3 = <u>glow</u>, freshness, lustre, radiance ≠ pallor

● VERB 1 = <u>flower</u>, blossom, open, bud ≠ wither 2 = <u>grow</u>, develop, wax 3 = <u>succeed</u>, flourish, thrive, prosper, fare well ≠ fail

blossom NOUN = <u>flower</u>, bloom, bud, efflorescence, floret

● VERB 1 = <u>bloom</u>, grow, develop, mature

2 = <u>succeed</u>, progress, thrive, flourish, prosper 3 = <u>flower</u>, bloom, bud

blow¹ VERB 1 = <u>move</u>, carry, drive, sweep, fling, buffet, waft 2 = <u>be carried</u>, flutter 3 = <u>exhale</u>, breathe, pant, puff 4 = <u>play</u>, sound, pipe, trumpet, blare, toot

● PHRASES **blow something up** 1 = <u>explode</u>, bomb, blast, detonate, blow sky-high 2 = <u>inflate</u>, pump up, fill, expand, swell, enlarge, puff up, distend 3 = <u>magnify</u>, increase, extend, expand, widen, broaden, amplify ◆ **blow up** 1 = <u>explode</u>, burst, shatter, erupt, detonate 2 (*Informal*) = <u>lose your temper</u>, rage, erupt, see red (*informal*), become angry, hit the roof (*informal*), fly off the handle (*informal*), go crook (*Austral. & N.Z. slang*), blow your top

blow² 1 = <u>knock</u>, stroke, punch, bang, sock (*slang*), smack, thump, clout (*informal*) 2 = <u>setback</u>, shock, disaster, reverse, disappointment, catastrophe, misfortune, bombshell

bludge (*Austral. & N.Z. informal*) = <u>slack</u>, skive (*Brit. informal*), idle, shirk

blue ADJECTIVE 1 = <u>depressed</u>, low, sad, unhappy, melancholy, dejected, despondent, downcast ≠ happy 2 = <u>smutty</u>, obscene, indecent, lewd, risqué, X-rated (*informal*) ≠ respectable

● PLURAL NOUN = <u>depression</u>, gloom, melancholy, unhappiness, low spirits, the dumps (*informal*), doldrums

blueprint 1 = <u>scheme</u>, plan, design, system, programme, proposal, strategy, pattern 2 = <u>plan</u>, scheme, pattern, draft, outline, sketch

bluff¹ NOUN = <u>deception</u>, fraud, sham, pretence, deceit, bravado, bluster, humbug

● VERB = <u>deceive</u>, trick, fool, pretend, cheat, con, fake, mislead

bluff² NOUN = <u>precipice</u>, bank, peak, cliff, ridge, crag, escarpment, promontory

● ADJECTIVE = <u>hearty</u>, open, blunt, outspoken, genial, ebullient, jovial, plain-spoken ≠ tactful

blunder NOUN = <u>mistake</u>, slip, fault, error, oversight, gaffe, slip-up (*informal*), indiscretion ≠ correctness

● VERB 1 = <u>make a mistake</u>, blow it (*slang*), err, slip up (*informal*), foul up, put your foot in it (*informal*) ≠ be correct 2 = <u>stumble</u>, fall, reel, stagger, lurch

blunt ADJECTIVE 1 = <u>frank</u>, forthright, straightforward, rude, outspoken, bluff, brusque, plain-spoken ≠ tactful 2 = <u>dull</u>, rounded, dulled, edgeless, unsharpened ≠ sharp

● VERB = <u>dull</u>, weaken, soften, numb, dampen, water down, deaden, take the edge off ≠ stimulate

blur NOUN = <u>haze</u>, confusion, fog, obscurity, indistinctness

● VERB 1 = <u>become indistinct</u>, become vague, become hazy, become fuzzy 2 = <u>obscure</u>, make indistinct, mask, obfuscate, make vague, make hazy

blush VERB = <u>turn red</u>, colour, glow, flush, redden, go red (as a beetroot), turn scarlet ≠ turn pale

● NOUN = <u>reddening</u>, colour, glow, flush, pink tinge, rosiness, ruddiness, rosy tint

board NOUN 1 = <u>plank</u>, panel, timber, slat, piece of timber 2 = <u>council</u>, directors, committee, congress, advisers, panel, assembly, trustees 3 = <u>meals</u>, provisions, victuals, daily meals

● VERB = <u>get on</u>, enter, mount, embark ≠ get off

boast VERB 1 = <u>brag</u>, crow, vaunt, talk big (*slang*), blow your own trumpet, show off, be proud of, congratulate yourself on, skite (*Austral. & N.Z. informal*) ≠ cover up 2 = <u>possess</u>, exhibit

● NOUN = <u>bragging</u> ≠ disclaimer

bob = <u>bounce</u>, duck, hop, oscillate

bodily = <u>physical</u>, material, actual, substantial, tangible, corporal, carnal, corporeal

body 1 = <u>physique</u>, build, form, figure, shape, frame, constitution 2 = <u>torso</u>, trunk 3 = <u>corpse</u>, dead body, remains, stiff (*slang*), carcass, cadaver 4 = <u>organization</u>, company, group, society, association, band, congress, institution 5 = <u>main part</u>, matter, material, mass, substance, bulk, essence 6 = <u>expanse</u>, mass, sweep

▆ RELATED WORDS
adjectives: corporal, physical

bog = <u>marsh</u>, swamp, slough, wetlands, fen, mire, quagmire, morass, pakihi (*N.Z.*)

bogey = <u>bugbear</u>, bête noire, horror, nightmare, bugaboo

bogus = <u>fake</u>, false, artificial, forged, imitation, sham, fraudulent, counterfeit ≠ genuine

Bohemian ADJECTIVE *often not cap.*

= <u>unconventional</u>, alternative, artistic, unorthodox, arty (*informal*), offbeat, left bank, nonconformist ≠ conventional

● NOUN *often not cap.* = <u>nonconformist</u>, rebel, radical, eccentric, maverick, hippy, dropout, individualist

boil¹ = <u>simmer</u>, bubble, foam, seethe, fizz, froth, effervesce

boil² = <u>pustule</u>, gathering, swelling, blister, carbuncle

bold 1 = <u>fearless</u>, enterprising, brave, daring, heroic, adventurous, courageous, audacious ≠ timid 2 = <u>impudent</u>, forward, confident, rude, cheeky, brazen, shameless, insolent ≠ shy

bolster = <u>support</u>, help, boost, strengthen, reinforce, shore up, augment

bolt NOUN 1 = <u>pin</u>, rod, peg, rivet 2 = <u>bar</u>, catch, lock, latch, fastener, sliding bar

● VERB 1 = <u>lock</u>, close, bar, secure, fasten, latch 2 = <u>dash</u>, fly 3 = <u>gobble</u>, stuff, wolf, cram, gorge, devour, gulp, guzzle

bomb NOUN = <u>explosive</u>, mine, shell, missile, device, rocket, grenade, torpedo

● VERB = <u>blow up</u>, attack, destroy, assault, shell, blitz, bombard, torpedo

bombard 1 = <u>attack</u>, assault, besiege, beset, assail 2 = <u>bomb</u>, shell, blitz, open fire, strafe, fire upon

bombardment = <u>bombing</u>, attack, assault, shelling, blitz, barrage, fusillade

bond NOUN 1 = <u>tie</u>, union, coupling, link, association, relation, connection, alliance 2 = <u>fastening</u>, tie, chain, cord, shackle, fetter, manacle 3 = <u>agreement</u>, word, promise, contract, guarantee, pledge, obligation, covenant

● VERB 1 = <u>form friendships</u>, connect 2 = <u>fix</u>, hold, bind, connect, glue, stick, paste, fasten

bonus 1 = <u>extra</u>, prize, gift, reward, premium, dividend 2 = <u>advantage</u>, benefit, gain, extra, plus, asset, icing on the cake

book NOUN 1 = <u>work</u>, title, volume, publication, tract, tome 2 = <u>notebook</u>, album, journal, diary, pad, notepad, exercise book, jotter

● VERB = <u>reserve</u>, schedule, engage, organize, charter, arrange for, make reservations

●PHRASES **book in** = <u>register</u>, enter

booklet = <u>brochure</u>, leaflet, hand-out, pamphlet, folder, mailshot, handbill

boom NOUN 1 = <u>expansion</u>, increase,

development, growth, jump, boost, improvement, upsurge ≠ decline **2** = <u>bang</u>, crash, clash, blast, burst, explosion, roar, thunder

● VERB **1** = <u>increase</u>, flourish, grow, develop, expand, strengthen, swell, thrive ≠ fall **2** = <u>bang</u>, roll, crash, blast, explode, roar, thunder, rumble

boon 1 = <u>benefit</u>, blessing, godsend, gift **2** = <u>gift</u>, favour

boost VERB **1** = <u>increase</u>, develop, raise, expand, add to, heighten, enlarge, amplify ≠ decrease

● NOUN **1** = <u>rise</u>, increase, jump, addition, improvement, expansion, upsurge, upturn ≠ fall **2** = <u>encouragement</u>, help

boot = <u>kick</u>, punt, put the boot in(to) (*slang*), drop-kick

border NOUN **1** = <u>frontier</u>, line, limit, bounds, boundary, perimeter, borderline **2** = <u>edge</u>, margin, verge, rim

● VERB = <u>edge</u>, bound, decorate, trim, fringe, rim, hem

bore¹ = <u>drill</u>, mine, sink, tunnel, pierce, penetrate, burrow, puncture

bore² VERB = <u>tire</u>, fatigue, weary, wear out, jade, be tedious, pall on, send to sleep ≠ excite

● NOUN = <u>nuisance</u>, pain (*informal*), yawn (*informal*), anorak (*informal*)

bored = <u>fed up</u>, tired, wearied, uninterested, sick and tired (*informal*), listless, brassed off (*Brit. slang*), hoha (*N.Z.*)

boredom = <u>tedium</u>, apathy, weariness, monotony, sameness, ennui, flatness, world-weariness ≠ excitement

boring = <u>uninteresting</u>, dull, tedious, tiresome, monotonous, flat, humdrum, mind-numbing

borrow 1 = <u>take on loan</u>, touch (someone) for (*slang*), scrounge (*informal*), cadge, use temporarily ≠ lend **2** = <u>steal</u>, take, copy, adopt, pinch (*informal*)

boss NOUN = <u>manager</u>, head, leader, director, chief, master, employer, supervisor, baas (*S. African*)

● PHRASES **boss someone around** (*Informal*) = <u>order around</u>, dominate, bully, oppress, push around (*slang*)

bother VERB **1** = <u>trouble</u>, concern, worry, alarm, disturb, disconcert, perturb **2** = <u>pester</u>, plague, harass, hassle (*informal*), inconvenience ≠ help

● NOUN = <u>trouble</u>, problem, worry,

difficulty, fuss, irritation, hassle (*informal*), nuisance, uphill (*S. African*) ≠ help

bottle shop (*Austral. & N.Z.*) = <u>off-licence</u> (*Brit.*), liquor store (*U.S. & Canad.*), bottle store (*S. African*), package store (*U.S. & Canad.*), offie or offy (*Brit. informal*)

bottle store (*S. African*) = <u>off-licence</u> (*Brit.*), liquor store (*U.S. & Canad.*), bottle shop (*Austral. & N.Z.*), package store (*U.S. & Canad.*), offie or offy (*Brit. informal*)

bottom NOUN **1** = <u>lowest part</u>, base, foot, bed, floor, foundation, depths ≠ top **2** = <u>underside</u>, sole, underneath, lower side **3** = <u>buttocks</u>, behind (*informal*), rear, backside, rump, seat, posterior

● ADJECTIVE = <u>lowest</u>, last ≠ higher

bounce VERB **1** = <u>rebound</u>, recoil, ricochet **2** = <u>bound</u>, spring, jump, leap, skip, gambol

● NOUN **1** = <u>springiness</u>, give, spring, resilience, elasticity, recoil **2** (*Informal*) = <u>life</u>, go (*informal*), energy, zip (*informal*), vigour, exuberance, dynamism, vivacity

bound¹ 1 = <u>compelled</u>, obliged, forced, committed, pledged, constrained, beholden, duty-bound **2** = <u>tied</u>, fixed, secured, attached, tied up, fastened, pinioned **3** = <u>certain</u>, sure, fated, doomed, destined

bound² 1 = <u>surround</u>, confine, enclose, encircle, hem in, demarcate **2** = <u>limit</u>, restrict, confine, restrain, circumscribe

bound³ VERB = <u>leap</u>, bob, spring, jump, bounce, skip, vault

● NOUN = <u>leap</u>, bob, spring, jump, bounce, hurdle, skip, vault

boundary 1 = <u>frontier</u>, edge, border, barrier, margin, brink **2** = <u>edges</u>, limits, fringes, extremities **3** = <u>dividing line</u>, borderline

bounds = <u>boundary</u>, limit, edge, border, confine, verge, rim, perimeter

bouquet 1 = <u>bunch of flowers</u>, spray, garland, wreath, posy, buttonhole, corsage, nosegay **2** = <u>aroma</u>, smell, scent, perfume, fragrance, savour, odour, redolence

bourgeois = <u>middle-class</u>, traditional, conventional, materialistic, hidebound

bout 1 = <u>period</u>, term, fit, spell, turn, interval **2** = <u>round</u>, series, session, cycle, sequence, stint **3** = <u>fight</u>, match, competition, struggle, contest, set-to, encounter, engagement

bow¹ VERB = <u>bend</u>, bob, nod, stoop, droop, genuflect
● NOUN = <u>bending</u>, bob, nod, obeisance, kowtow, genuflection

bow² (*Nautical*) = <u>prow</u>, head, stem, fore, beak

bowels 1 = <u>guts</u>, insides (*informal*), intestines, innards (*informal*), entrails, viscera, vitals 2 = <u>depths</u>, hold, inside, deep, interior, core, belly

bowl¹ = <u>basin</u>, plate, dish, vessel

bowl² = <u>throw</u>, hurl, launch, cast, pitch, toss, fling, chuck (*informal*)

box¹ NOUN = <u>container</u>, case, chest, trunk, pack, package, carton, casket
● VERB = <u>pack</u>, package, wrap, encase, bundle up

box² = <u>fight</u>, spar, exchange blows

boxer = <u>fighter</u>, pugilist, prizefighter

boy = <u>lad</u>, kid (*informal*), youth, fellow, youngster, schoolboy, junior, stripling

boycott = <u>embargo</u>, reject, snub, black ≠ support

boyfriend = <u>sweetheart</u>, man, lover, beloved, admirer, suitor, beau, date

brace VERB 1 = <u>steady</u>, support, secure, stabilize 2 = <u>support</u>, strengthen, steady, reinforce, bolster, fortify, buttress
● NOUN = <u>support</u>, stay, prop, bolster, bracket, reinforcement, strut, truss

bracing = <u>refreshing</u>, fresh, stimulating, crisp, brisk, exhilarating, invigorating ≠ tiring

brain = <u>intelligence</u>, understanding, sense, intellect

brake NOUN = <u>control</u>, check, curb, restraint, constraint, rein
● VERB = <u>slow</u>, decelerate, reduce speed

branch 1 = <u>bough</u>, shoot, arm, spray, limb, sprig, offshoot 2 = <u>office</u>, department, unit, wing, chapter, bureau 3 = <u>division</u>, part, section, subdivision, subsection 4 = <u>discipline</u>, section, subdivision

brand NOUN 1 = <u>trademark</u> 2 = <u>label</u>, mark, sign, stamp, symbol, logo, trademark, marker
● VERB 1 = <u>stigmatize</u>, mark, expose, denounce, disgrace, discredit, censure 2 = <u>mark</u>, burn, label, stamp, scar

brash = <u>bold</u>, rude, cocky, pushy (*informal*), brazen, impertinent, insolent, impudent ≠ timid

brave ADJECTIVE = <u>courageous</u>, daring, bold, heroic, adventurous, fearless, resolute, audacious ≠ timid
● VERB = <u>confront</u>, face, suffer, tackle, endure, defy, withstand, stand up to ≠ give in to

bravery = <u>courage</u>, nerve, daring, pluck, spirit, fortitude, heroism, mettle ≠ cowardice

brawl NOUN = <u>fight</u>, clash, fray, skirmish, scuffle, punch-up (*Brit. informal*), fracas, altercation, biffo (*Austral. slang*)
● VERB = <u>fight</u>, scrap (*informal*), wrestle, tussle, scuffle

breach 1 = <u>nonobservance</u>, abuse, violation, infringement, trespass, transgression, contravention, infraction ≠ compliance 2 = <u>opening</u>, crack, split, gap, rift, rupture, cleft, fissure

bread 1 = <u>food</u>, fare, kai (*N.Z. informal*), nourishment, sustenance 2 (*Slang*) = <u>money</u>, cash, dough (*slang*)

breadth 1 = <u>width</u>, spread, span, latitude, broadness, wideness 2 = <u>extent</u>, range, scale, scope, compass, expanse

break VERB 1 = <u>shatter</u>, separate, destroy, crack, snap, smash, crush, fragment ≠ repair 2 = <u>fracture</u>, crack, smash 3 = <u>burst</u>, tear, split 4 = <u>disobey</u>, breach, defy, violate, disregard, flout, infringe, contravene ≠ obey 5 = <u>stop</u>, cut, suspend, interrupt, cut short, discontinue 6 = <u>disturb</u>, interrupt 7 = <u>end</u>, stop, cut, drop, give up, abandon, suspend, interrupt 8 = <u>weaken</u>, undermine, tame, subdue, demoralize, dispirit 9 = <u>be revealed</u>, be published, be announced, be made public, be proclaimed, be let out 10 = <u>reveal</u>, tell, announce, declare, disclose, proclaim, make known 11 = <u>beat</u>, top, better, exceed, go beyond, excel, surpass, outstrip
● NOUN 1 = <u>fracture</u>, opening, tear, hole, split, crack, gap, fissure 2 = <u>interval</u>, pause, interlude, intermission 3 = <u>holiday</u>, leave, vacation, time off, recess, awayday 4 (*Informal*) = <u>stroke of luck</u>, chance, opportunity, advantage, fortune, opening
● PHRASES **break off** = <u>stop talking</u>, pause ◆ **break out** = <u>begin</u>, start, happen, occur, arise, set in, commence, spring up ◆ **break something off** = <u>detach</u>, separate, divide, cut off, pull off, sever, part, remove ◆ **break something up** = <u>stop</u>, end, suspend, dismantle, terminate, disband, diffuse ◆ **break up** 1 = <u>finish</u>, be

suspended, adjourn **2** = <u>split up</u>, separate, part, divorce

breakdown = <u>collapse</u>

break-in = <u>burglary</u>, robbery, breaking and entering

breakthrough = <u>development</u>, advance, progress, discovery, find, invention, step forward, leap forwards

breast = <u>bosom(s)</u>, front, chest, bust

breath = <u>inhalation</u>, breathing, pant, gasp, gulp, wheeze, exhalation, respiration

breathe 1 = <u>inhale and exhale</u>, pant, gasp, puff, gulp, wheeze, respire, draw in breath **2** = <u>whisper</u>, sigh, murmur

breathless 1 = <u>out of breath</u>, panting, gasping, gulping, wheezing, short-winded **2** = <u>excited</u>, curious, eager, enthusiastic, impatient, on tenterhooks, in suspense

breathtaking = <u>amazing</u>, exciting, stunning (*informal*), impressive, thrilling, magnificent, astonishing, sensational

breed NOUN **1** = <u>variety</u>, race, stock, type, species, strain, pedigree **2** = <u>kind</u>, sort, type, variety, brand, stamp

● VERB **1** = <u>rear</u>, tend, keep, raise, maintain, farm, look after, care for **2** = <u>reproduce</u>, multiply, propagate, procreate, produce offspring, bear young, bring forth young **3** = <u>produce</u>, cause, create, generate, bring about, arouse, give rise to, stir up

breeding = <u>refinement</u>, culture, taste, manners, polish, courtesy, sophistication, cultivation

breeze NOUN = <u>light wind</u>, air, draught, gust, waft, zephyr, breath of wind, current of air

● VERB = <u>sweep</u>, move briskly, pass, sail, hurry, glide, flit

brew VERB **1** = <u>boil</u>, make, soak, steep, stew, infuse (*tea*) **2** = <u>make</u>, ferment **3** = <u>start</u>, develop, gather, foment **4** = <u>develop</u>, form, gather, foment

● NOUN = <u>drink</u>, preparation, mixture, blend, liquor, beverage, infusion, concoction

bribe NOUN = <u>inducement</u>, pay-off (*informal*), sweetener (*slang*), kickback (*U.S.*), backhander (*slang*), enticement, allurement

● VERB = <u>buy off</u>, reward, pay off (*informal*), corrupt, suborn, grease the palm *or* hand of (*slang*)

bribery = <u>corruption</u>, inducement, buying off, payola (*informal*), palm-greasing

(*slang*)

bridge NOUN = <u>arch</u>, span, viaduct, flyover, overpass

● VERB **1** = <u>span</u>, cross **2** = <u>reconcile</u>, resolve

brief ADJECTIVE = <u>short</u>, quick, fleeting, swift, short-lived, momentary, ephemeral, transitory ≠ long

● VERB = <u>inform</u>, prime, prepare, advise, fill in (*informal*), instruct, put in the picture (*informal*), keep (someone) posted

● NOUN = <u>summary</u>, résumé, outline, sketch, abstract, digest, epitome, rundown

briefing 1 = <u>conference</u>, priming **2** = <u>instructions</u>, information, priming, directions, preparation, guidance, rundown

briefly 1 = <u>quickly</u>, shortly, hastily, momentarily, hurriedly **2** = <u>in outline</u>, in brief, in a nutshell, concisely

brigade 1 = <u>corps</u>, company, force, unit, division, troop, squad, team **2** = <u>group</u>, band, squad, organization

bright 1 = <u>vivid</u>, rich, brilliant, glowing, colourful **2** = <u>shining</u>, glowing, dazzling, gleaming, shimmering, radiant, luminous, lustrous **3** = <u>intelligent</u>, smart, clever, aware, sharp, enlightened, astute, wide-awake ≠ stupid **4** = <u>clever</u>, smart, ingenious **5** = <u>sunny</u>, clear, fair, pleasant, lucid, cloudless, unclouded ≠ cloudy

brighten 1 = <u>light up</u>, shine, glow, gleam, lighten ≠ dim **2** = <u>enliven</u>, animate, make brighter, vitalize **3** = <u>become brighter</u>, light up, glow, gleam

brilliance *or* **brilliancy 1** = <u>cleverness</u>, talent, wisdom, distinction, genius, excellence, greatness, inventiveness ≠ stupidity **2** = <u>brightness</u>, intensity, sparkle, dazzle, lustre, radiance, luminosity, vividness ≠ darkness **3** = <u>splendour</u>, glamour, grandeur, magnificence, éclat, illustriousness

brilliant 1 = <u>intelligent</u>, sharp, intellectual, clever, profound, penetrating, inventive, perspicacious ≠ stupid **2** = <u>expert</u>, masterly, talented, gifted, accomplished ≠ untalented **3** = <u>splendid</u>, famous, celebrated, outstanding, superb, magnificent, glorious, notable **4** = <u>bright</u>, shining, intense, sparkling, glittering, dazzling, vivid, radiant ≠ dark

brim NOUN = <u>rim</u>, edge, border, lip, margin, verge, brink

● VERB **1** = <u>be full</u>, spill, well over, run over

2 = <u>fill</u>, well over, fill up, overflow
bring VERB **1** = <u>fetch</u>, take, carry, bear, transfer, deliver, transport, convey **2** = <u>take</u>, guide, conduct, escort **3** = <u>cause</u>, produce, create, effect, occasion, result in, contribute to, inflict
● PHRASES **bring someone up** = <u>rear</u>, raise, support, train, develop, teach, breed, foster ◆ **bring something about** = <u>cause</u>, produce, create, effect, achieve, generate, accomplish, give rise to ◆ **bring something off** = <u>accomplish</u>, achieve, perform, succeed, execute, pull off, carry off ◆ **bring something up** = <u>mention</u>, raise, introduce, point out, refer to, allude to, broach
brink = <u>edge</u>, limit, border, lip, margin, boundary, skirt, frontier
brisk 1 = <u>quick</u>, lively, energetic, active, vigorous, bustling, sprightly, spry ≠ slow **2** = <u>short</u>, brief, blunt, abrupt, terse, gruff, brusque, monosyllabic
briskly = <u>quickly</u>, smartly, promptly, rapidly, readily, actively, efficiently, energetically
bristle NOUN = <u>hair</u>, spine, thorn, whisker, barb, stubble, prickle
● VERB **1** = <u>stand up</u>, rise, stand on end **2** = <u>be angry</u>, rage, seethe, flare up, bridle, see red
brittle = <u>fragile</u>, delicate, crisp, crumbling, frail, crumbly, breakable, friable ≠ tough
broad 1 = <u>wide</u>, large, ample, generous, expansive **2** = <u>large</u>, huge, vast, extensive, ample, spacious, expansive, roomy ≠ narrow **3** = <u>full</u>, general, comprehensive, complete, wide, sweeping, wide-ranging, thorough **4** = <u>universal</u>, general, common, wide, sweeping, worldwide, widespread, wide-ranging **5** = <u>general</u>, loose, vague, approximate, indefinite, ill-defined, inexact, unspecific
broadcast NOUN = <u>transmission</u>, show, programme, telecast
● VERB **1** = <u>transmit</u>, show, air, radio, cable, beam, send out, relay **2** = <u>make public</u>, report, announce, publish, spread, advertise, proclaim, circulate
broaden = <u>expand</u>, increase, develop, spread, extend, stretch, swell, supplement ≠ restrict
brochure = <u>booklet</u>, advertisement, leaflet, hand-out, circular, pamphlet, folder, mailshot

broekies (*S. African informal*) = <u>underpants</u>, pants, briefs, drawers, knickers, panties, boxer shorts, Y-fronts®, underdaks (*Austral. slang*)
broke (*Informal*) = <u>penniless</u>, short, ruined, bust (*informal*), bankrupt, impoverished, in the red, insolvent ≠ rich
broken 1 = <u>interrupted</u>, incomplete, erratic, intermittent, fragmentary, spasmodic, discontinuous **2** = <u>imperfect</u>, halting, hesitating, stammering, disjointed **3** = <u>smashed</u>, burst, shattered, fragmented, fractured, severed, ruptured, separated **4** = <u>defective</u>, not working, imperfect, out of order, on the blink (*slang*), kaput (*informal*)
broker = <u>dealer</u>, agent, trader, supplier, merchant, negotiator, mediator, intermediary
bronze = <u>reddish-brown</u>, copper, tan, rust, chestnut, brownish
brood NOUN **1** = <u>offspring</u>, issue, clutch, litter, progeny **2** = <u>children</u>, family, nearest and dearest, flesh and blood, ainga (*N.Z.*)
● VERB = <u>think</u>, obsess, muse, ponder, agonize, mull over, mope, ruminate
brook = <u>stream</u>, burn (*Scot. & Northern English*), rivulet, beck, watercourse, rill
brother 1 = <u>male sibling</u> **2** = <u>monk</u>, cleric, friar, religious

▦ RELATED WORD
adjective: fraternal

brotherly = <u>fraternal</u>, friendly, neighbourly, sympathetic, affectionate, benevolent, kind, amicable
brown ADJECTIVE **1** = <u>brunette</u>, bay, coffee, chocolate, chestnut, hazel, dun, auburn **2** = <u>tanned</u>, bronze, tan, sunburnt
● VERB = <u>fry</u>, cook, grill, sear, sauté
browse 1 = <u>skim</u>, scan, glance at, survey, look through, look round, dip into, leaf through **2** = <u>graze</u>, eat, feed, nibble
bruise NOUN = <u>discoloration</u>, mark, injury, blemish, contusion
● VERB **1** = <u>hurt</u>, injure, mark **2** = <u>damage</u>, mark, mar, discolour
brush¹ NOUN **1** = <u>broom</u>, sweeper, besom **2** = <u>conflict</u>, clash, confrontation, skirmish, tussle **3** = <u>encounter</u>, meeting, confrontation, rendezvous
● VERB **1** = <u>clean</u>, wash, polish, buff **2** = <u>touch</u>, sweep, kiss, stroke, glance, flick, scrape, graze
● PHRASES **brush someone off**

(*Slang*) = <u>ignore</u>, reject, dismiss, snub, disregard, scorn, disdain, spurn ♦ **brush something up** *or* **brush up on something** = <u>revise</u>, study, go over, cram, polish up, read up on, relearn, bone up on (*informal*)

brush² = <u>shrubs</u>, bushes, scrub, undergrowth, thicket, copse, brushwood

brutal 1 = <u>cruel</u>, savage, vicious, ruthless, callous, sadistic, heartless, inhuman ≠ kind **2** = <u>harsh</u>, tough, severe, rough, rude, indifferent, insensitive, callous ≠ sensitive

brutality = <u>cruelty</u>, atrocity, ferocity, savagery, ruthlessness, barbarism, inhumanity, viciousness

bubble NOUN = <u>air ball</u>, drop, bead, blister, blob, droplet, globule
● VERB **1** = <u>boil</u>, seethe **2** = <u>foam</u>, fizz, froth, percolate, effervesce **3** = <u>gurgle</u>, splash, murmur, trickle, ripple, babble, burble, lap

bubbly 1 = <u>lively</u>, happy, excited, animated, merry, bouncy, elated, sparky **2** = <u>frothy</u>, sparkling, fizzy, effervescent, carbonated, foamy

buckle NOUN = <u>fastener</u>, catch, clip, clasp, hasp
● VERB **1** = <u>fasten</u>, close, secure, hook, clasp **2** = <u>distort</u>, bend, warp, crumple, contort **3** = <u>collapse</u>, bend, twist, fold, give way, subside, cave in, crumple

bud NOUN = <u>shoot</u>, branch, sprout, sprig, offshoot
● VERB = <u>develop</u>, grow, shoot, sprout, burgeon, burst forth

budding = <u>developing</u>, beginning, growing, promising, potential, burgeoning, fledgling, embryonic

budge 1 = <u>move</u>, stir **2** = <u>dislodge</u>, move, push, transfer, shift, stir

budget NOUN = <u>allowance</u>, means, funds, income, finances, resources, allocation
● VERB = <u>plan</u>, estimate, allocate, cost, ration, apportion

buff¹ ADJECTIVE = <u>fawn</u>, tan, beige, yellowish, straw-coloured, sand-coloured, yellowish-brown
● VERB = <u>polish</u>, smooth, brush, shine, rub, wax, brighten, burnish

buff² (*Informal*) = <u>expert</u>, fan, addict, enthusiast, admirer, devotee, connoisseur, aficionado, fundi (*S. African*)

buffer = <u>safeguard</u>, screen, shield, cushion, intermediary, bulwark

buffet 1 = <u>smorgasbord</u> **2** = <u>snack bar</u>,

café, cafeteria, brasserie, refreshment counter

bug NOUN **1** (*Informal*) = <u>illness</u>, disease, virus, infection, disorder, sickness, ailment, affliction **2** = <u>fault</u>, error, defect, flaw, glitch, gremlin
● VERB **1** = <u>tap</u>, eavesdrop, listen in on **2** (*Informal*) = <u>annoy</u>, bother, disturb, irritate, hassle (*informal*), pester, vex, get on your nerves (*informal*)

build VERB = <u>construct</u>, make, raise, put up, assemble, erect, fabricate, form ≠ demolish
● NOUN = <u>physique</u>, form, body, figure, shape, structure, frame

building = <u>structure</u>, house, construction, dwelling, erection, edifice, domicile

build-up = <u>increase</u>, development, growth, expansion, accumulation, enlargement, escalation

bulge VERB **1** = <u>swell out</u>, project, expand, stick out, protrude, puff out, distend **2** = <u>stick out</u>, stand out, protrude
● NOUN **1** = <u>lump</u>, swelling, bump, projection, hump, protuberance, protrusion ≠ hollow **2** = <u>increase</u>, rise, boost, surge, intensification

bulk 1 = <u>size</u>, volume, dimensions, magnitude, substance, immensity, largeness **2** = <u>weight</u>, size, mass, heaviness, poundage **3** = <u>majority</u>, mass, most, body, best part, lion's share, better part, preponderance

bullet = <u>projectile</u>, ball, shot, missile, slug, pellet

bulletin = <u>report</u>, account, statement, message, communication, announcement, dispatch, communiqué

bully NOUN = <u>persecutor</u>, tough, oppressor, tormentor, bully boy, browbeater, coercer, ruffian
● VERB **1** = <u>persecute</u>, intimidate, torment, oppress, pick on, victimize, terrorize, push around (*slang*) **2** = <u>force</u>, coerce, browbeat, hector, domineer

bump VERB **1** = <u>knock</u>, hit, strike, crash, smash, slam, bang **2** = <u>jerk</u>, shake, bounce, rattle, jog, lurch, jolt
● NOUN **1** = <u>knock</u>, blow, impact, collision, thump **2** = <u>thud</u>, crash, knock, bang, smack, thump **3** = <u>lump</u>, swelling, bulge, hump, nodule, protuberance, contusion

bumper = <u>exceptional</u>, excellent, exo (*Austral. slang*), massive, jumbo (*informal*), abundant, whopping (*informal*), bountiful

bunch NOUN **1** = <u>group</u>, band, crowd, party, team, gathering, gang, flock **2** = <u>bouquet</u>, sheaf **3** = <u>cluster</u>, clump

●PHRASES **bunch together** *or* **up** = <u>group</u>, mass, collect, assemble, cluster, huddle

bundle NOUN = <u>bunch</u>, group, collection, mass, pile, stack, heap, batch

● VERB = <u>push</u>, thrust, shove, throw, rush, hurry, jostle, hustle

●PHRASES **bundle someone up** = <u>wrap up</u>, swathe

bungle = <u>mess up</u>, blow (*slang*), ruin, spoil, blunder, botch, make a mess of, muff, crool *or* cruel (*Austral. slang*) ≠ accomplish

bungling = <u>incompetent</u>, blundering, clumsy, inept, cack-handed (*informal*), maladroit, ham-fisted (*informal*), unco (*Austral. slang*)

bunk *or* **bunkum** (*Informal*) = <u>nonsense</u>, rubbish, garbage (*informal*), hot air (*informal*), twaddle, moonshine, baloney (*informal*), hogwash, bizzo (*Austral. slang*), bull's wool (*Austral. & N.Z. slang*), kak (*S. African taboo slang*)

buoy = <u>float</u>, guide, signal, marker, beacon

buoyant ADJECTIVE = <u>cheerful</u>, happy, upbeat (*informal*), carefree, jaunty, chirpy (*informal*), light-hearted ≠ gloomy

● ADJECTIVE = <u>floating</u>, light

burden NOUN **1** = <u>trouble</u>, worry, weight, responsibility, strain, affliction, onus, millstone **2** = <u>load</u>, weight, cargo, freight, consignment, encumbrance

● VERB = <u>weigh down</u>, worry, load, tax, bother, handicap, oppress, inconvenience

bureau 1 = <u>agency</u> **2** = <u>office</u>, department, section, branch, station, unit, division, subdivision **3** = <u>desk</u>, writing desk

bureaucracy 1 = <u>government</u>, officials, authorities, administration, the system, civil service, corridors of power **2** = <u>red tape</u>, regulations, officialdom

bureaucrat = <u>official</u>, officer, administrator, civil servant, public servant, functionary, mandarin

burglar = <u>housebreaker</u>, thief, robber, pilferer, filcher, cat burglar, sneak thief

burglary = <u>breaking and entering</u>, housebreaking, break-in

burial = <u>funeral</u>, interment, obsequies, entombment, exequies

burn 1 = <u>be on fire</u>, blaze, be ablaze,

smoke, flame, glow, flare, go up in flames **2** = <u>set on fire</u>, light, ignite, kindle, incinerate **3** = <u>scorch</u>, toast, sear, char, singe **4** = <u>be passionate</u>, be aroused, be inflamed **5** = <u>seethe</u>, fume, be angry, simmer, smoulder

burning 1 = <u>intense</u>, passionate, eager, ardent, fervent, impassioned, vehement ≠ mild **2** = <u>blazing</u>, fiery, smouldering, glowing **3** = <u>flashing</u>, blazing, flaming, gleaming, fiery **4** = <u>crucial</u>, important, pressing, significant, essential, vital, critical, acute

burrow NOUN = <u>hole</u>, shelter, tunnel, den, lair, retreat

● VERB **1** = <u>dig</u>, tunnel, excavate **2** = <u>delve</u>, search, probe, ferret, rummage, forage, fossick (*Austral. & N.Z.*)

burst VERB **1** = <u>explode</u>, blow up, break, split, crack, shatter, puncture, rupture **2** = <u>rush</u>, run, break, break out, erupt, spout, gush forth **3** = <u>barge</u>, charge, rush, shove

● NOUN **1** = <u>rush</u>, surge, outbreak, outburst, spate, gush, torrent, spurt **2** = <u>explosion</u>, crack, blast, bang, discharge

● ADJECTIVE = <u>ruptured</u>, flat, punctured, split, rent

bury 1 = <u>inter</u>, lay to rest, entomb, consign to the grave, inhume ≠ dig up **2** = <u>hide</u>, cover, conceal, stash (*informal*), secrete, stow away ≠ uncover **3** = <u>sink</u>, embed, immerse, enfold **4** = <u>forget</u>

bush NOUN = <u>shrub</u>, plant, hedge, thicket, shrubbery

● PHRASES **the bush** = <u>the wilds</u>, brush, scrub, woodland, backwoods, scrubland

business 1 = <u>trade</u>, selling, industry, manufacturing, commerce, dealings **2** = <u>establishment</u>, company, firm, concern, organization, corporation, venture, enterprise **3** = <u>profession</u>, work, job, line, trade, career, function, employment **4** = <u>matter</u>, issue, subject, point, problem, responsibility, task, duty **5** = <u>concern</u>, affair

businessman = <u>executive</u>, director, manager, merchant, capitalist, administrator, entrepreneur, tycoon

bust¹ = <u>bosom</u>, breasts, chest, front

bust² (*Informal*) VERB **1** = <u>break</u>, smash, split, burst, shatter, fracture, rupture **2** = <u>arrest</u>, catch, raid

● PHRASES **go bust** = <u>go bankrupt</u>, fail, be

ruined, become insolvent

bustle VERB = <u>hurry</u>, rush, fuss, hasten, scuttle, scurry, scamper ≠ idle

● NOUN = <u>activity</u>, to-do, stir, excitement, fuss, flurry, commotion, ado ≠ inactivity

bustling = <u>busy</u>, full, crowded, active, lively, buzzing, humming, swarming

busy ADJECTIVE 1 = <u>active</u>, industrious, rushed off your feet ≠ idle 2 = <u>occupied with</u>, working, engaged in, on duty, employed in, hard at work ≠ unoccupied 3 = <u>hectic</u>, full, exacting, energetic

●PHRASES **busy yourself** = <u>occupy yourself</u>, be engrossed, immerse yourself, involve yourself, absorb yourself, employ yourself, engage yourself

but CONJUNCTION = <u>however</u>, still, yet, nevertheless

● PREPOSITION = <u>except (for)</u>, save, bar, barring, excepting, excluding, with the exception of

● ADVERB = <u>only</u>, just, simply, merely

butcher NOUN = <u>murderer</u>, killer, slaughterer, slayer, destroyer, executioner, cut-throat, exterminator

● VERB 1 = <u>slaughter</u>, prepare, carve, cut up, dress, cut, clean, joint 2 = <u>kill</u>, slaughter, massacre, destroy, cut down, assassinate, slay, liquidate

butt¹ 1 = <u>end</u>, handle, shaft, stock, shank, hilt, haft 2 = <u>stub</u>, tip, leftover, fag end (*informal*)

butt² = <u>target</u>, victim, dupe, laughing stock, Aunt Sally

butt³ VERB = <u>knock</u>, push, bump, thrust, ram, shove, poke, prod

●PHRASES **butt in** 1 = <u>interfere</u>, meddle, intrude, heckle, barge in (*informal*), stick your nose in, put your oar in 2 = <u>interrupt</u>, cut in, break in, chip in (*informal*)

butt⁴ = <u>cask</u>, barrel

butterfly

  ▇▇▇RELATED WORDS

young: caterpillar, chrysalis *or* chrysalid

enthusiast: lepidopterist

buy VERB = <u>purchase</u>, get, pay for, obtain, acquire, invest in, shop for, procure ≠ sell

● NOUN = <u>purchase</u>, deal, bargain, acquisition, steal (*informal*), snip (*informal*), giveaway

by PREPOSITION 1 = <u>through</u>, through the agency of 2 = <u>via</u>, over, by way of 3 = <u>near</u>, past, along, close to, closest to, neighbouring, next to, beside

● ADVERB = <u>nearby</u>, close, handy, at hand, within reach

bypass 1 = <u>get round</u>, avoid 2 = <u>go round</u>, circumvent, depart from, deviate from, pass round, detour round ≠ cross

C

cab = <u>taxi</u>, minicab, taxicab, hackney carriage

cabin 1 = <u>room</u>, berth, quarters, compartment 2 = <u>hut</u>, shed, cottage, lodge, shack, chalet, shanty, whare (*N.Z.*)

cabinet 1 = <u>cupboard</u>, case, locker, dresser, closet, press, chiffonier 2 *often cap.* = <u>council</u>, committee, administration, ministry, assembly, board

cad (*Old-fashioned, informal*) = <u>scoundrel</u> (*slang*), rat (*informal*), bounder (*Brit. old-fashioned slang*), rotter (*slang, chiefly Brit.*), heel

café = <u>snack bar</u>, restaurant, cafeteria, coffee shop, brasserie, coffee bar, tearoom, lunchroom

cage = <u>enclosure</u>, pen, coop, hutch, pound

cake = <u>block</u>, bar, slab, lump, cube, loaf, mass

calculated = <u>deliberate</u>, planned, considered, intended, intentional, designed, aimed, purposeful ≠ unplanned

calculating = <u>scheming</u>, sharp, shrewd, cunning, sly, devious, manipulative, crafty ≠ direct

calculation 1 = <u>computation</u>, working out, reckoning, estimate, forecast, judgment, result, answer 2 = <u>planning</u>, intention, deliberation, foresight, contrivance, forethought, premeditation

calibre *or* (*U.S.*) **caliber** 1 = <u>worth</u>, quality, ability, talent, capacity, merit, distinction, stature 2 = <u>standard</u>, level, quality, grade 3 = <u>diameter</u>, bore, gauge, measure

call VERB 1 = <u>name</u>, entitle, dub, designate, term, style, label, describe as 2 = <u>cry</u>, shout,

scream, yell, whoop ≠ whisper **3** = <u>phone</u>, telephone, ring (up) (*informal, chiefly Brit.*) **4** = <u>hail</u>, summon **5** = <u>summon</u>, gather, rally, assemble, muster, convene ≠ dismiss **6** = <u>waken</u>, arouse, rouse
● NOUN **1** = <u>visit</u> **2** = <u>request</u>, order, demand, appeal, notice, command, invitation, plea **3** (usually used in a negative construction) = <u>need</u>, cause, reason, grounds, occasion, excuse, justification **4** = <u>attraction</u>, pull (*informal*), appeal, lure, allure, magnetism **5** = <u>cry</u>, shout, scream, yell, whoop ≠ whisper
● PHRASES **call for someone** = <u>fetch</u>, pick up, collect ✦ **call for something 1** = <u>demand</u>, order, request, insist on, cry out for **2** = <u>require</u>, need, involve, demand, occasion, entail, necessitate
calling = <u>profession</u>, trade, career, mission, vocation, life's work
calm ADJECTIVE **1** = <u>cool</u>, relaxed, composed, sedate, collected, dispassionate, unemotional, self-possessed ≠ excited **2** = <u>still</u>, quiet, smooth, mild, serene, tranquil, balmy, windless ≠ rough
● NOUN **1** = <u>peacefulness</u>, peace, serenity **2** = <u>stillness</u>, peace, quiet, hush, serenity, tranquillity, repose, peacefulness **3** = <u>peace</u>, calmness ≠ disturbance
● VERB **1** = <u>soothe</u>, quiet, relax, appease, still, allay, assuage, quieten ≠ excite **2** = <u>placate</u>, hush, pacify, mollify ≠ aggravate
camouflage NOUN **1** = <u>protective colouring</u> **2** = <u>disguise</u>, cover, screen, blind, mask, cloak, masquerade, subterfuge
● VERB = <u>disguise</u>, cover, screen, hide, mask, conceal, obscure, veil ≠ reveal
camp[1] = <u>camp site</u>, tents, encampment, bivouac, camping ground
camp[2] (*Informal*) = <u>affected</u>, mannered, artificial, posturing, ostentatious, effeminate
campaign 1 = <u>drive</u>, appeal, movement, push (*informal*), offensive, crusade **2** = <u>operation</u>, drive, attack, movement, push, offensive, expedition, crusade
canal = <u>waterway</u>, channel, passage, conduit, duct, watercourse
cancel VERB **1** = <u>call off</u>, drop, forget about **2** = <u>annul</u>, abolish, repeal, abort, do away with, revoke, eliminate
● PHRASES **cancel something out**

= <u>counterbalance</u>, offset, make up for, compensate for, neutralize, nullify, balance out
cancellation 1 = <u>abandonment</u> **2** = <u>annulment</u>, abolition, repeal, elimination, revocation
cancer 1 = <u>growth</u>, tumour, malignancy **2** = <u>evil</u>, corruption, sickness, pestilence
candidate = <u>contender</u>, competitor, applicant, nominee, entrant, claimant, contestant, runner
cannabis = <u>marijuana</u>, pot (*slang*), dope (*slang*), grass (*slang*), hemp, dagga (*S. African*)
cannon = <u>gun</u>, big gun, field gun, mortar
canon 1 = <u>rule</u>, standard, principle, regulation, formula, criterion, dictate, statute **2** = <u>list</u>, index, catalogue, roll
canopy = <u>awning</u>, covering, shade, sunshade
cap 1 (*Informal*) = <u>beat</u>, top, better, exceed, eclipse, surpass, transcend, outstrip **2** = <u>top</u>, crown **3** = <u>complete</u>, crown
capability = <u>ability</u>, means, power, potential, capacity, qualification(s), competence, proficiency ≠ inability
capable 1 = <u>able</u> ≠ incapable **2** = <u>accomplished</u>, qualified, talented, gifted, efficient, competent, proficient ≠ incompetent
capacity 1 = <u>ability</u>, facility, gift, genius, capability, aptitude, aptness, competence *or* competency **2** = <u>size</u>, room, range, space, volume, extent, dimensions, scope **3** = <u>function</u>, position, role, post, office
cape = <u>headland</u>, point, head, peninsula, promontory
capital NOUN = <u>money</u>, funds, investment(s), cash, finances, resources, assets, wealth
● ADJECTIVE (*Old-fashioned*) = <u>first-rate</u>, fine, excellent, superb
capitalism = <u>private enterprise</u>, free enterprise, private ownership, laissez faire *or* laisser faire
capsule 1 = <u>pill</u>, tablet, lozenge **2** (*Botany*) = <u>pod</u>, case, shell, vessel, sheath, receptacle, seed case
captain 1 = <u>leader</u>, boss, master, skipper, head, chief **2** = <u>commander</u>, skipper
captivate = <u>charm</u>, attract, fascinate, entrance, enchant, enthral, beguile, allure ≠ repel
captive ADJECTIVE = <u>confined</u>, caged,

imprisoned, locked up, enslaved, incarcerated, ensnared, subjugated
● NOUN = prisoner, hostage, convict, prisoner of war, detainee, internee

captivity = confinement, custody, detention, imprisonment, incarceration, internment

capture VERB = catch, arrest, take, bag, secure, seize, collar (*informal*), apprehend ≠ release
● NOUN = arrest, catching, trapping, imprisonment, seizure, apprehension, taking, taking captive

car 1 = vehicle, motor, wheels (*informal*), auto (*U.S.*), automobile, jalopy (*informal*), motorcar, machine 2 (*U.S. & Canad.*) = (railway) carriage, coach, cable car, dining car, sleeping car, buffet car, van

cardinal = principal, first, leading, chief, main, central, key, essential ≠ secondary

care VERB = be concerned, mind, bother, be interested, be bothered, give a damn, concern yourself
● NOUN 1 = custody, keeping, control, charge, management, protection, supervision, guardianship 2 = caution, attention, pains, consideration, heed, prudence, vigilance, forethought ≠ carelessness 3 = worry, concern, pressure, trouble, responsibility, stress, anxiety, disquiet ≠ pleasure
● PHRASES **care for someone** 1 = look after, mind, tend, attend, nurse, minister to, watch over 2 = love, desire, be fond of, want, prize ◆ **care for something** or **someone** = like, enjoy, take to, relish, be fond of, be keen on, be partial to ◆ **take care of** 1 = look after, mind, watch, protect, tend, nurse, care for, provide for 2 = deal with, manage, cope with, see to, handle

career NOUN = occupation, calling, employment, pursuit, vocation, livelihood, life's work
● VERB = rush, race, speed, tear, dash, barrel (along) (*informal*, (*chiefly U.S. & Canad.*), bolt, hurtle

careful 1 = cautious, scrupulous, circumspect, chary, thoughtful, discreet ≠ careless 2 = thorough, full, particular, precise, intensive, in-depth, meticulous, conscientious ≠ casual 3 = prudent, sparing, economical, canny, provident, frugal, thrifty

careless 1 = slapdash, irresponsible, sloppy (*informal*), cavalier, offhand, neglectful, slipshod, lackadaisical ≠ careful 2 = negligent, hasty, thoughtless, unthinking, forgetful, absent-minded, remiss ≠ careful 3 = nonchalant, casual, offhand, artless, unstudied ≠ careful

caretaker = warden, keeper, porter, superintendent, curator, custodian, watchman, janitor

cargo = load, goods, contents, shipment, freight, merchandise, baggage, consignment

caricature NOUN = parody, cartoon, distortion, satire, send-up (*Brit. informal*), travesty, takeoff (*informal*), lampoon
● VERB = parody, take off (*informal*), mock, distort, ridicule, mimic, send up (*Brit. informal*), lampoon

carnage = slaughter, murder, massacre, holocaust, havoc, bloodshed, shambles, mass murder

carnival = festival, fair, fête, celebration, gala, jubilee, jamboree, revelry

carol = song, hymn, Christmas song

carp = find fault, complain, criticize, reproach, quibble, cavil, pick holes ≠ praise

carpenter = joiner, cabinet-maker, woodworker

carriage 1 = vehicle, coach, trap, gig, cab, wagon, hackney, conveyance 2 = bearing, posture, gait, deportment, air

carry VERB 1 = convey, take, move, bring, bear, transfer, conduct, transport 2 = transport, take, transfer 3 = transmit, transfer, spread, pass on 4 = win, gain, secure, capture, accomplish
● PHRASES **carry on** 1 = continue, last, endure, persist, keep going, persevere 2 (*Informal*) = make a fuss, misbehave, create (*slang*), raise Cain ◆ **carry something on** = engage in, conduct, carry out, undertake, embark on, enter into ◆ **carry something out** = perform, effect, achieve, realize, implement, fulfil, accomplish, execute

carry-on (*Informal, chiefly Brit.*) = fuss, disturbance, racket, commotion

carton = box, case, pack, package, container

cartoon 1 = drawing, parody, satire, caricature, comic strip, takeoff (*informal*), lampoon, sketch 2 = animation, animated film, animated cartoon

carve 1 = <u>sculpt</u>, cut, chip, whittle, chisel, hew, fashion 2 = <u>etch</u>, engrave

cascade NOUN = <u>waterfall</u>, falls, torrent, flood, shower, fountain, avalanche, deluge
● VERB = <u>flow</u>, fall, flood, pour, plunge, surge, spill, tumble

case¹ 1 = <u>situation</u>, event, circumstance(s), state, position, condition, context, contingency 2 = <u>instance</u>, example, occasion, specimen, occurrence 3 (*Law*) = <u>lawsuit</u>, trial, suit, proceedings, dispute, action

case² 1 = <u>cabinet</u>, box, chest, holder 2 = <u>container</u>, carton, canister, casket, receptacle 3 = <u>suitcase</u>, bag, grip, holdall, portmanteau, valise 4 = <u>crate</u>, box 5 = <u>covering</u>, casing, shell, jacket, envelope, capsule, sheath, wrapper

cash = <u>money</u>, funds, notes, currency, silver, brass (*Northern English dialect*), dough (*slang*), coinage

cast NOUN 1 = <u>actors</u>, company, players, characters, troupe, dramatis personae 2 = <u>type</u>, sort, kind, style, stamp
● VERB 1 = <u>choose</u>, name, pick, select, appoint, assign, allot 2 = <u>bestow</u>, give, level, direct 3 = <u>give out</u>, spread, deposit, shed, distribute, scatter, emit, radiate 4 = <u>throw</u>, launch, pitch, toss, thrust, hurl, fling, sling 5 = <u>mould</u>, set, found, form, model, shape

caste = <u>class</u>, order, rank, status, stratum, social order

castle = <u>fortress</u>, keep, palace, tower, chateau, stronghold, citadel

casual 1 = <u>careless</u>, relaxed, unconcerned, blasé, offhand, nonchalant, lackadaisical ≠ serious 2 = <u>chance</u>, unexpected, random, accidental, incidental ≠ planned 3 = <u>informal</u>, leisure, sporty, non-dressy ≠ formal

casualty 1 = <u>fatality</u>, death, loss, wounded 2 = <u>victim</u>, sufferer

cat = <u>feline</u>, pussy (*informal*), moggy (*slang*), puss (*informal*), ballarat (*Austral. informal*), tabby

adjective: feline
male: tom
female: tabby
young: kitten

catalogue or (*U.S.*) **catalog** NOUN = <u>list</u>, record, schedule, index, register, directory, inventory, gazetteer
● VERB = <u>list</u>, file, index, register, classify, inventory, tabulate, alphabetize

catastrophe = <u>disaster</u>, tragedy, calamity, cataclysm, trouble, adversity, fiasco

catch VERB 1 = <u>capture</u>, arrest, trap, seize, snare, apprehend, ensnare, entrap ≠ free 2 = <u>trap</u>, capture, snare, ensnare, entrap 3 = <u>seize</u>, get, grab, snatch 4 = <u>grab</u>, take, grip, seize, grasp, clutch, lay hold of ≠ release 5 = <u>discover</u>, surprise, find out, expose, detect, catch in the act, take unawares 6 = <u>contract</u>, get, develop, suffer from, incur, succumb to, go down with ≠ escape
● NOUN 1 = <u>fastener</u>, clip, bolt, latch, clasp 2 (*Informal*) = <u>drawback</u>, trick, trap, disadvantage, hitch, snag, stumbling block, fly in the ointment ≠ advantage
● PHRASES **catch on** 1 (*Informal*) = <u>understand</u>, see, find out, grasp, see through, comprehend, twig (*Brit. informal*), get the picture 2 = <u>become popular</u>, take off, become trendy, come into fashion

catching = <u>infectious</u>, contagious, transferable, communicable, transmittable ≠ non-infectious

category = <u>class</u>, grouping, heading, sort, department, type, division, section

cater
● PHRASES **cater for something** or **someone** 1 = <u>provide for</u>, supply, purvey 2 = <u>take into account</u>, consider, bear in mind, make allowance for, have regard for

cattle = <u>cows</u>, stock, beasts, livestock, bovines

adjective: bovine
collective nouns: drove, herd

cause NOUN 1 = <u>origin</u>, source, spring, agent, maker, producer, root, beginning ≠ result 2 = <u>reason</u>, call, need, grounds, basis, incentive, motive, motivation 3 = <u>aim</u>, movement, principle, ideal, enterprise
● VERB = <u>produce</u>, create, lead to, result in, generate, induce, bring about, give rise to ≠ prevent

caution NOUN 1 = <u>care</u>, discretion, heed, prudence, vigilance, alertness, forethought, circumspection ≠ carelessness 2 = <u>reprimand</u>, warning, injunction, admonition

• VERB 1 = <u>warn</u>, urge, advise, alert, tip off, forewarn 2 = <u>reprimand</u>, warn, admonish, give an injunction to

cautious = <u>careful</u>, guarded, wary, tentative, prudent, judicious, circumspect, cagey (*informal*) ≠ careless

cavalry = <u>horsemen</u>, horse, mounted troops ≠ infantrymen

cave = <u>hollow</u>, cavern, grotto, den, cavity

cavity = <u>hollow</u>, hole, gap, pit, dent, crater

cease 1 = <u>stop</u>, end, finish, come to an end ≠ start 2 = <u>discontinue</u>, end, stop, finish, conclude, halt, terminate, break off ≠ begin

celebrate 1 = <u>rejoice</u>, party, enjoy yourself, carouse, live it up (*informal*), make merry, put the flags out, kill the fatted calf 2 = <u>commemorate</u>, honour, observe, toast, drink to, keep 3 = <u>perform</u>, observe, preside over, officiate at, solemnize

celebrated = <u>renowned</u>, popular, famous, distinguished, well-known, prominent, acclaimed, notable ≠ unknown

celebration 1 = <u>party</u>, festival, gala, jubilee, festivity, revelry, red-letter day, merrymaking 2 = <u>commemoration</u>, honouring, remembrance 3 = <u>performance</u>, observance, solemnization

celebrity 1 = <u>personality</u>, star, superstar, big name, dignitary, luminary, big shot (*informal*), V.I.P. ≠ nobody 2 = <u>fame</u>, reputation, distinction, prestige, prominence, stardom, renown, repute ≠ obscurity

cell 1 = <u>room</u>, chamber, lock-up, compartment, cavity, cubicle, dungeon, stall 2 = <u>unit</u>, group, section, core, nucleus, caucus, coterie

cement NOUN 1 = <u>mortar</u>, plaster, paste 2 = <u>sealant</u>, glue, gum, adhesive

• VERB = <u>stick</u>, join, bond, attach, seal, glue, plaster, weld

cemetery = <u>graveyard</u>, churchyard, burial ground, necropolis, God's acre

censor = <u>expurgate</u>, cut, blue-pencil, bowdlerize

censure VERB = <u>criticize</u>, blame, condemn, denounce, rebuke, reprimand, reproach, scold ≠ applaud

• NOUN = <u>disapproval</u>, criticism, blame, condemnation, rebuke, reprimand, reproach, stick (*slang*) ≠ approval

central 1 = <u>inner</u>, middle, mid, interior ≠ outer 2 = <u>main</u>, chief, key, essential, primary, principal, fundamental, focal ≠ minor

centre NOUN = <u>middle</u>, heart, focus, core, nucleus, hub, pivot, kernel ≠ edge

• VERB = <u>focus</u>, concentrate, cluster, revolve, converge

ceremonial ADJECTIVE = <u>formal</u>, public, official, ritual, stately, solemn, liturgical, courtly ≠ informal

• NOUN = <u>ritual</u>, ceremony, rite, formality, solemnity

ceremony 1 = <u>ritual</u>, service, rite, observance, commemoration, solemnities 2 = <u>formality</u>, ceremonial, propriety, decorum

certain 1 = <u>sure</u>, convinced, positive, confident, satisfied, assured ≠ unsure 2 = <u>bound</u>, sure, fated, destined ≠ unlikely 3 = <u>inevitable</u>, unavoidable, inescapable 4 = <u>known</u>, true, positive, conclusive, unequivocal, undeniable, irrefutable, unquestionable ≠ doubtful 5 = <u>fixed</u>, decided, established, settled, definite ≠ indefinite

certainly = <u>definitely</u>, surely, truly, undoubtedly, without doubt, undeniably, indisputably, assuredly

certainty 1 = <u>confidence</u>, trust, faith, conviction, assurance, sureness, positiveness ≠ doubt 2 = <u>inevitability</u> ≠ uncertainty 3 = <u>fact</u>, truth, reality, sure thing (*informal*), banker

certificate = <u>document</u>, licence, warrant, voucher, diploma, testimonial, authorization, credential(s)

certify = <u>confirm</u>, declare, guarantee, assure, testify, verify, validate, attest

chain NOUN 1 = <u>tether</u>, coupling, link, bond, shackle, fetter, manacle 2 = <u>series</u>, set, train, string, sequence, succession, progression

• VERB = <u>bind</u>, confine, restrain, handcuff, shackle, tether, fetter, manacle

chairman *or* **chairwoman** 1 = <u>director</u>, president, chief, executive, chairperson 2 = <u>master of ceremonies</u>, spokesman, chair, speaker, MC, chairperson

challenge NOUN 1 = <u>dare</u>, provocation, wero (*N.Z.*) 2 = <u>test</u>, trial, opposition, confrontation, ultimatum

• VERB 1 = <u>dispute</u>, question, tackle,

confront, defy, object to, disagree with, take issue with **2** = dare, invite, defy, throw down the gauntlet **3** = test **4** = question, interrogate

chamber **1** = hall, room **2** = council, assembly, legislature, legislative body **3** = room, bedroom, apartment, enclosure, cubicle **4** = compartment

champion NOUN **1** = winner, hero, victor, conqueror, title holder **2** = defender, guardian, patron, backer, protector, upholder

• VERB = support, back, defend, promote, advocate, fight for, uphold, espouse

chance NOUN **1** = probability, odds, possibility, prospect, likelihood ≠ certainty **2** = opportunity, opening, occasion, time **3** = accident, fortune, luck, fate, destiny, coincidence, providence ≠ design **4** = risk, speculation, gamble, hazard

• VERB = risk, try, stake, venture, gamble, hazard, wager

change NOUN **1** = alteration, innovation, transformation, modification, mutation, metamorphosis, difference, revolution **2** = variety, break (*informal*), departure, variation, novelty, diversion ≠ monotony **3** = exchange, trade, conversion, swap, substitution, interchange

• VERB **1** = alter, reform, transform, adjust, revise, modify, reorganize, restyle ≠ keep **2** = shift, vary, transform, alter, modify, mutate ≠ stay **3** = exchange, trade, replace, substitute, swap, interchange

channel NOUN **1** = means, way, course, approach, medium, route, path, avenue **2** = strait, sound, route, passage, canal, waterway **3** = duct, artery, groove, gutter, furrow, conduit

• VERB = direct, guide, conduct, transmit, convey

chant NOUN = song, carol, chorus, melody, psalm

• VERB = sing, chorus, recite, intone, carol

chaos NOUN = disorder, confusion, mayhem, anarchy, lawlessness, pandemonium, bedlam, tumult ≠ orderliness

chaotic = disordered, confused, uncontrolled, anarchic, tumultuous, lawless, riotous, topsy-turvy

chap (*Informal*) = fellow, man, person, individual, character, guy (*informal*), bloke (*Brit. informal*)

chapter **1** = section, part, stage, division,

episode, topic, segment, instalment **2** = period, time, stage, phase

character **1** = personality, nature, attributes, temperament, complexion, disposition **2** = nature, kind, quality, calibre **3** = reputation, honour, integrity, good name, rectitude **4** = role, part, persona **5** = eccentric, card (*informal*), original, oddball (*informal*) **6** = symbol, mark, sign, letter, figure, device, rune, hieroglyph

characteristic NOUN = feature, mark, quality, property, attribute, faculty, trait, quirk

• ADJECTIVE = typical, special, individual, representative, distinguishing, distinctive, peculiar, singular ≠ rare

characterize = distinguish, mark, identify, brand, stamp, typify

charge VERB **1** = accuse, indict, impeach, incriminate, arraign ≠ acquit **2** = attack, assault, assail ≠ retreat **3** = rush, storm, stampede **4** = fill, load

• NOUN **1** = price, rate, cost, amount, payment, expense, toll, expenditure **2** = accusation, allegation, indictment, imputation ≠ acquittal **3** = care, trust, responsibility, custody, safekeeping **4** = duty, office, responsibility, remit **5** = ward, pupil, protégé, dependant **6** = attack, rush, assault, onset, onslaught, stampede, sortie ≠ retreat

charisma = charm, appeal, personality, attraction, lure, allure, magnetism, force of personality

charismatic = charming, appealing, attractive, influential, magnetic, enticing, alluring

charitable **1** = benevolent, liberal, generous, lavish, philanthropic, bountiful, beneficent ≠ mean **2** = kind, understanding, forgiving, sympathetic, favourable, tolerant, indulgent, lenient ≠ unkind

charity **1** = charitable organization, fund, movement, trust, endowment **2** = donations, help, relief, gift, contributions, assistance, hand-out, philanthropy, koha (*N.Z.*) ≠ meanness **3** = kindness, humanity, goodwill, compassion, generosity, indulgence, altruism, benevolence, aroha (*N.Z.*) ≠ ill will

charm NOUN **1** = attraction, appeal,

fascination, allure, magnetism
≠ repulsiveness **2** = <u>talisman</u>, trinket, amulet, fetish **3** = <u>spell</u>, magic, enchantment, sorcery, makutu (*N.Z.*)
● **VERB 1** = <u>attract</u>, delight, fascinate, entrance, win over, enchant, captivate, beguile ≠ repel **2** = <u>persuade</u>, seduce, coax, beguile, sweet-talk (*informal*)

charming = <u>attractive</u>, pleasing, appealing, fetching, delightful, cute, seductive, captivating ≠ unpleasant

chart NOUN = <u>table</u>, diagram, blueprint, graph, plan, map
● **VERB 1** = <u>plot</u>, map out, delineate, sketch, draft, tabulate **2** = <u>monitor</u>, follow, record, note, document, register, trace, outline

charter NOUN **1** = <u>document</u>, contract, permit, licence, deed, prerogative **2** = <u>constitution</u>, laws, rules, code
● **VERB 1** = <u>hire</u>, commission, employ, rent, lease **2** = <u>authorize</u>, permit, sanction, entitle, license, empower, give authority

chase VERB **1** = <u>pursue</u>, follow, track, hunt, run after, course **2** = <u>drive away</u>, drive, expel, hound, send away, send packing, put to flight **3** = <u>rush</u>, run, race, shoot, fly, speed, dash, bolt
● **NOUN** = <u>pursuit</u>, race, hunt, hunting

chat VERB = <u>talk</u>, gossip, jaw (*slang*), natter, blather, blether (*Scot.*)
● **NOUN** = <u>talk</u>, tête-à-tête, conversation, gossip, heart-to-heart, natter, blather, blether (*Scot.*), korero (*N.Z.*)

chatter VERB = <u>prattle</u>, chat, rabbit on (*Brit. informal*), babble, gab (*informal*), natter, blather, schmooze (*slang*)
● **NOUN** = <u>prattle</u>, chat, gossip, babble, gab (*informal*), natter, blather, blether (*Scot.*)

cheap **1** = <u>inexpensive</u>, reduced, keen, reasonable, bargain, low-priced, low-cost, cut-price ≠ expensive **2** = <u>inferior</u>, poor, worthless, second-rate, shoddy, tawdry, tatty, trashy, bodger *or* bodgie (*Austral. slang*) ≠ good **3** (*Informal*) = <u>despicable</u>, mean, contemptible, scungy (*Austral. & N.Z.*) ≠ decent

cheat VERB = <u>deceive</u>, trick, fool, con (*informal*), mislead, rip off (*slang*), fleece, defraud
● **NOUN** = <u>deceiver</u>, sharper, shark, charlatan, trickster, con man (*informal*), double-crosser (*informal*), swindler, rorter (*Austral. slang*)

check VERB **1** *often with* **out** = <u>examine</u>,

test, study, look at, research, investigate, monitor, vet ≠ overlook **2** = <u>stop</u>, limit, delay, halt, restrain, inhibit, hinder, obstruct ≠ further
● **NOUN 1** = <u>examination</u>, test, research, investigation, inspection, scrutiny, once-over (*informal*) **2** = <u>control</u>, limitation, restraint, constraint, obstacle, curb, obstruction, stoppage

cheek (*Informal*) = <u>impudence</u>, nerve, disrespect, audacity, lip (*slang*), temerity, chutzpah (*U.S. & Canad. informal*), insolence

cheeky = <u>impudent</u>, rude, forward, insulting, saucy, audacious, pert, disrespectful ≠ respectful

cheer VERB **1** = <u>applaud</u>, hail, acclaim, clap ≠ boo **2** = <u>hearten</u>, encourage, comfort, uplift, brighten, cheer up, buoy up, gladden ≠ dishearten
● **NOUN** = <u>applause</u>, ovation, plaudits, acclamation
● **PHRASES cheer someone up** = <u>comfort</u>, encourage, hearten, enliven, gladden, gee up, jolly along (*informal*)
◆ **cheer up** = <u>take heart</u>, rally, perk up, buck up (*informal*)

cheerful **1** = <u>happy</u>, optimistic, enthusiastic, jolly, merry, upbeat (*informal*), buoyant, cheery ≠ sad **2** = <u>pleasant</u> ≠ gloomy

chemical = <u>compound</u>, drug, substance, synthetic substance, potion

chemist = <u>pharmacist</u>, apothecary (*obsolete*), dispenser

cherish **1** = <u>cling to</u>, prize, treasure, hold dear, cleave to ≠ despise **2** = <u>care for</u>, love, support, comfort, look after, shelter, nurture, hold dear ≠ neglect **3** = <u>harbour</u>, nurse, sustain, foster, entertain

chest **1** = <u>breast</u>, front **2** = <u>box</u>, case, trunk, crate, coffer, casket, strongbox
▬ **RELATED WORD**
adjective: pectoral

chew = <u>munch</u>, bite, grind, champ, crunch, gnaw, chomp, masticate

chic = <u>stylish</u>, smart, elegant, fashionable, trendy (*Brit. informal*) ≠ unfashionable

chief NOUN = <u>head</u>, leader, director, manager, boss (*informal*), captain, master, governor, baas (*S. African*), ariki (*N.Z.*) ≠ subordinate
● **ADJECTIVE** = <u>primary</u>, highest, leading, main, prime, key, premier, supreme

≠ minor

chiefly 1 = <u>especially</u>, essentially, principally, primarily, above all 2 = <u>mainly</u>, largely, usually, mostly, in general, on the whole, predominantly, in the main

child 1 = <u>youngster</u>, baby, kid (*informal*), infant, babe, juvenile, toddler, tot, littlie (*Austral. informal*), ankle-biter (*Austral. slang*), tacker (*Austral. slang*) 2 = <u>offspring</u>

■ RELATED WORDS
adjective: filial
prefix: paedo-

childbirth = <u>child-bearing</u>, labour, delivery, lying-in, confinement, parturition

childhood = <u>youth</u>, minority, infancy, schooldays, immaturity, boyhood *or* girlhood

childish 1 = <u>youthful</u>, young, boyish *or* girlish 2 = <u>immature</u>, juvenile, foolish, infantile, puerile ≠ mature

chill VERB 1 = <u>cool</u>, refrigerate, freeze 2 = <u>dishearten</u>, depress, discourage, dismay, dampen, deject
● NOUN 1 = <u>coldness</u>, bite, nip, sharpness, coolness, rawness, crispness, frigidity 2 = <u>shiver</u>, frisson
● ADJECTIVE = <u>chilly</u>, biting, sharp, freezing, raw, bleak, chilly, wintry

chilly 1 = <u>cool</u>, fresh, sharp, crisp, penetrating, brisk, draughty, nippy ≠ warm 2 = <u>unfriendly</u>, hostile, unsympathetic, frigid, unresponsive, unwelcoming ≠ friendly

china[1] = <u>pottery</u>, ceramics, ware, porcelain, crockery, tableware, service

china[2] (*Brit. & S. African informal*) = <u>friend</u>, pal, mate (*informal*), buddy (*informal*), companion, best friend, intimate, comrade, cobber (*Austral. & N.Z. old-fashioned informal*), E hoa (*N.Z.*)

chip NOUN 1 = <u>fragment</u>, shaving, wafer, sliver, shard 2 = <u>scratch</u>, nick, notch 3 = <u>counter</u>, disc, token
● VERB 1 = <u>nick</u>, damage, gash 2 = <u>chisel</u>, whittle

choice NOUN 1 = <u>range</u>, variety, selection, assortment 2 = <u>selection</u>, preference, pick 3 = <u>option</u>, say, alternative
● ADJECTIVE = <u>best</u>, prime, select, excellent, exclusive, elite, booshit (*Austral. slang*), exo (*Austral. slang*), sik (*Austral. slang*)

choke 1 = <u>suffocate</u>, stifle, smother, overpower, asphyxiate 2 = <u>strangle</u>, throttle, asphyxiate 3 = <u>block</u>, clog,

obstruct, bung, constrict, congest, stop, bar

choose 1 = <u>pick</u>, prefer, select, elect, adopt, opt for, designate, settle upon ≠ reject 2 = <u>wish</u>, want

chop = <u>cut</u>, fell, hack, sever, cleave, hew, lop

chore = <u>task</u>, job, duty, burden, hassle (*informal*), errand

chorus NOUN 1 = <u>refrain</u>, response, strain, burden 2 = <u>choir</u>, singers, ensemble, vocalists, choristers
● PHRASES **in chorus** = <u>in unison</u>, as one, all together, in concert, in harmony, in accord, with one voice

christen 1 = <u>baptize</u>, name 2 = <u>name</u>, call, term, style, title, dub, designate

Christmas = <u>festive season</u>, Noël, Xmas (*informal*), Yule (*archaic*), Yuletide (*archaic*)

chronicle VERB = <u>record</u>, tell, report, enter, relate, register, recount, set down
● NOUN = <u>record</u>, story, history, account, register, journal, diary, narrative

chuck (*Informal*) 1 = <u>throw</u>, cast, pitch, toss, hurl, fling, sling, heave 2 *often with* **away** *or* **out** = <u>throw out</u>, dump (*informal*), scrap, get rid of, ditch (*slang*), dispose of, dispense with, jettison 3 = <u>give up</u> *or* <u>over</u>, leave, abandon, cease, resign from, pack in 4 (*Austral. & N.Z. informal*) = <u>vomit</u>, throw up (*informal*), spew, heave (*slang*), puke (*slang*), barf (*U.S. slang*), chunder (*slang, chiefly Austral.*)

chuckle = <u>laugh</u>, giggle, snigger, chortle, titter

chum (*Informal*) = <u>friend</u>, mate (*informal*), pal (*informal*), companion, comrade, crony, cobber (*Austral. & N.Z. old-fashioned informal*), E hoa (*N.Z.*)

chunk = <u>piece</u>, block, mass, portion, lump, slab, hunk, nugget

churn 1 = <u>stir up</u>, beat, disturb, swirl, agitate 2 = <u>swirl</u>, toss

cinema 1 = <u>pictures</u>, movies, picture-house, flicks (*slang*) 2 = <u>films</u>, pictures, movies, big screen (*informal*), motion pictures, silver screen

circle NOUN 1 = <u>ring</u>, disc, hoop, halo 2 = <u>group</u>, company, set, club, society, clique, coterie
● VERB 1 = <u>go round</u>, ring, surround, enclose, envelop, encircle, circumscribe, circumnavigate 2 = <u>wheel</u>, spiral

circuit 1 = <u>course</u>, tour, track, route,

journey 2 = <u>racetrack</u>, course, track, racecourse 3 = <u>lap</u>, tour, revolution, orbit

circular ADJECTIVE 1 = <u>round</u>, ring-shaped 2 = <u>circuitous</u>, cyclical, orbital
● NOUN 1 = <u>advertisement</u>, notice, ad (*informal*), announcement, advert (*Brit. informal*), press release

circulate 1 = <u>spread</u>, issue, publish, broadcast, distribute, publicize, disseminate, promulgate 2 = <u>flow</u>, revolve, rotate, radiate

circulation 1 = <u>distribution</u>, currency, readership 2 = <u>bloodstream</u>, blood flow 3 = <u>flow</u>, circling, motion, rotation 4 = <u>spread</u>, distribution, transmission, dissemination

circumstance 1 *usually plural* = <u>situation</u>, condition, contingency, state of affairs, lie of the land 2 *usually plural* = <u>detail</u>, event, particular, respect 3 *usually plural* = <u>situation</u>, state, means, position, station, status 4 = <u>chance</u>, the times, accident, fortune, luck, fate, destiny, providence

cite = <u>quote</u>, name, advance, mention, extract, specify, allude to, enumerate

citizen = <u>inhabitant</u>, resident, dweller, denizen, subject, townsman
■ RELATED WORD
adjective: civil

city = <u>town</u>, metropolis, municipality, conurbation
■ RELATED WORD
adjective: civic

civic = <u>public</u>, municipal, communal, local

civil 1 = <u>civic</u>, political, domestic, municipal ≠ state 2 = <u>polite</u>, obliging, courteous, considerate, affable, well-mannered ≠ rude

civilization 1 = <u>society</u>, people, community, nation, polity 2 = <u>culture</u>, development, education, progress, enlightenment, sophistication, advancement, cultivation

civilize = <u>cultivate</u>, educate, refine, tame, enlighten, sophisticate

civilized 1 = <u>cultured</u>, educated, sophisticated, enlightened, humane ≠ primitive 2 = <u>polite</u>, mannerly, tolerant, gracious, courteous, well-behaved, well-mannered

claim VERB 1 = <u>assert</u>, insist, maintain, allege, uphold, profess 2 = <u>demand</u>, call for, ask for, insist on
● NOUN 1 = <u>assertion</u>, statement, allegation, declaration, pretension, affirmation, protestation 2 = <u>demand</u>, application, request, petition, call 3 = <u>right</u>, title, entitlement

clamour = <u>noise</u>, shouting, racket, outcry, din, uproar, commotion, hubbub

clamp NOUN = <u>vice</u>, press, grip, bracket, fastener
● VERB = <u>fasten</u>, fix, secure, brace, make fast

clan 1 = <u>family</u>, group, society, tribe, fraternity, brotherhood, ainga (*N.Z.*), ngai (*N.Z.*) 2 = <u>group</u>, set, circle, gang, faction, coterie, cabal

clap = <u>applaud</u>, cheer, acclaim ≠ boo

clarify 1 = <u>explain</u>, interpret, illuminate, clear up, simplify, make plain, elucidate, throw *or* shed light on

clarity 1 = <u>clearness</u>, precision, simplicity, transparency, lucidity, straightforwardness ≠ obscurity 2 = <u>transparency</u>, clearness ≠ cloudiness

clash VERB 1 = <u>conflict</u>, grapple, wrangle, lock horns, cross swords, war, feud, quarrel 2 = <u>disagree</u>, conflict, vary, counter, differ, contradict, diverge, run counter to 3 = <u>not go</u>, jar, not match 4 = <u>crash</u>, bang, rattle, jar, clatter, jangle, clang, clank
● NOUN 1 = <u>conflict</u>, fight, brush, confrontation, collision, showdown (*informal*) 2 = <u>disagreement</u>, difference, argument, dispute, dissent, difference of opinion

clasp VERB = <u>grasp</u>, hold, press, grip, seize, squeeze, embrace, clutch
● NOUN 1 = <u>grasp</u>, hold, grip, embrace, hug 2 = <u>fastening</u>, catch, grip, hook, pin, clip, buckle, brooch

class NOUN 1 = <u>group</u>, set, division, rank 2 = <u>type</u>, set, sort, kind, category, genre
● VERB = <u>classify</u>, group, rate, rank, brand, label, grade, designate

classic ADJECTIVE 1 = <u>typical</u>, standard, model, regular, usual, ideal, characteristic, definitive, dinki-di (*Austral. informal*) 2 = <u>masterly</u>, best, finest, world-class, consummate, first-rate ≠ second-rate 3 = <u>lasting</u>, enduring, abiding, immortal, undying, ageless, deathless
● NOUN = <u>standard</u>, masterpiece, prototype, paradigm, exemplar, model

classification = <u>categorization</u>, grading, taxonomy, sorting, analysis, arrangement

classify = <u>categorize</u>, sort, rank, arrange,

grade, catalogue, pigeonhole, tabulate

classy (*Informal*) = high-class, exclusive, superior, elegant, stylish, posh (*informal*, *chiefly Brit.*), up-market, top-drawer

clause = section, condition, article, chapter, passage, part, paragraph

claw NOUN 1 = nail, talon 2 = pincer
● VERB = scratch, tear, dig, rip, scrape, maul, mangulate (*Austral. slang*), lacerate

clean ADJECTIVE 1 = hygienic, fresh, sterile, pure, purified, antiseptic, sterilized, uncontaminated ≠ contaminated 2 = spotless, fresh, immaculate, impeccable, flawless, unblemished, unsullied ≠ dirty 3 = moral, good, pure, decent, innocent, respectable, upright, honourable ≠ immoral 4 = complete, final, whole, total, perfect, entire, decisive, thorough
● VERB = cleanse, wash, scrub, rinse, launder, scour, purify, disinfect ≠ dirty

cleanse = purify, clear, purge 1 = absolve, clear, purge, purify 2 = clean, wash, scrub, rinse, scour

clear ADJECTIVE 1 = comprehensible, explicit, understandable ≠ confused 2 = distinct ≠ indistinct 3 = obvious, plain, apparent, evident, distinct, pronounced, manifest, blatant ≠ ambiguous 4 = certain, sure, convinced, positive, satisfied, resolved, definite, decided ≠ confused 5 = transparent, see-through, translucent, crystalline, glassy, limpid, pellucid ≠ opaque 6 = unobstructed, open, free, empty, unhindered, unimpeded ≠ blocked 7 = bright, fine, fair, shining, sunny, luminous, cloudless, light ≠ cloudy 8 = untroubled, clean, pure, innocent, immaculate, unblemished, untarnished
● VERB 1 = unblock, free, loosen, extricate, open, disentangle 2 = remove, clean, wipe, cleanse, tidy (up), sweep away 3 = brighten, break up, lighten 4 = pass over, jump, leap, vault, miss 5 = absolve, acquit, vindicate, exonerate ≠ blame

clear-cut = straightforward, specific, plain, precise, black-and-white, explicit, definite, unequivocal

clearly 1 = obviously, undoubtedly, evidently, distinctly, markedly, overtly, undeniably, beyond doubt 2 = legibly, distinctly 3 = audibly, distinctly, intelligibly, comprehensibly

clergy = priesthood, ministry, clerics, clergymen, churchmen, the cloth, holy orders

clever 1 = intelligent, bright, talented, gifted, smart, knowledgeable, quick-witted ≠ stupid 2 = shrewd, bright, ingenious, resourceful, canny ≠ unimaginative 3 = skilful, talented, gifted ≠ inept

cliché = platitude, stereotype, commonplace, banality, truism, hackneyed phrase

client = customer, consumer, buyer, patron, shopper, patient

cliff = rock face, overhang, crag, precipice, escarpment, scar, bluff

climate = weather, temperature

climax = culmination, top, summit, height, highlight, peak, high point, zenith

climb VERB 1 = ascend, scale, mount, go up, clamber, shin up 2 = clamber, descend, scramble, dismount 3 = rise, go up, soar, ascend, fly up
● PHRASES **climb down** = back down, withdraw, yield, concede, retreat, surrender, give in, cave in (*informal*)

clinch 1 = secure, close, confirm, conclude, seal, sew up (*informal*), set the seal on 2 = settle, decide, determine

cling 1 = clutch, grip, embrace, grasp, hug, hold on to, clasp 2 = stick to, adhere to

clinical = unemotional, cold, scientific, objective, detached, analytic, impersonal, dispassionate

clip¹ VERB 1 = trim, cut, crop, prune, shorten, shear, snip, pare 2 (*Informal*) = smack, strike, knock, punch, thump, clout (*informal*), cuff, whack
● NOUN (*Informal*) = smack, strike, knock, punch, thump, clout (*informal*), cuff, whack

clip² = attach, fix, secure, connect, pin, staple, fasten, hold

cloak NOUN 1 = cape, coat, wrap, mantle 2 = covering, layer, blanket, shroud
● VERB 1 = cover, coat, wrap, blanket, shroud, envelop 2 = hide, cover, screen, mask, disguise, conceal, obscure, veil

clog = obstruct, block, jam, hinder, impede, congest

close¹ VERB 1 = shut, lock, fasten, secure ≠ open 2 = shut down, finish, cease 3 = wind up, finish, shut down, terminate 4 = block up, bar, seal ≠ open 5 = end, finish, complete, conclude, wind up,

terminate ≠ begin 6 = <u>clinch</u>, confirm, secure, conclude, seal, sew up (*informal*), set the seal on 7 = <u>come together</u>, join, connect ≠ separate
● NOUN = <u>end</u>, ending, finish, conclusion, completion, finale, culmination, denouement

close² 1 = <u>near</u>, neighbouring, nearby, handy, adjacent, adjoining, cheek by jowl ≠ far 2 = <u>intimate</u>, loving, familiar, thick (*informal*), attached, devoted, confidential, inseparable ≠ distant 3 = <u>noticeable</u>, marked, strong, distinct, pronounced 4 = <u>careful</u>, detailed, intense, minute, thorough, rigorous, painstaking 5 = <u>even</u>, level, neck and neck, fifty-fifty (*informal*), evenly matched 6 = <u>imminent</u>, near, impending, at hand, nigh ≠ far away 7 = <u>stifling</u>, oppressive, suffocating, stuffy, humid, sweltering, airless, muggy ≠ airy

closed 1 = <u>shut</u>, locked, sealed, fastened ≠ open 2 = <u>shut down</u>, out of service 3 = <u>exclusive</u>, select, restricted 4 = <u>finished</u>, over, ended, decided, settled, concluded, resolved, terminated

cloth = <u>fabric</u>, material, textiles

clothe = <u>dress</u>, array, robe, drape, swathe, attire, fit out, garb ≠ undress

clothes = <u>clothing</u>, wear, dress, gear (*informal*), outfit, costume, wardrobe, garments

clothing = <u>clothes</u>, wear, dress, gear (*informal*), outfit, costume, wardrobe, garments

cloud NOUN = <u>mist</u>, haze, vapour, murk, gloom
● VERB 1 = <u>confuse</u>, distort, impair, muddle, disorient 2 = <u>darken</u>, dim, be overshadowed

clout (*Informal*) VERB = <u>hit</u>, strike, punch, slap, sock (*slang*), smack, thump, clobber (*slang*)
● NOUN 1 = <u>thump</u>, blow, punch, slap, sock (*slang*), wallop (*informal*) 2 = <u>influence</u>, power, authority, pull, weight, prestige, mana (*N.Z.*)

clown NOUN 1 = <u>comedian</u>, fool, comic, harlequin, joker, jester, prankster, buffoon 2 = <u>fool</u>, idiot, twit (*informal*, *chiefly Brit.*), imbecile (*informal*), ignoramus, dolt, blockhead, dorba or dorb (*Austral. slang*), bogan (*Austral. slang*)
● VERB *usually with* **around** = <u>play the fool</u>, mess about, jest, act the fool

club NOUN 1 = <u>association</u>, company, group, union, society, lodge, guild, fraternity 2 = <u>stick</u>, bat, bludgeon, truncheon, cosh (*Brit.*), cudgel
● VERB = <u>beat</u>, strike, hammer, batter, bash, bludgeon, pummel, cosh (*Brit.*)

clue = <u>indication</u>, lead, sign, evidence, suggestion, trace, hint, suspicion

clump NOUN = <u>cluster</u>, group, bunch, bundle
● VERB = <u>stomp</u>, thump, lumber, tramp, plod, thud

clumsy = <u>awkward</u>, lumbering, bumbling, ponderous, ungainly, gauche, gawky, uncoordinated, unco (*Austral. slang*) ≠ skilful

cluster NOUN = <u>gathering</u>, group, collection, bunch, knot, clump, assemblage
● VERB = <u>gather</u>, group, collect, bunch, assemble, flock, huddle

clutch VERB 1 = <u>hold</u>, grip, embrace, grasp, cling to, clasp 2 = <u>seize</u>, catch, grab, grasp, snatch
● PLURAL NOUN = <u>power</u>, hands, control, grip, possession, grasp, custody, sway

clutter NOUN = <u>untidiness</u>, mess, disorder, confusion, litter, muddle, disarray, jumble ≠ order
● VERB = <u>litter</u>, scatter, strew, mess up ≠ tidy

coach NOUN 1 = <u>instructor</u>, teacher, trainer, tutor, handler 2 = <u>bus</u>, charabanc
● VERB = <u>instruct</u>, train, prepare, exercise, drill, tutor

coalition = <u>alliance</u>, union, association, combination, merger, conjunction, bloc, confederation

coarse 1 = <u>rough</u>, crude, unfinished, homespun, impure, unrefined, unprocessed, unpolished ≠ smooth 2 = <u>vulgar</u>, rude, indecent, improper, earthy, smutty, ribald, indelicate

coast NOUN = <u>shore</u>, border, beach, seaside, coastline, seaboard
● VERB = <u>cruise</u>, sail, drift, taxi, glide, freewheel

coat NOUN 1 = <u>fur</u>, hair, skin, hide, wool, fleece, pelt 2 = <u>layer</u>, covering, coating, overlay
● VERB = <u>cover</u>, spread, plaster, smear

coax = <u>persuade</u>, cajole, talk into, wheedle, sweet-talk (*informal*), prevail upon, entice, allure ≠ bully

cobber (*Austral. & N.Z. old-fashioned informal*) = <u>friend</u>, pal, mate (*informal*), buddy (*informal*), china (*Brit. & S. African informal*), best friend, intimate, comrade, E hoa (*N.Z.*)

cocktail = <u>mixture</u>, combination, compound, blend, mix

cocky *or* **cockie** (*Austral. & N.Z. informal*) = <u>farmer</u>, smallholder, crofter (*Scot.*), grazier, agriculturalist, rancher

code 1 = <u>principles</u>, rules, manners, custom, convention, ethics, maxim, etiquette, kawa (*N.Z.*), tikanga (*N.Z.*) 2 = <u>cipher</u>, cryptograph

coherent 1 = <u>consistent</u>, reasoned, organized, rational, logical, meaningful, systematic, orderly ≠ inconsistent 2 = <u>articulate</u>, lucid, comprehensible, intelligible ≠ unintelligible

coil 1 = <u>wind</u>, twist, curl, loop, spiral, twine 2 = <u>curl</u>, wind, twist, snake, loop, twine, wreathe

coin NOUN = <u>money</u>, change, cash, silver, copper, specie
• VERB = <u>invent</u>, create, make up, forge, originate, fabricate

coincide 1 = <u>occur simultaneously</u>, coexist, synchronize, be concurrent 2 = <u>agree</u>, match, accord, square, correspond, tally, concur, harmonize ≠ disagree

coincidence = <u>chance</u>, accident, luck, fluke, stroke of luck, happy accident

cold ADJECTIVE 1 = <u>chilly</u>, freezing, bleak, arctic, icy, frosty, wintry, frigid ≠ hot 2 = <u>distant</u>, reserved, indifferent, aloof, frigid, undemonstrative, standoffish ≠ emotional 3 = <u>unfriendly</u>, indifferent, frigid ≠ friendly
• NOUN = <u>coldness</u>, chill, frigidity, frostiness, iciness

collaborate 1 = <u>work together</u>, team up, join forces, cooperate, play ball (*informal*), participate 2 = <u>conspire</u>, cooperate, collude, fraternize

collaboration 1 = <u>teamwork</u>, partnership, cooperation, association, alliance 2 = <u>conspiring</u>, cooperation, collusion, fraternization

collaborator 1 = <u>co-worker</u>, partner, colleague, associate, team-mate, confederate 2 = <u>traitor</u>, turncoat, quisling, fraternizer

collapse VERB 1 = <u>fall down</u>, fall, give way, subside, cave in, crumple, fall apart at the seams 2 = <u>fail</u>, fold, founder, break down, fall through, come to nothing, go belly-up (*informal*)
• NOUN 1 = <u>falling down</u>, ruin, falling apart, cave-in, disintegration, subsidence 2 = <u>failure</u>, slump, breakdown, flop, downfall 3 = <u>faint</u>, breakdown, blackout, prostration

collar (*Informal*) = <u>seize</u>, catch, arrest, grab, capture, nail (*informal*), nab (*informal*), apprehend

colleague = <u>fellow worker</u>, partner, ally, associate, assistant, team-mate, comrade, helper

collect 1 = <u>gather</u>, save, assemble, heap, accumulate, amass, stockpile, hoard ≠ scatter 2 = <u>assemble</u>, meet, rally, cluster, come together, convene, converge, congregate ≠ disperse

collected = <u>calm</u>, cool, composed, poised, serene, unperturbed, unruffled, self-possessed ≠ nervous

collection 1 = <u>accumulation</u>, set, store, mass, pile, heap, stockpile, hoard 2 = <u>compilation</u>, accumulation, anthology 3 = <u>group</u>, company, crowd, assembly, cluster, assortment 4 = <u>gathering</u> 5 = <u>contribution</u>, donation, alms 6 = <u>offering</u>, offertory

collective 1 = <u>joint</u>, united, shared, combined, corporate, unified ≠ individual 2 = <u>combined</u>, aggregate, composite, cumulative ≠ separate

collide 1 = <u>crash</u>, clash, meet head-on, come into collision 2 = <u>conflict</u>, clash, be incompatible, be at variance

collision 1 = <u>crash</u>, impact, accident, smash, bump, pile-up (*informal*), prang (*informal*) 2 = <u>conflict</u>, opposition, clash, encounter, disagreement, incompatibility

colony = <u>settlement</u>, territory, province, possession, dependency, outpost, dominion, satellite state

colour *or* (*U.S.*) **color** NOUN 1 = <u>hue</u>, tone, shade, tint, colourway 2 = <u>paint</u>, stain, dye, tint, pigment, colorant
• VERB = <u>blush</u>, flush, redden

colourful 1 = <u>bright</u>, brilliant, psychedelic, variegated, multicoloured ≠ drab 2 = <u>interesting</u>, rich, graphic, lively, distinctive, vivid, picturesque ≠ boring

column 1 = <u>pillar</u>, support, post, shaft, upright, obelisk 2 = <u>line</u>, row, file, rank, procession, cavalcade

coma = <u>unconsciousness</u>, trance, oblivion, stupor

comb 1 = <u>untangle</u>, arrange, groom, dress 2 = <u>search</u>, hunt through, rake, sift, scour, rummage, ransack, forage, fossick (*Austral. & N.Z.*)

combat NOUN = <u>fight</u>, war, action, battle, conflict, engagement, warfare, skirmish ≠ peace
● VERB = <u>fight</u>, oppose, resist, defy, withstand, do battle with ≠ support

combination 1 = <u>mixture</u>, mix, blend, composite, amalgamation, coalescence 2 = <u>association</u>, union, alliance, coalition, federation, consortium, syndicate, confederation

combine 1 = <u>amalgamate</u>, mix, blend, integrate, merge ≠ separate 2 = <u>join together</u>, link, connect, integrate, merge, amalgamate 3 = <u>unite</u>, associate, team up, get together, collaborate, join forces, join together, pool resources ≠ split up

come VERB 1 = <u>approach</u>, near, advance, move towards, draw near 2 = <u>arrive</u>, turn up (*informal*), show up (*informal*) 3 = <u>reach</u>, extend, come up to, come as far as 4 = <u>happen</u>, fall, occur, take place, come about, come to pass 5 = <u>be available</u>, be made, be offered, be produced, be on offer
● PHRASES **come across as something** *or* **someone** = <u>seem</u>, look, seem to be, appear to be, give the impression of being ◆ **come across someone** = <u>meet</u>, encounter, run into, bump into (*informal*) ◆ **come across something** = <u>find</u>, discover, notice, unearth, stumble upon, chance upon = <u>be obtained</u>, be from, issue, emerge, flow, arise, originate, emanate

comeback 1 (*Informal*) = <u>return</u>, revival, rebound, resurgence, rally, recovery, triumph 2 = <u>response</u>, reply, retort, retaliation, riposte, rejoinder

comedian = <u>comic</u>, wit, clown, funny man, humorist, wag, joker, jester, dag (*N.Z. informal*)

comedy 1 = <u>light entertainment</u> ≠ tragedy, soapie (*Austral. slang*) 2 = <u>humour</u>, fun, joking, farce, jesting, hilarity ≠ seriousness

comfort NOUN 1 = <u>ease</u>, luxury, wellbeing, opulence 2 = <u>consolation</u>, succour, help, support, relief, compensation ≠ annoyance
● VERB = <u>console</u>, reassure, soothe, hearten, commiserate with ≠ distress

comfortable 1 = <u>pleasant</u>, homely, relaxing, cosy, agreeable, restful ≠ unpleasant 2 = <u>at ease</u>, happy, at home, contented, relaxed, serene ≠ uncomfortable 3 (*Informal*) = <u>well-off</u>, prosperous, affluent, well-to-do, comfortably-off, in clover (*informal*)

comforting = <u>consoling</u>, encouraging, cheering, reassuring, soothing, heart-warming ≠ upsetting

comic ADJECTIVE = <u>funny</u>, amusing, witty, humorous, farcical, comical, droll, jocular ≠ sad
● NOUN = <u>comedian</u>, funny man, humorist, wit, clown, wag, jester, dag (*N.Z. informal*), buffoon

coming ADJECTIVE = <u>approaching</u>, near, forthcoming, imminent, in store, impending, at hand, nigh
● NOUN = <u>arrival</u>, approach, advent

command VERB 1 = <u>order</u>, tell, charge, demand, require, direct, bid, compel ≠ beg 2 = <u>have authority over</u>, lead, head, control, rule, manage, handle, dominate ≠ be subordinate to
● NOUN 1 = <u>order</u>, demand, instruction, requirement, decree, directive, ultimatum, commandment 2 = <u>domination</u>, control, rule, mastery, power, government 3 = <u>management</u>, power, control, charge, authority, supervision

commander = <u>leader</u>, chief, officer, boss, head, captain, bass (*S. African*), ruler

commanding = <u>dominant</u>, controlling, dominating, superior, decisive, advantageous

commemorate = <u>celebrate</u>, remember, honour, recognize, salute, pay tribute to, immortalize ≠ ignore

commence 1 = <u>embark on</u>, start, open, begin, initiate, originate, instigate, enter upon ≠ stop 2 = <u>start</u>, open, begin, go ahead ≠ end

commend 1 = <u>praise</u>, acclaim, applaud, compliment, extol, approve, speak highly of ≠ criticize 2 = <u>recommend</u>, suggest, approve, advocate, endorse

comment VERB 1 = <u>remark</u>, say, note,

mention, point out, observe, utter
2 *usually with* **on** = remark on, explain, talk about, discuss, speak about, say something about, allude to, elucidate
● NOUN **1** = remark, statement, observation **2** = note, explanation, illustration, commentary, exposition, annotation, elucidation

commentary 1 = narration, report, review, explanation, description, voice-over **2** = analysis, notes, review, critique, treatise

commentator 1 = reporter, special correspondent, sportscaster **2** = critic, interpreter, annotator

commercial 1 = mercantile, trading **2** = materialistic, mercenary, profit-making

commission VERB = appoint, order, contract, select, engage, delegate, nominate, authorize
● NOUN **1** = duty, task, mission, mandate, errand **2** = fee, cut, percentage, royalties, rake-off (*slang*) **3** = committee, board, representatives, commissioners, delegation, deputation

commit 1 = do, perform, carry out, execute, enact, perpetrate **2** = put in custody, confine, imprison ≠ release

commitment 1 = dedication, loyalty, devotion
≠ indecisiveness **2** = responsibility, tie, duty, obligation, liability, engagement

common 1 = usual, standard, regular, ordinary, familiar, conventional, routine, frequent ≠ rare **2** = popular, general, accepted, standard, routine, widespread, universal, prevailing **3** = shared, collective **4** = ordinary, average, typical, dinki-di (*Austral. informal*) ≠ important **5** = vulgar, inferior, coarse, plebeian ≠ refined **6** = collective, public, community, social, communal ≠ personal

commonplace ADJECTIVE = everyday, common, ordinary, widespread, mundane, banal, run-of-the-mill, humdrum ≠ rare
● NOUN = cliché, platitude, banality, truism

common sense = good sense, sound judgment, level-headedness, prudence, gumption (*Brit. informal*), horse sense, native intelligence, wit

communal = public, shared, general, joint, collective
≠ private

commune = community, collective, cooperative, kibbutz

communicate 1 = contact, talk, speak, make contact, get in contact **2** = make known, declare, disclose, pass on, proclaim, transmit, convey, impart ≠ keep secret **3** = pass on, transfer, spread, transmit

communication 1 = contact, conversation, correspondence, link, relations **2** = passing on, circulation, transmission, disclosure, imparting, dissemination, conveyance **3** = message, news, report, word, information, statement, announcement, disclosure

communism *usually cap.* = socialism, Marxism, collectivism, Bolshevism, state socialism

communist *often cap.* = socialist, Red (*informal*), Marxist, Bolshevik, collectivist

community = society, people, public, residents, commonwealth, general public, populace, state

commuter = daily traveller, passenger, suburbanite

compact¹ ADJECTIVE **1** = closely packed, solid, thick, dense, compressed, condensed, pressed together ≠ loose **2** = concise, brief, to the point, succinct, terse ≠ lengthy
● VERB = pack closely, stuff, cram, compress, condense, tamp ≠ loosen

compact² = agreement, deal, understanding, contract, bond, arrangement, treaty, bargain

companion 1 = friend, partner, ally, colleague, associate, mate (*informal*), comrade, accomplice, cobber (*Austral. & N.Z. old-fashioned informal*) **2** = assistant, aide, escort, attendant

company 1 = business, firm, association, corporation, partnership, establishment, syndicate, house **2** = group, set, community, band, crowd, collection, gathering, assembly **3** = troop, unit, squad, team **4** = companionship, society, presence, fellowship **5** = guests, party, visitors, callers

comparable 1 = equal, equivalent, on a par, tantamount, a match for, proportionate, commensurate, as good as ≠ unequal **2** = similar, related, alike, corresponding, akin, analogous, of a piece, cognate

comparative = <u>relative</u>, qualified, by comparison

compare VERB = <u>contrast</u>, balance, weigh, set against, juxtapose
  ● PHRASES **compare to something** = <u>liken to</u>, parallel, identify with, equate to, correlate to, mention in the same breath as ◆ **compare with something** = <u>be as good as</u>, match, approach, equal, compete with, be on a par with, be the equal of, hold a candle to

comparison 1 = <u>contrast</u>, distinction, differentiation, juxtaposition 2 = <u>similarity</u>, analogy, resemblance, correlation, likeness, comparability

compartment 1 = <u>section</u>, carriage, berth 2 = <u>bay</u>, booth, locker, niche, cubicle, alcove, pigeonhole, cubbyhole

compass = <u>range</u>, field, area, reach, scope, limit, extent, boundary

compassion = <u>sympathy</u>, understanding, pity, humanity, mercy, sorrow, kindness, tenderness, aroha (N.Z.) ≠ indifference

compassionate = <u>sympathetic</u>, understanding, pitying, humanitarian, charitable, humane, benevolent, merciful ≠ uncaring

compatible 1 = <u>consistent</u>, in keeping, congruous ≠ inappropriate 2 = <u>like-minded</u>, harmonious, in harmony ≠ incompatible

compel = <u>force</u>, make, railroad (*informal*), oblige, constrain, coerce, impel, dragoon

compelling 1 = <u>convincing</u>, telling, powerful, forceful, conclusive, weighty, cogent, irrefutable 2 = <u>pressing</u>, binding, urgent, overriding, imperative, unavoidable, coercive, peremptory 3 = <u>fascinating</u>, gripping, irresistible, enchanting, enthralling, hypnotic, spellbinding, mesmeric ≠ boring

compensate 1 = <u>recompense</u>, repay, refund, reimburse, remunerate, make good 2 = <u>make amends</u>, make up for, atone, make it up to someone, pay for, do penance, cancel out, make reparation 3 = <u>balance</u>, cancel (out), offset, make up for, redress, counteract, counterbalance

compensation 1 = <u>reparation</u>, damages, recompense, remuneration, restitution, reimbursement 2 = <u>recompense</u>, amends, reparation, atonement

compete 1 = <u>contend</u>, fight, vie, challenge, struggle, contest, strive 2 = <u>take part</u>, participate, be in the running, be a competitor, be a contestant, play

competence 1 = <u>ability</u>, skill, talent, capacity, expertise, proficiency, capability ≠ incompetence 2 = <u>fitness</u>, suitability, adequacy, appropriateness ≠ inadequacy

competent 1 = <u>able</u>, skilled, capable, proficient ≠ incompetent 2 = <u>fit</u>, qualified, suitable, adequate ≠ unqualified

competition 1 = <u>rivalry</u>, opposition, struggle, strife 2 = <u>opposition</u>, field, rivals, challengers 3 = <u>contest</u>, event, championship, tournament, head-to-head

competitive 1 = <u>cut-throat</u>, aggressive, fierce, ruthless, relentless, antagonistic, dog-eat-dog 2 = <u>ambitious</u>, pushing, opposing, aggressive, vying, contentious, combative

competitor 1 = <u>rival</u>, adversary, antagonist 2 = <u>contestant</u>, participant, contender, challenger, entrant, player, opponent

compilation = <u>collection</u>, treasury, accumulation, anthology, assortment, assemblage

compile = <u>put together</u>, collect, gather, organize, accumulate, marshal, garner, amass

complacency = <u>smugness</u>, satisfaction, contentment, self-congratulation, self-satisfaction

complacent = <u>smug</u>, self-satisfied, pleased with yourself, resting on your laurels, contented, satisfied, serene, unconcerned ≠ insecure

complain = <u>find fault</u>, moan, grumble, whinge (*informal*), carp, groan, lament, whine

complaint 1 = <u>protest</u>, objection, grievance, charge 2 = <u>grumble</u>, criticism, moan, lament, grievance, grouse, gripe (*informal*) 3 = <u>disorder</u>, problem, disease, upset, illness, sickness, ailment, affliction

complement VERB = <u>enhance</u>, complete, improve, boost, crown, add to, set off, heighten
  ● NOUN 1 = <u>accompaniment</u>, companion, accessory, completion, finishing touch, rounding-off, adjunct, supplement 2 = <u>total</u>, capacity, quota, aggregate, contingent, entirety

complementary = <u>matching</u>,

companion, corresponding, compatible, reciprocal, interrelating, interdependent, harmonizing ≠ incompatible

complete ADJECTIVE 1 = total, perfect, absolute, utter, outright, thorough, consummate, out-and-out 2 = whole, full, entire ≠ partial 3 = entire, full, whole, intact, unbroken, faultless ≠ incomplete 4 = unabridged, full, entire 5 = finished, done, ended, achieved, concluded, fulfilled, accomplished ≠ unfinished 6 = perfect, finish off, round off, crown ≠ spoil
● VERB 1 = finish, conclude, end, close, settle, wrap up (*informal*), finalize ≠ start 2 = fill in, fill out

completely = totally, entirely, wholly, utterly, perfectly, fully, absolutely, altogether

completion = finishing, end, close, conclusion, fulfilment, culmination, fruition

complex ADJECTIVE 1 = compound, multiple, composite, manifold, heterogeneous, multifarious 2 = complicated, difficult, involved, elaborate, tangled, intricate, tortuous, convoluted ≠ simple
● NOUN 1 = structure, system, scheme, network, organization, aggregate, composite 2 (*Informal*) = obsession, preoccupation, phobia, fixation, fixed idea, idée fixe (*French*)

complexion 1 = skin, colour, colouring, hue, skin tone, pigmentation 2 = nature, character, make-up 3 = perspective, look, light, appearance, aspect, angle, slant

complexity = complication, involvement, intricacy, entanglement

complicate = make difficult, confuse, muddle, entangle, involve ≠ simplify

complicated 1 = involved, difficult, puzzling, troublesome, problematic, perplexing ≠ simple 2 = complex, involved, elaborate, intricate, convoluted, labyrinthine ≠ understandable

complication 1 = problem, difficulty, obstacle, drawback, snag, uphill (*S. African*) 2 = complexity, web, confusion, intricacy, entanglement

compliment NOUN = praise, honour, tribute, bouquet, flattery, eulogy

≠ criticism
● PLURAL NOUN 1 = greetings, regards, respects, good wishes, salutation ≠ insult 2 = congratulations, praise, commendation
● VERB = praise, flatter, salute, congratulate, pay tribute to, commend, extol, wax lyrical about ≠ criticize

complimentary 1 = flattering, approving, appreciative, congratulatory, commendatory ≠ critical 2 = free, donated, courtesy, honorary, on the house, gratuitous, gratis

comply = obey, follow, observe, submit to, conform to, adhere to, abide by, acquiesce with ≠ defy

component NOUN = part, piece, unit, item, element, ingredient, constituent
● ADJECTIVE = constituent, inherent, intrinsic

compose VERB 1 = put together, make up, constitute, comprise, make, build, form, fashion ≠ destroy 2 = create, write, produce, invent, devise, contrive 3 = arrange, make up, construct, put together, order, organize
● PHRASES **compose yourself** = calm, control, collect, quiet, soothe, pull yourself together

composed = calm, cool, collected, relaxed, poised, at ease, serene, sedate ≠ agitated

composition 1 = design, structure, make-up, organization, arrangement, formation, layout, configuration 2 = creation, work, piece, production, opus, masterpiece 3 = essay, exercise, treatise, literary work 4 = production, creation, making, fashioning, formation, putting together, compilation, formulation

compound NOUN = combination, mixture, blend, composite, fusion, synthesis, alloy, medley ≠ element
● ADJECTIVE = complex, multiple, composite, intricate ≠ simple
● VERB 1 = intensify, add to, complicate, worsen, heighten, exacerbate, aggravate, magnify ≠ lessen 2 = combine, unite, mix, blend, synthesize, amalgamate, intermingle ≠ divide

comprehend = understand, see, take in, perceive, grasp, conceive, make out, fathom ≠ misunderstand

comprehension = understanding,

grasp, conception, realization, intelligence, perception, discernment ≠ incomprehension

comprehensive = <u>broad</u>, full, complete, blanket, thorough, inclusive, exhaustive, all-inclusive ≠ limited

compress 1 = <u>squeeze</u>, crush, squash, press 2 = <u>condense</u>, contract, concentrate, shorten, abbreviate

comprise 1 = <u>be composed of</u>, include, contain, consist of, take in, embrace, encompass 2 = <u>make up</u>, form, constitute, compose

compromise NOUN = <u>give-and-take</u>, agreement, settlement, accommodation, concession, adjustment, trade-off ≠ disagreement

● VERB 1 = <u>meet halfway</u>, concede, make concessions, give and take, strike a balance, strike a happy medium, go fifty-fifty (*informal*) ≠ disagree 2 = <u>undermine</u>, expose, embarrass, weaken, prejudice, discredit, jeopardize, dishonour ≠ support

compulsive 1 = <u>obsessive</u>, confirmed, chronic, persistent, addictive, uncontrollable, incurable, inveterate 2 = <u>fascinating</u>, gripping, absorbing, compelling, captivating, enthralling, hypnotic, engrossing 3 = <u>irresistible</u>, overwhelming, compelling, urgent, neurotic, uncontrollable, driving

compulsory = <u>obligatory</u>, forced, required, binding, mandatory, imperative, requisite, de rigueur (*French*) ≠ voluntary

compute = <u>calculate</u>, total, count, reckon, figure out, add up, tally, enumerate

comrade = <u>companion</u>, friend, partner, ally, colleague, associate, fellow, co-worker, cobber (*Austral. & N.Z. old-fashioned informal*)

con (*Informal*) VERB = <u>swindle</u>, trick, cheat, rip off (*slang*), deceive, defraud, dupe, hoodwink

● NOUN = <u>swindle</u>, trick, fraud, deception, scam (*slang*), sting (*informal*)

conceal 1 = <u>hide</u>, bury, cover, screen, disguise, obscure, camouflage ≠ reveal 2 = <u>keep secret</u>, hide, disguise, mask, suppress, veil ≠ show

concede 1 = <u>admit</u>, allow, accept, acknowledge, own, grant, confess ≠ deny 2 = <u>give up</u>, yield, hand over, surrender, relinquish, cede ≠ conquer

conceive 1 = <u>imagine</u>, envisage,

comprehend, visualize, think, believe, suppose, fancy 2 = <u>think up</u>, create, design, devise, formulate, contrive 3 = <u>become pregnant</u>, get pregnant, become impregnated

concentrate 1 = <u>focus your attention on</u>, focus on, pay attention to, be engrossed in, put your mind to, keep your mind on, apply yourself to, give your mind to ≠ pay no attention to 2 = <u>focus</u>, centre, converge, bring to bear 3 = <u>gather</u>, collect, cluster, accumulate, congregate ≠ scatter

concentrated 1 = <u>condensed</u>, rich, undiluted, reduced, evaporated, thickened, boiled down 2 = <u>intense</u>, hard, deep, intensive, all-out (*informal*)

concentration 1 = <u>attention</u>, application, absorption, single-mindedness, intentness ≠ inattention 2 = <u>focusing</u>, centring, consolidation, convergence, bringing to bear, intensification, centralization 3 = <u>convergence</u>, collection, mass, cluster, accumulation, aggregation ≠ scattering

concept = <u>idea</u>, view, image, theory, notion, conception, hypothesis, abstraction

conception 1 = <u>idea</u>, plan, design, image, concept, notion 2 = <u>impregnation</u>, insemination, fertilization, germination

concern NOUN 1 = <u>anxiety</u>, fear, worry, distress, unease, apprehension, misgiving, disquiet 2 = <u>worry</u>, care, anxiety 3 = <u>affair</u>, issue, matter, consideration 4 = <u>care</u>, interest, attentiveness 5 = <u>business</u>, job, affair, responsibility, task 6 = <u>company</u>, business, firm, organization, corporation, enterprise, establishment 7 = <u>importance</u>, interest, bearing, relevance

● VERB 1 = <u>worry</u>, trouble, bother, disturb, distress, disquiet, perturb, make anxious 2 = <u>be about</u>, cover, deal with, go into, relate to, have to do with 3 = <u>be relevant to</u>, involve, affect, regard, apply to, bear on, have something to do with, pertain to

concerned 1 = <u>worried</u>, troubled, upset, bothered, disturbed, anxious, distressed, uneasy ≠ indifferent 2 = <u>involved</u>, interested, active, mixed up, implicated, privy to

concerning = <u>regarding</u>, about, re, touching, respecting, relating to, on the subject of, with reference to

concession 1 = <u>compromise</u>, agreement, settlement, accommodation, adjustment,

trade-off, give-and-take **2** = <u>privilege</u>,
right, permit, licence, entitlement,
indulgence, prerogative **3** = <u>reduction</u>,
saving, grant, discount, allowance
4 = <u>surrender</u>, yielding, conceding,
renunciation, relinquishment

conclude 1 = <u>decide</u>, judge, assume,
gather, work out, infer, deduce, surmise
2 = <u>come to an end</u>, end, close, finish,
wind up ≠ begin **3** = <u>bring to an end</u>, end,
close, finish, complete, wind up, terminate,
round off ≠ begin **4** = <u>accomplish</u>, effect,
bring about, carry out, pull off

conclusion 1 = <u>decision</u>, opinion,
conviction, verdict, judgment, deduction,
inference **2** = <u>end</u>, ending, close, finish,
completion, finale, termination, bitter end
3 = <u>outcome</u>, result, upshot, consequence,
culmination, end result

concrete 1 = <u>specific</u>, precise, explicit,
definite, clear-cut, unequivocal ≠ vague
2 = <u>real</u>, material, actual, substantial,
sensible, tangible, factual ≠ abstract

condemn 1 = <u>denounce</u>, damn, criticize,
disapprove, censure, reprove, upbraid,
blame ≠ approve **2** = <u>sentence</u>, convict,
damn, doom, pass sentence on ≠ acquit

condemnation = <u>denunciation</u>, blame,
censure, disapproval, reproach, stricture,
reproof

condition NOUN **1** = <u>state</u>, order, shape,
nick (*Brit. informal*), trim **2** = <u>situation</u>,
state, position, status, circumstances
3 = <u>requirement</u>, terms, rider, restriction,
qualification, limitation, prerequisite,
proviso **4** = <u>health</u>, shape, fitness,
trim, form, kilter, state of health, fettle
5 = <u>ailment</u>, problem, complaint,
weakness, malady, infirmity
• PLURAL NOUN = <u>circumstances</u>, situation,
environment, surroundings, way of life,
milieu
• VERB = <u>train</u>, teach, adapt, accustom

conditional = <u>dependent</u>, limited,
qualified, subject to, contingent,
provisional, with reservations
≠ unconditional

condone = <u>overlook</u>, excuse, forgive,
pardon, turn a blind eye to, look the
other way, make allowance for, let pass
≠ condemn

conduct VERB **1** = <u>carry out</u>, run, control,
manage, direct, handle, organize,
administer **2** = <u>accompany</u>, lead, escort,
guide, steer, convey, usher
• NOUN **1** = <u>management</u>, running, control,
handling, administration, direction,
organization, guidance **2** = <u>behaviour</u>,
ways, bearing, attitude, manners,
demeanour, deportment
• PHRASES **conduct yourself** = <u>behave</u>
<u>yourself</u>, act, carry yourself, acquit yourself,
deport yourself, comport yourself

confer 1 = <u>discuss</u>, talk, consult,
deliberate, discourse, converse **2** = <u>grant</u>,
give, present, accord, award, hand out,
bestow

conference = <u>meeting</u>, congress,
discussion, convention, forum,
consultation, seminar, symposium, hui
(*N.Z.*)

confess 1 = <u>admit</u>, acknowledge, disclose,
confide, own up, come clean (*informal*),
divulge ≠ cover up **2** = <u>declare</u>, allow,
reveal, confirm, concede, assert, affirm,
profess

confession = <u>admission</u>, revelation,
disclosure, acknowledgment, exposure,
unbosoming

confidant *or* **confidante** = <u>close friend</u>,
familiar, intimate, crony, alter ego, bosom
friend

confide = <u>tell</u>, admit, reveal, confess,
whisper, disclose, impart, divulge

confidence NOUN **1** = <u>trust</u>, belief, faith,
dependence, reliance, credence ≠ distrust
2 = <u>self-assurance</u>, courage, assurance,
aplomb, boldness, self-possession, nerve
≠ shyness **3** = <u>secret</u>
• PHRASES **in confidence** = <u>in secrecy</u>,
privately, confidentially, between you and
me (and the gatepost), (just) between
ourselves

confident 1 = <u>certain</u>, sure, convinced,
positive, secure, satisfied, counting
on ≠ unsure **2** = <u>self-assured</u>, positive,
assured, bold, self-confident, self-reliant,
sure of yourself ≠ insecure

confidential 1 = <u>secret</u>, private, intimate,
classified, privy, off the record, hush-hush
(*informal*) **2** = <u>secretive</u>, low, soft, hushed

confine VERB **1** = <u>imprison</u>, enclose, shut
up, intern, incarcerate, hem in, keep, cage
2 = <u>restrict</u>, limit
• PLURAL NOUN = <u>limits</u>, bounds,
boundaries, compass, precincts,
circumference, edge

confirm 1 = <u>prove</u>, support, establish,

back up, verify, validate, bear out, substantiate **2** = <u>ratify</u>, establish, sanction, endorse, authorize **3** = <u>strengthen</u>, establish, fix, secure, reinforce, fortify

confirmation 1 = <u>proof</u>, evidence, testimony, verification, ratification, validation, corroboration, authentication ≠ repudiation **2** = <u>affirmation</u>, approval, acceptance, endorsement, ratification, assent, agreement ≠ disapproval

confirmed = <u>long-established</u>, seasoned, chronic, hardened, habitual, ingrained, inveterate, dyed-in-the-wool

confiscate = <u>seize</u>, appropriate, impound, commandeer, sequester ≠ give back

conflict NOUN **1** = <u>dispute</u>, difference, opposition, hostility, disagreement, friction, strife, fighting ≠ agreement **2** = <u>struggle</u>, battle, clash, strife **3** = <u>battle</u>, war, fight, clash, contest, encounter, combat, strife ≠ peace
● VERB = <u>be incompatible</u>, clash, differ, disagree, collide, be at variance ≠ agree

conflicting = <u>incompatible</u>, opposing, clashing, contrary, contradictory, inconsistent, paradoxical, discordant ≠ agreeing

conform 1 = <u>fit in</u>, follow, adjust, adapt, comply, obey, fall in with, toe the line **2** = <u>fulfil</u>, meet, match, suit, satisfy, agree with, obey, abide by

confound = <u>bewilder</u>, baffle, confuse, astound, perplex, mystify, flummox, dumbfound

confront 1 = <u>tackle</u>, deal with, cope with, meet head-on **2** = <u>trouble</u>, face, perturb, bedevil **3** = <u>challenge</u>, face, oppose, tackle, encounter, defy, stand up to, accost ≠ evade

confrontation = <u>conflict</u>, fight, contest, set-to (*informal*), encounter, showdown (*informal*), head-to-head

confuse 1 = <u>mix up with</u>, take for, muddle with **2** = <u>bewilder</u>, puzzle, baffle, perplex, mystify, fluster, faze, flummox **3** = <u>obscure</u>, cloud, make more difficult

confused 1 = <u>bewildered</u>, puzzled, baffled, at sea, muddled, perplexed, taken aback, disorientated ≠ enlightened **2** = <u>disorderly</u>, disordered, chaotic, mixed up, jumbled, untidy, in disarray, topsy-turvy ≠ tidy

confusing = <u>bewildering</u>, puzzling, misleading, unclear, baffling, contradictory, perplexing ≠ clear

confusion 1 = <u>bewilderment</u>, doubt, uncertainty ≠ enlightenment **2** = <u>disorder</u>, chaos, turmoil, upheaval, muddle, shambles, commotion ≠ order

congestion 1 = <u>overcrowding</u>, crowding, jam, clogging, bottleneck

congratulate = <u>compliment</u>, pat on the back, wish joy to

congratulations PLURAL NOUN = <u>good wishes</u>, greetings, compliments, best wishes, felicitations
● INTERJECTION = <u>good wishes</u>, greetings, compliments, best wishes, felicitations

congregation = <u>parishioners</u>, brethren, crowd, assembly, flock, fellowship, multitude, throng

congress 1 = <u>meeting</u>, council, conference, assembly, convention, conclave, hui (*N.Z.*), runanga (*N.Z.*) **2** = <u>legislature</u>, council, parliament, House of Representatives (*N.Z.*)

conjure VERB = <u>produce</u>, generate, bring about, give rise to, make, create, effect, produce as if by magic
● PHRASES **conjure something up** = <u>bring to mind</u>, recall, evoke, recreate, recollect, produce as if by magic

connect 1 = <u>link</u>, join, couple, attach, fasten, affix, unite ≠ separate **2** = <u>associate</u>, join, link, identify, lump together

connected = <u>linked</u>, united, joined, coupled, related, allied, associated, combined

connection 1 = <u>association</u>, relationship, link, bond, relevance, tie-in **2** = <u>communication</u>, alliance, attachment, liaison, affinity, union **3** = <u>link</u>, coupling, junction, fastening, tie **4** = <u>contact</u>, friend, ally, associate, acquaintance

conquer 1 = <u>seize</u>, obtain, acquire, occupy, overrun, annex, win **2** = <u>defeat</u>, overcome, overthrow, beat, master, crush, overpower, quell ≠ lose to **3** = <u>overcome</u>, beat, defeat, master, overpower

conquest 1 = <u>takeover</u>, coup, invasion, occupation, annexation, subjugation **2** = <u>defeat</u>, victory, triumph, overthrow, rout, mastery

conscience 1 = <u>principles</u>, scruples, moral sense, sense of right and wrong, still small voice **2** = <u>guilt</u>, shame, regret, remorse, contrition, self-reproach

conscious 1 *often with of* = <u>aware</u> <u>of</u>, alert to, responsive to, sensible of ≠ unaware 2 = <u>deliberate</u>, knowing, studied, calculated, self-conscious, intentional, wilful, premeditated ≠ unintentional 3 = <u>awake</u>, wide-awake, sentient, alive ≠ asleep

consciousness = <u>awareness</u>, understanding, knowledge, recognition, sensibility, realization, apprehension

consecutive = <u>successive</u>, running, succeeding, in turn, uninterrupted, sequential, in sequence

consensus = <u>agreement</u>, general agreement, unanimity, common consent, unity, harmony, assent, concord, kotahitanga (*N.Z.*)

consent NOUN = <u>agreement</u>, sanction, approval, go-ahead (*informal*), permission, compliance, assent, acquiescence ≠ refusal
● VERB = <u>agree</u>, approve, permit, concur, assent, acquiesce ≠ refuse

consequence 1 = <u>result</u>, effect, outcome, repercussion, issue, sequel, end result, upshot 2 = <u>importance</u>, concern, moment, value, account, weight, import, significance

consequently = <u>as a result</u>, thus, therefore, hence, subsequently, accordingly, for that reason, thence

conservation 1 = <u>preservation</u>, saving, protection, maintenance, safeguarding, upkeep, guardianship, safekeeping 2 = <u>economy</u>, saving, thrift, husbandry

conservative ADJECTIVE = <u>traditional</u>, conventional, cautious, sober, reactionary, die-hard, hidebound ≠ radical
● NOUN = <u>traditionalist</u>, reactionary, die-hard, stick-in-the-mud (*informal*) ≠ radical

Conservative ADJECTIVE = <u>Tory</u>, Republican (*U.S.*), right-wing
● NOUN = <u>Tory</u>, Republican (*U.S.*), right-winger

conserve 1 = <u>save</u>, husband, take care of, hoard, store up, use sparingly ≠ waste 2 = <u>protect</u>, keep, save, preserve

consider 1 = <u>think</u>, see, believe, rate, judge, suppose, deem, view as 2 = <u>think about</u>, reflect on, weigh, contemplate, deliberate, ponder, meditate, ruminate 3 = <u>bear in mind</u>, remember, respect, think about, take into account, reckon with, take into consideration, make allowance for

considerable = <u>large</u>, goodly, great, marked, substantial, noticeable, plentiful, appreciable ≠ small

considerably = <u>greatly</u>, very much, significantly, remarkably, substantially, markedly, noticeably, appreciably

consideration 1 = <u>thought</u>, review, analysis, examination, reflection, scrutiny, deliberation 2 = <u>thoughtfulness</u>, concern, respect, kindness, tact, considerateness 3 = <u>factor</u>, point, issue, concern, element, aspect 4 = <u>payment</u>, fee, reward, remuneration, recompense, tip

considering = <u>taking into account</u>, in the light of, bearing in mind, in view of, keeping in mind, taking into consideration

consist VERB
● PHRASES **consist in something** = <u>lie in</u>, involve, reside in, be expressed by, subsist in, be found *or* contained in
◆ **consist of something** = <u>be made up</u> <u>of</u>, include, contain, incorporate, amount to, comprise, be composed of

consistency 1 = <u>agreement</u>, regularity, uniformity, constancy, steadiness, steadfastness, evenness 2 = <u>texture</u>, density, thickness, firmness, viscosity, compactness

consistent 1 = <u>steady</u>, even, regular, stable, constant, persistent, dependable, unchanging ≠ erratic 2 = <u>compatible</u>, agreeing, in keeping, harmonious, in harmony, consonant, in accord, congruous ≠ incompatible 3 = <u>coherent</u>, logical, compatible, harmonious, consonant ≠ contradictory

consolation = <u>comfort</u>, help, support, relief, cheer, encouragement, solace, succour

console = <u>comfort</u>, cheer, soothe, support, encourage, calm, succour, express sympathy for ≠ distress

consolidate 1 = <u>strengthen</u>, secure, reinforce, fortify, stabilize 2 = <u>combine</u>, unite, join, merge, unify, amalgamate, federate

conspicuous = <u>obvious</u>, clear, patent, evident, noticeable, blatant, salient ≠ inconspicuous

conspiracy = <u>plot</u>, scheme, intrigue, collusion, machination

conspire 1 = <u>plot</u>, scheme, intrigue,

manoeuvre, contrive, machinate, plan
2 = <u>work together</u>, combine, contribute, cooperate, concur, tend

constant 1 = <u>continuous</u>, sustained, perpetual, interminable, unrelenting, incessant, ceaseless, nonstop ≠ occasional **2** = <u>unchanging</u>, even, fixed, permanent, stable, steady, uniform, invariable ≠ changing **3** = <u>faithful</u>, true, devoted, loyal, stalwart, staunch, trustworthy, trusty ≠ undependable

constantly = <u>continuously</u>, always, all the time, invariably, continually, endlessly, perpetually, incessantly ≠ occasionally

constituent NOUN 1 = <u>voter</u>, elector, member of the electorate **2** = <u>component</u>, element, ingredient, part, unit, factor
● **ADJECTIVE** = <u>component</u>, basic, essential, integral, elemental

constitute 1 = <u>represent</u>, be, consist of, embody, exemplify, be equivalent to **2** = <u>make up</u>, form, compose, comprise

constitution 1 = <u>state of health</u>, build, body, frame, physique, physical condition **2** = <u>structure</u>, form, nature, make-up, composition, character, disposition

constitutional = <u>legitimate</u>, official, legal, chartered, statutory, vested

constrain 1 = <u>restrict</u>, confine, curb, restrain, constrict, straiten, check **2** = <u>force</u>, bind, compel, oblige, necessitate, coerce, impel, pressurize

constraint 1 = <u>restriction</u>, limitation, curb, rein, deterrent, hindrance, check **2** = <u>force</u>, pressure, necessity, restraint, compulsion, coercion

construct 1 = <u>build</u>, make, form, create, fashion, shape, manufacture, assemble ≠ demolish **2** = <u>create</u>, make, form, compose, put together

construction 1 = <u>building</u>, creation, composition **2** (*Formal*) = <u>interpretation</u>, reading, explanation, rendering, inference

constructive = <u>helpful</u>, positive, useful, practical, valuable, productive ≠ unproductive

consult 1 = <u>ask</u>, refer to, turn to, take counsel, pick (someone's) brains, question **2** = <u>confer</u>, talk, compare notes **3** = <u>refer to</u>, check in, look in

consultant = <u>specialist</u>, adviser, counsellor, authority

consultation 1 = <u>discussion</u>, talk, council, conference, dialogue **2** = <u>meeting</u>, interview, session, appointment, examination, deliberation, hearing

consume 1 = <u>eat</u>, swallow, devour, put away, gobble (up), eat up **2** = <u>use up</u>, spend, waste, absorb, exhaust, squander, dissipate, expend **3** = <u>destroy</u>, devastate, demolish, ravage, annihilate, lay waste **4** *often passive* = <u>obsess</u>, dominate, absorb, preoccupy, eat up, monopolize, engross

consumer = <u>buyer</u>, customer, user, shopper, purchaser

consumption 1 = <u>using up</u>, use, loss, waste, expenditure, exhaustion, depletion, dissipation **2** (*Old-fashioned*) = <u>tuberculosis</u>, T.B.

contact NOUN 1 = <u>communication</u>, link, association, connection, correspondence **2** = <u>touch</u>, contiguity **3** = <u>connection</u>, colleague, associate, liaison, acquaintance, confederate
● **VERB** = <u>get</u> *or* be in touch with, call, reach, approach, write to, speak to, communicate with

contain 1 = <u>hold</u>, incorporate, accommodate, enclose, have capacity for **2** = <u>include</u>, consist of, embrace, comprise, embody, comprehend **3** = <u>restrain</u>, control, hold in, curb, suppress, hold back, stifle, repress

container = <u>holder</u>, vessel, repository, receptacle

contaminate = <u>pollute</u>, infect, stain, corrupt, taint, defile, adulterate, befoul ≠ purify

contamination = <u>pollution</u>, infection, corruption, poisoning, taint, impurity, contagion, defilement

contemplate 1 = <u>consider</u>, plan, think of, intend, envisage, foresee **2** = <u>think about</u>, consider, ponder, reflect upon, ruminate (upon), muse over, deliberate over **3** = <u>look at</u>, examine, inspect, gaze at, eye up, view, study, regard

contemporary ADJECTIVE 1 = <u>modern</u>, recent, current, up-to-date, present-day, à la mode, newfangled, present ≠ old-fashioned **2** = <u>coexisting</u>, concurrent, contemporaneous
● **NOUN** = <u>peer</u>, fellow, equal

contempt = <u>scorn</u>, disdain, mockery, derision, disrespect, disregard ≠ respect

contend 1 = <u>argue</u>, hold, maintain, allege, assert, affirm **2** = <u>compete</u>, fight, struggle, clash, contest, strive, vie, jostle

content¹ NOUN 1 = <u>subject matter</u>, material, theme, substance, essence, gist 2 = <u>amount</u>, measure, size, load, volume, capacity
● PLURAL NOUN = <u>constituents</u>, elements, load, ingredients
content² ADJECTIVE = <u>satisfied</u>, happy, pleased, contented, comfortable, fulfilled, at ease, gratified
● NOUN = <u>satisfaction</u>, ease, pleasure, comfort, peace of mind, gratification, contentment
● PHRASES **content yourself with something** = <u>satisfy yourself with</u>, be happy with, be satisfied with, be content with
contented = <u>satisfied</u>, happy, pleased, content, comfortable, glad, thankful, gratified ≠ discontented
contentious = <u>argumentative</u>, wrangling, bickering, quarrelsome, querulous, cavilling, disputatious, captious
contest NOUN 1 = <u>competition</u>, game, match, trial, tournament 2 = <u>struggle</u>, fight, battle, conflict, dispute, controversy, combat
● VERB 1 = <u>compete in</u>, take part in, fight in, go in for, contend for, vie in 2 = <u>oppose</u>, question, challenge, argue, debate, dispute, object to, call in or into question
contestant = <u>competitor</u>, candidate, participant, contender, entrant, player
context 1 = <u>circumstances</u>, conditions, situation, ambience 2 = <u>frame of reference</u>, background, framework, relation, connection
contingency = <u>possibility</u>, happening, chance, event, incident, accident, emergency, eventuality
continual 1 = <u>constant</u>, interminable, incessant, unremitting ≠ erratic 2 = <u>frequent</u>, regular, repeated, recurrent ≠ occasional
continually 1 = <u>constantly</u>, always, all the time, forever, incessantly, nonstop, interminably 2 = <u>repeatedly</u>, often, frequently, many times, over and over, persistently
continuation 1 = <u>continuing</u>, lasting, carrying on, keeping up, endurance, perpetuation, prolongation 2 = <u>addition</u>, extension, supplement, sequel, resumption, postscript
continue 1 = <u>keep on</u>, go on, maintain,

sustain, carry on, persist in, persevere, stick at ≠ stop 2 = <u>go on</u>, progress, proceed, carry on, keep going 3 = <u>resume</u>, return to, take up again, proceed, carry on, recommence, pick up where you left off ≠ stop 4 = <u>remain</u>, last, stay, survive, carry on, live on, endure, persist ≠ quit
continuing = <u>lasting</u>, sustained, enduring, ongoing, in progress
continuity = <u>cohesion</u>, flow, connection, sequence, succession, progression
continuous = <u>constant</u>, extended, prolonged, unbroken, uninterrupted, unceasing ≠ occasional
contract NOUN = <u>agreement</u>, commitment, arrangement, settlement, bargain, pact, covenant
● VERB 1 = <u>agree</u>, negotiate, pledge, bargain, undertake, come to terms, covenant, make a deal ≠ refuse 2 = <u>constrict</u>, confine, tighten, shorten, compress, condense, shrivel 3 = <u>tighten</u>, narrow, shorten ≠ stretch 4 = <u>lessen</u>, reduce, shrink, diminish, decrease, dwindle ≠ increase 5 = <u>catch</u>, get, develop, acquire, incur, be infected with, go down with, be afflicted with ≠ avoid
contraction 1 = <u>tightening</u>, narrowing, shortening, constricting, shrinkage 2 = <u>abbreviation</u>, reduction, shortening, compression
contradict 1 = <u>dispute</u>, deny, challenge, belie, fly in the face of, be at variance with 2 = <u>negate</u>, deny, rebut, controvert ≠ confirm
contradiction 1 = <u>conflict</u>, inconsistency, contravention, incongruity 2 = <u>negation</u>, opposite, denial
contradictory = <u>inconsistent</u>, conflicting, opposed, opposite, contrary, incompatible, paradoxical
contrary ADJECTIVE 1 = <u>opposite</u>, different, opposed, clashing, counter, reverse, adverse, contradictory ≠ in agreement 2 = <u>perverse</u>, difficult, awkward, intractable, obstinate, stroppy (*Brit. slang*), cantankerous, disobliging ≠ cooperative
● NOUN = <u>opposite</u>, reverse, converse, antithesis
contrast NOUN = <u>difference</u>, opposition, comparison, distinction, foil, disparity, divergence, dissimilarity
● VERB 1 = <u>differentiate</u>, compare, oppose, distinguish, set in opposition 2 = <u>differ</u>, be

contrary, be at variance, be dissimilar

contribute VERB = give, provide, supply, donate, subscribe, chip in (*informal*), bestow

● PHRASES **contribute to something** = be partly responsible for, lead to, be instrumental in, be conducive to, help

contribution = gift, offering, grant, donation, input, subscription, koha (*N.Z.*)

contributor = donor, supporter, patron, subscriber, giver

contrive 1 = devise, plan, fabricate, create, design, scheme, manufacture, plot 2 = manage, succeed, arrange, manoeuvre

contrived = forced, planned, laboured, strained, artificial, elaborate, unnatural, overdone ≠ natural

control NOUN 1 = power, authority, management, command, guidance, supervision, supremacy, charge 2 = restraint, check, regulation, brake, limitation, curb 3 = self-discipline, self-restraint, restraint, self-command 4 = switch, instrument, button, dial, lever, knob

● PLURAL NOUN = instruments, dash, dials, console, dashboard, control panel

● VERB 1 = have power over, manage, direct, handle, command, govern, administer, supervise 2 = limit, restrict, curb 3 = restrain, limit, check, contain, curb, hold back, subdue, repress

controversial = disputed, contentious, at issue, debatable, under discussion, open to question, disputable

controversy = argument, debate, row, dispute, quarrel, squabble, wrangling, altercation

convene 1 = call, gather, assemble, summon, bring together, convoke 2 = meet, gather, assemble, come together, congregate

convenience 1 = benefit, good, advantage 2 = suitability, fitness, appropriateness 3 = usefulness, utility ≠ uselessness 4 = accessibility, availability, nearness 5 = appliance, facility, comfort, amenity, labour-saving device, help

convenient 1 = suitable, fit, handy, satisfactory 2 = useful, practical, handy, serviceable, labour-saving ≠ useless 3 = nearby, available, accessible, handy, at hand, within reach, close at hand, just round the corner ≠ inaccessible

4 = appropriate, timely, suitable, helpful

convention 1 = custom, practice, tradition, code, usage, protocol, etiquette, propriety, kawa (*N.Z.*), tikanga (*N.Z.*) 2 = agreement, contract, treaty, bargain, pact, protocol 3 = assembly, meeting, council, conference, congress, convocation, hui (*N.Z.*), runanga (*N.Z.*)

conventional 1 = proper, conservative, respectable, genteel, conformist 2 = ordinary, standard, normal, regular, usual 3 = traditional, accepted, orthodox, customary 4 = unoriginal, routine, stereotyped, banal, prosaic, run-of-the-mill, hackneyed ≠ unconventional

converge VERB = come together, meet, join, combine, gather, merge, coincide, intersect

● PHRASES **converge on something** = close in on, arrive at, move towards, home in on, come together at

conversation = talk, discussion, dialogue, tête-à-tête, conference, chat, gossip, discourse, korero (*N.Z.*)

▩ RELATED WORD
adjective: colloquial

conversion 1 = change, transformation, metamorphosis 2 = adaptation, reconstruction, modification, alteration, remodelling, reorganization

convert VERB 1 = change, turn, transform, alter, transpose 2 = adapt, modify, remodel, reorganize, customize, restyle 3 = reform, convince, proselytize

● NOUN = neophyte, disciple, proselyte

convey 1 = communicate, impart, reveal, relate, disclose, make known, tell 2 = carry, transport, move, bring, bear, conduct, fetch

convict VERB = find guilty, sentence, condemn, imprison, pronounce guilty

● NOUN = prisoner, criminal, lag (*slang*), felon, jailbird

conviction 1 = belief, view, opinion, principle, faith, persuasion, creed, tenet, kaupapa (*N.Z.*) 2 = certainty, confidence, assurance, firmness, certitude

convince 1 = assure, persuade, satisfy, reassure 2 = persuade, induce, coax, talk into, prevail upon, bring round to the idea of

convincing = persuasive, credible, conclusive, telling, powerful, impressive, plausible, cogent ≠ unconvincing

cool ADJECTIVE 1 = cold, chilled, refreshing, chilly, nippy ≠ warm 2 = calm, collected, relaxed, composed, sedate, self-controlled, unruffled, unemotional ≠ agitated 3 = unfriendly, distant, indifferent, aloof, lukewarm, offhand, unenthusiastic, unwelcoming ≠ friendly 4 = unenthusiastic, indifferent, lukewarm, unwelcoming
• VERB 1 = lose heat, cool off ≠ warm (up) 2 = make cool, freeze, chill, refrigerate, cool off ≠ warm (up)
• NOUN 1 = coldness, chill, coolness 2 (*Slang*) = calmness, control, temper, composure, self-control, poise, self-discipline, self-possession

cooperate = work together, collaborate, coordinate, join forces, conspire, pull together, pool resources, combine your efforts ≠ conflict

cooperation = teamwork, unity, collaboration, give-and-take, combined effort, esprit de corps, kotahitanga (*N.Z.*) ≠ opposition

cooperative 1 = shared, joint, combined, collective, collaborative 2 = helpful, obliging, accommodating, supportive, responsive, onside (*informal*)

cope VERB = manage, get by (*informal*), struggle through, survive, carry on, make the grade, hold your own
• PHRASES **cope with something** = deal with, handle, struggle with, grapple with, wrestle with, contend with, weather

copy NOUN = reproduction, duplicate, replica, imitation, forgery, counterfeit, likeness, facsimile ≠ original
• VERB 1 = reproduce, replicate, duplicate, transcribe, counterfeit ≠ create 2 = imitate, act like, emulate, behave like, follow, repeat, mirror, ape

cord = rope, line, string, twine

cordon NOUN = chain, line, ring, barrier, picket line
• PHRASES **cordon something off** = surround, isolate, close off, fence off, separate, enclose, picket, encircle

core 1 = centre 2 = heart, essence, nucleus, kernel, crux, gist, nub, pith

corner NOUN 1 = angle, joint, crook 2 = bend, curve 3 = space, hideaway, nook, hide-out
• VERB 1 = trap, catch, run to earth 2 (usually with *market* as object)

= monopolize, take over, dominate, control, hog (*slang*), engross

corporation 1 = business, company, concern, firm, society, association, organization, enterprise 2 = town council, council, municipal authorities, civic authorities

corps = team, unit, regiment, detachment, company, band, division, troop

corpse = body, remains, carcass, cadaver, stiff (*slang*)

correct ADJECTIVE 1 = accurate, right, true, exact, precise, flawless, faultless, O.K. *or* okay (*informal*) ≠ inaccurate 2 = right, standard, appropriate, acceptable, proper, precise 3 = proper, seemly, standard, fitting, kosher (*informal*) ≠ inappropriate
• VERB 1 = rectify, remedy, redress, right, reform, cure, adjust, amend ≠ spoil 2 = rebuke, discipline, reprimand, chide, admonish, chastise, chasten, reprove ≠ praise

correction 1 = rectification, improvement, amendment, adjustment, modification, alteration, emendation 2 = punishment, discipline, reformation, admonition, chastisement, reproof, castigation

correctly = rightly, right, perfectly, properly, precisely, accurately

correctness 1 = truth, accuracy, precision, exactitude, exactness, faultlessness 2 = decorum, propriety, good manners, civility, good breeding

correspond 1 = be consistent, match, agree, accord, fit, square, tally, conform ≠ differ 2 = communicate, write, keep in touch, exchange letters

correspondence 1 = communication, writing, contact 2 = letters, post, mail 3 = relation, match, agreement, comparison, harmony, coincidence, similarity, correlation

correspondent 1 = reporter, journalist, contributor, hack 2 = letter writer, pen friend *or* pen pal

corresponding = equivalent, matching, similar, related, complementary, reciprocal, analogous

corridor = passage, alley, aisle, hallway, passageway

corrupt ADJECTIVE 1 = dishonest, bent (*slang*), crooked (*informal*), fraudulent, unscrupulous, venal, unprincipled

≠ honest 2 = <u>depraved</u>, vicious, degenerate, debased, profligate, dissolute 3 = <u>distorted</u>, doctored, altered, falsified

● VERB 1 = <u>bribe</u>, fix (*informal*), buy off, suborn, grease (someone's) palm (*slang*) 2 = <u>deprave</u>, pervert, subvert, debauch ≠ reform 3 = <u>distort</u>, doctor, tamper with

corruption 1 = <u>dishonesty</u>, fraud, bribery, extortion, venality, shady dealings (*informal*) 2 = <u>depravity</u>, vice, evil, perversion, decadence, wickedness, immorality 3 = <u>distortion</u>, doctoring, falsification

cosmetic = <u>superficial</u>, surface, nonessential

cosmic 1 = <u>extraterrestrial</u>, stellar 2 = <u>universal</u>, general, overarching

cosmopolitan = <u>sophisticated</u>, cultured, refined, cultivated, urbane, well-travelled, worldly-wise ≠ unsophisticated

cost NOUN 1 = <u>price</u>, worth, expense, charge, damage (*informal*), amount, payment, outlay 2 = <u>loss</u>, suffering, damage, injury, penalty, hurt, expense, harm

● PLURAL NOUN = <u>expenses</u>, spending, expenditure, overheads, outgoings, outlay, budget

● VERB 1 = <u>sell at</u>, come to, set (someone) back (*informal*), be priced at, command a price of 2 = <u>lose</u>, deprive of, cheat of

costly 1 = <u>expensive</u>, dear, stiff, steep (*informal*), highly-priced, exorbitant, extortionate ≠ inexpensive 2 = <u>damaging</u>, disastrous, harmful, catastrophic, loss-making, ruinous, deleterious

costume = <u>outfit</u>, dress, clothing, uniform, ensemble, livery, apparel, attire

cosy 1 = <u>comfortable</u>, homely, warm, intimate, snug, comfy (*informal*), sheltered 2 = <u>snug</u>, warm, comfortable, sheltered, comfy (*informal*), tucked up 3 = <u>intimate</u>, friendly, informal

cottage = <u>cabin</u>, lodge, hut, shack, chalet, whare (*N.Z.*)

cough VERB = <u>clear your throat</u>, bark, hack

● NOUN = <u>frog</u> or <u>tickle in your throat</u>, bark, hack

council 1 = <u>committee</u>, governing body, board 2 = <u>governing body</u>, parliament, congress, cabinet, panel, assembly, convention, conference, runanga (*N.Z.*)

counsel NOUN 1 = <u>advice</u>, information, warning, direction, suggestion,

recommendation, guidance 2 = <u>legal adviser</u>, lawyer, attorney, solicitor, advocate, barrister

● VERB = <u>advise</u>, recommend, advocate, warn, urge, instruct, exhort

count VERB 1 *often with* up = <u>add (up)</u>, total, reckon (up), tot up = calculate, compute, tally, number 2 = <u>matter</u>, be important, carry weight, tell, rate, weigh, signify 3 = <u>consider</u>, judge, regard, deem, think of, rate, look upon 4 = <u>include</u>, number among, take into account *or* consideration

● NOUN = <u>calculation</u>, poll, reckoning, sum, tally, numbering, computation, enumeration

● PHRASES **count on** *or* **upon something** *or* **someone** = <u>depend on</u>, trust, rely on, bank on, take for granted, lean on, reckon on, take on trust

counter VERB 1 = <u>oppose</u>, meet, block, resist, parry, deflect, repel, rebuff 2 = <u>retaliate</u>, answer, reply, respond, retort, hit back, rejoin, strike back ≠ yield

● ADVERB = <u>opposite to</u>, against, versus, conversely, in defiance of, at variance with, contrariwise ≠ in accordance with

counterpart = <u>opposite number</u>, equal, twin, equivalent, match, fellow, mate

countless = <u>innumerable</u>, legion, infinite, myriad, untold, limitless, incalculable, immeasurable ≠ limited

country 1 = <u>nation</u>, state, land, commonwealth, kingdom, realm, people 2 = <u>people</u>, community, nation, society, citizens, inhabitants, populace, public 3 = <u>countryside</u>, provinces, sticks (*informal*), farmland, outback (*Austral. & N.Z.*), green belt, backwoods, bush (*N.Z. & S. African*) ≠ town 4 = <u>territory</u>, land, region, terrain

countryside = <u>country</u>, rural areas, outback (*Austral. & N.Z.*), green belt, sticks (*informal*)

county = <u>province</u>, district, shire

coup = <u>masterstroke</u>, feat, stunt, action, exploit, manoeuvre, deed, accomplishment

couple NOUN = <u>pair</u>, two, brace, duo, twosome

● PHRASES **couple something to something** = <u>link to</u>, connect to, pair with, unite with, join to, hitch to, yoke to

coupon = <u>slip</u>, ticket, certificate, token,

voucher, card

courage = <u>bravery</u>, nerve, resolution, daring, pluck, heroism, mettle, gallantry ≠ cowardice

courageous = <u>brave</u>, daring, bold, gritty, fearless, gallant, intrepid, valiant ≠ cowardly

courier 1 = <u>messenger</u>, runner, carrier, bearer, envoy 2 = <u>guide</u>, representative, escort, conductor

course NOUN 1 = <u>route</u>, way, line, road, track, direction, path, passage 2 = <u>procedure</u>, plan, policy, programme, method, conduct, behaviour, manner 3 = <u>progression</u>, order, unfolding, development, movement, progress, flow, sequence 4 = <u>classes</u>, programme, schedule, lectures, curriculum 5 = <u>racecourse</u>, circuit 6 = <u>period</u>, time, duration, term, passing
● VERB 1 = <u>run</u>, flow, stream, gush, race, speed, surge 2 = <u>hunt</u>, follow, chase, pursue
● PHRASES **of course** = <u>naturally</u>, certainly, obviously, definitely, undoubtedly, needless to say, without a doubt, indubitably

court NOUN 1 = <u>law court</u>, bar, bench, tribunal 2 = <u>palace</u>, hall, castle, manor 3 = <u>royal household</u>, train, suite, attendants, entourage, retinue, cortege
● VERB 1 = <u>cultivate</u>, seek, flatter, solicit, pander to, curry favour with, fawn upon 2 = <u>invite</u>, seek, attract, prompt, provoke, bring about, incite 3 = <u>woo</u>, go (out) with, date, take out, run after, walk out with, set your cap at

courtesy 1 = <u>politeness</u>, good manners, civility, gallantry, graciousness, affability, urbanity 2 = <u>favour</u>, kindness, indulgence

courtyard = <u>yard</u>, square, piazza, quadrangle, plaza, enclosure, cloister, quad (*informal*)

cove = <u>bay</u>, sound, inlet, anchorage

covenant = <u>promise</u>, contract, agreement, commitment, arrangement, pledge, pact

cover VERB 1 = <u>conceal</u>, hide, mask, disguise, obscure, veil, cloak, shroud ≠ reveal 2 = <u>clothe</u>, dress, wrap, envelop ≠ uncover 3 = <u>overlay</u>, blanket 4 = <u>coat</u>, cake, plaster, smear, envelop, spread, encase, daub 5 = <u>submerge</u>, flood, engulf, overrun, wash over 6 = <u>travel over</u>, cross, traverse, pass through *or* over 7 = <u>protect</u>, guard, defend, shield 8 = <u>consider</u>, deal with, investigate, describe, tell of 9 = <u>report on</u>, write about, commentate on, relate, tell of, narrate, write up 10 = <u>pay for</u>, fund, provide for, offset, be enough for
● NOUN 1 = <u>protection</u>, shelter, shield, defence, guard, camouflage, concealment 2 = <u>insurance</u>, protection, compensation, indemnity, reimbursement 3 = <u>covering</u>, case, top, coating, envelope, lid, canopy, wrapper 4 = <u>bedclothes</u>, bedding, sheets, blankets, quilt, duvet, eiderdown 5 = <u>jacket</u>, case, wrapper 6 = <u>disguise</u>, front, screen, mask, veil, façade, pretext, smoke screen

covering NOUN = <u>cover</u>, coating, casing, wrapping, layer, blanket
● ADJECTIVE = <u>explanatory</u>, accompanying, introductory, descriptive

covet = <u>long for</u>, desire, envy, crave, aspire to, yearn for, lust after, set your heart on

coward = <u>wimp</u>, chicken (*slang*), scaredy-cat (*informal*), yellow-belly (*slang*)

cowardly = <u>faint-hearted</u>, scared, spineless, soft, yellow (*informal*), weak, chicken (*slang*), fearful, sookie (*N.Z.*) ≠ brave

cowboy = <u>cowhand</u>, drover, rancher, stockman, cattleman, herdsman, gaucho (*S. American*)

crack VERB 1 = <u>break</u>, split, burst, snap, fracture, splinter 2 = <u>snap</u>, ring, crash, burst, explode, pop, detonate 3 (*Informal*) = <u>hit</u>, clip (*informal*), slap, smack, clout (*informal*), cuff, whack 4 = <u>break</u>, cleave 5 = <u>solve</u>, work out, resolve, clear up, fathom, decipher, suss (out) (*slang*), get to the bottom of 6 = <u>break down</u>, collapse, yield, give in, give way, succumb, lose control, be overcome
● NOUN 1 = <u>break</u>, chink, gap, fracture, rift, cleft, crevice, fissure 2 = <u>split</u>, break, fracture 3 = <u>snap</u>, pop, crash, burst, explosion, clap, report 4 (*Informal*) = <u>blow</u>, slap, smack, clout (*informal*), cuff, whack, clip (*informal*) 5 (*Informal*) = <u>joke</u>, dig, gag (*informal*), quip, jibe, wisecrack, witticism, funny remark
● ADJECTIVE (*Slang*) = <u>first-class</u>, choice, excellent, ace, elite, superior, world-class, first-rate

crackdown = <u>clampdown</u>, crushing, repression, suppression

cracked = broken, damaged, split, chipped, flawed, faulty, defective, imperfect

cradle NOUN 1 = crib, cot, Moses basket, bassinet 2 = birthplace, beginning, source, spring, origin, fount, fountainhead, wellspring

● VERB = hold, support, rock, nurse, nestle

craft 1 = vessel, boat, ship, plane, aircraft, spacecraft 2 = occupation, work, business, trade, employment, pursuit, vocation, handicraft 3 = skill, art, ability, technique, know-how (informal), expertise, aptitude, artistry

craftsman = skilled worker, artisan, master, maker, wright, technician, smith

cram 1 = stuff, force, jam, shove, compress 2 = pack, fill, stuff 3 = squeeze, press, pack in 4 = study, revise, swot, bone up (informal), mug up (slang)

cramp[1] = spasm, pain, ache, contraction, pang, stitch, convulsion, twinge

cramp[2] = restrict, hamper, inhibit, hinder, handicap, constrain, obstruct, impede

cramped = restricted, confined, overcrowded, crowded, packed, uncomfortable, closed in, congested ≠ spacious

crash NOUN 1 = collision, accident, smash, wreck, prang (informal), bump, pile-up (informal) 2 = smash, clash, boom, bang, thunder, racket, din, clatter 3 = collapse, failure, depression, ruin, downfall

● VERB 1 = fall, plunge, topple, lurch, hurtle, overbalance, fall headlong 2 = plunge, hurtle 3 = collapse, fail, go under, be ruined, go bust (informal), fold up, go to the wall, go belly up (informal)

● PHRASES **crash into** = collide with, hit, bump into, drive into, plough into

crate = container, case, box, packing case, tea chest

crater = hollow, hole, depression, dip, cavity

crave 1 = long for, yearn for, hanker after, want, desire, hope for, lust after 2 (Informal) = beg, ask for, seek, petition, pray for, plead for, solicit, implore

craving = longing, hope, desire, yen (informal), hunger, appetite, yearning, thirst

crawl VERB = creep, slither, inch, wriggle, writhe, worm your way, advance slowly ≠ run

● PHRASES **crawl to someone** = grovel, creep, fawn, toady, humble yourself

craze = fad, fashion, trend, rage, enthusiasm, vogue, mania, infatuation

crazed = mad, crazy, raving, insane, lunatic, berko (Austral. slang), off the air (Austral. slang), porangi (N.Z.)

crazy 1 (Informal) = ridiculous, absurd, foolish, ludicrous, senseless, preposterous, idiotic, nonsensical, porangi (N.Z.) ≠ sensible 2 = insane, mad, unbalanced, deranged, nuts (slang), crazed, demented, off the air (Austral. slang), out of your mind, porangi (N.Z.) ≠ sane 3 = fanatical, wild (informal), mad, devoted, enthusiastic, passionate, infatuated ≠ uninterested

cream NOUN 1 = lotion, ointment, oil, essence, cosmetic, paste, emulsion, salve 2 = best, elite, prime, pick, flower, crème de la crème (French)

● NOUN or ADJECTIVE = off-white, ivory, yellowish-white

creamy 1 = milky, buttery 2 = smooth, soft, velvety, rich

crease NOUN 1 = fold, line, ridge, groove, corrugation 2 = wrinkle, line, crow's-foot

● VERB 1 = crumple, rumple, fold, double up, corrugate 2 = wrinkle, crumple, screw up

create 1 = cause, lead to, occasion, bring about 2 = make, produce, invent, compose, devise, originate, formulate, spawn ≠ destroy 3 = appoint, make, establish, set up, invest, install, constitute

creation 1 = universe, world, nature, cosmos 2 = invention, production, achievement, brainchild (informal), concoction, handiwork, pièce de résistance (French), magnum opus 3 = making, generation, formation, conception, genesis 4 = setting up, development, production, institution, foundation, establishment, formation, inception

creative = imaginative, gifted, artistic, inventive, original, inspired, clever, ingenious

creativity = imagination, inspiration, ingenuity, originality, inventiveness, cleverness

creator 1 = maker, father, author, designer, architect, inventor, originator 2 usually with cap. = God, Maker

creature 1 = <u>living thing</u>, being, animal, beast, brute 2 = <u>person</u>, man, woman, individual, soul, human being, mortal

credentials 1 = <u>qualifications</u>, ability, skill, fitness, attribute, capability, eligibility, aptitude 2 = <u>certification</u>, document, reference(s), papers, licence, passport, testimonial, authorization

credibility = <u>believability</u>, reliability, plausibility, trustworthiness

credible 1 = <u>believable</u>, possible, likely, reasonable, probable, plausible, conceivable, imaginable ≠ unbelievable 2 = <u>reliable</u>, honest, dependable, trustworthy, sincere, trusty ≠ unreliable

credit NOUN 1 = <u>praise</u>, honour, recognition, approval, tribute, acclaim, acknowledgment, kudos 2 = <u>source of satisfaction</u> or pride, asset, honour, feather in your cap 3 = <u>prestige</u>, reputation, standing, position, influence, regard, status, esteem 4 = <u>belief</u>, trust, confidence, faith, reliance, credence

● VERB = <u>believe</u>, rely on, have faith in, trust, accept

● PHRASES **credit someone with something** = <u>attribute to</u>, assign to, ascribe to, impute to

creed = <u>belief</u>, principles, doctrine, dogma, credo, catechism, articles of faith

creek 1 = <u>inlet</u>, bay, cove, bight, firth or frith (*Scot.*) 2 (*U.S., Canad., Austral., & N.Z.*) = <u>stream</u>, brook, tributary, bayou, rivulet, watercourse, runnel

creep VERB = <u>sneak</u>, steal, tiptoe, slink, skulk, approach unnoticed

● NOUN (*Slang*) = <u>bootlicker</u> (*informal*), sneak, sycophant, crawler (*slang*), toady

● PHRASES **give someone the creeps** (*Informal*) = <u>disgust</u>, frighten, scare, repel, repulse, make your hair stand on end, make you squirm

crescent = <u>meniscus</u>, sickle, new moon

crest 1 = <u>top</u>, summit, peak, ridge, highest point, pinnacle, apex, crown 2 = <u>tuft</u>, crown, comb, plume, mane 3 = <u>emblem</u>, badge, symbol, insignia, bearings, device

crew 1 = <u>(ship's) company</u>, hands, (ship's) complement 2 = <u>team</u>, squad, gang, corps, posse 3 (*Informal*) = <u>crowd</u>, set, bunch (*informal*), band, pack, gang, mob, horde

crime 1 = <u>offence</u>, violation, trespass, felony, misdemeanour, misdeed, transgression, unlawful act

2 = <u>lawbreaking</u>, corruption, illegality, vice, misconduct, wrongdoing

criminal NOUN = <u>lawbreaker</u>, convict, offender, crook (*informal*), villain, culprit, sinner, felon, rorter (*Austral. slang*), skelm (*S. African*)

● ADJECTIVE 1 = <u>unlawful</u>, illicit, lawless, wrong, illegal, corrupt, crooked (*informal*), immoral ≠ lawful 2 (*Informal*) = <u>disgraceful</u>, ridiculous, foolish, senseless, scandalous, preposterous, deplorable

cripple 1 = <u>disable</u>, paralyse, lame, maim, incapacitate, weaken, hamstring 2 = <u>damage</u>, destroy, ruin, spoil, impair, put paid to, put out of action ≠ help

crippled = <u>disabled</u>, handicapped, paralysed, lame, incapacitated

crisis 1 = <u>emergency</u>, plight, predicament, trouble, deep water, meltdown (*informal*), dire straits 2 = <u>critical point</u>, climax, height, crunch (*informal*), turning point, culmination, crux, moment of truth

crisp 1 = <u>firm</u>, crunchy, crispy, crumbly, fresh, brittle, unwilted ≠ soft 2 = <u>bracing</u>, fresh, refreshing, brisk, invigorating ≠ warm 3 = <u>clean</u>, smart, trim, neat, tidy, spruce, well-groomed, well-pressed

criterion = <u>standard</u>, test, rule, measure, principle, gauge, yardstick, touchstone

critic 1 = <u>judge</u>, authority, expert, analyst, commentator, pundit, reviewer, connoisseur 2 = <u>fault-finder</u>, attacker, detractor, knocker (*informal*)

critical 1 = <u>crucial</u>, decisive, pressing, serious, vital, urgent, all-important, pivotal ≠ unimportant 2 = <u>grave</u>, serious, acute, precarious ≠ safe 3 = <u>disparaging</u>, disapproving, scathing, derogatory, nit-picking (*informal*), censorious, fault-finding, captious ≠ complimentary 4 = <u>analytical</u>, penetrating, discriminating, discerning, perceptive, judicious ≠ undiscriminating

criticism 1 = <u>fault-finding</u>, censure, disapproval, disparagement, stick (*slang*), flak (*informal*), bad press, character assassination 2 = <u>analysis</u>, assessment, judgment, commentary, evaluation, appreciation, appraisal, critique

criticize = <u>find fault with</u>, censure, disapprove of, knock (*informal*), condemn, carp, put down, slate (*informal*) ≠ praise

crook NOUN (*Informal*) = <u>criminal</u>, rogue, cheat, thief, shark, villain, robber, racketeer,

skelm (*S. African*)
● **ADJECTIVE** (*Austral. & N.Z. informal*) = ill,
sick, poorly (*informal*), unhealthy, seedy
(*informal*), unwell, queasy, out of sorts
(*informal*)
● **PHRASES** **go (off) crook** (*Austral. & N.Z. informal*) = lose your temper, be furious,
rage, go mad, lose it (*informal*), crack up
(*informal*), see red (*informal*), blow your
top

crooked 1 = bent, twisted, curved,
irregular, warped, out of shape, misshapen
≠ straight 2 = deformed, distorted
3 = zigzag, winding, twisting 4 = at an
angle, uneven, slanting, squint, awry,
lopsided, askew, off-centre 5 (*Informal*)
= dishonest, criminal, illegal, corrupt,
unlawful, shady (*informal*), fraudulent,
bent (*slang*) ≠ honest

crop NOUN = yield, produce, gathering,
fruits, harvest, vintage, reaping
● **VERB** 1 = graze, eat, browse, feed on,
nibble 2 = cut, trim, clip, prune, shear, snip,
pare, lop
● **PHRASES** **crop up** (*Informal*) = happen,
appear, emerge, occur, arise, turn up,
spring up

cross VERB 1 = go across, pass over,
traverse, cut across, move across, travel
across 2 = span, bridge, go across, extend
over 3 = intersect, intertwine, crisscross
4 = oppose, interfere with, obstruct, block,
resist, impede 5 = interbreed, mix, blend,
cross-pollinate, crossbreed, hybridize,
cross-fertilize, intercross
● NOUN 1 = crucifix 2 = trouble, worry,
trial, load, burden, grief, woe, misfortune
3 = mixture, combination, blend,
amalgam, amalgamation 4 = crossroads,
crossing, junction, intersection
● **ADJECTIVE** = angry, annoyed, put out,
grumpy, short, ill-tempered, irascible,
tooshie (*Austral. slang*), in a bad mood,
hoha (*N.Z.*) ≠ good-humoured
● **PHRASES** **cross something out** *or* **off**
= strike off *or* out, eliminate, cancel, delete,
blue-pencil, score off *or* out

crouch = bend down, kneel, squat, stoop,
bow, duck, hunch

crow = gloat, triumph, boast, swagger,
brag, exult, blow your own trumpet

crowd NOUN 1 = multitude, mass, throng,
army, host, pack, mob, swarm 2 = group,
set, lot, circle, gang, bunch (*informal*),

clique 3 = audience, spectators, house,
gate, attendance
● **VERB** 1 = flock, mass, collect, gather,
stream, surge, swarm, throng 2 = squeeze,
pack, pile, bundle, cram 3 = congest, pack,
cram

crowded = packed, full, busy, cramped,
swarming, teeming, congested, jam-
packed

crown NOUN 1 = coronet, tiara, diadem,
circlet 2 = laurel wreath, trophy, prize,
honour, garland, laurels, wreath 3 = high
point, top, tip, summit, crest, pinnacle,
apex
● **VERB** 1 = install, honour, dignify, ordain,
inaugurate 2 = top, cap, be on top of,
surmount 3 = cap, finish, complete,
perfect, round off, put the finishing
touch to, be the climax *or* culmination of
4 (*Slang*) = strike, belt (*informal*), bash, hit
over the head, box, punch, cuff, biff (*slang*)
● **PHRASES** **the Crown** 1 = monarch, ruler,
sovereign, emperor *or* empress, king *or*
queen 2 = monarchy, sovereignty, royalty

crucial 1 (*Informal*) = vital, important,
pressing, essential, urgent, momentous,
high-priority 2 = critical, central, key,
psychological, decisive, pivotal

crude 1 = rough, basic, makeshift
2 = simple, rudimentary, basic, primitive,
coarse, clumsy, rough-and-ready
3 = vulgar, dirty, rude, obscene, coarse,
indecent, tasteless, smutty ≠ tasteful
4 = unrefined, natural, raw, unprocessed
≠ processed

crudely 1 = roughly, basically 2 = simply,
roughly, basically, coarsely 3 = vulgarly,
rudely, coarsely, crassly, obscenely, lewdly,
impolitely, tastelessly

cruel 1 = brutal, ruthless, callous, sadistic,
inhumane, vicious, monstrous, unkind
≠ kind 2 = bitter, ruthless, traumatic,
grievous, unrelenting, merciless, pitiless

cruelly 1 = brutally, severely, mercilessly,
in cold blood, callously, monstrously,
sadistically, pitilessly 2 = bitterly, deeply,
severely, ruthlessly, mercilessly, grievously,
pitilessly, traumatically

cruelty = brutality, ruthlessness, depravity,
inhumanity, barbarity, callousness,
spitefulness, mercilessness

cruise NOUN = sail, voyage, boat trip, sea
trip
● **VERB** 1 = sail, coast, voyage 2 = travel

along, coast, drift, keep a steady pace

crumb 1 = <u>bit</u>, grain, fragment, shred, morsel 2 = <u>morsel</u>, scrap, shred, snippet, soupçon (*French*)

crumble 1 = <u>disintegrate</u>, collapse, deteriorate, decay, fall apart, degenerate, tumble down, go to pieces 2 = <u>crush</u>, fragment, pulverize, pound, grind, powder, granulate 3 = <u>collapse</u>, deteriorate, decay, fall apart, degenerate, go to pieces, go to wrack and ruin

crumple 1 = <u>crush</u>, squash, screw up, scrumple 2 = <u>crease</u>, wrinkle, rumple, ruffle, pucker 3 = <u>collapse</u>, sink, go down, fall 4 = <u>break down</u>, fall, collapse, give way, cave in, go to pieces 5 = <u>screw up</u>

crunch VERB = <u>chomp</u>, champ, munch, chew noisily, grind
● NOUN (*Informal*) = <u>critical point</u>, test, crisis, emergency, crux, moment of truth

crusade NOUN 1 = <u>campaign</u>, drive, movement, cause, push 2 = <u>holy war</u>
● VERB = <u>campaign</u>, fight, push, struggle, lobby, agitate, work

crush VERB 1 = <u>squash</u>, break, squeeze, compress, press, pulverize 2 = <u>crease</u>, wrinkle, crumple 3 = <u>overcome</u>, overwhelm, put down, subdue, overpower, quash, quell, stamp out 4 = <u>demoralize</u>, depress, devastate, discourage, humble, put down (*slang*), humiliate, squash
● NOUN = <u>crowd</u>, mob, horde, throng, pack, mass, jam, huddle

crust = <u>layer</u>, covering, coating, skin, surface, shell

cry VERB 1 = <u>weep</u>, sob, shed tears, blubber, snivel ≠ laugh 2 = <u>shout</u>, scream, roar, yell, howl, call out, exclaim, shriek ≠ whisper
● NOUN 1 = <u>weep</u>, sob, bawl, blubber 2 = <u>shout</u>, call, scream, roar, yell, howl, shriek, bellow 3 = <u>appeal</u>, plea
● PLURAL NOUN = <u>weeping</u>, sobbing, blubbering, snivelling
● PHRASES **cry off** (*Informal*) = <u>back out</u>, withdraw, quit, excuse yourself

cuddle VERB 1 = <u>hug</u>, embrace, fondle, cosset 2 = <u>pet</u>, hug, bill and coo
● PHRASES **cuddle up** = <u>snuggle</u>

cue = <u>signal</u>, sign, hint, prompt, reminder, suggestion

culminate = <u>end up</u>, close, finish, conclude, wind up, climax, come to a head, come to a climax

culprit = <u>offender</u>, criminal, felon, guilty party, wrongdoer, miscreant, evildoer, transgressor

cult 1 = <u>sect</u>, faction, school, religion, clique, hauhau (*N.Z.*) 2 = <u>craze</u>, fashion, trend, fad 3 = <u>obsession</u>, worship, devotion, idolization

cultivate 1 = <u>farm</u>, work, plant, tend, till, plough 2 = <u>develop</u>, establish, foster 3 = <u>court</u>, seek out, run after, dance attendance upon 4 = <u>improve</u>, refine

cultural 1 = <u>ethnic</u>, national, native, folk, racial 2 = <u>artistic</u>, educational, aesthetic, enriching, enlightening, civilizing, edifying

culture 1 = <u>the arts</u> 2 = <u>civilization</u>, society, customs, way of life 3 = <u>lifestyle</u>, habit, way of life, mores 4 = <u>refinement</u>, education, enlightenment, sophistication, good taste, urbanity

cultured = <u>refined</u>, intellectual, educated, sophisticated, enlightened, well-informed, urbane, highbrow ≠ uneducated

cunning ADJECTIVE 1 = <u>crafty</u>, sly, devious, artful, sharp, wily, Machiavellian, shifty ≠ frank 2 = <u>ingenious</u>, imaginative, sly, devious, artful, Machiavellian 3 = <u>skilful</u>, clever ≠ clumsy
● NOUN 1 = <u>craftiness</u>, guile, trickery, deviousness, artfulness, slyness ≠ candour 2 = <u>skill</u>, subtlety, ingenuity, artifice, cleverness ≠ clumsiness

cup 1 = <u>mug</u>, goblet, chalice, teacup, beaker, bowl 2 = <u>trophy</u>

cupboard = <u>cabinet</u>, press

curb VERB = <u>restrain</u>, control, check, restrict, suppress, inhibit, hinder, retard
● NOUN = <u>restraint</u>, control, check, brake, limitation, rein, deterrent, bridle

cure VERB 1 = <u>make better</u>, correct, heal, relieve, remedy, mend, ease 2 = <u>restore to health</u>, restore, heal 3 = <u>preserve</u>, smoke, dry, salt, pickle
● NOUN = <u>remedy</u>, treatment, antidote, panacea, nostrum

curiosity 1 = <u>inquisitiveness</u>, interest, prying, snooping (*informal*), nosiness (*informal*) 2 = <u>oddity</u>, wonder, sight, phenomenon, spectacle, freak, novelty, rarity

curious ADJECTIVE 1 = <u>inquisitive</u>, interested, questioning, searching, inquiring, meddling, prying, nosy (*informal*) ≠ uninterested 2 = <u>strange</u>, unusual, bizarre, odd, novel, rare,

extraordinary, unexpected
● ADJECTIVE ≠ ordinary

curl NOUN 1 = <u>ringlet</u>, lock 2 = <u>twist</u>, spiral, coil, kink, whorl 3 = <u>crimp</u>, wave, perm
● VERB 1 = <u>twirl</u>, turn, bend, twist, curve, loop, spiral, coil 2 = <u>wind</u>

curly = <u>wavy</u>, curled, curling, fuzzy, frizzy

currency 1 = <u>money</u>, coinage, legal tender, notes, coins 2 = <u>acceptance</u>, popularity, circulation, vogue, prevalence

current NOUN 1 = <u>flow</u>, course, undertow, jet, stream, tide, progression, river 2 = <u>draught</u>, flow, breeze, puff 3 = <u>mood</u>, feeling, spirit, atmosphere, trend, tendency, undercurrent
● ADJECTIVE 1 = <u>present</u>, fashionable, up-to-date, contemporary, trendy (*Brit. informal*), topical, present-day, in fashion ≠ out-of-date 2 = <u>prevalent</u>, common, accepted, popular, widespread, customary, in circulation

curse VERB 1 = <u>swear</u>, cuss (*informal*), blaspheme, take the Lord's name in vain 2 = <u>abuse</u>, damn, scold, vilify
● NOUN 1 = <u>oath</u>, obscenity, blasphemy, expletive, profanity, imprecation, swearword 2 = <u>malediction</u>, jinx, anathema, hoodoo (*informal*), excommunication 3 = <u>affliction</u>, plague, scourge, trouble, torment, hardship, bane

cursed = <u>under a curse</u>, damned, doomed, jinxed, bedevilled, accursed, ill-fated

curtail = <u>reduce</u>, diminish, decrease, dock, cut back, shorten, lessen, cut short

curtain = <u>hanging</u>, drape (*chiefly U.S.*), portière

curve NOUN = <u>bend</u>, turn, loop, arc, curvature
● VERB = <u>bend</u>, turn, wind, twist, arch, snake, arc, coil

curved = <u>bent</u>, rounded, twisted, bowed, arched, serpentine, sinuous

cushion NOUN = <u>pillow</u>, pad, bolster, headrest, beanbag, hassock
● VERB 1 = <u>protect</u> 2 = <u>soften</u>, dampen, muffle, mitigate, deaden, suppress, stifle

custody 1 = <u>care</u>, charge, protection, supervision, safekeeping, keeping 2 = <u>imprisonment</u>, detention, confinement, incarceration

custom 1 = <u>tradition</u>, practice, convention, ritual, policy, rule, usage, kaupapa (*N.Z.*) 2 = <u>habit</u>, way, practice,

procedure, routine, wont 3 = <u>customers</u>, business, trade, patronage

customary 1 = <u>usual</u>, common, accepted, established, traditional, normal, ordinary, conventional ≠ unusual 2 = <u>accustomed</u>, regular, usual

customer = <u>client</u>, consumer, regular (*informal*), buyer, patron, shopper, purchaser

customs = <u>import charges</u>, tax, duty, toll, tariff

cut VERB 1 = <u>slit</u>, score, slice, slash, pierce, penetrate 2 = <u>chop</u>, split, slice, dissect 3 = <u>carve</u>, slice 4 = <u>sever</u>, cut in two 5 = <u>shape</u>, carve, engrave, chisel, form, score, fashion, whittle 6 = <u>slash</u>, wound 7 = <u>clip</u>, mow, trim, prune, snip, pare, lop 8 = <u>trim</u>, shave, snip 9 = <u>reduce</u>, lower, slim (down), diminish, slash, decrease, cut back ≠ increase 10 = <u>abridge</u>, edit, shorten, curtail, condense, abbreviate ≠ extend 11 = <u>delete</u>, take out, expurgate 12 = <u>hurt</u>, wound, upset, sting, hurt someone's feelings 13 (*Informal*) = <u>ignore</u>, avoid, slight, blank (*slang*), snub, spurn, cold-shoulder, turn your back on ≠ greet 14 = <u>cross</u>, bisect
● NOUN 1 = <u>incision</u>, nick, stroke, slash, slit 2 = <u>gash</u>, nick, wound, slash, laceration 3 = <u>reduction</u>, fall, lowering, slash, decrease, cutback 4 (*Informal*) = <u>share</u>, piece, slice, percentage, portion 5 = <u>style</u>, look, fashion, shape

cutback = <u>reduction</u>, cut, retrenchment, economy, decrease, lessening

cute = <u>appealing</u>, sweet, attractive, engaging, charming, delightful, lovable, winsome

cutting = <u>hurtful</u>, wounding, bitter, malicious, scathing, acrimonious, barbed, sarcastic ≠ kind

cycle = <u>series of events</u>, circle, revolution, rotation

cynic = <u>sceptic</u>, doubter, pessimist, misanthrope, misanthropist, scoffer

cynical 1 = <u>sceptical</u>, mocking, pessimistic, scoffing, contemptuous, scornful, distrustful, derisive ≠ trusting 2 = <u>unbelieving</u>, sceptical, disillusioned, pessimistic, disbelieving, mistrustful ≠ optimistic

cynicism 1 = <u>scepticism</u>, pessimism, misanthropy 2 = <u>disbelief</u>, doubt, scepticism, mistrust

d

dab VERB 1 = <u>pat</u>, touch, tap 2 = <u>apply</u>, daub, stipple
● NOUN 1 = <u>spot</u>, bit, drop, pat, smudge, speck 2 = <u>touch</u>, stroke, flick

daft (*Informal, chiefly Brit.*) 1 = <u>stupid</u>, crazy, silly, absurd, foolish, idiotic, witless, crackpot (*informal*), off the air (*Austral. slang*) 2 = <u>crazy</u>, mad, touched, nuts (*slang*), crackers (*Brit. slang*), insane, demented, deranged, off the air (*Austral. slang*), porangi (*N.Z.*)

dag NOUN (*N.Z. informal*) = <u>joker</u>, comic, wag, wit, comedian, clown, humorist, prankster
● PHRASES **rattle your dags** (*N.Z. informal*) = <u>hurry up</u>, get a move on, step on it (*informal*), get your skates on (*informal*), make haste

dagga (*S. African*) = <u>cannabis</u>, marijuana, pot (*slang*), dope (*slang*), hash (*slang*), grass (*slang*), weed (*slang*), hemp

daily ADVERB = <u>every day</u>, day by day, once a day
● ADJECTIVE = <u>everyday</u>, diurnal, quotidian

dam NOUN = <u>barrier</u>, wall, barrage, obstruction, embankment
● VERB = <u>block up</u>, restrict, hold back, barricade, obstruct

damage VERB = <u>spoil</u>, hurt, injure, harm, ruin, crush, devastate, wreck ≠ fix
● NOUN 1 = <u>destruction</u>, harm, loss, injury, suffering, hurt, ruin, devastation ≠ improvement 2 (*Informal*) = <u>cost</u>, price, charge, bill, amount, payment, expense, outlay
● PLURAL NOUN (*Law*) = <u>compensation</u>, fine, satisfaction, amends, reparation, restitution, reimbursement, atonement

damaging = <u>harmful</u>, detrimental, hurtful, ruinous, deleterious, injurious, disadvantageous ≠ helpful

dame = <u>lady</u>, baroness, dowager, grande dame (*French*), noblewoman, peeress

damn = <u>criticize</u>, condemn, blast, denounce, put down, censure ≠ praise

damned (*Slang*) = <u>infernal</u>, detestable, confounded, hateful, loathsome

damp ADJECTIVE = <u>moist</u>, wet, soggy, humid, dank, sopping, clammy, dewy ≠ dry
● NOUN = <u>moisture</u>, liquid, drizzle, dampness, wetness, dankness ≠ dryness
● VERB = <u>moisten</u>, wet, soak, dampen, moisturize
● PHRASES **damp something down** = <u>curb</u>, reduce, check, diminish, inhibit, stifle, allay, pour cold water on

dampen 1 = <u>reduce</u>, check, moderate, dull, restrain, stifle, lessen 2 = <u>moisten</u>, wet, spray, make damp

dance VERB 1 = <u>prance</u>, trip, hop, skip, sway, whirl, caper, jig 2 = <u>caper</u>, trip, spring, jump, bound, skip, frolic, cavort
● NOUN = <u>ball</u>, social, hop (*informal*), disco, knees-up (*Brit. informal*), discotheque, B and S (*Austral. informal*)

dancer = <u>ballerina</u>, Terpsichorean

danger 1 = <u>jeopardy</u>, vulnerability 2 = <u>hazard</u>, risk, threat, menace, peril, pitfall

dangerous = <u>perilous</u>, risky, hazardous, vulnerable, insecure, unsafe, precarious, breakneck ≠ safe

dangerously = <u>perilously</u>, alarmingly, precariously, recklessly, riskily, hazardously, unsafely

dangle 1 = <u>hang</u>, swing, trail, sway, flap, hang down 2 = <u>wave</u> 3 = <u>offer</u>, flourish, brandish, flaunt

dare 1 = <u>risk doing</u>, venture, presume, make bold (*archaic*), hazard doing 2 = <u>challenge</u>, provoke, defy, taunt, goad, throw down the gauntlet

daring ADJECTIVE = <u>brave</u>, bold, adventurous, reckless, fearless, audacious, intrepid, daredevil ≠ timid
● NOUN = <u>bravery</u>, nerve (*informal*), courage, spirit, bottle (*Brit. slang*), pluck, audacity, boldness ≠ timidity

dark ADJECTIVE 1 = <u>dim</u>, murky, shady, shadowy, grey, dingy, unlit, poorly lit 2 = <u>black</u>, brunette, ebony, dark-skinned, sable, dusky, swarthy ≠ fair 3 = <u>evil</u>, foul, sinister, vile, wicked, infernal 4 = <u>secret</u>, hidden, mysterious, concealed 5 = <u>gloomy</u>, sad, grim, miserable, bleak, dismal, pessimistic, melancholy ≠ cheerful
● NOUN 1 = <u>darkness</u>, shadows, gloom, dusk, obscurity, murk, dimness, semi-

darkness 2 = night, twilight, evening, evo (*Austral. slang*), dusk, night-time, nightfall

darken 1 = cloud, obscure, dim, overshadow, blacken ≠ brighten 2 = make dark, blacken

darkness = dark, shadows, shade, gloom, blackness, murk, duskiness

darling NOUN = beloved, love, dear, dearest, angel, treasure, precious, sweetheart
● ADJECTIVE = beloved, dear, treasured, precious, adored, cherished

dart = dash, run, race, shoot, fly, speed, spring, tear

dash VERB 1 = rush, run, race, shoot, fly, career, speed, tear ≠ dawdle 2 = throw, cast, pitch, slam, toss, hurl, fling, chuck (*informal*) 3 = crash, break, smash, shatter, splinter
● NOUN 1 = rush, run, race, sprint, dart, spurt, sortie 2 = drop, little, bit, shot (*informal*), touch, spot, trace, hint ≠ lot 3 (*Old-fashioned*) = style, spirit, flair, flourish, verve, panache, élan, brio

dashing 1 (*Old-fashioned*) = stylish, smart, elegant, flamboyant, sporty, jaunty, showy 2 = bold, spirited, gallant, swashbuckling, debonair ≠ dull

data = information, facts, figures, details, intelligence, statistics

date NOUN 1 = time, stage, period 2 = appointment, meeting, arrangement, commitment, engagement, rendezvous, tryst, assignation 3 = partner, escort, friend
● VERB 1 = put a date on, assign a date to, fix the period of 2 = become dated, become old-fashioned
● PHRASES **date from** *or* **date back to** (with a *time* or *date* as object) = come from, belong to, originate in, exist from, bear a date of

dated = old-fashioned, outdated, out of date, obsolete, unfashionable, outmoded, passé, old hat ≠ modern

daunting = intimidating, alarming, frightening, discouraging, unnerving, disconcerting, demoralizing, off-putting (*Brit. informal*) ≠ reassuring

dawn NOUN 1 = daybreak, morning, sunrise, daylight, aurora (*poetic*), crack of dawn, sunup, cockcrow 2 (*Literary*) = beginning, start, birth, rise, origin, emergence, advent, genesis

● VERB 1 = begin, start, rise, develop, emerge, unfold, originate 2 = grow light, break, brighten, lighten
● PHRASES **dawn on** *or* **upon someone** = hit, strike, occur to, register (*informal*), become apparent, come to mind, come into your head

day 1 = twenty-four hours 2 = daytime, daylight 3 = date 4 = time, age, era, period, epoch

daylight = sunlight, sunshine, light of day

daze VERB = stun, shock, paralyse, numb, stupefy, benumb
● NOUN (usually used in the phrase *in a daze*) = shock, confusion, distraction, trance, bewilderment, stupor, trancelike state

dazzle VERB 1 = impress, amaze, overwhelm, astonish, overpower, bowl over (*informal*), take your breath away 2 = blind, confuse, daze, bedazzle
● NOUN = splendour, sparkle, glitter, brilliance, magnificence, razzmatazz (*slang*)

dazzling = splendid, brilliant, stunning, glorious, sparkling, glittering, sensational (*informal*), virtuoso ≠ ordinary

dead ADJECTIVE 1 = deceased, departed, late, perished, extinct, defunct, passed away ≠ alive 2 = boring, dull, dreary, flat, plain, humdrum, uninteresting 3 = not working, useless, inactive, inoperative ≠ working 4 = numb, frozen, paralysed, insensitive, inert, deadened, immobilized, unfeeling 5 (usually used of *centre, silence*, or *stop*) = total, complete, absolute, utter, outright, thorough, unqualified 6 (*Informal*) = exhausted, tired, worn out, spent, done in (*informal*), all in (*slang*), drained, knackered (*slang*)
● NOUN = middle, heart, depth, midst
● ADVERB (*Informal*) = exactly, completely, totally, directly, fully, entirely, absolutely, thoroughly

deadline = time limit, cutoff point, target date *or* time, limit

deadlock 1 = impasse, stalemate, standstill, gridlock, standoff 2 = tie, draw, stalemate, impasse, standstill, gridlock, standoff, dead heat

deadly 1 = lethal, fatal, deathly, dangerous, devastating, mortal, murderous, malignant 2 (*Informal*) = boring, dull, tedious, flat, monotonous,

uninteresting, mind-numbing, wearisome
deaf 1 = <u>hard of hearing</u>, without hearing,
stone deaf **2** = <u>oblivious</u>, indifferent,
unmoved, unconcerned, unsympathetic,
impervious, unhearing
deal NOUN **1** (*Informal*) = <u>agreement</u>,
understanding, contract, arrangement,
bargain, transaction, pact **2** = <u>amount</u>,
quantity, measure, degree, mass, volume,
share, portion
● PHRASES **deal in something** = <u>sell</u>,
trade in, stock, traffic in, buy and sell
◆ **deal something out** = <u>distribute</u>,
give, share, assign, allocate, dispense,
allot, mete out ◆ **deal with something**
= <u>be concerned with</u>, involve, concern,
touch, regard, apply to, bear on, pertain to
◆ **deal with something** *or* **someone**
= <u>handle</u>, manage, treat, cope with, take
care of, see to, attend to, get to grips with
dealer = <u>trader</u>, merchant, supplier,
wholesaler, purveyor, tradesman
dear ADJECTIVE **1** = <u>beloved</u>, close, valued,
favourite, prized, treasured, precious,
intimate ≠ hated **2** (*Brit. informal*)
= <u>expensive</u>, costly, high-priced, pricey
(*informal*), at a premium, overpriced,
exorbitant ≠ cheap
● NOUN = <u>darling</u>, love, dearest, angel,
treasure, precious, beloved, loved one
dearly (*Formal*) **1** = <u>very much</u>, greatly,
extremely, profoundly **2** = <u>at great cost</u>, at
a high price
death 1 = <u>dying</u>, demise, end, passing,
departure ≠ birth **2** = <u>destruction</u>, finish,
ruin, undoing, extinction, downfall
≠ beginning
RELATED WORDS
adjectives: fatal, lethal, mortal
deathly = <u>deathlike</u>, white, pale, ghastly,
wan, pallid, ashen
debacle *or* **débâcle** = <u>disaster</u>,
catastrophe, fiasco
debate NOUN = <u>discussion</u>, talk, argument,
dispute, analysis, conversation, controversy,
dialogue
● VERB **1** = <u>discuss</u>, question, talk about,
argue about, dispute, examine, deliberate
2 = <u>consider</u>, reflect, think about, weigh,
contemplate, deliberate, ponder, ruminate
debris = <u>remains</u>, bits, waste, ruins,
fragments, rubble, wreckage, detritus
debt NOUN = <u>debit</u>, commitment,
obligation, liability

● PHRASES **in debt** = <u>owing</u>, liable, in the
red (*informal*), in arrears
debtor = <u>borrower</u>, mortgagor
debut = <u>entrance</u>, beginning, launch,
coming out, introduction, presentation,
first appearance, initiation
decay VERB **1** = <u>rot</u>, spoil, crumble,
deteriorate, perish, decompose, moulder,
go bad **2** = <u>decline</u>, diminish, crumble,
deteriorate, fall off, dwindle, lessen, wane
≠ grow
● NOUN **1** = <u>rot</u>, corruption, mould, blight,
decomposition, gangrene, canker, caries
2 = <u>decline</u>, collapse, deterioration, failing,
fading, degeneration ≠ growth
deceased = <u>dead</u>, late, departed, expired,
defunct, lifeless
deceive = <u>take in</u>, trick, fool (*informal*),
cheat, con (*informal*), mislead, dupe,
swindle
decency 1 = <u>propriety</u>, correctness,
decorum, respectability, etiquette
2 = <u>courtesy</u>, politeness, civility,
graciousness, urbanity, courteousness
decent 1 = <u>satisfactory</u>, fair, all right,
reasonable, sufficient, good enough,
adequate, ample ≠ unsatisfactory
2 = <u>proper</u>, becoming, seemly, fitting,
appropriate, suitable, respectable,
befitting ≠ improper **3** (*Informal*) = <u>good</u>,
kind, friendly, neighbourly, generous,
helpful, obliging, accommodating
4 = <u>respectable</u>, pure, proper, modest,
chaste, decorous
deception 1 = <u>trickery</u>, fraud, deceit,
cunning, treachery, guile, legerdemain
≠ honesty **2** = <u>trick</u>, lie, bluff, hoax, decoy,
ruse, subterfuge
decide 1 = <u>make a decision</u>, make up
your mind, reach *or* come to a decision,
choose, determine, conclude ≠ hesitate
2 = <u>resolve</u>, answer, determine, conclude,
clear up, ordain, adjudicate, adjudge
3 = <u>settle</u>, determine, resolve
decidedly = <u>definitely</u>, clearly, positively,
distinctly, downright, unequivocally,
unmistakably
decision 1 = <u>judgment</u>, finding, ruling,
sentence, resolution, conclusion, verdict,
decree **2** = <u>decisiveness</u>, purpose,
resolution, resolve, determination,
firmness, forcefulness, strength of mind
or will
decisive 1 = <u>crucial</u>, significant, critical,

influential, momentous, conclusive, fateful ≠ uncertain 2 = resolute, decided, firm, determined, forceful, incisive, trenchant, strong-minded ≠ indecisive

deck = decorate, dress, clothe, array, adorn, embellish, festoon, beautify

declaration 1 = announcement, proclamation, decree, notice, notification, edict, pronouncement 2 = affirmation, profession, assertion, revelation, disclosure, acknowledgment, protestation, avowal 3 = statement, testimony

declare 1 = state, claim, announce, voice, express, maintain, assert, proclaim 2 = testify, state, swear, assert, affirm, bear witness, vouch 3 = make known, reveal, show, broadcast, confess, communicate, disclose

decline VERB 1 = fall, drop, lower, sink, fade, shrink, diminish, decrease ≠ rise 2 = deteriorate, weaken, pine, decay, worsen, languish, degenerate, droop ≠ improve 3 = refuse, reject, turn down, avoid, spurn, abstain, say 'no' ≠ accept ● NOUN 1 = depression, recession, slump, falling off, downturn, dwindling, lessening ≠ rise 2 = deterioration, failing, weakening, decay, worsening, degeneration ≠ improvement

décor or **decor** = decoration, colour scheme, ornamentation, furnishing style

decorate 1 = adorn, trim, embroider, ornament, embellish, festoon, beautify, grace 2 = do up, paper, paint, wallpaper, renovate (informal), furbish 3 = pin a medal on, cite, confer an honour on or upon

decoration 1 = adornment, trimming, enhancement, elaboration, embellishment, ornamentation, beautification 2 = ornament, trimmings, garnish, frill, bauble 3 = medal, award, star, ribbon, badge

decorative = ornamental, fancy, pretty, attractive, for show, embellishing, showy, beautifying

decrease VERB 1 = drop, decline, lessen, lower, shrink, diminish, dwindle, subside 2 = reduce, cut, lower, moderate, weaken, diminish, cut down, shorten ≠ increase ● NOUN = lessening, decline, reduction, loss, falling off, dwindling, contraction, cutback ≠ growth

decree NOUN 1 = law, order, ruling, act,

command, statute, proclamation, edict 2 = judgment, finding, ruling, decision, verdict, arbitration ● VERB = order, rule, command, demand, proclaim, prescribe, pronounce, ordain

dedicate 1 = devote, give, apply, commit, pledge, surrender, give over to 2 = offer, address, inscribe

dedicated = committed, devoted, enthusiastic, single-minded, zealous, purposeful, wholehearted ≠ indifferent

dedication 1 = commitment, loyalty, devotion, allegiance, adherence, single-mindedness, faithfulness, wholeheartedness ≠ indifference 2 = inscription, message, address

deduct = subtract, remove, take off, take away, reduce by, knock off (informal), decrease by ≠ add

deduction 1 = conclusion, finding, verdict, judgment, assumption, inference 2 = reasoning, thinking, thought, analysis, logic 3 = discount, reduction, cut, concession, decrease, rebate, diminution 4 = subtraction, reduction, concession

deed 1 = action, act, performance, achievement, exploit, feat 2 (Law) = document, title, contract

deep ADJECTIVE 1 = big, wide, broad, profound, yawning, bottomless, unfathomable ≠ shallow 2 = intense, great, serious (informal), acute, extreme, grave, profound, heartfelt ≠ superficial 3 = sound, profound, unbroken, undisturbed, untroubled 4 = absorbed, lost, gripped, preoccupied, immersed, engrossed, rapt 5 = dark, strong, rich, intense, vivid ≠ light 6 = low, booming, bass, resonant, sonorous, low-pitched ≠ high 7 = secret, hidden, mysterious, obscure, abstract, esoteric, mystifying, arcane 8 = far, a long way, a good way, miles, a great distance ● NOUN = middle, heart, midst, dead ● PHRASES **the deep** (Poetic) = the ocean, the sea, the waves, the main, the high seas, the briny (informal)

deepen 1 = intensify, increase, grow, strengthen, reinforce, escalate, magnify 2 = dig out, excavate, scoop out, hollow out

deeply = thoroughly, completely, seriously, sadly, severely, gravely, profoundly, intensely

de facto ADJECTIVE = <u>actual</u>, real, existing
 ● ADVERB = <u>in fact</u>, really, actually, in effect, in reality
default VERB = <u>fail to pay</u>, dodge, evade, neglect
 ● NOUN 1 (usually in phrase *by default* or *in default of*) = <u>failure</u>, neglect, deficiency, lapse, omission, dereliction 2 = <u>nonpayment</u>, evasion
defeat VERB 1 = <u>beat</u>, crush, overwhelm, conquer, master, rout, trounce, vanquish ≠ surrender 2 = <u>frustrate</u>, foil, thwart, ruin, baffle, confound, balk, get the better of
 ● NOUN 1 = <u>conquest</u>, beating, overthrow, rout ≠ victory 2 = <u>frustration</u>, failure, reverse, setback, thwarting
defect NOUN = <u>deficiency</u>, failing, fault, error, flaw, imperfection
 ● VERB = <u>desert</u>, rebel, quit, revolt, change sides
defence *or* (*U.S.*) **defense** NOUN
 1 = <u>protection</u>, cover, security, guard, shelter, safeguard, immunity 2 = <u>armaments</u>, weapons 3 = <u>argument</u>, explanation, excuse, plea, justification, vindication, rationalization 4 = <u>plea</u> (*Law*), testimony, denial, alibi, rebuttal
 ● PLURAL NOUN = <u>shield</u>, barricade, fortification, buttress, rampart, bulwark, fortified pa (*N.Z.*)
defend 1 = <u>protect</u>, cover, guard, screen, preserve, look after, shelter, shield 2 = <u>support</u>, champion, justify, endorse, uphold, vindicate, stand up for, speak up for
defendant = <u>the accused</u>, respondent, prisoner at the bar
defender 1 = <u>supporter</u>, champion, advocate, sponsor, follower 2 = <u>protector</u>, guard, guardian, escort, bodyguard
defensive 1 = <u>protective</u>, watchful, on the defensive, on guard 2 = <u>oversensitive</u>, uptight (*informal*)
defer = <u>postpone</u>, delay, put off, suspend, shelve, hold over, procrastinate, put on ice (*informal*)
defiance = <u>resistance</u>, opposition, confrontation, contempt, disregard, disobedience, insolence, insubordination ≠ obedience
defiant = <u>resisting</u>, rebellious, daring, bold, provocative, audacious, antagonistic, insolent ≠ obedient
deficiency 1 = <u>lack</u>, want, deficit, absence,

shortage, scarcity, dearth ≠ sufficiency 2 = <u>failing</u>, fault, weakness, defect, flaw, drawback, shortcoming, imperfection
deficit = <u>shortfall</u>, shortage, deficiency, loss, arrears
define 1 = <u>mark out</u>, outline, limit, bound, delineate, circumscribe, demarcate 2 = <u>describe</u>, interpret, characterize, explain, spell out, expound 3 = <u>establish</u>, specify, designate
definite 1 = <u>specific</u>, exact, precise, clear, particular, fixed, black-and-white, cut-and-dried (*informal*) ≠ vague 2 = <u>clear</u>, black-and-white, unequivocal, unambiguous, guaranteed, cut-and-dried (*informal*) 3 = <u>noticeable</u>, marked, clear, decided, striking, particular, distinct, conspicuous 4 = <u>certain</u>, decided, sure, settled, convinced, positive, confident, assured ≠ uncertain
definitely = <u>certainly</u>, clearly, surely, absolutely, positively, without doubt, unquestionably, undeniably
definition 1 = <u>description</u>, interpretation, explanation, clarification, exposition, elucidation, statement of meaning 2 = <u>sharpness</u>, focus, clarity, contrast, precision, distinctness
definitive 1 = <u>final</u>, convincing, absolute, clinching, decisive, definite, conclusive, irrefutable 2 = <u>authoritative</u>, greatest, ultimate, reliable, exhaustive, superlative
deflect = <u>turn aside</u>, bend
defy = <u>resist</u>, oppose, confront, brave, disregard, stand up to, spurn, flout
degenerate VERB = <u>decline</u>, slip, sink, decrease, deteriorate, worsen, decay, lapse
 ● ADJECTIVE = <u>depraved</u>, corrupt, low, perverted, immoral, decadent, debauched, dissolute
degrade = <u>demean</u>, disgrace, humiliate, shame, humble, discredit, debase, dishonour ≠ ennoble
degree = <u>amount</u>, stage, grade
delay VERB 1 = <u>put off</u>, suspend, postpone, shelve, defer, hold over 2 = <u>hold up</u>, detain, hold back, hinder, obstruct, impede, bog down, set back ≠ speed (up)
 ● NOUN = <u>hold-up</u>, wait, setback, interruption, stoppage, impediment, hindrance
delegate NOUN = <u>representative</u>, agent, deputy, ambassador, commissioner, envoy, proxy, legate

● VERB 1 = <u>entrust</u>, transfer, hand over, give, pass on, assign, consign, devolve 2 = <u>appoint</u>, commission, select, contract, engage, nominate, designate, mandate

delegation 1 = <u>deputation</u>, envoys, contingent, commission, embassy, legation 2 = <u>commissioning</u>, assignment, devolution, committal

delete = <u>remove</u>, cancel, erase, strike out, obliterate, efface, cross out, expunge

deliberate ADJECTIVE 1 = <u>intentional</u>, meant, planned, intended, conscious, calculated, wilful, purposeful ≠ accidental 2 = <u>careful</u>, measured, slow, cautious, thoughtful, circumspect, methodical, unhurried ≠ hurried

● VERB = <u>consider</u>, think, ponder, discuss, debate, reflect, consult, weigh

deliberately = <u>intentionally</u>, on purpose, consciously, knowingly, wilfully, by design, in cold blood, wittingly

deliberation 1 = <u>consideration</u>, thought, reflection, calculation, meditation, forethought, circumspection 2 = <u>discussion</u>, talk, conference, debate, analysis, conversation, dialogue, consultation

delicacy 1 = <u>fragility</u>, flimsiness 2 = <u>daintiness</u>, charm, grace, elegance, neatness, prettiness, slenderness, exquisiteness 3 = <u>difficulty</u> 4 = <u>sensitivity</u>, understanding, consideration, diplomacy, discretion, tact, thoughtfulness, sensitiveness 5 = <u>treat</u>, luxury, savoury, dainty, morsel, titbit 6 = <u>lightness</u>, accuracy, precision, elegance, sensibility, purity, subtlety, refinement

delicate 1 = <u>fine</u>, elegant, exquisite, graceful 2 = <u>subtle</u>, fine, delicious, faint, refined, understated, dainty ≠ bright 3 = <u>fragile</u>, weak, frail, brittle, tender, flimsy, dainty, breakable 4 = <u>skilled</u>, precise, deft 5 = <u>diplomatic</u>, sensitive, thoughtful, discreet, considerate, tactful ≠ insensitive

delicious = <u>delectable</u>, tasty, choice, savoury, dainty, mouthwatering, scrumptious (*informal*), appetizing, lekker (*S. African slang*), yummo (*Austral. slang*) ≠ unpleasant

delight NOUN = <u>pleasure</u>, joy, satisfaction, happiness, ecstasy, enjoyment, bliss, glee ≠ displeasure

● VERB = <u>please</u>, satisfy, thrill, charm, cheer, amuse, enchant, gratify ≠ displease

● PHRASES **delight in** *or* **take (a) delight in something** *or* **someone** = <u>like</u>, love, enjoy, appreciate, relish, savour, revel in, take pleasure in

delightful = <u>pleasant</u>, charming, thrilling, enjoyable, enchanting, agreeable, pleasurable, rapturous ≠ unpleasant

deliver 1 = <u>bring</u>, carry, bear, transport, distribute, convey, cart 2 *sometimes with* **up** = <u>hand over</u>, commit, give up, yield, surrender, turn over, relinquish, make over 3 = <u>give</u>, read, present, announce, declare, utter 4 = <u>strike</u>, give, deal, launch, direct, aim, administer, inflict 5 (*Dated*) = <u>release</u>, free, save, rescue, loose, liberate, ransom, emancipate

delivery 1 = <u>handing over</u>, transfer, distribution, transmission, dispatch, consignment, conveyance 2 = <u>consignment</u>, goods, shipment, batch 3 = <u>speech</u>, utterance, articulation, intonation, elocution, enunciation 4 = <u>childbirth</u>, labour, confinement, parturition

delusion = <u>misconception</u>, mistaken idea, misapprehension, fancy, illusion, hallucination, fallacy, false impression

demand VERB 1 = <u>request</u>, ask (for), order, expect, claim, seek, insist on, exact 2 = <u>challenge</u>, ask, question, inquire 3 = <u>require</u>, want, need, involve, call for, entail, necessitate, cry out for ≠ provide ● NOUN 1 = <u>request</u>, order 2 = <u>need</u>, want, call, market, claim, requirement

demanding = <u>difficult</u>, trying, hard, taxing, wearing, challenging, tough, exacting ≠ easy

demise 1 = <u>failure</u>, end, fall, defeat, collapse, ruin, breakdown, overthrow 2 (*Euphemistic*) = <u>death</u>, end, dying, passing, departure, decease

democracy = <u>self-government</u>, republic, commonwealth

Democrat ADJECTIVE = <u>left-wing</u>, Labour ● NOUN = <u>left-winger</u>

democratic = <u>self-governing</u>, popular, representative, autonomous, populist, egalitarian

demolish 1 = <u>knock down</u>, level, destroy, dismantle, flatten, tear down, bulldoze, raze ≠ build 2 = <u>destroy</u>, wreck, overturn, overthrow, undo

demolition = <u>knocking down</u>, levelling, destruction, explosion, wrecking, tearing down, bulldozing, razing

demon 1 = <u>evil spirit</u>, devil, fiend, goblin, ghoul, malignant spirit, atua (*N.Z.*), wairua (*N.Z.*) 2 = <u>wizard</u>, master, ace (*informal*), fiend

demonstrate 1 = <u>prove</u>, show, indicate, make clear, manifest, testify to 2 = <u>show</u>, express, display, indicate, exhibit, manifest 3 = <u>march</u>, protest, rally, object, parade, picket, remonstrate, express disapproval, hikoi (*N.Z.*) 4 = <u>describe</u>, show, explain, teach, illustrate

demonstration 1 = <u>march</u>, protest, rally, sit-in, parade, picket, mass lobby, hikoi (*N.Z.*) 2 = <u>display</u>, show, performance, explanation, description, presentation, exposition 3 = <u>indication</u>, proof, testimony, confirmation, substantiation 4 = <u>exhibition</u>, display, expression, illustration

den 1 = <u>lair</u>, hole, shelter, cave, haunt, cavern, hide-out 2 (*Chiefly U.S.*) = <u>study</u>, retreat, sanctuary, hideaway, sanctum, cubbyhole

denial 1 = <u>negation</u>, contradiction, dissent, retraction, repudiation ≠ admission 2 = <u>refusal</u>, veto, rejection, prohibition, rebuff, repulse 3 = <u>renunciation</u>, giving up, rejection, abdication, repudiation, forswearing, disavowal, relinquishment

denomination 1 = <u>religious group</u>, belief, sect, persuasion, creed, school, hauhau (*N.Z.*) 2 = <u>unit</u>, value, size, grade

denounce 1 = <u>condemn</u>, attack, censure, revile, vilify, stigmatize 2 = <u>report</u>, dob in (*Austral. slang*)

dense 1 = <u>thick</u>, heavy, solid, compact, condensed, impenetrable, close-knit ≠ thin 2 = <u>heavy</u>, thick, opaque, impenetrable 3 = <u>stupid</u> (*Informal*), thick, dull, dumb (*informal*), dozy (*Brit. informal*), stolid, dopey (*informal*), moronic ≠ bright

density 1 = <u>tightness</u>, thickness, compactness, impenetrability, denseness 2 = <u>mass</u>, bulk, consistency, solidity

dent VERB = <u>make a dent in</u>, press in, gouge, hollow, push in
● NOUN = <u>hollow</u>, chip, indentation, depression, impression, pit, dip, crater, ding (*Austral. & N.Z. dated informal*)

deny 1 = <u>contradict</u>, disagree with, rebuff, negate, rebut, refute ≠ admit 2 = <u>renounce</u>, reject, retract, repudiate,

disown, recant, disclaim 3 = <u>refuse</u>, forbid, reject, rule out, turn down, prohibit, withhold, preclude ≠ permit

depart 1 = <u>leave</u>, go, withdraw, retire, disappear, quit, retreat, exit ≠ arrive 2 = <u>deviate</u>, vary, differ, stray, veer, swerve, diverge, digress

department = <u>section</u>, office, unit, station, division, branch, bureau, subdivision

departure 1 = <u>leaving</u>, going, retirement, withdrawal, exit, going away, removal, exodus ≠ arrival 2 = <u>retirement</u>, going, withdrawal, exit, going away, removal 3 = <u>shift</u>, change, difference, variation, innovation, novelty, deviation, divergence

depend 1 = <u>be determined by</u>, be based on, be subject to, hang on, rest on, revolve around, hinge on, be subordinate to 2 = <u>count on</u>, turn to, trust in, bank on, lean on, rely upon, reckon on

dependent *or* (*U.S. sometimes*)
dependant ADJECTIVE = <u>reliant</u>, vulnerable, helpless, powerless, weak, defenceless ≠ independent
● PHRASES **dependent on** *or* **upon** 1 = <u>reliant on</u>, relying on 2 = <u>determined by</u>, depending on, subject to, influenced by, conditional on, contingent on

depict 1 = <u>illustrate</u>, portray, picture, paint, outline, draw, sketch, delineate 2 = <u>describe</u>, present, represent, outline, characterize

deplete = <u>use up</u>, reduce, drain, exhaust, consume, empty, lessen, impoverish ≠ increase

deplore = <u>disapprove of</u>, condemn, object to, denounce, censure, abhor, take a dim view of

deploy (used of troops or military resources) = <u>use</u>, station, position, arrange, set out, utilize

deployment (used of troops or military resources) = <u>use</u>, stationing, spread, organization, arrangement, positioning, utilization

deport = <u>expel</u>, exile, throw out, oust, banish, expatriate, extradite, evict

depose = <u>oust</u>, dismiss, displace, demote, dethrone, remove from office

deposit NOUN 1 = <u>down payment</u>, security, stake, pledge, instalment, retainer, part payment 2 = <u>accumulation</u>, mass, build-up, layer 3 = <u>sediment</u>, grounds, residue,

lees, precipitate, silt, dregs
● VERB 1 = put, place, lay, drop 2 = store, keep, put, bank, lodge, entrust, consign

depot 1 = arsenal, warehouse, storehouse, repository, depository 2 (*Chiefly U.S. & Canad.*) = bus station, station, garage, terminus

depreciation = devaluation, fall, drop, depression, slump, deflation

depress 1 = sadden, upset, distress, discourage, grieve, oppress, weigh down, make sad ≠ cheer 2 = lower, cut, reduce, diminish, decrease, lessen ≠ raise 3 = devalue, depreciate, cheapen 4 = press down, push, squeeze, lower, flatten, compress, push down

depressed 1 = sad, blue, unhappy, discouraged, fed up, mournful, dejected, despondent 2 = poverty-stricken, poor, deprived, disadvantaged, run-down, impoverished, needy 3 = lowered, devalued, weakened, depreciated, cheapened 4 = sunken, hollow, recessed, indented, concave

depressing = bleak, sad, discouraging, gloomy, dismal, harrowing, saddening, dispiriting

depression 1 = despair, misery, sadness, dumps (*informal*), the blues, melancholy, unhappiness, despondency 2 = recession, slump, economic decline, stagnation, inactivity, hard *or* bad times 3 = hollow, pit, dip, bowl, valley, dent, cavity, indentation

deprivation 1 = lack, denial, withdrawal, removal, expropriation, dispossession 2 = want, need, hardship, suffering, distress, privation, destitution

deprive = dispossess, rob, strip, despoil, bereave

deprived = poor, disadvantaged, needy, in need, lacking, bereft, destitute, down at heel ≠ prosperous

depth 1 = deepness, drop, measure, extent 2 = insight, wisdom, penetration, profundity, discernment, sagacity, astuteness, profoundness ≠ superficiality 3 = breadth

deputy = substitute, representative, delegate, lieutenant, proxy, surrogate, second-in-command, legate

derelict ADJECTIVE = abandoned, deserted, ruined, neglected, discarded, forsaken, dilapidated

● NOUN = tramp, outcast, drifter, down-and-out, vagrant, bag lady, derro (*Austral. slang*)

descend VERB 1 = fall, drop, sink, go down, plunge, dive, tumble, plummet ≠ rise 2 = get off 3 = go down, come down, walk down, move down, climb down 4 = slope, dip, incline, slant
● PHRASES **be descended from** = originate from, derive from, spring from, proceed from, issue from

descent 1 = fall, drop, plunge, coming down, swoop 2 = slope, drop, dip, incline, slant, declivity 3 = decline, deterioration, degeneration 4 = origin, extraction, ancestry, lineage, family tree, parentage, genealogy, derivation

describe 1 = relate, tell, report, explain, express, recount, recite, narrate 2 = portray, depict 3 = trace, draw, outline, mark out, delineate

description 1 = account, report, explanation, representation, sketch, narrative, portrayal, depiction 2 = calling, naming, branding, labelling, dubbing, designation 3 = kind, sort, type, order, class, variety, brand, category

desert[1] – wilderness, waste, wilds, wasteland

desert[2] 1 = abandon, leave, quit (*informal*), forsake 2 = leave, abandon, strand, maroon, walk out on (*informal*), forsake, jilt, leave stranded ≠ take care of 3 = abscond

deserted 1 = empty, abandoned, desolate, neglected, vacant, derelict, unoccupied 2 = abandoned, neglected, forsaken

deserve = merit, warrant, be entitled to, have a right to, rate, earn, justify, be worthy of

deserved = well-earned, fitting, due, earned, justified, merited, proper, warranted

deserving = worthy, righteous, commendable, laudable, praiseworthy, meritorious, estimable ≠ undeserving

design VERB 1 = plan, draw, draft, trace, outline, devise, sketch, formulate 2 = create, plan, fashion, propose, invent, conceive, originate, fabricate 3 = intend, mean, plan, aim, purpose
● NOUN 1 = pattern, form, style, shape, organization, arrangement, construction

2 = plan, drawing, model, scheme, draft, outline, sketch, blueprint 3 = intention, end, aim, goal, target, purpose, object, objective

designate 1 = name, call, term, style, label, entitle, dub 2 = choose, reserve, select, label, flag, assign, allocate, set aside 3 = appoint, name, choose, commission, select, elect, delegate, nominate

designer 1 = couturier 2 = producer, architect, deviser, creator, planner, inventor, originator

desirable 1 = advantageous, useful, valuable, helpful, profitable, of service, convenient, worthwhile ≠ disadvantageous 2 = popular ≠ unpopular 3 = attractive, appealing, pretty, fair, inviting, lovely, charming, sexy (*informal*) ≠ unattractive

desire NOUN 1 = wish, want, longing, hope, urge, aspiration, craving, thirst 2 = lust, passion, libido, appetite, lasciviousness
● VERB = want, long for, crave, hope for, ache for, wish for, yearn for, thirst for

despair NOUN = despondency, depression, misery, gloom, desperation, anguish, hopelessness, dejection
● VERB = lose hope, give up, lose heart

desperate 1 = grave, pressing, serious, severe, extreme, urgent, drastic 2 = last-ditch, daring, furious, risky, frantic, audacious

desperately = gravely, badly, seriously, severely, dangerously, perilously

desperation 1 = misery, worry, trouble, despair, agony, anguish, unhappiness, hopelessness 2 = recklessness, madness, frenzy, impetuosity, rashness, foolhardiness

despise = look down on, loathe, scorn, detest, revile, abhor ≠ admire

despite = in spite of, in the face of, regardless of, even with, notwithstanding, in the teeth of, undeterred by

destination = stop, station, haven, resting-place, terminus, journey's end

destined = fated, meant, intended, certain, bound, doomed, predestined

destiny 1 = fate, fortune, lot, portion, doom, nemesis 2 *usually cap.* = fortune, chance, karma, providence, kismet, predestination, divine will

destroy 1 = ruin, crush, devastate, wreck, shatter, wipe out, demolish, eradicate

2 = slaughter, kill

destruction 1 = ruin, havoc, wreckage, demolition, devastation, annihilation 2 slaughter, extermination, eradication 3 = slaughter

destructive = devastating, fatal, deadly, lethal, harmful, damaging, catastrophic, ruinous

detach 1 = separate, remove, divide, cut off, sever, disconnect, tear off, disengage ≠ attach 2 = free, remove, separate, isolate, cut off, disengage

detached 1 = objective, neutral, impartial, reserved, impersonal, disinterested, unbiased, dispassionate ≠ subjective 2 = separate, disconnected, discrete, unconnected, undivided

detachment 1 = indifference, fairness, neutrality, objectivity, impartiality, coolness, remoteness, nonchalance 2 (*Military*) = unit, party, force, body, squad, patrol, task force

detail NOUN 1 = point, fact, feature, particular, respect, factor, element, aspect 2 = fine point, particular, nicety, triviality 3 (*Military*) = party, force, body, duty, squad, assignment, fatigue, detachment
● VERB = list, relate, catalogue, recount, rehearse, recite, enumerate, itemize

detailed = comprehensive, full, complete, minute, particular, thorough, exhaustive, all-embracing ≠ brief

detain 1 = hold, arrest, confine, restrain, imprison, intern, take prisoner, hold in custody 2 = delay, hold up, hamper, hinder, retard, impede, keep back, slow up *or* down

detect 1 = discover, find, uncover, track down, unmask 2 = notice, see, spot, note, identify, observe, recognize, perceive

detective = investigator, cop (*slang*), private eye, sleuth (*informal*), private investigator, gumshoe (*U.S. slang*)

detention = imprisonment, custody, quarantine, confinement, incarceration ≠ release

deter 1 = discourage, inhibit, put off, frighten, intimidate, dissuade, talk out of 2 = prevent, stop

deteriorate = decline, worsen, degenerate, slump, go downhill ≠ improve

determination = resolution, purpose, resolve, dedication, fortitude, persistence, tenacity, perseverance ≠ indecision

determine 1 = <u>affect</u>, decide, regulate, ordain 2 = <u>settle</u>, learn, establish, discover, find out, work out, detect, verify 3 = <u>decide on</u>, choose, elect, resolve 4 = <u>decide</u>, conclude, resolve, make up your mind

determined = <u>resolute</u>, firm, dogged, intent, persistent, persevering, single-minded, tenacious

deterrent = <u>discouragement</u>, obstacle, curb, restraint, impediment, check, hindrance, disincentive ≠ incentive

devastate = <u>destroy</u>, ruin, sack, wreck, demolish, level, ravage, raze

devastation = <u>destruction</u>, ruin, havoc, demolition, desolation

develop 1 = <u>grow</u>, advance, progress, mature, evolve, flourish, ripen 2 = <u>establish</u>, set up, promote, generate, undertake, initiate, embark on, cultivate 3 = <u>form</u>, establish, breed, generate, originate 4 = <u>expand</u>, extend, work out, elaborate, unfold, enlarge, broaden, amplify

development 1 = <u>growth</u>, increase, advance, progress, spread, expansion, evolution, enlargement 2 = <u>establishment</u>, forming, generation, institution, invention, initiation, inauguration, instigation 3 = <u>event</u>, happening, result, incident, improvement, evolution, unfolding, occurrence

deviant ADJECTIVE = <u>perverted</u>, sick (*informal*), twisted, warped, kinky (*slang*) ≠ normal
● NOUN = <u>pervert</u>, freak, misfit

device 1 = <u>gadget</u>, machine, tool, instrument, implement, appliance, apparatus, contraption 2 = <u>ploy</u>, scheme, plan, trick, manoeuvre, gambit, stratagem, wile

devil NOUN 1 = <u>evil spirit</u>, demon, fiend, atua (*N.Z.*), wairua (*N.Z.*) 2 = <u>brute</u>, monster, beast, barbarian, fiend, terror, swine, ogre 3 = <u>person</u>, individual, soul, creature, thing, beggar 4 = <u>scamp</u>, rogue, rascal, scoundrel, scallywag (*informal*), nointer (*Austral. slang*)
● PHRASES **the Devil** = Satan, Lucifer, Prince of Darkness, Mephistopheles, Evil One, Beelzebub, Old Nick (*informal*)

devise = <u>work out</u>, design, construct, invent, conceive, formulate, contrive,

dream up

devoid *with of* = <u>lacking in</u>, without, free from, wanting in, bereft of, empty of, deficient in

devote = <u>dedicate</u>, give, commit, apply, reserve, pledge, surrender, assign

devoted = <u>dedicated</u>, committed, true, constant, loyal, faithful, ardent, staunch ≠ disloyal

devotee = <u>enthusiast</u>, fan, supporter, follower, admirer, buff (*informal*), fanatic, adherent

devotion NOUN 1 = <u>love</u>, passion, affection, attachment, fondness 2 = <u>dedication</u>, commitment, loyalty, allegiance, fidelity, adherence, constancy, faithfulness ≠ indifference 3 = <u>worship</u>, reverence, spirituality, holiness, piety, godliness, devoutness ≠ irreverence
● PLURAL NOUN = <u>prayers</u>, religious observance, church service, divine office

devour 1 = <u>eat</u>, consume, swallow, wolf, gulp, gobble, guzzle, polish off (*informal*) 2 = <u>enjoy</u>, take in, read compulsively *or* voraciously

devout = <u>religious</u>, godly, pious, pure, holy, orthodox, saintly, reverent ≠ irreverent

diagnose = <u>identify</u>, determine, recognize, distinguish, interpret, pronounce, pinpoint

diagnosis = <u>identification</u>, discovery, recognition, detection

diagram = <u>plan</u>, figure, drawing, chart, representation, sketch, graph

dialogue 1 = <u>discussion</u>, conference, exchange, debate 2 = <u>conversation</u>, discussion, communication, discourse

diary 1 = <u>journal</u>, chronicle 2 = <u>engagement book</u>, Filofax®, appointment book

dictate VERB = <u>speak</u>, say, utter, read out
● NOUN 1 = <u>command</u>, order, decree, demand, direction, injunction, fiat, edict 2 = <u>principle</u>, law, rule, standard, code, criterion, maxim
● PHRASES **dictate to someone** = <u>order (about)</u>, direct, lay down the law, pronounce to

dictator = <u>absolute ruler</u>, tyrant, despot, oppressor, autocrat, absolutist, martinet

dictatorship = <u>absolute rule</u>, tyranny, totalitarianism, authoritarianism, despotism, autocracy, absolutism

dictionary = <u>wordbook</u>, vocabulary,

glossary, lexicon

die VERB 1 = <u>pass away</u>, expire, perish, croak (*slang*), give up the ghost, snuff it (*slang*), peg out (*informal*), kick the bucket (*slang*), cark it (*Austral. & N.Z. slang*) ≠ live 2 = <u>stop</u>, fail, halt, break down, run down, stop working, peter out, fizzle out 3 = <u>dwindle</u>, decline, sink, fade, diminish, decrease, decay, wither ≠ increase

● PHRASES **be dying for something** = <u>long for</u>, want, desire, crave, yearn for, hunger for, pine for, hanker after

diet¹ NOUN 1 = <u>food</u>, provisions, fare, rations, kai (*N.Z. informal*), nourishment, sustenance, victuals 2 = <u>fast</u>, regime, abstinence, regimen

● VERB = <u>slim</u>, fast, lose weight, abstain, eat sparingly ≠ overindulge

diet² *often cap.* = <u>council</u>, meeting, parliament, congress, chamber, convention, legislature

differ 1 = <u>be dissimilar</u>, contradict, contrast with, vary, belie, depart from, diverge, negate ≠ accord 2 = <u>disagree</u>, clash, dispute, dissent ≠ agree

difference 1 = <u>dissimilarity</u>, contrast, variation, change, variety, diversity, alteration, discrepancy ≠ similarity 2 = <u>remainder</u>, rest, balance, remains, excess 3 = <u>disagreement</u>, conflict, argument, clash, dispute, quarrel, contretemps ≠ agreement

different 1 = <u>dissimilar</u>, opposed, contrasting, changed, unlike, altered, inconsistent, disparate 2 = <u>various</u>, varied, diverse, assorted, miscellaneous, sundry 3 = <u>unusual</u>, special, strange, extraordinary, distinctive, peculiar, uncommon, singular

differentiate 1 = <u>distinguish</u>, separate, discriminate, contrast, mark off, make a distinction, tell apart, set off *or* apart 2 = <u>make different</u>, separate, distinguish, characterize, single out, segregate, individualize, mark off 3 = <u>become different</u>, change, convert, transform, alter, adapt, modify

difficult 1 = <u>hard</u>, tough, taxing, demanding, challenging, exacting, formidable, uphill ≠ easy 2 = <u>problematical</u>, involved, complex, complicated, obscure, baffling, intricate, knotty ≠ simple 3 = <u>troublesome</u>, demanding, perverse, fussy,

fastidious, hard to please, refractory, unaccommodating ≠ cooperative

difficulty 1 = <u>problem</u>, trouble, obstacle, hurdle, dilemma, complication, snag, uphill (*S. African*) 2 = <u>hardship</u>, strain, awkwardness, strenuousness, arduousness, laboriousness

dig VERB 1 = <u>hollow out</u>, mine, quarry, excavate, scoop out 2 = <u>delve</u>, tunnel, burrow 3 = <u>turn over</u> 4 = <u>search</u>, hunt, root, delve, forage, dig down, fossick (*Austral. & N.Z.*) 5 = <u>poke</u>, drive, push, stick, punch, stab, thrust, shove

● NOUN 1 = <u>cutting remark</u>, crack (*slang*), insult, taunt, sneer, jeer, barb, wisecrack (*informal*) 2 = <u>poke</u>, thrust, nudge, prod, jab, punch

digest VERB 1 = <u>ingest</u>, absorb, incorporate, dissolve, assimilate 2 = <u>take in</u>, absorb, grasp, soak up

● NOUN = <u>summary</u>, résumé, abstract, epitome, synopsis, précis, abridgment

dignity 1 = <u>decorum</u>, gravity, majesty, grandeur, respectability, nobility, solemnity, courtliness 2 = <u>self-importance</u>, pride, self-esteem, self-respect

dilemma = <u>predicament</u>, problem, difficulty, spot (*informal*), mess, puzzle, plight, quandary

dilute 1 = <u>water down</u>, thin (out), weaken, adulterate, make thinner, cut (*informal*) ≠ condense 2 = <u>reduce</u>, weaken, diminish, temper, decrease, lessen, diffuse, mitigate ≠ intensify

dim ADJECTIVE 1 = <u>poorly lit</u>, dark, gloomy, murky, shady, shadowy, dusky, tenebrous 2 = <u>cloudy</u>, grey, gloomy, dismal, overcast, leaden ≠ bright 3 = <u>unclear</u>, obscured, faint, blurred, fuzzy, shadowy, hazy, bleary ≠ distinct 4 = <u>stupid</u> (*Informal*), thick, dull, dense, dumb (*informal*), daft (*informal*), dozy (*Brit. informal*), obtuse ≠ bright

● VERB 1 = <u>turn down</u>, fade, dull 2 = <u>grow or become faint</u>, fade, dull, grow *or* become dim 3 = <u>darken</u>, dull, cloud over

dimension 1 = <u>aspect</u>, side, feature, angle, facet 2 = <u>extent</u>, size

diminish 1 = <u>decrease</u>, decline, lessen, shrink, dwindle, wane, recede, subside ≠ grow 2 = <u>reduce</u>, cut, decrease, lessen, lower, curtail ≠ increase

din = <u>noise</u>, row, racket, crash, clamour, clatter, uproar, commotion ≠ silence

dine = <u>eat</u>, lunch, feast, sup

dinkum (*Austral. & N.Z. informal*)
= <u>genuine</u>, honest, natural, frank, sincere,
candid, upfront (*informal*), artless

dinner 1 = <u>meal</u>, main meal, spread
(*informal*), repast **2** = <u>banquet</u>, feast,
repast, hakari (*N.Z.*)

dip VERB **1** = <u>plunge</u>, immerse, bathe, duck,
douse, dunk **2** = <u>drop (down)</u>, fall, lower,
sink, descend, subside **3** = <u>slope</u>, drop
(down), descend, fall, decline, sink, incline,
drop away
● NOUN **1** = <u>plunge</u>, ducking, soaking,
drenching, immersion, douche **2** = <u>nod</u>,
drop, lowering, slump, sag **3** = <u>hollow</u>,
hole, depression, pit, basin, trough,
concavity
● PHRASES **dip into something** = <u>sample</u>,
skim, glance at, browse, peruse

diplomacy 1 = <u>statesmanship</u>, statecraft,
international negotiation **2** = <u>tact</u>, skill,
sensitivity, craft, discretion, subtlety,
delicacy, finesse ≠ tactlessness

diplomat 1 = <u>official</u>, ambassador, envoy,
statesman, consul, attaché, emissary,
chargé d'affaires

diplomatic 1 = <u>consular</u>, official,
foreign-office, ambassadorial, foreign-
politic **2** = <u>tactful</u>, politic, sensitive,
subtle, delicate, polite, discreet, prudent
≠ tactless

dire = <u>desperate</u>, pressing, critical, terrible,
crucial, extreme, awful, urgent

direct ADJECTIVE = <u>quickest</u>, shortest
● ADVERB **1** = <u>straight</u>, through
≠ circuitous **2** = <u>first-hand</u>, personal,
immediate ≠ indirect **3** = <u>clear</u>, specific,
plain, absolute, definite, explicit,
downright, point-blank ≠ ambiguous
4 = <u>straightforward</u>, open, straight, frank,
blunt, honest, candid, forthright ≠ indirect
5 = <u>verbatim</u>, exact, word-for-word, strict,
accurate, faithful, letter-for-letter **6** = <u>non-
stop</u>, straight
● VERB **1** = <u>aim</u>, point, level, train, focus
2 = <u>guide</u>, show, lead, point the way,
point in the direction of **3** = <u>control</u>, run,
manage, lead, guide, handle, conduct,
oversee **4** = <u>order</u>, command, instruct,
charge, demand, require, bid **5** = <u>address</u>,
send, mail, route, label

direction NOUN **1** = <u>way</u>, course,
line, road, track, bearing, route, path
2 = <u>management</u>, control, charge,
administration, leadership, command,

guidance, supervision
● PLURAL NOUN = <u>instructions</u>, rules,
information, plan, briefing, regulations,
recommendations, guidelines

directive = <u>order</u>, ruling, regulation,
command, instruction, decree, mandate,
injunction

directly 1 = <u>straight</u>, unswervingly,
without deviation, by the shortest
route, in a beeline **2** = <u>immediately</u>,
promptly, right away, straightaway **3** (*Old-
fashioned*) = <u>at once</u>, as soon as possible,
straightaway, forthwith **4** = <u>honestly</u>,
openly, frankly, plainly, point-blank,
unequivocally, truthfully, unreservedly

director = <u>controller</u>, head, leader,
manager, chief, executive, governor,
administrator, baas (*S. African*)

dirt 1 = <u>filth</u>, muck, grime, dust, mud,
impurity, kak (*S. African taboo slang*)
2 = <u>soil</u>, ground, earth, clay, turf, loam

dirty ADJECTIVE **1** = <u>filthy</u>, soiled, grubby,
foul, muddy, polluted, messy, grimy, festy
(*Austral. slang*) ≠ clean **2** = <u>dishonest</u>,
illegal, unfair, cheating, crooked,
fraudulent, treacherous, unscrupulous
≠ honest **3** = <u>obscene</u>, indecent, blue,
offensive, filthy, pornographic, sleazy, lewd
≠ decent
● VERB = <u>soil</u>, foul, stain, spoil, muddy,
pollute, blacken, defile ≠ clean

disability = <u>handicap</u>, affliction, disorder,
defect, impairment, infirmity

disable = <u>handicap</u>, cripple, damage,
paralyse, impair, incapacitate, immobilize,
enfeeble

disabled = <u>differently abled</u>, physically
challenged, handicapped, weakened,
crippled, paralysed, lame, incapacitated
≠ able-bodied

disadvantage 1 = <u>drawback</u>, trouble,
handicap, nuisance, snag, inconvenience,
downside ≠ advantage **2** = <u>harm</u>, loss,
damage, injury, hurt, prejudice, detriment,
disservice ≠ benefit

disagree 1 = <u>differ (in opinion)</u>, argue,
clash, dispute, dissent, quarrel, take issue
with, cross swords ≠ agree **2** = <u>make
ill</u>, upset, sicken, trouble, hurt, bother,
distress, discomfort

disagreement = <u>argument</u>, row, conflict,
clash, dispute, dissent, quarrel, squabble
≠ agreement

disappear 1 = <u>vanish</u>, recede, evanesce

≠ appear **2** = <u>pass</u>, fade away **3** = <u>cease</u>, dissolve, evaporate, perish, die out, pass away, melt away, leave no trace

disappearance **1** = <u>vanishing</u>, going, passing, melting, eclipse, evaporation, evanescence **2** = <u>flight</u>, departure **3** = <u>loss</u>, losing, mislaying

disappoint = <u>let down</u>, dismay, fail, disillusion, dishearten, disenchant, dissatisfy, disgruntle

disappointment **1** = <u>regret</u>, discontent, dissatisfaction, disillusionment, chagrin, disenchantment, dejection, despondency **2** = <u>letdown</u>, blow, setback, misfortune, calamity, choker (*informal*) **3** = <u>frustration</u>

disapproval = <u>displeasure</u>, criticism, objection, condemnation, dissatisfaction, censure, reproach, denunciation

disapprove = <u>condemn</u>, object to, dislike, deplore, frown on, take exception to, take a dim view of, find unacceptable ≠ approve

disarm **1** = <u>demilitarize</u>, disband, demobilize, deactivate **2** = <u>win over</u>, persuade

disarmament = <u>arms reduction</u>, demobilization, arms limitation, demilitarization, de-escalation

disarming = <u>charming</u>, winning, irresistible, persuasive, likable *or* likeable

disarray **1** = <u>confusion</u>, disorder, indiscipline, disunity, disorganization, unruliness ≠ order **2** = <u>untidiness</u>, mess, chaos, muddle, clutter, shambles, jumble, hotchpotch ≠ tidiness

disaster **1** = <u>catastrophe</u>, trouble, tragedy, ruin, misfortune, adversity, calamity, cataclysm **2** = <u>failure</u>, mess, flop (*informal*), catastrophe, debacle, cock-up (*Brit. slang*), washout (*informal*)

disastrous **1** = <u>terrible</u>, devastating, tragic, fatal, catastrophic, ruinous, calamitous, cataclysmic **2** = <u>unsuccessful</u>

disbelief = <u>scepticism</u>, doubt, distrust, mistrust, incredulity, unbelief, dubiety ≠ belief

discard = <u>get rid of</u>, drop, throw away *or* out, reject, abandon, dump (*informal*), dispose of, dispense with ≠ keep

discharge VERB **1** = <u>release</u>, free, clear, liberate, pardon, allow to go, set free **2** = <u>dismiss</u>, sack (*informal*), fire (*informal*), remove, expel, discard, oust, cashier **3** = <u>carry out</u>, perform, fulfil, accomplish,

do, effect, realize, observe **4** = <u>pay</u>, meet, clear, settle, square (up), honour, satisfy, relieve **5** = <u>pour forth</u>, release, leak, emit, dispense, ooze, exude, give off **6** = <u>fire</u>, shoot, set off, explode, let off, detonate, let loose (*informal*)

● NOUN **1** = <u>release</u>, liberation, clearance, pardon, acquittal **2** = <u>dismissal</u>, notice, removal, the boot (*slang*), expulsion, the push (*slang*), marching orders (*informal*), ejection **3** = <u>emission</u>, ooze, secretion, excretion, pus, seepage, suppuration **4** = <u>firing</u>, report, shot, blast, burst, explosion, volley, salvo

disciple **1** = <u>apostle</u> **2** = <u>follower</u>, student, supporter, pupil, devotee, apostle, adherent ≠ teacher

discipline NOUN **1** = <u>control</u>, authority, regulation, supervision, orderliness, strictness **2** = <u>punishment</u>, penalty, correction, chastening, chastisement, castigation **3** = <u>self-control</u>, control, restraint, self-discipline, willpower, self-restraint, orderliness **4** = <u>training</u>, practice, exercise, method, regulation, drill, regimen **5** = <u>field of study</u>, area, subject, theme, topic, course, curriculum, speciality

● VERB **1** = <u>punish</u>, correct, reprimand, castigate, chastise, chasten, penalize, bring to book **2** = <u>train</u>, educate

disclose **1** = <u>make known</u>, reveal, publish, relate, broadcast, confess, communicate, divulge ≠ keep secret **2** = <u>show</u>, reveal, expose, unveil, uncover, lay bare, bring to light ≠ hide

disclosure **1** = <u>revelation</u>, announcement, publication, leak, admission, declaration, confession, acknowledgment **2** = <u>uncovering</u>, publication, revelation, divulgence

discomfort **1** = <u>pain</u>, hurt, ache, throbbing, irritation, tenderness, pang, malaise ≠ comfort **2** = <u>uneasiness</u>, worry, anxiety, doubt, distress, misgiving, qualms, trepidation ≠ reassurance **3** = <u>inconvenience</u>, trouble, difficulty, bother, hardship, irritation, nuisance, uphill (*S. African*)

discontent = <u>dissatisfaction</u>, unhappiness, displeasure, regret, envy, restlessness, uneasiness

discontented = <u>dissatisfied</u>, unhappy, fed up, disgruntled, disaffected, vexed, displeased ≠ satisfied

discount NOUN = deduction, cut, reduction, concession, rebate
● VERB 1 = mark down, reduce, lower 2 = disregard, reject, ignore, overlook, discard, set aside, dispel, pass over

discourage 1 = dishearten, depress, intimidate, overawe, demoralize, put a damper on, dispirit, deject ≠ hearten 2 = put off, deter, prevent, dissuade, talk out of ≠ encourage

discourse 1 = conversation, talk, discussion, speech, communication, chat, dialogue 2 = speech, essay, lecture, sermon, treatise, dissertation, homily, oration, whaikorero (N.Z.)

discover 1 = find out, learn, notice, realize, recognize, perceive, detect, uncover 2 = find, come across, uncover, unearth, turn up, dig up, come upon

discovery 1 = finding out, news, revelation, disclosure, realization 2 = invention, launch, institution, pioneering, innovation, inauguration 3 = breakthrough, find, development, advance, leap, invention, step forward, quantum leap 4 = finding, revelation, uncovering, disclosure, detection

discredit VERB 1 = disgrace, shame, smear, humiliate, taint, disparage, vilify, slander ≠ honour 2 = dispute, question, challenge, deny, reject, discount, distrust, mistrust
● NOUN = disgrace, scandal, shame, disrepute, stigma, ignominy, dishonour, ill-repute ≠ honour

discreet = tactful, diplomatic, guarded, careful, cautious, wary, prudent, considerate ≠ tactless

discrepancy = disagreement, difference, variation, conflict, contradiction, inconsistency, disparity, divergence

discretion 1 = tact, consideration, caution, diplomacy, prudence, wariness, carefulness, judiciousness ≠ tactlessness 2 = choice, will, pleasure, preference, inclination, volition

discriminate VERB = differentiate, distinguish, separate, tell the difference, draw a distinction
● PHRASES **discriminate against someone** = treat differently, single out, victimize, treat as inferior, show bias against, show prejudice against

discriminating = discerning, particular, refined, cultivated, selective, tasteful,

fastidious ≠ undiscriminating

discrimination 1 = prejudice, bias, injustice, intolerance, bigotry, favouritism, unfairness 2 = discernment, taste, judgment, perception, subtlety, refinement

discuss = talk about, consider, debate, examine, argue about, deliberate about, converse about, confer about

discussion 1 = talk, debate, argument, conference, conversation, dialogue, consultation, discourse, korero (N.Z.) 2 = examination, investigation, analysis, scrutiny, dissection

disdain NOUN = contempt, scorn, arrogance, derision, haughtiness, superciliousness
● VERB = scorn, reject, slight, disregard, spurn, deride, look down on, sneer at

disease = illness, condition, complaint, infection, disorder, sickness, ailment, affliction

diseased = unhealthy, sick, infected, rotten, ailing, sickly, unwell, crook (Austral. & N.Z. informal), unsound

disgrace NOUN 1 = shame, degradation, disrepute, ignominy, dishonour, infamy, opprobrium, odium ≠ honour 2 = scandal, stain, stigma, blot, blemish
● VERB = shame, humiliate, discredit, degrade, taint, sully, dishonour, bring shame upon ≠ honour

disgraceful = shameful, shocking, scandalous, unworthy, ignominious, disreputable, contemptible, dishonourable

disgruntled = discontented, dissatisfied, annoyed, irritated, put out, grumpy, vexed, displeased, hoha (N.Z.)

disguise NOUN = costume, mask, camouflage
● VERB = hide, cover, conceal, screen, mask, suppress, withhold, veil

disguised 1 = in disguise, masked, camouflaged, undercover, incognito 2 = false, artificial, forged, fake, mock, imitation, sham, counterfeit

disgust NOUN 1 = loathing, revulsion, hatred, dislike, nausea, distaste, aversion, repulsion ≠ liking 2 = outrage, shock, anger, hurt, fury, resentment, wrath, indignation
● VERB = sicken, offend, revolt, put off, repel, nauseate ≠ delight

disgusting 1 = <u>sickening</u>, foul, revolting, gross, repellent, nauseating, repugnant, loathsome, festy (*Austral. slang*), yucko (*Austral. slang*) **2** = <u>appalling</u>, shocking, awful, offensive, dreadful, horrifying

dish 1 = <u>bowl</u>, plate, platter, salver **2** = <u>food</u>, fare, recipe

dishonest = <u>deceitful</u>, corrupt, crooked (*informal*), lying, bent (*slang*), false, cheating, treacherous ≠ honest

disintegrate = <u>break up</u>, crumble, fall apart, separate, shatter, splinter, break apart, go to pieces

dislike VERB = <u>hate</u>, object to, loathe, despise, disapprove of, detest, recoil from, take a dim view of ≠ like
● NOUN = <u>hatred</u>, hostility, disapproval, distaste, animosity, aversion, displeasure, antipathy ≠ liking

dismal 1 = <u>bad</u>, awful, dreadful, rotten (*informal*), terrible, poor, dire, abysmal **2** = <u>sad</u>, gloomy, dark, depressing, discouraging, bleak, dreary, sombre ≠ happy **3** = <u>gloomy</u>, depressing, dull, dreary ≠ cheerful

dismantle = <u>take apart</u>, strip, demolish, disassemble, take to pieces *or* bits

dismay NOUN **1** = <u>alarm</u>, fear, horror, anxiety, dread, apprehension, nervousness, consternation **2** = <u>disappointment</u>, frustration, dissatisfaction, disillusionment, chagrin, disenchantment, discouragement
● VERB **1** = <u>alarm</u>, frighten, scare, panic, distress, terrify, appal, startle **2** = <u>disappoint</u>, upset, discourage, daunt, disillusion, let down, dishearten, dispirit

dismiss 1 = <u>reject</u>, disregard **2** = <u>banish</u>, dispel, discard, set aside, cast out, lay aside, put out of your mind **3** = <u>sack</u>, fire (*informal*), remove (*informal*), axe (*informal*), discharge, lay off, cashier, give notice to **4** = <u>let go</u>, free, release, discharge, dissolve, liberate, disperse, send away

dismissal = <u>the sack</u>, removal, notice, the boot (*slang*), expulsion (*informal*), the push (*slang*), marching orders (*informal*)

disobey 1 = <u>defy</u>, ignore, rebel, disregard, refuse to obey **2** = <u>infringe</u>, defy, refuse to obey, flout, violate, contravene, overstep, transgress

disorder 1 = <u>illness</u>, disease, complaint, condition, sickness, ailment, affliction, malady **2** = <u>untidiness</u>, mess, confusion, chaos, muddle, clutter, shambles, disarray **3** = <u>disturbance</u>, riot, turmoil, unrest, uproar, commotion, unruliness, biffo (*Austral. slang*)

disorderly 1 = <u>untidy</u>, confused, chaotic, messy, jumbled, shambolic (*informal*), disorganized, higgledy-piggledy (*informal*) ≠ tidy **2** = <u>unruly</u>, disruptive, rowdy, turbulent, tumultuous, lawless, riotous, ungovernable

dispatch *or* **despatch** VERB **1** = <u>send</u>, consign **2** = <u>kill</u>, murder, destroy, execute, slaughter, assassinate, slay, liquidate **3** = <u>carry out</u>, perform, fulfil, effect, finish, achieve, settle, dismiss
● NOUN = <u>message</u>, news, report, story, account, communication, bulletin, communiqué

dispel = <u>drive away</u>, dismiss, eliminate, expel, disperse, banish, chase away

dispense VERB **1** = <u>distribute</u>, assign, allocate, allot, dole out, share out, apportion, deal out **2** = <u>prepare</u>, measure, supply, mix **3** = <u>administer</u>, operate, carry out, implement, enforce, execute, apply, discharge
● PHRASES **dispense with something** *or* **someone 1** = <u>do away with</u>, give up, cancel, abolish, brush aside, forgo **2** = <u>do without</u>, get rid of, dispose of, relinquish

disperse 1 = <u>scatter</u>, spread, distribute, strew, diffuse, disseminate, throw about **2** = <u>break up</u>, separate, scatter, dissolve, disband ≠ gather **3** = <u>dissolve</u>, break up

displace 1 = <u>replace</u>, succeed, supersede, oust, usurp, supplant, take the place of **2** = <u>move</u>, shift, disturb, budge, misplace

display VERB **1** = <u>show</u>, present, exhibit, put on view ≠ conceal **2** = <u>expose</u>, show, reveal, exhibit, uncover **3** = <u>demonstrate</u>, show, reveal, register, expose, disclose, manifest **4** = <u>show off</u>, parade, exhibit, sport (*informal*), flash (*informal*), flourish, brandish, flaunt
● NOUN **1** = <u>proof</u>, exhibition, demonstration, evidence, expression, illustration, revelation, testimony **2** = <u>exhibition</u>, show, demonstration, presentation, array **3** = <u>ostentation</u>, show, flourish, fanfare, pomp **4** = <u>show</u>, exhibition, parade, spectacle, pageant

disposable 1 = <u>throwaway</u>, nonreturnable **2** = <u>available</u>, expendable, consumable

disposal NOUN = <u>throwing away</u>, dumping (*informal*), scrapping, removal, discarding, jettisoning, ejection, riddance
● PHRASES **at your disposal** = <u>available</u>, ready, to hand, accessible, handy, at hand, on tap, expendable

dispose VERB = <u>arrange</u>, put, place, group, order, distribute, array
● PHRASES **dispose of someone** = <u>kill</u>, murder, destroy, execute, slaughter, assassinate, slay, liquidate ◆ **dispose of something** 1 = <u>get rid of</u>, destroy, dump (*informal*), scrap, discard, unload, jettison, throw out *or* away 2 = <u>deal with</u>, manage, treat, handle, settle, cope with, take care of, see to

disposition 1 = <u>character</u>, nature, spirit, make-up, constitution, temper, temperament 2 = <u>tendency</u>, inclination, propensity, habit, leaning, bent, bias, proclivity 3 = <u>arrangement</u>, grouping, ordering, organization, distribution, placement

dispute NOUN 1 = <u>disagreement</u>, conflict, argument, dissent, altercation 2 = <u>argument</u>, row, clash, controversy, contention, feud, quarrel, squabble
● VERB 1 = <u>contest</u>, question, challenge, deny, doubt, oppose, object to, contradict 2 = <u>argue</u>, fight, clash, disagree, fall out (*informal*), quarrel, squabble, bicker

disqualify = <u>ban</u>, rule out, prohibit, preclude, debar, declare ineligible

disregard VERB = <u>ignore</u>, discount, overlook, neglect, pass over, turn a blind eye to, make light of, pay no heed to ≠ pay attention to
● NOUN = <u>ignoring</u>, neglect, contempt, indifference, negligence, disdain, disrespect

disrupt 1 = <u>interrupt</u>, stop, upset, hold up, interfere with, unsettle, obstruct, cut short 2 = <u>disturb</u>, upset, confuse, disorder, spoil, disorganize, disarrange

disruption = <u>disturbance</u>, interference, interruption, stoppage

disruptive = <u>disturbing</u>, upsetting, disorderly, unsettling, troublesome, unruly ≠ well-behaved

dissatisfaction = <u>discontent</u>, frustration, resentment, disappointment, irritation, unhappiness, annoyance, displeasure

dissatisfied = <u>discontented</u>, frustrated,

unhappy, disappointed, fed up, disgruntled, displeased, unsatisfied ≠ satisfied

dissent = <u>disagreement</u>, opposition, protest, resistance, refusal, objection, discord, demur ≠ assent

dissident NOUN = <u>protester</u>, rebel, dissenter, demonstrator, agitator
● ADJECTIVE = <u>dissenting</u>, disagreeing, nonconformist, heterodox

dissolve 1 = <u>melt</u>, soften, thaw, liquefy, deliquesce 2 = <u>end</u>, suspend, break up, wind up, terminate, discontinue, dismantle, disband

distance 1 = <u>space</u>, length, extent, range, stretch, gap, interval, span 2 = <u>aloofness</u>, reserve, detachment, restraint, stiffness, coolness, coldness, standoffishness

distant 1 = <u>far-off</u>, far, remote, abroad, out-of-the-way, far-flung, faraway, outlying ≠ close 2 = <u>remote</u> 3 = <u>reserved</u>, withdrawn, cool, remote, detached, aloof, unfriendly, reticent ≠ friendly 4 = <u>faraway</u>, blank, vague, distracted, vacant, preoccupied, oblivious, absent-minded

distinct 1 = <u>different</u>, individual, separate, discrete, unconnected ≠ similar 2 = <u>striking</u>, dramatic, outstanding, noticeable, well-defined 3 = <u>definite</u>, marked, clear, decided, obvious, evident, noticeable, conspicuous ≠ vague

distinction 1 = <u>difference</u>, contrast, variation, differential, discrepancy, disparity, dissimilarity 2 = <u>excellence</u>, importance, fame, merit, prominence, greatness, eminence, repute 3 = <u>feature</u>, quality, characteristic, mark, individuality, peculiarity, distinctiveness, particularity 4 = <u>merit</u>, honour, integrity, excellence, rectitude

distinctive = <u>characteristic</u>, special, individual, unique, typical, peculiar, singular, idiosyncratic ≠ ordinary

distinctly 1 = <u>definitely</u>, clearly, obviously, plainly, patently, decidedly, markedly, noticeably 2 = <u>clearly</u>, plainly

distinguish 1 = <u>differentiate</u>, determine, separate, discriminate, decide, judge, ascertain, tell the difference 2 = <u>characterize</u>, mark, separate, single out, set apart 3 = <u>make out</u>, recognize, perceive, know, see, tell, pick out, discern

distinguished = <u>eminent</u>, noted, famous, celebrated, well-known, prominent, esteemed, acclaimed ≠ unknown

distort 1 = misrepresent, twist, bias, disguise, pervert, slant, colour, misinterpret 2 = deform, bend, twist, warp, buckle, mangle, mangulate (*Austral. slang*), disfigure, contort

distortion 1 = misrepresentation, bias, slant, perversion, falsification 2 = deformity, bend, twist, warp, buckle, contortion, malformation, crookedness

distract 1 = divert, sidetrack, draw away, turn aside, lead astray, draw *or* lead away from 2 = amuse, occupy, entertain, beguile, engross

distracted = agitated, troubled, puzzled, at sea, perplexed, flustered, in a flap (*informal*)

distraction 1 = disturbance, interference, diversion, interruption 2 = entertainment, recreation, amusement, diversion, pastime

distraught = frantic, desperate, distressed, distracted, worked-up, agitated, overwrought, out of your mind

distress NOUN 1 = suffering, pain, worry, grief, misery, torment, sorrow, heartache 2 = need, trouble, difficulties, poverty, hard times, hardship, misfortune, adversity
● VERB = upset, worry, trouble, disturb, grieve, torment, harass, agitate

distressed 1 = upset, worried, troubled, distracted, tormented, distraught, agitated, wretched 2 = poverty-stricken, poor, impoverished, needy, destitute, indigent, down at heel, straitened

distressing = upsetting, worrying, disturbing, painful, sad, harrowing, heart-breaking

distribute 1 = hand out, pass round 2 = circulate, deliver, convey 3 = share, deal, allocate, dispense, allot, dole out, apportion

distribution 1 = delivery, mailing, transportation, handling 2 = sharing, division, assignment, rationing, allocation, allotment, apportionment 3 = spread, organization, arrangement, placement

district = area, region, sector, quarter, parish, neighbourhood, vicinity, locality

distrust VERB = suspect, doubt, be wary of, mistrust, disbelieve, be suspicious of ≠ trust
● NOUN = suspicion, question, doubt, disbelief, scepticism, mistrust, misgiving, wariness ≠ trust

disturb 1 = interrupt, trouble, bother, plague, disrupt, interfere with, hassle, inconvenience 2 = upset, concern, worry, trouble, alarm, distress, unsettle, unnerve ≠ calm 3 = muddle, disorder, mix up, mess up, jumble up, disarrange

disturbance 1 = disorder, fray, brawl, fracas, commotion, rumpus 2 = upset, bother, distraction, intrusion, interruption, annoyance

disturbed 1 (*Psychiatry*) = unbalanced, troubled, disordered, unstable, neurotic, upset, deranged, maladjusted ≠ balanced 2 = worried, concerned, troubled, upset, bothered, nervous, anxious, uneasy ≠ calm

disturbing = worrying, upsetting, alarming, frightening, distressing, startling, unsettling, harrowing

ditch NOUN = channel, drain, trench, dyke, furrow, gully, moat, watercourse
● VERB 1 (*Slang*) = get rid of, dump (*informal*), scrap, discard, dispose of, dispense with, jettison, throw out *or* overboard 2 (*Slang*) = leave, drop, abandon, dump (*informal*), get rid of, forsake

dive VERB 1 = plunge, drop, duck, dip, descend, plummet 2 = go underwater 3 = nose-dive, plunge, crash, swoop, plummet
● NOUN = plunge, spring, jump, leap, lunge, nose dive

diverse 1 = various, mixed, varied, assorted, miscellaneous, several, sundry, motley 2 = different, unlike, varying, separate, distinct, disparate, discrete, dissimilar

diversify = vary, change, expand, spread out, branch out

diversion 1 = distraction, deviation, digression 2 = pastime, game, sport, entertainment, hobby, relaxation, recreation, distraction 3 (*Chiefly Brit.*) = detour, roundabout way, indirect course 4 (*Chiefly Brit.*) = deviation, departure, straying, divergence, digression

diversity 1 = difference, multiplicity, heterogeneity, diverseness 2 = range, variety, scope, sphere

divert 1 = redirect, switch, avert, deflect, deviate, turn aside 2 = distract, sidetrack, lead astray, draw *or* lead away from 3 = entertain, delight, amuse, please, charm, gratify, beguile, regale

divide 1 = separate, split, segregate, bisect ≠ join 2 *sometimes with* ***up*** = share, distribute, allocate, dispense, allot, mete, deal out 3 = split, break up, come between, estrange, cause to disagree

dividend = bonus, share, cut (*informal*), gain, extra, plus, portion, divvy (*informal*)

divine ADJECTIVE 1 = heavenly, spiritual, holy, immortal, supernatural, celestial, angelic, superhuman 2 = sacred, religious, holy, spiritual, blessed, revered, hallowed, consecrated 3 (*Informal*) = wonderful, perfect, beautiful, excellent, lovely, glorious, marvellous, splendid

● VERB = guess, suppose, perceive, discern, infer, deduce, apprehend, surmise

division 1 = separation, dividing, splitting up, partition, cutting up 2 = sharing, sharing, distribution, assignment, rationing, allocation, allotment, apportionment 3 = disagreement, split, rift, rupture, abyss, chasm, variance, discord ≠ unity 4 = department, group, branch 5 = part, bit, piece, section, class, category, fraction

divorce NOUN = separation, split, break-up, parting, split-up, rift, dissolution, annulment

● VERB = separate, split up, part company, dissolve your marriage

dizzy 1 = giddy, faint, light-headed, swimming, reeling, shaky, wobbly, off balance 2 = confused, dazzled, at sea, bewildered, muddled, bemused, dazed, disorientated

do VERB 1 = perform, achieve, carry out, complete, accomplish, execute, pull off 2 = make, prepare, fix, arrange, look after, see to, get ready 3 = solve, work out, resolve, figure out, decode, decipher, puzzle out 4 = be adequate, be sufficient, satisfy, suffice, pass muster, cut the mustard, meet requirements 5 = produce, make, create, develop, manufacture, construct, invent, fabricate

● NOUN (*Informal*, *chiefly Brit. & N.Z.*) = party, gathering, function, event, affair, occasion, celebration, reception

● PHRASES **do away with something** = get rid of, remove, eliminate, abolish, discard, put an end to, dispense with, discontinue ◆ **do without something** *or* **someone** = manage without, give up, dispense with, forgo, kick (*informal*), abstain from, get along without

dock¹ NOUN = port, haven, harbour, pier, wharf, quay, waterfront, anchorage

● VERB 1 = moor, land, anchor, put in, tie up, berth, drop anchor 2 (*of spacecraft*) = link up, unite, join, couple, rendezvous, hook up

dock² 1 = cut, reduce, decrease, diminish, lessen ≠ increase 2 = deduct, subtract 3 = cut off, crop, clip, shorten, curtail, cut short

doctor NOUN = physician, medic (*informal*), general practitioner, medical practitioner, G.P.

● VERB 1 = change, alter, interfere with, disguise, pervert, tamper with, tinker with, misrepresent 2 = add to, spike, cut, mix something with something, dilute, water down, adulterate

doctrine = teaching, principle, belief, opinion, conviction, creed, dogma, tenet, kaupapa (*N.Z.*)

document NOUN = paper, form, certificate, report, record, testimonial, authorization

● VERB = support, certify, verify, detail, validate, substantiate, corroborate, authenticate

dodge VERB 1 = duck, dart, swerve, sidestep, shoot, turn aside 2 = evade, avoid, escape, get away from, elude 3 = avoid, evade, shirk

● NOUN = trick, scheme, ploy, trap, device, fraud, manoeuvre, deception

dodgy 1 (*Brit., Austral., & N.Z.*) = nasty, offensive, unpleasant, revolting, distasteful, repellent, obnoxious, repulsive 2 (*Brit., Austral., & N.Z.*) = risky, difficult, tricky, dangerous, delicate, uncertain, dicey (*informal, chiefly Brit.*), chancy (*informal*) 3 = second rate, poor, inferior, mediocre, shoddy, bush-league (*Austral. & N.Z. informal*), half-pie (*N.Z. informal*), bodger *or* bodgie (*Austral. slang*)

dog NOUN = hound, canine, pooch (*slang*), cur, man's best friend, kuri *or* goorie (*N.Z.*), brak (*S. African*)

● VERB 1 = plague, follow, trouble, haunt, hound, torment 2 = pursue, follow, track, chase, trail, hound, stalk

● PHRASES **go to the dogs** (*Informal*) = deteriorate, degenerate, be in decline, go downhill (*informal*), go down the drain, go to pot, go to ruin

▬▬ RELATED WORDS

adjective: canine
female: bitch
young: pup, puppy
dogged = <u>determined</u>, persistent, stubborn, resolute, tenacious, steadfast, obstinate, indefatigable ≠ irresolute
dole NOUN = <u>share</u>, grant, gift, allowance, handout, koha (*N.Z.*)
● PHRASES **dole something out** = <u>give out</u>, distribute, assign, allocate, hand out, dispense, allot, apportion
dolphin

▰▰▰ RELATED WORD
collective noun: school
domestic ADJECTIVE 1 = <u>home</u>, internal, native, indigenous 2 = <u>household</u>, home, family, private 3 = <u>home-loving</u>, homely, housewifely, stay-at-home, domesticated 4 = <u>domesticated</u>, trained, tame, pet, house-trained
● NOUN = <u>servant</u>, help, maid, daily, char (*informal*), charwoman
dominant 1 = <u>main</u>, chief, primary, principal, prominent, predominant, pre-eminent ≠ minor 2 = <u>controlling</u>, ruling, commanding, supreme, governing, superior, authoritative
dominate 1 = <u>control</u>, rule, direct, govern, monopolize, tyrannize, have the whip hand over 2 = <u>tower above</u>, overlook, survey, stand over, loom over, stand head and shoulders above
domination = <u>control</u>, power, rule, authority, influence, command, supremacy, ascendancy
don = <u>put on</u>, get into, dress in, pull on, change into, get dressed in, clothe yourself in, slip on or into
donate = <u>give</u>, present, contribute, grant, subscribe, endow, entrust, impart
donation = <u>contribution</u>, gift, subscription, offering, present, grant, hand-out, koha (*N.Z.*)
donor = <u>giver</u>, contributor, benefactor, philanthropist, donator ≠ recipient
doom NOUN 1 = <u>destruction</u>, ruin, catastrophe, downfall 2 = <u>fate</u>, fortune
● VERB = <u>condemn</u>, sentence, consign, destine
doomed = <u>hopeless</u>, condemned, ill-fated, fated, unhappy, unfortunate, cursed, unlucky
door = <u>opening</u>, entry, entrance, exit, doorway

dope NOUN 1 (*Slang*) = <u>drugs</u>, narcotics, opiates, dadah (*Austral. slang*) 2 (*Informal*) = <u>idiot</u>, fool, twit (*informal*, *chiefly Brit.*), dunce, simpleton, dimwit (*informal*), nitwit (*informal*), dumb-ass (*slang*), dorba or dorb (*Austral. slang*), bogan (*Austral. slang*)
● VERB = <u>drug</u>, knock out, sedate, stupefy, anaesthetize, narcotize
dorp (*S. African*) = <u>town</u>, village, settlement, municipality, kainga or kaika (*N.Z.*)
dose 1 = <u>measure</u>, amount, allowance, portion, prescription, ration, draught, dosage 2 = <u>quantity</u>, measure, supply, portion
dot NOUN = <u>spot</u>, point, mark, fleck, jot, speck, speckle
● VERB = <u>spot</u>, stud, fleck, speckle
● PHRASES **on the dot** = <u>on time</u>, promptly, precisely, exactly (*informal*), to the minute, on the button (*informal*), punctually
double ADJECTIVE 1 = <u>matching</u>, coupled, paired, twin, duplicate, in pairs 2 = <u>dual</u>, enigmatic, twofold
● VERB 1 = <u>multiply by two</u>, duplicate, increase twofold, enlarge, magnify 2 = <u>fold up</u> or over
● NOUN = <u>twin</u>, lookalike, spitting image, clone, replica, dead ringer (*slang*), Doppelgänger, duplicate
● PHRASES **at** or **on the double** = <u>at once</u>, now, immediately, directly, quickly, promptly, straight away, right away
♦ **double as something** or **someone** = <u>function as</u>, serve as
doubt NOUN 1 = <u>uncertainty</u>, confusion, hesitation, suspense, indecision, hesitancy, lack of conviction, irresolution ≠ certainty 2 = <u>suspicion</u>, scepticism, distrust, apprehension, mistrust, misgivings, qualms ≠ belief
● VERB 1 = <u>be uncertain</u>, be sceptical, be dubious 2 = <u>waver</u>, hesitate, vacillate, fluctuate 3 = <u>disbelieve</u>, question, suspect, query, distrust, mistrust, lack confidence in ≠ believe
doubtful 1 = <u>unlikely</u>, unclear, dubious, questionable, improbable, debatable, equivocal ≠ certain 2 = <u>unsure</u>, uncertain, hesitant, suspicious, hesitating, sceptical, tentative, wavering ≠ certain
doubtless = <u>probably</u>, presumably, most

likely

down ADJECTIVE = <u>depressed</u>, low, sad, unhappy, discouraged, miserable, fed up, dejected
● VERB (*Informal*) = <u>swallow</u>, drink (down), drain, gulp (down), put away (*informal*), toss off

downfall = <u>ruin</u>, fall, destruction, collapse, disgrace, overthrow, undoing, comeuppance (*slang*)

downgrade = <u>demote</u>, degrade, take down a peg (*informal*), lower or reduce in rank ≠ promote

downright = <u>complete</u>, absolute, utter, total, plain, outright, unqualified, out-and-out

down-to-earth = <u>sensible</u>, practical, realistic, matter-of-fact, sane, no-nonsense, unsentimental, plain-spoken

downward = <u>descending</u>, declining, heading down, earthward

draft NOUN 1 = <u>outline</u>, plan, sketch, version, rough, abstract 2 = <u>money order</u>, bill (of exchange), cheque, postal order
● VERB = <u>outline</u>, write, plan, produce, create, design, draw, compose

drag VERB = <u>pull</u>, draw, haul, trail, tow, tug, jerk, lug
● NOUN (*Slang*) = <u>nuisance</u>, bore, bother, pest, hassle (*informal*), inconvenience, annoyance

drain VERB 1 = <u>remove</u>, draw, empty, withdraw, tap, pump, bleed 2 = <u>empty</u> 3 = <u>flow out</u>, leak, trickle, ooze, seep, exude, well out, effuse 4 = <u>drink up</u>, swallow, finish, put away (*informal*), quaff, gulp down 5 = <u>exhaust</u>, wear out, strain, weaken, fatigue, debilitate, tire out, enfeeble 6 = <u>consume</u>, exhaust, empty, use up, sap, dissipate
● NOUN 1 = <u>sewer</u>, channel, pipe, sink, ditch, trench, conduit, duct 2 = <u>reduction</u>, strain, drag, exhaustion, sapping, depletion

drama 1 = <u>play</u>, show, stage show, dramatization 2 = <u>theatre</u>, acting, stagecraft, dramaturgy 3 = <u>excitement</u>, crisis, spectacle, turmoil, histrionics

dramatic 1 = <u>exciting</u>, thrilling, tense, sensational, breathtaking, electrifying, melodramatic, climactic 2 = <u>theatrical</u>, Thespian, dramaturgical 3 = <u>expressive</u> 4 = <u>powerful</u>, striking, impressive, vivid, jaw-dropping ≠ ordinary

drape = <u>cover</u>, wrap, fold, swathe

drastic = <u>extreme</u>, strong, radical, desperate, severe, harsh

draught 1 = <u>breeze</u>, current, movement, flow, puff, gust, current of air 2 = <u>drink</u>

draw VERB 1 = <u>sketch</u>, design, outline, trace, portray, paint, depict, mark out 2 = <u>pull</u>, drag, haul, tow, tug 3 = <u>extract</u>, take. remove 4 = <u>deduce</u>, make, take, derive, infer 5 = <u>attract</u> 6 = <u>entice</u>
● NOUN 1 = <u>tie</u>, deadlock, stalemate, impasse, dead heat 2 (*Informal*) = <u>appeal</u>, pull (*informal*), charm, attraction, lure, temptation, fascination, allure
● PHRASES **draw on** or **upon something** = <u>make use of</u>, use, employ, rely on, exploit, extract, take from, fall back on

drawback = <u>disadvantage</u>, difficulty, handicap, deficiency, flaw, hitch, snag, downside ≠ advantage

drawing = <u>picture</u>, illustration, representation, cartoon, sketch, portrayal, depiction, study

drawn = <u>tense</u>, worn, stressed, tired, pinched, haggard

dread VERB = <u>fear</u>, shrink from, cringe at the thought of, quail from, shudder to think about, have cold feet about (*informal*), tremble to think about
● NOUN = <u>fear</u>, alarm, horror, terror, dismay, fright, apprehension, trepidation

dreadful 1 = <u>terrible</u>, shocking, awful, appalling, horrible, fearful, hideous, atrocious 2 = <u>serious</u>, terrible, awful, horrendous, monstrous, abysmal 3 = <u>awful</u>, terrible, horrendous, frightful

dream NOUN 1 = <u>vision</u>, illusion, delusion, hallucination 2 = <u>ambition</u>, wish, fantasy, desire, pipe dream 3 = <u>daydream</u> 4 = <u>delight</u>, pleasure, joy, beauty, treasure, gem, marvel, pearler (*Austral. slang*)
● VERB 1 = <u>have dreams</u>, hallucinate 2 = <u>daydream</u>, stargaze, build castles in the air or in Spain
● PHRASES **dream of something** or **someone** = <u>daydream about</u>, fantasize about

dreamer = <u>idealist</u>, visionary, daydreamer, utopian, escapist, Walter Mitty, fantasist

dreary = <u>dull</u>, boring, tedious, drab, tiresome, monotonous, humdrum, uneventful ≠ exciting

drench = <u>soak</u>, flood, wet, drown, steep, swamp, saturate, inundate

dress NOUN 1 = <u>frock</u>, gown, robe

2 = clothing, clothes, costume, garments, apparel, attire, garb, togs
• VERB **1** = put on clothes, don clothes, slip on *or* into something ≠ undress **2** = clothe **3** = bandage, treat, plaster, bind up **4** = arrange, prepare, get ready

dribble 1 = run, drip, trickle, drop, leak, ooze, seep, fall in drops **2** = drool, drivel, slaver, slobber

drift VERB **1** = float, go (aimlessly), bob, coast, slip, sail, slide, glide **2** = wander, stroll, stray, roam, meander, rove, range **3** = stray, wander, digress, get off the point **4** = pile up, gather, accumulate, amass, bank up
• NOUN **1** = pile, bank, mass, heap, mound, accumulation **2** = meaning, point, gist, direction, import, intention, tendency, significance

drill NOUN **1** = bit, borer, gimlet, boring tool **2** = training, exercise, discipline, instruction, preparation, repetition **3** = practice
• VERB **1** = bore, pierce, penetrate, sink in, puncture, perforate **2** = train, coach, teach, exercise, discipline, practise, instruct, rehearse

drink VERB **1** = swallow, sip, suck, gulp, sup, guzzle, imbibe, quaff **2** = booze (*informal*), tipple, tope, hit the bottle (*informal*)
• NOUN **1** = glass, cup, draught **2** = beverage, refreshment, potion, liquid **3** = alcohol, booze (*informal*), liquor, spirits, the bottle (*informal*), hooch *or* hootch (*informal, chiefly U.S. & Canad.*)

drip VERB = drop, splash, sprinkle, trickle, dribble, exude, plop
• NOUN **1** = drop, bead, trickle, dribble, droplet, globule, pearl **2** (*Informal*) = weakling, wet (*Brit. informal*), weed (*informal*), softie (*informal*), mummy's boy (*informal*), namby-pamby

drive VERB **1** = go (by car), ride (by car), motor, travel by car **2** = operate, manage, direct, guide, handle, steer **3** = push, propel **4** = thrust, push, hammer, ram **5** = herd, urge, impel **6** = force, press, prompt, spur, prod, constrain, coerce, goad
• NOUN **1** = run, ride, trip, journey, spin (*informal*), outing, excursion, jaunt **2** = initiative, energy, enterprise, ambition, motivation, zip (*informal*), vigour, get-up-and-go (*informal*) **3** = campaign, push (*informal*), crusade, action, effort, appeal

drop VERB **1** = fall, decline, diminish **2** *often with away* = decline, fall, sink **3** = plunge, fall, tumble, descend, plummet **4** = drip, trickle, dribble, fall in drops **5** = sink, fall, descend **6** = quit, give up, axe (*informal*), kick (*informal*), relinquish, discontinue
• NOUN **1** = decrease, fall, cut, lowering, decline, reduction, slump, fall-off **2** = droplet, bead, globule, bubble, pearl, drip **3** = dash, shot (*informal*), spot, trace, sip, tot, trickle, mouthful **4** = fall, plunge, descent
• PHRASES **drop off 1** = fall asleep, nod (off), doze (off), snooze (*informal*), have forty winks (*informal*) **2** = decrease, lower, decline, shrink, diminish, dwindle, lessen, subside ♦ **drop out** = leave, stop, give up, withdraw, quit, pull out, fall by the wayside ♦ **drop out of something** = discontinue, give up, quit

drought = water shortage, dryness, dry spell, aridity ≠ flood

drove *often plural* = herd, company, crowds, collection, mob, flocks, swarm, horde

drown 1 = go down, go under **2** = drench, flood, soak, steep, swamp, saturate, engulf, submerge **3** = overwhelm, overcome, wipe out, overpower, obliterate, swallow up

drug NOUN **1** = medication, medicine, remedy, physic, medicament **2** = dope (*slang*), narcotic (*slang*), stimulant, opiate, dadah (*Austral. slang*)
• VERB = knock out, dope (*slang*), numb, deaden, stupefy, anaesthetize

drum VERB = pound, beat, tap, rap, thrash, tattoo, throb, pulsate
• PHRASES **drum something into someone** = drive into, hammer into, instil into, din into, harp on about to

drunk ADJECTIVE = intoxicated, plastered (*slang*), drunken, merry (*Brit. informal*), under the influence (*informal*), tipsy, legless (*informal*), inebriated, out to it (*Austral. & N.Z. slang*), babalas (*S. African*)
• NOUN = drunkard, alcoholic, lush (*slang*), boozer (*informal*), wino (*informal*), inebriate, alko *or* alco (*Austral. slang*)

dry ADJECTIVE **1** = dehydrated, dried-up, arid, parched, desiccated ≠ wet **2** = thirsty, parched **3** = sarcastic, cynical, low-key, sly, sardonic, deadpan, droll, ironical **4** = dull, boring, tedious, dreary, tiresome, monotonous, run-of-the-mill, humdrum ≠ interesting **5** = plain, simple, bare, basic, stark, unembellished

● VERB **1** = drain, make dry **2** often with **out** = dehydrate, make dry, desiccate, sear, parch, dehumidify ≠ wet

● PHRASES **dry up** or **out** = become dry, harden, wither, shrivel up, wizen

dual = twofold, double, twin, matched, paired, duplicate, binary, duplex

dubious 1 = suspect, suspicious, crooked, dodgy (Brit., Austral., & N.Z. informal), questionable, unreliable, fishy (informal), disreputable ≠ trustworthy **2** = unsure, uncertain, suspicious, hesitating, doubtful, sceptical, tentative, wavering ≠ sure

duck 1 = bob, drop, lower, bend, bow, dodge, crouch, stoop **2** (Informal) = dodge, avoid, escape, evade, elude, sidestep, shirk **3** = dunk, wet, plunge, dip, submerge, immerse, douse, souse

due ADJECTIVE **1** = expected, scheduled **2** = fitting, deserved, appropriate, justified, suitable, merited, proper, rightful **3** = payable, outstanding, owed, owing, unpaid, in arrears

● ADVERB = directly, dead, straight, exactly, undeviatingly

● NOUN = right(s), privilege, deserts, merits, comeuppance (informal)

● PLURAL NOUN = membership fee, charges, fee, contribution, levy

duel NOUN **1** = single combat, affair of honour **2** = contest, fight, competition, clash, encounter, engagement, rivalry

● VERB = fight, struggle, clash, compete, contest, contend, vie with, lock horns

duff (Brit., Austral., & N.Z. informal) = bad, poor, useless, inferior, unsatisfactory, defective, imperfect, substandard, bodger or bodgie (Austral. slang)

dull ADJECTIVE **1** = boring, tedious, dreary, flat, plain, monotonous, run-of-the-mill, humdrum ≠ exciting **2** = lifeless, indifferent, apathetic, listless, unresponsive, passionless ≠ lively **3** = cloudy, dim, gloomy, dismal, overcast, leaden ≠ bright **4** = blunt, blunted, unsharpened ≠ sharp

● VERB = relieve, blunt, lessen, moderate, soften, alleviate, allay, take the edge off

duly 1 = properly, fittingly, correctly, appropriately, accordingly, suitably, deservedly, rightfully **2** = on time,
promptly, punctually, at the proper time

dumb 1 = unable to speak, mute ≠ articulate **2** = silent, mute, speechless, tongue-tied, wordless, voiceless, soundless, mum **3** (Informal) = stupid, thick, dull, foolish, dense, unintelligent, asinine, dim-witted (informal) ≠ clever

dummy NOUN **1** = model, figure, mannequin, form, manikin **2** = imitation, copy, duplicate, sham, counterfeit, replica **3** (Slang) = fool, idiot, dunce, oaf, simpleton, nitwit (informal), blockhead, dumb-ass (slang), dorba or dorb (Austral. slang), bogan (Austral. slang)

● ADJECTIVE = imitation, false, fake, artificial, mock, bogus, simulated, sham

dump VERB **1** = drop, deposit, throw down, let fall, fling down **2** = get rid of, tip, dispose of, unload, jettison, empty out, throw away or out **3** = scrap, get rid of, abolish, put an end to, discontinue, jettison, put paid to

● NOUN **1** = rubbish tip, tip, junkyard, rubbish heap, refuse heap **2** (Informal) = pigsty, hole (informal), slum, hovel

dunny (Austral. & N.Z. old-fashioned informal) = toilet, lavatory, bathroom, loo (Brit. informal), W.C., bog (slang), Gents or Ladies, can (U.S. & Canad. slang), bogger (Austral. slang), brasco (Austral. slang)

duplicate VERB **1** = repeat, reproduce, copy, clone, replicate **2** = copy

● ADJECTIVE = identical, matched, matching, twin, corresponding, twofold

● NOUN **1** = copy, facsimile **2** = photocopy, copy, reproduction, replica, carbon copy

durable 1 = hard-wearing, strong, tough, reliable, resistant, sturdy, long-lasting ≠ fragile **2** = enduring, continuing, dependable, unwavering, unfaltering

duration = length, time, period, term, stretch, extent, spell, span

dusk = twilight, evening, evo (Austral. slang), nightfall, sunset, dark, sundown, eventide, gloaming (Scot. poetic) ≠ dawn

dust NOUN **1** = grime, grit, powder **2** = particles

● VERB = sprinkle, cover, powder, spread, spray, scatter, sift, dredge

dusty = dirty, grubby, unclean, unswept

duty NOUN **1** = responsibility, job, task, work, role, function, obligation, assignment **2** = tax, toll, levy, tariff, excise

● PHRASES **on duty** = at work, busy,

engaged, on active service

dwarf VERB 1 = tower above or over, dominate, overlook, stand over, loom over, stand head and shoulders above 2 = eclipse, tower above or over, put in the shade, diminish
● ADJECTIVE = miniature, small, baby, tiny, diminutive, bonsai, undersized
● NOUN = gnome, midget, Lilliputian, Tom Thumb, pygmy or pigmy

dwell (*Formal or literary*) = live, reside, lodge, abide

dwelling (*Formal or literary*) = home, house, residence, abode, quarters, lodging, habitation, domicile, whare (*N.Z.*)

dwindle = lessen, decline, fade, shrink, diminish, decrease, wane, subside ≠ increase

dye VERB = colour, stain, tint, tinge, pigment
● NOUN = colouring, colour, pigment, stain, tint, tinge, colorant

dying 1 = near death, moribund, in extremis (*Latin*), at death's door, not long for this world 2 = final, last, parting, departing 3 = failing, declining, foundering, diminishing, decreasing, dwindling, subsiding

dynamic = energetic, powerful, vital, go-ahead, lively, animated, high-powered, forceful ≠ apathetic

dynasty = empire, house, rule, regime, sovereignty

e

each DETERMINER = every, every single
● PRONOUN = every one, all, each one, each and every one, one and all
● ADVERB = apiece, individually, for each, to each, respectively, per person, per head, per capita

eager 1 = anxious, keen, hungry, impatient, itching, thirsty ≠ unenthusiastic 2 = keen, interested, intense, enthusiastic,

passionate, avid (*informal*), fervent ≠ uninterested

ear = sensitivity, taste, discrimination, appreciation
▬▬ RELATED WORD
adjective: aural

early ADVERB 1 = in good time, beforehand, ahead of schedule, in advance, with time to spare ≠ late 2 = too soon, before the usual time, prematurely, ahead of time ≠ late
● ADJECTIVE 1 = first, opening, initial, introductory 2 = premature, forward, advanced, untimely, unseasonable ≠ belated 3 = primitive, first, earliest, young, original, undeveloped, primordial, primeval ≠ developed

earmark 1 = set aside, reserve, label, flag, allocate, designate, mark out 2 = mark out, identify, designate

earn 1 = be paid, make, get, receive, gain, net, collect, bring in 2 = deserve, win, gain, attain, justify, merit, warrant, be entitled to

earnest 1 = serious, grave, intense, dedicated, sincere, thoughtful, solemn, ardent ≠ frivolous 2 = determined, dogged, intent, persistent, persevering, resolute, wholehearted ≠ half-hearted

earnings = income, pay, wages, revenue, proceeds, salary, receipts, remuneration

earth 1 = world, planet, globe, sphere, orb, earthly sphere 2 = ground, land, dry land, terra firma 3 = soil, ground, land, dust, clay, dirt, turf, silt

earthly 1 = worldly, material, secular, mortal, temporal, human ≠ spiritual 2 = sensual, worldly, physical, fleshly, bodily, carnal 3 (*Informal*) = possible, likely, practical, feasible, conceivable, imaginable

ease NOUN 1 = straightforwardness, simplicity, readiness 2 = comfort, luxury, leisure, relaxation, prosperity, affluence, rest, repose ≠ hardship 3 = peace of mind, peace, content, quiet, comfort, happiness, serenity, tranquillity ≠ agitation
● VERB 1 = relieve, calm, soothe, lessen, alleviate, lighten, lower, relax ≠ aggravate 2 = reduce, diminish, lessen, slacken 3 = move carefully, edge, slip, inch, slide, creep, manoeuvre

easily = without difficulty, smoothly, readily, comfortably, effortlessly, with ease, straightforwardly

easy 1 = <u>simple</u>, straightforward, no trouble, not difficult, effortless, painless, uncomplicated, child's play (*informal*) ≠ hard 2 = <u>untroubled</u>, relaxed, peaceful, serene, tranquil, quiet 3 = <u>carefree</u>, comfortable, leisurely, trouble-free, untroubled, cushy (*informal*) ≠ difficult 4 = <u>tolerant</u>, soft, mild, laid-back (*informal*), indulgent, easy-going, lenient, permissive ≠ strict

eat 1 = <u>consume</u>, swallow, chew, scoff (*slang*), devour, munch, tuck into (*informal*), put away 2 = <u>have a meal</u>, lunch, breakfast, dine, snack, feed, graze (*informal*), have lunch

ebb VERB 1 = <u>flow back</u>, go out, withdraw, retreat, wane, recede 2 = <u>decline</u>, flag, diminish, decrease, dwindle, lessen, subside, fall away
● NOUN = <u>flowing back</u>, going out, withdrawal, retreat, wane, low water, low tide, outgoing tide

eccentric ADJECTIVE = <u>odd</u>, strange, peculiar, irregular, quirky, unconventional, idiosyncratic, outlandish ≠ normal
● NOUN = <u>crank</u> (*informal*), character (*informal*), oddball (*informal*), nonconformist, weirdo or weirdie (*informal*)

echo NOUN 1 = <u>reverberation</u>, ringing, repetition, answer, resonance, resounding 2 = <u>copy</u>, reflection, clone, reproduction, imitation, duplicate, double, reiteration
● VERB 1 = <u>reverberate</u>, repeat, resound, ring, resonate 2 = <u>recall</u>, reflect, copy, mirror, resemble, imitate, ape

eclipse NOUN = <u>obscuring</u>, covering, blocking, shading, dimming, extinction, darkening, blotting out
● VERB = <u>surpass</u>, exceed, overshadow, excel, transcend, outdo, outclass, outshine

economic 1 = <u>financial</u>, industrial, commercial 2 = <u>profitable</u>, successful, commercial, rewarding, productive, lucrative, worthwhile, viable 3 (*Informal*) = <u>economical</u>, cheap, reasonable, modest, low-priced, inexpensive

economical 1 = <u>thrifty</u>, sparing, careful, prudent, provident, frugal, parsimonious, scrimping ≠ extravagant 2 = <u>efficient</u>, sparing, cost-effective, money-saving, time-saving ≠ wasteful

economy 1 = <u>financial system</u>, financial state 2 = <u>thrift</u>, restraint, prudence, husbandry, frugality, parsimony

ecstasy = <u>rapture</u>, delight, joy, bliss, euphoria, fervour, elation ≠ agony

ecstatic = <u>rapturous</u>, entranced, joyous, elated, overjoyed, blissful, euphoric, enraptured

edge NOUN 1 = <u>border</u>, side, limit, outline, boundary, fringe, verge, brink 2 = <u>verge</u>, point, brink, threshold 3 = <u>advantage</u>, lead, dominance, superiority, upper hand, head start, ascendancy, whip hand 4 = <u>power</u>, force, bite, effectiveness, incisiveness, powerful quality 5 = <u>sharpness</u>, point, bitterness, keenness
● VERB 1 = <u>inch</u>, ease, creep, slink, steal, sidle, move slowly 2 = <u>border</u>, fringe, hem, pipe
● PHRASES **on edge** = <u>tense</u>, nervous, impatient, irritable, apprehensive, edgy, ill at ease, on tenterhooks

edit = <u>revise</u>, improve, correct, polish, adapt, rewrite, condense, redraft

edition = <u>version</u>, copy, issue, programme (*TV, Radio*), printing, volume, impression, publication

educate = <u>teach</u>, school, train, develop, improve, inform, discipline, tutor

educated 1 = <u>cultured</u>, intellectual, learned, sophisticated, refined, cultivated, enlightened, knowledgeable ≠ uncultured 2 = <u>taught</u>, schooled, coached, informed, tutored, instructed, nurtured, well-informed ≠ uneducated

education 1 = <u>teaching</u>, schooling, training, development, discipline, instruction, nurture, tuition 2 = <u>learning</u>, schooling, cultivation, refinement

educational 1 = <u>academic</u>, school, learning, teaching, scholastic, pedagogical, pedagogic 2 = <u>instructive</u>, useful, cultural, illuminating, enlightening, informative, instructional, edifying

eerie = <u>uncanny</u>, strange, frightening, ghostly, weird, mysterious, scary (*informal*), sinister

effect NOUN 1 = <u>result</u>, consequence, conclusion, outcome, event, end result, upshot 2 = <u>impression</u>, feeling, impact, influence 3 = <u>purpose</u>, impression, sense, intent, essence, thread, tenor
● PLURAL NOUN = <u>belongings</u>, goods, things, property, stuff, gear, possessions, paraphernalia
● VERB = <u>bring about</u>, produce, complete,

achieve, perform, fulfil, accomplish, execute

effective 1 = <u>efficient</u>, successful, useful, active, capable, valuable, helpful, adequate ≠ ineffective **2** = <u>powerful</u>, strong, convincing, persuasive, telling, impressive, compelling, forceful ≠ weak **3** = <u>virtual</u>, essential, practical, implied, implicit, tacit, unacknowledged **4** = <u>in operation</u>, official, current, active, in effect, valid, operative ≠ inoperative

efficiency 1 = <u>effectiveness</u>, power, economy, productivity, organization, cost-effectiveness, orderliness **2** = <u>competence</u>, expertise, capability, professionalism, proficiency, adeptness

efficient 1 = <u>effective</u>, successful, structured, productive, systematic, streamlined, cost-effective, methodical ≠ inefficient **2** = <u>competent</u>, professional, capable, organized, productive, proficient, businesslike, well-organized ≠ incompetent

effort 1 = <u>attempt</u>, try, endeavour, shot (*informal*), bid, essay, go (*informal*), stab (*informal*) **2** = <u>exertion</u>, work, trouble, energy, struggle, application, graft, toil

egg NOUN = <u>ovum</u>, gamete, germ cell
● PHRASES **egg someone on** = <u>incite</u>, push, encourage, urge, prompt, spur, provoke, prod

eject 1 = <u>throw out</u>, remove, turn out, expel (*slang*), oust, banish, drive out, evict **2** = <u>bail out</u>, escape, get out

elaborate ADJECTIVE **1** = <u>complicated</u>, detailed, studied, complex, precise, thorough, intricate, painstaking **2** = <u>ornate</u>, involved, complex, fancy, complicated, intricate, baroque, ornamented ≠ plain
● VERB **1** = <u>develop</u>, flesh out **2** = <u>expand (upon)</u>, extend, enlarge (on), amplify, embellish, flesh out, add detail (to) ≠ simplify

elastic 1 = <u>flexible</u>, supple, rubbery, pliable, plastic, springy, pliant, tensile ≠ rigid **2** = <u>adaptable</u>, yielding, variable, flexible, accommodating, tolerant, adjustable, supple ≠ inflexible

elbow = <u>joint</u>, angle, curve

elder ADJECTIVE = <u>older</u>, first, senior, first-born
● NOUN = <u>older person</u>, senior

elect 1 = <u>vote for</u>, choose, pick, determine,

select, appoint, opt for, settle on **2** = <u>choose</u>, decide, prefer, select, opt

election 1 = <u>vote</u>, poll, ballot, referendum, franchise, plebiscite, show of hands **2** = <u>appointment</u>, picking, choice, selection

electric 1 = <u>electric-powered</u>, powered, cordless, battery-operated, electrically-charged, mains-operated **2** = <u>charged</u>, exciting, stirring, thrilling, stimulating, dynamic, tense, rousing

elegance = <u>style</u>, taste, grace, dignity, sophistication, grandeur, refinement, gracefulness

elegant = <u>stylish</u>, fine, sophisticated, delicate, handsome, refined, chic, exquisite ≠ inelegant

element NOUN **1** = <u>component</u>, part, unit, section, factor, principle, aspect, foundation **2** = <u>group</u>, faction, clique, set, party, circle **3** = <u>trace</u>, suggestion, hint, dash, suspicion, tinge, smattering, soupçon
● PLURAL NOUN = <u>weather conditions</u>, climate, the weather, wind and rain, atmospheric conditions, powers of nature
● PHRASES **be in your element** = <u>be in a situation you enjoy</u>, be in your natural environment, be in familiar surroundings

elementary = <u>simple</u>, clear, easy, plain, straightforward, rudimentary, uncomplicated, undemanding ≠ complicated

elevate 1 = <u>promote</u>, raise, advance, upgrade, exalt, kick upstairs (*informal*), aggrandize, give advancement to **2** = <u>increase</u>, lift, raise, step up, intensify, move up, hoist, raise high **3** = <u>raise</u>, lift, heighten, uplift, hoist, lift up, raise up, hike up

elevated 1 = <u>exalted</u>, important, august, grand, superior, noble, dignified, high-ranking **2** = <u>high-minded</u>, fine, grand, noble, inflated, dignified, sublime, lofty ≠ humble **3** = <u>raised</u>, high, lifted up, upraised

elicit 1 = <u>bring about</u>, cause, derive, bring out, evoke, give rise to, draw out, bring forth **2** = <u>obtain</u>, extract, exact, evoke, wrest, draw out, extort

eligible 1 = <u>entitled</u>, fit, qualified, suitable ≠ ineligible **2** = <u>available</u>, free, single, unmarried, unattached

eliminate 1 = <u>remove</u>, end, stop, withdraw,

get rid of, abolish, cut out, dispose of

elite = aristocracy, best, pick, cream, upper class, nobility, crème de la crème (*French*), flower ≠ rabble

eloquent 1 = silver-tongued, moving, powerful, effective, stirring, articulate, persuasive, forceful ≠ inarticulate 2 = expressive, telling, pointed, significant, vivid, meaningful, indicative, suggestive

elsewhere = in *or* to another place, away, abroad, hence (*archaic*), somewhere else, not here, in other places, in *or* to a different place

elude 1 = evade, escape, lose, avoid, flee, duck (*informal*), dodge, get away from 2 = escape, baffle, frustrate, puzzle, stump, foil, be beyond (someone), thwart

elusive 1 = difficult to catch, tricky, slippery, difficult to find, evasive, shifty 2 = indefinable, fleeting, subtle, indefinite, transient, intangible, indescribable, transitory

emanate = flow, emerge, spring, proceed, arise, stem, derive, originate

embargo NOUN = ban, bar, restriction, boycott, restraint, prohibition, moratorium, stoppage, rahui (*N.Z.*)
● VERB = block, stop, bar, ban, restrict, boycott, prohibit, blacklist

embark VERB = go aboard, climb aboard, board ship, step aboard, go on board, take ship ≠ get off
● PHRASES **embark on something** = begin, start, launch, enter, take up, set out, set about, plunge into

embarrass = shame, distress, show up (*informal*), humiliate, disconcert, fluster, mortify, discomfit

embarrassed = ashamed, shamed, uncomfortable, awkward, abashed, humiliated, uneasy, unsettled

embarrassing = humiliating, upsetting, compromising, delicate, uncomfortable, awkward, sensitive, troublesome, barro (*Austral. slang*)

embarrassment 1 = shame, distress, showing up (*informal*), humiliation, discomfort, unease, self-consciousness, awkwardness 2 = problem, difficulty, nuisance, source of trouble, thorn in your flesh 3 = predicament, problem, difficulty (*informal*), mess, jam (*informal*), plight, scrape (*informal*), pickle (*informal*)

embody 1 = personify, represent, stand

for, manifest, exemplify, symbolize, typify, actualize 2 = incorporate, include, contain, combine, collect, take in, encompass

embrace VERB 1 = hug, hold, cuddle, seize, squeeze, clasp, envelop, canoodle (*slang*) 2 = accept, support, welcome, adopt, take up, seize, espouse, take on board 3 = include, involve, cover, contain, take in, incorporate, comprise, encompass
● NOUN = hug, hold, cuddle, squeeze, clinch (*slang*), clasp

embroil = involve, mix up, implicate, entangle, mire, ensnare, enmesh

embryo 1 = foetus, unborn child, fertilized egg 2 = germ, beginning, source, root, seed, nucleus, rudiment

emerge 1 = come out, appear, surface, rise, arise, turn up, spring up, emanate ≠ withdraw 2 = become apparent, come out, become known, come to light, crop up, transpire, become evident, come out in the wash

emergence 1 = coming, development, arrival, surfacing, rise, appearance, arising, turning up 2 = disclosure, publishing, broadcasting, broadcast, publication, declaration, revelation, becoming known

emergency NOUN = crisis, danger, difficulty, accident, disaster, necessity, plight, scrape (*informal*)
● ADJECTIVE 1 = urgent, crisis, immediate 2 = alternative, extra, additional, substitute, replacement, temporary, makeshift, stopgap

emigrate = move abroad, move, relocate, migrate, resettle, leave your country

eminent = prominent, noted, respected, famous, celebrated, distinguished, well-known, esteemed ≠ unknown

emission = giving off *or* out, release, shedding, leak, radiation, discharge, transmission, ejaculation

emit 1 = give off, release, leak, transmit, discharge, send out, radiate, eject ≠ absorb 2 = utter, produce, voice, give out, let out

emotion 1 = feeling, spirit, soul, passion, excitement, sensation, sentiment, fervour 2 = instinct, sentiment, sensibility, intuition, tenderness, gut feeling, soft-heartedness

emotional 1 = psychological, private, personal, hidden, spiritual, inner 2 = moving, touching, affecting, stirring, sentimental, poignant, emotive, heart-rending **3** = <u>passionate</u>, sentimental, temperamental, excitable, demonstrative, hot-blooded **4** = <u>emotive</u>, sensitive, controversial, delicate, contentious, heated, inflammatory, touchy

emphasis 1 = <u>importance</u>, attention, weight, significance, stress, priority, prominence **2** = <u>stress</u>, accent, force, weight

emphasize 1 = <u>highlight</u>, stress, underline, draw attention to, dwell on, play up, make a point of, give priority to ≠ minimize **2** = <u>stress</u>, accentuate, lay stress on

emphatic 1 = <u>forceful</u>, positive, definite, vigorous, unmistakable, insistent, unequivocal, vehement ≠ hesitant **2** = <u>significant</u>, pronounced, decisive, resounding, conclusive

empire 1 = <u>kingdom</u>, territory, province, federation, commonwealth, realm, domain **2** = <u>organization</u>, company, business, firm, concern, corporation, consortium, syndicate

■ RELATED WORD
adjective: imperial

empirical *or* **empiric** = <u>first-hand</u>, direct, observed, practical, actual, experimental, pragmatic, factual ≠ hypothetical

employ 1 = <u>hire</u>, commission, appoint, take on, retain, engage, recruit, sign up **2** = <u>use</u>, apply, exercise, exert, make use of, utilize, ply, bring to bear **3** = <u>spend</u>, fill, occupy, involve, engage, take up, make use of, use up

employed 1 = <u>working</u>, in work, having a job, in employment, in a job, earning your living ≠ out of work **2** = <u>busy</u>, active, occupied, engaged, hard at work, in harness, rushed off your feet ≠ idle

employee = <u>worker</u>, labourer, workman, staff member, member of staff, hand, wage-earner, white-collar worker

employer 1 = <u>boss</u> (*informal*), manager, head, leader, director, chief, owner, master, baas (*S. African*) **2** = <u>company</u>, business, firm, organization, establishment, outfit (*informal*)

employment 1 = <u>job</u>, work, position, trade, post, situation, profession, occupation **2** = <u>taking on</u>, commissioning, appointing, hire, hiring, retaining, engaging, appointment **3** = <u>use</u>,

application, exertion, exercise, utilization

empower 1 = <u>authorize</u>, allow, commission, qualify, permit, sanction, entitle, delegate **2** = <u>enable</u>, equip, emancipate, give means to, enfranchise

empty ADJECTIVE **1** = <u>bare</u>, clear, abandoned, deserted, vacant, free, void, desolate ≠ full **2** = <u>meaningless</u>, cheap, hollow, vain, idle, futile, insincere **3** = <u>worthless</u>, meaningless, hollow, pointless, futile, senseless, fruitless, inane ≠ meaningful

● VERB **1** = <u>clear</u>, drain, void, unload, pour out, unpack, remove the contents of ≠ fill **2** = <u>exhaust</u>, consume the contents of, void, deplete, use up ≠ replenish **3** = <u>evacuate</u>, clear, vacate

emulate = <u>imitate</u>, follow, copy, mirror, echo, mimic, model yourself on

enable 1 = <u>allow</u>, permit, empower, give someone the opportunity, give someone the means ≠ prevent **2** = <u>authorize</u>, allow, permit, qualify, sanction, entitle, license, warrant ≠ stop

enact 1 = <u>establish</u>, order, command, approve, sanction, proclaim, decree, authorize **2** = <u>perform</u>, play, present, stage, represent, put on, portray, depict

enchant = <u>fascinate</u>, delight, charm, entrance, dazzle, captivate, enthral, beguile

enclose *or* **inclose 1** = <u>surround</u>, circle, bound, fence, confine, close in, wall in, encircle **2** = <u>send with</u>, include, put in, insert

encompass 1 = <u>include</u>, hold, cover, admit, deal with, contain, take in, embrace **2** = <u>surround</u>, circle, enclose, close in, envelop, encircle, fence in, ring

encounter VERB **1** = <u>experience</u>, meet, face, suffer, have, go through, sustain, endure **2** = <u>meet</u>, confront, come across, bump into (*informal*), run across, come upon, chance upon, meet by chance

● NOUN **1** = <u>meeting</u>, brush, confrontation, rendezvous, chance meeting **2** = <u>battle</u>, conflict, clash, contest, run-in (*informal*), confrontation, head-to-head

encourage 1 = <u>inspire</u>, comfort, cheer, reassure, console, hearten, cheer up, embolden ≠ discourage **2** = <u>urge</u>, persuade, prompt, spur, coax, egg on ≠ dissuade **3** = <u>promote</u>, back, support, increase, foster, advocate, stimulate, endorse ≠ prevent

encouragement 1 = <u>inspiration</u>, support, comfort, comforting, cheer, cheering, reassurance, morale boosting 2 = <u>urging</u>, prompting, stimulus, persuasion, coaxing, egging on, incitement 3 = <u>promotion</u>, backing, support, endorsement, stimulation, furtherance

end NOUN 1 = <u>close</u>, ending, finish, expiry, expiration ≠ beginning 2 = <u>conclusion</u>, ending, climax, completion, finale, culmination, denouement, consummation ≠ start 3 = <u>finish</u>, close, stop, resolution, conclusion, closure, completion, termination 4 = <u>extremity</u>, limit, edge, border, extent, extreme, margin, boundary 5 = <u>tip</u>, point, head, peak, extremity 6 = <u>purpose</u>, point, reason, goal, target, aim, object, mission 7 = <u>outcome</u>, resolution, conclusion 8 = <u>death</u>, dying, ruin, destruction, passing on, doom, demise, extinction 9 = <u>remnant</u>, butt, stub, scrap, fragment, stump, remainder, leftover

● VERB 1 = <u>stop</u>, finish, halt, cease, wind up, terminate, call off, discontinue ≠ start 2 = <u>finish</u>, close, conclude, wind up, culminate, terminate, come to an end, draw to a close ≠ begin

▨ RELATED WORDS

adjectives: final, terminal, ultimate

endanger = <u>put at risk</u>, risk, threaten, compromise, jeopardize, imperil, put in danger, expose to danger ≠ save

endearing = <u>attractive</u>, winning, pleasing, appealing, sweet, engaging, charming, pleasant

endeavour (*Formal*) VERB = <u>try</u>, labour, attempt, aim, struggle, venture, strive, aspire

● NOUN = <u>attempt</u>, try, effort, trial, bid, venture, enterprise, undertaking

ending = <u>finish</u>, end, close, conclusion, summing up, completion, finale, culmination ≠ start

endless = <u>eternal</u>, infinite, continual, unlimited, interminable, incessant, boundless, everlasting ≠ temporary

endorse 1 = <u>approve</u>, back, support, champion, promote, recommend, advocate, uphold 2 = <u>sign</u>, initial, countersign, sign on the back of

endorsement = <u>approval</u>, backing, support, favour, recommendation, acceptance, agreement, upholding

endow 1 = <u>provide</u>, favour, grace, bless, supply, furnish, endue 2 = <u>finance</u>, fund, pay for, award, confer, bestow, bequeath, donate money to 3 = <u>imbue</u>

endowment = <u>provision</u>, funding, award, grant, gift, contribution, subsidy, donation, koha (*N.Z.*)

endurance 1 = <u>staying power</u>, strength, resolution, determination, patience, stamina, fortitude, persistence 2 = <u>permanence</u>, stability, continuity, duration, longevity, durability, continuance

endure 1 = <u>experience</u>, suffer, bear, meet, encounter, cope with, sustain, undergo 2 = <u>last</u>, continue, remain, stay, stand, go on, survive, live on

enemy = <u>foe</u>, rival, opponent, the opposition, competitor, the other side, adversary, antagonist ≠ friend

energetic 1 = <u>forceful</u>, determined, active, aggressive, dynamic, vigorous, hard-hitting, strenuous 2 = <u>lively</u>, active, dynamic, vigorous, animated, tireless, bouncy, indefatigable ≠ lethargic 3 = <u>strenuous</u>, hard, taxing, demanding, tough, exhausting, vigorous, arduous

energy 1 = <u>strength</u>, might, stamina, forcefulness 2 = <u>liveliness</u>, drive, determination, pep, vitality, vigour, verve, resilience 3 = <u>power</u>

enforce 1 = <u>carry out</u>, apply, implement, fulfil, execute, administer, put into effect, put into action 2 = <u>impose</u>, force, insist on

engage 1 *with in* = <u>participate in</u>, join in, take part in, undertake, embark on, enter into, become involved in, set about 2 = <u>captivate</u>, catch, arrest, fix, capture 3 = <u>occupy</u>, involve, draw, grip, absorb, preoccupy, immerse, engross 4 = <u>employ</u>, appoint, take on, hire, retain, recruit, enlist, enrol ≠ dismiss 5 = <u>set going</u>, apply, trigger, activate, switch on, energize, bring into operation 6 (*Military*) = <u>begin battle with</u>, attack, take on, encounter, fall on, battle with, meet, assail

engaged 1 = <u>occupied</u>, working, employed, busy, tied up 2 = <u>betrothed</u>, promised, pledged, affianced, promised in marriage ≠ unattached 3 = <u>in use</u>, busy, tied up, unavailable ≠ free

engagement 1 = <u>appointment</u>, meeting, interview, date, commitment, arrangement, rendezvous **2** = betrothal, marriage contract, troth (*archaic*), agreement to marry **3** = battle, fight, conflict, action, struggle, clash, encounter, combat **4** = participation, joining, taking part, involvement

engaging = charming, interesting, pleasing, attractive, lovely, entertaining, winning, fetching (*informal*) ≠ unpleasant

engine = machine, motor, mechanism, generator, dynamo

engineer NOUN **1** = designer, producer, architect, developer, deviser, creator, planner, inventor **2** = worker, specialist, operator, practitioner, operative, driver, conductor, technician
● VERB **1** = design, plan, create, construct, devise **2** = bring about, plan, effect, set up (*informal*), scheme, arrange, plot, mastermind

engraving = print, carving, etching, inscription, plate, woodcut, dry point

engulf 1 = immerse, swamp, submerge, overrun, inundate, envelop, swallow up **2** = overwhelm, overcome, crush, swamp

enhance = improve, better, increase, lift, boost, add to, strengthen, reinforce ≠ reduce

enjoy 1 = take pleasure in *or* from, like, love, appreciate, relish, delight in, be pleased with, be fond of ≠ hate **2** = have, use, own, experience, possess, have the benefit of, reap the benefits of, be blessed *or* favoured with

enjoyable = pleasurable, good, great, fine, nice, satisfying, lovely, entertaining ≠ unpleasant

enjoyment 1 = pleasure, liking, fun, delight, entertainment, joy, happiness, relish **2** – benefit, use, advantage, favour, possession, blessing

enlarge VERB **1** = expand, increase, extend, add to, build up, widen, intensify, broaden ≠ reduce **2** = grow, increase, extend, expand, swell, become bigger, puff up, grow larger
● PHRASES **enlarge on something** = expand on, develop, add to, fill out, elaborate on, flesh out, expatiate on, give further details about

enlighten = inform, tell, teach, advise, counsel, educate, instruct, illuminate

enlightened = informed, aware, reasonable, educated, sophisticated,

cultivated, open-minded, knowledgeable ≠ ignorant

enlightenment = understanding, learning, education, knowledge, instruction, awareness, wisdom, insight

enlist 1 = join up, join, enter (into), register, volunteer, sign up, enrol **2** = recruit, take on, hire, sign up, call up, muster, mobilize, conscript **3** = obtain, get, gain, secure, engage, procure

enormous = huge, massive, vast, extensive, tremendous, gross, immense, gigantic ≠ tiny

enough DETERMINER = sufficient, adequate, ample, abundant, as much as you need, as much as is necessary
● PRONOUN = sufficiency, plenty, sufficient, abundance, adequacy, right amount, ample supply
● ADVERB = sufficiently, amply, reasonably, adequately, satisfactorily, abundantly, tolerably

enrage = anger, infuriate, incense, madden, inflame, exasperate, antagonize, make you angry ≠ calm

enrich 1 = enhance, develop, improve, boost, supplement, refine, heighten, augment **2** = make rich, make wealthy, make affluent, make prosperous, make well-off

enrol 1 = enlist, register, be accepted, be admitted, join up, put your name down for, sign up *or* on **2** = recruit, take on, enlist

en route = on *or* along the way, travelling, on the road, in transit, on the journey

ensemble 1 = group, company, band, troupe, cast, orchestra, chorus **2** = collection, set, body, whole, total, sum, combination, entity **3** = outfit, suit, get-up (*informal*), costume

ensue = follow, result, develop, proceed, arise, stem, derive, issue ≠ come first

ensure 1 = make certain, guarantee, secure, make sure, confirm, warrant, certify **2** = protect, defend, secure, safeguard, guard, make safe

entail = involve, require, produce, demand, call for, occasion, need, bring about

enter 1 = come *or* go in *or* into, arrive, set foot in somewhere, cross the threshold of somewhere, make an entrance ≠ exit **2** = penetrate, get in, pierce, pass into, perforate **3** = join, start work at,

begin work at, enrol in, enlist in ≠ leave
4 = participate in, join (in), be involved
in, get involved in, play a part in, partake
in, associate yourself with, start to be
in **5** = begin, start, take up, move into,
commence, set out on, embark upon
6 = compete in, contest, join in, fight, sign
up for, go in for **7** = record, note, register,
log, list, write down, take down, inscribe

enterprise 1 = firm, company, business,
concern, operation, organization,
establishment, commercial undertaking
2 = venture, operation, project, adventure,
undertaking, programme, pursuit,
endeavour **3** = initiative, energy, daring,
enthusiasm, imagination, drive, ingenuity,
originality

enterprising = resourceful, original,
spirited, daring, bold, enthusiastic,
imaginative, energetic

entertain 1 = amuse, interest, please,
delight, charm, enthral, cheer, regale
2 = show hospitality to, receive,
accommodate, treat, put up, lodge, be
host to, have company of **3** = consider,
imagine, think about, contemplate,
conceive of, bear in mind, keep in mind,
give thought to

entertainment 1 = enjoyable, fun,
pleasure, leisure, relaxation, recreation,
enjoyment, amusement **2** = pastime,
show, sport, performance, treat,
presentation, leisure activity

enthusiasm = keenness, interest,
passion, motivation, relish, zeal, zest,
fervour

enthusiast = fan, supporter, lover,
follower, addict, buff (*informal*), fanatic,
devotee

enthusiastic = keen, committed, eager,
passionate, vigorous, avid, fervent, zealous
≠ apathetic

entice = lure, attract, invite, persuade,
tempt, induce, seduce, lead on

entire = whole, full, complete, total, gross

entirely = completely, totally, absolutely,
fully, altogether, thoroughly, wholly,
utterly ≠ partly

entitle 1 = give the right to, allow, enable,
permit, sanction, license, authorize,
empower **2** = call, name, title, term, label,
dub, christen, give the title of

entity = thing, being, individual, object,
substance, creature, organism

entrance[1] **1** = way in, opening, door,
approach, access, entry, gate, passage
≠ exit **2** = appearance, coming in, entry,
arrival, introduction ≠ exit **3** = admission,
access, entry, entrée, admittance,
permission to enter, right of entry

entrance[2] **1** = enchant, delight, charm,
fascinate, dazzle, captivate, enthral,
beguile ≠ bore **2** = mesmerize, bewitch,
hypnotize, put a spell on, cast a spell on,
put in a trance

entrant = competitor, player, candidate,
entry, participant, applicant, contender,
contestant

entrenched *or* **intrenched** = fixed,
set, rooted, well-established, ingrained,
deep-seated, deep-rooted, unshakeable *or*
unshakable

entrepreneur = businessman *or*
businesswoman, tycoon, executive,
industrialist, speculator, magnate,
impresario, business executive

entrust *or* **intrust 1** = give custody of,
deliver, commit, delegate, hand over, turn
over, confide **2** = assign

entry 1 = admission, access, entrance,
admittance, entrée, permission to enter,
right of entry **2** = coming in, entering,
appearance, arrival, entrance ≠ exit
3 = introduction, presentation, initiation,
inauguration, induction, debut, investiture
4 = record, listing, account, note,
statement, item **5** = way in, opening, door,
approach, access, gate, passage, entrance

envelope = wrapping, casing, case,
covering, cover, jacket, sleeve, wrapper

environment 1 = surroundings,
setting, conditions, situation, medium,
circumstances, background, atmosphere
2 = habitat, home, surroundings, territory,
terrain, locality, natural home

environmental = ecological, green

environmentalist = conservationist,
ecologist, green

envisage 1 = imagine, contemplate,
conceive (of), visualize, picture, fancy,
think up, conceptualize **2** = foresee, see,
expect, predict, anticipate, envision

envoy 1 = ambassador, diplomat, emissary
2 = messenger, agent, representative,
delegate, courier, intermediary, emissary

envy NOUN = covetousness, resentment,
jealousy, bitterness, resentfulness,
enviousness (*informal*)

● VERB 1 = <u>be jealous (of)</u>, resent, begrudge, be envious (of) 2 = <u>covet</u>, desire, crave, aspire to, yearn for, hanker after

epidemic 1 = <u>outbreak</u>, plague, growth, spread, scourge, contagion 2 = <u>spate</u>, plague, outbreak, wave, rash, eruption, upsurge

episode 1 = <u>event</u>, experience, happening, matter, affair, incident, adventure, occurrence 2 = <u>instalment</u>, part, act, scene, section, chapter, passage 3 = <u>period</u>, attack, spell, phase, bout

equal ADJECTIVE 1 = <u>identical</u>, the same, matching, equivalent, uniform, alike, corresponding ≠ unequal 2 = <u>fair</u>, just, impartial, egalitarian, unbiased, even-handed ≠ unfair 3 = <u>even</u>, balanced, fifty-fifty (*informal*), evenly matched ≠ uneven ● NOUN 1 = <u>match</u>, equivalent, twin, counterpart ● VERB 1 = <u>amount to</u>, make, come to, total, level, parallel, tie with, equate ≠ be unequal to 2 = <u>be equal to</u>, match, reach 3 = <u>be as good as</u>, match, compare with, equate with, measure up to, be as great as

equality 1 = <u>fairness</u>, equal opportunity, equal treatment, egalitarianism, fair treatment, justness ≠ inequality 2 = <u>sameness</u>, balance, identity, similarity, correspondence, parity, likeness, uniformity ≠ disparity

equate 1 = <u>identify</u>, associate, connect, compare, relate, mention in the same breath, think of in connection with 2 = <u>make equal</u>, match, even up 3 = <u>be equal to</u>, parallel, compare with, liken, be commensurate with, correspond with *or* to

equation = <u>equating</u>, comparison, parallel, correspondence

equilibrium = <u>stability</u>, balance, symmetry, steadiness, evenness, equipoise

equip 1 = <u>supply</u>, provide for, stock, arm, array, furnish, fit out, kit out 2 = <u>prepare</u>, qualify, educate, get ready

equipment = <u>apparatus</u>, stock, supplies, stuff, tackle, gear, tools, provisions

equitable = <u>even-handed</u>, just, fair, reasonable, proper, honest, impartial, unbiased

equivalent NOUN = <u>equal</u>, counterpart, twin, parallel, match, opposite number ● ADJECTIVE = <u>equal</u>, same, comparable,

parallel, identical, alike, corresponding, tantamount ≠ different

era = <u>age</u>, time, period, date, generation, epoch, day *or* days

eradicate = <u>wipe out</u>, eliminate, remove, destroy, get rid of, erase, extinguish, obliterate

erase 1 = <u>delete</u>, cancel out, wipe out, remove, eradicate, obliterate, blot out, expunge 2 = <u>rub out</u>, remove, wipe out, delete

erect VERB 1 = <u>build</u>, raise, set up, construct, put up, assemble, put together ≠ demolish 2 = <u>found</u>, establish, form, create, set up, institute, organize, put up ● ADJECTIVE = <u>upright</u>, straight, stiff, vertical, elevated, perpendicular, pricked-up ≠ bent

erode 1 = <u>disintegrate</u>, crumble, deteriorate, corrode, break up, grind down, waste away, wear down *or* away 2 = <u>destroy</u>, consume, crumble, eat away, corrode, break up, grind down, abrade 3 = <u>weaken</u>, destroy, undermine, diminish, impair, lessen, wear away

erosion 1 = <u>disintegration</u>, deterioration, wearing down *or* away, grinding down 2 = <u>deterioration</u>, undermining, destruction, weakening, attrition, eating away, abrasion, grinding down

erotic = <u>sexual</u>, sexy (*informal*), crude, explicit, sensual, seductive, vulgar, voluptuous

erratic = <u>unpredictable</u>, variable, unstable, irregular, inconsistent, uneven, unreliable, wayward ≠ regular

error = <u>mistake</u>, slip, blunder, oversight, howler (*informal*), bloomer (*Brit. informal*), miscalculation, solecism

erupt 1 = <u>explode</u>, blow up, emit lava 2 = <u>discharge</u>, expel, emit, eject, spout, throw off, pour forth, spew forth *or* out 3 = <u>gush</u>, burst out, pour forth, belch forth, spew forth *or* out 4 = <u>start</u>, break out, began, explode, flare up, burst out, boil over 5 (*Medical*) = <u>break out</u>, appear, flare up

escalate 1 = <u>grow</u>, increase, extend, intensify, expand, surge, mount, heighten ≠ decrease 2 = <u>increase</u>, develop, extend, intensify, expand, build up, heighten ≠ lessen

escape VERB 1 = <u>get away</u>, flee, take off, fly, bolt, slip away, abscond, make a break for it **2** = <u>avoid</u>, miss, evade, dodge, shun, elude, duck, steer clear of **3** = <u>leak out</u>, flow out, gush out, emanate, seep out, exude, spill out, pour forth

● NOUN **1** = <u>getaway</u>, break, flight, breakout **2** = <u>avoidance</u>, evasion, circumvention **3** = <u>relaxation</u>, recreation, distraction, diversion, pastime **4** = <u>leak</u>, emission, outpouring, seepage, issue, emanation

escort NOUN **1** = <u>guard</u>, bodyguard, train, convoy, entourage, retinue, cortege **2** = <u>companion</u>, partner, attendant, guide, beau, chaperon

● VERB = <u>accompany</u>, lead, partner, conduct, guide, shepherd, usher, chaperon

especially 1 = <u>notably</u>, mostly, strikingly, conspicuously, outstandingly **2** = <u>very</u>, specially, extremely, remarkably, unusually, exceptionally, markedly, uncommonly

espionage = <u>spying</u>, intelligence, surveillance, counter-intelligence, undercover work

essay NOUN = <u>composition</u>, study, paper, article, piece, assignment, discourse, tract

● VERB (*Formal*) = <u>attempt</u>, try, undertake, endeavour

essence 1 = <u>fundamental nature</u>, nature, being, heart, spirit, soul, core, substance **2** = <u>concentrate</u>, spirits, extract, tincture, distillate

essential ADJECTIVE **1** = <u>vital</u>, important, needed, necessary, critical, crucial, key, indispensable ≠ unimportant **2** = <u>fundamental</u>, main, basic, principal, cardinal, elementary, innate, intrinsic ≠ secondary

● NOUN = <u>prerequisite</u>, fundamental, necessity, must, basic, sine qua non (*Latin*), rudiment

establish 1 = <u>set up</u>, found, create, institute, constitute, inaugurate **2** = <u>prove</u>, confirm, demonstrate, certify, verify, substantiate, corroborate, authenticate **3** = <u>secure</u>, form, ground, settle

establishment NOUN **1** = <u>creation</u>, founding, setting up, foundation, institution, organization, formation, installation **2** = <u>organization</u>, company, business, firm, concern, operation, institution, corporation

● PHRASES **the Establishment** = <u>the</u> <u>authorities</u>, the system, the powers that be, the ruling class

estate 1 = <u>lands</u>, property, area, grounds,

domain, manor, holdings **2** = <u>area</u>, centre, park, development, site, zone, plot **3** (*Law*) = <u>property</u>, capital, assets, fortune, goods, effects, wealth, possessions

esteem NOUN = <u>respect</u>, regard, honour, admiration, reverence, estimation, veneration

● VERB = <u>respect</u>, admire, think highly of, love, value, prize, treasure, revere

estimate VERB **1** = <u>calculate roughly</u>, value, guess, judge, reckon, assess, evaluate, gauge **2** = <u>think</u>, believe, consider, rate, judge, hold, rank, reckon

● NOUN **1** = <u>approximate calculation</u>, guess, assessment, judgment, valuation, guesstimate (*informal*), rough calculation, ballpark figure (*informal*) **2** = <u>assessment</u>, opinion, belief, appraisal, evaluation, judgment, estimation

estuary = <u>inlet</u>, mouth, creek, firth, fjord

etch 1 = <u>engrave</u>, cut, impress, stamp, carve, imprint, inscribe **2** = <u>corrode</u>, eat into, burn into

etching = <u>print</u>, impression, carving, engraving, imprint, inscription

eternal 1 = <u>everlasting</u>, lasting, permanent, enduring, endless, perpetual, timeless, unending ≠ transitory **2** = <u>interminable</u>, endless, infinite, continual, immortal, never-ending, everlasting ≠ occasional

eternity 1 (*Theology*) = <u>the afterlife</u>, heaven, paradise, the next world, the hereafter **2** = <u>perpetuity</u>, immortality, infinity, timelessness, endlessness **3** = <u>ages</u>

ethical 1 = <u>moral</u>, behavioural **2** = <u>right</u>, morally acceptable, good, just, fair, responsible, principled ≠ unethical

ethics = <u>moral code</u>, standards, principles, morals, conscience, morality, moral values, moral principles, tikanga (*N.Z.*)

ethnic *or* **ethnical** = <u>cultural</u>, national, traditional, native, folk, racial, genetic, indigenous

euphoria = <u>elation</u>, joy, ecstasy, rapture, exhilaration, jubilation ≠ despondency

evacuate 1 = <u>remove</u>, clear, withdraw, expel, move out, send to a safe place **2** = <u>abandon</u>, leave, clear, desert, quit, withdraw from, pull out of, move out of

evade 1 = <u>avoid</u>, escape, dodge, get away from, elude, steer clear of, sidestep, duck ≠ face **2** = <u>avoid answering</u>, parry, fend off, fudge, hedge, equivocate

evaluate = assess, rate, judge, estimate, reckon, weigh, calculate, gauge

evaporate 1 = disappear, vaporize, dematerialize, vanish, dissolve, dry up, fade away, melt away 2 = dry up, dry, dehydrate, vaporize, desiccate 3 = fade away, disappear, vanish, dissolve, melt away

eve 1 = night before, day before, vigil 2 = brink, point, edge, verge, threshold

even 1 = regular, stable, constant, steady, smooth, uniform, unbroken, uninterrupted ≠ variable 2 = level, straight, flat, smooth, true, steady, uniform, parallel ≠ uneven 3 = equal, like, matching, similar, identical, comparable ≠ unequal 4 = equally matched, level, tied, on a par, neck and neck, fifty-fifty (*informal*), all square ≠ ill-matched 5 = square, quits, on the same level, on an equal footing 6 = calm, composed, cool, well-balanced, placid, unruffled, imperturbable, even-tempered ≠ excitable

evening = dusk (*archaic*), night, sunset, twilight, sundown, gloaming (*Scot. poetic*), close of day, evo (*Austral. slang*)

event 1 = incident, happening, experience, affair, occasion, proceeding, business, circumstance 2 = competition, game, tournament, contest, bout

eventual = final, overall, concluding, ultimate

eventually = in the end, finally, one day, after all, some time, ultimately, at the end of the day, when all is said and done

ever 1 = at any time, at all, in any case, at any point, by any chance, on any occasion, at any period 2 = always, for ever, at all times, evermore 3 = constantly, continually, perpetually

every = each, each and every, every single

everybody = everyone, each one, the whole world, each person, every person, all and sundry, one and all

everyday = ordinary, common, usual, routine, stock, customary, mundane, run-of-the-mill ≠ unusual

everyone = everybody, each one, the whole world, each person, every person, all and sundry, one and all

everything = all, the lot, the whole lot, each thing

everywhere 1 = all over, all around, the world over, high and low, in every nook and cranny, far and wide *or* near, to *or* in every place 2 = all around, all over, in every nook and cranny, ubiquitously, far and wide *or* near, to *or* in every place

evidence NOUN 1 = proof, grounds, demonstration, confirmation, verification, corroboration, authentication, substantiation 2 = sign(s), suggestion, trace, indication 3 = testimony, statement, submission, avowal

● VERB = show, prove, reveal, display, indicate, witness, demonstrate, exhibit

evident = obvious, clear, plain, apparent, visible, manifest, noticeable, unmistakable ≠ hidden

evidently 1 = obviously, clearly, plainly, undoubtedly, manifestly, without question, unmistakably 2 = apparently, seemingly, outwardly, ostensibly, so it seems, to all appearances

evil NOUN 1 = wickedness, bad, vice, sin, wrongdoing, depravity, badness, villainy 2 = harm, suffering, hurt, woe 3 = act of cruelty, crime, ill, horror, outrage, misfortune, mischief, affliction

● ADJECTIVE 1 = wicked, bad, malicious, immoral, sinful, malevolent, depraved, villainous 2 = harmful, disastrous, destructive, dire, catastrophic, pernicious, ruinous 3 = demonic, satanic, diabolical, hellish, devilish, infernal, fiendish 4 = offensive, nasty, foul, unpleasant, vile, noxious, disagreeable, pestilential 5 = unfortunate, unfavourable, ruinous, calamitous

evoke = arouse, cause, induce, awaken, give rise to, stir up, rekindle, summon up ≠ suppress

evolution 1 = rise, development, adaptation, natural selection, Darwinism, survival of the fittest 2 = development, growth, advance, progress, working out, expansion, extension, unfolding

evolve 1 = develop, metamorphose, adapt yourself 2 = grow, develop, advance, progress, mature 3 = work out, develop, progress, expand, unfold

exact ADJECTIVE = accurate, correct, true, right, specific, precise, definite, faultless ≠ approximate

● VERB 1 = demand, claim, force, command, extract, compel, extort 2 = inflict, apply, administer, mete out, deal out

exacting 1 = demanding, hard, taxing,

difficult, tough ≠ easy **2** = <u>strict</u>, severe, harsh, rigorous, stringent

exactly 1 = <u>accurately</u>, correctly, precisely, faithfully, explicitly, scrupulously, truthfully, unerringly **2** = <u>precisely</u>, specifically, bang on (*informal*), to the letter

exaggerate = <u>overstate</u>, enlarge, embroider, amplify, embellish, overestimate, overemphasize, pile it on about (*informal*)

examination 1 = <u>checkup</u>, analysis, going-over (*informal*), exploration, health check, check **2** = <u>exam</u>, test, research, paper, investigation, practical, assessment, quiz

examine 1 = <u>inspect</u>, study, survey, investigate, explore, analyse, scrutinize, peruse **2** = <u>check</u>, analyse, check over **3** = <u>test</u>, question, assess, quiz, evaluate, appraise **4** = <u>question</u>, quiz, interrogate, cross-examine, grill (*informal*), give the third degree to (*informal*)

example 1 = <u>instance</u>, specimen, case, sample, illustration, particular case, particular instance, typical case **2** = <u>illustration</u>, model, ideal, standard, prototype, paradigm, archetype, paragon **3** = <u>warning</u>, lesson, caution, deterrent

exceed 1 = <u>surpass</u>, better, pass, eclipse, beat, cap (*informal*), top, be over **2** = <u>go over the limit of</u>, go beyond, overstep

excel VERB = <u>be superior</u>, eclipse, beat, surpass, transcend, outdo, outshine
● PHRASES **excel in** *or* **at something** = <u>be good at</u>, shine at, be proficient in, show talent in, be skilful at, be talented at

excellence = <u>high quality</u>, merit, distinction, goodness, superiority, greatness, supremacy, eminence

excellent = <u>outstanding</u>, good, great, fine, cool (*informal*), brilliant, very good, superb, booshit (*Austral. slang*), exo (*Austral. slang*), sik (*Austral. slang*) ≠ terrible

except *or* **except for** PREPOSITION = <u>apart from</u>, but for, saving, barring, excepting, other than, excluding, omitting
● VERB = <u>exclude</u>, leave out, omit, disregard, pass over

exception = <u>special case</u>, freak, anomaly, inconsistency, deviation, oddity, peculiarity, irregularity

exceptional 1 = <u>remarkable</u>, special, excellent, extraordinary, outstanding, superior, first-class, marvellous ≠ average **2** = <u>unusual</u>, special, odd, strange, extraordinary, unprecedented, peculiar, abnormal ≠ ordinary

excerpt = <u>extract</u>, part, piece, section, selection, passage, fragment, quotation

excess 1 = <u>surfeit</u>, surplus, overload, glut, superabundance, superfluity ≠ shortage **2** = <u>overindulgence</u>, extravagance, profligacy, debauchery, dissipation, intemperance, indulgence, prodigality ≠ moderation

excessive 1 = <u>immoderate</u>, too much, extreme, exaggerated, unreasonable, disproportionate, undue, uncontrolled **2** = <u>inordinate</u>, unfair, unreasonable, disproportionate, undue, unwarranted, exorbitant, extortionate

exchange VERB = <u>interchange</u>, change, trade, switch, swap, barter, give to each other, give to one another
● NOUN **1** = <u>conversation</u>, talk, word, discussion, chat, dialogue, natter, powwow **2** = <u>interchange</u>, trade, switch, swap, trafficking, swapping, substitution, barter

excite 1 = <u>thrill</u>, inspire, stir, provoke, animate, rouse, exhilarate, inflame **2** = <u>arouse</u>, provoke, rouse, stir up **3** = <u>titillate</u>, thrill, stimulate, turn on (*slang*), arouse, get going (*informal*), electrify

excitement = <u>exhilaration</u>, action, activity, passion, thrill, animation, furore, agitation

exciting 1 = <u>stimulating</u>, dramatic, gripping, stirring, thrilling, sensational, rousing, exhilarating ≠ boring **2** = <u>titillating</u>, stimulating, arousing, erotic

exclaim = <u>cry out</u>, declare, shout, proclaim, yell, utter, call out

exclude 1 = <u>keep out</u>, bar, ban, refuse, forbid, boycott, prohibit, disallow ≠ let in **2** = <u>omit</u>, reject, eliminate, rule out, miss out, leave out ≠ include **3** = <u>eliminate</u>, reject, ignore, rule out, leave out, set aside, omit, pass over

exclusion 1 = <u>ban</u>, bar, veto, boycott, embargo, prohibition, disqualification **2** = <u>elimination</u>, missing out, rejection, leaving out, omission

exclusive 1 = <u>select</u>, fashionable, stylish, restricted, posh (*informal, chiefly Brit.*), chic, high-class, up-market ≠ unrestricted **2** = <u>sole</u>, full, whole, complete, total, entire, absolute, undivided ≠ shared **3** = <u>entire</u>, full, whole, complete, total, absolute, undivided **4** = <u>limited</u>, unique, restricted, confined, peculiar

excursion = <u>trip</u>, tour, journey, outing, expedition, ramble, day trip, jaunt

excuse NOUN = <u>justification</u>, reason, explanation, defence, grounds, plea, apology, vindication ≠ accusation
● VERB **1** = <u>justify</u>, explain, defend, vindicate, mitigate, apologize for, make excuses for ≠ blame **2** = <u>forgive</u>, pardon, overlook, tolerate, acquit, turn a blind eye to, exonerate, make allowances for **3** = <u>free</u>, relieve, exempt, release, spare, discharge, let off, absolve ≠ convict

execute 1 = <u>put to death</u>, kill, shoot, hang, behead, decapitate, guillotine, electrocute **2** = <u>carry out</u>, effect, implement, accomplish, discharge, administer, prosecute, enact **3** = <u>perform</u>, carry out, accomplish

execution 1 = <u>killing</u>, hanging, the death penalty, the rope, capital punishment, beheading, the electric chair, the guillotine **2** = <u>carrying out</u>, performance, operation, administration, prosecution, enforcement, implementation, accomplishment

executive NOUN **1** = <u>administrator</u>, official, director, manager, chairman, managing director, controller, chief executive officer **2** = <u>administration</u>, government, directors, management, leadership, hierarchy, directorate
● ADJECTIVE = <u>administrative</u>, controlling, directing, governing, regulating, decision-making, managerial

exemplify = <u>show</u>, represent, display, demonstrate, illustrate, exhibit, embody, serve as an example of

exempt ADJECTIVE = <u>immune</u>, free, excepted, excused, released, spared, not liable to ≠ liable
● VERB = <u>grant immunity</u>, free, excuse, release, spare, relieve, discharge, let off

exemption = <u>immunity</u>, freedom, relief, exception, discharge, release, dispensation, absolution

exercise VERB **1** = <u>put to use</u>, use, apply, employ, exert, utilize, bring to bear, avail yourself of **2** = <u>train</u>, work out, practise, keep fit, do exercises
● NOUN **1** = <u>use</u>, practice, application,

operation, discharge, implementation, fulfilment, utilization **2** = <u>exertion</u>, training, activity, work, labour, effort, movement, toil **3** = <u>manoeuvre</u>, campaign, operation, movement, deployment **4** = <u>task</u>, problem, lesson, assignment, practice

exert VERB = <u>apply</u>, use, exercise, employ, wield, make use of, utilize, bring to bear
● PHRASES **exert yourself** = <u>make an effort</u>, work, labour, struggle, strain, strive, endeavour, toil

exhaust 1 = <u>tire out</u>, fatigue, drain, weaken, weary, sap, wear out, debilitate **2** = <u>use up</u>, spend, consume, waste, go through, run through, deplete, squander

exhausted 1 = <u>worn out</u>, tired out, drained, spent, bushed (*informal*), done in (*informal*), all in (*slang*), fatigued ≠ invigorated **2** = <u>used up</u>, consumed, spent, finished, depleted, dissipated, expended ≠ replenished

exhaustion 1 = <u>tiredness</u>, fatigue, weariness, debilitation **2** = <u>depletion</u>, emptying, consumption, using up

exhibit 1 = <u>show</u>, reveal, display, demonstrate, express, indicate, manifest **2** = <u>display</u>, show, set out, parade, unveil, put on view

exhibition 1 = <u>show</u>, display, representation, presentation, spectacle, showcase, exposition **2** = <u>display</u>, show, performance, demonstration, revelation

exile NOUN **1** = <u>banishment</u>, expulsion, deportation, eviction, expatriation **2** = <u>expatriate</u>, refugee, outcast, émigré, deportee
● VERB = <u>banish</u>, expel, throw out, deport, drive out, eject, expatriate, cast out

exist 1 = <u>live</u>, be present, survive, endure, be in existence, be, have breath **2** = <u>occur</u>, be present **3** = <u>survive</u>, stay alive, make ends meet, subsist, eke out a living, scrape by, scrimp and save, support yourself

existence 1 = <u>reality</u>, being, life, subsistence, actuality **2** = <u>life</u>, situation, way of life, life style

existent = <u>in existence</u>, living, existing, surviving, standing, present, alive, extant

exit NOUN **1** = <u>way out</u>, door, gate, outlet, doorway, gateway, escape route ≠ entry **2** = <u>departure</u>, withdrawal, retreat, farewell, going, goodbye, exodus, decamping
● VERB = <u>depart</u>, leave, go out, withdraw,

retire, quit, retreat, go away ≠ enter

exodus = departure, withdrawal, retreat, leaving, flight, exit, migration, evacuation

exotic 1 = unusual, striking, strange, fascinating, mysterious, colourful, glamorous, unfamiliar ≠ ordinary 2 = foreign, alien, tropical, external, naturalized

expand VERB 1 = get bigger, increase, grow, extend, swell, widen, enlarge, become bigger ≠ contract 2 = make bigger, increase, develop, extend, widen, enlarge, broaden, magnify ≠ reduce 3 = spread (out), stretch (out), unfold, unravel, diffuse, unfurl, unroll
● PHRASES **expand on something** = go into detail about, embellish, elaborate on, develop, flesh out, expound on, enlarge on, expatiate on

expansion 1 = increase, development, growth, spread, magnification, amplification 2 = enlargement, increase, growth, opening out

expatriate NOUN = exile, refugee, emigrant, émigré
● ADJECTIVE = exiled, refugee, banished, emigrant, émigré, expat

expect 1 = think, believe, suppose, assume, trust, imagine, reckon, presume 2 = anticipate, look forward to, predict, envisage, await, hope for, contemplate 3 = require, demand, want, call for, ask for, hope for, insist on

expectation 1 = projection, supposition, assumption, belief, forecast, likelihood, probability, presumption 2 = anticipation, hope, promise, excitement, expectancy, apprehension, suspense

expedition = journey, mission, voyage, tour, quest, trek

expel 1 = throw out, exclude, ban, dismiss, kick out (informal), ask to leave, turf out (informal), debar ≠ let in 2 = banish, exile, deport, evict, force to leave ≠ take in 3 = drive out, discharge, force out, let out, eject, issue, spew, belch

expenditure 1 = spending, payment, expense, outgoings, cost, outlay 2 = consumption, using, output

expense = cost, charge, expenditure, payment, spending, outlay

expensive = costly, high-priced, lavish, extravagant, dear, stiff, steep (informal), pricey ≠ cheap

experience NOUN 1 = knowledge, practice, skill, contact, expertise, involvement, exposure, participation 2 = event, affair, incident, happening, encounter, episode, adventure, occurrence
● VERB = undergo, feel, face, taste, go through, sample, encounter, endure

experienced = knowledgeable, skilled, tried, tested, seasoned, expert, veteran, practised ≠ inexperienced

experiment NOUN 1 = test, trial, investigation, examination, procedure, demonstration, observation, try-out 2 = research, investigation, analysis, observation, research and development, experimentation
● VERB = test, investigate, trial, research, try, examine, pilot, sample

experimental 1 = test, trial, pilot, preliminary, provisional, tentative, speculative, exploratory 2 = innovative, new, original, radical, creative, ingenious, avant-garde, inventive

expert NOUN = specialist, authority, professional, master, genius, guru, pundit, maestro, fundi (S. African) ≠ amateur
● ADJECTIVE = skilful, experienced, professional, masterly, qualified, talented, outstanding, practised ≠ unskilled

expertise = skill, knowledge, know-how (informal), facility, judgment, mastery, proficiency, adroitness

expire 1 = become invalid, end, finish, conclude, close, stop, run out, cease 2 = die, depart, perish, kick the bucket (informal), depart this life, meet your maker, cark it (Austral. & N.Z. slang), pass away or on

explain 1 = make clear or plain, describe, teach, define, resolve, clarify, clear up, simplify 2 = account for, excuse, justify, give a reason for

explanation 1 = reason, answer, account, excuse, motive, justification, vindication 2 = description, report, definition, teaching, interpretation, illustration, clarification, simplification

explicit 1 = clear, obvious, specific, direct, precise, straightforward, definite, overt ≠ vague 2 = frank, specific, graphic, unambiguous, unrestricted, unrestrained, uncensored ≠ indirect

explode 1 = blow up, erupt, burst, go off, shatter 2 = detonate, set off, discharge, let off **3** = <u>lose your temper</u>, rage, erupt, become angry, hit the roof (*informal*), go crook (*Austral. & N.Z. slang*) **4** = <u>increase</u>, grow, develop, extend, advance, shoot up, soar, boost **5** = <u>disprove</u>, discredit, refute, demolish, repudiate, put paid to, invalidate, debunk

exploit VERB **1** = <u>take advantage of</u>, abuse, use, manipulate, milk, misuse, ill-treat, play on *or* upon **2** = <u>make the best use of</u>, use, make use of, utilize, cash in on (*informal*), capitalize on, use to good advantage, profit by *or* from
● NOUN = <u>feat</u>, act, achievement, enterprise, adventure, stunt, deed, accomplishment

exploitation = <u>misuse</u>, abuse, manipulation, using, ill-treatment

exploration **1** = <u>expedition</u>, tour, trip, survey, travel, journey, reconnaissance **2** = <u>investigation</u>, research, survey, search, inquiry, analysis, examination, inspection

explore **1** = <u>travel around</u>, tour, survey, scout, reconnoitre **2** = <u>investigate</u>, consider, research, survey, search, examine, probe, look into

explosion **1** = <u>blast</u>, crack, burst, bang, discharge, report, blowing up, clap **2** = <u>increase</u>, rise, development, growth, boost, expansion, enlargement, escalation **3** = <u>outburst</u>, fit, storm, attack, surge, flare-up, eruption **4** = <u>outbreak</u>, flare-up, eruption, upsurge

explosive NOUN = <u>bomb</u>, mine, shell, missile, rocket, grenade, charge, torpedo
● ADJECTIVE **1** = <u>unstable</u>, dangerous, volatile, hazardous, unsafe, perilous, combustible, inflammable **2** = <u>sudden</u>, rapid, marked, unexpected, startling, swift, abrupt **3** = <u>fiery</u>, violent, volatile, stormy, touchy, vehement

expose **1** = <u>uncover</u>, show, reveal, display, exhibit, present, unveil, lay bare ≠ hide **2** = <u>make vulnerable</u>, subject, endanger, leave open, jeopardize, put at risk, imperil, lay open

exposure **1** = <u>hypothermia</u>, frostbite, extreme cold, intense cold **2** = <u>uncovering</u>, showing, display, exhibition, revelation, presentation, unveiling

express VERB **1** = <u>state</u>, communicate, convey, articulate, say, word, voice, declare **2** = <u>show</u>, indicate, exhibit, demonstrate, reveal, intimate, convey, signify
● ADJECTIVE **1** = <u>explicit</u>, clear, plain, distinct,

definite, unambiguous, categorical **2** = <u>specific</u>, exclusive, particular, sole, special, singular, clear-cut, especial **3** = <u>fast</u>, direct, rapid, priority, prompt, swift, high-speed, speedy

expression **1** = <u>statement</u>, declaration, announcement, communication, utterance, articulation **2** = <u>indication</u>, demonstration, exhibition, display, showing, show, sign, symbol **3** = <u>look</u>, countenance, face, air, appearance, aspect **4** = <u>phrase</u>, saying, word, term, remark, maxim, idiom, adage

expressive = <u>vivid</u>, striking, telling, moving, poignant, eloquent ≠ impassive

expulsion **1** = <u>ejection</u>, exclusion, dismissal, removal, eviction, banishment **2** = <u>discharge</u>, emission, spewing, secretion, excretion, ejection, seepage, suppuration

exquisite **1** = <u>beautiful</u>, elegant, graceful, pleasing, attractive, lovely, charming, comely ≠ unattractive **2** = <u>fine</u>, beautiful, lovely, elegant, precious, delicate, dainty **3** = <u>intense</u>, acute, severe, sharp, keen, extreme

extend **1** = <u>spread out</u>, reach, stretch **2** = <u>stretch</u>, stretch out, spread out, straighten out **3** = <u>last</u>, continue, go on, stretch, carry on **4** = <u>protrude</u>, project, stand out, bulge, stick out, hang, overhang, jut out **5** = <u>widen</u>, increase, expand, add to, enhance, supplement, enlarge, broaden ≠ reduce **6** = <u>make longer</u>, prolong, lengthen, draw out, spin out, drag out ≠ shorten **7** = <u>offer</u>, present, confer, stick out, impart, proffer ≠ withdraw

extension **1** = <u>annexe</u>, addition, supplement, appendix, appendage **2** = <u>lengthening</u>, extra time, continuation, additional period of time **3** = <u>development</u>, expansion, widening, increase, broadening, enlargement, diversification

extensive ADJECTIVE = <u>large</u>, considerable, substantial, spacious, wide, broad, expansive
● ADJECTIVE ≠ confined **2** = <u>comprehensive</u>, complete, wide, pervasive ≠ restricted **3** = <u>great</u>, vast, widespread, large-scale, far-reaching, far-flung, voluminous ≠ limited

extent **1** = <u>magnitude</u>, amount, scale, level, stretch, expanse **2** = <u>size</u>, area, length, width, breadth

exterior NOUN = <u>outside</u>, face, surface, covering, skin, shell, coating, façade
● ADJECTIVE = <u>outer</u>, outside, external, surface, outward, outermost ≠ inner

external 1 = <u>outer</u>, outside, surface, outward, exterior, outermost ≠ internal
2 = <u>foreign</u>, international, alien, extrinsic ≠ domestic 3 = <u>outside</u>, visiting ≠ inside

extinct = <u>dead</u>, lost, gone, vanished, defunct ≠ living

extinction = <u>dying out</u>, destruction, abolition, oblivion, extermination, annihilation, eradication, obliteration

extra ADJECTIVE 1 = <u>additional</u>, more, added, further, supplementary, auxiliary, ancillary ≠ vital 2 = <u>surplus</u>, excess, spare, redundant, unused, leftover, superfluous
● NOUN = <u>addition</u>, bonus, supplement, accessory ≠ necessity
● ADVERB 1 = <u>in addition</u>, additionally, over and above 2 = <u>exceptionally</u>, very, specially, especially, particularly, extremely, remarkably, unusually

extract VERB 1 = <u>take out</u>, draw, pull, remove, withdraw, pull out, bring out
2 = <u>pull out</u>, remove, take out, draw, uproot, pluck out 3 = <u>elicit</u>, obtain, force, draw, derive, glean, coerce
● NOUN 1 = <u>passage</u>, selection, excerpt, cutting, clipping, quotation, citation
2 = <u>essence</u>, solution, concentrate, juice, distillation

extraordinary 1 = <u>remarkable</u>, outstanding, amazing, fantastic, astonishing, exceptional, phenomenal, extremely good ≠ unremarkable
2 = <u>unusual</u>, strange, remarkable, uncommon ≠ ordinary

extravagant 1 = <u>wasteful</u>, lavish, prodigal, profligate, spendthrift ≠ economical 2 = <u>excessive</u>, outrageous, over the top (*slang*), unreasonable, preposterous ≠ moderate

extreme ADJECTIVE 1 = <u>great</u>, highest, supreme, acute, severe, maximum, intense, ultimate ≠ mild 2 = <u>severe</u>, radical, strict, harsh, rigid, drastic, uncompromising
3 = <u>radical</u>, excessive, fanatical, immoderate ≠ moderate 4 = <u>farthest</u>, furthest, far, remotest, far-off, outermost, most distant ≠ nearest
● NOUN = <u>limit</u>, end, edge, opposite, pole, boundary, antithesis, extremity

extremely = <u>very</u>, particularly, severely, terribly, unusually, exceptionally, extraordinarily, tremendously

extremist NOUN = <u>radical</u>, activist, militant, fanatic, die-hard, bigot, zealot
● ADJECTIVE = <u>extreme</u>, wild, passionate, frenzied, obsessive, fanatical, fervent, zealous

eye NOUN 1 = <u>eyeball</u>, optic (*informal*), organ of vision, organ of sight 2 *often plural* = <u>eyesight</u>, sight, vision, perception, ability to see, power of seeing
3 = <u>appreciation</u>, taste, recognition, judgment, discrimination, perception, discernment 4 = <u>observance</u>, observation, surveillance, vigil, watch, lookout
5 = <u>centre</u>, heart, middle, mid, core, nucleus
● VERB = <u>look at</u>, view, study, watch, survey, observe, contemplate, check out (*informal*)
▇▇▇ RELATED WORDS
adjectives: ocular, ophthalmic, optic

f

fable 1 = <u>legend</u>, myth, parable, allegory, story, tale 2 = <u>fiction</u>, fantasy, myth, invention, yarn (*informal*), fabrication, urban myth, tall story (*informal*) ≠ fact

fabric 1 = <u>cloth</u>, material, stuff, textile, web 2 = <u>framework</u>, structure, make-up, organization, frame, foundations, construction, constitution 3 = <u>structure</u>, foundations, construction, framework

fabulous 1 (*Informal*) = <u>wonderful</u>, excellent, brilliant, superb, spectacular, fantastic (*informal*), marvellous, sensational (*informal*) ≠ ordinary
2 = <u>astounding</u>, amazing, extraordinary, remarkable, incredible, astonishing, unbelievable, breathtaking 3 = <u>legendary</u>, imaginary, mythical, fictitious, made-up, fantastic, invented, unreal

façade 1 = <u>front</u>, face, exterior 2 = <u>show</u>, front, appearance, mask, exterior, guise, pretence, semblance

face NOUN 1 = <u>countenance</u>, features, profile, mug (*slang*), visage 2 = <u>expression</u>, look, air, appearance, aspect, countenance 3 = <u>side</u>, front, outside, surface, exterior, elevation, vertical surface
● VERB 1 = <u>look onto</u>, overlook, be opposite, look out on, front onto 2 = <u>confront</u>, meet, encounter, deal with, oppose, tackle, experience, brave 3 *often with* **up to** = <u>accept</u>, deal with, tackle, acknowledge, cope with, confront, come to terms with, meet head-on

facilitate = <u>further</u>, help, forward, promote, speed up, pave the way for, make easy, expedite ≠ hinder

facility 1 *often plural* = <u>amenity</u>, means, aid, opportunity, advantage, resource, equipment, provision 2 = <u>opportunity</u>, possibility, convenience 3 = <u>ability</u>, skill, efficiency, fluency, proficiency, dexterity, adroitness 4 = <u>ease</u>, fluency, effortlessness ≠ difficulty

fact 1 = <u>truth</u>, reality, certainty, verity ≠ fiction 2 = <u>event</u>, happening, act, performance, incident, deed, occurrence, fait accompli (*French*)

faction 1 = <u>group</u>, set, party, gang, bloc, contingent, clique, coterie 2 = <u>dissension</u>, division, conflict, rebellion, disagreement, variance, discord, infighting ≠ agreement

factor = <u>element</u>, part, cause, influence, item, aspect, characteristic, consideration

factory = <u>works</u>, plant, mill, workshop, assembly line, shop floor

factual = <u>true</u>, authentic, real, correct, genuine, exact, precise, dinkum (*Austral. & N.Z. informal*), true-to-life ≠ fictitious

faculty NOUN 1 = <u>ability</u>, power, skill, facility, capacity, propensity, aptitude ≠ failing 2 = <u>department</u>, school 3 = <u>teaching staff</u>, staff, teachers, professors, lecturers (*chiefly U.S.*)
● PLURAL NOUN = <u>powers</u>, reason, senses, intelligence, wits, capabilities, mental abilities, physical abilities

fad = <u>craze</u>, fashion, trend, rage, vogue, whim, mania

fade 1 = <u>become pale</u>, bleach, wash out, discolour, lose colour, decolour 2 = <u>make pale</u>, dim, bleach, wash out, blanch, discolour, decolour 3 = <u>grow dim</u>, fade away, become less loud 4 = <u>dwindle</u>,

disappear, vanish, melt away, decline, dissolve, wane, die away

fail VERB 1 = <u>be unsuccessful</u>, founder, fall, break down, flop (*informal*), fizzle out (*informal*), come unstuck, miscarry ≠ succeed 2 = <u>disappoint</u>, abandon, desert, neglect, omit, let down, forsake, be disloyal to 3 = <u>stop working</u>, stop, die, break down, stall, cut out, malfunction, conk out (*informal*) 4 = <u>wither</u>, perish, sag, waste away, shrivel up 5 = <u>go bankrupt</u>, collapse, fold (*informal*), close down, go under, go bust (*informal*), go out of business, be wound up 6 = <u>decline</u>, deteriorate, degenerate 7 = <u>give out</u>, dim, peter out, die away, grow dim
● PHRASES **without fail** = <u>without exception</u>, regularly, constantly, invariably, religiously, unfailingly, conscientiously, like clockwork

failing NOUN = <u>shortcoming</u>, fault, weakness, defect, deficiency, flaw, drawback, blemish ≠ strength
● PREPOSITION = <u>in the absence of</u>, lacking, in default of

failure 1 = <u>lack of success</u>, defeat, collapse, breakdown, overthrow, miscarriage, fiasco, downfall ≠ success 2 = <u>loser</u>, disappointment, flop (*informal*), write-off, no-hoper (*chiefly Austral.*), dud (*informal*), black sheep, washout (*informal*), dead duck (*slang*) 3 = <u>bankruptcy</u>, crash, collapse, ruin, closure, winding up, downfall, going under ≠ prosperity

faint ADJECTIVE 1 = <u>dim</u>, low, soft, faded, distant, vague, unclear, muted ≠ clear 2 = <u>slight</u>, weak, feeble, unenthusiastic, remote, slim, vague, slender 3 = <u>dizzy</u>, giddy, light-headed, weak, exhausted, wobbly, muzzy, woozy (*informal*) ≠ energetic
● VERB = <u>pass out</u>, black out, lose consciousness, keel over (*informal*), go out, collapse, swoon (*literary*), flake out (*informal*)
● NOUN = <u>blackout</u>, collapse, coma, swoon (*literary*), unconsciousness

faintly 1 = <u>slightly</u>, rather, a little, somewhat, dimly 2 = <u>softly</u>, weakly, feebly, in a whisper, indistinctly, unclearly

fair¹ 1 = <u>unbiased</u>, impartial, even-handed, unprejudiced, just, reasonable, proper, legitimate ≠ unfair 2 = <u>respectable</u>, average, reasonable, decent, acceptable, moderate, adequate, satisfactory **3** = light, golden, blonde, blond, yellowish, fair-haired, light-coloured, flaxen-haired **4** = fine, clear, dry, bright, pleasant, sunny, cloudless, unclouded **5** = beautiful, pretty, attractive, lovely, handsome, good-looking, bonny, comely ≠ ugly

fair² = carnival, show, fête, festival, exhibition, mart, bazaar, gala

fairly 1 = equitably, objectively, legitimately, honestly, justly, lawfully, without prejudice, dispassionately **2** = moderately, rather, quite, somewhat, reasonably, adequately, pretty well, tolerably **3** = positively, really, simply, absolutely **4** = deservedly, objectively, honestly, justifiably, justly, impartially, equitably, without fear or favour

fairness = impartiality, justice, equity, legitimacy, decency, disinterestedness, rightfulness, equitableness

fairy = sprite, elf, brownie, pixie, puck, imp, leprechaun, peri

fairy tale or **fairy story 1** = folk tale, romance, traditional story **2** = lie, fiction, invention, fabrication, untruth, urban myth, tall story, urban legend

faith 1 = confidence, trust, credit, conviction, assurance, dependence, reliance, credence ≠ distrust **2** = religion, church, belief, persuasion, creed, communion, denomination, dogma ≠ agnosticism

faithful 1 = loyal, true, committed, constant, devoted, dedicated, reliable, staunch ≠ disloyal **2** = accurate, close, true, strict, exact, precise

fake ADJECTIVE = artificial, false, forged, counterfeit, put-on, pretend (*informal*), mock, imitation ≠ genuine
● NOUN **1** = forgery, copy, fraud, reproduction, dummy, imitation, hoax, counterfeit **2** = charlatan, deceiver, sham, quack
● VERB **1** = forge, copy, reproduce, fabricate, counterfeit, falsify **2** = sham, put on, pretend, simulate, feign, go through the motions of

fall VERB **1** = drop, plunge, tumble, plummet, collapse, sink, go down, come down ≠ rise **2** = decrease, drop, decline, go down, slump, diminish, dwindle, lessen ≠ increase **3** = be overthrown, surrender, succumb, submit, capitulate,

be conquered, pass into enemy hands ≠ triumph **4** = be killed, die, perish, meet your end ≠ survive **5** = occur, happen, come about, chance, take place, befall, come to pass
● NOUN **1** = drop, slip, plunge, dive, tumble, descent, plummet, nose dive **2** = decrease, drop, lowering, decline, reduction, slump, dip, lessening **3** = collapse, defeat, downfall, ruin, destruction, overthrow, submission, capitulation

false 1 = incorrect, wrong, mistaken, misleading, faulty, inaccurate, invalid, erroneous ≠ correct **2** = untrue, fraudulent, trumped up, fallacious, untruthful ≠ true **3** = artificial, forged, fake, reproduction, replica, imitation, bogus, simulated ≠ real

falter 1 = hesitate, delay, waver, vacillate ≠ persevere **2** = tumble, totter **3** = stutter, pause, stumble, hesitate, stammer

fame = prominence, glory, celebrity, stardom, reputation, honour, prestige, stature ≠ obscurity

familiar 1 = well-known, recognized, common, ordinary, routine, frequent, accustomed, customary ≠ unfamiliar **2** = friendly, close, dear, intimate, amicable ≠ formal **3** = relaxed, easy, friendly, comfortable, intimate, casual, amicable **4** = disrespectful, forward, bold, intrusive, presumptuous, impudent, overfamiliar

familiarity 1 = acquaintance, experience, understanding, knowledge, awareness, grasp ≠ unfamiliarity **2** = friendliness, intimacy, ease, openness, informality, sociability ≠ formality **3** = disrespect, forwardness, overfamiliarity, cheek, presumption, boldness ≠ respect

family 1 = relations, relatives, household, folk (*informal*), kin, nuclear family, next of kin, kith and kin, ainga (*N.Z.*) **2** = children, kids (*informal*), offspring, little ones, littlies (*Austral. informal*) **3** = ancestors, house, race, tribe, clan, dynasty, line of descent **4** = species, group, class, system, order, network, genre, subdivision

famine = hunger, want, starvation, deprivation, scarcity, dearth

famous = well-known, celebrated, acclaimed, noted, distinguished, prominent, legendary, renowned ≠ unknown

fan¹ NOUN = blower, ventilator, air

conditioner

● VERB = blow, cool, refresh, air-condition, ventilate

fan² = supporter, lover, follower, enthusiast, admirer, buff (*informal*), devotee, aficionado

fanatic = extremist, activist, militant, bigot, zealot

fancy ADJECTIVE = elaborate, decorative, extravagant, intricate, baroque, ornamental, ornate, embellished ≠ plain

● NOUN 1 = whim, thought, idea, desire, urge, notion, humour, impulse 2 = delusion, dream, vision, fantasy, daydream, chimera

● VERB 1 = wish for, want, desire, hope for, long for, crave, yearn for, thirst for 2 (*Informal*) = be attracted to, find attractive, lust after, like, take to, be captivated by, have a thing about (*informal*), have eyes for 3 = suppose, think, believe, imagine, reckon, conjecture, think likely

fantastic 1 (*Informal*) = wonderful, great, excellent, very good, smashing (*informal*), superb, tremendous (*informal*), magnificent, booshit (*Austral. slang*), exo (*Austral. slang*), sik (*Austral. slang*) ≠ ordinary 2 = strange, bizarre, grotesque, fanciful, outlandish 3 = implausible, unlikely, incredible, absurd, preposterous, cock-and-bull (*informal*)

fantasy or (*Archaic*) **phantasy** 1 = daydream, dream, wish, reverie, flight of fancy, pipe dream 2 = imagination, fancy, invention, creativity, originality

far ADVERB 1 = a long way, miles, deep, a good way, afar, a great distance 2 = much, greatly, very much, extremely, significantly, considerably, decidedly, markedly

● ADJECTIVE *often with* **off** = remote, distant, far-flung, faraway, out-of-the-way, far-off, outlying, off the beaten track ≠ near

farce 1 = comedy, satire, slapstick, burlesque, buffoonery 2 = mockery, joke, nonsense, parody, shambles, sham, travesty

fare NOUN 1 = charge, price, ticket price, ticket money 2 = food, provisions, board, rations, kai (*N.Z. informal*), nourishment, sustenance, victuals, nutriment

● VERB = get on, do, manage, make out, prosper, get along

farewell INTERJECTION = goodbye, bye (*informal*), so long, see you, take care, good morning, bye-bye (*informal*), good day, haere ra (*N.Z.*)

● NOUN = goodbye, parting, departure, leave-taking, adieu, valediction, sendoff (*informal*)

farm NOUN = smallholding, ranch (*chiefly U.S. & Canad.*), farmstead, station (*Austral. & N.Z.*), vineyard, plantation, croft (*Scot.*), grange, homestead

● VERB = cultivate, work, plant, grow crops on, keep animals on

fascinate = entrance, absorb, intrigue, rivet, captivate, enthral, beguile, transfix ≠ bore

fascinating = captivating, engaging, gripping, compelling, intriguing, very interesting, irresistible, enticing ≠ boring

fascination = attraction, pull, magic, charm, lure, allure, magnetism, enchantment

fashion NOUN 1 = style, look, trend, rage, custom, mode, vogue, craze 2 = method, way, style, manner, mode

● VERB = make, shape, cast, construct, form, create, manufacture, forge

fashionable = popular, in fashion, trendy (*Brit. informal*), in (*informal*), modern, with it (*informal*), stylish, chic ≠ unfashionable

fast¹ ADJECTIVE 1 = quick, flying, rapid, fleet, swift, speedy, brisk, hasty ≠ slow 2 = fixed, firm, sound, stuck, secure, tight, jammed, fastened ≠ unstable 3 = dissipated, wild, exciting, loose, extravagant, reckless, self-indulgent, wanton 4 = close, firm, devoted, faithful, steadfast

● ADVERB 1 = quickly, rapidly, swiftly, hastily, hurriedly, speedily, in haste, at full speed ≠ slowly 2 = securely, firmly, tightly, fixedly 3 = fixedly, firmly, soundly, deeply, securely, tightly

fast² VERB = go hungry, abstain, go without food, deny yourself

● NOUN = fasting, diet, abstinence

fasten 1 = secure, close, do up 2 = tie, bind, tie up 3 = fix, join, link, connect, attach, affix

fat ADJECTIVE 1 = overweight, large, heavy, plump, stout, obese, tubby, portly ≠ thin 2 = fatty, greasy, adipose, oleaginous, oily ≠ lean

● NOUN = fatness, flesh, bulk, obesity, flab, blubber, paunch, fatty tissue

fatal 1 = <u>disastrous</u>, devastating, crippling, catastrophic, ruinous, calamitous, baleful, baneful ≠ minor 2 = <u>lethal</u>, deadly, mortal, causing death, final, killing, terminal, malignant ≠ harmless

fate 1 = <u>destiny</u>, chance, fortune, luck, the stars, providence, nemesis, kismet 2 = <u>fortune</u>, destiny, lot, portion, cup, horoscope

fated = <u>destined</u>, doomed, predestined, preordained, foreordained

father NOUN 1 = <u>daddy</u> (*informal*), dad (*informal*), male parent, pop (*U.S. informal*), old man (*Brit. informal*), pa (*informal*), papa (*old-fashioned informal*), pater 2 = <u>founder</u>, author, maker, architect, creator, inventor, originator, prime mover 3 *usually cap.* = <u>priest</u>, minister, vicar, parson, pastor, cleric, churchman, padre (*informal*) 4 *usually plural* = <u>forefather</u>, predecessor, ancestor, forebear, progenitor, tupuna *or* tipuna (*N.Z.*)
● VERB = <u>sire</u>, parent, conceive, bring to life, beget, procreate, bring into being, give life to
▪ RELATED WORD
adjective: paternal

fatherly = <u>paternal</u>, kindly, protective, supportive, benign, affectionate, patriarchal, benevolent

fatigue NOUN = <u>tiredness</u>, lethargy, weariness, heaviness, languor, listlessness ≠ freshness
● VERB = <u>tire</u>, exhaust, weaken, weary, drain, wear out, take it out of (*informal*), tire out ≠ refresh

fatty = <u>greasy</u>, fat, creamy, oily, adipose, oleaginous, suety, rich

fault NOUN 1 = <u>responsibility</u>, liability, guilt, accountability, culpability 2 = <u>mistake</u>, slip, error, blunder, lapse, oversight, indiscretion, howler (*informal*) 3 = <u>failing</u>, weakness, defect, deficiency, flaw, shortcoming, blemish, imperfection ≠ strength
● VERB = <u>criticize</u>, blame, complain, condemn, moan about, censure, hold (someone) responsible, find fault with
● PHRASES **find fault with something** *or* **someone** = <u>criticize</u>, complain about, whinge about (*informal*), quibble, carp at, take to task, pick holes in ◆ **to a fault** = <u>excessively</u>, unduly, in the extreme, overmuch,

immoderately

faulty 1 = <u>defective</u>, damaged, malfunctioning, broken, flawed, impaired, imperfect, out of order 2 = <u>incorrect</u>, flawed, unsound

favour NOUN 1 = <u>approval</u>, goodwill, commendation, approbation ≠ disapproval 2 = <u>favouritism</u>, preferential treatment 3 = <u>support</u>, backing, aid, assistance, patronage, good opinion 4 = <u>good turn</u>, service, benefit, courtesy, kindness, indulgence, boon, good deed ≠ wrong
● VERB 1 = <u>prefer</u>, opt for, like better, incline towards, choose, pick, desire, go for ≠ object to 2 = <u>indulge</u>, reward, side with, smile upon 3 = <u>support</u>, champion, encourage, approve, advocate, subscribe to, commend, stand up for ≠ oppose 4 = <u>help</u>, benefit

favourable 1 = <u>positive</u>, encouraging, approving, praising, reassuring, enthusiastic, sympathetic, commending ≠ disapproving 2 = <u>affirmative</u>, agreeing, confirming, positive, assenting, corroborative 3 = <u>advantageous</u>, promising, encouraging, suitable, helpful, beneficial, auspicious, opportune ≠ disadvantageous

favourite ADJECTIVE = <u>preferred</u>, favoured, best-loved, most-liked, special, choice, dearest, pet
● NOUN = <u>darling</u>, pet, blue-eyed boy (*informal*), beloved, idol, fave (*informal*), teacher's pet, the apple of your eye

fear NOUN 1 = <u>dread</u>, horror, panic, terror, fright, alarm, trepidation, fearfulness 2 = <u>bugbear</u>, bête noire, horror, nightmare, anxiety, terror, dread, spectre
● VERB 1 = <u>be afraid of</u>, dread, shudder at, be fearful of, tremble at, be terrified by, take fright at, shake in your shoes about 2 = <u>regret</u>, feel, suspect, have a feeling, have a hunch, have a sneaking suspicion, have a funny feeling
● PHRASES **fear for something** *or* **someone** = <u>worry about</u>, be anxious about, feel concern for

fearful 1 = <u>scared</u>, afraid, alarmed, frightened, nervous, terrified, petrified ≠ unafraid 2 = <u>timid</u>, afraid, frightened, scared, alarmed, nervous, uneasy, jumpy ≠ brave 3 = <u>frightful</u>, terrible, awful, dreadful, horrific, dire, horrendous, gruesome

feasible = practicable, possible, reasonable, viable, workable, achievable, attainable, likely ≠ impracticable

feast NOUN 1 = banquet, repast, spread (*informal*), dinner, treat, hakari (*N.Z.*) 2 = festival, holiday, fête, celebration, holy day, red-letter day, religious festival, saint's day

● VERB = eat your fill, wine and dine, overindulge, consume, indulge, gorge, devour, pig out (*slang*)

feat = accomplishment, act, performance, achievement, enterprise, undertaking, exploit, deed

feather NOUN = plume

● PLURAL NOUN = plumage, plumes, down

feature NOUN 1 = aspect, quality, characteristic, property, factor, trait, hallmark, facet 2 = article, report, story, piece, item, column 3 = highlight, attraction, speciality, main item

● PLURAL NOUN = face, countenance, physiognomy, lineaments

● VERB 1 = spotlight, present, emphasize, play up, foreground, give prominence to 2 = star, appear, participate, play a part

federation = union, league, association, alliance, combination, coalition, partnership, consortium

fed up = cheesed off, depressed, bored, tired, discontented, dissatisfied, glum, sick and tired (*informal*), hoha (*N.Z.*)

fee = charge, price, cost, bill, payment, wage, salary, toll

feeble 1 = weak, frâil, debilitated, sickly, puny, weedy (*informal*), infirm, effete ≠ strong 2 = inadequate, pathetic, insufficient, lame 3 = unconvincing, poor, thin, tame, pathetic, lame, flimsy, paltry ≠ effective

feed VERB 1 = cater for, provide for, nourish, provide with food, supply, sustain, cook for, wine and dine 2 = graze, eat, browse, pasture 3 = eat, drink milk

● NOUN 1 = food, fodder, provender, pasturage 2 (*Informal*) = meal, spread (*informal*), dinner, lunch, tea, breakfast, feast, supper

feel VERB 1 = experience, bear 2 = touch, handle, manipulate, finger, stroke, paw, caress, fondle 3 = be aware of 4 = perceive, detect, discern, experience, notice, observe 5 = sense, be aware,

be convinced, have a feeling, intuit 6 = believe, consider, judge, deem, think, hold

● NOUN 1 = texture, finish, touch, surface, surface quality 2 = impression, feeling, air, sense, quality, atmosphere, mood, aura

feeling 1 = emotion, sentiment 2 = opinion, view, attitude, belief, point of view, instinct, inclination 3 = passion, emotion, intensity, warmth 4 = ardour, love, care, warmth, tenderness, fervour 5 = sympathy, understanding, concern, pity, sensitivity, compassion, sorrow, sensibility 6 = sensation, sense, impression, awareness 7 = sense of touch, perception, sensation 8 = impression, idea, sense, notion, suspicion, hunch, inkling, presentiment 9 = atmosphere, mood, aura, ambience, feel, air, quality

fell 1 = cut down, cut, level, demolish, knock down, hew 2 = knock down

fellow 1 (*Old-fashioned*) = man, person, individual, character, guy (*informal*), bloke (*Brit. informal*), chap (*informal*) 2 = associate, colleague, peer, partner, companion, comrade, crony

fellowship 1 = society, club, league, association, organization, guild, fraternity, brotherhood 2 = camaraderie, brotherhood, companionship, sociability

feminine = womanly, pretty, soft, gentle, tender, delicate, ladylike ≠ masculine

fence NOUN = barrier, wall, defence, railings, hedge, barricade, hedgerow, rampart

● VERB *often with* **in** *or* **off** = enclose, surround, bound, protect, pen, confine, encircle

ferocious 1 = fierce, violent, savage, ravening, predatory, rapacious, wild ≠ gentle 2 = cruel, bitter, brutal, vicious, ruthless, bloodthirsty

ferry NOUN = ferry boat, boat, ship, passenger boat, packet boat, packet

● VERB = transport, bring, carry, ship, take, run, shuttle, convey

fertile = productive, rich, lush, prolific, abundant, plentiful, fruitful, teeming ≠ barren

fertility = fruitfulness, abundance, richness, fecundity, luxuriance, productiveness

fertilizer = compost, muck, manure, dung, bone meal, dressing

festival 1 = <u>celebration</u>, fair, carnival, gala, fête, entertainment, jubilee, fiesta 2 = <u>holy day</u>, holiday, feast, commemoration, feast day, red-letter day, saint's day, fiesta

festive = <u>celebratory</u>, happy, merry, jubilant, cheery, joyous, joyful, jovial ≠ mournful

fetch 1 = <u>bring</u>, pick up, collect, go and get, get, carry, deliver, transport 2 = <u>sell for</u>, make, raise, earn, realize, go for, yield, bring in

fetching = <u>attractive</u>, charming, cute, enticing, captivating, alluring, winsome

feud NOUN = <u>hostility</u>, row, conflict, argument, disagreement, rivalry, quarrel, vendetta

● VERB = <u>quarrel</u>, row, clash, dispute, fall out, contend, war, squabble

fever = <u>excitement</u>, frenzy, ferment, agitation, fervour, restlessness, delirium

few = <u>not many</u>, one or two, scarcely any, rare, meagre, negligible, sporadic, sparse

fiasco = <u>flop</u>, failure, disaster, mess (*informal*), catastrophe, debacle, cock-up (*Brit. slang*), washout (*informal*)

fibre – <u>thread</u>, strand, filament, tendril, pile, texture, wisp

fiction 1 = <u>tale</u>, story, novel, legend, myth, romance, narration, creative writing 2 = <u>lie</u>, invention, fabrication, falsehood, untruth, urban myth, tall story, urban legend

fictional = <u>imaginary</u>, made-up, invented, legendary, unreal, nonexistent

fiddle VERB 1 *usually with* **with** = <u>fidget</u>, play, finger, tamper, mess about *or* around 2 *usually with* **with** = <u>tinker</u>, adjust, interfere, mess about *or* around 3 (*Informal*) = <u>cheat</u>, cook (*informal*), fix, diddle (*informal*), wangle (*informal*)

● NOUN 1 (*Brit. informal*) = <u>fraud</u>, racket, scam (*slang*), fix, swindle 2 = <u>violin</u>

fiddling = <u>trivial</u>, small, petty, trifling, insignificant, unimportant, pettifogging, futile

fidelity 1 = <u>loyalty</u>, devotion, allegiance, constancy, faithfulness, dependability, trustworthiness, staunchness ≠ disloyalty 2 = <u>accuracy</u>, precision, correspondence, closeness, faithfulness, exactness, scrupulousness ≠ inaccuracy

field NOUN 1 = <u>meadow</u>, land, green, lea (*poetic*), pasture 2 = <u>speciality</u>, line, area, department, territory, discipline, province, sphere 3 = <u>line</u>, reach, sweep 4 = <u>competitors</u>, competition, candidates, runners, applicants, entrants, contestants

● VERB 1 (*Informal*) = <u>deal with</u>, answer, handle, respond to, reply to, deflect, turn aside 2 (*Sport*) = <u>retrieve</u>, return, stop, catch, pick up

fierce 1 = <u>ferocious</u>, wild, dangerous, cruel, savage, brutal, aggressive, menacing, aggers (*Austral. slang*), biffo (*Austral. slang*) ≠ gentle 2 = <u>intense</u>, strong, keen, relentless, cut-throat 3 = <u>stormy</u>, strong, powerful, violent, intense, raging, furious, howling ≠ tranquil

fiercely = <u>ferociously</u>, savagely, passionately, furiously, viciously, tooth and nail, tigerishly, with no holds barred

fiery 1 = <u>burning</u>, flaming, blazing, on fire, ablaze, aflame, afire 2 = <u>excitable</u>, fierce, passionate, irritable, impetuous, irascible, hot-headed

fight VERB 1 = <u>oppose</u>, campaign against, dispute, contest, resist, defy, contend, withstand 2 = <u>battle</u>, combat, do battle 3 = <u>engage in</u>, conduct, wage, pursue, carry on

● NOUN 1 = <u>battle</u>, campaign, movement, struggle 2 = <u>conflict</u>, clash, contest, encounter 3 = <u>brawl</u>, scrap (*informal*), confrontation, rumble (*U.S. & N.Z. slang*), duel, skirmish, tussle, biffo (*Austral. slang*) 4 = <u>row</u>, argument, dispute, quarrel, squabble 5 = <u>resistance</u>, spirit, pluck, militancy, belligerence, pluckiness

fighter 1 = <u>boxer</u>, wrestler, pugilist, prize fighter 2 = <u>soldier</u>, warrior, fighting man, man-at-arms

figure NOUN 1 = <u>digit</u>, character, symbol, number, numeral 2 = <u>shape</u>, build, body, frame, proportions, physique 3 = <u>personage</u>, person, individual, character, personality, celebrity, big name, dignitary 4 = <u>diagram</u>, drawing, picture, illustration, representation, sketch 5 = <u>design</u>, shape, pattern 6 = <u>price</u>, cost, value, amount, total, sum

● VERB 1 *usually with* **in** = <u>feature</u>, act, appear, contribute to, play a part, be featured 2 = <u>calculate</u>, work out, compute, tot up, total, count, reckon, tally

● PHRASES **figure something** *or* **someone out** = <u>understand</u>, make out, fathom, see, solve, comprehend, make sense of, decipher

figurehead = nominal head, titular head, front man, puppet, mouthpiece

file¹ NOUN 1 = folder, case, portfolio, binder 2 = dossier, record, information, data, documents, case history, report, case 3 = line, row, chain, column, queue, procession
● VERB 1 = arrange, order, classify, put in place, categorize, pigeonhole, put in order 2 = register, record, enter, log, put on record 3 = march, troop, parade, walk in line, walk behind one another

file² = smooth, shape, polish, rub, scrape, rasp, abrade

fill 1 = top up, fill up, make full, become full, brim over 2 = swell, expand, become bloated, extend, balloon, fatten 3 = pack, crowd, squeeze, cram, throng 4 = stock, supply, pack, load 5 = plug, close, stop, seal, cork, bung, block up, stop up 6 = saturate, charge, pervade, permeate, imbue, impregnate, suffuse 7 = fulfil, hold, perform, carry out, occupy, execute, discharge 8 often with **up** = satisfy, stuff, glut

filling NOUN = stuffing, padding, filler, wadding, inside, insides, contents
● ADJECTIVE = satisfying, heavy, square, substantial, ample

film NOUN 1 = movie, picture, flick (slang), motion picture 2 = cinema, the movies 3 = layer, covering, cover, skin, coating, dusting, tissue, membrane
● VERB 1 = photograph, record, shoot, video, videotape, take 2 = adapt for the screen, make into a film

filter VERB 1 = purify, treat, strain, refine, riddle, sift, sieve, winnow 2 = trickle, seep, percolate, escape, leak, penetrate, ooze, dribble
● NOUN = sieve, mesh, gauze, strainer, membrane, riddle, sifter

filthy 1 = dirty, foul, polluted, squalid, slimy, unclean, putrid, festy (Austral. slang) 2 = grimy, muddy, blackened, grubby, begrimed, festy (Austral. slang) 3 = obscene, corrupt, indecent, pornographic, lewd, depraved, impure, smutty

final 1 = last, latest, closing, finishing, concluding, ultimate, terminal ≠ first 2 = irrevocable, absolute, definitive, decided, settled, definite, conclusive, irrefutable

finale = climax, ending, close, conclusion, culmination, denouement, last part, epilogue ≠ opening

finally 1 = eventually, at last, in the end, ultimately, at length, at long last, after a long time 2 = lastly, in the end, ultimately 3 = in conclusion, lastly, in closing, to conclude, to sum up, in summary

finance VERB = fund, back, support, pay for, guarantee, invest in, underwrite, endow
● NOUN = economics, business, money, banking, accounts, investment, commerce
● PLURAL NOUN = resources, money, funds, capital, cash, affairs, budgeting, assets

financial = economic, business, commercial, monetary, fiscal, pecuniary

find VERB 1 = discover, uncover, spot, locate, detect, come across, hit upon, put your finger on ≠ lose 2 = encounter, meet, recognize 3 = observe, learn, note, discover, notice, realize, come up with, perceive
● NOUN = discovery, catch, asset, bargain, acquisition, good buy
● PHRASES **find something out** = learn, discover, realize, observe, perceive, detect, become aware, come to know

fine¹ 1 = excellent, good, striking, masterly, very good, impressive, outstanding, magnificent ≠ poor 2 = satisfactory, good, all right, suitable, acceptable, convenient, fair, O.K. or okay (informal) 3 = thin, light, narrow, wispy 4 = delicate, light, thin, sheer, flimsy, wispy, gossamer, diaphanous ≠ coarse 5 = stylish, expensive, elegant, refined, tasteful, quality 6 = exquisite, delicate, fragile, dainty 7 = minute, exact, precise, nice 8 = keen, minute, nice, sharp, acute, subtle, precise, hairsplitting 9 = brilliant, quick, keen, alert, clever, penetrating, astute 10 = sunny, clear, fair, dry, bright, pleasant, clement, balmy ≠ cloudy

fine² NOUN = penalty, damages, punishment, forfeit, financial penalty
● VERB = penalize, charge, punish

finger = touch, feel, handle, play with, manipulate, paw (informal), maul, toy with

finish VERB 1 = stop, close, complete, conclude, cease, wrap up (informal), terminate, round off ≠ start 2 = get done, complete, conclude 3 = end, stop, conclude, wind up, terminate

4 = <u>consume</u>, dispose of, devour, polish off, eat, get through **5** = <u>use up</u>, empty, exhaust **6** = <u>coat</u>, polish, stain, texture, wax, varnish, gild, veneer **7** *usually with* ***off*** = <u>destroy</u>, defeat, overcome, bring down, ruin, dispose of, rout, put an end to **8** *usually with* ***off*** = <u>kill</u>, murder, destroy, massacre, butcher, slaughter, slay, exterminate

● NOUN **1** = <u>end</u>, close, conclusion, run-in, completion, finale, culmination, cessation ≠ beginning **2** = <u>surface</u>, polish, shine, texture, glaze, veneer, lacquer, lustre

finished 1 = <u>over</u>, done, through, ended, closed, complete, executed, finalized ≠ begun **2** = <u>ruined</u>, done for (*informal*), doomed, through, lost, defeated, wiped out, undone

fire NOUN **1** = <u>flames</u>, blaze, combustion, inferno, conflagration, holocaust **2** = <u>passion</u>, energy, spirit, enthusiasm, excitement, intensity, sparkle, vitality **3** = <u>bombardment</u>, shooting, firing, shelling, hail, volley, barrage, gunfire

● VERB **1** = <u>let off</u>, shoot, shell, set off, discharge, detonate **2** = <u>shoot</u>, explode, discharge, detonate, pull the trigger **3** (*Informal*) = <u>dismiss</u>, sack (*informal*), get rid of, discharge, lay off, make redundant, cashier, give notice **4** *sometimes with* ***up*** = <u>inspire</u>, excite, stir, stimulate, motivate, awaken, animate, rouse

fireworks 1 = <u>pyrotechnics</u>, illuminations, feux d'artifice **2** (*Informal*) = <u>trouble</u>, row, storm, rage, uproar, hysterics

firm¹ 1 = <u>hard</u>, solid, dense, set, stiff, compacted, rigid, inflexible ≠ soft **2** = <u>secure</u>, fixed, rooted, stable, steady, fast, embedded, immovable ≠ unstable **3** = <u>strong</u>, close, tight, steady **4** = <u>strict</u>, unshakeable, resolute, inflexible, unyielding, unbending **5** = <u>determined</u>, resolved, definite, set on, adamant, resolute, inflexible, unyielding ≠ wavering **6** = <u>definite</u>, hard, clear, confirmed, settled, fixed, hard-and-fast, cut-and-dried (*informal*)

firm² = <u>company</u>, business, concern, association, organization, corporation, venture, enterprise

firmly 1 = <u>securely</u>, safely, tightly **2** = <u>immovably</u>, securely, steadily, like a rock, unflinchingly, unshakeably **3** = <u>steadily</u>, securely, tightly, unflinchingly

4 = <u>resolutely</u>, staunchly, steadfastly, definitely, unwaveringly, unchangeably

first ADJECTIVE **1** = <u>earliest</u>, original, primordial **2** = <u>initial</u>, opening, earliest, maiden, introductory **3** = <u>top</u>, best, winning, premier **4** = <u>elementary</u>, key, basic, primary, fundamental, cardinal, rudimentary, elemental **5** = <u>foremost</u>, highest, greatest, leading, head, ruling, chief, prime

● ADVERB = <u>to begin with</u>, firstly, initially, at the beginning, in the first place, beforehand, to start with, at the outset

● NOUN = <u>novelty</u>, innovation, originality, new experience

● PHRASES **from the first** = <u>from the start</u>, from the beginning, from the outset, from the very beginning, from the introduction, from the starting point, from the inception, from the commencement

fish = <u>angle</u>, net, cast, trawl

fit¹ VERB **1** = <u>adapt</u>, shape, arrange, alter, adjust, modify, tweak (*informal*), customize **2** = <u>place</u>, insert **3** = <u>suit</u>, meet, match, belong to, conform to, correspond to, accord with, be appropriate to **4** = <u>equip</u>, provide, arm, prepare, fit out, kit out

● ADJECTIVE **1** = <u>appropriate</u>, suitable, right, becoming, seemly, fitting, skilled, correct ≠ inappropriate **2** = <u>healthy</u>, strong, robust, sturdy, well, trim, strapping, hale ≠ unfit

fit² **1** = <u>seizure</u>, attack, bout, spasm, convulsion, paroxysm **2** = <u>bout</u>, burst, outbreak, outburst, spell

fitness 1 = <u>appropriateness</u>, competence, readiness, eligibility, suitability, propriety, aptness **2** = <u>health</u>, strength, good health, vigour, good condition, wellness, robustness

fitting NOUN = <u>accessory</u>, part, piece, unit, component, attachment

● ADJECTIVE = <u>appropriate</u>, suitable, proper, apt, right, becoming, seemly, correct ≠ unsuitable

fix VERB **1** = <u>place</u>, join, stick, attach, set, position, plant, link **2** = <u>decide</u>, set, choose, establish, determine, settle, arrange, arrive at **3** = <u>arrange</u>, organize, sort out, see to, fix up, make arrangements for **4** = <u>repair</u>, mend, service, correct, restore, see to, overhaul, patch up **5** = <u>focus</u>, direct at, fasten on **6** (*Informal*) = <u>rig</u>, set up (*informal*), influence, manipulate, fiddle (*informal*)

● NOUN (*Informal*) = <u>mess</u>, corner, difficulty, dilemma, embarrassment, plight, pickle (*informal*), uphill (*S. African*)

● PHRASES **fix someone up** = <u>provide</u>, supply, bring about, lay on, arrange for

◆ **fix something up** = <u>arrange</u>, plan, settle, fix, organize, sort out, agree on, make arrangements for

fixed 1 = <u>inflexible</u>, set, steady, resolute, unwavering ≠ wavering 2 = <u>immovable</u>, set, established, secure, rooted, permanent, rigid ≠ mobile 3 = <u>agreed</u>, set, planned, decided, established, settled, arranged, resolved

fizz 1 = <u>bubble</u>, froth, fizzle, effervesce, produce bubbles 2 = <u>sputter</u>, buzz, sparkle, hiss, crackle

flag[1] NOUN = <u>banner</u>, standard, colours, pennant, ensign, streamer, pennon

● VERB = <u>mark</u>, identify, indicate, label, pick out, note

● PHRASES **flag something** *or* **someone down** = <u>hail</u>, stop, signal, wave down

flag[2] = <u>weaken</u>, fade, weary, falter, wilt, wane, sag, languish

flagging = <u>weakening</u>, declining, waning, fading, deteriorating, wearying, faltering, wilting

flair 1 = <u>ability</u>, feel, talent, gift, genius, faculty, mastery, knack 2 = <u>style</u>, taste, dash, chic, elegance, panache, discernment, stylishness

flake NOUN = <u>chip</u>, scale, layer, peeling, shaving, wafer, sliver

● VERB = <u>chip</u>, peel (off), blister

flamboyant 1 = <u>camp</u> (*informal*), dashing, theatrical, swashbuckling 2 = <u>showy</u>, elaborate, extravagant, ornate, ostentatious 3 = <u>colourful</u>, striking, brilliant, glamorous, stylish, dazzling, glitzy (*slang*), showy

flame NOUN 1 = <u>fire</u>, light, spark, glow, blaze, brightness, inferno 2 (*Informal*) = <u>sweetheart</u>, partner, lover, girlfriend, boyfriend, heart-throb (*Brit.*), beau

● VERB = <u>burn</u>, flash, shine, glow, blaze, flare, glare

flank 1 = <u>side</u>, hip, thigh, loin 2 = <u>wing</u>, side, sector, aspect

flap VERB 1 = <u>flutter</u>, wave, flail 2 = <u>beat</u>, wave, thrash, flutter, wag, vibrate, shake

● NOUN 1 = <u>flutter</u>, beating, waving,

shaking, swinging, swish 2 (*Informal*) = <u>panic</u>, state (*informal*), agitation, commotion, sweat (*informal*), dither (*chiefly Brit.*), fluster, tizzy (*informal*)

flare NOUN = <u>flame</u>, burst, flash, blaze, glare, flicker

● VERB 1 = <u>blaze</u>, flame, glare, flicker, burn up 2 = <u>widen</u>, spread, broaden, spread out, dilate, splay

flash NOUN = <u>blaze</u>, burst, spark, beam, streak, flare, dazzle, glare

● VERB 1 = <u>blaze</u>, shine, beam, sparkle, flare, glare, gleam, light up 2 = <u>speed</u>, race, shoot, fly, tear, dash, whistle, streak 3 (*Informal*) = <u>show quickly</u>, display, expose, exhibit, flourish, show off, flaunt

● ADJECTIVE (*Informal*) = <u>ostentatious</u>, smart, trendy, showy

flat[1] ADJECTIVE 1 = <u>even</u>, level, levelled, smooth, horizontal ≠ uneven 2 = <u>punctured</u>, collapsed, burst, blown out, deflated, empty 3 = <u>used up</u>, finished, empty, drained, expired 4 = <u>absolute</u>, firm, positive, explicit, definite, outright, downright, unequivocal 5 = <u>dull</u>, dead, empty, boring, depressing, tedious, lacklustre, tiresome ≠ exciting 6 = <u>without energy</u>, empty, weak, tired, depressed, drained, weary, worn out 7 = <u>monotonous</u>, boring, dull, tedious, tiresome, unchanging

● ADVERB = <u>completely</u>, directly, absolutely, categorically, precisely, exactly, utterly, outright

● PHRASES **flat out** (*Informal*) = <u>at full speed</u>, all out, to the full, hell for leather (*informal*), as hard as possible, at full tilt, for all you are worth

flat[2] = <u>apartment</u>, rooms, quarters, digs, suite, penthouse, living quarters

flatly = <u>absolutely</u>, completely, positively, categorically, unequivocally, unhesitatingly

flatten 1 = <u>level</u>, squash, compress, trample, iron out, even out, smooth off 2 = <u>destroy</u>, level, ruin, demolish, knock down, pull down, raze

flatter 1 = <u>praise</u>, compliment, pander to, sweet-talk (*informal*), wheedle, soft-soap (*informal*), butter up 2 = <u>suit</u>, become, enhance, set off, embellish, do something for, show to advantage

flattering 1 = <u>becoming</u>, kind, effective, enhancing, well-chosen ≠ unflattering

2 = ingratiating, complimentary, fawning, fulsome, laudatory, adulatory ≠ uncomplimentary

flavour NOUN 1 = taste, seasoning, flavouring, savour, relish, smack, aroma, zest ≠ blandness 2 = quality, feeling, feel, style, character, tone, essence, tinge
● VERB = season, spice, add flavour to, enrich, infuse, imbue, pep up, leaven

flaw = weakness, failing, defect, weak spot, fault, blemish, imperfection, chink in your armour

flawed 1 = damaged, defective, imperfect, blemished, faulty 2 = erroneous, incorrect, invalid, wrong, mistaken, false, faulty, unsound

flee = run away, escape, bolt, fly, take off (informal), depart, run off, take flight

fleet = navy, task force, flotilla, armada

fleeting = momentary, passing, brief, temporary, short-lived, transient, ephemeral, transitory ≠ lasting

flesh NOUN 1 = fat, muscle, tissue, brawn 2 = fatness, fat, adipose tissue, corpulence, weight 3 = meat 4 = physical nature, carnality, human nature, flesh and blood, sinful nature
● PHRASES **your own flesh and blood** = family, blood, relations, relatives, kin, kith and kin, blood relations, kinsfolk, ainga (N.Z.)

flexibility 1 = elasticity, pliability, springiness, pliancy, give (informal) 2 = adaptability, openness, versatility, adjustability 3 = complaisance, accommodation, give and take, amenability

flexible 1 = pliable, plastic, elastic, supple, lithe, springy, pliant, stretchy ≠ rigid 2 = adaptable, open, variable, adjustable, discretionary ≠ inflexible

flick VERB 1 = jerk, pull, tug, lurch, jolt 2 = strike, tap, remove quickly, hit, touch, stroke, flip, whisk
● PHRASES **flick through something** = browse, glance at, skim, leaf through, flip through, thumb through, skip through

flicker VERB 1 = twinkle, flash, sparkle, flare, shimmer, gutter, glimmer 2 = flutter, waver, quiver, vibrate
● NOUN 1 = glimmer, flash, spark, flare, gleam 2 = trace, breath, spark, glimmer, iota

flight¹ 1 = journey, trip, voyage

2 = aviation, flying, aeronautics 3 = flock, group, unit, cloud, formation, squadron, swarm, flying group

flight² = escape, fleeing, departure, retreat, exit, running away, exodus, getaway

fling VERB = throw, toss, hurl, launch, cast, propel, sling, catapult
● NOUN = binge, good time, bash, party, spree, night on the town, rave-up (Brit. slang)

flip VERB 1 = flick, switch, snap, slick 2 = spin, turn, overturn, turn over, roll over 3 = toss, throw, flick, fling, sling
● NOUN = toss, throw, spin, snap, flick

flirt VERB 1 = chat up, lead on (informal), make advances at, make eyes at, philander, make sheep's eyes at 2 usually with **with** = toy with, consider, entertain, play with, dabble in, trifle with, give a thought to, expose yourself to
● NOUN = tease, philanderer, coquette, heart-breaker

float 1 = glide, sail, drift, move gently, bob, coast, slide, be carried 2 = be buoyant, hang, hover ≠ sink 3 = launch, offer, sell, set up, promote, get going ≠ dissolve

floating 1 = uncommitted, wavering, undecided, indecisive, vacillating, sitting on the fence (informal), unaffiliated, independent 2 = free, wandering, variable, fluctuating, unattached, movable

flock NOUN 1 = herd, group, flight, drove, colony, gaggle, skein 2 = crowd, company, group, host, collection, mass, gathering, herd
● VERB 1 = stream, crowd, mass, swarm, throng 2 = gather, crowd, mass, collect, assemble, herd, huddle, converge

flog = beat, whip, lash, thrash, whack, scourge, hit hard, trounce

flood NOUN 1 = deluge, downpour, inundation, tide, overflow, torrent, spate 2 = torrent, flow, rush, stream, tide, abundance, glut, profusion 3 = series, stream, avalanche, barrage, spate, torrent 4 = outpouring, rush, stream, surge, torrent
● VERB 1 = immerse, swamp, submerge, inundate, drown, cover with water 2 = pour over, swamp, run over, overflow, inundate 3 = engulf, sweep into, overwhelm, surge into, swarm into, pour into 4 = saturate, fill, choke, swamp, glut, oversupply, overfill 5 = stream, flow, rush,

pour, surge

floor NOUN 1 = <u>ground</u> 2 = <u>storey</u>, level, stage, tier

● VERB 1 (*Informal*) = <u>disconcert</u>, stump, baffle, confound, throw (*informal*), defeat, puzzle, bewilder 2 = <u>knock down</u>, fell, knock over, prostrate, deck (*slang*)

flop VERB 1 = <u>slump</u>, fall, drop, collapse, sink 2 = <u>hang down</u>, hang, dangle, sag, droop 3 (*Informal*) = <u>fail</u>, fold (*informal*), founder, fall flat, come unstuck, misfire, go belly-up (*slang*) ≠ succeed

● NOUN (*Informal*) = <u>failure</u>, disaster, fiasco, debacle, washout (*informal*), nonstarter ≠ success

floppy = <u>droopy</u>, soft, loose, limp, sagging, baggy, flaccid, pendulous

floral = <u>flowery</u>, flower-patterned

flounder 1 = <u>falter</u>, struggle, stall, slow down, run into trouble, come unstuck (*informal*), be in difficulties, hit a bad patch 2 = <u>dither</u>, struggle, blunder, be confused, falter, be in the dark, be out of your depth 3 = <u>struggle</u>, struggle, toss, thrash, stumble, fumble, grope

flourish VERB 1 = <u>thrive</u>, increase, advance, progress, boom, bloom, blossom, prosper ≠ fail 2 = <u>succeed</u>, move ahead, go places (*informal*) 3 = <u>grow</u>, thrive, flower, succeed, bloom, blossom, prosper 4 = <u>wave</u>, brandish, display, shake, wield, flaunt

● NOUN 1 = <u>wave</u>, sweep, brandish, swish, swing, twirl 2 = <u>show</u>, display, parade, fanfare 3 = <u>curlicue</u>, sweep, decoration, swirl, plume, embellishment, ornamentation

flourishing = <u>thriving</u>, successful, blooming, prospering, rampant, going places, in the pink

flow VERB 1 = <u>run</u>, course, rush, sweep, move, pass, roll, flood 2 = <u>pour</u>, move, sweep, flood, stream 3 = <u>issue</u>, follow, result, emerge, spring, proceed, arise, derive

● NOUN = <u>stream</u>, current, movement, motion, course, flood, drift, tide

flower NOUN 1 = <u>bloom</u>, blossom, efflorescence 2 = <u>elite</u>, best, prime, finest, pick, choice, cream, crème de la crème (*French*) 3 = <u>height</u>, prime, peak

● VERB 1 = <u>bloom</u>, open, mature, flourish, unfold, blossom 2 = <u>blossom</u>, grow, develop, progress, mature, thrive, flourish,

bloom

adjective: floral

fluctuate 1 = <u>change</u>, swing, vary, alternate, waver, veer, seesaw 2 = <u>shift</u>, oscillate

fluent = <u>effortless</u>, natural, articulate, well-versed, voluble

fluid NOUN = <u>liquid</u>, solution, juice, liquor, sap

● ADJECTIVE = <u>liquid</u>, flowing, watery, molten, melted, runny, liquefied ≠ solid

flurry 1 = <u>commotion</u>, stir, bustle, flutter, excitement, fuss, disturbance, ado 2 = <u>gust</u>, shower, gale, swirl, squall, storm

flush¹ VERB 1 = <u>blush</u>, colour, glow, redden, turn red, go red 2 *often with out* = <u>cleanse</u>, wash out, rinse out, flood, swill, hose down 3 = <u>expel</u>, drive, dislodge

● NOUN = <u>blush</u>, colour, glow, reddening, redness, rosiness

flush² 1 = <u>level</u>, even, true, flat, square 2 (*Informal*) = <u>wealthy</u>, rich, well-off, in the money (*informal*), well-heeled (*informal*), replete, moneyed

flutter VERB 1 = <u>beat</u>, flap, tremble, ripple, waver, quiver, vibrate, palpitate 2 = <u>flit</u>

● NOUN 1 = <u>tremor</u>, tremble, shiver, shudder, palpitation 2 = <u>vibration</u>, twitching, quiver 3 = <u>agitation</u>, state (*informal*), confusion, excitement, flap (*informal*), dither (*chiefly Brit.*), commotion, fluster

fly 1 = <u>take wing</u>, soar, glide, wing, sail, hover, flutter, flit 2 = <u>pilot</u>, control, operate, steer, manoeuvre, navigate 3 = <u>airlift</u>, send by plane, take by plane, take in an aircraft 4 = <u>flutter</u>, wave, float, flap 5 = <u>display</u>, show, flourish, brandish 6 = <u>rush</u>, race, shoot, career, speed, tear, dash, hurry 7 = <u>pass swiftly</u>, pass, glide, slip away, roll on, flit, elapse, run its course 8 = <u>leave</u>, get away, escape, flee, run for it, skedaddle (*informal*), take to your heels

flying = <u>hurried</u>, brief, rushed, fleeting, short-lived, hasty, transitory

foam NOUN = <u>froth</u>, spray, bubbles, lather, suds, spume, head

● VERB = <u>bubble</u>, boil, fizz, froth, lather, effervesce

focus VERB 1 = <u>concentrate</u>, centre, spotlight, direct, aim, pinpoint, zoom in 2 = <u>fix</u>, train, direct, aim

● NOUN 1 = <u>centre</u>, focal point, central point 2 = <u>focal point</u>, heart, target, hub

foe = <u>enemy</u>, rival, opponent, adversary, antagonist ≠ friend

fog = <u>mist</u>, gloom, haze, smog, murk, miasma, peasouper (*informal*)

foil[1] = <u>thwart</u>, stop, defeat, disappoint, counter, frustrate, hamper, balk

foil[2] = <u>complement</u>, relief, contrast, antithesis

fold VERB 1 = <u>bend</u>, crease, double over 2 (*Informal*) = <u>go bankrupt</u>, fail, crash, collapse, founder, shut down, go under, go bust (*informal*)

● NOUN = <u>crease</u>, gather, bend, overlap, wrinkle, pleat, ruffle, furrow

folk 1 = <u>people</u>, persons, individuals, men and women, humanity, inhabitants, mankind, mortals 2 *usually plural* = <u>family</u>, parents, relations, relatives, tribe, clan, kin, kindred, ainga (*N.Z.*)

follow 1 = <u>accompany</u>, attend, escort, go behind, tag along behind, come behind 2 = <u>pursue</u>, track, dog, hunt, chase, shadow, trail, hound ≠ avoid 3 = <u>come after</u>, go after, come next ≠ precede 4 = <u>result</u>, issue, develop, spring, flow, proceed, arise, ensue 5 = <u>obey</u>, observe, adhere to, stick to, heed, conform to, keep to, pay attention to ≠ ignore 6 = <u>succeed</u>, replace, come after, take over from, come next, supersede, supplant, take the place of 7 = <u>understand</u>, realize, appreciate, take in, grasp, catch on (*informal*), comprehend, fathom 8 = <u>keep up with</u>, support, be interested in, cultivate, be a fan of, keep abreast of

follower = <u>supporter</u>, fan, disciple, devotee, apostle, pupil, adherent, groupie (*slang*) ≠ leader

following ADJECTIVE 1 = <u>next</u>, subsequent, successive, ensuing, later, succeeding, consequent 2 = <u>coming</u>, about to be mentioned

● NOUN = <u>supporters</u>, backing, train, fans, suite, clientele, entourage, coterie

folly = <u>foolishness</u>, nonsense, madness, stupidity, indiscretion, lunacy, imprudence, rashness ≠ wisdom

fond ADJECTIVE 1 = <u>loving</u>, caring, warm, devoted, tender, adoring, affectionate, indulgent ≠ indifferent 2 = <u>unrealistic</u>, empty, naive, vain, foolish, deluded, overoptimistic, delusive ≠ sensible

● PHRASES **fond of** 1 = <u>attached to</u>, in love with, keen on, attracted to, having a soft spot for, enamoured of 2 = <u>keen on</u>, into (*informal*), hooked on, partial to, having a soft spot for, addicted to

fondly 1 = <u>lovingly</u>, tenderly, affectionately, amorously, dearly, possessively, with affection, indulgently 2 = <u>unrealistically</u>, stupidly, vainly, foolishly, naively, credulously

food = <u>nourishment</u>, fare, diet, tucker (*Austral. & N.Z. informal*), rations, nutrition, cuisine, refreshment, nibbles, kai (*N.Z. informal*)

fool NOUN 1 = <u>simpleton</u>, idiot, mug (*Brit. slang*), dummy (*slang*), git (*Brit. slang*), twit (*informal, chiefly Brit.*), dunce, imbecile (*informal*), dorba or dorb (*Austral. slang*), bogan (*Austral. slang*) ≠ genius 2 = <u>dupe</u>, mug (*Brit. slang*), sucker (*slang*), stooge (*slang*), laughing stock, pushover (*informal*), fall guy (*informal*) 3 = <u>jester</u>, clown, harlequin, buffoon, court jester

● VERB = <u>deceive</u>, mislead, delude, trick, take in, con (*informal*), dupe, beguile

foolish = <u>unwise</u>, silly, absurd, rash, senseless, foolhardy, ill-judged, imprudent ≠ sensible

footing 1 = <u>basis</u>, foundation, base position, groundwork 2 = <u>relationship</u>, position, basis, standing, rank, status, grade

footpath (*Austral. & N.Z.*) = <u>pavement</u>, sidewalk (*U.S. & Canad.*)

footstep = <u>step</u>, tread, footfall

foray = <u>raid</u>, sally, incursion, inroad, attack, assault, invasion, swoop

forbid = <u>prohibit</u>, ban, disallow, exclude, rule out, veto, outlaw, preclude ≠ permit

forbidden = <u>prohibited</u>, banned, vetoed, outlawed, taboo, out of bounds, proscribed

forbidding = <u>threatening</u>, severe, frightening, hostile, menacing, sinister, daunting, ominous ≠ inviting

force VERB 1 = <u>compel</u>, make, drive, press, oblige, constrain, coerce, impel 2 = <u>push</u>, thrust, propel 3 = <u>break open</u>, blast, wrench, prise, wrest

● NOUN 1 = <u>compulsion</u>, pressure, violence, constraint, oppression, coercion, duress, arm-twisting (*informal*) 2 = <u>power</u>, might,

pressure, energy, strength, momentum, impulse, vigour ≠ weakness 3 = intensity, vigour, vehemence, fierceness, emphasis 4 = army, unit, company, host, troop, squad, patrol, regiment
● PHRASES **in force 1** = valid, working, current, effective, binding, operative, operational, in operation **2** = in great numbers, all together, in full strength

forced 1 = compulsory, enforced, mandatory, obligatory, involuntary, conscripted ≠ voluntary **2** = false, affected, strained, wooden, stiff, artificial, contrived, unnatural ≠ natural

forceful 1 = dynamic, powerful, assertive ≠ weak **2** = powerful, strong, convincing, effective, compelling, persuasive, cogent

forecast NOUN = prediction, prognosis, guess, prophecy, conjecture, forewarning
● VERB = predict, anticipate, foresee, foretell, divine, prophesy, augur, forewarn

forefront = lead, centre, front, fore, spearhead, prominence, vanguard, foreground

foreign = alien, exotic, unknown, strange, imported, remote, external, unfamiliar ≠ native

foreigner = alien, incomer, immigrant, non-native, stranger, settler

foremost = leading, best, highest, chief, prime, primary, supreme, most important

foresee = predict, forecast, anticipate, envisage, prophesy, foretell

forever 1 = evermore, always, ever, for good, for keeps, for all time, in perpetuity, till the cows come home (*informal*) **2** = constantly, always, all the time, continually, endlessly, persistently, eternally, perpetually

forfeit VERB = relinquish, lose, give up, surrender, renounce, be deprived of, say goodbye to, be stripped of
● NOUN = penalty, fine, damages, forfeiture, loss, mulct

forge 1 = form, build, create, establish, set up, fashion, shape, frame **2** = fake, copy, reproduce, imitate, counterfeit, feign, falsify **3** = create, make, work, found, form, model, fashion, shape

forget 1 = neglect, overlook, omit, not remember, be remiss, fail to remember **2** = leave behind, lose, lose sight of, mislay

forgive = excuse, pardon, not hold something against, understand, acquit,

condone, let off (*informal*), turn a blind eye to ≠ blame

forgiveness = pardon, mercy, absolution, exoneration, amnesty, acquittal, remission

forgotten = unremembered, lost, past, left behind, omitted, bygone, past recall

fork = branch, part, separate, split, divide, diverge, subdivide, bifurcate

forked = branching, split, branched, divided, angled, pronged, zigzag, Y-shaped

form NOUN **1** = type, sort, kind, variety, class, style **2** = shape, formation, configuration, structure, pattern, appearance **3** = condition, health, shape, nick (*informal*), fitness, trim, fettle **4** = document, paper, sheet, questionnaire, application **5** = procedure, etiquette, use, custom, convention, usage, protocol, wont, kawa (*N.Z.*), tikanga (*N.Z.*) **6** = class, year, set, rank, grade, stream
● VERB **1** = arrange, combine, line up, organize, assemble, draw up **2** = make, produce, fashion, build, create, shape, construct, forge **3** = constitute, make up, compose, comprise **4** = establish, start, launch **5** = take shape, grow, develop, materialize, rise, appear, come into being, crystallize **6** = draw up, devise, formulate, organize **7** = develop, pick up, acquire, cultivate, contract

formal 1 = serious, stiff, detached, official, correct, conventional, remote, precise ≠ informal **2** = official, authorized, endorsed, certified, solemn **3** = ceremonial, traditional, solemn, ritualistic, dressy **4** = conventional, established, traditional

formality 1 = correctness, seriousness, decorum, protocol, etiquette **2** = convention, procedure, custom, ritual, rite

format = arrangement, form, style, make-up, look, plan, design, type

formation 1 = establishment, founding, forming, setting up, starting, production, generation, manufacture **2** = development, shaping, constitution, moulding, genesis **3** = arrangement, grouping, design, structure, pattern, organization, array, configuration

former = previous, one-time, erstwhile, earlier, prior, sometime, foregoing ≠ current

formerly = <u>previously</u>, earlier, in the past, at one time, before, lately, once

formidable 1 = <u>impressive</u>, great, powerful, tremendous, mighty, terrific, awesome, invincible 2 = <u>intimidating</u>, threatening, terrifying, menacing, dismaying, fearful, daunting, frightful ≠ encouraging

formula = <u>method</u>, plan, policy, rule, principle, procedure, recipe, blueprint

formulate 1 = <u>devise</u>, plan, develop, prepare, work out, invent, forge, draw up 2 = <u>express</u>, detail, frame, define, specify, articulate, set down, put into words

fort NOUN = <u>fortress</u>, keep, camp, tower, castle, garrison, stronghold, citadel, fortified pa (*N.Z.*)
● PHRASES **hold the fort** (*Informal*) = <u>take responsibility</u>, cover, stand in, carry on, take over the reins, deputize, keep things on an even keel

forte = <u>speciality</u>, strength, talent, strong point, métier, long suit (*informal*), gift ≠ weak point

forth 1 (*Formal or old-fashioned*) = <u>forward</u>, out, away, ahead, onward, outward 2 = <u>out</u>

forthcoming 1 = <u>approaching</u>, coming, expected, future, imminent, prospective, impending, upcoming 2 = <u>available</u>, ready, accessible, at hand, in evidence, obtainable, on tap (*informal*) 3 = <u>communicative</u>, open, free, informative, expansive, sociable, chatty, talkative

fortify 1 = <u>protect</u>, defend, strengthen, reinforce, support, shore up, augment, buttress 2 = <u>strengthen</u>, add alcohol to ≠ dishearten

fortitude = <u>courage</u>, strength, resolution, grit, bravery, backbone, perseverance, valour

fortress = <u>castle</u>, fort, stronghold, citadel, redoubt, fastness, fortified pa (*N.Z.*)

fortunate 1 = <u>lucky</u>, favoured, jammy (*Brit. slang*), in luck ≠ unfortunate 2 = <u>well-off</u>, rich, successful, wealthy, prosperous, affluent, opulent, well-heeled (*informal*) 3 = <u>providential</u>, fortuitous, felicitous, timely, helpful, convenient, favourable, advantageous

fortunately = <u>luckily</u>, happily, as luck would have it, providentially, by good luck, by a happy chance

fortune NOUN 1 = <u>wealth</u>, means, property, riches, resources, assets, possessions, treasure ≠ poverty 2 = <u>luck</u>, fluke (*informal*), stroke of luck, serendipity, twist of fate, run of luck 3 = <u>chance</u>, fate, destiny, providence, the stars, Lady Luck, kismet
● PLURAL NOUN = <u>destiny</u>, lot, experiences, history, condition, success, means, adventures

forward ADVERB 1 = <u>forth</u>, on, ahead, onwards ≠ backward(s) 2 = <u>on</u>, onward, onwards
● ADJECTIVE 1 = <u>leading</u>, first, head, front, advance, foremost 2 = <u>future</u>, advanced, premature, prospective 3 = <u>presumptuous</u>, familiar, bold, cheeky, brash, pushy (*informal*), brazen, shameless ≠ shy
● VERB 1 = <u>further</u>, advance, promote, assist, hurry, hasten, expedite 2 = <u>send on</u>, send, post, pass on, dispatch, redirect

fossick (*Austral. & N.Z.*) = <u>search</u>, hunt, explore, ferret, check, forage, rummage

foster 1 = <u>bring up</u>, mother, raise, nurse, look after, rear, care for, take care of 2 = <u>develop</u>, support, further, encourage, feed, promote, stimulate, uphold ≠ suppress

foul ADJECTIVE 1 = <u>dirty</u>, unpleasant, stinking, filthy, grubby, repellent, squalid, repulsive, festy (*Austral. slang*), yucko (*Austral. slang*) ≠ clean 2 = <u>obscene</u>, crude, indecent, blue, abusive, coarse, vulgar, lewd 3 = <u>unfair</u>, illegal, crooked, shady (*informal*), fraudulent, dishonest, unscrupulous, underhand 4 = <u>offensive</u>, bad, wrong, evil, corrupt, disgraceful, shameful, immoral ≠ admirable
● VERB = <u>dirty</u>, stain, contaminate, pollute, taint, sully, defile, besmirch ≠ clean

found = <u>establish</u>, start, set up, begin, create, institute, organize, constitute

foundation 1 = <u>basis</u> 2 often plural = <u>substructure</u>, underpinning, groundwork, bedrock, base, footing, bottom 3 = <u>setting up</u>, institution, instituting, organization, settlement, establishment, initiating, originating

founder[1] = <u>initiator</u>, father, author, architect, creator, beginner, inventor, originator

founder[2] 1 = <u>fail</u>, collapse, break down, fall through, be unsuccessful, come unstuck, miscarry, misfire **2** = <u>sink</u>, go down, be lost, submerge, capsize, go to the bottom

fountain 1 = <u>font</u>, spring, reservoir, spout, fount, water feature, well **2** = <u>jet</u>, stream, spray, gush **3** = <u>source</u>, fount, wellspring, cause, origin, derivation, fountainhead

fowl = <u>poultry</u>

foyer = <u>entrance hall</u>, lobby, reception area, vestibule, anteroom, antechamber

fraction = <u>percentage</u>, share, section, slice, portion

fracture NOUN **1** = <u>break</u>, split, crack **2** = <u>cleft</u>, opening, split, crack, rift, rupture, crevice, fissure
● VERB **1** = <u>break</u>, crack **2** = <u>split</u>, separate, divide, rend, fragment, splinter, rupture

fragile 1 = <u>unstable</u>, weak, vulnerable, delicate, uncertain, insecure, precarious, flimsy **2** = <u>fine</u>, weak, delicate, frail, brittle, flimsy, dainty, easily broken ≠ durable **3** = <u>delicate</u>, fine, charming, elegant, neat, exquisite, graceful, petite **4** = <u>unwell</u>, poorly, weak, delicate, crook (*Austral. & N.Z. informal*), shaky, frail, feeble, sickly

fragment NOUN **1** = <u>piece</u>, bit, scrap, particle, portion, shred, speck, sliver
● VERB **1** = <u>break</u>, shatter, crumble, disintegrate, splinter, come apart, break into pieces, come to pieces ≠ fuse **2** = <u>break up</u>, split up

fragrance 1 = <u>scent</u>, smell, perfume, bouquet, aroma, sweet smell, sweet odour, redolence ≠ stink **2** = <u>perfume</u>, scent, cologne, eau de toilette, eau de Cologne, toilet water, Cologne water

fragrant = <u>aromatic</u>, perfumed, balmy, redolent, sweet-smelling, sweet-scented, odorous ≠ stinking

frail 1 = <u>feeble</u>, weak, puny, infirm ≠ strong **2** = <u>flimsy</u>, weak, vulnerable, delicate, fragile, insubstantial

frame NOUN **1** = <u>casing</u>, framework, structure, shell, construction, skeleton, chassis **2** = <u>physique</u>, build, form, body, figure, anatomy, carcass
● VERB **1** = <u>mount</u>, case, enclose **2** = <u>surround</u>, ring, enclose, encompass, envelop, encircle, hem in **3** = <u>devise</u>, draft, compose, sketch, put together, draw up, formulate, map out
● PHRASES **frame of mind** = <u>mood</u>, state, attitude, humour, temper, outlook, disposition, mind-set

framework 1 = <u>system</u>, plan, order,

scheme, arrangement, the bare bones **2** = <u>structure</u>, body, frame, foundation, shell, skeleton

frank = <u>candid</u>, open, direct, straightforward, blunt, sincere, outspoken, honest ≠ secretive

frankly 1 = <u>honestly</u>, sincerely, in truth, candidly, to tell you the truth, to be frank, to be frank with someone, to be honest **2** = <u>openly</u>, freely, directly, plainly, bluntly, candidly, without reserve

frantic 1 = <u>frenzied</u>, wild, furious, distracted, distraught, berserk, at the end of your tether, beside yourself, berko (*Austral. slang*) ≠ calm **2** = <u>hectic</u>, desperate, frenzied, fraught (*informal*), frenetic

fraternity 1 = <u>companionship</u>, fellowship, brotherhood, kinship, camaraderie **2** = <u>circle</u>, company, guild **3** = <u>brotherhood</u>, club, union, society, league, association

fraud 1 = <u>deception</u>, deceit, treachery, swindling, trickery, duplicity, double-dealing, chicanery ≠ honesty **2** = <u>scam</u>, deception (*slang*) **3** = <u>hoax</u>, trick, con (*informal*), deception, sham, spoof (*informal*), prank, swindle **4** (*Informal*) = <u>impostor</u>, fake, hoaxer, pretender, charlatan, fraudster, swindler, phoney *or* phony (*informal*)

fraudulent = <u>deceitful</u>, crooked (*informal*), untrue, sham, treacherous, dishonest, swindling, double-dealing ≠ genuine

fray = <u>wear thin</u>, wear, rub, wear out, chafe

freak ADJECTIVE = <u>abnormal</u>, chance, unusual, exceptional, unparalleled
● NOUN **1** (*Informal*) = <u>enthusiast</u>, fan, nut (*slang*), addict, buff (*informal*), fanatic, devotee, fiend (*informal*) **2** = <u>aberration</u>, eccentric, anomaly, oddity, monstrosity, malformation **3** = <u>weirdo</u> *or* weirdie (*informal*), eccentric, character (*informal*), oddball (*informal*), nonconformist

free ADJECTIVE **1** = <u>complimentary</u>, for free (*informal*), for nothing, unpaid, for love, free of charge, on the house, without charge **2** = <u>allowed</u>, permitted, unrestricted, unimpeded, clear, able **3** = <u>at liberty</u>, loose, liberated, at large, on the loose ≠ confined **4** = <u>independent</u>, unfettered, footloose **5** = <u>available</u>, empty, spare, vacant, unused, unoccupied,

untaken 6 = generous, liberal, lavish, unstinting, unsparing ≠ mean
● VERB 1 = clear, disengage, cut loose, release, rescue, extricate 2 = release, liberate, let out, set free, deliver, loose, untie, unchain ≠ confine 3 = disentangle, extricate, disengage, loose, unravel, disconnect, untangle

freedom 1 = independence, democracy, sovereignty, self-determination, emancipation, autarchy, rangatiratanga (N.Z.) 2 = liberty, release, discharge, emancipation, deliverance ≠ captivity 3 = licence, latitude, free rein, opportunity, discretion, carte blanche, blank cheque ≠ restriction

freely 1 = abundantly, liberally, lavishly, extravagantly, copiously, unstintingly, amply 2 = openly, frankly, plainly, candidly, unreservedly, straightforwardly, without reserve 3 = willingly, readily, voluntarily, spontaneously, without prompting, of your own free will, of your own accord

freeway (U.S. & Austral.) = motorway (Brit.), autobahn (German), autoroute (French), autostrada (Italian)

freeze 1 = ice over or up, harden, stiffen, solidify, become solid 2 = chill 3 = fix, hold, limit, hold up 4 = suspend, stop, shelve, curb, cut short, discontinue

freezing 1 = icy, biting, bitter, raw, chill, arctic, frosty, glacial 2 = frozen, very cold

freight 1 = transportation, traffic, delivery, carriage, shipment, haulage, conveyance, transport 2 = cargo, goods, load, delivery, burden, shipment, merchandise, consignment

French = Gallic

frenzied = uncontrolled, wild, crazy, furious, frantic, frenetic, feverish, rabid

frenzy = fury, passion, rage, seizure, hysteria, paroxysm, derangement ≠ calm

frequent ADJECTIVE = common, repeated, usual, familiar, everyday, persistent, customary, recurrent ≠ infrequent
● VERB = visit, attend, haunt, be found at, patronize, hang out at (informal), visit often, go to regularly ≠ keep away

frequently = often, commonly, repeatedly, many times, habitually, not infrequently, much ≠ infrequently

fresh 1 = additional, more, new, other, added, further, extra, supplementary 2 = natural, unprocessed, unpreserved

≠ preserved 3 = new, original, novel, different, recent, modern, up-to-date, unorthodox ≠ old 4 = invigorating, clean, pure, crisp, bracing, refreshing, brisk, unpolluted ≠ stale 5 = cool, cold, refreshing, brisk, chilly, nippy 6 = lively, keen, alert, refreshed, vigorous, energetic, sprightly, spry ≠ weary 7 = cheeky (Informal), impertinent, forward, familiar, audacious, disrespectful, presumptuous, insolent ≠ well-mannered

fret = worry, brood, agonize, obsess, lose sleep, upset yourself, distress yourself

friction 1 = conflict, hostility, resentment, disagreement, animosity, discord, bad blood, dissension 2 = resistance, rubbing, scraping, grating, rasping, chafing, abrasion 3 = rubbing, scraping, grating, rasping, chafing, abrasion

friend 1 = companion, pal, mate (informal), buddy (informal), best friend, close friend, comrade, chum (informal), cobber (Austral. & N.Z.), E hoa (N.Z. old-fashioned informal) ≠ foe 2 = supporter, ally, associate, sponsor, patron, well-wisher

friendly = amiable, welcoming, warm, neighbourly, pally (informal), helpful, sympathetic, affectionate = amicable, warm, familiar, pleasant, intimate, informal, cordial, congenial ≠ unfriendly

friendship 1 = attachment, relationship, bond, link, association, tie 2 = friendliness, affection, harmony, goodwill, intimacy, familiarity, rapport, companionship ≠ unfriendliness

fright 1 = fear, shock, alarm, horror, panic, dread, consternation, trepidation ≠ courage 2 = scare, start, turn, surprise, shock, jolt, the creeps (informal), the willies (slang)

frighten = scare, shock, alarm, terrify, startle, intimidate, unnerve, petrify ≠ reassure

frightened = afraid, alarmed, scared, terrified, shocked, startled, petrified, flustered

frightening = terrifying, shocking, alarming, startling, horrifying, menacing, scary (informal), fearful

fringe NOUN 1 = border, edging, edge, trimming, hem, frill, flounce 2 = edge, limits, border, margin, outskirts, perimeter, periphery, borderline
● ADJECTIVE = unofficial, alternative, radical,

innovative, avant-garde, unconventional, unorthodox

front NOUN 1 = <u>head</u>, start, lead, forefront 2 = <u>exterior</u>, face, façade, frontage 3 = <u>foreground</u>, fore, forefront, nearest part 4 = <u>front line</u>, trenches, vanguard, firing line 5 (*Informal*) = <u>disguise</u>, cover, blind, mask, cover-up, cloak, façade, pretext
● ADJECTIVE 1 = <u>foremost</u>, at the front ≠ back 2 = <u>leading</u>, first, lead, head, foremost, topmost
● VERB = <u>face onto</u>, overlook, look out on, have a view of, look over *or* onto

frontier = <u>border</u>, limit, edge, boundary, verge, perimeter, borderline, dividing line

frost = <u>hoarfrost</u>, freeze, rime

frown VERB = <u>glare</u>, scowl, glower, make a face, look daggers, knit your brows, lour *or* lower
● NOUN = <u>scowl</u>, glare, glower, dirty look

frozen 1 = <u>icy</u>, hard, solid, frosted, arctic, ice-covered, icebound 2 = <u>chilled</u>, cold, iced, refrigerated, ice-cold 3 = <u>ice-cold</u>, freezing, numb, very cold, frigid, frozen stiff

fruit 1 = <u>produce</u>, crop, yield, harvest 2 *often plural* = <u>result</u>, reward, outcome, end result, return, effect, benefit, profit

frustrate = <u>thwart</u>, stop, check, block, defeat, disappoint, counter, spoil, crool *or* cruel (*Austral. slang*) ≠ further

frustrated = <u>disappointed</u>, discouraged, infuriated, exasperated, resentful, embittered, disheartened

frustration 1 = <u>annoyance</u>, disappointment, resentment, irritation, grievance, dissatisfaction, exasperation, vexation 2 = <u>obstruction</u>, blocking, foiling, spoiling, thwarting, circumvention

fudge = <u>misrepresent</u>, hedge, stall, flannel (*Brit. informal*), equivocate

fuel = <u>incitement</u>, ammunition, provocation, incentive

fugitive = <u>runaway</u>, refugee, deserter, escapee

fulfil 1 = <u>carry out</u>, perform, complete, achieve, accomplish ≠ neglect 2 = <u>achieve</u>, realize, satisfy, attain, consummate, bring to fruition 3 = <u>satisfy</u>, please, content, cheer, refresh, gratify, make happy 4 = <u>comply with</u>, meet, fill, satisfy, observe, obey, conform to, answer

fulfilment = <u>achievement</u>, implementation, completion, accomplishment, realization, attainment, consummation

full 1 = <u>filled</u>, stocked, brimming, replete, complete, loaded, saturated ≠ empty 2 = <u>satiated</u>, having had enough, replete 3 = <u>extensive</u>, complete, generous, adequate, ample, abundant, plentiful ≠ incomplete 4 = <u>comprehensive</u>, complete, exhaustive, all-embracing 5 = <u>rounded</u>, strong, rich, powerful, intense, pungent 6 = <u>plump</u>, rounded, voluptuous, shapely, well-rounded, buxom, curvaceous 7 = <u>voluminous</u>, large, loose, baggy, billowing, puffy, capacious, loose-fitting ≠ tight 8 = <u>rich</u>, strong, deep, loud, distinct, resonant, sonorous, clear ≠ thin

full-scale = <u>major</u>, wide-ranging, all-out, sweeping, comprehensive, thorough, in-depth, exhaustive

fully 1 = <u>completely</u>, totally, perfectly, entirely, altogether, thoroughly, wholly, utterly 2 = <u>in all respects</u>, completely, totally, entirely, altogether, thoroughly, wholly

fumble = <u>grope</u>, flounder, scrabble, feel around

fume VERB = <u>rage</u>, seethe, see red (*informal*), storm, rant, smoulder, get hot under the collar (*informal*)
● PLURAL NOUN = <u>smoke</u>, gas, exhaust, pollution, vapour, smog

fun NOUN 1 = <u>amusement</u>, sport, pleasure, entertainment, recreation, enjoyment, merriment, jollity 2 = <u>enjoyment</u>, pleasure, mirth ≠ gloom
● ADJECTIVE = <u>enjoyable</u>, entertaining, pleasant, amusing, lively, diverting, witty, convivial
● PHRASES **make fun of something** *or* **someone** = <u>mock</u>, tease, ridicule, poke fun at, laugh at, mimic, parody, send up (*Brit. informal*)

function NOUN 1 = <u>purpose</u>, business, job, use, role, responsibility, task, duty 2 = <u>reception</u>, party, affair, gathering, bash (*informal*), social occasion, soiree, do (*informal*)
● VERB 1 = <u>work</u>, run, operate, perform, go 2 = <u>act</u>, operate, perform, behave, do duty, have the role of

functional 1 = <u>practical</u>, utilitarian, serviceable, hard-wearing, useful

2 = <u>working</u>, operative, operational, going, prepared, ready, viable, up and running

fund NOUN = <u>reserve</u>, stock, supply, store, collection, pool

● PLURAL NOUN = <u>money</u>, capital, cash, finance, means, savings, resources, assets

● VERB = <u>finance</u>, back, support, pay for, subsidize, provide money for, put up the money for

fundamental 1 = <u>central</u>, key, basic, essential, primary, principal, cardinal ≠ incidental **2** = <u>basic</u>, essential, underlying, profound, elementary, rudimentary

fundamentally 1 = <u>basically</u>, at heart, at bottom **2** = <u>essentially</u>, radically, basically, primarily, profoundly, intrinsically

fundi (*S. African*) = <u>expert</u>

funeral = <u>burial</u>, committal, laying to rest, cremation, interment, obsequies, entombment

funny 1 = <u>humorous</u>, amusing, comical, entertaining, comic, witty, hilarious, riotous ≠ unfunny **2** = <u>comic</u>, comical **3** = <u>peculiar</u>, odd, strange, unusual, bizarre, curious, weird, mysterious **4** = <u>ill</u>, poorly (*informal*), sick, odd, crook (*Austral. & N.Z. informal*), ailing, unhealthy, unwell, off-colour (*informal*)

furious 1 = <u>angry</u>, raging, fuming, infuriated, incensed, enraged, inflamed, very angry, tooshie (*Austral. slang*) ≠ pleased **2** = <u>violent</u>, intense, fierce, savage, turbulent, vehement, unrestrained

furnish 1 = <u>decorate</u>, fit out, stock, equip **2** = <u>supply</u>, give, offer, provide, present, grant, hand out

furniture = <u>household goods</u>, furnishings, fittings, house fittings, goods, things (*informal*), possessions, appliances

furore = <u>commotion</u>, to-do, stir, disturbance, outcry, uproar, hullabaloo

further *or* **farther** ADVERB = <u>in addition</u>, moreover, besides, furthermore, also, to boot, additionally, into the bargain

● ADJECTIVE = <u>additional</u>, more, new, other, extra, fresh, supplementary

● VERB = <u>promote</u>, help, develop, forward, encourage, advance, work for, assist ≠ hinder

furthermore = <u>moreover</u>, further, in addition, besides, too, as well, to boot, additionally

furthest *or* **farthest** = <u>most distant</u>,

extreme, ultimate, remotest, furthermost, outmost

fury 1 = <u>anger</u>, passion, rage, madness, frenzy, wrath, impetuosity ≠ calmness **2** = <u>violence</u>, force, intensity, severity, ferocity, savagery, vehemence, fierceness ≠ peace

fuss NOUN **1** = <u>commotion</u>, to-do, bother, stir, excitement, ado, hue and cry, palaver **2** = <u>bother</u>, trouble, struggle, hassle (*informal*), nuisance, inconvenience, hindrance **3** = <u>complaint</u>, row, protest, objection, trouble, argument, squabble, furore

● VERB = <u>worry</u>, flap (*informal*), fret, fidget, take pains, be agitated, get worked up

futile = <u>useless</u>, vain, unsuccessful, pointless, worthless, fruitless, ineffectual, unprofitable ≠ useful

future NOUN **1** = <u>time to come</u>, hereafter, what lies ahead **2** = <u>prospect</u>, expectation, outlook

● ADJECTIVE = <u>forthcoming</u>, coming, later, approaching, to come, succeeding, fated, subsequent ≠ past

fuzzy 1 = <u>frizzy</u>, fluffy, woolly, downy **2** = <u>indistinct</u>, blurred, vague, distorted, unclear, bleary, out of focus, ill-defined ≠ distinct

g

gadget = <u>device</u>, thing, appliance, machine, tool, implement, invention, instrument

gag¹ NOUN = <u>muzzle</u>, tie, restraint

● VERB **1** = <u>suppress</u>, silence, muffle, curb, stifle, muzzle, quieten **2** = <u>retch</u>, heave

gag² (*Informal*) = <u>joke</u>, crack (*slang*), funny (*informal*), quip, pun, jest, wisecrack (*informal*), witticism

gain VERB **1** = <u>acquire</u>, get, receive, pick up, secure, collect, gather, obtain **2** = <u>profit</u>, get, land, secure, collect, gather, capture, acquire ≠ lose **3** = <u>put on</u>, increase in, gather, build up **4** = <u>attain</u>, get, reach, get to, secure, obtain, acquire, arrive at

● NOUN **1** = <u>rise</u>, increase, growth, advance, improvement, upsurge, upturn, upswing **2** = <u>profit</u>, return, benefit, advantage, yield, dividend ≠ loss

● PLURAL NOUN = <u>profits</u>, earnings, revenue, proceeds, winnings, takings

● PHRASES **gain on something** or **someone** = <u>get nearer to</u>, close in on, approach, catch up with, narrow the gap on

gala = <u>festival</u>, fête, celebration, carnival, festivity, pageant, jamboree

gale 1 = <u>storm</u>, hurricane, tornado, cyclone, blast, typhoon, tempest, squall **2** (*Informal*) = <u>outburst</u>, scream, roar, fit, storm, shout, burst, explosion

gall = <u>annoy</u>, provoke, irritate, trouble, disturb, madden, exasperate, vex

gallop 1 = <u>run</u>, race, career, speed, bolt **2** = <u>dash</u>, run, race, career, speed, rush, sprint

gamble NOUN **1** = <u>risk</u>, chance, venture, lottery, speculation, uncertainty, leap in the dark ≠ certainty **2** = <u>bet</u>, flutter (*informal*), punt (*chiefly Brit.*), wager

● VERB **1** = <u>take a chance</u>, speculate, stick your neck out (*informal*) **2** = <u>risk</u>, chance, hazard, wager **3** = <u>bet</u>, play, game, speculate, punt, wager, have a flutter (*informal*)

game NOUN **1** = <u>pastime</u>, sport, activity, entertainment, recreation, distraction, amusement, diversion ≠ job **2** = <u>match</u>, meeting, event, competition, tournament, clash, contest, head-to-head **3** = <u>amusement</u>, joke, entertainment, diversion **4** = <u>wild animals</u> or birds, prey, quarry **5** = <u>scheme</u>, plan, design, trick, plot, tactic, manoeuvre, ploy

● ADJECTIVE **1** = <u>willing</u>, prepared, ready, keen, eager, interested, desirous **2** = <u>brave</u>, courageous, spirited, daring, persistent, gritty, intrepid, plucky ≠ cowardly

gang = <u>group</u>, crowd, pack, company, band, bunch, mob

gangster = <u>hoodlum</u> (*chiefly U.S.*), crook (*informal*), bandit, hood (*U.S. slang*), robber, mobster (*U.S. slang*), racketeer, ruffian, tsotsi (*S. African*)

gap 1 = <u>opening</u>, space, hole, break, crack, slot, aperture, cleft **2** = <u>interval</u>, pause, interruption, respite, lull, interlude,

breathing space, hiatus **3** = <u>difference</u>, gulf, contrast, disagreement, discrepancy, inconsistency, disparity, divergence

gape 1 = <u>stare</u>, wonder, goggle, gawp (*Brit. slang*), gawk **2** = <u>open</u>, split, crack, yawn

gaping = <u>wide</u>, great, open, broad, vast, yawning, wide open, cavernous

garland NOUN = <u>wreath</u>, band, bays, crown, honours, laurels, festoon, chaplet

● VERB = <u>adorn</u>, crown, deck, festoon, wreathe

garment *often plural* = <u>clothes</u>, dress, clothing, gear (*slang*), uniform, outfit, costume, apparel

garnish NOUN = <u>decoration</u>, embellishment, adornment, ornamentation, trimming

● VERB = <u>decorate</u>, adorn, ornament, embellish, trim ≠ strip

garrison NOUN **1** = <u>troops</u>, group, unit, section, command, armed force, detachment **2** = <u>fort</u>, fortress, camp, base, post, station, stronghold, fortification, fortified pa (*N.Z.*)

● VERB = <u>station</u>, position, post, install, assign, put on duty

gas 1 = <u>fumes</u>, vapour **2** (*U.S., Canad., & N.Z.*) = <u>petrol</u>, gasoline

gasp VERB = <u>pant</u>, blow, puff, choke, gulp, catch your breath

● NOUN = <u>pant</u>, puff, gulp, sharp intake of breath

gate = <u>barrier</u>, opening, door, entrance, exit, gateway, portal

gather 1 = <u>congregate</u>, assemble, collect, meet, mass, come together, muster, converge ≠ scatter **2** = <u>assemble</u>, collect, bring together, muster, call together ≠ disperse **3** = <u>collect</u>, assemble, accumulate, mass, muster, garner, amass, stockpile **4** = <u>pick</u>, harvest, pluck, reap, garner, glean **5** = <u>build up</u>, rise, increase, grow, expand, swell, intensify, heighten **6** = <u>understand</u>, believe, hear, learn, assume, conclude, presume, infer **7** = <u>fold</u>, tuck, pleat

gathering 1 = <u>assembly</u>, group, crowd, meeting, conference, company, congress, mass, hui (*N.Z.*), runanga (*N.Z.*) **2** = <u>collecting</u>, obtaining, attainment

gauge VERB **1** = <u>measure</u>, calculate, evaluate, value, determine, count, weigh, compute **2** = <u>judge</u>, estimate, guess, assess, evaluate, rate, appraise, reckon

● NOUN = meter, dial, measuring instrument

gay ADJECTIVE 1 = homosexual, lesbian, queer (*informal or derogatory*), moffie (*S. African slang*) 2 = cheerful, lively, sparkling, merry, upbeat (*informal*), buoyant, cheery, carefree ≠ sad 3 = colourful, rich, bright, brilliant, vivid, flamboyant, flashy, showy ≠ drab
● NOUN = homosexual, lesbian, auntie *or* aunty (*Austral. slang*), lily (*Austral. slang*) ≠ heterosexual

gaze VERB = stare, look, view, watch, regard, gape
● NOUN = stare, look, fixed look

gazette = newspaper, paper, journal, periodical, news-sheet

gear NOUN 1 = mechanism, works, machinery, cogs, cogwheels, gearwheels 2 = equipment, supplies, tackle, tools, instruments, apparatus, paraphernalia, accoutrements 3 = clothing, wear, dress, clothes, outfit, costume, garments, togs
● VERB *with* **to** *or* **towards** = equip, fit, adjust, adapt

gem 1 = precious stone, jewel, stone 2 = treasure, prize, jewel, pearl, masterpiece, humdinger (*slang*), taonga (*N.Z.*)

general 1 = widespread, accepted, popular, public, common, broad, extensive, universal ≠ individual 2 = overall, complete, total, global, comprehensive, blanket, inclusive, all-embracing ≠ restricted 3 = universal, overall, widespread, collective, across-the-board ≠ exceptional 4 = vague, loose, blanket, sweeping, unclear, approximate, woolly, indefinite ≠ specific

generally 1 = usually, commonly, typically, normally, on the whole, by and large, ordinarily, as a rule ≠ occasionally 2 = commonly, widely, publicly, universally, extensively, popularly, conventionally, customarily ≠ individually

generate = produce, create, make, cause, give rise to, engender ≠ end

generation 1 = age group, peer group 2 = age, period, era, time, lifetime, span, epoch

generic = collective, general, common, wide, comprehensive, universal, blanket, inclusive ≠ specific

generosity 1 = liberality, charity, bounty, munificence, beneficence, largesse *or* largess 2 = magnanimity, goodness, kindness, selflessness, charity, unselfishness, high-mindedness, nobleness

generous 1 = liberal, lavish, charitable, hospitable, bountiful, open-handed, unstinting, beneficent ≠ mean 2 = magnanimous, kind, noble, good, high-minded, unselfish, big-hearted 3 = plentiful, lavish, ample, abundant, full, rich, liberal, copious ≠ meagre

genesis = beginning, origin, start, birth, creation, formation, inception ≠ end

genius 1 = brilliance, ability, talent, capacity, gift, bent, excellence, flair 2 = master, expert, mastermind, maestro, virtuoso, whiz (*informal*), hotshot (*informal*), brainbox, fundi (*S. African*) ≠ dunce

genre = type, group, order, sort, kind, class, style, species

gentle 1 = kind, kindly, tender, mild, humane, compassionate, meek, placid ≠ unkind 2 = slow, easy, slight, moderate, gradual, imperceptible 3 = moderate, light, soft, slight, mild, soothing ≠ violent

gentlemanly = chivalrous, refined, polite, civil, courteous, gallant, genteel, well-mannered

genuine 1 = authentic, real, actual, true, valid, legitimate, veritable, bona fide, dinkum (*Austral. & N.Z. informal*) ≠ counterfeit 2 = heartfelt, sincere, honest, earnest, real, true, frank, unaffected ≠ affected 3 = sincere, honest, frank, candid, dinkum (*Austral. & N.Z. informal*), guileless ≠ hypocritical

germ 1 = microbe, virus, bug (*informal*), bacterium, bacillus, microorganism 2 = beginning, root, seed, origin, spark, embryo, rudiment

gesture NOUN = sign, action, signal, motion, indication, gesticulation
● VERB = signal, sign, wave, indicate, motion, beckon, gesticulate

get VERB 1 = become, grow, turn, come to be 2 = persuade, convince, induce, influence, entice, incite, impel, prevail upon 3 (*Informal*) = annoy, upset, anger, disturb, trouble, bug (*informal*), irritate, gall 4 = obtain, receive, gain, acquire, win, land, net, pick up 5 = fetch, bring, collect 6 = understand, follow, catch, see, realize, take in, perceive, grasp **7** = <u>catch</u>, develop, contract, succumb to, fall victim to, go down with, come down with **8** = <u>arrest</u>, catch, grab, capture, seize, take, nab (*informal*), apprehend

● PHRASES **get at someone** = <u>criticize</u>, attack, blame, put down, knock (*informal*), nag, pick on, disparage ◆ **get at something 1** = <u>reach</u>, touch, grasp, get (a) hold of, stretch to **2** = <u>find out</u>, learn, reach, reveal, discover, acquire, detect, uncover **3** = <u>imply</u>, mean, suggest, hint, intimate, lead up to, insinuate ◆ **get by** = <u>manage</u>, survive, cope, fare, exist, get along, make do, muddle through ◆ **get something across** = <u>communicate</u>, pass on, transmit, convey, impart, bring home, make known, put over

ghastly = <u>horrible</u>, shocking, terrible, awful, dreadful, horrendous, hideous, frightful ≠ lovely

ghost 1 = <u>spirit</u>, soul, phantom, spectre, spook (*informal*), apparition, wraith, atua (*N.Z.*), kehua (*N.Z.*), wairua (*N.Z.*) **2** = <u>trace</u>, shadow, suggestion, hint, suspicion, glimmer, semblance

▌RELATED WORD
adjective: spectral

ghostly = <u>unearthly</u>, phantom, eerie, supernatural, spooky (*informal*), spectral

giant ADJECTIVE = <u>huge</u>, vast, enormous, tremendous, immense, titanic, gigantic, monumental ≠ tiny
● NOUN = <u>ogre</u>, monster, titan, colossus

gidday *or* **g'day** (*Austral. & N.Z.*) = <u>hello</u>, hi (*informal*), greetings, how do you do?, good morning, good evening, good afternoon, welcome, kia ora (*N.Z.*)

gift 1 = <u>donation</u>, offering, present, contribution, grant, legacy, hand-out, endowment, bonsela (*S. African*), koha (*N.Z.*) **2** = <u>talent</u>, ability, capacity, genius, power, capability, flair, knack

gifted = <u>talented</u>, able, skilled, expert, masterly, brilliant, capable, clever ≠ talentless

gigantic = <u>huge</u>, large, giant, massive, enormous, tremendous, immense, titanic ≠ tiny

giggle VERB = <u>laugh</u>, chuckle, snigger, chortle, titter, twitter
● NOUN = <u>laugh</u>, chuckle, snigger, chortle, titter, twitter

girl = <u>female child</u>, lass, lassie (*informal*),

miss, maiden (*archaic*), maid (*archaic*)

give VERB **1** = <u>perform</u>, do, carry out, execute **2** = <u>communicate</u>, announce, transmit, pronounce, utter, issue **3** = <u>produce</u>, make, cause, occasion, engender **4** = <u>present</u>, contribute, donate, provide, supply, award, grant, deliver ≠ take **5** = <u>concede</u>, allow, grant **6** = <u>surrender</u>, yield, devote, hand over, relinquish, part with

● PHRASES **give in** = <u>admit defeat</u>, yield, concede, collapse, quit, submit, surrender, succumb ◆ **give something away** = <u>reveal</u>, expose, leak, disclose, betray, uncover, let out, divulge ◆ **give something off** *or* **out** = <u>emit</u>, produce, release, discharge, send out, throw out, exude ◆ **give something up** = <u>abandon</u>, stop, quit, cease, renounce, leave off, desist

glad 1 = <u>happy</u>, pleased, delighted, contented, gratified, joyful, overjoyed ≠ unhappy **2** (*Archaic*) = <u>pleasing</u>, happy, cheering, pleasant, cheerful, gratifying

gladly 1 = <u>happily</u>, cheerfully, gleefully **2** = <u>willingly</u>, freely, happily, readily, cheerfully, with pleasure ≠ reluctantly

glamorous 1 = <u>attractive</u>, elegant, dazzling ≠ unglamorous **2** = <u>exciting</u>, glittering, prestigious, glossy ≠ unglamorous

glamour 1 = <u>charm</u>, appeal, beauty, attraction, fascination, allure, enchantment **2** = <u>excitement</u>, magic, thrill, romance, prestige, glitz (*slang*)

glance VERB = <u>peek</u>, look, view, glimpse, peep ≠ scrutinize
● NOUN = <u>peek</u>, look, glimpse, peep, dekko (*slang*) ≠ good look

glare VERB **1** = <u>scowl</u>, frown, glower, look daggers, lour *or* lower **2** = <u>dazzle</u>, blaze, flare, flame
● NOUN **1** = <u>scowl</u>, frown, glower, dirty look, black look, lour *or* lower **2** = <u>dazzle</u>, glow, blaze, flame, brilliance

glaring 1 = <u>obvious</u>, gross, outrageous, manifest, blatant, conspicuous, flagrant, unconcealed ≠ inconspicuous **2** = <u>dazzling</u>, strong, bright, glowing, blazing ≠ subdued

glaze NOUN = <u>coat</u>, finish, polish, shine, gloss, varnish, enamel, lacquer
● VERB = <u>coat</u>, polish, gloss, varnish, enamel, lacquer

gleam VERB = <u>shine</u>, flash, glow, sparkle, glitter, shimmer, glint, glimmer

● NOUN 1 = <u>glimmer</u>, flash, beam, glow, sparkle 2 = <u>trace</u>, suggestion, hint, flicker, glimmer, inkling

glide = <u>slip</u>, sail, slide

glimpse NOUN = <u>look</u>, sighting, sight, glance, peep, peek

● VERB = <u>catch sight of</u>, spot, sight, view, spy, espy

glitter VERB = <u>shine</u>, flash, sparkle, glare, gleam, shimmer, twinkle, glint

● NOUN 1 = <u>glamour</u>, show, display, splendour, tinsel, pageantry, gaudiness, showiness 2 = <u>sparkle</u>, flash, shine, glare, gleam, sheen, shimmer, brightness

global 1 = <u>worldwide</u>, world, international, universal 2 = <u>comprehensive</u>, general, total, unlimited, exhaustive, all-inclusive ≠ limited

globe = <u>planet</u>, world, earth, sphere, orb

gloom 1 = <u>darkness</u>, dark, shadow, shade, twilight, dusk, obscurity, blackness ≠ light 2 = <u>depression</u>, sorrow, woe, melancholy, unhappiness, despondency, dejection, low spirits ≠ happiness

gloomy 1 = <u>dark</u>, dull, dim, dismal, black, grey, murky, dreary ≠ light 2 = <u>miserable</u>, sad, pessimistic, melancholy, glum, dejected, dispirited, downcast ≠ happy 3 = <u>depressing</u>, bad, dreary, sombre, dispiriting, disheartening, cheerless

glorious 1 = <u>splendid</u>, beautiful, brilliant, shining, superb, gorgeous, dazzling ≠ dull 2 = <u>delightful</u>, fine, wonderful, excellent, marvellous, gorgeous 3 = <u>illustrious</u>, famous, celebrated, distinguished, honoured, magnificent, renowned, eminent ≠ ordinary

glory NOUN 1 = <u>honour</u>, praise, fame, distinction, acclaim, prestige, eminence, renown ≠ shame 2 = <u>splendour</u>, majesty, greatness, grandeur, nobility, pomp, magnificence, pageantry

● VERB = <u>triumph</u>, boast, relish, revel, exult, take delight, pride yourself

gloss[1] = <u>shine</u>, gleam, sheen, polish, brightness, veneer, lustre, patina

gloss[2] NOUN = <u>interpretation</u>, comment, note, explanation, commentary, translation, footnote, elucidation

● VERB = <u>interpret</u>, explain, comment, translate, annotate, elucidate

glossy = <u>shiny</u>, polished, shining, glazed, bright, silky, glassy, lustrous ≠ dull

glow NOUN = <u>light</u>, gleam, splendour, glimmer, brilliance, brightness, radiance, luminosity ≠ dullness

● VERB 1 = <u>shine</u>, burn, gleam, brighten, glimmer, smoulder 2 = <u>be pink</u>

glowing 1 = <u>complimentary</u>, enthusiastic, rave (*informal*), ecstatic, rhapsodic, laudatory, adulatory ≠ scathing 2 = <u>aglow</u>, bright, radiant ≠ pale

glue NOUN = <u>adhesive</u>, cement, gum, paste

● VERB = <u>stick</u>, fix, seal, cement, gum, paste, affix

go VERB 1 = <u>move</u>, travel, advance, journey, proceed, pass, set off ≠ stay 2 = <u>leave</u>, withdraw, depart, move out, slope off, make tracks 3 = <u>elapse</u>, pass, flow, fly by, expire, lapse, slip away 4 = <u>be given</u>, be spent, be awarded, be allotted 5 = <u>function</u>, work, run, move, operate, perform ≠ fail 6 = <u>match</u>, blend, correspond, fit, suit, chime, harmonize 7 = <u>serve</u>, help, tend

● NOUN 1 = <u>attempt</u>, try, effort, bid, shot (*informal*), crack (*informal*) 2 = <u>turn</u>, shot (*informal*), stint 3 (*Informal*) = <u>energy</u>, life, drive, spirit, vitality, vigour, verve, force

● PHRASES **go off** 1 = <u>depart</u>, leave, quit, go away, move out, decamp, slope off 2 = <u>explode</u>, fire, blow up, detonate, come about 3 (*Informal*) = <u>go bad</u>, turn, spoil, rot, go stale ◆ **go out** 1 = <u>see someone</u>, court, date (*informal*, *chiefly U.S.*), woo, go steady (*informal*), be romantically involved with 2 = <u>be extinguished</u>, die out, fade out ◆ **go through something** 1 = <u>suffer</u>, experience, bear, endure, brave, undergo, tolerate, withstand 2 = <u>search</u>, look through, rummage through, rifle through, hunt through, fossick through (*Austral. & N.Z.*), ferret about in 3 = <u>examine</u>, check, search, explore, look through

goal = <u>aim</u>, end, target, purpose, object, intention, objective, ambition

god = <u>deity</u>, immortal, divinity, divine being, supreme being, atua (*N.Z.*)

godly = <u>devout</u>, religious, holy, righteous, pious, good, saintly, god-fearing

gogga (*S. African*) = <u>insect</u>, bug, creepy-crawly (*Brit. informal*)

golden 1 = <u>yellow</u>, blonde, blond, flaxen ≠ dark 2 = <u>successful</u>, glorious, prosperous, rich, flourishing, halcyon ≠ worst

3 = promising, excellent, favourable, opportune ≠ unfavourable

gone 1 = missing, lost, away, vanished, absent, astray **2** = past, over, ended, finished, elapsed

good ADJECTIVE **1** = excellent, great, fine, pleasing, acceptable, first-class, splendid, satisfactory, booshit (*Austral. slang*), exo (*Austral. slang*), sik (*Austral. slang*) ≠ bad **2** = proficient, able, skilled, expert, talented, clever, accomplished, first-class ≠ bad **3** = beneficial, useful, helpful, favourable, wholesome, advantageous ≠ harmful **4** = honourable, moral, worthy, ethical, upright, admirable, honest, righteous ≠ bad **5** = well-behaved, polite, orderly, obedient, dutiful, well-mannered ≠ naughty **6** = kind, kindly, friendly, obliging, charitable, humane, benevolent, merciful ≠ unkind **7** = true, real, genuine, proper, dinkum (*Austral. & N.Z. informal*) **8** = full, complete, extensive ≠ scant **9** = considerable, large, substantial, sufficient, adequate, ample **10** = valid, convincing, compelling, legitimate, authentic, persuasive, bona fide ≠ invalid **11** = convenient, timely, fitting, appropriate, suitable ≠ inconvenient

● NOUN **1** = benefit, interest, gain, advantage, use, profit, welfare, usefulness ≠ disadvantage **2** = virtue, goodness, righteousness, worth, merit, excellence, morality, rectitude ≠ evil

● PHRASES **for good** = permanently, finally, for ever, once and for all, irrevocably

goodbye NOUN = farewell, parting, leave-taking

● INTERJECTION = farewell, see you, see you later, ciao (*Italian*), cheerio, adieu, ta-ta, au revoir (*French*), haere ra (*N.Z.*)

goodness 1 = virtue, honour, merit, integrity, morality, honesty, righteousness, probity ≠ badness **2** = excellence, value, quality, worth, merit, superiority **3** = nutrition, benefit, advantage, wholesomeness, salubriousness **4** = kindness, charity, humanity, goodwill, mercy, compassion, generosity, friendliness

goods 1 = merchandise, stock, products, stuff, commodities, wares **2** = property, things, effects, gear, possessions, belongings, trappings, paraphernalia

goodwill = friendliness, friendship, benevolence, amity, kindliness

gore¹ = blood, slaughter, bloodshed, carnage, butchery

gore² = pierce, wound, transfix, impale

gorge NOUN = ravine, canyon, pass, chasm, cleft, fissure, defile, gulch

● VERB **1** = overeat, devour, gobble, wolf, gulp, guzzle **2** *usually reflexive* = stuff, feed, cram, glut

gorgeous 1 = magnificent, beautiful, superb, spectacular, splendid, dazzling, sumptuous ≠ shabby **2** = delightful, good, great, wonderful, excellent, lovely, fantastic, pleasant ≠ awful **3** (*Informal*) = beautiful, lovely, stunning (*informal*), elegant, handsome, exquisite, ravishing ≠ ugly

gospel 1 = doctrine, news, teachings, message, revelation, creed, credo, tidings **2** = truth, fact, certainty, the last word

gossip NOUN **1** = idle talk, scandal, hearsay, tittle-tattle, small talk, chitchat, blether, chinwag (*Brit. informal*) **2** = busybody, chatterbox (*informal*), chatterer, scandalmonger, gossipmonger

● VERB = chat, chatter, jaw (*slang*), blether

gourmet = connoisseur, foodie (*informal*), bon vivant (*French*), epicure, gastronome

govern 1 = rule, lead, control, command, manage, direct, guide, handle **2** = restrain, control, check, master, discipline, regulate, curb, tame

government 1 = administration, executive, ministry, regime, powers-that-be **2** = rule, authority, administration, sovereignty, governance, statecraft

governor = leader, administrator, ruler, head, director, manager, chief, executive, baas (*S. African*)

gown = dress, costume, garment, robe, frock, garb, habit

grab = snatch, catch, seize, capture, grip, grasp, clutch, snap up

grace NOUN **1** = elegance, poise, ease, polish, refinement, fluency, suppleness, gracefulness ≠ ungainliness **2** = manners, decency, etiquette, consideration, propriety, tact, decorum ≠ bad manners **3** = indulgence, mercy, pardon, reprieve **4** = benevolence, favour, goodness, goodwill, generosity, kindness, kindliness ≠ ill will **5** = prayer, thanks, blessing, thanksgiving, benediction **6** = favour, regard, respect, approval, approbation, good opinion ≠ disfavour

● VERB 1 = <u>adorn</u>, enhance, decorate, enrich, set off, ornament, embellish 2 = <u>honour</u>, favour, dignify ≠ insult

graceful 1 = <u>elegant</u>, easy, pleasing, beautiful ≠ inelegant 2 = <u>polite</u>, mannerly, charming, gracious, civil, courteous, well-mannered

gracious = <u>courteous</u>, polite, civil, accommodating, kind, friendly, cordial, well-mannered ≠ ungracious

grade VERB = <u>classify</u>, rate, order, class, group, sort, range, rank

● NOUN 1 = <u>class</u> 2 degree 3 = <u>level</u>, rank, group, class, stage, category, echelon

gradual = <u>steady</u>, slow, regular, gentle, progressive, piecemeal, unhurried ≠ sudden

gradually = <u>steadily</u>, slowly, progressively, gently, step by step, little by little, by degrees, unhurriedly

graduate 1 = <u>mark off</u>, grade, proportion, regulate, gauge, calibrate, measure out 2 = <u>classify</u>, rank, grade, group, order, sort, arrange

graft NOUN 1 = <u>shoot</u>, bud, implant, sprout, splice, scion 2 (*Informal*) = <u>labour</u>, work, effort, struggle, sweat, toil, slog, exertion

● VERB 1 = <u>join</u>, insert, transplant, implant, splice, affix 2 = <u>work</u>, labour, struggle, sweat (*informal*), slave, strive, toil

grain 1 = <u>seed</u>, kernel, grist 2 = <u>cereal</u>, corn 3 = <u>bit</u>, piece, trace, scrap, particle, fragment, speck, morsel 4 = <u>texture</u>, pattern, surface, fibre, weave, nap

grand 1 = <u>impressive</u>, great, large, magnificent, imposing, splendid, regal, stately ≠ unimposing 2 = <u>ambitious</u>, great, grandiose 3 = <u>superior</u>, great, dignified, stately 4 = <u>excellent</u>, great (*informal*), fine, wonderful, outstanding, smashing (*informal*), first-class, splendid ≠ bad

grandeur = <u>splendour</u>, glory, majesty, nobility, pomp, magnificence, sumptuousness, sublimity

grant NOUN = <u>award</u>, allowance, donation, endowment, gift, subsidy, hand-out

● VERB 1 = <u>give</u>, allow, present, award, permit, assign, allocate, hand out 2 = <u>accept</u>, allow, admit, acknowledge, concede

graphic 1 = <u>vivid</u>, clear, detailed, striking, explicit, expressive ≠ vague 2 = <u>pictorial</u>,

visual, diagrammatic ≠ impressionistic

grapple 1 = <u>deal</u>, tackle, struggle, take on, confront, get to grips, address yourself to 2 = <u>struggle</u>, fight, combat, wrestle, battle, clash, tussle, scuffle

grasp VERB 1 = <u>grip</u>, hold, catch, grab, seize, snatch, clutch, clinch 2 = <u>understand</u>, realize, take in, get, see, catch on, comprehend, catch *or* get the drift of

● NOUN 1 = <u>grip</u>, hold, possession, embrace, clutches, clasp 2 = <u>understanding</u>, knowledge, grip, awareness, mastery, comprehension 3 = <u>reach</u>, power, control, scope

grasping = <u>greedy</u>, acquisitive, rapacious, avaricious, covetous, snoep (*S. African informal*) ≠ generous

grate 1 = <u>shred</u>, mince, pulverize 2 = <u>scrape</u>, grind, rub, scratch, creak, rasp

grateful = <u>thankful</u>, obliged, in (someone's) debt, indebted, appreciative, beholden

grating[1] = <u>grille</u>, grid, grate, lattice, trellis, gridiron

grating[2] = <u>irritating</u>, harsh, annoying, jarring, unpleasant, raucous, strident, discordant ≠ pleasing

gratitude = <u>thankfulness</u>, thanks, recognition, obligation, appreciation, indebtedness, gratefulness ≠ ingratitude

grave[1] = <u>tomb</u>, vault, crypt, mausoleum, sepulchre, pit, burying place

grave[2] 1 = <u>serious</u>, important, critical, pressing, threatening, dangerous, acute, severe ≠ trifling 2 = <u>solemn</u>, sober, sombre, dour, unsmiling ≠ carefree

graveyard = <u>cemetery</u>, churchyard, burial ground, charnel house, necropolis

gravity 1 = <u>seriousness</u>, importance, significance, urgency, severity, acuteness, weightiness, momentousness ≠ triviality 2 = <u>solemnity</u>, seriousness, gravitas ≠ frivolity

graze[1] = <u>feed</u>, crop, browse, pasture

graze[2] VERB 1 = <u>scratch</u>, skin, scrape, chafe, abrade 2 = <u>touch</u>, brush, rub, scrape, shave, skim, glance off

● NOUN = <u>scratch</u>, scrape, abrasion

greasy = <u>fatty</u>, slippery, oily, slimy, oleaginous

great 1 = <u>large</u>, big, huge, vast, enormous, immense, gigantic, prodigious ≠ small 2 = <u>important</u>, serious, significant, critical, crucial, momentous ≠ unimportant

3 = famous, outstanding, remarkable, prominent, renowned, eminent, illustrious, noteworthy **4** (*Informal*) = excellent, fine, wonderful, superb, fantastic (*informal*), tremendous (*informal*), marvellous (*informal*), terrific (*informal*), booshit (*Austral. slang*), exo (*Austral. slang*), sik (*Austral. slang*) ≠ poor **5** = very, really, extremely, exceedingly

greatly = very much, hugely, vastly, considerably, remarkably, enormously, immensely, tremendously

greatness 1 = grandeur, glory, majesty, splendour, pomp, magnificence **2** = fame, glory, celebrity, distinction, eminence, note, renown, illustriousness

greed *or* **greediness 1** = gluttony, voracity **2** = avarice, longing, desire, hunger, craving, selfishness, acquisitiveness, covetousness ≠ generosity

greedy 1 = gluttonous, insatiable, voracious, ravenous, piggish **2** = avaricious, grasping, selfish, insatiable, acquisitive, rapacious, materialistic, desirous ≠ generous

green ADJECTIVE **1** = verdant, leafy, grassy **2** = ecological, conservationist, environment-friendly, ozone-friendly, non-polluting **3** = inexperienced, new, raw, naive, immature, gullible, untrained, wet behind the ears (*informal*) **4** = jealous, grudging, resentful, envious, covetous
● NOUN = lawn, common, turf, sward

greet 1 = salute, hail, say hello to, address, accost **2** = welcome, meet, receive, karanga (*N.Z.*), mihi (*N.Z.*) **3** = receive, take, respond to, react to

greeting = welcome, reception, salute, address, salutation, hongi (*N.Z.*), kia ora (*N.Z.*)

grey 1 = dull, dark, dim, gloomy, drab **2** = boring, dull, anonymous, faceless, colourless, nondescript, characterless **3** = pale, wan, pallid, ashen **4** = ambiguous, uncertain, neutral, unclear, debatable

grief = sadness, suffering, regret, distress, misery, sorrow, woe, anguish ≠ joy

grievance = complaint, gripe (*informal*), axe to grind

grieve 1 = mourn, suffer, weep, lament **2** = sadden, hurt, injure, distress, wound, pain, afflict, upset ≠ gladden

grim = terrible, severe, harsh, forbidding, formidable, sinister

grind VERB **1** = crush, mill, powder, grate, pulverize, pound, abrade, granulate **2** = press, push, crush, jam, mash, force down **3** = grate, scrape, gnash **4** = sharpen, polish, sand, smooth, whet
● NOUN = hard work (*Informal*), labour, sweat (*informal*), chore, toil, drudgery

grip VERB **1** = grasp, hold, catch, seize, clutch, clasp, take hold of **2** = engross, fascinate, absorb, entrance, hold, compel, rivet, enthral
● NOUN **1** = clasp, hold, grasp **2** = control, rule, influence, command, power, possession, domination, mastery **3** = hold, purchase, friction, traction **4** = understanding, sense, command, awareness, grasp, appreciation, mastery, comprehension

gripping = fascinating, exciting, thrilling, entrancing, compelling, riveting, enthralling, engrossing

grit NOUN **1** = gravel, sand, dust, pebbles **2** = courage, spirit, resolution, determination, guts (*informal*), backbone, fortitude, tenacity
● VERB = clench, grind, grate, gnash

gritty 1 = rough, sandy, dusty, rasping, gravelly, granular **2** = courageous, dogged, determined, spirited, brave, resolute, tenacious, plucky

groan VERB **1** = moan, cry, sigh **2** (*Informal*) = complain, object, moan, grumble, gripe (*informal*), carp, lament, whine
● NOUN **1** = moan, cry, sigh, whine **2** (*Informal*) = complaint, protest, objection, grumble, grouse, gripe (*informal*)

groom NOUN **1** = stableman, stableboy, hostler *or* ostler (*archaic*) **2** = newly-wed, husband, bridegroom, marriage partner
● VERB **1** = brush, clean, tend, rub down, curry **2** = smarten up, clean, tidy, preen, spruce up, primp **3** = train, prime, prepare, coach, ready, educate, drill, nurture

groove = indentation, cut, hollow, channel, trench, flute, trough, furrow

grope = feel, search, fumble, flounder, fish, scrabble, cast about, fossick (*Austral. & N.Z.*)

gross ADJECTIVE **1** = flagrant, blatant, rank, sheer, utter, grievous, heinous, unmitigated ≠ qualified **2** = vulgar, offensive, crude, obscene, coarse,

indelicate ≠ decent 3 = <u>fat</u>, obese,
overweight, hulking, corpulent ≠ slim
4 = <u>total</u>, whole, entire, aggregate, before
tax, before deductions ≠ net
● VERB = <u>earn</u>, make, take, bring in, rake in
(*informal*)

grotesque 1 = <u>unnatural</u>, bizarre,
strange, fantastic, distorted, deformed,
outlandish, freakish ≠ natural 2 = <u>absurd</u>,
preposterous ≠ natural

ground NOUN 1 = <u>earth</u>, land, dry land,
terra firma 2 = <u>arena</u>, pitch, stadium, park
(*informal*), field, enclosure
● PLURAL NOUN 1 = <u>estate</u>, land, fields,
gardens, territory 2 = <u>reason</u>, cause, basis,
occasion, foundation, excuse, motive,
justification 3 = <u>dregs</u>, lees, deposit,
sediment
● VERB 1 = <u>base</u>, found, establish, set, settle,
fix 2 = <u>instruct</u>, train, teach, initiate, tutor,
acquaint with, familiarize with

group NOUN = <u>crowd</u>, party, band, pack,
gang, bunch
● VERB = <u>arrange</u>, order, sort, class, classify,
marshal, bracket

grove = <u>wood</u>, plantation, covert, thicket,
copse, coppice, spinney

grow 1 = <u>develop</u>, get bigger ≠ shrink
2 = <u>get bigger</u>, spread, swell, stretch,
expand, enlarge, multiply 3 = <u>cultivate</u>,
produce, raise, farm, breed, nurture,
propagate 4 = <u>become</u>, get, turn, come to
be 5 = <u>originate</u>, spring, arise, stem, issue
6 = <u>improve</u>, advance, progress, succeed,
thrive, flourish, prosper

grown-up NOUN = <u>adult</u>, man, woman
● ADJECTIVE = <u>mature</u>, adult, of age, fully-
grown

growth 1 = <u>increase</u>, development,
expansion, proliferation, enlargement,
multiplication ≠ decline 2 = <u>progress</u>,
success, improvement, expansion,
advance, prosperity ≠ failure 3 (*Medical*)
= <u>tumour</u>, cancer, swelling, lump,
carcinoma (*Pathology*), sarcoma (*Medical*)

grudge NOUN = <u>resentment</u>, bitterness,
grievance, dislike, animosity, antipathy,
enmity, rancour ≠ goodwill
● VERB = <u>resent</u>, mind, envy, covet,
begrudge ≠ welcome

gruelling = <u>exhausting</u>, demanding,
tiring, taxing, severe, punishing, strenuous,
arduous ≠ easy

gruesome = <u>horrific</u>, shocking, terrible,

horrible, grim, ghastly, grisly, macabre
≠ pleasant

grumble VERB 1 = <u>complain</u>, moan, gripe
(*informal*), whinge (*informal*), carp, whine,
grouse, bleat 2 = <u>rumble</u>, growl, gurgle
● NOUN 1 = <u>complaint</u>, protest, objection,
moan, grievance, grouse, gripe (*informal*),
grouch (*informal*) 2 = <u>rumble</u>, growl,
gurgle

guarantee VERB 1 = <u>ensure</u>, secure,
assure, warrant, make certain 2 = <u>promise</u>,
pledge, undertake
● NOUN 1 = <u>promise</u>, pledge, assurance,
certainty, word of honour 2 = <u>warranty</u>,
contract, bond

guard VERB 1 = <u>protect</u>, defend, secure,
mind, preserve, shield, safeguard, watch
over
● NOUN 1 = <u>sentry</u>, warder, warden,
custodian, watch, lookout, watchman,
sentinel 2 = <u>shield</u>, security, defence,
screen, protection, safeguard, buffer

guarded = <u>cautious</u>, reserved, careful,
suspicious, wary, prudent, reticent,
circumspect

guardian = <u>keeper</u>, champion, defender,
guard, warden, curator, protector,
custodian

guerrilla = <u>freedom fighter</u>, partisan,
underground fighter

guess VERB 1 = <u>estimate</u>, predict, work
out, speculate, conjecture, postulate,
hypothesize ≠ know 2 = <u>suppose</u>, think,
believe, suspect, judge, imagine, reckon,
fancy
● NOUN 1 = <u>estimate</u>, speculation,
judgment, hypothesis, conjecture, shot in
the dark ≠ certainty 2 = <u>supposition</u>, idea,
theory, hypothesis

guest = <u>visitor</u>, company, caller,
manu(w)hiri (*N.Z.*)

guidance = <u>advice</u>, direction, leadership,
instruction, help, management, teaching,
counselling

guide NOUN 1 = <u>handbook</u>, manual,
guidebook, instructions, catalogue
2 = <u>directory</u>, street map 3 = <u>escort</u>, leader,
usher 4 = <u>pointer</u>, sign, landmark, marker,
beacon, signpost, guiding light, lodestar
5 = <u>model</u>, example, standard, ideal,
inspiration, paradigm
● VERB 1 = <u>lead</u>, direct, escort, conduct,
accompany, shepherd, usher, show
the way 2 = <u>steer</u>, control, manage,

direct, handle, command, manoeuvre
3 = <u>supervise</u>, train, teach, influence,
advise, counsel, instruct, oversee

guild = <u>society</u>, union, league, association,
company, club, order, organization

guilt 1 = <u>shame</u>, regret, remorse,
contrition, guilty conscience, self-
reproach ≠ pride **2** = <u>culpability</u>, blame,
responsibility, misconduct, wickedness,
sinfulness, guiltiness ≠ innocence

guilty 1 = <u>ashamed</u>, sorry, rueful, sheepish,
contrite, remorseful, regretful, shamefaced
≠ proud **2** = <u>culpable</u>, responsible,
to blame, offending, erring, at fault,
reprehensible, blameworthy ≠ innocent

guise 1 = <u>form</u>, appearance, shape, aspect,
mode, semblance **2** = <u>pretence</u>, disguise,
aspect, semblance

gulf 1 = <u>bay</u>, bight, sea inlet **2** = <u>chasm</u>,
opening, split, gap, separation, void, rift, abyss

gum NOUN = <u>glue</u>, adhesive, resin, cement,
paste
● VERB = <u>stick</u>, glue, affix, cement, paste

gun = <u>firearm</u>, shooter (*slang*), piece
(*slang*), handgun

gunman = <u>armed man</u>, gunslinger (*U.S.
slang*)

guru 1 = <u>authority</u>, expert, leader, master,
pundit, Svengali, fundi (*S. African*)
2 = <u>teacher</u>, mentor, sage, master, tutor

gush VERB **1** = <u>flow</u>, run, rush, flood, pour,
stream, cascade, spurt **2** = <u>enthuse</u>, rave,
spout, overstate, effuse
● NOUN = <u>stream</u>, flow, rush, flood, jet,
cascade, torrent, spurt

gut NOUN = <u>paunch</u> (*Informal*), belly, spare
tyre (*Brit. slang*), potbelly, puku (*N.Z.*)
● PLURAL NOUN **1** = <u>intestines</u>, insides
(*informal*), stomach, belly, bowels, innards
(*informal*), entrails **2** (*Informal*) = <u>courage</u>,
spirit, nerve, daring, pluck, backbone,
bottle (*slang*), audacity
● VERB **1** = <u>disembowel</u>, clean **2** = <u>ravage</u>,
empty, clean out, despoil
● ADJECTIVE = <u>instinctive</u>, natural, basic,
spontaneous, intuitive, involuntary,
heartfelt, unthinking

gutter = <u>drain</u>, channel, ditch, trench,
trough, conduit, sluice

guy (*Informal*) = <u>man</u>, person, fellow, lad,
bloke (*Brit. informal*), chap

Gypsy or **Gipsy** = <u>traveller</u>, roamer,
wanderer, Bohemian, rover, rambler,
nomad, Romany

h

habit 1 = <u>mannerism</u>, custom, way,
practice, characteristic, tendency, quirk,
propensity **2** = <u>addiction</u>, dependence,
compulsion

hack¹ = <u>cut</u>, chop, slash, mutilate, mangle,
mangulate (*Austral. slang*), hew, lacerate

hack² = <u>reporter</u>, writer, correspondent,
journalist, scribbler, contributor, literary
hack

hail¹ VERB **1** = <u>acclaim</u>, honour,
acknowledge, cheer, applaud ≠ condemn
2 = <u>salute</u>, greet, address, welcome, say
hello to, halloo ≠ snub **3** = <u>flag down</u>,
summon, signal to, wave down
● PHRASES **hail from somewhere**
= <u>come from</u>, be born in, originate in, be a
native of, have your roots in

hail² NOUN **1** = <u>hailstones</u>, sleet, hailstorm,
frozen rain **2** = <u>shower</u>, rain, storm, battery,
volley, barrage, bombardment, downpour
● VERB **1** = <u>rain</u>, shower, pelt **2** = <u>batter</u>, rain,
bombard, pelt, rain down on, beat down
upon

hair = <u>locks</u>, mane, tresses, shock, mop,
head of hair

hairdresser = <u>stylist</u>, barber, coiffeur *or*
coiffeuse

hairy 1 = <u>shaggy</u>, woolly, furry, stubbly,
bushy, unshaven, hirsute **2** (*Slang*)
= <u>dangerous</u>, risky, unpredictable,
hazardous, perilous

hale (*Old-fashioned*) = <u>healthy</u>, well,
strong, sound, fit, flourishing, robust,
vigorous

half NOUN = <u>fifty per cent</u>, equal part
● ADJECTIVE = <u>partial</u>, limited, moderate,
halved
● ADVERB = <u>partially</u>, partly, in part
■ RELATED WORDS
prefixes: bi-, demi-, hemi-, semi-

halfway ADVERB = <u>midway</u>, to *or* in the
middle
● ADJECTIVE = <u>midway</u>, middle, mid, central,
intermediate, equidistant

hall 1 = <u>passage</u>, lobby, corridor, hallway,

foyer, entry, passageway, entrance hall
2 = meeting place, chamber, auditorium, concert hall, assembly room

hallmark 1 = trademark, sure sign, telltale sign **2** (*Brit.*) = mark, sign, device, stamp, seal, symbol

halt VERB **1** = stop, break off, stand still, wait, rest ≠ continue **2** = come to an end, stop, cease **3** = hold back, end, check, block, curb, terminate, cut short, bring to an end ≠ aid
● NOUN = stop, end, close, pause, standstill, stoppage ≠ continuation

halting = faltering, stumbling, awkward, hesitant, laboured, stammering, stuttering

halve 1 = cut in half, reduce by fifty per cent, decrease by fifty per cent, lessen by fifty per cent **2** = split in two, cut in half, bisect, divide in two, share equally, divide equally

hammer 1 = hit, drive, knock, beat, strike, tap, bang **2** (*Informal*) = defeat, beat, thrash, trounce, run rings around (*informal*), wipe the floor with (*informal*), drub

hamper = hinder, handicap, prevent, restrict, frustrate, hamstring, interfere with, obstruct ≠ help

hand NOUN **1** = palm, fist, paw (*informal*), mitt (*slang*) **2** = worker, employee, labourer, workman, operative, craftsman, artisan, hired man **3** = round of applause, clap, ovation, big hand **4** = writing, script, handwriting, calligraphy
● VERB = give, pass, hand over, present to, deliver

handbook = guidebook, guide, manual, instruction book

handcuff VERB = shackle, secure, restrain, fetter, manacle
● PLURAL NOUN = shackles, cuffs (*informal*), fetters, manacles

handful = few, sprinkling, small amount, smattering, small number ≠ a lot

handicap NOUN **1** = disability, defect, impairment, physical abnormality **2** = disadvantage, barrier, restriction, obstacle, limitation, drawback, stumbling block, impediment ≠ advantage **3** = advantage, head start
● VERB = hinder, limit, restrict, burden, hamstring, hamper, hold back, impede ≠ help

handle NOUN = grip, hilt, haft, stock

● VERB **1** = manage, deal with, tackle, cope with **2** = deal with, manage **3** = control, manage, direct, guide, manipulate, manoeuvre **4** = hold, feel, touch, pick up, finger, grasp

handsome 1 = good-looking, attractive, gorgeous, elegant, personable, dishy (*informal, chiefly Brit.*), comely ≠ ugly **2** = generous, large, princely, liberal, considerable, lavish, ample, abundant ≠ mean

handy 1 = useful, practical, helpful, neat, convenient, easy to use, manageable, user-friendly ≠ useless **2** = convenient, close, available, nearby, accessible, on hand, at hand, within reach ≠ inconvenient **3** = skilful, skilled, expert, adept, deft, proficient, adroit, dexterous ≠ unskilled

hang VERB **1** = dangle, swing, suspend **2** = lower, suspend, dangle **3** = lean **4** – execute, lynch, string up (*informal*)
● PHRASES **get the hang of something** = grasp, understand, learn, master, comprehend, catch on to, acquire the technique of ◆ **hang back** = be reluctant, hesitate, hold back, recoil, demur

hangover = aftereffects, morning after (*informal*)

hang-up (*Informal*) = preoccupation, thing (*informal*), problem, block, difficulty, obsession, mania, inhibition

hank = coil, roll, length, bunch, piece, loop, clump, skein

happen 1 = occur, take place, come about, result, develop, transpire (*informal*), come to pass **2** = chance, turn out (*informal*)

happening = event, incident, experience, affair, proceeding, episode, occurrence

happily 1 = luckily, fortunately, providentially, opportunely **2** = joyfully, cheerfully, gleefully, blithely, merrily, gaily, joyously **3** = willingly, freely, gladly, with pleasure

happiness = pleasure, delight, joy, satisfaction, ecstasy, bliss, contentment, elation ≠ unhappiness

happy 1 = pleased, delighted, content, thrilled, glad, cheerful, merry, ecstatic **2** = contented, joyful, blissful ≠ sad **3** = fortunate, lucky, timely, favourable, auspicious, propitious, advantageous ≠ unfortunate

harass = <u>annoy</u>, trouble, bother, harry, plague, hound, hassle (*informal*), persecute

harassed = <u>hassled</u>, worried, troubled, strained, under pressure, tormented, distraught (*informal*), vexed

harassment = <u>hassle</u>, trouble, bother, irritation, persecution (*informal*), nuisance, annoyance, pestering

harbour NOUN = <u>port</u>, haven, dock, mooring, marina, pier, wharf, anchorage
● VERB 1 = <u>hold</u>, bear, maintain, nurse, retain, foster, entertain, nurture 2 = <u>shelter</u>, protect, hide, shield, provide refuge, give asylum

hard ADJECTIVE 1 = <u>tough</u>, strong, firm, solid, stiff, rigid, resistant, compressed ≠ soft 2 = <u>difficult</u>, involved, complicated, puzzling, intricate, perplexing, impenetrable, thorny ≠ easy 3 = <u>exhausting</u>, tough, exacting, rigorous, gruelling, strenuous, arduous, laborious ≠ easy 4 = <u>harsh</u>, cold, cruel, stern, callous, unkind, unsympathetic, pitiless ≠ kind 5 = <u>grim</u>, painful, distressing, harsh, unpleasant, intolerable, grievous, disagreeable
● ADVERB 1 = <u>strenuously</u>, steadily, persistently, doggedly, diligently, energetically, industriously, untiringly 2 = <u>intently</u>, closely, carefully, sharply, keenly 3 = <u>forcefully</u>, strongly, heavily, sharply, severely, fiercely, vigorously, intensely ≠ softly

harden 1 = <u>solidify</u>, set, freeze, cake, bake, clot, thicken, stiffen 2 = <u>accustom</u>, season, toughen, train, inure, habituate

hardened 1 = <u>habitual</u>, chronic, shameless, inveterate, incorrigible ≠ occasional 2 = <u>seasoned</u>, experienced, accustomed, toughened, inured, habituated ≠ naive

hardly 1 = <u>barely</u>, only just, scarcely, just, with difficulty, with effort ≠ completely 2 = <u>only just</u>, just, barely, scarcely

hardship = <u>suffering</u>, need, difficulty, misfortune, adversity, tribulation, privation ≠ ease

hardy = <u>strong</u>, tough, robust, sound, rugged, sturdy, stout ≠ frail

harm VERB 1 = <u>injure</u>, hurt, wound, abuse, ill-treat, maltreat ≠ heal 2 = <u>damage</u>, hurt, ruin, spoil
● NOUN 1 = <u>injury</u>, suffering, damage, ill, hurt, distress 2 = <u>damage</u>, loss, ill, hurt, misfortune, mischief ≠ good

harmful = <u>damaging</u>, dangerous, negative, destructive, hazardous, unhealthy, detrimental, hurtful ≠ harmless

harmless 1 = <u>safe</u>, benign, wholesome, innocuous, nontoxic ≠ dangerous 2 = <u>inoffensive</u>, innocent, innocuous, gentle, tame, unobjectionable

harmony 1 = <u>accord</u>, peace, agreement, friendship, sympathy, cooperation, rapport, compatibility ≠ conflict 2 = <u>tune</u>, melody, unison, tunefulness, euphony ≠ discord

harness VERB = <u>exploit</u>, control, channel, employ, utilize, mobilize
● NOUN = <u>equipment</u>, tackle, gear, tack

harrowing = <u>distressing</u>, disturbing, painful, terrifying, traumatic, tormenting, agonizing, nerve-racking

harry = <u>pester</u>, bother, plague, harass, hassle (*informal*), badger, chivvy

harsh 1 = <u>severe</u>, hard, tough, stark, austere, inhospitable 2 = <u>bleak</u>, freezing, severe, icy 3 = <u>cruel</u>, savage, ruthless, barbarous, pitiless 4 = <u>hard</u>, severe, cruel, stern, pitiless ≠ kind 5 = <u>drastic</u>, punitive, Draconian 6 = <u>raucous</u>, rough, grating, strident, rasping, discordant, guttural, dissonant ≠ soft

harshly = <u>severely</u>, roughly, cruelly, strictly, sternly, brutally

harvest NOUN 1 = <u>harvesting</u>, picking, gathering, collecting, reaping, harvest-time 2 = <u>crop</u>, yield, year's growth, produce
● VERB = <u>gather</u>, pick, collect, bring in, pluck, reap

hassle (*Informal*) NOUN = <u>trouble</u>, problem, difficulty, bother, grief (*informal*), uphill (*S. African*), inconvenience
● VERB = <u>bother</u>, bug (*informal*), annoy, hound, harass, badger, pester

hasten = <u>rush</u>, race, fly, speed, dash, hurry (up), scurry, make haste ≠ dawdle

hastily 1 = <u>quickly</u>, rapidly, promptly, speedily 2 = <u>hurriedly</u>, rashly, precipitately, impetuously

hatch 1 = <u>incubate</u>, breed, sit on, brood, bring forth 2 = <u>devise</u>, design, invent, put together, conceive, brew, formulate, contrive

hate VERB 1 = <u>detest</u>, loathe, despise, dislike, abhor, recoil from, not be able to

bear ≠ love **2** = <u>dislike</u>, detest, shrink from, recoil from, not be able to bear ≠ like **3** = <u>be unwilling</u>, regret, be reluctant, hesitate, be sorry, be loath, feel disinclined
● NOUN = <u>dislike</u>, hostility, hatred, loathing, animosity, aversion, antipathy, enmity ≠ love

hatred = <u>hate</u>, dislike, animosity, aversion, revulsion, antipathy, enmity, repugnance ≠ love

haul VERB = <u>drag</u>, draw, pull, heave
● NOUN = <u>yield</u>, gain, spoils, catch, harvest, loot, takings, booty

haunt VERB = <u>plague</u>, trouble, obsess, torment, possess, stay with, recur, prey on
● NOUN = <u>meeting place</u>, hangout (*informal*), rendezvous, stamping ground

haunted 1 = <u>possessed</u>, ghostly, cursed, eerie, spooky (*informal*), jinxed **2** = <u>preoccupied</u>, worried, troubled, plagued, obsessed, tormented

haunting = <u>evocative</u>, poignant, unforgettable

have VERB **1** = <u>own</u>, keep, possess, hold, retain, boast, be the owner of **2** = <u>get</u>, obtain, take, receive, accept, gain, secure, acquire **3** = <u>suffer</u>, experience, undergo, sustain, endure, be suffering from **4** = <u>give birth to</u>, bear, deliver, bring forth, beget **5** = <u>experience</u>, go through, undergo, meet with, come across, run into, be faced with
● PHRASES **have someone on** = <u>tease</u>, kid (*informal*), wind up (*Brit. slang*), trick, deceive, take the mickey, pull someone's leg ◆ **have something on** = <u>wear</u>, be wearing, be dressed in, be clothed in, be attired in ◆ **have to 1** = <u>must</u>, should, be forced, ought, be obliged, be bound, have got to, be compelled **2** = <u>have got to</u>, must

haven = <u>sanctuary</u>, shelter, retreat, asylum, refuge, oasis, sanctum

havoc 1 = <u>devastation</u>, damage, destruction, ruin **2** (*Informal*) = <u>disorder</u>, confusion, chaos, disruption, mayhem, shambles

hazard NOUN = <u>danger</u>, risk, threat, problem, menace, peril, jeopardy, pitfall
● VERB = <u>jeopardize</u>, risk, endanger, threaten, expose, imperil, put in jeopardy
● PHRASES **hazard a guess** = <u>guess</u>, conjecture, presume, take a guess

hazardous = <u>dangerous</u>, risky, difficult, insecure, unsafe, precarious, perilous, dicey (*informal, chiefly Brit.*) ≠ safe

haze = <u>mist</u>, cloud, fog, obscurity, vapour

head NOUN **1** = <u>skull</u>, crown, pate, nut (*slang*), loaf (*slang*) **2** = <u>mind</u>, reasoning, understanding, thought, sense, brain, brains (*informal*), intelligence **3** = <u>top</u>, crown, summit, peak, crest, pinnacle **4** (*Informal*) = <u>head teacher</u>, principal **5** = <u>leader</u>, president, director, manager, chief, boss (*informal*), captain, master
● ADJECTIVE = <u>chief</u>, main, leading, first, prime, premier, supreme, principal
● VERB **1** = <u>lead</u>, precede, be the leader of, be *or* go first, be *or* go at the front of, lead the way **2** = <u>top</u>, lead, crown, cap **3** = <u>be in charge of</u>, run, manage, lead, control, direct, guide, command
● PHRASES **go to your head 1** = <u>intoxicate</u> **2** = <u>make someone conceited</u>, puff someone up, make someone full of themselves ◆ **head over heels** = <u>completely</u>, thoroughly, utterly, intensely, wholeheartedly, uncontrollably

headache 1 = <u>migraine</u>, head (*informal*), neuralgia **2** = <u>problem</u> (*Informal*), worry, trouble, bother, nuisance, inconvenience, bane, vexation

heading = <u>title</u>, name, caption, headline, rubric

heady 1 = <u>exciting</u>, thrilling, stimulating, exhilarating, intoxicating **2** = <u>intoxicating</u>, strong, potent, inebriating

heal 1 *sometimes with* **up** = <u>mend</u>, get better, get well, cure, regenerate, show improvement **2** = <u>cure</u>, restore, mend, make better, remedy, make good, make well ≠ injure

health 1 = <u>condition</u>, state, shape, constitution, fettle **2** = <u>wellbeing</u>, strength, fitness, vigour, good condition, soundness, robustness, healthiness ≠ illness **3** = <u>state</u>, condition, shape

healthy 1 = <u>well</u>, fit, strong, active, robust, in good shape (*informal*), in the pink, in fine fettle ≠ ill **2** = <u>wholesome</u>, beneficial, nourishing, nutritious, salutary, hygienic, salubrious ≠ unwholesome **3** = <u>invigorating</u>, beneficial, salutary, salubrious

heap NOUN **1** = <u>pile</u>, lot, collection, mass, stack, mound, accumulation, hoard **2** *often plural* (*Informal*) = <u>a lot</u>, lots (*informal*), plenty, masses, load(s) (*informal*), great

deal, tons, stack(s)
- VERB *sometimes with* **up** = pile, collect, gather, stack, accumulate, amass, hoard
- PHRASES **heap something on someone** = load with, confer on, assign to, bestow on, shower upon

hear 1 = overhear, catch, detect 2 = listen to 3 (*Law*) = try, judge, examine, investigate 4 = learn, discover, find out, pick up, gather, ascertain, get wind of (*informal*)

hearing = inquiry, trial, investigation, industrial tribunal

heart NOUN 1 = emotions, feelings, love, affection 2 = nature, character, soul, constitution, essence, temperament, disposition 3 = root, core, centre, nucleus, hub, gist, nitty-gritty (*informal*), nub 4 = courage, will, spirit, purpose, bottle (*Brit. informal*), resolution, resolve, stomach
- PHRASES **by heart** = from or by memory, verbatim, word for word, pat, word-perfect, by rote, off by heart, off pat

▓▓ RELATED WORD
adjective: cardiac

heat VERB *sometimes with* **up** = warm (up), cook, boil, roast, reheat, make hot ≠ chill
- NOUN 1 = warmth, hotness, temperature ≠ cold 2 = hot weather, warmth, closeness, high temperature, heatwave, warm weather, hot climate, mugginess 3 = passion, excitement, intensity, fury, fervour, vehemence ≠ calmness

▓▓ RELATED WORD
adjective: thermal

heated 1 = impassioned, intense, spirited, excited, angry, furious, fierce, lively ≠ calm 2 = wound up, worked up, keyed up, het up (*informal*)

heaven NOUN 1 = paradise, next world, hereafter, nirvana (*Buddhism, Hinduism*), bliss, Zion (*Christianity*), life everlasting, Elysium *or* Elysian fields (*Greek myth*) 2 (*Informal*) = happiness, paradise, ecstasy, bliss, utopia, rapture, seventh heaven
- PHRASES **the heavens** (*Old-fashioned*) = sky, ether, firmament

heavenly 1 = celestial, holy, divine, blessed, immortal, angelic ≠ earthly 2 (*Informal*) = wonderful, lovely, delightful, beautiful, divine (*informal*), exquisite, sublime, blissful ≠ awful

heavily 1 = excessively, to excess,

very much, a great deal, considerably, copiously, without restraint, immoderately 2 = densely, closely, thickly, compactly 3 = hard, clumsily, awkwardly, weightily

heavy 1 = weighty, large, massive, hefty, bulky, ponderous ≠ light 2 = intensive, severe, serious, concentrated, fierce, excessive, relentless 3 = considerable, large, huge, substantial, abundant, copious, profuse ≠ slight

hectic = frantic, chaotic, heated, animated, turbulent, frenetic, feverish ≠ peaceful

hedge VERB = prevaricate, evade, sidestep, duck, dodge, flannel (*Brit. informal*), equivocate, temporize
- PHRASES **hedge against something** = protect against, insure against, guard against, safeguard against, shield against, cover against

heed (*Formal*) VERB = pay attention to, listen to, take notice of, follow, consider, note, observe, obey ≠ ignore
- NOUN = thought, care, mind, attention, regard, respect, notice ≠ disregard

heel (*Slang*) = swine, cad (*Brit. informal*), bounder (*Brit. old-fashioned slang*), rotter (*slang, chiefly Brit.*)

hefty (*Informal*) = big, strong, massive, strapping, robust, muscular, burly, hulking ≠ small

height 1 = tallness, stature, highness, loftiness ≠ shortness 2 = altitude, measurement, highness, elevation, tallness ≠ depth 3 = peak, top, crown, summit, crest, pinnacle, apex ≠ valley 4 = culmination, climax, zenith, limit, maximum, ultimate ≠ low point

heighten = intensify, increase, add to, improve, strengthen, enhance, sharpen, magnify

heir = successor, beneficiary, inheritor, heiress (*fem.*), next in line

hell 1 = the underworld, the abyss, Hades (*Greek myth*), hellfire, the inferno, fire and brimstone, the nether world, the bad fire (*informal*) 2 (*Informal*) = torment, suffering, agony, nightmare, misery, ordeal, anguish, wretchedness

hello = hi (*informal*), greetings, how do you do?, good morning, good evening, good afternoon, welcome, kia ora (*N.Z.*), gidday *or* g'day (*Austral. & N.Z.*)

helm (*Nautical*) = tiller, wheel, rudder

help VERB 1 *sometimes with* **out** = aid,

support, assist, cooperate with, abet, lend a hand, succour ≠ hinder **2** = improve, ease, relieve, facilitate, alleviate, mitigate, ameliorate ≠ make worse **3** = assist, aid, support **4** = resist, refrain from, avoid, prevent, keep from

● NOUN = assistance, aid, support, advice, guidance, cooperation, helping hand ≠ hindrance

helper = assistant, ally, supporter, mate, second, aide, attendant, collaborator

helpful 1 = cooperative, accommodating, kind, friendly, neighbourly, sympathetic, supportive, considerate **2** = useful, practical, profitable, constructive **3** = beneficial, advantageous

helping = portion, serving, ration, piece, dollop (*informal*), plateful

helpless = powerless, weak, disabled, incapable, paralysed, impotent, infirm ≠ powerful

hem NOUN = edge, border, margin, trimming, fringe

● PHRASES **hem something or someone in 1** = surround, confine, enclose, shut in **2** = restrict, confine, beset, circumscribe

hence = therefore, thus, consequently, for this reason, in consequence, ergo, on that account

herald VERB = indicate, promise, usher in, presage, portend, foretoken

● NOUN **1** (*Often literary*) = forerunner, sign, signal, indication, token, omen, precursor, harbinger **2** = messenger, courier, proclaimer, announcer, crier, town crier

herd = flock, crowd, collection, mass, drove, mob, swarm, horde

hereditary 1 = genetic, inborn, inbred, transmissible, inheritable **2** (*Law*) = inherited, passed down, traditional, ancestral

heritage = inheritance, legacy, birthright, tradition, endowment, bequest

hero 1 = protagonist, leading man **2** = star, champion, victor, superstar, conqueror **3** = idol, favourite, pin-up (*slang*), fave (*informal*)

heroic = courageous, brave, daring, fearless, gallant, intrepid, valiant, lion-hearted ≠ cowardly

heroine 1 = protagonist, leading lady, diva, prima donna **2** = idol, favourite, pin-up (*slang*), fave (*informal*)

hesitate 1 = waver, delay, pause, wait, doubt, falter, dither (*chiefly Brit.*), vacillate ≠ be decisive **2** = be reluctant, be unwilling, shrink from, think twice, scruple, demur, hang back, be disinclined ≠ be determined

hesitation = reluctance, reservation(s), misgiving(s), ambivalence, qualm(s), unwillingness, scruple(s), compunction

hidden 1 = secret, veiled, latent **2** = concealed, secret, covert, unseen, clandestine, secreted, under wraps

hide¹ 1 = conceal, stash (*informal*), secrete, put out of sight ≠ display **2** = go into hiding, take cover, keep out of sight, hole up, lie low, go underground, go to ground, go to earth **3** = keep secret, suppress, withhold, keep quiet about, hush up, draw a veil over, keep dark, keep under your hat ≠ disclose **4** = obscure, cover, mask, disguise, conceal, veil, cloak, shroud ≠ reveal

hide² = skin, leather, pelt

hideous = ugly, revolting, ghastly, monstrous, grotesque, gruesome, grisly, unsightly ≠ beautiful

hiding (*Informal*) = beating, whipping, thrashing, licking (*informal*), spanking, walloping (*informal*), drubbing

hierarchy = grading, ranking, social order, pecking order, class system, social stratum

high ADJECTIVE **1** = tall, towering, soaring, steep, elevated, lofty ≠ short **2** = extreme, great, acute, severe, extraordinary, excessive ≠ low **3** = strong, violent, extreme, blustery, squally, sharp **4** = important, chief, powerful, superior, eminent, exalted ≠ lowly **5** = high-pitched, piercing, shrill, penetrating, strident, sharp, acute, piping ≠ deep **6** (*Informal*) = intoxicated, stoned (*slang*), tripping (*informal*)

● ADVERB = way up, aloft, far up, to a great height

high-flown = extravagant, elaborate, pretentious, exaggerated, inflated, lofty, grandiose, overblown ≠ straightforward

highlight VERB = emphasize, stress, accent, show up, underline, spotlight, accentuate, call attention to ≠ play down

● NOUN = high point, peak, climax, feature, focus, focal point, high spot ≠ low point

highly = extremely, very, greatly, vastly, exceptionally, immensely, tremendously

hijack = <u>seize</u>, take over, commandeer, expropriate

hike NOUN = <u>walk</u>, march, trek, ramble, tramp, traipse

● VERB = <u>walk</u>, march, trek, ramble, tramp, back-pack

hilarious 1 = <u>funny</u>, entertaining, amusing, hysterical, humorous, comical, side-splitting 2 = <u>merry</u>, uproarious, rollicking ≠ serious

hill = <u>mount</u>, fell, height, mound, hilltop, tor, knoll, hillock, kopje *or* koppie (*S. African*)

hinder = <u>obstruct</u>, stop, check, block, delay, frustrate, handicap, interrupt ≠ help

hint NOUN 1 = <u>clue</u>, suggestion, implication, indication, pointer, allusion, innuendo, intimation 2 *often plural* = <u>advice</u>, help, tip(s), suggestion(s), pointer(s) 3 = <u>trace</u>, touch, suggestion, dash, suspicion, tinge, undertone

● VERB *sometimes with at* = <u>suggest</u>, indicate, imply, intimate, insinuate

hire VERB 1 = <u>employ</u>, commission, take on, engage, appoint, sign up, enlist 2 = <u>rent</u>, charter, lease, let, engage

● NOUN 1 = <u>rental</u>, hiring, rent, lease 2 = <u>charge</u>, rental, price, cost, fee

hiss VERB 1 = <u>whistle</u>, wheeze, whiz, whirr, sibilate 2 = <u>jeer</u>, mock, deride

● NOUN 1 = <u>fizz</u>, buzz, hissing, fizzing, sibilation

historic = <u>significant</u>, notable, momentous, famous, extraordinary, outstanding, remarkable, ground-breaking ≠ unimportant

historical = <u>factual</u>, real, documented, actual, authentic, attested ≠ contemporary

history 1 = <u>the past</u>, antiquity, yesterday, yesteryear, olden days 2 = <u>chronicle</u>, record, story, account, narrative, recital, annals

hit VERB 1 = <u>strike</u>, beat, knock, bang, slap, smack, thump, clout (*informal*) 2 = <u>collide with</u>, run into, bump into, clash with, smash into, crash against, bang into 3 = <u>affect</u>, damage, harm, ruin, devastate, overwhelm, touch, impact on 4 = <u>reach</u>, gain, achieve, arrive at, accomplish, attain

● NOUN 1 = <u>shot</u>, blow 2 = <u>blow</u>, knock, stroke, belt (*informal*), rap, slap, smack, clout (*informal*) 3 = <u>success</u>, winner, triumph, smash (*informal*), sensation

● PHRASES **hit it off** (*Informal*) = <u>get on (well) with</u>, click (*slang*), be on good terms, get on like a house on fire (*informal*)

◆ **hit on** *or* **upon something** = <u>think up</u>, discover, arrive at, invent, stumble on, light upon, strike upon

hitch NOUN = <u>problem</u>, catch, difficulty, hold-up, obstacle, drawback, snag, uphill (*S. African*), impediment

● VERB 1 (*Informal*) = <u>hitchhike</u>, thumb a lift 2 = <u>fasten</u>, join, attach, couple, tie, connect, harness, tether

● PHRASES **hitch something up** = <u>pull up</u>, tug, jerk, yank

hitherto (*Formal*) = <u>previously</u>, so far, until now, thus far, heretofore

hobby = <u>pastime</u>, relaxation, leisure pursuit, diversion, avocation, (leisure) activity

hoist VERB = <u>raise</u>, lift, erect, elevate, heave

● NOUN = <u>lift</u>, crane, elevator, winch

hold VERB 1 = <u>embrace</u>, grasp, clutch, hug, squeeze, cradle, clasp, enfold 2 = <u>restrain</u> ≠ release 3 = <u>accommodate</u>, take, contain, seat, have a capacity for 4 = <u>consider</u>, think, believe, judge, regard, assume, reckon, deem ≠ have 5 = <u>occupy</u>, have, fill, maintain, retain, possess, hold down (*informal*) 6 = <u>conduct</u>, convene, call, run, preside over ≠ cancel 7 = <u>detain</u>, confine, imprison, impound ≠ release

● NOUN 1 = <u>grip</u>, grasp, clasp 2 = <u>foothold</u>, footing 3 = <u>control</u>, influence, mastery, mana (*N.Z.*)

holder 1 = <u>owner</u>, bearer, possessor, keeper, proprietor 2 = <u>case</u>, cover, container

hold-up 1 = <u>robbery</u>, theft, mugging (*informal*), stick-up (*slang, chiefly U.S.*) 2 – <u>delay</u>, wait, hitch, setback, snag, traffic jam, stoppage, bottleneck

hole 1 = <u>cavity</u>, pit, hollow, chamber, cave, cavern 2 = <u>opening</u>, crack, tear, gap, breach, vent, puncture, aperture 3 = <u>burrow</u>, den, earth, shelter, lair 4 (*Informal*) = <u>hovel</u>, dump (*informal*), dive (*slang*), slum 5 (*Informal*) = <u>predicament</u>, spot (*informal*), fix (*informal*), mess, jam (*informal*), dilemma, scrape (*informal*), hot water (*informal*)

holiday 1 = <u>vacation</u>, leave, break, time off, recess 2 = <u>festival</u>, fête, celebration, feast, gala

hollow ADJECTIVE 1 = <u>empty</u>, vacant, void,

unfilled ≠ solid 2 = <u>worthless</u>, useless, vain, meaningless, pointless, futile, fruitless ≠ meaningful 3 = <u>dull</u>, low, deep, muted, toneless, reverberant ≠ vibrant

● NOUN 1 = <u>cavity</u>, hole, bowl, depression, pit, basin, crater, trough ≠ mound 2 = <u>valley</u>, dale, glen, dell, dingle ≠ hill

● VERB *often followed by* **out** = <u>scoop out</u>, dig out, excavate, gouge out

holocaust 1 = <u>devastation</u>, destruction, genocide, annihilation, conflagration 2 = <u>genocide</u>, massacre, annihilation

holy 1 = <u>sacred</u>, blessed, hallowed, venerable, consecrated, sacrosanct, sanctified ≠ unsanctified 2 = <u>devout</u>, godly, religious, pure, righteous, pious, virtuous, saintly ≠ sinful

homage = <u>respect</u>, honour, worship, devotion, reverence, deference, adulation, adoration ≠ contempt

home NOUN 1 = <u>dwelling</u>, house, residence, abode, habitation, pad (*slang*), domicile 2 = <u>birthplace</u>, homeland, home town, native land

● ADJECTIVE 1 = <u>domestic</u>, local, internal, native

● PHRASES **at home** 1 = <u>in</u>, present, available 2 = <u>at ease</u>, relaxed, comfortable, content, at peace ◆ **bring something home to someone** = <u>make clear</u>, emphasize, drive home, press home, impress upon

homeland = <u>native land</u>, birthplace, motherland, fatherland, country of origin, mother country

homeless = <u>destitute</u>, displaced, dispossessed, down-and-out

homely 1 = <u>comfortable</u>, welcoming, friendly, cosy, homespun 2 = <u>plain</u>, simple, ordinary, modest ≠ elaborate

homicide = <u>murder</u>, killing, manslaughter, slaying, bloodshed

hone 1 = <u>improve</u>, better, enhance, upgrade, refine, sharpen, help 2 = <u>sharpen</u>, point, grind, edge, file, polish, whet

honest 1 = <u>trustworthy</u>, upright, ethical, honourable, reputable, truthful, virtuous, law-abiding ≠ dishonest 2 = <u>open</u>, direct, frank, plain, sincere, candid, forthright, upfront (*informal*) ≠ secretive

honestly 1 = <u>ethically</u>, legally, lawfully, honourably, by fair means 2 = <u>frankly</u>, plainly, candidly, straight (out), truthfully, to your face, in all sincerity

honesty 1 = <u>integrity</u>, honour, virtue, morality, probity, rectitude, truthfulness, trustworthiness 2 = <u>frankness</u>, openness, sincerity, candour, bluntness, outspokenness, straightforwardness

honorary = <u>nominal</u>, unofficial, titular, in name *or* title only

honour NOUN 1 = <u>integrity</u>, morality, honesty, goodness, fairness, decency, probity, rectitude ≠ dishonour 2 = <u>prestige</u>, credit, reputation, glory, fame, distinction, dignity, renown ≠ disgrace 3 = <u>reputation</u>, standing, prestige, image, status, stature, good name, cachet 4 = <u>acclaim</u>, praise, recognition, compliments, homage, accolades, commendation ≠ contempt 5 = <u>privilege</u>, credit, pleasure, compliment

● VERB 1 = <u>acclaim</u>, praise, decorate, commemorate, commend 2 = <u>respect</u>, value, esteem, prize, appreciate, adore ≠ scorn 3 = <u>fulfil</u>, keep, carry out, observe, discharge, live up to, be true to 4 = <u>pay</u>, take, accept, pass, acknowledge ≠ refuse

honourable 1 = <u>principled</u>, moral, ethical, fair, upright, honest, virtuous, trustworthy 2 = <u>proper</u>, respectable, virtuous, creditable

hook NOUN = <u>fastener</u>, catch, link, peg, clasp

● VERB 1 = <u>fasten</u>, fix, secure, clasp 2 = <u>catch</u>, land, trap, entrap

hooked 1 = <u>bent</u>, curved, aquiline, hook-shaped 2 (*Informal*) = <u>obsessed</u>, addicted, taken, devoted, turned on (*slang*), enamoured 3 (*Informal*) = <u>addicted</u>, dependent, using (*informal*), having a habit

hooligan = <u>delinquent</u>, vandal, hoon (*Austral. & N.Z.*), ruffian, lager lout, yob *or* yobbo (*Brit. slang*), cougan (*Austral. slang*), scozza (*Austral. slang*), bogan (*Austral. slang*)

hoop = <u>ring</u>, band, loop, wheel, round, girdle, circlet

hop VERB = <u>jump</u>, spring, bound, leap, skip, vault, caper

● NOUN = <u>jump</u>, step, spring, bound, leap, bounce, skip, vault

hope VERB = <u>believe</u>, look forward to, cross your fingers

● NOUN = <u>belief</u>, confidence, expectation, longing, dream, desire, ambition, assumption ≠ despair

hopeful 1 = optimistic, confident, looking forward to, buoyant, sanguine, expectant ≠ despairing **2** = promising, encouraging, bright, reassuring, rosy, heartening, auspicious ≠ unpromising

hopefully = optimistically, confidently, expectantly, with anticipation

hopeless = impossible, pointless, futile, useless, vain, no-win, unattainable

horde = crowd, mob, swarm, host, band, pack, drove, gang

horizon = skyline, view, vista

horizontal = level, flat, parallel

horrible 1 (*Informal*) = dreadful, terrible, awful, nasty, cruel, mean, unpleasant, horrid ≠ wonderful **2** = terrible, appalling, terrifying, shocking, grim, dreadful, revolting, ghastly

horrific = horrifying, shocking, appalling, awful, terrifying, dreadful, horrendous, ghastly

horrify 1 = terrify, alarm, frighten, scare, intimidate, petrify, make your hair stand on end ≠ comfort **2** = shock, appal, dismay, sicken, outrage ≠ delight

horror 1 = terror, fear, alarm, panic, dread, fright, consternation, trepidation **2** = hatred, disgust, loathing, aversion, revulsion, repugnance, odium, detestation ≠ love

horse = nag, mount, mare, colt, filly, stallion, steed (*archaic or literary*), moke (*Austral. slang*), yarraman *or* yarramin (*Austral.*), gee-gee (*slang*)

▆ RELATED WORDS
adjectives: equestrian, equine
male: stallion
female: mare
young: foal, colt, filly

hospitality = welcome, warmth, kindness, friendliness, sociability, conviviality, neighbourliness, cordiality

host¹ *or* **hostess** NOUN **1** = master of ceremonies, proprietor, innkeeper, landlord *or* landlady **2** = presenter, compere (*Brit.*), anchorman *or* anchorwoman
● VERB = present, introduce, compere (*Brit.*), front (*informal*)

host² **1** = multitude, lot, load (*informal*), wealth, array, myriad, great quantity, large number **2** = crowd, army, pack, drove, mob, herd, legion, swarm

hostage = captive, prisoner, pawn

hostile 1 = antagonistic, opposed, contrary, ill-disposed **2** = unfriendly, belligerent, antagonistic, rancorous, ill-disposed ≠ friendly **3** = inhospitable, adverse, uncongenial, unsympathetic, unwelcoming ≠ hospitable

hostility NOUN **1** = unfriendliness, hatred, animosity, spite, bitterness, malice, venom, enmity ≠ friendliness **2** = opposition, resentment, antipathy, aversion, antagonism, ill feeling, ill-will, animus ≠ approval
● PLURAL NOUN = warfare, war, fighting, conflict, combat, armed conflict ≠ peace

hot 1 = heated, boiling, steaming, roasting, searing, scorching, scalding **2** = warm, close, stifling, humid, torrid, sultry, sweltering, balmy ≠ cold **3** = spicy, pungent, peppery, piquant, biting, sharp ≠ mild **4** = intense, passionate, heated, spirited, fierce, lively, animated, ardent **5** = new, latest, fresh, recent, up to date, just out, up to the minute, bang up to date (*informal*) ≠ old **6** = popular, hip, fashionable, cool, in demand, sought-after, must-see, in vogue ≠ unpopular **7** = fierce, intense, strong, keen, competitive, cut-throat **8** = fiery, violent, raging, passionate, stormy ≠ calm

hound = harass, harry, bother, provoke, annoy, torment, hassle (*informal*), badger
▆ RELATED WORD
collective noun: pack

house NOUN **1** = home, residence, dwelling, pad (*slang*), homestead, abode, habitation, domicile, whare (*N.Z.*) **2** = household, family **3** = firm, company, business, organization, outfit (*informal*) **4** = assembly, parliament, Commons, legislative body **5** = dynasty, tribe, clan
● VERB **1** = accommodate, quarter, take in, put up, lodge, harbour, billet **2** = contain, keep, hold, cover, store, protect, shelter **3** = take, accommodate, sleep, provide shelter for, give a bed to
● PHRASES **on the house** = free, for free (*informal*), for nothing, free of charge, gratis

household = family, home, house, family circle, ainga (*N.Z.*)

housing 1 = accommodation, homes, houses, dwellings, domiciles **2** = case, casing, covering, cover, shell, jacket, holder, container

hover 1 = float, fly, hang, drift, flutter **2** = linger, loiter, hang about or around (*informal*) **3** = waver, fluctuate, dither (*chiefly Brit.*), oscillate, vacillate

however = but, nevertheless, still, though, yet, nonetheless, notwithstanding, anyhow

howl VERB 1 = bay, cry **2** = cry, scream, roar, weep, yell, wail, shriek, bellow
● **NOUN 1** = baying, cry, bay, bark, barking, yelping **2** = cry, scream, roar, bay, wail, shriek, clamour, bawl

hub = centre, heart, focus, core, middle, focal point, nerve centre

huddle VERB 1 = curl up, crouch, hunch up **2** = crowd, press, gather, collect, squeeze, cluster, flock, herd
● **NOUN** (*Informal*) = discussion, conference, meeting, hui (*N.Z.*), powwow, confab (*informal*), korero (*N.Z.*)

hue = colour, tone, shade, dye, tint, tinge

hug VERB = embrace, cuddle, squeeze, clasp, enfold, hold close, take in your arms
● **NOUN** = embrace, squeeze, bear hug, clinch (*slang*), clasp

huge = enormous, large, massive, vast, tremendous, immense, gigantic, monumental ≠ tiny

hui (*N.Z.*) = meeting, gathering, assembly, conference, congress, rally, convention, get-together (*informal*)

hull = framework, casing, body, covering, frame

hum 1 = drone, buzz, murmur, throb, vibrate, purr, thrum, whir **2** (*Informal*) = be busy, buzz, bustle, stir, pulse, pulsate

human ADJECTIVE = mortal, manlike ≠ nonhuman
● **NOUN** = human being, person, individual, creature, mortal, man or woman ≠ nonhuman

humane = kind, compassionate, understanding, forgiving, tender, sympathetic, benign, merciful ≠ cruel

humanitarian ADJECTIVE
1 = compassionate, charitable, humane, benevolent, altruistic **2** = charitable, philanthropic, public-spirited
● **NOUN** = philanthropist, benefactor, Good Samaritan, altruist

humanity 1 = the human race, man, mankind, people, mortals, humankind, Homo sapiens **2** = human nature, mortality **3** = kindness, charity,

compassion, sympathy, mercy, philanthropy, fellow feeling, kind-heartedness

humble ADJECTIVE 1 = modest, meek, unassuming, unpretentious, self-effacing, unostentatious ≠ proud **2** = lowly, poor, mean, simple, ordinary, modest, obscure, undistinguished ≠ distinguished
● **VERB** = humiliate, disgrace, crush, subdue, chasten, put (someone) in their place, take down a peg (*informal*) ≠ exalt

humidity = damp, moisture, dampness, wetness, moistness, dankness, clamminess, mugginess

humiliate = embarrass, shame, humble, crush, put down, degrade, chasten, mortify ≠ honour

humiliating = embarrassing, shaming, humbling, mortifying, crushing, degrading, ignominious, barro (*Austral. slang*)

humiliation = embarrassment, shame, disgrace, humbling, put-down, degradation, indignity, ignominy

humorous = funny, comic, amusing, entertaining, witty, comical, droll, jocular ≠ serious

humour NOUN 1 = comedy, funniness, fun, amusement, funny side, jocularity, facetiousness, ludicrousness ≠ seriousness **2** = mood, spirits, temper, disposition, frame of mind **3** = joking, comedy, wit, farce, jesting, wisecracks (*informal*), witticisms
● **VERB** = indulge, accommodate, go along with, flatter, gratify, pander to, mollify ≠ oppose

hunch NOUN = feeling, idea, impression, suspicion, intuition, premonition, inkling, presentiment
● **VERB** = crouch, bend, curve, arch, draw in

hunger NOUN 1 = appetite, emptiness, hungriness, ravenousness **2** = starvation, famine, malnutrition, undernourishment **3** = desire, appetite, craving, ache, lust, yearning, itch, thirst
● **PHRASES hunger for or after something** = want, desire, crave, long for, wish for, yearn for, hanker after, ache for

hungry 1 = starving, ravenous, famished, starved, empty, voracious, peckish (*informal, chiefly Brit.*) **2** = eager, keen, craving, yearning, greedy, avid, desirous, covetous

hunk = lump, piece, chunk, block, mass, wedge, slab, nugget

hunt VERB = stalk, track, chase, pursue, trail, hound

● NOUN = search, hunting, investigation, chase, pursuit, quest

● PHRASES **hunt for something** or **someone** = search for, look for, seek for, forage for, scour for, fossick for (*Austral. & N.Z.*), ferret about for

hurdle 1 = obstacle, difficulty, barrier, handicap, hazard, uphill (*S. African*), obstruction, stumbling block 2 = fence, barrier, barricade

hurl = throw, fling, launch, cast, pitch, toss, propel, sling

hurricane = storm, gale, tornado, cyclone, typhoon, tempest, twister (*U.S. informal*), willy-willy (*Austral.*)

hurried 1 = hasty, quick, brief, rushed, short, swift, speedy 2 = rushed, perfunctory, speedy, hasty, cursory

hurry VERB 1 = rush, fly, dash, scurry, scoot ≠ dawdle 2 = make haste, rush, get a move on (*informal*), step on it (*informal*)

● NOUN = rush, haste, speed, urgency, flurry, quickness ≠ slowness

hurt VERB 1 = injure, damage, wound, cut, disable, bruise, scrape, impair ≠ heal 2 = ache, be sore, be painful, burn, smart, sting, throb, be tender 3 = harm, injure, ill-treat, maltreat 4 = upset, distress, pain, wound, annoy, grieve, sadden

● NOUN = distress, suffering, pain, grief, misery, sorrow, heartache, wretchedness ≠ happiness

● ADJECTIVE 1 = injured, wounded, damaged, harmed, cut, bruised, scarred ≠ healed 2 = upset, wounded, crushed, offended, aggrieved, tooshie (*Austral. slang*) ≠ calmed

hurtle = rush, charge, race, shoot, fly, speed, tear, crash

husband NOUN = partner, spouse, mate, better half (*humorous*)

● VERB = conserve, budget, save, store, hoard, economize on, use economically ≠ squander

hush VERB = quieten, silence, mute, muzzle, shush

● NOUN = quiet, silence, calm, peace, tranquillity, stillness

hut 1 = cabin, shack, shanty, hovel, whare (*N.Z.*) 2 = shed, outhouse, lean-to, lockup

hybrid 1 = crossbreed, cross, mixture, compound, composite, amalgam, mongrel, half-breed 2 = mixture, compound, composite, amalgam

hygiene = cleanliness, sanitation, disinfection, sterility

hymn 1 = religious song, song of praise, carol, chant, anthem, psalm, paean 2 = song of praise, anthem, paean

hype (*Slang*) = publicity, promotion, plugging (*informal*), razzmatazz (*slang*), brouhaha, ballyhoo (*informal*)

hypocrisy = insincerity, pretence, deception, cant, duplicity, deceitfulness ≠ sincerity

hypothesis = theory, premise, proposition, assumption, thesis, postulate, supposition

hysteria = frenzy, panic, madness, agitation, delirium, hysterics

hysterical 1 = frenzied, frantic, raving, distracted, distraught, crazed, overwrought, berko (*Austral. slang*) ≠ calm 2 (*Informal*) = hilarious, uproarious, side-splitting, comical ≠ serious

icy 1 = cold, freezing, bitter, biting, raw, chill, chilly, frosty ≠ hot 2 = slippery, glassy, slippy (*informal* or *dialect*), like a sheet of glass 3 = unfriendly, cold, distant, aloof, frosty, frigid, unwelcoming ≠ friendly

idea 1 = notion, thought, view, teaching, opinion, belief, conclusion, hypothesis 2 = understanding, thought, view, opinion, concept, impression, perception 3 = intention, aim, purpose, object, plan, objective

ideal NOUN 1 = epitome, standard, dream, pattern, perfection, last word, paragon 2 = model, prototype, paradigm

● ADJECTIVE = perfect, best, model, classic, supreme, ultimate, archetypal, exemplary

≠ imperfect

ideally = in a perfect world, all things being equal, if you had your way

identical = alike, matching, twin, duplicate, indistinguishable, interchangeable ≠ different

identification 1 = discovery, recognition, determining, establishment, diagnosis, confirmation, divination 2 = recognition, naming, distinguishing, confirmation, pinpointing 3 = connection, relationship, association 4 = understanding, relationship, involvement, unity, sympathy, empathy, rapport, fellow feeling

identify VERB 1 = recognize, place, name, remember, spot, diagnose, make out, pinpoint 2 = establish, spot, confirm, demonstrate, pick out, certify, verify, mark out
● PHRASES **identify something** or **someone with something** or **someone** = equate with, associate with
◆ **identify with someone** = relate to, respond to, feel for, empathize with

identity = individuality, self, character, personality, existence, originality, separateness

idiot = fool, moron, twit (*informal*, *chiefly Brit.*), chump, imbecile, cretin, simpleton, halfwit, galah (*Austral. & N.Z. informal*), dorba or dorb (*Austral. slang*), bogan (*Austral. slang*)

idle ADJECTIVE 1 = unoccupied, unemployed, redundant, inactive ≠ occupied 2 = unused, inactive, out of order, out of service 3 = lazy, slow, slack, sluggish, lax, negligent, inactive, inert ≠ busy 4 = useless, vain, pointless, unsuccessful, ineffective, worthless, futile, fruitless ≠ useful
● VERB *often with* **away** = fritter, lounge, potter, loaf, dally, loiter, dawdle, laze

idol 1 = hero, pin-up, favourite, pet, darling, beloved (*slang*), fave (*informal*) 2 = graven image, god, deity

if 1 = provided, assuming, given that, providing, supposing, presuming, on condition that, as long as 2 = when, whenever, every time, any time

ignite 1 = catch fire, burn, burst into flames, inflame, flare up, take fire 2 = set fire to, light, set alight, torch, kindle

ignorance 1 = lack of education, stupidity, foolishness ≠ knowledge

2 *with of* = unawareness of, inexperience of, unfamiliarity with, innocence of, unconsciousness of

ignorant 1 = uneducated, illiterate ≠ educated 2 = insensitive, rude, crass 3 *with of* = uninformed of, unaware of, oblivious to, innocent of, unconscious of, inexperienced of, uninitiated about, unenlightened about ≠ informed

ignore 1 = pay no attention to, neglect, disregard, slight, overlook, scorn, spurn, rebuff ≠ pay attention to 2 = overlook, discount, disregard, reject, neglect, shrug off, pass over, brush aside 3 = snub, slight, rebuff

ill ADJECTIVE 1 = unwell, sick, poorly (*informal*), diseased, weak, crook (*Austral. & N.Z. slang*), ailing, frail ≠ healthy 2 = harmful, bad, damaging, evil, foul, unfortunate, destructive, detrimental ≠ favourable
● NOUN = problem, trouble, suffering, worry, injury, hurt, strain, harm ≠ good
● ADVERB 1 = badly, unfortunately, unfavourably, inauspiciously 2 = hardly, barely, scarcely, just, only just, by no means, at a push ≠ well

illegal = unlawful, banned, forbidden, prohibited, criminal, outlawed, illicit, unlicensed ≠ legal

illicit 1 = illegal, criminal, prohibited, unlawful, illegitimate, unlicensed, unauthorized, felonious ≠ legal 2 = forbidden, improper, immoral, guilty, clandestine, furtive

illness = sickness, disease, infection, disorder, bug (*informal*), ailment, affliction, malady

illuminate 1 = light up, brighten ≠ darken 2 = explain, interpret, make clear, clarify, clear up, enlighten, shed light on, elucidate ≠ obscure

illuminating = informative, revealing, enlightening, helpful, explanatory, instructive ≠ confusing

illusion 1 = delusion, misconception, misapprehension, fancy, fallacy, false impression, false belief 2 = false impression, appearance, impression, deception, fallacy ≠ reality 3 = fantasy, vision, hallucination, trick, spectre, mirage, daydream, apparition

illustrate 1 = demonstrate, emphasize 2 = explain, sum up, summarize, bring home, point up, elucidate

illustrated = pictured, decorated, pictorial

illustration 1 = example, case, instance, sample, specimen, exemplar **2** = picture, drawing, painting, image, print, plate, figure, portrait

image 1 = thought, idea, vision, concept, impression, perception, mental picture, conceptualization **2** = figure of speech **3** = reflection, likeness, mirror image **4** = figure, idol, icon, fetish, talisman **5** = replica, copy, reproduction, counterpart, clone, facsimile, spitting image (*informal*), Doppelgänger **6** = picture, photo, photograph, representation, reproduction, snapshot

imaginary = fictional, made-up, invented, imagined, unreal, hypothetical, fictitious, illusory ≠ real

imagination 1 = creativity, vision, invention, ingenuity, enterprise, originality, inventiveness, resourcefulness **2** = mind's eye, fancy

imaginative = creative, original, inspired, enterprising, clever, ingenious, inventive ≠ unimaginative

imagine 1 = envisage, see, picture, plan, think of, conjure up, envision, visualize **2** = believe, think, suppose, assume, suspect, guess (*informal, chiefly U.S. & Canad.*), take it, reckon

imitate 1 = copy, follow, repeat, echo, emulate, ape, simulate, mirror **2** = do an impression of, mimic, copy

imitation NOUN **1** = replica, fake, reproduction, sham, forgery, counterfeiting, likeness, duplication **2** = copying, resemblance, mimicry **3** = impression, impersonation
● ADJECTIVE = artificial, mock, reproduction, dummy, synthetic, man-made, simulated, sham ≠ real

immaculate 1 = clean, spotless, neat, spruce, squeaky-clean, spick-and-span ≠ dirty **2** = pure, perfect, impeccable, flawless, faultless, above reproach ≠ corrupt **3** = perfect, flawless, impeccable, faultless, unblemished, untarnished, unexceptionable ≠ tainted

immediate 1 = instant, prompt, instantaneous, quick, on-the-spot, split-second ≠ later **2** = nearest, next, direct, close, near ≠ far

immediately = at once, now, instantly, straight away, directly, promptly, right away, without delay

immense = huge, great, massive, vast, enormous, extensive, tremendous, very big ≠ tiny

immerse 1 = engross, involve, absorb, busy, occupy, engage **2** = plunge, dip, submerge, sink, duck, bathe, douse, dunk

immigrant = settler, incomer, alien, stranger, outsider, newcomer, migrant, emigrant

imminent = near, coming, close, approaching, gathering, forthcoming, looming, impending ≠ remote

immoral = wicked, bad, wrong, corrupt, indecent, sinful, unethical, depraved ≠ moral

immortal ADJECTIVE **1** = timeless, eternal, everlasting, lasting, traditional, classic, enduring, perennial ≠ ephemeral **2** = undying, eternal, imperishable, deathless ≠ mortal
● NOUN **1** = hero, genius, great **2** = god, goddess, deity, divine being, immortal being, atua (*N.Z.*)

immune
● PHRASES **immune from** = exempt from, free from ◆ **immune to 1** = resistant to, free from, protected from, safe from, not open to, spared from, secure against, invulnerable to **2** = unaffected by, invulnerable to

immunity 1 = exemption, amnesty, indemnity, release, freedom, invulnerability **2** *with* **to** = resistance to, protection from, resilience to, inoculation against, immunization from ≠ susceptibility to

impact NOUN **1** = effect, influence, consequences, impression, repercussions, ramifications **2** = collision, contact, crash, knock, stroke, smash, bump, thump
● VERB = hit, strike, crash, clash, crush, ram, smack, collide

impair = worsen, reduce, damage, injure, harm, undermine, weaken, diminish ≠ improve

impaired = damaged, flawed, faulty, defective, imperfect, unsound

impasse = deadlock, stalemate, standstill, dead end, standoff

impatient 1 = cross, annoyed, irritated, prickly, touchy, bad-tempered, intolerant, ill-tempered ≠ easy-going 2 = **eager**, longing, keen, anxious, hungry, enthusiastic, restless, avid ≠ calm

impeccable = **faultless**, perfect, immaculate, flawless, squeaky-clean, unblemished, unimpeachable, irreproachable ≠ flawed

impending = **looming**, coming, approaching, near, forthcoming, imminent, upcoming, in the pipeline

imperative = **urgent**, essential, pressing, vital, crucial ≠ unnecessary

imperial = **royal**, regal, kingly, queenly, princely, sovereign, majestic, monarchial

impetus 1 = **incentive**, push, spur, motivation, impulse, stimulus, catalyst, goad 2 = **force**, power, energy, momentum

implant 1 = **insert**, fix, graft 2 = **instil**, infuse, inculcate

implement VERB = **carry out**, effect, carry through, complete, apply, perform, realize, fulfil ≠ hinder
● NOUN = **tool**, machine, device, instrument, appliance, apparatus, gadget, utensil

implicate VERB = **incriminate**, involve, embroil, entangle, inculpate ≠ dissociate
● PHRASES **implicate something** or **someone in something** = **involve in**, associate with

implication NOUN = **suggestion**, hint, inference, meaning, significance, presumption, overtone, innuendo
● PLURAL NOUN = **consequences**, result, developments, upshot

implicit 1 = **implied**, understood, suggested, hinted at, taken for granted, unspoken, inferred, tacit ≠ explicit 2 = **inherent**, underlying, intrinsic, latent, ingrained, inbuilt 3 = **absolute**, full, complete, firm, fixed, constant, utter, outright

implied = **suggested**, indirect, hinted at, implicit, unspoken, tacit, undeclared, unstated

imply 1 = **suggest**, hint, insinuate, indicate, intimate, signify 2 = **involve**, mean, entail, require, indicate, point to, signify, presuppose

import VERB = **bring in**, buy in, ship in, introduce
● NOUN 1 (*Formal*) = **significance**, concern, value, weight, consequence, substance, moment, magnitude 2 = **meaning**,

implication, significance, sense, intention, substance, drift, thrust

importance 1 = **significance**, interest, concern, moment, value, weight, import, consequence 2 = **prestige**, standing, status, rule, authority, influence, distinction, esteem, mana (*N.Z.*)

important 1 = **significant**, critical, substantial, urgent, serious, far-reaching, momentous, seminal ≠ unimportant 2 = **powerful**, prominent, commanding, dominant, influential, eminent, high-ranking, authoritative

impose
● PHRASES **impose something on** or **upon someone** 1 = **levy**, introduce, charge, establish, fix, institute, decree, ordain 2 = **inflict**, force, enforce, visit, press, apply, thrust, saddle (someone) with

imposing = **impressive**, striking, grand, powerful, commanding, awesome, majestic, dignified ≠ unimposing

imposition 1 = **application**, introduction, levying 2 = **intrusion**, liberty, presumption

impossible 1 = **not possible**, out of the question, impracticable, unfeasible 2 = **unachievable**, out of the question, vain, unthinkable, inconceivable, far-fetched, unworkable, implausible ≠ possible 3 = **absurd**, crazy (*informal*), ridiculous, outrageous, ludicrous, unreasonable, preposterous, farcical

impotence = **powerlessness**, inability, helplessness, weakness, incompetence, paralysis, frailty, incapacity ≠ powerfulness

impoverish 1 = **bankrupt**, ruin, beggar, break 2 = **deplete**, drain, exhaust, diminish, use up, sap, wear out, reduce

impoverished = **poor**, needy, destitute, bankrupt, poverty-stricken, impecunious, penurious ≠ rich

impress VERB = **excite**, move, strike, touch, affect, inspire, amaze, overcome
● PHRASES **impress something on** or **upon someone** = **stress**, bring home to, instil in, drum into, knock into, emphasize to, fix in, inculcate in

impression 1 = **idea**, feeling, thought, sense, view, assessment, judgment, reaction 2 = **effect**, influence, impact 3 = **imitation**, parody, impersonation, send-up (*Brit. informal*), takeoff (*informal*) 4 = **mark**, imprint, stamp, outline, hollow, dent, indentation

impressive = grand, striking, splendid, good, great (*informal*), fine, powerful, exciting ≠ unimpressive

imprint NOUN = mark, impression, stamp, indentation
● VERB = engrave, print, stamp, impress, etch, emboss

imprison = jail, confine, detain, lock up, put away, intern, incarcerate, send down (*informal*) ≠ free

imprisoned = jailed, confined, locked up, inside (*slang*), in jail, captive, behind bars, incarcerated

imprisonment = confinement, custody, detention, captivity, incarceration

improbable 1 = doubtful, unlikely, dubious, questionable, fanciful, far-fetched, implausible ≠ probable
2 = unconvincing, weak, unbelievable, preposterous ≠ convincing

improper 1 = inappropriate, unfit, unsuitable, out of place, unwarranted, uncalled-for ≠ appropriate 2 = indecent, vulgar, suggestive, unseemly, untoward, risqué, smutty, unbecoming ≠ decent

improve 1 = enhance, better, add to, upgrade, touch up, ameliorate ≠ worsen
2 = get better, pick up, develop, advance

improvement 1 = enhancement, advancement, betterment 2 = advance, development, progress, recovery, upswing

improvise 1 = devise, contrive, concoct, throw together 2 = ad-lib, invent, busk, wing it (*informal*), play it by ear (*informal*), extemporize, speak off the cuff (*informal*)

impulse = urge, longing, wish, notion, yearning, inclination, itch, whim

inaccurate = incorrect, wrong, mistaken, faulty, unreliable, defective, erroneous, unsound ≠ accurate

inadequacy 1 = shortage, poverty, dearth, paucity, insufficiency, meagreness, scantiness 2 = incompetence, inability, deficiency, incapacity, ineffectiveness
3 = shortcoming, failing, weakness, defect, imperfection

inadequate 1 = insufficient, meagre, poor, lacking, scant, sparse, sketchy ≠ adequate 2 = incapable, incompetent, faulty, deficient, unqualified, not up to scratch (*informal*) ≠ capable

inadvertently = unintentionally, accidentally, by accident, mistakenly, unwittingly, by mistake, involuntarily

≠ deliberately

inaugural = first, opening, initial, maiden, introductory

incarnation = embodiment, manifestation, epitome, type, personification

incense = anger, infuriate, enrage, irritate, madden, inflame, rile (*informal*), make your blood boil (*informal*)

incensed = angry, furious, fuming, infuriated, enraged, maddened, indignant, irate, tooshie (*Austral. slang*), off the air (*Austral. slang*)

incentive = inducement, encouragement, spur, lure, bait, motivation, carrot (*informal*), stimulus ≠ disincentive

incident 1 = disturbance, scene, clash, disorder, confrontation, brawl, fracas, commotion 2 = adventure, drama, excitement, crisis, spectacle
3 = happening, event, affair, business, fact, matter, occasion, episode

incidentally = by the way, in passing, en passant, parenthetically, by the bye

inclination 1 = desire, longing, aspiration, craving, hankering 2 = tendency, liking, disposition, penchant, propensity, predisposition, predilection, proclivity
≠ aversion

incline VERB = predispose, influence, persuade, prejudice, sway, dispose
● NOUN = slope, rise, dip, grade, descent, ascent, gradient

inclined 1 = disposed, given, prone, likely, liable, apt, predisposed 2 = willing, minded, disposed

include 1 = contain, involve, incorporate, cover, consist of, take in, embrace, comprise ≠ exclude 2 = count 3 = add, enter, put in, insert

inclusion = addition, incorporation, introduction, insertion ≠ exclusion

inclusive = comprehensive, general, global, sweeping, blanket, umbrella, across-the-board, all-embracing ≠ limited

income = revenue, earnings, pay, returns, profits, wages, yield, proceeds

incoming 1 = arriving, landing, approaching, entering, returning, homeward ≠ departing 2 = new

incompatible = inconsistent, conflicting, contradictory, incongruous, unsuited, mismatched ≠ compatible

incompetence = ineptitude, inability,

inadequacy, incapacity, ineffectiveness, uselessness, unfitness, incapability

incompetent = <u>inept</u>, useless, incapable, floundering, bungling, unfit, ineffectual, inexpert ≠ competent

incomplete = <u>unfinished</u>, partial, wanting, deficient, imperfect, fragmentary, half-pie (*N.Z. informal*) ≠ complete

inconsistency 1 = <u>unreliability</u>, instability, unpredictability, fickleness, unsteadiness 2 = <u>incompatibility</u>, discrepancy, disparity, disagreement, variance, divergence, incongruity

inconsistent 1 = <u>changeable</u>, variable, unpredictable, unstable, erratic, fickle, capricious, unsteady ≠ consistent 2 = <u>incompatible</u>, conflicting, at odds, contradictory, incongruous, discordant, out of step, irreconcilable ≠ compatible

inconvenience NOUN = <u>trouble</u>, difficulty, bother, fuss, disadvantage, disturbance, disruption, nuisance, uphill (*S. African*)
● VERB = <u>trouble</u>, bother, disturb, upset, disrupt, put out, discommode

incorporate 1 = <u>include</u>, contain, take in, embrace, integrate, encompass, assimilate, comprise of 2 = <u>integrate</u>, include, absorb, merge, fuse, assimilate, subsume 3 = <u>blend</u>, combine, compound, mingle

incorrect = <u>false</u>, wrong, mistaken, flawed, faulty, inaccurate, untrue, erroneous ≠ correct

increase VERB 1 = <u>raise</u>, extend, boost, expand, develop, advance, strengthen, widen ≠ decrease 2 = <u>grow</u>, develop, spread, expand, swell, enlarge, escalate, multiply ≠ shrink
● NOUN = <u>growth</u>, rise, development, gain, expansion, extension, proliferation, enlargement

increasingly = <u>progressively</u>, more and more

incredible 1 (*Informal*) = <u>amazing</u>, wonderful, stunning, extraordinary, overwhelming, astonishing, staggering, sensational (*informal*) 2 = <u>unbelievable</u>, unthinkable, improbable, inconceivable, preposterous, unconvincing, unimaginable, far-fetched

incumbent NOUN = <u>holder</u>, keeper, bearer
● ADJECTIVE (*Formal*) = <u>obligatory</u>, required, necessary, essential, binding, compulsory, mandatory, imperative

incur = <u>sustain</u>, experience, suffer, gain,

earn, collect, meet with, provoke

indecent 1 = <u>obscene</u>, lewd, dirty, inappropriate, rude, crude, filthy, improper ≠ decent 2 = <u>unbecoming</u>, unsuitable, vulgar, unseemly, undignified, indecorous ≠ proper

indeed 1 = <u>certainly</u>, yes, definitely, surely, truly, undoubtedly, without doubt, indisputably 2 = <u>really</u>, actually, in fact, certainly, genuinely, in truth, in actuality

indefinitely = <u>endlessly</u>, continually, for ever, ad infinitum

independence = <u>freedom</u>, liberty, autonomy, sovereignty, self-rule, self-sufficiency, self-reliance, rangatiratanga (*N.Z.*) ≠ subjugation

independent 1 = <u>separate</u>, unattached, uncontrolled, unconstrained ≠ controlled 2 = <u>self-sufficient</u>, free, liberated, self-contained, self-reliant, self-supporting 3 = <u>self-governing</u>, free, autonomous, liberated, sovereign, self-determining, nonaligned ≠ subject

independently = <u>separately</u>, alone, solo, on your own, by yourself, unaided, individually, autonomously

indicate 1 = <u>show</u>, suggest, reveal, display, demonstrate, point to, imply, manifest 2 = <u>imply</u>, suggest, hint, intimate, signify, insinuate 3 = <u>point to</u>, point out, specify, gesture towards, designate 4 = <u>register</u>, show, record, read, express, display, demonstrate

indication = <u>sign</u>, mark, evidence, suggestion, symptom, hint, clue, manifestation

indicator = <u>sign</u>, mark, measure, guide, signal, symbol, meter, gauge

indict = <u>charge</u>, accuse, prosecute, summon, impeach, arraign

indictment = <u>charge</u>, allegation, prosecution, accusation, impeachment, summons, arraignment

indifference = <u>disregard</u>, apathy, negligence, detachment, coolness, coldness, nonchalance, aloofness ≠ concern

indifferent 1 = <u>unconcerned</u>, detached, cold, cool, callous, aloof, unmoved, unsympathetic ≠ concerned 2 = <u>mediocre</u>, ordinary, moderate, so-so (*informal*), passable, undistinguished, no great shakes (*informal*), half-pie (*N.Z. informal*) ≠ excellent

indignation = resentment, anger, rage, exasperation, pique, umbrage

indirect 1 = related, secondary, subsidiary, incidental, unintended **2** = circuitous, roundabout, curving, wandering, rambling, deviant, meandering, tortuous ≠ direct

indispensable = essential, necessary, needed, key, vital, crucial, imperative, requisite ≠ dispensable

individual ADJECTIVE **1** = separate, independent, isolated, lone, solitary ≠ collective **2** = unique, special, fresh, novel, exclusive, singular, idiosyncratic, unorthodox ≠ conventional
● NOUN = person, being, human, unit, character, soul, creature

individually = separately, independently, singly, one by one, one at a time

induce 1 = cause, produce, create, effect, lead to, occasion, generate, bring about ≠ prevent **2** = persuade, encourage, influence, convince, urge, prompt, sway, entice ≠ dissuade

indulge VERB **1** = gratify, satisfy, feed, give way to, yield to, pander to, gladden **2** = spoil, pamper, cosset, humour, give in to, coddle, mollycoddle, overindulge
● PHRASES **indulge yourself** = treat yourself, splash out, spoil yourself, luxuriate in something, overindulge yourself

indulgence 1 = luxury, treat, extravagance, favour, privilege **2** = gratification, satisfaction, fulfilment, appeasement, satiation

industrialist = capitalist, tycoon, magnate, manufacturer, captain of industry, big businessman

industry 1 = business, production, manufacturing, trade, commerce **2** = trade, world, business, service, line, field, profession, occupation **3** = diligence, effort, labour, hard work, trouble, activity, application, endeavour

ineffective 1 = unproductive, useless, futile, vain, unsuccessful, pointless, fruitless, ineffectual ≠ effective **2** = inefficient, useless, poor, powerless, unfit, worthless, inept, impotent

inefficient 1 = wasteful, uneconomical, profligate **2** = incompetent, inept, weak, bungling, ineffectual, disorganized ≠ efficient

inequality = disparity, prejudice, difference, bias, diversity, irregularity, unevenness, disproportion

inevitable = unavoidable, inescapable, inexorable, sure, certain, fixed, assured, fated ≠ avoidable

inevitably = unavoidably, naturally, necessarily, surely, certainly, as a result, automatically, consequently

inexpensive = cheap, reasonable, budget, bargain, modest, economical ≠ expensive

inexperienced = new, green, raw, callow, immature, untried, unpractised, unversed ≠ experienced

infamous = notorious, ignominious, disreputable, ill-famed ≠ esteemed

infancy = beginnings, start, birth, roots, seeds, origins, dawn, outset ≠ end

infant = baby, child, babe, toddler, tot, bairn (Scot.), littlie (Austral. informal), ankle-biter (Austral. slang), tacker (Austral. slang)

infect 1 = contaminate **2** = pollute, poison, corrupt, contaminate, taint, defile **3** = affect, move, upset, overcome, stir, disturb

infection = disease, condition, complaint, illness, virus, disorder, corruption, poison

infectious = catching, spreading, contagious, communicable, virulent, transmittable

inferior ADJECTIVE = lower, minor, secondary, subsidiary, lesser, humble, subordinate, lowly ≠ superior
● NOUN = underling, junior, subordinate, lesser, menial, minion

infertility = sterility, barrenness, unproductiveness, infecundity

infiltrate = penetrate, pervade, permeate, percolate, filter through to, make inroads into, sneak into (informal), insinuate yourself

infinite 1 = vast, enormous, immense, countless, measureless **2** = limitless, endless, unlimited, eternal, never-ending, boundless, everlasting, inexhaustible ≠ finite

inflame = enrage, stimulate, provoke, excite, anger, arouse, rouse, infuriate ≠ calm

inflamed = swollen, sore, red, hot, infected, fevered

inflate 1 = blow up, pump up, swell, dilate,

distend, bloat, puff up *or* out ≠ deflate
2 = increase, expand, enlarge ≠ diminish
3 = exaggerate, embroider, embellish, enlarge, amplify, overstate, overestimate, overemphasize

inflated = exaggerated, swollen, overblown

inflation = increase, expansion, extension, swelling, escalation, enlargement

inflict = impose, administer, visit, apply, deliver, levy, wreak, mete *or* deal out

influence NOUN **1** = control, power, authority, direction, command, domination, supremacy, mastery, mana (*N.Z.*) **2** = power, authority, pull (*informal*), importance, prestige, clout (*informal*), leverage **3** = spell, hold, power, weight, magic, sway, allure, magnetism
● VERB **1** = affect, have an effect on, have an impact on, control, concern, direct, guide, bear upon **2** = persuade, prompt, urge, induce, entice, coax, incite, instigate

influential 1 = important, powerful, telling, leading, inspiring, potent, authoritative, weighty ≠ unimportant **2** = instrumental, important, significant, crucial

influx = arrival, rush, invasion, incursion, inundation, inrush

inform VERB = tell, advise, notify, instruct, enlighten, communicate to, tip someone off
● PHRASES **inform on someone** = betray, denounce, shop (*slang, chiefly Brit.*), give someone away, incriminate, blow the whistle on (*informal*), grass on (*Brit. slang*), double-cross (*informal*), dob someone in (*Austral. & N.Z. slang*)

informal 1 = natural, relaxed, casual, familiar, unofficial, laid-back, easy-going, colloquial **2** = relaxed, easy, comfortable, simple, natural, casual, cosy, laid-back (*informal*) ≠ formal **3** = casual, comfortable, leisure, everyday, simple **4** = unofficial, irregular ≠ official

information = facts, news, report, message, notice, knowledge, data, intelligence, drum (*Austral. informal*)

informative = instructive, revealing, educational, forthcoming, illuminating, enlightening, chatty, communicative

informed = knowledgeable, up to date, enlightened, learned, expert, familiar, versed, in the picture

infuriate = enrage, anger, provoke, irritate, incense, madden, exasperate, rile ≠ soothe

infuriating = annoying, irritating, provoking, galling, maddening, exasperating, vexatious

ingenious = creative, original, brilliant, clever, bright, shrewd, inventive, crafty ≠ unimaginative

ingredient = component, part, element, feature, piece, unit, item, aspect

inhabit = live in, occupy, populate, reside in, dwell in, abide in

inhabitant = occupant, resident, citizen, local, native, tenant, inmate, dweller

inhabited = populated, peopled, occupied, developed, settled, tenanted, colonized

inhale = breathe in, gasp, draw in, suck in, respire ≠ exhale

inherent = intrinsic, natural, essential, native, fundamental, hereditary, instinctive, innate ≠ extraneous

inherit = be left, come into, be willed, succeed to, fall heir to

inheritance = legacy, heritage, bequest, birthright, patrimony

inhibit 1 = hinder, check, frustrate, curb, restrain, constrain, obstruct, impede ≠ further **2** = prevent, stop, frustrate ≠ allow

inhibited = shy, reserved, guarded, subdued, repressed, constrained, self-conscious, reticent ≠ uninhibited

initial = opening, first, earliest, beginning, primary, maiden, introductory, embryonic ≠ final

initially = at first, first, firstly, originally, primarily, in the beginning, at *or* in the beginning

initiate VERB **1** = begin, start, open, launch, kick off (*informal*), embark on, originate, set about **2** = introduce, admit, enlist, enrol, launch, establish, invest, recruit
● NOUN = novice, member, pupil, convert, amateur, newcomer, beginner, trainee
● PHRASES **initiate someone into something** = instruct in, train in, coach in, acquaint with, drill in, make aware of, teach about, tutor in

initiative 1 = advantage, start, lead, upper hand **2** = enterprise, drive, energy, leadership, ambition, daring, enthusiasm, dynamism

inject 1 = <u>vaccinate</u>, administer, inoculate
2 = <u>introduce</u>, bring in, insert, instil, infuse, breathe

injection 1 = <u>vaccination</u>, shot (*informal*), jab (*informal*), dose, booster, immunization, inoculation
2 = <u>introduction</u>, investment, insertion, advancement, dose, infusion

injunction = <u>order</u>, ruling, command, instruction, mandate, precept, exhortation

injure 1 = <u>hurt</u>, wound, harm, damage, smash, crush, mar, shatter, mangulate (*Austral. slang*) 2 = <u>damage</u>, harm, ruin, wreck, spoil, impair, crool *or* cruel (*Austral. slang*) 3 = <u>undermine</u>, damage

injured = <u>hurt</u>, damaged, wounded, broken, cut, crushed, disabled, weakened, crook (*Austral. & N.Z. slang*)

injury 1 = <u>wound</u>, cut, damage, trauma (*Pathology*), gash, lesion, laceration
2 = <u>harm</u>, suffering, damage, ill, hurt, disability, misfortune, affliction 3 = <u>wrong</u>, offence, insult, detriment, disservice

injustice 1 = <u>unfairness</u>, discrimination, prejudice, bias, inequality, oppression, intolerance, bigotry ≠ justice 2 = <u>wrong</u>, injury, crime, error, offence, sin, misdeed, transgression

inland = <u>interior</u>, internal, upcountry

inner 1 = <u>inside</u>, internal, interior, inward ≠ outer 2 = <u>central</u>, middle, internal, interior 3 = <u>hidden</u>, deep, secret, underlying, obscure, repressed, unrevealed ≠ obvious

innocence 1 = <u>naiveté</u>, simplicity, inexperience, credulity, gullibility, ingenuousness, artlessness, unworldliness ≠ worldliness 2 = <u>blamelessness</u>, clean hands, uprightness, irreproachability, guiltlessness ≠ guilt 3 = <u>chastity</u>, virtue, purity, modesty, celibacy, continence, maidenhood

innocent 1 = <u>not guilty</u>, in the clear, blameless, clean, honest, uninvolved, irreproachable, guiltless ≠ guilty 2 = <u>naive</u>, open, trusting, simple, childlike, gullible, unsophisticated, unworldly ≠ worldly
3 = <u>harmless</u>, innocuous, inoffensive, well-meant, unobjectionable, well-intentioned

innovation 1 = <u>change</u>, revolution, departure, introduction, variation, transformation, upheaval, alteration
2 = <u>newness</u>, novelty, originality, freshness, modernization, uniqueness

inquest = <u>inquiry</u>, investigation, probe, inquisition

inquire *or* **enquire** VERB = <u>ask</u>, question, query, quiz
● PHRASES **inquire into something**
= <u>investigate</u>, study, examine, research, explore, look into, probe into, make inquiries into

inquiry *or* **enquiry** 1 = <u>question</u>, query, investigation 2 = <u>investigation</u>, study, review, survey, examination, probe, inspection, exploration 3 = <u>research</u>, investigation, analysis, inspection, exploration, interrogation

insane 1 = <u>mad</u>, crazy, mentally ill, crazed, demented, deranged, out of your mind, off the air (*Austral. slang*), porangi (*N.Z.*) ≠ sane 2 = <u>stupid</u>, foolish, daft (*informal*), irresponsible, irrational, senseless, preposterous, impractical ≠ reasonable

insect = <u>bug</u>, creepy-crawly (*Brit. informal*), gogga (*S. African informal*)

insecure 1 = <u>unconfident</u>, worried, anxious, afraid, shy, uncertain, unsure, timid ≠ confident 2 = <u>unsafe</u>, exposed, vulnerable, wide-open, unprotected, defenceless, unguarded ≠ safe

insecurity = <u>anxiety</u>, fear, worry, uncertainty ≠ confidence

insert = <u>put</u>, place, position, slip, slide, slot, thrust, stick in

inside NOUN = <u>interior</u>, contents, core, nucleus
● PLURAL NOUN (*Informal*) = <u>stomach</u>, guts, belly, bowels, innards (*informal*), entrails, viscera, vitals
● ADJECTIVE 1 = <u>inner</u>, internal, interior, inward ≠ outside 2 = <u>confidential</u>, private, secret, internal, exclusive, restricted, privileged, classified
● ADVERB = <u>indoors</u>, in, within, under cover

insight 1 = <u>understanding</u>, perception, sense, knowledge, vision, judgment, awareness, grasp 2 *with* **into**
= <u>understanding of</u>, perception of, awareness of, experience of, description of, introduction to, observation of, judgment of

insignificant = <u>unimportant</u>, minor, irrelevant, petty, trivial, meaningless, trifling, paltry ≠ important

insist 1 lay down the law, put your foot down (*informal*) 2 = <u>demand</u>, order, require, command, dictate, entreat

3 = <u>assert</u>, state, maintain, claim, declare, repeat, vow, swear

insistence 1 = <u>demand</u>, command, dictate, entreaty, importunity **2** = <u>assertion</u>, claim, statement, declaration, persistence, pronouncement

inspect 1 = <u>examine</u>, check, look at, view, survey, look over, scrutinize, go over or through **2** = <u>check</u>, examine, investigate, look at, survey, vet, look over, go over or through

inspection 1 = <u>examination</u>, investigation, scrutiny, once-over (*informal*) **2** = <u>check</u>, search, investigation, review, survey, examination, scrutiny, once-over (*informal*)

inspector = <u>examiner</u>, investigator, supervisor, monitor, superintendent, auditor, censor, surveyor

inspiration 1 = <u>imagination</u>, creativity, ingenuity, insight, originality, inventiveness, cleverness **2** = <u>motivation</u>, example, model, boost, spur, incentive, revelation, stimulus ≠ deterrent **3** = <u>influence</u>, spur, stimulus, muse

inspire 1 = <u>motivate</u>, stimulate, encourage, influence, spur, animate, enliven, galvanize ≠ discourage **2** = <u>give rise to</u>, produce, result in, engender

inspired 1 = <u>brilliant</u>, wonderful, impressive, outstanding, thrilling, memorable, dazzling, superlative **2** = <u>stimulated</u>, uplifted, exhilarated, enthused, elated

inspiring = <u>uplifting</u>, exciting, moving, stirring, stimulating, rousing, exhilarating, heartening ≠ uninspiring

instability 1 = <u>uncertainty</u>, insecurity, vulnerability, volatility, unpredictability, fluctuation, impermanence, unsteadiness ≠ stability **2** = <u>imbalance</u>, variability, unpredictability, unsteadiness, changeableness

install 1 = <u>set up</u>, put in, place, position, station, establish, lay, fix **2** = <u>institute</u>, establish, introduce, invest, ordain, inaugurate, induct **3** = <u>settle</u>, position, plant, establish, lodge, ensconce

installation 1 = <u>setting up</u>, fitting, instalment, placing, positioning, establishment **2** = <u>appointment</u>, ordination, inauguration, induction, investiture

instalment 1 = <u>payment</u>, repayment, part payment **2** = <u>part</u>, section, chapter, episode, portion, division

instance NOUN = <u>example</u>, case, occurrence, occasion, sample, illustration
● VERB = <u>name</u>, mention, identify, point out, advance, quote, refer to, point to

instant NOUN **1** = <u>moment</u>, second, flash, split second, jiffy (*informal*), trice, twinkling of an eye (*informal*) **2** = <u>time</u>, point, hour, moment, stage, occasion, phase, juncture
● ADJECTIVE **1** = <u>immediate</u>, prompt, instantaneous, direct, quick, on-the-spot, split-second **2** = <u>ready-made</u>, fast, convenience, ready-mixed, ready-cooked, precooked

instantly = <u>immediately</u>, at once, straight away, now, directly, right away, instantaneously, this minute

instead ADVERB = <u>rather</u>, alternatively, preferably, in preference, in lieu, on second thoughts
● PHRASES **instead of** = <u>in place of</u>, rather than, in preference to, in lieu of, in contrast with

instinct 1 = <u>natural inclination</u>, talent, tendency, faculty, inclination, knack, predisposition, proclivity **2** = <u>talent</u>, skill, gift, capacity, bent, genius, faculty, knack **3** = <u>intuition</u>, impulse

instinctive = <u>natural</u>, inborn, automatic, unconscious, inherent, spontaneous, reflex, innate ≠ acquired

instinctively = <u>intuitively</u>, naturally, automatically, without thinking, involuntarily, by instinct

institute NOUN = <u>establishment</u>, body, centre, school, university, society, association, college
● VERB = <u>establish</u>, start, found, launch, set up, introduce, fix, organize ≠ end

institution 1 = <u>establishment</u>, body, centre, school, university, society, association, college **2** = <u>custom</u>, practice, tradition, law, rule, procedure, convention, ritual

institutional = <u>conventional</u>, accepted, established, formal, routine, orthodox, procedural

instruct 1 = <u>order</u>, tell, direct, charge, bid, command, mandate, enjoin **2** = <u>teach</u>, school, train, coach, educate, drill, tutor

instruction NOUN **1** = <u>order</u>, ruling, command, rule, demand, regulation,

dictate, decree **2** = <u>teaching</u>, schooling, training, grounding, education, coaching, lesson(s), guidance
● **PLURAL NOUN** = <u>information</u>, rules, advice, directions, recommendations, guidance, specifications
instructor = <u>teacher</u>, coach, guide, adviser, trainer, demonstrator, tutor, mentor
instrument 1 = <u>tool</u>, device, implement, mechanism, appliance, apparatus, gadget, contraption (*informal*) **2** = <u>agent</u>, means, medium, agency, vehicle, mechanism, organ
instrumental = <u>active</u>, involved, influential, useful, helpful, contributory
insufficient = <u>inadequate</u>, scant, meagre, short, sparse, deficient, lacking ≠ ample
insulate = <u>isolate</u>, protect, screen, defend, shelter, shield, cut off, cushion
insult VERB = <u>offend</u>, abuse, wound, slight, put down, snub, malign, affront ≠ praise
● **NOUN 1** = <u>jibe</u>, slight, put-down, abuse, snub, barb, affront, abusive remark
2 = <u>offence</u>, slight, snub, slur, affront, slap in the face (*informal*), kick in the teeth (*informal*), insolence
insulting = <u>offensive</u>, rude, abusive, degrading, contemptuous, disparaging, scurrilous, insolent ≠ complimentary
insurance 1 = <u>assurance</u>, cover, security, protection, safeguard, indemnity
2 = <u>protection</u>, security, guarantee, shelter, safeguard, warranty
insure 1 = <u>assure</u>, cover, protect, guarantee, warrant, underwrite, indemnify
2 = <u>protect</u>, cover, safeguard
intact = <u>undamaged</u>, whole, complete, sound, perfect, entire, unscathed, unbroken ≠ damaged
integral = <u>essential</u>, basic, fundamental, necessary, component, constituent, indispensable, intrinsic ≠ inessential
integrate = <u>join</u>, unite, combine, blend, incorporate, merge, fuse, assimilate ≠ separate
integrity 1 = <u>honesty</u>, principle, honour, virtue, goodness, morality, purity, probity ≠ dishonesty **2** = <u>unity</u>, unification, cohesion, coherence, wholeness, soundness, completeness
intellect = <u>intelligence</u>, mind, reason, understanding, sense, brains (*informal*), judgment

intellectual ADJECTIVE = <u>scholarly</u>, learned, academic, lettered, intelligent, cerebral, erudite, scholastic ≠ stupid
● **NOUN** = <u>academic</u>, expert, genius, thinker, master, mastermind, maestro, highbrow, fundi (*S. African*), acca (*Austral. slang*) ≠ idiot
intelligence 1 = <u>intellect</u>, understanding, brains (*informal*), sense, knowledge, judgment, wit, perception ≠ stupidity
2 = <u>information</u>, news, facts, report, findings, knowledge, data, notification ≠ misinformation
intelligent = <u>clever</u>, bright, smart, sharp, enlightened, knowledgeable, well-informed, brainy (*informal*) ≠ stupid
intend = <u>plan</u>, mean, aim, propose, purpose, have in mind *or* view
intense 1 = <u>extreme</u>, great, severe, fierce, deep, powerful, supreme, acute ≠ mild **2** = <u>fierce</u>, tough **3** = <u>passionate</u>, emotional, fierce, heightened, ardent, fanatical, fervent, heartfelt ≠ indifferent
intensify 1 = <u>increase</u>, raise, add to, strengthen, reinforce, widen, heighten, sharpen ≠ decrease **2** = <u>escalate</u>, increase, widen, deepen
intensity 1 = <u>force</u>, strength, fierceness **2** = <u>passion</u>, emotion, fervour, force, strength, fanaticism, ardour, vehemence
intensive = <u>concentrated</u>, thorough, exhaustive, full, demanding, detailed, complete, serious
intent ADJECTIVE = <u>absorbed</u>, intense, fascinated, preoccupied, enthralled, attentive, watchful, engrossed ≠ indifferent
● **NOUN** = <u>intention</u>, aim, purpose, meaning, end, plan, goal, design ≠ chance
intention = <u>aim</u>, plan, idea, goal, end, design, target, wish
inter = <u>bury</u>, lay to rest, entomb, consign to the grave
intercept = <u>catch</u>, stop, block, seize, cut off, interrupt, head off, obstruct
intercourse 1 = <u>sexual intercourse</u>, sex (*informal*), copulation, coitus, carnal knowledge **2** = <u>contact</u>, communication, commerce, dealings
interest NOUN 1 *often plural* = <u>hobby</u>, activity, pursuit, entertainment, recreation, amusement, preoccupation, diversion
2 *often plural* = <u>advantage</u>, good, benefit, profit **3** = <u>stake</u>, investment

● VERB = <u>arouse your curiosity</u>, fascinate, attract, grip, entertain, intrigue, divert, captivate ≠ bore

interested 1 = <u>curious</u>, attracted, excited, drawn, keen, gripped, fascinated, captivated ≠ uninterested 2 = <u>involved</u>, concerned, affected, implicated

interesting = <u>intriguing</u>, absorbing, appealing, attractive, engaging, gripping, entrancing, stimulating ≠ uninteresting

interface = <u>connection</u>, link, boundary, border, frontier

interfere VERB = <u>meddle</u>, intervene, intrude, butt in, tamper, pry, encroach, stick your oar in (*informal*)

● PHRASES **interfere with something** *or* **someone** = <u>conflict with</u>, check, clash, handicap, hamper, disrupt, inhibit, thwart

interference = <u>intrusion</u>, intervention, meddling, opposition, conflict, obstruction, prying

interim = <u>temporary</u>, provisional, makeshift, acting, caretaker, improvised, stopgap

interior NOUN = <u>inside</u>, centre, heart, middle, depths, core, nucleus

● ADJECTIVE 1 = <u>inside</u>, internal, inner ≠ exterior 2 = <u>mental</u>, emotional, psychological, private, personal, secret, hidden, spiritual

intermediary = <u>mediator</u>, agent, middleman, broker, go-between

intermediate = <u>middle</u>, mid, halfway, in-between (*informal*), midway, intervening, transitional, median

internal 1 = <u>domestic</u>, home, national, local, civic, in-house, intramural 2 = <u>inner</u>, inside, interior ≠ external

international = <u>global</u>, world, worldwide, universal, cosmopolitan, intercontinental

Internet

● PHRASES **the Internet** = <u>the information superhighway</u>, the net (*informal*), the web (*informal*), the World Wide Web, cyberspace

interpret 1 = <u>take</u>, understand, explain, construe 2 = <u>translate</u>, transliterate 3 = <u>explain</u>, make sense of, decode, decipher, elucidate 4 = <u>understand</u>, read, crack, solve, figure out (*informal*), comprehend, decode, deduce 5 = <u>portray</u>, present, perform, render, depict, enact, act out

interpretation 1 = <u>explanation</u>, analysis,

exposition, elucidation 2 = <u>performance</u>, portrayal, presentation, reading, rendition 3 = <u>reading</u>, study, review, version, analysis, explanation, examination, evaluation

interpreter = <u>translator</u>

interrogation = <u>questioning</u>, inquiry, examination, grilling (*informal*), cross-examination, inquisition, third degree (*informal*)

interrupt 1 = <u>intrude</u>, disturb, intervene, interfere (with), break in, heckle, butt in, barge in (*informal*) 2 = <u>suspend</u>, stop, end, delay, cease, postpone, shelve, put off

interruption 1 = <u>disruption</u>, break, disturbance, hitch, intrusion 2 = <u>stoppage</u>, pause, suspension

interval 1 = <u>period</u>, spell, space, stretch, pause, span 2 = <u>break</u>, interlude, intermission, rest, gap, pause, respite, lull 3 = <u>delay</u>, gap, hold-up, stoppage 4 = <u>stretch</u>, space

intervene 1 = <u>step in</u> (*informal*), interfere, mediate, intrude, intercede, arbitrate, take a hand (*informal*) 2 = <u>interrupt</u>, involve yourself 3 = <u>happen</u>, occur, take place, follow, arise, ensue, befall, materialize

intervention = <u>mediation</u>, interference, intrusion, arbitration, conciliation, agency

interview NOUN 1 = <u>meeting</u> 2 = <u>audience</u>, talk, conference, exchange, dialogue, consultation, press conference

● VERB 1 = <u>examine</u>, talk to 2 = <u>question</u>, interrogate, examine, investigate, pump, grill (*informal*), quiz, cross-examine

interviewer = <u>questioner</u>, reporter, investigator, examiner, interrogator

intimacy = <u>familiarity</u>, closeness, confidentiality ≠ aloofness

intimate¹ ADJECTIVE 1 = <u>close</u>, dear, loving, near, familiar, thick (*informal*), devoted, confidential ≠ distant 2 = <u>private</u>, personal, confidential, special, individual, secret, exclusive ≠ public 3 = <u>detailed</u>, minute, full, deep, particular, immediate, comprehensive, profound 4 = <u>cosy</u>, relaxed, friendly, informal, harmonious, snug, comfy (*informal*), warm

● NOUN = <u>friend</u>, close friend, crony, cobber (*Austral. & N.Z. old-fashioned informal*), confidant *or* confidante, (constant) companion, E hoa (*N.Z.*) ≠ stranger

intimate² 1 = <u>suggest</u>, indicate, hint, imply, insinuate 2 = <u>announce</u>, state,

declare, communicate, make known
intimately 1 = <u>closely</u>, personally, warmly, familiarly, tenderly, affectionately, confidentially, confidingly 2 = <u>fully</u>, very well, thoroughly, in detail, inside out
intimidate = <u>frighten</u>, pressure, threaten, scare, bully, plague, hound, daunt
intimidation = <u>bullying</u>, pressure, threat(s), menaces, coercion, arm-twisting (*informal*), browbeating, terrorization
intricate = <u>complicated</u>, involved, complex, fancy, elaborate, tangled, tortuous, convoluted ≠ simple
intrigue NOUN 1 = <u>plot</u>, scheme, conspiracy, manoeuvre, collusion, stratagem, chicanery, wile 2 = <u>affair</u>, romance, intimacy, liaison, amour
● VERB 1 = <u>interest</u>, fascinate, attract, rivet, titillate 2 = <u>plot</u>, scheme, manoeuvre, conspire, connive, machinate
intriguing = <u>interesting</u>, fascinating, absorbing, exciting, engaging, gripping, stimulating, compelling
introduce 1 = <u>bring in</u>, establish, set up, start, found, launch, institute, pioneer 2 = <u>present</u>, acquaint, make known, familiarize 3 = <u>suggest</u>, air, advance, submit, bring up, put forward, broach, moot 4 = <u>add</u>, insert, inject, throw in (*informal*), infuse
introduction 1 = <u>launch</u>, institution, pioneering, inauguration ≠ elimination 2 = <u>opening</u>, prelude, preface, lead-in, preamble, foreword, prologue, intro (*informal*) ≠ conclusion
introductory 1 = <u>preliminary</u>, first, initial, inaugural, preparatory ≠ concluding 2 = <u>starting</u>, opening, initial
intruder = <u>trespasser</u>, invader, prowler, interloper, infiltrator, gate-crasher (*informal*)
intrusion 1 = <u>interruption</u>, interference, infringement, trespass, encroachment 2 = <u>invasion</u>, breach, infringement, encroachment, infraction, usurpation
intuition 1 = <u>instinct</u>, perception, insight, sixth sense 2 = <u>feeling</u>, idea, impression, suspicion, premonition, inkling, presentiment
invade 1 = <u>attack</u>, storm, assault, capture, occupy, seize, raid, overwhelm 2 = <u>infest</u>, swarm, overrun, ravage, beset, pervade, permeate
invader = <u>attacker</u>, raider, plunderer,

aggressor, trespasser
invalid¹ NOUN = <u>patient</u>, sufferer, convalescent, valetudinarian
● ADJECTIVE = <u>disabled</u>, ill, sick, ailing, frail, infirm, bedridden
invalid² 1 = <u>null and void</u>, void, worthless, inoperative ≠ valid 2 = <u>unfounded</u>, false, illogical, irrational, unsound, fallacious ≠ sound
invaluable = <u>precious</u>, valuable, priceless, inestimable, worth your *or* its weight in gold ≠ worthless
invariably = <u>always</u>, regularly, constantly, repeatedly, consistently, continually, eternally, habitually
invasion 1 = <u>attack</u>, assault, capture, takeover, raid, offensive, occupation, conquering 2 = <u>intrusion</u>, breach, violation, disturbance, disruption, infringement, encroachment, infraction
invent 1 = <u>create</u>, make, produce, design, discover, manufacture, devise, conceive 2 = <u>make up</u>, devise, concoct, forge, fake, fabricate, feign, falsify
invention 1 = <u>creation</u>, machine, device, design, instrument, discovery, innovation, gadget 2 = <u>development</u>, design, production, setting up, foundation, construction, creation, discovery 3 = <u>fiction</u>, fantasy, lie, yarn, fabrication, falsehood, untruth 4 = <u>creativity</u>, imagination, initiative, enterprise, genius, ingenuity, originality, inventiveness
inventive = <u>creative</u>, original, innovative, imaginative, inspired, fertile, ingenious, resourceful ≠ uninspired
inventor = <u>creator</u>, maker, author, designer, architect, coiner, originator
inventory = <u>list</u>, record, catalogue, listing, account, roll, file, register
invest VERB 1 = <u>spend</u>, expend, advance, venture, put in, devote, lay out, sink in 2 = <u>empower</u>, provide, charge, sanction, license, authorize, vest
● PHRASES **invest in something** = <u>buy</u>, get, purchase, pay for, obtain, acquire, procure
investigate = <u>examine</u>, study, research, go into, explore, look into, inspect, probe into
investigation = <u>examination</u>, study, inquiry, review, search, survey, probe, inspection
investigator = <u>examiner</u>, researcher,

monitor, detective, analyser, explorer, scrutinizer, inquirer

investment 1 = investing, backing, funding, financing, contribution, speculation, transaction, expenditure 2 = stake, interest, share, concern, portion, ante (*informal*) 3 = buy, asset, acquisition, venture, risk, gamble

invisible = unseen, imperceptible, indiscernible, unseeable ≠ visible

invitation = request, call, invite (*informal*), summons

invite 1 = ask 2 = request, look for, bid for, appeal for 3 = encourage, attract, cause, court, ask for (*informal*), generate, foster, tempt

inviting = tempting, appealing, attractive, welcoming, enticing, seductive, alluring, mouthwatering ≠ uninviting

invoke 1 = apply, use, implement, initiate, resort to, put into effect 2 = call upon, appeal to, pray to, petition, beseech, entreat, supplicate

involve 1 = entail, mean, require, occasion, imply, give rise to, necessitate 2 = concern, draw in, bear on

involved = complicated, complex, intricate, hard, confused, confusing, elaborate, tangled ≠ straightforward

involvement = connection, interest, association, commitment, attachment

inward 1 = incoming, entering, inbound, ingoing 2 = internal, inner, private, personal, inside, secret, hidden, interior ≠ outward

Ireland = Hibernia (*Latin*)

iron ADJECTIVE 1 = ferrous, ferric 2 = inflexible, hard, strong, tough, rigid, adamant, unconditional, steely ≠ weak
● PHRASES **iron something out** = settle, resolve, sort out, get rid of, reconcile, clear up, put right, straighten out
▇ RELATED WORDS
adjectives: ferric, ferrous

ironic or **ironical** 1 = sarcastic, dry, acid, bitter, mocking, wry, satirical, tongue-in-cheek 2 = paradoxical, contradictory, puzzling, baffling, confounding, enigmatic, incongruous

irony 1 = sarcasm, mockery, ridicule, satire, cynicism, derision 2 = paradox, incongruity

irrational = illogical, crazy, absurd, unreasonable, preposterous, nonsensical ≠ rational

irregular 1 = variable, erratic, occasional, random, casual, shaky, sporadic, haphazard ≠ steady 2 = uneven, rough, ragged, crooked, jagged, bumpy, contorted, lopsided ≠ even 3 = inappropriate, unconventional, unethical, unusual, extraordinary, exceptional, peculiar, unofficial 4 = unofficial, underground, guerrilla, resistance, partisan, rogue, paramilitary, mercenary

irrelevant = unconnected, unrelated, unimportant, inappropriate, peripheral, immaterial, extraneous, beside the point ≠ relevant

irresistible = overwhelming, compelling, overpowering, urgent, compulsive

irresponsible = thoughtless, reckless, careless, unreliable, untrustworthy, shiftless, scatterbrained ≠ responsible

irritate 1 = annoy, anger, bother, needle (*informal*), infuriate, exasperate, nettle, irk ≠ placate 2 = inflame, pain, rub, scratch, scrape, chafe

irritated = annoyed, cross, angry, bothered, put out, exasperated, nettled, vexed, tooshie (*Austral. slang*), hoha (*N.Z.*)

irritating = annoying, trying, infuriating, disturbing, nagging, troublesome, maddening, irksome ≠ pleasing

irritation 1 = annoyance, anger, fury, resentment, gall, indignation, displeasure, exasperation ≠ pleasure 2 = nuisance, irritant, drag (*informal*), pain in the neck (*informal*), thorn in your flesh

island = underline{isle}, atoll, islet, ait or eyot (*dialect*), cay or key
▇ RELATED WORD
adjective: insular

isolate 1 = separate, break up, cut off, detach, split up, insulate, segregate, disconnect 2 = quarantine

isolated = remote, far, distant, lonely, out-of-the-way, hidden, secluded, inaccessible

isolation = separation, segregation, detachment, solitude, seclusion, remoteness

issue NOUN 1 = topic, point, matter, problem, question, subject, theme 2 = point, question, bone of contention 3 = edition, printing, copy, publication, number, version 4 = children, offspring, babies, kids (*informal*), heirs, descendants,

progeny ≠ parent

● VERB = <u>give out</u>, release, publish, announce, deliver, spread, broadcast, distribute

● PHRASES **take issue with something** or **someone** = <u>disagree with</u>, question, challenge, oppose, dispute, object to, argue with, take exception to

itch VERB 1 = <u>prickle</u>, tickle, tingle 2 = <u>long</u>, ache, crave, pine, hunger, lust, yearn, hanker

● NOUN 1 = <u>irritation</u>, tingling, prickling, itchiness 2 = <u>desire</u>, longing, craving, passion, yen (*informal*), hunger, lust, yearning

item 1 = <u>article</u>, thing, object, piece, unit, component 2 = <u>matter</u>, point, issue, case, question, concern, detail, subject 3 = <u>report</u>, story, piece, account, note, feature, notice, article

itinerary = <u>schedule</u>, programme, route, timetable

jab VERB = <u>poke</u>, dig, punch, thrust, tap, stab, nudge, prod

● NOUN = <u>poke</u>, dig, punch, thrust, tap, stab, nudge, prod

jacket = <u>covering</u>, casing, case, cover, skin, shell, coat, wrapping

jackpot = <u>prize</u>, winnings, award, reward, bonanza

jail NOUN = <u>prison</u>, penitentiary (*U.S.*), confinement, dungeon, nick (*Brit. slang*), slammer (*slang*), reformatory, boob (*Austral. slang*)

● VERB = <u>imprison</u>, confine, detain, lock up, put away, intern, incarcerate, send down

jam NOUN = <u>predicament</u>, tight spot, situation, trouble, hole (*slang*), fix (*informal*), mess, pinch

● VERB 1 = <u>pack</u>, force, press, stuff, squeeze, ram, wedge, cram 2 = <u>crowd</u>, throng, crush, mass, surge, flock, swarm,

congregate 3 = <u>congest</u>, block, clog, stick, stall, obstruct

jar¹ = <u>pot</u>, container, drum, vase, jug, pitcher, urn, crock

jar² 1 *usually with on* = <u>irritate</u>, annoy, offend, nettle, irk, grate on, get on your nerves (*informal*) 2 = <u>jolt</u>, rock, shake, bump, rattle, vibrate, convulse

jargon = <u>parlance</u>, idiom, usage, argot

jaw PLURAL NOUN = <u>opening</u>, entrance, mouth

● VERB (*Informal*) = <u>talk</u>, chat, gossip, chatter, spout, natter

jealous 1 = <u>suspicious</u>, protective, wary, doubtful, sceptical, vigilant, watchful, possessive ≠ trusting 2 = <u>envious</u>, grudging, resentful, green, green with envy, desirous, covetous ≠ satisfied

jealousy = <u>suspicion</u>, mistrust, possessiveness, doubt, spite, resentment, wariness, dubiety

jeer VERB = <u>mock</u>, deride, heckle, barrack, ridicule, taunt, scoff, gibe ≠ cheer

● NOUN = <u>mockery</u>, abuse, ridicule, taunt, boo, derision, gibe, catcall ≠ applause

jeopardy = <u>danger</u>, risk, peril, vulnerability, insecurity

jerk VERB = <u>jolt</u>, bang, bump, lurch

● NOUN = <u>lurch</u>, movement, thrust, twitch, jolt

jet NOUN = <u>stream</u>, current, spring, flow, rush, flood, burst, spray

● VERB = <u>fly</u>, wing, cruise, soar, zoom

jewel 1 = <u>gemstone</u>, gem, ornament, sparkler (*informal*), rock (*slang*) 2 = <u>treasure</u>, wonder, darling, pearl, gem, paragon, pride and joy, taonga (*N.Z.*)

jewellery = <u>jewels</u>, treasure, gems, trinkets, ornaments, finery, regalia

job 1 = <u>position</u>, work, calling, business, field, career, employment, profession 2 = <u>task</u>, duty, work, venture, enterprise, undertaking, assignment, chore

jobless = <u>unemployed</u>, redundant, out of work, inactive, unoccupied, idle

jog 1 = <u>run</u>, trot, canter, lope 2 = <u>nudge</u>, push, shake, prod 3 = <u>stimulate</u>, stir, prod

join 1 = <u>enrol in</u>, enter, sign up for, enlist in 2 = <u>connect</u>, unite, couple, link, combine, attach, fasten, add ≠ detach

joint ADJECTIVE = <u>shared</u>, mutual, collective, communal, united, joined, allied, combined

● NOUN = <u>junction</u>, connection, brace,

bracket, hinge, intersection, node, nexus

jointly = <u>collectively</u>, together, in conjunction, as one, in common, mutually, in partnership, in league ≠ separately

joke NOUN 1 = <u>jest</u>, gag (*informal*), wisecrack (*informal*), witticism, crack (*informal*), quip, pun, one-liner (*informal*) 2 = <u>laugh</u>, jest, jape 3 = <u>prank</u>, trick, practical joke, lark (*informal*), escapade, jape 4 = <u>laughing stock</u>, clown, buffoon

● VERB = <u>jest</u>, kid (*informal*), mock, tease, taunt, quip, banter, play the fool

joker = <u>comedian</u>, comic, wit, clown, wag, jester, prankster, buffoon

jolly = <u>happy</u>, cheerful, merry, upbeat (*informal*), playful, cheery, genial, chirpy (*informal*) ≠ miserable

jolt VERB 1 = <u>jerk</u>, push, shake, knock, jar, shove, jog, jostle 2 = <u>surprise</u>, stun, disturb, stagger, startle, perturb, discompose

● NOUN 1 = <u>jerk</u>, start, jump, shake, bump, jar, jog, lurch 2 = <u>surprise</u>, blow, shock, setback, bombshell, bolt from the blue

journal 1 = <u>magazine</u>, publication, gazette, periodical 2 = <u>newspaper</u>, paper, daily, weekly, monthly 3 = <u>diary</u>, record, history, log, notebook, chronicle, annals, yearbook

journalist = <u>reporter</u>, writer, correspondent, newsman *or* newswoman, commentator, broadcaster, hack (*derogatory*), columnist

journey NOUN 1 = <u>trip</u>, drive, tour, flight, excursion, trek, expedition, voyage 2 = <u>progress</u>, voyage, pilgrimage, odyssey

● VERB = <u>travel</u>, go, move, tour, progress, proceed, wander, trek, go walkabout (*Austral.*)

joy = <u>delight</u>, pleasure, satisfaction, ecstasy, enjoyment, bliss, glee, rapture ≠ sorrow

jubilee = <u>celebration</u>, holiday, festival, festivity

judge NOUN 1 = <u>magistrate</u>, justice, beak (*Brit. slang*), His, Her *or* Your Honour 2 = <u>referee</u>, expert, specialist, umpire, mediator, examiner, connoisseur, assessor 3 = <u>critic</u>, assessor, arbiter

● VERB 1 = <u>adjudicate</u>, referee, umpire, mediate, officiate, arbitrate 2 = <u>evaluate</u>, rate, consider, view, value, esteem 3 = <u>estimate</u>, guess, assess, calculate,

evaluate, gauge

▬▬ RELATED WORD
adjective: judicial

judgment 1 = <u>opinion</u>, view, estimate, belief, assessment, diagnosis, valuation, appraisal 2 = <u>verdict</u>, finding, ruling, decision, sentence, decree, arbitration, adjudication 3 = <u>sense</u>, good sense, understanding, discrimination, perception, wisdom, wit, prudence

judicial = <u>legal</u>, official

jug = <u>container</u>, pitcher, urn, carafe, creamer (*U.S. & Canad.*), vessel, jar, crock

juggle = <u>manipulate</u>, change, alter, modify, manoeuvre

juice 1 = <u>liquid</u>, extract, fluid, liquor, sap, nectar 2 = <u>secretion</u>

juicy 1 = <u>moist</u>, lush, succulent 2 (*Informal*) = <u>interesting</u>, colourful, sensational, vivid, provocative, spicy (*informal*), suggestive, racy

jumble NOUN = <u>muddle</u>, mixture, mess, disorder, confusion, clutter, disarray, mishmash

● VERB = <u>mix</u>, mistake, confuse, disorder, shuffle, muddle, disorganize

jumbo = <u>giant</u>, large, huge, immense, gigantic, oversized ≠ tiny

jump VERB 1 = <u>leap</u>, spring, bound, bounce, hop, skip 2 = <u>vault</u>, hurdle, go over, sail over, hop over 3 = <u>spring</u>, bound, bounce 4 = <u>recoil</u>, start, jolt, flinch, shake, jerk, quake, shudder 5 = <u>increase</u>, rise, climb, escalate, advance, soar, surge, spiral 6 = <u>miss</u>, avoid, skip, omit, evade

● NOUN 1 = <u>leap</u>, spring, skip, bound, hop, vault 2 = <u>rise</u>, increase, upswing, advance, upsurge, upturn, increment

jumped-up = <u>conceited</u>, arrogant, pompous, overbearing, presumptuous, insolent

jumper = <u>sweater</u>, top, jersey, cardigan, woolly, pullover

junior 1 = <u>minor</u>, lower, secondary, lesser, subordinate, inferior 2 = <u>younger</u> ≠ senior

junk = <u>rubbish</u>, refuse, waste, scrap, litter, debris, garbage (*chiefly U.S.*), trash

jurisdiction 1 = <u>authority</u>, power, control, rule, influence, command, mana (*N.Z.*) 2 = <u>range</u>, area, field, bounds, province, scope, sphere, compass

just ADVERB 1 = <u>recently</u>, lately, only now 2 = <u>merely</u>, only, simply, solely 3 = <u>barely</u>, hardly, by a whisker, by the skin of your

teeth **4** = <u>exactly</u>, really, quite, completely, totally, perfectly, entirely, truly
● ADJECTIVE **1** = <u>fair</u>, good, legitimate, upright, honest, equitable, conscientious, virtuous ≠ unfair **2** = <u>fitting</u>, due, correct, deserved, appropriate, justified, decent, merited ≠ inappropriate

justice 1 = <u>fairness</u>, equity, integrity, honesty, decency, rightfulness, right ≠ injustice **2** = <u>justness</u>, fairness, legitimacy, right, integrity, honesty, legality, rightfulness **3** = <u>judge</u>, magistrate, beak (*Brit. slang*), His, Her or Your Honour

justification = <u>reason</u>, grounds, defence, basis, excuse, warrant, rationale, vindication

justify = <u>explain</u>, support, warrant, defend, excuse, uphold, vindicate, exonerate

juvenile NOUN = <u>child</u>, youth, minor, girl, boy, teenager, infant, adolescent ≠ adult
● ADJECTIVE **1** = <u>young</u>, junior, adolescent, youthful, immature ≠ adult **2** = <u>immature</u>, childish, infantile, puerile, young, youthful, inexperienced, callow

k

kai (*N.Z. informal*) = <u>food</u>, grub (*slang*), provisions, fare, tucker (*Austral. & N.Z. informal*), refreshment, foodstuffs

kak (*S. African taboo*) = <u>faeces</u>, excrement, manure, dung, droppings, waste matter **2** = <u>rubbish</u>, nonsense, garbage (*informal*), rot, drivel, tripe (*informal*), bizzo (*Austral. slang*), bull's wool (*Austral. & N.Z. slang*)

keen 1 = <u>eager</u>, intense, enthusiastic, passionate, ardent, avid, fervent, impassioned ≠ unenthusiastic **2** = <u>earnest</u>, fierce, intense, vehement, passionate, heightened, ardent, fanatical **3** = <u>sharp</u>, incisive, cutting, edged, razor-like ≠ dull **4** = <u>perceptive</u>, quick, sharp, acute, smart, wise, clever, shrewd ≠ obtuse **5** = <u>intense</u>,

strong, fierce, relentless, cut-throat

keep¹ VERB **1** *usually with from* = <u>prevent</u>, restrain, hinder, keep back **2** = <u>hold on to</u>, maintain, retain, save, preserve, nurture, cherish, conserve ≠ lose **3** = <u>store</u>, put, place, house, hold, deposit, stack, stow **4** = <u>carry</u>, stock, sell, supply, handle **5** = <u>support</u>, maintain, sustain, provide for, mind, fund, finance, feed **6** = <u>raise</u>, own, maintain, tend, farm, breed, look after, rear **7** = <u>manage</u>, run, administer, be in charge (of), direct, handle, supervise **8** = <u>delay</u>, detain, hinder, impede, obstruct, set back ≠ release
● NOUN = <u>board</u>, food, maintenance, living, kai (*N.Z. informal*)
● PHRASES **keep something up 1** = <u>continue</u>, make, maintain, carry on, persist in, persevere with **2** = <u>maintain</u>, sustain, perpetuate, retain, preserve, prolong ◆ **keep up** = <u>keep pace</u>

keep² = <u>tower</u>, castle

keeper = <u>curator</u>, guardian, steward, attendant, caretaker, preserver

keeping NOUN = <u>care</u>, charge, protection, possession, custody, guardianship, safekeeping
● PHRASES **in keeping with** = <u>in agreement with</u>, in harmony with, in accord with, in compliance with, in conformity with, in balance with, in correspondence with, in proportion with

key NOUN **1** = <u>opener</u>, door key, latchkey **2** = <u>answer</u>
● ADJECTIVE = <u>essential</u>, leading, major, main, important, necessary, vital, crucial ≠ minor

kia ora (*N.Z.*) = <u>hello</u>, hi (*informal*), greetings, gidday *or* g'day (*Austral. & N.Z.*), how do you do?, good morning, good evening, good afternoon

kick VERB **1** = <u>boot</u>, knock, punt **2** (*Informal*) = <u>give up</u>, break, stop, abandon, quit, cease, eschew, leave off
● NOUN (*Informal*) = <u>thrill</u>, buzz (*slang*), tingle, high (*slang*)
● PHRASES **kick off** (*Informal*) = <u>begin</u>, start, open, commence, initiate, get on the road ◆ **kick someone out** (*Informal*) = <u>dismiss</u>, remove, get rid of, expel, eject, evict, sack (*informal*)

kid¹ (*Informal*) = <u>child</u>, baby, teenager, youngster, infant, adolescent, juvenile, toddler, littlie (*Austral. informal*), ankle-biter (*Austral. slang*), tacker (*Austral. slang*)

kid² = <u>tease</u>, joke, trick, fool, pretend, wind up (*Brit. slang*), hoax, delude

kidnap = <u>abduct</u>, capture, seize, snatch (*slang*), hijack, hold to ransom

kill 1 = <u>slay</u>, murder, execute, slaughter, destroy, massacre, butcher, cut down **2** (*Informal*) = <u>destroy</u>, crush, scotch, stop, halt, wreck, shatter, suppress

killer = <u>murderer</u>, slayer, hit man (*slang*), butcher, gunman, assassin, terminator, executioner

killing NOUN = <u>murder</u>, massacre, slaughter, dispatch, manslaughter, elimination, slaying, homicide
● ADJECTIVE (*Informal*) = <u>tiring</u>, taxing, exhausting, punishing, fatiguing, gruelling, sapping, debilitating
● PHRASES **make a killing** (*Informal*) = <u>profit</u>, gain, clean up (*informal*), be lucky, be successful, make a fortune, strike it rich (*informal*), make a bomb (*slang*)

kind¹ 1 = <u>class</u>, sort, type, variety, brand, category, genre **2** = <u>sort</u>, set, type, family, species, breed

kind² = <u>considerate</u>, kindly, concerned, friendly, generous, obliging, charitable, benign ≠ unkind

kindly ADJECTIVE = <u>benevolent</u>, kind, caring, warm, helpful, pleasant, sympathetic, benign ≠ cruel
● ADVERB = <u>benevolently</u>, politely, generously, thoughtfully, tenderly, lovingly, cordially, affectionately ≠ unkindly

kindness = <u>goodwill</u>, understanding, charity, humanity, compassion, generosity, philanthropy, benevolence ≠ malice

king = <u>ruler</u>, monarch, sovereign, leader, lord, Crown, emperor, head of state

kingdom = <u>country</u>, state, nation, territory, realm

kiss VERB **1** = <u>peck</u> (*informal*), osculate, neck (*informal*) **2** = <u>brush</u>, touch, shave, scrape, graze, glance off, stroke
● NOUN = <u>peck</u> (*informal*), snog (*Brit. slang*), smacker (*slang*), French kiss, osculation

kit NOUN **1** = <u>equipment</u>, materials, tackle, tools, apparatus, paraphernalia **2** = <u>gear</u>, things, stuff, equipment, uniform
● PHRASES **kit something** or **someone out** or **up** = <u>equip</u>, fit, supply, provide with, arm, stock, costume, furnish

knack = <u>skill</u>, art, ability, facility, talent, gift, capacity, trick ≠ ineptitude

kneel = <u>genuflect</u>, stoop

knickers = <u>underwear</u>, smalls, briefs, drawers, panties, bloomers

knife NOUN = <u>blade</u>, carver, cutter
● VERB = <u>cut</u>, wound, stab, slash, thrust, pierce, spear, jab

knit 1 = <u>join</u>, unite, link, tie, bond, combine, bind, weave **2** = <u>heal</u>, unite, join, link, bind, fasten, intertwine **3** = <u>furrow</u>, tighten, knot, wrinkle, crease, screw up, pucker, scrunch up

knob = <u>ball</u>, stud, knot, lump, bump, projection, hump, protrusion

knock VERB **1** = <u>bang</u>, strike, tap, rap, thump, pummel **2** = <u>hit</u>, strike, punch, belt (*informal*), smack, thump, cuff **3** (*Informal*) = <u>criticize</u>, condemn, put down, run down, abuse, slate (*informal*), censure, denigrate
● NOUN **1** = <u>knocking</u>, pounding, beating, tap, bang, banging, rap, thump **2** = <u>bang</u>, blow, impact, jar, collision, jolt, smash **3** = <u>blow</u>, hit, punch, crack, clip, slap, bash, smack hit **4** (*Informal*) = <u>setback</u>, check, defeat, blow, reverse, disappointment, hold-up, hitch
● PHRASES **knock about** or **around** = <u>wander</u>, travel, roam, rove, range, drift, stray, ramble, go walkabout (*Austral.*)
◆ **knock about** or **around with someone** = <u>mix with</u>, associate with, mingle with, consort with, hobnob with, socialize with, accompany ◆ **knock off** (*Informal*) = <u>stop work</u>, get out, call it a day (*informal*), finish work, clock off, clock out ◆ **knock someone about** or **around** = <u>hit</u>, attack, beat, strike, abuse, injure, assault, batter ◆ **knock someone down** = <u>run over</u>, hit, run down, knock over, mow down ◆ **knock something down** = <u>demolish</u>, destroy, flatten, tear down, level, fell, dismantle, bulldoze
◆ **knock something off** (*Slang*) = <u>steal</u>, take, nick (*slang, chiefly Brit.*), thieve, rob, pinch

knockout 1 = <u>killer blow</u>, coup de grâce (*French*), KO or K.O. (*slang*) **2** (*Informal*) = <u>success</u>, hit, winner, triumph, smash, sensation, smash hit ≠ failure

knot NOUN = <u>connection</u>, tie, bond, joint, loop, ligature
● VERB = <u>tie</u>, secure, bind, loop, tether

know 1 = <u>have knowledge of</u>, see,

understand, recognize, perceive, be aware of, be conscious of **2** = be acquainted with, recognize, be familiar with, be friends with, be friendly with, have knowledge of, have dealings with, socialize with ≠ be unfamiliar with **3** *sometimes with **about** or **of*** = be familiar with, understand, comprehend, have knowledge of, be acquainted with, feel certain of, have dealings in, be versed in ≠ be ignorant of

know-how (*Informal*) = expertise, ability, skill, knowledge, facility, talent, command, capability

knowing = meaningful, significant, expressive, enigmatic, suggestive

knowledge 1 = understanding, sense, judgment, perception, awareness, insight, grasp, appreciation **2** = learning, education, intelligence, instruction, wisdom, scholarship, enlightenment, erudition ≠ ignorance **3** = acquaintance, intimacy, familiarity ≠ unfamiliarity

knowledgeable 1 = well-informed, conversant, au fait (*French*), experienced, aware, familiar, in the know (*informal*), cognizant **2** = intelligent, learned, educated, scholarly, erudite

known = famous, well-known, celebrated, noted, acknowledged, recognized, avowed ≠ unknown

kopje *or* **koppie** (*S. African*) = hill, down (*archaic*), fell, mount, hilltop, knoll, hillock, brae (*Scot.*)

label NOUN = tag, ticket, tab, marker, sticker
● VERB = tag, mark, stamp, ticket, tab
labour NOUN **1** = workers, employees, workforce, labourers, hands **2** = work, effort, employment, toil, industry **3** = childbirth, birth, delivery, parturition

● VERB **1** = work, toil, strive, work hard, sweat (*informal*), slave, endeavour, slog away (*informal*) ≠ rest **2** = struggle, work, strain, work hard, strive, grapple, toil, make an effort **3** = overemphasize, stress, elaborate, exaggerate, strain, dwell on, overdo, go on about **4** *usually with **under*** = be disadvantaged by, suffer from, be a victim of, be burdened by

Labour = left-wing, Democrat (*U.S.*)

laboured = difficult, forced, strained, heavy, awkward

labourer = worker, manual worker, hand, blue-collar worker, drudge, navvy (*Brit. informal*)

lace NOUN **1** = netting, net, filigree, meshwork, openwork **2** = cord, tie, string, lacing, shoelace, bootlace
● VERB **1** = fasten, tie, tie up, do up, secure, bind, thread **2** = mix, drug, doctor, add to, spike, contaminate, fortify, adulterate **3** = intertwine, interweave, entwine, twine, interlink

lack NOUN = shortage, want, absence, deficiency, need, inadequacy, scarcity, dearth ≠ abundance
● VERB = miss, want, need, require, not have, be without, be short of, be in need of ≠ have

lad = boy, kid (*informal*), guy (*informal*), youth, fellow, youngster, juvenile, nipper (*informal*)

laden = loaded, burdened, full, charged, weighed down, encumbered

lady 1 = gentlewoman, duchess, noble, dame, baroness, countess, aristocrat, viscountess **2** = woman, female, girl, damsel, charlie (*Austral. slang*), chook (*Austral. slang*), wahine (*N.Z.*)

lag = hang back, delay, trail, linger, loiter, straggle, dawdle, tarry

laid-back = relaxed, calm, casual, easy-going, unflappable (*informal*), unhurried, free and easy ≠ tense

lake = pond, pool, reservoir, loch (*Scot.*), lagoon, mere, lough (*Irish*), tarn

lame 1 = disabled, handicapped, crippled, limping, hobbling, game **2** = unconvincing, poor, pathetic, inadequate, thin, weak, feeble, unsatisfactory

lament VERB = bemoan, grieve, mourn, weep over, complain about, regret, wail

about, deplore
● NOUN 1 = <u>complaint</u>, moan, wailing, lamentation 2 = <u>dirge</u>, requiem, elegy, threnody

land NOUN 1 = <u>ground</u>, earth, dry land, terra firma 2 = <u>soil</u>, ground, earth, clay, dirt, sod, loam 3 = <u>countryside</u>, farmland 4 (*Law*) = <u>property</u>, grounds, estate, real estate, realty, acreage 5 = <u>country</u>, nation, region, state, district, territory, province, kingdom
● VERB 1 = <u>arrive</u>, dock, put down, moor, alight, touch down, disembark, come to rest 2 (*Informal*) = <u>gain</u>, get, win, secure, acquire
● PHRASES **land up** = <u>end up</u>, turn up, wind up, finish up, fetch up (*informal*)
■■■ RELATED WORD
adjective: terrestrial

landlord 1 = <u>owner</u>, landowner, proprietor, freeholder, lessor, landholder 2 = <u>innkeeper</u>, host, hotelier

landmark 1 = <u>feature</u>, spectacle, monument 2 = <u>milestone</u>, turning point, watershed, critical point

landscape = <u>scenery</u>, country, view, land, scene, prospect, countryside, outlook

landslide = <u>landslip</u>, avalanche, rockfall

lane = <u>road</u>, street, track, path, way, passage, trail, pathway

language 1 = <u>tongue</u>, dialect, vernacular, patois 2 = <u>speech</u>, communication, expression, speaking, talk, talking, discourse, parlance

languish 1 = <u>decline</u>, fade away, wither away, flag, weaken, wilt ≠ flourish 2 (*Literary*) = <u>waste away</u>, suffer, rot, be abandoned, be neglected ≠ thrive 3 *often with for* = <u>pine</u>, long, desire, hunger, yearn, hanker

lap¹ = <u>circuit</u>, tour, leg, stretch, circle, orbit, loop

lap² VERB 1 = <u>ripple</u>, wash, splash, swish, gurgle, slosh, purl, plash 2 = <u>drink</u>, sip, lick, swallow, gulp, sup
● PHRASES **lap something up** = <u>relish</u>, like, enjoy, delight in, savour, revel in, wallow in, accept eagerly

lapse NOUN 1 = <u>decline</u>, fall, drop, deterioration 2 = <u>mistake</u>, failing, fault, failure, error, slip, negligence, omission 3 = <u>interval</u>, break, gap, pause, interruption, lull, breathing space, intermission

● VERB 1 = <u>slip</u>, fall, decline, sink, drop, slide, deteriorate, degenerate 2 = <u>end</u>, stop, run out, expire, terminate

lapsed = <u>expired</u>, ended, finished, run out, invalid, out of date, discontinued

large ADJECTIVE 1 = <u>big</u>, great, huge, heavy, massive, vast, enormous, tall ≠ small 2 = <u>massive</u>, great, big, huge, vast, enormous, considerable, substantial ≠ small
● PHRASES **at large** 1 = <u>in general</u>, generally, chiefly, mainly, as a whole, in the main 2 = <u>free</u>, on the run, fugitive, at liberty, on the loose, unchained, unconfined ◆ **by and large** = <u>on the whole</u>, generally, mostly, in general, all things considered, predominantly, in the main, all in all

largely = <u>mainly</u>, generally, chiefly, mostly, principally, primarily, predominantly, by and large

large-scale = <u>wide-ranging</u>, global, sweeping, broad, wide, vast, extensive, wholesale

lash¹ VERB 1 = <u>pound</u>, beat, strike, hammer, drum, smack (*dialect*) 2 = <u>censure</u>, attack, blast, put down, criticize, slate (*informal, chiefly Brit.*), scold, tear into (*informal*) 3 = <u>whip</u>, beat, thrash, birch, flog, scourge
● NOUN = <u>blow</u>, hit, strike, stroke, stripe, swipe (*informal*)

lash² = <u>fasten</u>, tie, secure, bind, strap, make fast

last¹ ADJECTIVE 1 = <u>most recent</u>, latest, previous 2 = <u>hindmost</u>, final, at the end, remotest, furthest behind, most distant, rearmost ≠ foremost 3 = <u>final</u>, closing, concluding, ultimate ≠ first
● ADVERB = <u>in</u> *or* at the end, after, behind, in the rear, bringing up the rear
● PHRASES **the last word** 1 = <u>final decision</u>, final say, final statement, conclusive comment 2 = <u>leading</u>, finest, cream, supreme, elite, foremost, pre-eminent, unsurpassed

last² = <u>continue</u>, remain, survive, carry on, endure, persist, keep on, abide ≠ end

lasting = <u>continuing</u>, long-term, permanent, enduring, remaining, abiding, long-standing, perennial ≠ passing

latch NOUN = fastening, catch, bar, lock, hook, bolt, hasp

● VERB = fasten, bar, secure, bolt, make fast

late ADJECTIVE 1 = overdue, delayed, last-minute, belated, tardy, behind time, behindhand ≠ early 2 = dead, deceased, departed, passed on, former, defunct ≠ alive 3 = recent, new, advanced, fresh ≠ old

● ADVERB = behind time, belatedly, tardily, behindhand, dilatorily ≠ early

lately = recently, of late, just now, in recent times, not long ago, latterly

later ADVERB = afterwards, after, eventually, in time, subsequently, later on, thereafter, in a while

● ADJECTIVE = subsequent, next, following, ensuing

latest = up-to-date, current, fresh, newest, modern, most recent, up-to-the-minute

latitude = scope, liberty, freedom, play, space, licence, leeway, laxity

latter PRONOUN = second, last, last-mentioned, second-mentioned

● ADJECTIVE = last, ending, closing, final, concluding ≠ earlier

laugh VERB = chuckle, giggle, snigger, cackle, chortle, guffaw, titter, be in stitches

● NOUN 1 = chortle, giggle, chuckle, snigger, guffaw, titter 2 (*Informal*) = joke, scream (*informal*), hoot (*informal*), lark, prank 3 (*Informal*) = clown, character (*informal*), scream (*informal*), entertainer, card (*informal*), joker, hoot (*informal*)

● PHRASES **laugh something off** = disregard, ignore, dismiss, overlook, shrug off, minimize, brush aside, make light of

laughter = amusement, entertainment, humour, glee, fun, mirth, hilarity, merriment

launch VERB 1 = propel, fire, dispatch, discharge, project, send off, set in motion, send into orbit 2 = begin, start, open, initiate, introduce, found, set up, originate

● PHRASES **launch into something** = start enthusiastically, begin, initiate, embark on, instigate, inaugurate, embark upon

laurel

● PHRASES **rest on your laurels** = sit back, relax, take it easy, relax your efforts

lavatory = toilet, bathroom, loo (*Brit.* *informal*), privy, cloakroom (*Brit.*), urinal, latrine, washroom, dunny (*Austral. & N.Z. old-fashioned informal*), bogger (*Austral. slang*), brasco (*Austral. slang*)

lavish ADJECTIVE 1 = grand, magnificent, splendid, abundant, copious, profuse ≠ stingy 2 = extravagant, wild, excessive, exaggerated, wasteful, prodigal, unrestrained, immoderate ≠ thrifty 3 = generous, free, liberal, bountiful, open-handed, unstinting, munificent ≠ stingy

● VERB = shower, pour, heap, deluge, dissipate ≠ stint

law 1 = constitution, code, legislation, charter 2 = statute, act, bill, rule, order, command, regulation, resolution 3 = principle, code, canon, precept, axiom, kaupapa (*N.Z.*) 4 = the legal profession, the bar, barristers

▓▓ RELATED WORDS
adjectives: legal, judicial

lawsuit = case, action, trial, suit, proceedings, dispute, prosecution, legal action

lawyer = legal adviser, attorney, solicitor, counsel, advocate, barrister, counsellor, legal representative

lay¹ VERB 1 = place, put, set, spread, plant, leave, deposit, put down 2 = devise, plan, design, prepare, work out, plot, hatch, contrive 3 = produce, bear, deposit 4 = arrange, prepare, make, organize, position, set out, devise, put together 5 = attribute, assign, allocate, allot, ascribe, impute 6 = put forward, offer, present, advance, lodge, submit, bring forward 7 = bet, stake, venture, gamble, chance, risk, hazard, wager

● PHRASES **lay someone off** = dismiss, fire (*informal*), release, sack (*informal*), pay off, discharge, let go, make redundant ◆ **lay someone out** (*Informal*) = knock out, fell, floor, knock unconscious, knock for six ◆ **lay something out** 1 = arrange, order, design, display, exhibit, put out, spread out 2 (*Informal*) = spend, pay, invest, fork out (*slang*), expend, shell out (*informal*), disburse

lay² 1 = nonclerical, secular, non-ordained 2 = nonspecialist, amateur, unqualified, untrained, inexpert, nonprofessional

layer = tier, level, seam, stratum

layout = arrangement, design, outline, format, plan, formation

lazy 1 = idle, inactive, indolent, slack, negligent, inert, workshy, slothful ≠ industrious **2** = lethargic, languorous, slow-moving, languid, sleepy, sluggish, drowsy, somnolent ≠ quick

leach = extract, strain, drain, filter, seep, percolate

lead VERB **1** = go in front (of), head, be in front, be at the head (of), walk in front (of) **2** = guide, conduct, steer, escort, precede, usher, pilot, show the way **3** = connect to, link, open onto **4** = be ahead (of), be first, exceed, be winning, excel, surpass, come first, transcend **5** = command, rule, govern, preside over, head, control, manage, direct **6** = live, have, spend, experience, pass, undergo **7** = result in, cause, produce, contribute, generate, bring about, bring on, give rise to **8** = cause, prompt, persuade, move, draw, influence, motivate, prevail

● NOUN **1** = first place, winning position, primary position, vanguard **2** = advantage, start, edge, margin, winning margin **3** = example, direction, leadership, guidance, model, pattern **4** = clue, suggestion, hint, indication, pointer, tip-off **5** = leading role, principal, protagonist, title role, principal part **6** = leash, line, cord, rein, tether

● ADJECTIVE = main, prime, top, leading, first, head, chief, premier

● PHRASES **lead someone on** = entice, tempt, lure, mislead, draw on, seduce, deceive, beguile ◆ **lead up to something** = introduce, prepare for, pave the way for

leader = principal, president, head, chief, boss (*informal*), director, manager, chairman, baas (*S. African*) ≠ follower

leadership 1 = authority, control, influence, command, premiership, captaincy, governance, headship **2** = guidance, government, authority, management, direction, supervision, domination, superintendency

leading = principal, top, major, main, first, highest, greatest, chief ≠ minor

leaf NOUN **1** = frond, blade, cotyledon **2** = page, sheet, folio

● PHRASES **leaf through something** (with *book*, *magazine* etc. as object) = skim, glance, scan, browse, look through, dip into, flick through, flip through

leaflet = booklet, notice, brochure, circular, flyer, tract, pamphlet, handout

leafy = green, shaded, shady, verdant

league 1 = association, union, alliance, coalition, group, corporation, partnership, federation **2** (*Informal*) = class, group, level, category

leak VERB **1** = escape, pass, spill, release, drip, trickle, ooze, seep **2** = disclose, tell, reveal, pass on, give away, make public, divulge, let slip

● NOUN **1** = leakage, discharge, drip, seepage, percolation **2** = hole, opening, crack, puncture, aperture, chink, crevice, fissure **3** = disclosure, exposé, exposure, admission, revelation, uncovering, betrayal, unearthing

lean¹ VERB **1** = bend, tip, slope, incline, tilt, heel, slant **2** = rest, prop, be supported, recline, repose **3** = tend, prefer, favour, incline, be prone to, be disposed to

● PHRASES **lean on someone** = depend on, trust, rely on, cling to, count on, have faith in

lean² = thin, slim, slender, skinny, angular, trim, spare, gaunt ≠ fat

leaning = tendency, bias, inclination, bent, disposition, penchant, propensity, predilection

leap VERB = jump, spring, bound, bounce, hop, skip

● NOUN **1** = jump, spring, bound, vault **2** = rise, change, increase, soaring, surge, escalation, upsurge, upswing

● PHRASES **leap at something** = accept eagerly, seize on, jump at

learn 1 = master, grasp, pick up, take in, familiarize yourself with **2** = discover, hear, understand, find out about, become aware, discern, ascertain, come to know **3** = memorize, commit to memory, learn by heart, learn by rote, learn parrot-fashion, get off pat

learned = scholarly, academic, intellectual, versed, well-informed, erudite, highbrow, well-read ≠ uneducated

learner = student, novice, beginner, apprentice, neophyte, tyro ≠ expert

learning = knowledge, study, education, scholarship, enlightenment

lease = hire, rent, let, loan, charter, rent out, hire out

least = smallest, meanest, fewest, lowest,

tiniest, minimum, slightest, minimal

leave VERB 1 = <u>depart from</u>, withdraw from, go from, escape from, quit, flee, exit, pull out of ≠ arrive 2 = <u>quit</u>, give up, get out of, resign from, drop out of 3 = <u>give up</u>, abandon, dump (*informal*), drop, surrender, ditch (*informal*), chuck (*informal*), discard ≠ stay with 4 = <u>entrust</u>, commit, delegate, refer, hand over, assign, consign, allot 5 = <u>bequeath</u>, will, transfer, endow, confer, hand down 6 = <u>forget</u>, leave behind, mislay 7 = <u>cause</u>, produce, result in, generate, deposit

• NOUN 1 = <u>holiday</u>, break, vacation, time off, sabbatical, leave of absence, furlough 2 = <u>permission</u>, freedom, sanction, liberty, concession, consent, allowance, warrant ≠ refusal 3 = <u>departure</u>, parting, withdrawal, goodbye, farewell, retirement, leave-taking, adieu ≠ arrival

• PHRASES **leave something** or **someone out** = <u>omit</u>, exclude, miss out, forget, reject, ignore, overlook, neglect

lecture NOUN 1 = <u>talk</u>, address, speech, lesson, instruction, presentation, discourse, sermon 2 = <u>telling-off</u> (*informal*), rebuke, reprimand, talking-to (*informal*), scolding, dressing-down (*informal*), reproof

• VERB 1 = <u>talk</u>, speak, teach, address, discourse, spout, expound, hold forth 2 = <u>tell off</u> (*informal*), berate, scold, reprimand, censure, castigate, admonish, reprove

lees = <u>sediment</u>, grounds, deposit, dregs

left 1 = <u>left-hand</u>, port, larboard (*Nautical*) 2 (*of politics*) = <u>socialist</u>, radical, left-wing, leftist

left-wing = <u>socialist</u>, communist, red (*informal*), radical, revolutionary, militant, Bolshevik, Leninist

leg NOUN 1 = <u>limb</u>, member, shank, lower limb, pin (*informal*), stump (*informal*) 2 = <u>support</u>, prop, brace, upright 3 = <u>stage</u>, part, section, stretch, lap, segment, portion

• PHRASES **pull someone's leg** (*Informal*) = <u>tease</u>, trick, fool, kid (*informal*), wind up (*Brit. slang*), hoax, make fun of, lead up the garden path

legacy = <u>bequest</u>, inheritance, gift, estate, heirloom

legal 1 = <u>judicial</u>, judiciary, forensic, juridical, jurisdictive 2 = <u>lawful</u>, allowed, sanctioned, constitutional, valid, legitimate, authorized, permissible

legend 1 = <u>myth</u>, story, tale, fiction, saga, fable, folk tale, folk story 2 = <u>celebrity</u>, star, phenomenon, genius, prodigy, luminary, megastar (*informal*) 3 = <u>inscription</u>, title, caption, device, motto, rubric

legendary 1 = <u>famous</u>, celebrated, well-known, acclaimed, renowned, famed, immortal, illustrious ≠ unknown 2 = <u>mythical</u>, fabled, traditional, romantic, fabulous, fictitious, storybook, apocryphal ≠ factual

legion 1 = <u>army</u>, company, force, division, troop, brigade 2 = <u>multitude</u>, host, mass, drove, number, horde, myriad, throng

legislation 1 = <u>law</u>, act, ruling, rule, bill, measure, regulation, charter 2 = <u>lawmaking</u>, regulation, prescription, enactment

legislative = <u>law-making</u>, judicial, law-giving

legislator = <u>lawmaker</u>, lawgiver

legislature = <u>parliament</u>, congress, senate, assembly, chamber

legitimate ADJECTIVE 1 = <u>lawful</u>, legal, genuine, authentic, authorized, rightful, kosher (*informal*), dinkum (*Austral. & N.Z. informal*), licit ≠ unlawful 2 = <u>reasonable</u>, correct, sensible, valid, warranted, logical, justifiable, well-founded ≠ unreasonable

• VERB = <u>legitimize</u>, allow, permit, sanction, authorize, legalize, pronounce lawful

leisure = <u>spare</u>, free, rest, ease, relaxation, recreation ≠ work

lekker (*S. African slang*) = <u>delicious</u>, tasty, luscious, palatable, delectable, mouthwatering, scrumptious (*informal*), appetizing, yummo (*Austral. slang*)

lemon

■ RELATED WORDS
adjectives: citric, citrous

lend VERB 1 = <u>loan</u>, advance, sub (*Brit. informal*) 2 = <u>give</u>, provide, add, supply, grant, confer, bestow, impart

• PHRASES **lend itself to something** = <u>be appropriate for</u>, suit, be suitable for, be appropriate to, be serviceable for

length NOUN 1 = <u>distance</u>, reach, measure, extent, span, longitude 2 = <u>duration</u>, term, period, space, stretch, span, expanse 3 = <u>piece</u>, measure, section, segment, portion

• PHRASES **at length** 1 = <u>at last</u>, finally, eventually, in time, in the end, at long last **2** = for a long time, completely, fully, thoroughly, for hours, in detail, for ages, in depth

lengthen 1 = extend, continue, increase, stretch, expand, elongate ≠ shorten **2** = protract, extend, prolong, draw out, spin out, make longer ≠ cut down

lengthy 1 = protracted, long, prolonged, tedious, drawn-out, interminable, long-winded, long-drawn-out **2** = very long, rambling, interminable, long-winded, wordy, discursive, extended ≠ brief

lesbian 1 = homosexual, gay, les (slang), sapphic, lesbo (slang)

less DETERMINER = smaller, shorter, not so much

● **PREPOSITION** = minus, without, lacking, excepting, subtracting

lessen 1 = reduce, lower, diminish, decrease, ease, narrow, minimize ≠ increase **2** = grow less, diminish, decrease, contract, ease, shrink

lesser = lower, secondary, subsidiary, inferior, less important ≠ greater

lesson 1 = class, schooling, period, teaching, coaching, session, instruction, lecture **2** = example, warning, message, moral, deterrent **3** = Bible reading, reading, text, Bible passage, Scripture passage

let VERB 1 = allow, permit, authorize, give the go-ahead, give permission **2** = lease, hire, rent, rent out, hire out, sublease

● **PHRASES let on** (Informal) **1** = reveal, disclose, say, tell, admit, give away, divulge, let slip ◆ **let someone down** = disappoint, fail, abandon, desert, disillusion, fall short, leave stranded, leave in the lurch ◆ **let someone off** = excuse, release, discharge, pardon, spare, forgive, exempt, exonerate ◆ **let something or someone in** = admit, include, receive, welcome, greet, take in, incorporate, give access to ◆ **let something down** = deflate, empty, exhaust, flatten, puncture ◆ **let something off 1** = fire, explode, set off, discharge, detonate **2** = emit, release, leak, exude, give off ◆ **let something out 1** = release, discharge **2** = emit, make, produce, give vent to ◆ **let up** = stop, diminish, decrease, subside, relax, ease (up), moderate, lessen

lethal = deadly, terminal, fatal, dangerous, devastating, destructive, mortal, murderous ≠ harmless

letter 1 = message, line, note, communication, dispatch, missive, epistle **2** = character, mark, sign, symbol

level NOUN = position, standard, degree, grade, standing, stage, rank, status

● **ADJECTIVE 1** = equal, balanced, at the same height **2** = horizontal, even, flat, smooth, uniform ≠ slanted **3** = even, tied, equal, drawn, neck and neck, all square, level pegging

● **VERB 1** = equalize, balance, even up **2** = destroy, devastate, demolish, flatten, knock down, pull down, tear down, bulldoze ≠ build **3** = direct, point, turn, train, aim, focus **4** = flatten, plane, smooth, even off or out

● **PHRASES on the level** (Informal) = honest, genuine, straight, fair, square, dinkum (Austral. & N.Z. informal), above board

lever NOUN = handle, bar

● **VERB** = prise, force

leverage 1 = influence, authority, pull (informal), weight, clout (informal) **2** = force, hold, pull, strength, grip, grasp

levy NOUN = tax, fee, toll, tariff, duty, excise, exaction

● **VERB** = impose, charge, collect, demand, exact

liability 1 = disadvantage, burden, drawback, inconvenience, handicap, nuisance, hindrance, millstone **2** = responsibility, accountability, culpability, answerability

liable 1 = likely, tending, inclined, disposed, prone, apt **2** = vulnerable, subject, exposed, prone, susceptible, open, at risk of **3** = responsible, accountable, answerable, obligated

liaison 1 = contact, communication, connection, interchange **2** = intermediary, contact, hook-up **3** = affair, romance, intrigue, fling, love affair, amour, entanglement

liar = falsifier, perjurer, fibber, fabricator

libel NOUN = defamation, misrepresentation, denigration, smear, calumny, aspersion

● **VERB** = defame, smear, slur, blacken, malign, denigrate, revile, vilify

liberal 1 = tolerant, open-minded, permissive, indulgent, easy-going, broad-minded ≠ intolerant **2** = <u>progressive</u>, radical, reformist, libertarian, forward-looking, free-thinking ≠ conservative **3** = <u>abundant</u>, generous, handsome, lavish, ample, rich, plentiful, copious ≠ limited **4** = <u>generous</u>, kind, charitable, extravagant, open-hearted, bountiful, magnanimous, open-handed ≠ stingy

liberate = <u>free</u>, release, rescue, save, deliver, let out, set free, let loose ≠ imprison

liberty NOUN = <u>independence</u>, sovereignty, liberation, autonomy, immunity, self-determination, emancipation, self-government ≠ restraint
● PHRASES **at liberty 1** = <u>free</u>, escaped, unlimited, at large, not confined, untied, on the loose, unchained **2** = <u>able</u>, free, allowed, permitted, entitled, authorized
◆ **take liberties** or **a liberty** = <u>not show enough respect</u>, show disrespect, act presumptuously, behave too familiarly, behave impertinently

licence NOUN **1** = <u>certificate</u>, document, permit, charter, warrant **2** = <u>permission</u>, the right, authority, leave, sanction, liberty, immunity, entitlement ≠ denial **3** = <u>freedom</u>, creativity, latitude, independence, liberty, deviation, leeway, free rein ≠ restraint **4** = <u>laxity</u>, excess, indulgence, irresponsibility, licentiousness, immoderation ≠ moderation
● PHRASES **under licence** = <u>with permission</u>, under a charter, under warrant, under a permit, with authorization, under a patent

license = <u>permit</u>, sanction, allow, warrant, authorize, empower, certify, accredit ≠ forbid

lick VERB **1** = <u>taste</u>, lap, tongue **2** (*Informal*) = <u>beat</u>, defeat, overcome, rout, outstrip, outdo, trounce, vanquish **3** (*of flames*) = <u>flicker</u>, touch, flick, dart, ripple, play over
● NOUN **1** = <u>dab</u>, bit, touch, stroke **2** (*Informal*) = <u>pace</u>, rate, speed, clip (*informal*)

lie¹ NOUN = <u>falsehood</u>, deceit, fabrication, fib, fiction, invention, deception, untruth
● VERB = <u>fib</u>, fabricate, falsify, prevaricate, not tell the truth, equivocate, dissimulate, tell untruths
● PHRASES **give the lie to something** = <u>disprove</u>, expose, discredit, contradict, refute, negate, invalidate, rebut

lie² **1** = <u>recline</u>, rest, lounge, sprawl, stretch out, loll, repose **2** = <u>be placed</u>, be, rest, exist, be situated **3** = <u>be situated</u>, sit, be located, be positioned **4** = <u>be buried</u>, remain, rest, be, be entombed

life 1 = <u>being</u>, existence, vitality, sentience **2** = <u>existence</u>, being, lifetime, time, days, span **3** = <u>way of life</u>, situation, conduct, behaviour, life style **4** = <u>liveliness</u>, energy, spirit, vitality, animation, vigour, verve, zest **5** = <u>biography</u>, story, history, profile, confessions, autobiography, memoirs, life story
▬ RELATED WORDS
adjectives: animate, vital

lifelong = <u>long-lasting</u>, enduring, lasting, persistent, long-standing, perennial

lifetime = <u>existence</u>, time, day(s), span

lift VERB **1** = <u>raise</u>, pick up, hoist, draw up, elevate, uplift, heave up, upraise ≠ lower **2** = <u>revoke</u>, end, remove, withdraw, stop, cancel, terminate, rescind ≠ impose **3** = <u>disappear</u>, clear, vanish, disperse, dissipate, rise, be dispelled
● NOUN **1** = <u>boost</u>, encouragement, stimulus, pick-me-up, fillip, shot in the arm (*informal*), gee-up ≠ blow **2** = <u>elevator</u> (*chiefly U.S.*), hoist, paternoster **3** = <u>ride</u>, run, drive, hitch (*informal*)
● PHRASES **lift off** = <u>take off</u>, be launched, blast off, take to the air

light¹ NOUN **1** = <u>brightness</u>, illumination, luminosity, shining, glow, glare, gleam, brilliance ≠ dark **2** = <u>lamp</u>, torch, candle, flare, beacon, lantern, taper **3** = <u>match</u>, spark, flame, lighter **4** = <u>aspect</u>, context, angle, point of view, interpretation, viewpoint, slant, standpoint
● ADJECTIVE **1** = <u>bright</u>, brilliant, shining, illuminated, luminous, well-lit, lustrous, well-illuminated ≠ dark **2** = <u>pale</u>, fair, faded, blonde, blond, bleached, pastel, light-coloured ≠ dark
● VERB **1** = <u>illuminate</u>, light up, brighten ≠ darken **2** = <u>ignite</u>, inflame, kindle, touch off, set alight ≠ put out
● PHRASES **light up 1** = <u>cheer</u>, shine, blaze, sparkle, animate, brighten, lighten, irradiate **2** = <u>shine</u>, flash, beam, blaze, sparkle, flare, glare, gleam

light² ADJECTIVE **1** = <u>insubstantial</u>, thin, slight, portable, buoyant, airy, flimsy, underweight ≠ heavy **2** = <u>weak</u>, soft, gentle, moderate, slight, mild, faint, indistinct ≠ strong 3 = digestible, modest, frugal ≠ substantial 4 = insignificant, small, slight, petty, trivial, trifling, inconsequential, inconsiderable ≠ serious 5 = light-hearted, funny, entertaining, amusing, witty, humorous, frivolous, unserious ≠ serious 6 = nimble, graceful, deft, agile, sprightly, lithe, limber, lissom ≠ clumsy

● PHRASES **light on** or **upon something** 1 = settle, land, perch, alight 2 = come across, find, discover, encounter, stumble on, hit upon, happen upon

lighten¹ = brighten, illuminate, light up, irradiate, become light

lighten² 1 = ease, relieve, alleviate, allay, reduce, lessen, mitigate, assuage ≠ intensify 2 = cheer, lift, revive, brighten, perk up, buoy up ≠ depress

lightly 1 = moderately, thinly, slightly, sparsely, sparingly ≠ heavily 2 = gently, softly, slightly, faintly, delicately ≠ forcefully 3 = carelessly, breezily, thoughtlessly, flippantly, frivolously, heedlessly ≠ seriously 4 = easily, simply, readily, effortlessly, unthinkingly, without thought, flippantly, heedlessly ≠ with difficulty

lightweight 1 = thin, fine, delicate, sheer, flimsy, gossamer, diaphanous, filmy 2 = unimportant, shallow, trivial, insignificant, slight, petty, worthless, trifling ≠ significant

like¹ = similar to, same as, equivalent to, parallel to, identical to, alike, corresponding to, comparable to ≠ different

like² 1 = enjoy, love, delight in, go for, relish, savour, revel in, be fond of ≠ dislike 2 = admire, approve of, appreciate, prize, take to, esteem, cherish, hold dear ≠ dislike 3 = wish, want, choose, prefer, desire, fancy, care, feel inclined

likelihood = probability, chance, possibility, prospect

likely 1 = inclined, disposed, prone, liable, tending, apt 2 = probable, expected, anticipated, odds-on, on the cards, to be expected 3 = plausible, possible, reasonable, credible, feasible, believable

liken = compare, match, relate, parallel, equate, set beside

likewise = similarly, the same, in the same way, in similar fashion, in like manner

liking = fondness, love, taste, weakness, preference, affection, inclination, penchant ≠ dislike

limb 1 = part, member, arm, leg, wing, extremity, appendage 2 = branch, spur, projection, offshoot, bough

limelight = publicity, recognition, fame, the spotlight, attention, prominence, stardom, public eye

limit NOUN 1 = end, ultimate, deadline, breaking point, extremity 2 = boundary, edge, border, frontier, perimeter
● VERB = restrict, control, check, bound, confine, curb, restrain, ration

limitation 1 = restriction, control, check, curb, restraint, constraint 2 = weakness, failing, qualification, reservation, defect, flaw, shortcoming, imperfection

limited = restricted, controlled, checked, bounded, confined, curbed, constrained, finite ≠ unlimited

limp¹ VERB = hobble, stagger, stumble, shuffle, hop, falter, shamble, totter
● NOUN = lameness, hobble

limp² = floppy, soft, slack, drooping, flabby, pliable, flaccid ≠ stiff

line NOUN 1 = stroke, mark, score, band, scratch, slash, streak, stripe 2 = wrinkle, mark, crease, furrow, crow's foot 3 = row, queue, rank, file, column, convoy, procession 4 = string, cable, wire, rope, thread, cord 5 = trajectory, way, course, track, channel, direction, route, path 6 = boundary, limit, edge, border, frontier, partition, borderline 7 = occupation, work, calling, business, job, area, trade, field
● VERB 1 = border, edge, bound, fringe 2 = mark, crease, furrow, rule, score
● PHRASES **in line for** = due for, shortlisted for, in the running for

lined 1 = wrinkled, worn, furrowed, wizened 2 = ruled, feint

line-up = arrangement, team, row, selection, array

linger = stay, remain, stop, wait, delay, hang around, idle, dally

link NOUN 1 = connection, relationship, association, tie-up, affinity 2 = relationship, association, bond, connection, attachment, affinity 3 = component, part, piece, element, constituent
● VERB 1 = associate, relate, identify, connect, bracket 2 = connect, join, unite,

couple, tie, bind, attach, fasten ≠ separate

lip 1 = <u>edge</u>, rim, brim, margin, brink 2 (*Slang*) = <u>impudence</u>, insolence, impertinence, cheek (*informal*), effrontery, backchat (*informal*), brass neck (*informal*)

liquid NOUN = <u>fluid</u>, solution, juice, sap
• ADJECTIVE 1 = <u>fluid</u>, running, flowing, melted, watery, molten, runny, aqueous 2 (*of assets*) = <u>convertible</u>, disposable, negotiable, realizable

liquor 1 = <u>alcohol</u>, drink, spirits, booze (*informal*), hard stuff (*informal*), strong drink 2 = <u>juice</u>, stock, liquid, extract, broth

list¹ NOUN = <u>inventory</u>, record, series, roll, index, register, catalogue, directory
• VERB = <u>itemize</u>, record, enter, register, catalogue, enumerate, note down, tabulate

list² VERB = <u>lean</u>, tip, incline, tilt, heel over, careen
• NOUN = <u>tilt</u>, leaning, slant, cant

listen 1 = <u>hear</u>, attend, pay attention, lend an ear, prick up your ears 2 = <u>pay attention</u>, observe, obey, mind, heed, take notice, take note of, take heed of

literacy = <u>education</u>, learning, knowledge

literal 1 = <u>exact</u>, close, strict, accurate, faithful, verbatim, word for word 2 = <u>actual</u>, real, true, simple, plain, genuine, bona fide, unvarnished

literally = <u>exactly</u>, really, closely, actually, truly, precisely, strictly, faithfully

literary = <u>well-read</u>, learned, formal, intellectual, scholarly, erudite, bookish

literate = <u>educated</u>, informed, knowledgeable

literature = <u>writings</u>, letters, compositions, lore, creative writing

litigation = <u>lawsuit</u>, case, action, prosecution

litter NOUN 1 = <u>rubbish</u>, refuse, waste, junk, debris, garbage (*chiefly U.S.*), trash, muck 2 = <u>brood</u>, young, offspring, progeny
• VERB 1 = <u>clutter</u>, mess up, clutter up, be scattered about, disorder, disarrange, derange 2 = <u>scatter</u>, spread, shower, strew

little ADJECTIVE 1 = <u>small</u>, minute, short, tiny, wee, compact, miniature, diminutive ≠ big 2 = <u>young</u>, small, junior, infant, immature, undeveloped, babyish
• ADVERB 1 = <u>hardly</u>, barely, scarcely ≠ much 2 = <u>rarely</u>, seldom, scarcely, not often, infrequently, hardly ever ≠ always
• NOUN = <u>bit</u>, touch, spot, trace, hint,

particle, fragment, speck ≠ lot
• PHRASES **a little** = <u>to a small extent</u>, slightly, to some extent, to a certain extent, to a small degree

live¹ 1 = <u>dwell</u>, board, settle, lodge, occupy, abide, inhabit, reside 2 = <u>exist</u>, last, prevail, be, have being, breathe, persist, be alive 3 = <u>survive</u>, get along, make a living, make ends meet, subsist, eke out a living, support yourself, maintain yourself 4 = <u>thrive</u>, flourish, prosper, have fun, enjoy yourself, live life to the full

live² 1 = <u>living</u>, alive, breathing, animate 2 = <u>active</u>, unexploded 3 = <u>topical</u>, important, pressing, current, hot, burning, controversial, prevalent

livelihood = <u>occupation</u>, work, employment, living, job, bread and butter (*informal*)

lively 1 = <u>animated</u>, spirited, quick, keen, active, alert, dynamic, vigorous ≠ dull 2 = <u>vivid</u>, strong, striking, bright, exciting, stimulating, bold, colourful ≠ dull 3 = <u>enthusiastic</u>, strong, keen, stimulating, eager, formidable, vigorous, animated

living NOUN = <u>lifestyle</u>, ways, situation, conduct, behaviour, customs, lifestyle, way of life
• ADJECTIVE 1 = <u>alive</u>, existing, moving, active, breathing, animate ≠ dead 2 = <u>current</u>, present, active, contemporary, in use, extant ≠ obsolete

load VERB 1 = <u>fill</u>, stuff, pack, pile, stack, heap, cram, freight 2 = <u>make ready</u>, charge, prime
• NOUN 1 = <u>cargo</u>, delivery, haul, shipment, batch, freight, consignment 2 = <u>oppression</u>, charge, worry, trouble, weight, responsibility, burden, onus
• PHRASES **load someone down** = <u>burden</u>, worry, oppress, weigh down, saddle with, encumber, snow under

loaded 1 = <u>tricky</u>, charged, sensitive, delicate, manipulative, emotive, insidious, artful 2 = <u>biased</u>, weighted, rigged, distorted 3 (*Slang*) = <u>rich</u>, wealthy, affluent, well off, flush (*informal*), well-heeled (*informal*), well-to-do, moneyed

loaf¹ 1 = <u>lump</u>, block, cake, cube, slab 2 (*Slang*) = <u>head</u>, mind, sense, common sense, nous (*Brit. slang*), gumption (*Brit. informal*)

loaf² = <u>idle</u>, hang around, take it easy, lie around, loiter, laze, lounge around

loan NOUN = <u>advance</u>, credit, overdraft
• VERB = <u>lend</u>, advance, let out

loathe = <u>hate</u>, dislike, despise, detest, abhor, abominate

loathing = <u>hatred</u>, hate, disgust, aversion, revulsion, antipathy, repulsion, abhorrence

lobby VERB = <u>campaign</u>, press, pressure, push, influence, promote, urge, persuade
• NOUN 1 = <u>pressure group</u>, group, camp, faction, lobbyists, interest group, special-interest group, ginger group 2 = <u>corridor</u>, passage, entrance, porch, hallway, foyer, entrance hall, vestibule

lobola (*S. African*) = <u>dowry</u>, portion, marriage settlement, dot (*archaic*)

local ADJECTIVE 1 = <u>community</u>, regional 2 = <u>confined</u>, limited, restricted
• NOUN = <u>resident</u>, native, inhabitant

locate 1 = <u>find</u>, discover, detect, come across, track down, pinpoint, unearth, pin down 2 = <u>place</u>, put, set, position, seat, site, establish, settle

location = <u>place</u>, point, setting, position, situation, spot, venue, locale

lock¹ VERB 1 = <u>fasten</u>, close, secure, shut, bar, seal, bolt 2 = <u>unite</u>, join, link, engage, clench, entangle, interlock, entwine 3 = <u>embrace</u>, press, grasp, clutch, hug, enclose, clasp, encircle
• NOUN = <u>fastening</u>, catch, bolt, clasp, padlock
• PHRASES **lock someone up** = <u>imprison</u>, jail, confine, cage, detain, shut up, incarcerate, send down (*informal*)

lock² = <u>strand</u>, curl, tuft, tress, ringlet

lodge NOUN 1 = <u>cabin</u>, shelter, cottage, hut, chalet, gatehouse 2 = <u>society</u>, group, club, section, wing, chapter, branch
• VERB 1 = <u>register</u>, enter, file, submit, put on record 2 = <u>stay</u>, room, board, reside 3 = <u>stick</u>, remain, implant, come to rest, imbed

lodging *often plural* = <u>accommodation</u>, rooms, apartments, quarters, digs (*Brit. informal*), shelter, residence, abode

lofty 1 = <u>noble</u>, grand, distinguished, renowned, elevated, dignified, illustrious, exalted ≠ humble 2 = <u>high</u>, raised, towering, soaring, elevated ≠ low 3 = <u>haughty</u>, proud, arrogant, patronizing, condescending, disdainful, supercilious ≠ modest

log NOUN 1 = <u>stump</u>, block, branch, chunk,

trunk 2 = <u>record</u>, account, register, journal, diary, logbook
• VERB = <u>record</u>, enter, note, register, chart, put down, set down

logic = <u>reason</u>, reasoning, sense, good sense

logical 1 = <u>rational</u>, clear, reasoned, sound, consistent, valid, coherent, well-organized ≠ illogical 2 = <u>reasonable</u>, sensible, natural, wise, plausible ≠ unlikely

lone = <u>solitary</u>, single, one, only, sole, unaccompanied

loneliness = <u>solitude</u>, isolation, desolation, seclusion

lonely 1 = <u>solitary</u>, alone, isolated, abandoned, lone, withdrawn, single, forsaken ≠ accompanied 2 = <u>desolate</u>, deserted, remote, isolated, out-of-the-way, secluded, uninhabited, godforsaken ≠ crowded

lonesome (*Chiefly U.S. & Canad.*) = <u>lonely</u>, gloomy, dreary, desolate, forlorn, friendless, companionless

long¹ 1 = <u>elongated</u>, extended, stretched, expanded, extensive, lengthy, far-reaching, spread out ≠ short 2 = <u>prolonged</u>, sustained, lengthy, lingering, protracted, interminable, spun out, long-drawn-out ≠ brief

long² = <u>desire</u>, want, wish, burn, pine, lust, crave, yearn

longing = <u>desire</u>, hope, wish, burning, urge, ambition, hunger, yen (*informal*) ≠ indifference

long-standing = <u>established</u>, fixed, enduring, abiding, long-lasting, long-established, time-honoured

look VERB 1 = <u>see</u>, view, consider, watch, eye, study, survey, examine 2 = <u>search</u>, seek, hunt, forage, fossick (*Austral. & N.Z.*) 3 = <u>consider</u>, contemplate 4 = <u>face</u>, overlook 5 = <u>hope</u>, expect, await, anticipate, reckon on 6 = <u>seem</u>, appear, look like, strike you as
• NOUN 1 = <u>glimpse</u>, view, glance, observation, sight, examination, gaze, inspection 2 = <u>appearance</u>, bearing, air, style, aspect, manner, expression, impression
• PHRASES **look after something** *or* **someone** = <u>take care of</u>, mind, protect, tend, guard, nurse, care for, supervise
♦ **look down on** *or* **upon someone** = <u>disdain</u>, despise, scorn, sneer at, spurn,

contemn (*formal*) ◆ **look forward to something** = anticipate, expect, look for, wait for, await, hope for, long for ◆ **look out for something** = be careful of, beware, watch out for, pay attention to, be wary of, keep an eye out for ◆ **look someone up** = visit, call on, drop in on (*informal*), look in on ◆ **look something up** = research, find, search for, hunt for, track down, seek out ◆ **look up** = improve, develop, advance, pick up, progress, get better, shape up (*informal*), perk up ◆ **look up to someone** = respect, honour, admire, esteem, revere, defer to, think highly of

lookout 1 = watchman, guard, sentry, sentinel 2 = watch, guard, vigil 3 = watchtower, post, observatory, observation post 4 (*Informal*) = concern, business, worry

loom = appear, emerge, hover, take shape, threaten, bulk, menace, come into view

loop NOUN = curve, ring, circle, twist, curl, spiral, coil, twirl
● VERB = twist, turn, roll, knot, curl, spiral, coil, wind round

loophole = let-out, escape, excuse

loose ADJECTIVE 1 = free, detached, insecure, unfettered, unrestricted, untied, unattached, unfastened 2 = slack, easy, relaxed, sloppy, loose-fitting ≠ tight 3 (*Old-fashioned*) = promiscuous, fast, abandoned, immoral, dissipated, profligate, debauched, dissolute ≠ chaste 4 = vague, random, inaccurate, rambling, imprecise, ill-defined, indistinct, inexact ≠ precise
● VERB = free, release, liberate, detach, unleash, disconnect, set free, untie ≠ fasten

loosen VERB = untie, undo, release, separate, detach, unloose
● PHRASES **loosen up** = relax, chill (*slang*), soften, unwind, go easy (*informal*), hang loose, outspan (*S. African*), ease up or off

loot VERB = plunder, rob, raid, sack, rifle, ravage, ransack, pillage
● NOUN = plunder, goods, prize, haul, spoils, booty, swag (*slang*)

lord NOUN 1 = peer, nobleman, count, duke, gentleman, earl, noble, baron 2 = ruler, leader, chief, master, governor, commander, superior, liege
● PHRASES **lord it over someone** = boss around or about (*informal*), order around, threaten, bully, menace, intimidate, hector, bluster ◆ **the Lord** or **Our Lord** = Jesus Christ, God, Christ, Messiah, Jehovah, the Almighty

lose 1 = be defeated, be beaten, lose out, come to grief 2 = mislay, drop, forget, be deprived of, lose track of, misplace 3 = forfeit, miss, yield, be deprived of, pass up (*informal*)

loser = failure, flop (*informal*), also-ran, no-hoper (*Austral. slang*), dud (*informal*), non-achiever

loss NOUN 1 = losing, waste, squandering, forfeiture ≠ gain 2 *sometimes plural* = deficit, debt, deficiency, debit, depletion ≠ gain 3 = damage, cost, injury, hurt, harm ≠ advantage
● PHRASES **at a loss** = confused, puzzled, baffled, bewildered, helpless, stumped, perplexed, mystified

lost = missing, disappeared, vanished, wayward, misplaced, mislaid

lot NOUN 1 = bunch (*informal*), group, crowd, crew, set, band, quantity, assortment 2 = destiny, situation, circumstances, fortune, chance, accident, fate, doom
● PHRASES **a lot** or **lots** 1 = plenty, scores, masses (*informal*), load(s) (*informal*), wealth, piles (*informal*), a great deal, stack(s) 2 = often, regularly, a great deal, frequently, a good deal

lotion = cream, solution, balm, salve, liniment, embrocation

lottery 1 = raffle, draw, lotto (*Brit., N.Z., & S. African*), sweepstake 2 = gamble, chance, risk, hazard, toss-up (*informal*)

loud 1 = noisy, booming, roaring, thundering, forte (*Music*), resounding, deafening, thunderous ≠ quiet 2 = garish, bold, glaring, flamboyant, brash, flashy, lurid, gaudy ≠ sombre

loudly = noisily, vigorously, vehemently, vociferously, uproariously, lustily, shrilly, fortissimo.(*Music*)

lounge VERB = relax, loaf, sprawl, lie about, take it easy, loiter, loll, laze, outspan (*S. African*)
● NOUN = sitting room, living room, parlour, drawing room, front room, reception room, television room

love VERB 1 = adore, care for, treasure, cherish, prize, worship, be devoted to, dote on ≠ hate 2 = enjoy, like, appreciate, relish, delight in, savour, take pleasure in, have a soft spot for ≠ dislike

● NOUN 1 = passion, affection, warmth, attachment, intimacy, devotion, tenderness, adoration, aroha (N.Z.) ≠ hatred 2 = liking, taste, bent for, weakness for, relish for, enjoyment, devotion to, penchant for 3 = beloved, dear, dearest, lover, darling, honey, sweetheart, truelove ≠ enemy 4 = sympathy, understanding, pity, humanity, warmth, mercy, sorrow, kindness, aroha (N.Z.)

● PHRASES make love = have sexual intercourse, have sex, go to bed, sleep together, do it (informal), mate, have sexual relations, have it off (slang)

love affair = romance, relationship, affair, intrigue, liaison, amour

lovely 1 = beautiful, appealing, attractive, charming, pretty, handsome, good-looking, exquisite ≠ ugly 2 = wonderful, pleasing, nice, pleasant, engaging, marvellous, delightful, enjoyable ≠ horrible

lover = sweetheart, beloved, loved one, flame (informal), mistress, admirer, suitor, woman friend

loving 1 = affectionate, dear, devoted, tender, fond, doting, amorous, warm-hearted ≠ cruel 2 = tender, kind, caring, warm, gentle, sympathetic, considerate

low 1 = small, little, short, stunted, squat ≠ tall 2 = inferior, bad, poor, inadequate, unsatisfactory, deficient, second-rate, shoddy, half-pie (N.Z. informal), bodger or bodgie (Austral. slang) 3 = quiet, soft, gentle, whispered, muted, subdued, hushed, muffled ≠ loud 4 = dejected, depressed, miserable, fed up, moody, gloomy, glum, despondent ≠ happy 5 = coarse, common, rough, crude, rude, vulgar, undignified, disreputable 6 = ill, weak, frail, stricken, debilitated ≠ strong

lower ADJECTIVE 1 = subordinate, under, smaller, junior, minor, secondary, lesser, inferior 2 = reduced, cut, diminished, decreased, lessened, curtailed ≠ increased

● VERB 1 = drop, sink, depress, let down, submerge, take down, let fall ≠ raise 2 = lessen, cut, reduce, diminish, slash, decrease, prune, minimize ≠ increase

low-key = subdued, quiet, restrained, muted, understated, toned down

loyal = faithful, true, devoted, dependable, constant, staunch, trustworthy, trusty ≠ disloyal

loyalty = faithfulness, commitment, devotion, allegiance, fidelity, homage, obedience, constancy

luck NOUN 1 = good fortune, success, advantage, prosperity, blessing, windfall, godsend, serendipity 2 = fortune, lot, stars, chance, accident, fate, destiny, twist of fate

● PHRASES in luck = fortunate, successful, favoured, well-off, jammy (Brit. slang)

◆ out of luck = unfortunate, cursed, unlucky, unsuccessful

luckily = fortunately, happily, opportunely

lucky = fortunate, successful, favoured, charmed, blessed, jammy (Brit. slang), serendipitous ≠ unlucky

lucrative = profitable, rewarding, productive, fruitful, well-paid, advantageous, remunerative

ludicrous = ridiculous, crazy, absurd, preposterous, silly, laughable, farcical, outlandish ≠ sensible

luggage = baggage, things, cases, bags, gear, suitcases, paraphernalia, impedimenta

lull NOUN = respite, pause, quiet, silence, calm, hush, let-up (informal)

● VERB = calm, soothe, subdue, quell, allay, pacify, tranquillize

lumber¹ VERB (Brit. informal) = burden, land, load, saddle, encumber

● NOUN (Brit.) = junk, refuse, rubbish, trash, clutter, jumble

lumber² = plod, shuffle, shamble, trudge, stump, waddle, trundle

lumbering = awkward, heavy, hulking, ponderous, ungainly

lump NOUN 1 = piece, ball, block, mass, chunk, hunk, nugget 2 = swelling, growth, bump, tumour, bulge, hump, protrusion

● VERB = group, throw, mass, combine, collect, pool, consolidate, conglomerate

lunatic NOUN = madman, maniac, psychopath, nutcase (slang)

● ADJECTIVE = mad, crazy, insane, irrational, daft, deranged, crackpot (informal), crackbrained, off the air (Austral. slang)

lunge VERB = pounce, charge, dive, leap, plunge, thrust

● NOUN = thrust, charge, pounce, spring, swing, jab

lurch 1 = tilt, roll, pitch, list, rock, lean, heel
2 = stagger, reel, stumble, weave, sway,
totter

lure VERB = tempt, draw, attract, invite,
trick, seduce, entice, allure
● NOUN = temptation, attraction, incentive,
bait, carrot (*informal*), inducement,
enticement, allurement

lurk = hide, sneak, prowl, lie in wait, slink,
skulk, conceal yourself

lush 1 = abundant, green, flourishing,
dense, rank, verdant **2** = luxurious, grand,
elaborate, lavish, extravagant, sumptuous,
plush (*informal*), ornate

lust NOUN **1** = lechery, sensuality, lewdness,
lasciviousness **2** = desire, longing, passion,
appetite, craving, greed, thirst
● PHRASES **lust for** *or* **after someone**
= desire, want, crave, yearn for, covet,
hunger for *or* after ◆ **lust for** *or* **after
something** = desire, crave, yearn for,
covet

luxurious = sumptuous, expensive,
comfortable, magnificent, splendid, lavish,
plush (*informal*), opulent

luxury 1 = opulence, splendour, richness,
extravagance, affluence, hedonism, a
bed of roses, the life of Riley ≠ poverty
2 = extravagance, treat, extra, indulgence,
frill ≠ necessity

lying NOUN = dishonesty, perjury,
deceit, misrepresentation, mendacity,
untruthfulness
● ADJECTIVE = deceitful, false, deceiving,
treacherous, dishonest, two-faced,
mendacious, perfidious ≠ truthful

lyrical = enthusiastic, inspired, poetic,
impassioned, effusive, rhapsodic

m

machine 1 = appliance, device, apparatus,
engine, tool, instrument, mechanism,
gadget **2** = system, structure, organization,
machinery, setup (*informal*)

machinery = equipment, gear,
instruments, apparatus, technology,
tackle, tools, gadgetry

macho = manly, masculine, chauvinist,
virile

mad 1 = insane, crazy (*informal*), nuts
(*slang*), raving, unstable, psychotic,
demented, deranged, off the air (*Austral.
slang*) ≠ sane **2** = foolish, absurd, wild,
stupid, daft (*informal*), irrational, senseless,
preposterous ≠ sensible **3** (*Informal*)
= angry, furious, incensed, enraged, livid
(*informal*), berserk, berko (*Austral. slang*),
tooshie (*Austral. slang*), off the air (*Austral.
slang*) ≠ calm **4** = enthusiastic, wild,
crazy (*informal*), ardent, fanatical, avid,
impassioned, infatuated ≠ nonchalant
5 = frenzied, wild, excited, frenetic,
uncontrolled, unrestrained

madden = infuriate, irritate, incense,
enrage, upset, annoy, inflame, drive you
crazy ≠ calm

madly 1 (*Informal*) = passionately, wildly,
desperately, intensely, to distraction,
devotedly **2** = foolishly, wildly, absurdly,
ludicrously, irrationally, senselessly
3 = energetically, wildly, furiously,
excitedly, recklessly, speedily, like mad
(*informal*) **4** = insanely, frantically,
hysterically, crazily, deliriously, distractedly,
frenziedly

madness 1 = insanity, mental illness,
delusion, mania, dementia, distraction,
aberration, psychosis **2** = foolishness,
nonsense, folly, absurdity, idiocy, wildness,
daftness (*informal*), foolhardiness

magazine = journal, publication,
supplement, rag (*informal*), issue, glossy
(*informal*), pamphlet, periodical

magic NOUN **1** = sorcery, wizardry,
witchcraft, enchantment, black art,
necromancy **2** = conjuring, illusion,
trickery, sleight of hand, legerdemain,
prestidigitation **3** = charm, power,
glamour, fascination, magnetism,
enchantment, allurement
● ADJECTIVE = miraculous, entrancing,
charming, fascinating, marvellous,
magical, enchanting, bewitching

magician 1 = conjuror, illusionist,
prestidigitator **2** = sorcerer, witch,
wizard, illusionist, warlock, necromancer,
enchanter *or* enchantress

magistrate = judge, justice, justice of the

peace, J.P.

magnetic = attractive, irresistible, seductive, captivating, charming, fascinating, charismatic, hypnotic ≠ repulsive

magnificent 1 = splendid, impressive, imposing, glorious, gorgeous, majestic, regal, sublime ≠ ordinary 2 = brilliant, fine, excellent, outstanding, superb, splendid

magnify 1 = enlarge, increase, boost, expand, intensify, blow up (*informal*), heighten, amplify ≠ reduce 2 = make worse, exaggerate, intensify, worsen, exacerbate, increase, inflame 3 = exaggerate, overstate, inflate, overplay, overemphasize ≠ understate

magnitude 1 = importance, consequence, significance, moment, note, weight, greatness ≠ unimportance 2 = immensity, size, extent, enormity, volume, vastness ≠ smallness 3 = intensity, amplitude

maid 1 = servant, chambermaid, housemaid, menial, maidservant, female servant, domestic (*archaic*), parlourmaid 2 (*Literary*) = girl, maiden, lass, damsel, lassie (*informal*), wench

maiden NOUN (*Literary*) = girl, maid, lass, damsel, virgin, lassie (*informal*), wench
● ADJECTIVE 1 = first, initial, inaugural, introductory 2 = unmarried, unwed

mail NOUN = letters, post, correspondence
● VERB = post, send, forward, e-mail, dispatch

main ADJECTIVE = chief, leading, head, central, essential, primary, principal, foremost ≠ minor
● PLURAL NOUN 1 = pipeline, channel, pipe, conduit, duct 2 = cable, line, electricity supply, mains supply
● PHRASES **in the main** = on the whole, generally, mainly, mostly, in general, for the most part

mainly = chiefly, mostly, largely, principally, primarily, on the whole, predominantly, in the main

mainstream = conventional, general, established, received, accepted, current, prevailing, orthodox ≠ unconventional

maintain 1 = continue, retain, preserve, sustain, carry on, keep up, prolong, perpetuate ≠ end 2 = assert, state, claim, insist, declare, contend, profess, avow ≠ disavow 3 = look after, care for, take care

of, conserve, keep in good condition

maintenance 1 = upkeep, keeping, care, repairs, conservation, nurture, preservation 2 = allowance, support, keep, alimony 3 = continuation, carrying-on, perpetuation, prolongation

majestic = grand, magnificent, impressive, superb, splendid, regal, stately, monumental ≠ modest

majesty = grandeur, glory, splendour, magnificence, nobility ≠ triviality

major 1 = important, critical, significant, great, serious, crucial, outstanding, notable 2 = main, higher, greater, bigger, leading, chief, senior, supreme ≠ minor

majority 1 = most, mass, bulk, best part, better part, lion's share, preponderance, greater number 2 = adulthood, maturity, age of consent, seniority, manhood *or* womanhood

make VERB 1 = produce, cause, create, effect, lead to, generate, bring about, give rise to 2 = perform, do, effect, carry out, execute 3 = force, cause, compel, drive, require, oblige, induce, constrain 4 = create, build, produce, manufacture, form, fashion, construct, assemble 5 = earn, get, gain, net, win, clear, obtain, bring in 6 = amount to, total, constitute, add up to, count as, tot up to (*informal*)
● NOUN = brand, sort, style, model, kind, type, variety, marque
● PHRASES **make for something** = head for, aim for, head towards, be bound for
◆ **make it** (*Informal*) = succeed, prosper, arrive (*informal*), get on, crack it (*informal*)
◆ **make off** = flee, clear out (*informal*), bolt, take to your heels, run away *or* off
◆ **make something up** = invent, create, construct, compose, frame, coin, devise, originate ◆ **make up** = settle your differences, bury the hatchet, call it quits, declare a truce, be friends again ◆ **make up for something** = compensate for, make amends for, atone for, balance out, offset, make recompense for ◆ **make up something** 1 = form, account for, constitute, compose, comprise 2 = complete, supply, fill, round off

maker = manufacturer, producer, builder, constructor

makeshift = temporary, provisional, substitute, expedient, stopgap

make-up 1 = cosmetics, paint (*informal*),

powder, face (*informal*), greasepaint
(*Theatre*) **2** = <u>nature</u>, character,
constitution, temperament, disposition
3 = <u>structure</u>, organization, arrangement,
construction, assembly, constitution,
format, composition

making NOUN = <u>creation</u>, production,
manufacture, construction, assembly,
composition, fabrication
● PLURAL NOUN = <u>beginnings</u>, potential,
capacity, ingredients

male = <u>masculine</u>, manly, macho, virile
≠ female

malicious = <u>spiteful</u>, malevolent,
resentful, vengeful, rancorous, ill-disposed,
ill-natured ≠ benevolent

mammoth = <u>colossal</u>, huge, giant,
massive, enormous, immense, gigantic,
monumental ≠ tiny

man NOUN **1** = <u>male</u>, guy (*informal*),
fellow (*informal*), gentleman, bloke (*Brit.
informal*), chap (*Brit. informal*), dude (*U.S.
informal*), geezer (*informal*) **2** = <u>human</u>,
human being, person, individual, soul
3 = <u>mankind</u>, humanity, people, human
race, humankind, Homo sapiens
● VERB = <u>staff</u>, people, crew, occupy,
garrison

mana (*N.Z.*) = <u>authority</u>, influence, power,
might, standing, status, importance,
eminence

manage 1 = <u>be in charge of</u>, run, handle,
direct, conduct, command, administer,
supervise **2** = <u>organize</u>, use, handle,
regulate **3** = <u>cope</u>, survive, succeed, carry
on, make do, get by (*informal*), muddle
through **4** = <u>perform</u>, do, achieve, carry
out, undertake, cope with, accomplish,
contrive **5** = <u>control</u>, handle, manipulate

management 1 = <u>administration</u>, control,
running, operation, handling, direction,
command, supervision **2** = <u>directors</u>,
board, executive(s), administration,
employers

manager = <u>supervisor</u>, head, director,
executive, boss (*informal*), governor,
administrator, organizer, baas (*S. African*)

mandate = <u>command</u>, order, commission,
instruction, decree, directive, edict

mandatory = <u>compulsory</u>, required,
binding, obligatory, requisite ≠ optional

manhood = <u>manliness</u>, masculinity, virility

manifest ADJECTIVE = <u>obvious</u>, apparent,
patent, evident, clear, glaring, noticeable,

blatant ≠ concealed
● VERB = <u>display</u>, show, reveal, express,
demonstrate, expose, exhibit ≠ conceal

manifestation 1 = <u>sign</u>, symptom,
indication, mark, example, evidence, proof,
testimony **2** = <u>display</u>, show, exhibition,
expression, demonstration

manipulate 1 = <u>influence</u>, control, direct,
negotiate, exploit, manoeuvre **2** = <u>work</u>,
use, operate, handle

mankind = <u>people</u>, man, humanity,
human race, humankind, Homo sapiens

manly = <u>virile</u>, masculine, strong, brave,
bold, strapping, vigorous, courageous
≠ effeminate

man-made = <u>artificial</u>, manufactured,
mock, synthetic, ersatz

manner NOUN **1** = <u>style</u>, way, fashion,
method, custom, mode **2** = <u>behaviour</u>,
air, bearing, conduct, aspect, demeanour
3 = <u>type</u>, form, sort, kind, variety, brand,
category
● PLURAL NOUN **1** = <u>conduct</u>, behaviour,
demeanour **2** = <u>politeness</u>, courtesy,
etiquette, refinement, decorum, p's and q's
3 = <u>protocol</u>, customs, social graces

mannered = <u>affected</u>, artificial,
pretentious, stilted, arty-farty (*informal*)
≠ natural

manoeuvre VERB **1** = <u>scheme</u>, wangle
(*informal*), machinate **2** = <u>manipulate</u>,
arrange, organize, set up, engineer, fix,
orchestrate, contrive
● NOUN **1** = <u>stratagem</u>, scheme, trick, tactic,
intrigue, dodge, ploy, ruse **2** *often plural*
= <u>movement</u>, operation, exercise, war
game

mansion = <u>residence</u>, manor, hall, villa,
seat

mantle 1 = <u>covering</u>, screen, curtain,
blanket, veil, shroud, canopy, pall
2 = <u>cloak</u>, wrap, cape, hood, shawl

manual ADJECTIVE **1** = <u>physical</u>, human
2 = <u>hand-operated</u>, hand, non-automatic
● NOUN = <u>handbook</u>, guide, instructions,
bible

manufacture VERB **1** = <u>make</u>, build,
produce, construct, create, turn out,
assemble, put together **2** = <u>concoct</u>, make
up, invent, devise, fabricate, think up, cook
up (*informal*), trump up
● NOUN = <u>making</u>, production,
construction, assembly, creation

manufacturer = <u>maker</u>, producer,

builder, creator, industrialist, constructor

many DETERMINER = <u>numerous</u>, various, countless, abundant, myriad, innumerable, manifold, umpteen (*informal*)
● PRONOUN = <u>a lot</u>, lots (*informal*), plenty, scores, heaps (*informal*)

mar 1 = <u>harm</u>, damage, hurt, spoil, stain, taint, tarnish 2 = <u>ruin</u>, spoil, scar, flaw, impair, detract from, deform, blemish ≠ improve

march VERB 1 = <u>parade</u>, walk, file, pace, stride, swagger 2 = <u>walk</u>, strut, storm, sweep, stride, flounce
● NOUN 1 = <u>walk</u>, trek, slog, yomp (*Brit. informal*), routemarch 2 = <u>progress</u>, development, advance, evolution, progression

margin = <u>edge</u>, side, border, boundary, verge, brink, rim, perimeter

marginal 1 = <u>insignificant</u>, small, minor, slight, minimal, negligible 2 = <u>borderline</u>, bordering, on the edge, peripheral

marijuana = <u>cannabis</u>, pot (*slang*), dope (*slang*), grass (*slang*), hemp, dagga (*S. African*)

marine = <u>nautical</u>, maritime, naval, seafaring, seagoing

mariner = <u>sailor</u>, seaman, sea dog, seafarer, salt

marital = <u>matrimonial</u>, nuptial, conjugal, connubial

maritime 1 = <u>nautical</u>, marine, naval, oceanic, seafaring 2 = <u>coastal</u>, seaside, littoral

mark NOUN 1 = <u>spot</u>, stain, streak, smudge, line, scratch, scar, blot 2 = <u>characteristic</u>, feature, standard, quality, measure, stamp, attribute, criterion 3 = <u>indication</u>, sign, symbol, token 4 = <u>brand</u>, impression, label, device, flag, symbol, token, emblem 5 = <u>target</u>, goal, aim, purpose, object, objective
● VERB 1 = <u>scar</u>, scratch, stain, streak, blot, smudge, blemish 2 = <u>label</u>, identify, brand, flag, stamp, characterize 3 = <u>grade</u>, correct, assess, evaluate, appraise 4 = <u>distinguish</u>, show, illustrate, exemplify, denote 5 = <u>observe</u>, mind, note, notice, attend to, pay attention to, pay heed to

marked = <u>noticeable</u>, clear, decided, striking, obvious, prominent, patent, distinct ≠ imperceptible

markedly = <u>noticeably</u>, clearly, obviously, considerably, distinctly, decidedly,

strikingly, conspicuously

market NOUN = <u>fair</u>, mart, bazaar, souk (*Arabic*)
● VERB = <u>sell</u>, promote, retail, peddle, vend

maroon = <u>abandon</u>, leave, desert, strand, leave high and dry (*informal*)

marriage = <u>wedding</u>, match, nuptials, wedlock, matrimony
▬▬ RELATED WORDS
adjectives: conjugal, marital, nuptial

marry 1 = <u>tie the knot</u> (*informal*), wed, get hitched (*slang*) 2 = <u>unite</u>, join, link, bond, ally, merge, knit, unify

marsh = <u>swamp</u>, bog, slough, fen, quagmire, morass

marshal 1 = <u>conduct</u>, take, lead, guide, steer, escort, shepherd, usher 2 = <u>arrange</u>, group, order, line up, organize, deploy, array, draw up

martial = <u>military</u>, belligerent, warlike, bellicose

marvel VERB = <u>be amazed</u>, wonder, gape, be awed
● NOUN 1 = <u>wonder</u>, phenomenon, miracle, portent 2 = <u>genius</u>, prodigy

marvellous = <u>excellent</u>, great (*informal*), wonderful, brilliant, amazing, extraordinary, superb, spectacular, booshit (*Austral. slang*), exo (*Austral. slang*), sik (*Austral. slang*) ≠ terrible

masculine = <u>male</u>, manly, mannish, manlike, virile

mask NOUN = <u>façade</u>, disguise, front, cover, screen, veil, guise, camouflage
● VERB = <u>disguise</u>, hide, conceal, obscure, cover (up), screen, blanket, veil

mass NOUN 1 = <u>lot</u>, collection, load, pile, quantity, bunch, stack, heap 2 = <u>piece</u>, block, lump, chunk, hunk 3 = <u>size</u>, matter, weight, extent, bulk, magnitude, greatness
● ADJECTIVE = <u>large-scale</u>, general, widespread, extensive, universal, wholesale, indiscriminate
● VERB = <u>gather</u>, assemble, accumulate, collect, rally, swarm, throng, congregate

massacre NOUN = <u>slaughter</u>, murder, holocaust, carnage, extermination, annihilation, butchery, blood bath
● VERB = <u>slaughter</u>, kill, murder, butcher, wipe out, exterminate, mow down, cut to pieces

massage NOUN = <u>rub-down</u>, manipulation
● VERB 1 = <u>rub down</u>, manipulate, knead 2 = <u>manipulate</u>, alter, distort, doctor,

cook (*informal*), fix (*informal*), rig, fiddle (*informal*)

massive = huge, big, enormous, immense, hefty, gigantic, monumental, mammoth ≠ tiny

master NOUN 1 = lord, ruler, commander, chief, director, manager, boss (*informal*), head, baas (*S. African*) ≠ servant 2 = expert, maestro, ace (*informal*), genius, wizard, virtuoso, doyen, past master, fundi (*S. African*) ≠ amateur 3 = teacher, tutor, instructor ≠ student

● ADJECTIVE = main, principal, chief, prime, foremost, predominant ≠ lesser

● VERB 1 = learn, understand, pick up, grasp, get the hang of (*informal*), know inside out, know backwards 2 = overcome, defeat, conquer, tame, triumph over, vanquish ≠ give in to

masterly = skilful, expert, crack (*informal*), supreme, world-class, consummate, first-rate, masterful

mastermind VERB = plan, manage, direct, organize, devise, conceive

● NOUN = organizer, director, manager, engineer, brain(s) (*informal*), architect, planner

masterpiece = classic, tour de force (*French*), pièce de résistance (*French*), magnum opus, jewel

mastery 1 = understanding, skill, know-how, expertise, prowess, finesse, proficiency, virtuosity 2 = control, command, domination, superiority, supremacy, upper hand, ascendancy, mana (*N.Z.*), whip hand

match NOUN 1 = game, test, competition, trial, tie, contest, fixture, bout 2 = marriage, pairing, alliance, partnership 3 = equal, rival, peer, counterpart

● VERB 1 = correspond with, go with, fit with, harmonize with 2 = correspond, agree, accord, square, coincide, tally, conform, match up 3 = rival, equal, compete with, compare with, emulate, measure up to

matching = identical, like, twin, equivalent, corresponding, coordinating ≠ different

mate NOUN 1 (*Informal*) = friend, pal (*informal*), companion, buddy (*informal*), comrade, chum (*informal*), mucker (*Brit. informal*), crony, cobber (*Austral. & N.Z. old-fashioned informal*), E hoa (*N.Z.*)

2 = partner, lover, companion, spouse, consort, helpmeet, husband *or* wife 3 = assistant, subordinate, apprentice, helper, accomplice, sidekick (*informal*) 4 = colleague, associate, companion

● VERB = pair, couple, breed

material NOUN 1 = substance, matter, stuff 2 = cloth, fabric, textile 3 = information, details, facts, notes, evidence, particulars, data, info (*informal*)

● ADJECTIVE 1 = physical, solid, substantial, concrete, bodily, tangible, palpable, corporeal 2 = relevant, important, significant, essential, vital, serious, meaningful, applicable

materially = significantly, much, greatly, essentially, seriously, gravely, substantially ≠ insignificantly

maternal = motherly, protective, nurturing, maternalistic

maternity = motherhood, parenthood, motherliness

matted = tangled, knotted, unkempt, knotty, tousled, ratty, uncombed

matter NOUN 1 = situation, concern, business, question, event, subject, affair, incident 2 = substance, material, body, stuff

● VERB = be important, make a difference, count, be relevant, make any difference, carry weight, cut any ice (*informal*), be of account

matter-of-fact = unsentimental, plain, sober, down-to-earth, mundane, prosaic, deadpan, unimaginative

mature VERB = develop, grow up, bloom, blossom, come of age, age

● ADJECTIVE 1 = matured, seasoned, ripe, mellow 2 = grown-up, adult, of age, fully fledged, full-grown ≠ immature

maturity 1 = adulthood, puberty, coming of age, pubescence, manhood *or* womanhood ≠ immaturity 2 = ripeness

maul 1 = mangle, claw, lacerate, tear, mangulate (*Austral. slang*) 2 = ill-treat, abuse, batter, molest, manhandle

maverick NOUN = rebel, radical, dissenter, individualist, protester, eccentric, heretic, nonconformist ≠ traditionalist

● ADJECTIVE = rebel, radical, dissenting, individualistic, eccentric, heretical, iconoclastic, nonconformist

maximum ADJECTIVE = greatest, highest, supreme, paramount, utmost, most, topmost ≠ minimal

● NOUN = <u>top</u>, peak, ceiling, utmost, upper limit ≠ minimum

maybe = <u>perhaps</u>, possibly, perchance (*archaic*)

mayhem = <u>chaos</u>, trouble, violence, disorder, destruction, confusion, havoc, fracas

maze = <u>web</u>, confusion, tangle, labyrinth, imbroglio, complex network

meadow = <u>field</u>, pasture, grassland, lea (*poetic*)

mean¹ 1 = <u>signify</u>, indicate, represent, express, stand for, convey, spell out, symbolize **2** = <u>imply</u>, suggest, intend, hint at, insinuate **3** = <u>intend</u>, want, plan, expect, design, aim, wish, think

mean² 1 = <u>miserly</u>, stingy, parsimonious, niggardly, mercenary, penny-pinching, ungenerous, tight-fisted, snoep (*S. African informal*) ≠ generous **2** = <u>dishonourable</u>, petty, shameful, shabby, vile, callous, sordid, despicable, scungy (*Austral. & N.Z.*) ≠ honourable

mean³ NOUN = <u>average</u>, middle, balance, norm, midpoint

● ADJECTIVE = <u>average</u>, middle, standard

meaning 1 = <u>significance</u>, message, substance, drift, connotation, gist **2** = <u>definition</u>, sense

meaningful = <u>significant</u>, important, material, useful, relevant, valid, worthwhile, purposeful ≠ trivial

meaningless = <u>nonsensical</u>, senseless, inconsequential, inane ≠ worthwhile

means PLURAL NOUN 1 = <u>method</u>, way, process, medium, agency, instrument, mode **2** = <u>money</u>, funds, capital, income, resources, fortune, wealth, affluence

● PHRASES **by all means** = <u>certainly</u>, surely, of course, definitely, doubtlessly

◆ **by no means** = <u>in no way</u>, definitely not, not in the least, on no account

meantime *or* **meanwhile** = <u>at the same time</u>, simultaneously, concurrently

meanwhile *or* **meantime** = <u>for now</u>, in the interim

measure VERB = <u>quantify</u>, determine, assess, weigh, calculate, evaluate, compute, gauge

● NOUN **1** = <u>quantity</u>, share, amount, allowance, portion, quota, ration, allotment **2** = <u>action</u>, act, step, procedure, means, control, initiative, manoeuvre

3 = <u>gauge</u>, rule, scale, metre, ruler, yardstick **4** = <u>law</u>, act, bill, legislation, resolution, statute

measured 1 = <u>steady</u>, even, slow, regular, dignified, stately, solemn, leisurely **2** = <u>considered</u>, reasoned, studied, calculated, deliberate, sober, well-thought-out

measurement = <u>calculation</u>, assessment, evaluation, valuation, computation, calibration, mensuration

meat = <u>food</u>, flesh, kai (*N.Z. informal*)

mechanical 1 = <u>automatic</u>, automated, mechanized, power-driven, motor-driven ≠ manual **2** = <u>unthinking</u>, routine, automatic, instinctive, involuntary, impersonal, cursory, perfunctory ≠ conscious

mechanism 1 = <u>process</u>, way, means, system, operation, agency, method, technique **2** = <u>machine</u>, device, tool, instrument, appliance, apparatus, contrivance

mediate = <u>intervene</u>, step in (*informal*), intercede, referee, umpire, reconcile, arbitrate, conciliate

mediation = <u>arbitration</u>, intervention, reconciliation, conciliation, intercession

mediator = <u>negotiator</u>, arbitrator, referee, umpire, intermediary, middleman, arbiter, peacemaker

medicine = <u>remedy</u>, drug, cure, prescription, medication, nostrum, medicament

mediocre = <u>second-rate</u>, average, ordinary, indifferent, middling, pedestrian, inferior, so-so (*informal*), half-pie (*N.Z. informal*) ≠ excellent

meditation = <u>reflection</u>, thought, study, musing, pondering, contemplation, rumination, cogitation

medium ADJECTIVE = <u>average</u>, mean, middle, middling, fair, intermediate, midway, mediocre ≠ extraordinary

● NOUN **1** = <u>spiritualist</u>, seer, clairvoyant, fortune teller, channeller **2** = <u>middle</u>, mean, centre, average, compromise, midpoint

meet 1 = <u>encounter</u>, come across, run into, happen on, find, contact, confront, bump into (*informal*) ≠ avoid **2** = <u>gather</u>, collect, assemble, get together, come together, muster, convene, congregate ≠ disperse **3** = <u>fulfil</u>, match (up to), answer, satisfy, discharge, comply with, come up to, conform to ≠ **fall short of 4** = experience, face, suffer, bear, go through, encounter, endure, undergo **5** = converge, join, cross, touch, connect, come together, link up, intersect ≠ diverge

meeting 1 = conference, gathering, assembly, congress, session, convention, get-together (*informal*), reunion, hui (*N.Z.*) **2** = encounter, introduction, confrontation, engagement, rendezvous, tryst, assignation

melancholy ADJECTIVE = sad, depressed, miserable, gloomy, glum, mournful, despondent, dispirited ≠ happy

● NOUN = sadness, depression, misery, gloom, sorrow, unhappiness, despondency, dejection ≠ happiness

mellow ADJECTIVE **1** = full-flavoured, rich, sweet, delicate **2** = ripe, mature, ripened ≠ unripe

● VERB **1** = relax, improve, settle, calm, mature, soften, sweeten **2** = season, develop, improve, ripen

melody 1 = tune, song, theme, air, music, strain **2** = tunefulness, harmony, musicality, euphony, melodiousness

melt 1 = dissolve, run, soften, fuse, thaw, defrost, liquefy, unfreeze **2** *often with away* = disappear, fade, vanish, dissolve, disperse, evaporate, evanesce **3** = soften, relax, disarm, mollify

member = representative, associate, supporter, fellow, subscriber, comrade, disciple

membership 1 = participation, belonging, fellowship, enrolment **2** = members, body, associates, fellows

memoir = account, life, record, journal, essay, biography, narrative, monograph

memoirs = autobiography, diary, life story, experiences, memories, journals, recollections, reminiscences

memorable = noteworthy, celebrated, historic, striking, famous, significant, remarkable, notable ≠ forgettable

memorandum = note, minute, message, communication, reminder, memo, jotting

memorial NOUN = monument, shrine, plaque, cenotaph

● ADJECTIVE = commemorative, remembrance, monumental

memory 1 = recall, mind, retention, ability to remember, powers of recall,

powers of retention **2** = recollection, reminder, reminiscence, impression, echo, remembrance **3** = commemoration, respect, honour, recognition, tribute, remembrance, observance

menace NOUN **1** (*Informal*) = nuisance, plague, pest, annoyance, troublemaker **2** = threat, warning, intimidation, ill-omen, ominousness

● VERB = bully, threaten, intimidate, terrorize, frighten, scare

menacing = threatening, frightening, forbidding, looming, intimidating, ominous, louring *or* lowering ≠ encouraging

mend VERB **1** = repair, fix, restore, renew, patch up, renovate, refit, retouch **2** = darn, repair, patch, stitch, sew **3** = heal, improve, recover, get better, be all right, be cured, recuperate, pull through **4** = improve, reform, correct, revise, amend, rectify, ameliorate, emend

● PHRASES **on the mend** = convalescent, improving, recovering, getting better, recuperating

mental 1 = intellectual, rational, theoretical, cognitive, brain, conceptual, cerebral **2** (*Informal*) = insane, mad, disturbed, unstable, mentally ill, psychotic, unbalanced, deranged

mentality = attitude, character, personality, psychology, make-up, outlook, disposition, cast of mind

mentally = psychologically, intellectually, inwardly

mention VERB = refer to, point out, bring up, state, reveal, declare, disclose, intimate

● NOUN **1** *often with of* = reference to, observation, indication, remark on, allusion to **2** = acknowledgment, recognition, tribute, citation, honourable mention

mentor = guide, teacher, coach, adviser, tutor, instructor, counsellor, guru

menu = bill of fare, tariff (*chiefly Brit.*), set menu, table d'hôte, carte du jour (*French*)

merchandise = goods, produce, stock, products, commodities, wares

merchant = tradesman, dealer, trader, broker, retailer, supplier, seller, salesman

mercy 1 = compassion, pity, forgiveness, grace, kindness, clemency, leniency, forbearance ≠ cruelty **2** = blessing, boon, godsend

mere 1 = <u>simple</u>, nothing more than, common, plain, pure 2 = <u>bare</u>, slender, trifling, meagre, just, only, basic, no more than

merge 1 = <u>combine</u>, blend, fuse, amalgamate, unite, join, mix, mingle ≠ separate 2 = <u>join</u>, unite, combine, fuse ≠ separate 3 = <u>melt</u>, blend, mingle

merger = <u>union</u>, fusion, consolidation, amalgamation, combination, coalition, incorporation

merit NOUN = <u>advantage</u>, value, quality, worth, strength, asset, virtue, strong point
• VERB = <u>deserve</u>, warrant, be entitled to, earn, have a right to, be worthy of

merry 1 = <u>cheerful</u>, happy, carefree, jolly, festive, joyous, convivial, blithe ≠ gloomy 2 (*Brit. informal*) = <u>tipsy</u>, happy, mellow, tiddly (*slang, chiefly Brit.*), squiffy (*Brit. informal*)

mesh NOUN = <u>net</u>, netting, network, web, tracery
• VERB = <u>engage</u>, combine, connect, knit, coordinate, interlock, dovetail, harmonize

mess NOUN 1 = <u>untidiness</u>, disorder, confusion, chaos, litter, clutter, disarray, jumble 2 = <u>shambles</u> 3 = <u>difficulty</u>, dilemma, plight, hole (*informal*), fix (*informal*), jam (*informal*), muddle, pickle (*informal*), uphill (*S. African*)
• PHRASES **mess about** or **around** = <u>potter about</u>, dabble, amuse yourself, fool about or around, muck about or around (*informal*), play about or around, trifle ♦ **mess something up** 1 = <u>botch</u>, muck something up (*Brit. slang*), muddle something up 2 = <u>dirty</u>, pollute, clutter, disarrange, dishevel ♦ **mess with something** or **someone** = <u>interfere</u>, play, fiddle (*informal*), tamper, tinker, meddle

message 1 = <u>communication</u>, note, bulletin, word, letter, dispatch, memorandum, communiqué 2 = <u>point</u>, meaning, idea, moral, theme, import, purport

messenger = <u>courier</u>, runner, carrier, herald, envoy, go-between, emissary, delivery boy

messy 1 = <u>disorganized</u>, sloppy (*informal*), untidy 2 = <u>dirty</u> 3 = <u>untidy</u>, disordered, chaotic, muddled, cluttered, shambolic, disorganized ≠ tidy 4 = <u>dishevelled</u>, ruffled, untidy, rumpled, bedraggled,

tousled, uncombed 5 = <u>confusing</u>, difficult, complex, confused, tangled, chaotic, tortuous

metaphor = <u>figure of speech</u>, image, symbol, analogy, conceit (*literary*), allegory, trope, figurative expression

method 1 = <u>manner</u>, process, approach, technique, way, system, style, procedure 2 = <u>orderliness</u>, planning, order, system, purpose, pattern, organization, regularity

midday = <u>noon</u>, twelve o'clock, noonday

middle NOUN = <u>centre</u>, heart, midst, halfway point, midpoint, midsection
• ADJECTIVE 1 = <u>central</u>, medium, mid, intervening, halfway, intermediate, median 2 = <u>intermediate</u>, intervening

middle-class = <u>bourgeois</u>, traditional, conventional

middling 1 = <u>mediocre</u>, all right, indifferent, so-so (*informal*), unremarkable, tolerable, run-of-the-mill, passable, half-pie (*N.Z. informal*) 2 = <u>moderate</u>, medium, average, fair, ordinary, modest, adequate

midnight = <u>twelve o'clock</u>, middle of the night, dead of night, the witching hour

midst
PHRASES **in the midst of** = <u>among</u>, during, in the middle of, surrounded by, amidst, in the thick of

midway ADJECTIVE or ADVERB = <u>halfway</u>, in the middle of, part-way, equidistant, at the midpoint, betwixt and between

might NOUN = <u>power</u>, force, energy, strength, vigour
• PHRASES **with all your might** = <u>forcefully</u>, vigorously, mightily, manfully, lustily

mighty = <u>powerful</u>, strong, strapping, robust, vigorous, sturdy, forceful, lusty ≠ weak

migrant NOUN = <u>wanderer</u>, immigrant, traveller, rover, nomad, emigrant, itinerant, drifter
• ADJECTIVE = <u>itinerant</u>, wandering, drifting, roving, travelling, shifting, immigrant, transient

migrate = <u>move</u>, travel, journey, wander, trek, voyage, roam, emigrate

migration = <u>wandering</u>, journey, voyage, travel, movement, trek, emigration, roving

mild 1 = <u>gentle</u>, calm, easy going, meek, placid, docile, peaceable, equable ≠ harsh 2 = <u>temperate</u>, warm, calm, moderate, tranquil, balmy ≠ cold **3** = **bland**, thin, smooth, tasteless, insipid, flavourless

militant = **aggressive**, active, vigorous, assertive, combative ≠ peaceful

military ADJECTIVE = **warlike**, armed, soldierly, martial

● NOUN = **armed forces**, forces, services, army

milk = **exploit**, pump, take advantage of

■ RELATED WORD

adjective: lactic

mill NOUN **1** = **grinder**, crusher, quern **2** = **factory**, works, plant, workshop, foundry

● VERB = **grind**, pound, crush, powder, grate

● PHRASES **mill about** *or* **around** = **swarm**, crowd, stream, surge, throng

mimic VERB = **imitate**, do (*informal*), take off (*informal*), ape, parody, caricature, impersonate

● NOUN = **imitator**, impressionist, copycat (*informal*), impersonator, caricaturist

mince 1 = **cut**, grind, crumble, dice, hash, chop up **2** = **tone down**, spare, moderate, weaken, soften

mincing = **affected**, camp (*informal*), precious, pretentious, dainty, sissy, effeminate, foppish

mind NOUN **1** = **memory**, recollection, remembrance, powers of recollection **2** = **intelligence**, reason, reasoning, understanding, sense, brain(s) (*informal*), wits, intellect **3** = **intention**, wish, desire, urge, fancy, leaning, notion, inclination **4** = **sanity**, reason, senses, judgment, wits, marbles (*informal*), rationality, mental balance

● VERB **1** = **take offence at**, dislike, care about, object to, resent, disapprove of, be bothered by, be affronted by **2** = **be careful**, watch, take care, be wary, be cautious, be on your guard **3** = **look after**, watch, protect, tend, guard, take care of, attend to, keep an eye on **4** = **pay attention to**, mark, note, listen to, observe, obey, heed, take heed of

■ RELATED WORD

adjective: mental

mine NOUN **1** = **pit**, deposit, shaft, colliery, excavation **2** = **source**, store, fund, stock, supply, reserve, treasury, wealth

● VERB = **dig up**, extract, quarry, unearth, excavate, hew, dig for

miner = **coalminer**, pitman (*Brit.*), collier (*Brit.*)

mingle 1 = **mix**, combine, blend, merge, unite, join, interweave, intermingle ≠ separate **2** = **associate**, consort, socialize, rub shoulders (*informal*), hobnob, fraternize, hang about *or* around ≠ dissociate

miniature = **small**, little, minute, tiny, toy, scaled-down, diminutive, minuscule ≠ giant

minimal = **minimum**, smallest, least, slightest, token, nominal, negligible, least possible

minimize 1 = **reduce**, decrease, shrink, diminish, prune, curtail, miniaturize ≠ increase **2** = **play down**, discount, belittle, disparage, decry, underrate, deprecate, make light *or* little of ≠ praise

minimum ADJECTIVE = **lowest**, smallest, least, slightest, minimal, least possible ≠ maximum

● NOUN = **lowest**, least, lowest level, nadir

minister NOUN = **clergyman**, priest, vicar, parson, preacher, pastor, cleric, rector

● VERB *often with* **to** = **attend**, serve, tend, take care of, cater to, pander to, administer to

ministry 1 = **department**, office, bureau, government department **2** = **administration**, council **3** = **the priesthood**, the church, the cloth, holy orders

minor = **small**, lesser, slight, petty, trivial, insignificant, unimportant, inconsequential ≠ major

mint = **make**, produce, strike, cast, stamp, punch, coin

minute¹ NOUN = **moment**, second, bit, flash, instant, tick (*Brit. informal*), sec (*informal*), short time

● PLURAL NOUN = **record**, notes, proceedings, transactions, transcript, memorandum

minute² **1** = **small**, little, tiny, miniature, microscopic, diminutive, minuscule, infinitesimal ≠ huge **2** = **precise**, close, detailed, critical, exact, meticulous, exhaustive, painstaking ≠ imprecise

miracle = **wonder**, phenomenon, sensation, marvel, amazing achievement, astonishing feat

miraculous = **wonderful**, amazing, extraordinary, incredible, astonishing, unbelievable, phenomenal, astounding ≠ ordinary

mirror NOUN = <u>looking-glass</u>, glass (*Brit.*), reflector
● VERB = <u>reflect</u>, follow, copy, echo, emulate

miscarriage = <u>failure</u>, error, breakdown, mishap, perversion

misconduct = <u>immorality</u>, wrongdoing, mismanagement, malpractice, impropriety

miserable 1 = <u>sad</u>, depressed, gloomy, forlorn, dejected, despondent, sorrowful, wretched ≠ happy 2 = <u>pathetic</u>, sorry, shameful, despicable, deplorable, lamentable ≠ respectable

misery 1 = <u>unhappiness</u>, distress, despair, grief, suffering, depression, gloom, torment ≠ happiness 2 (*Brit. informal*) = <u>moaner</u>, pessimist, killjoy, spoilsport, prophet of doom, wet blanket (*informal*), sourpuss (*informal*), wowser (*Austral. & N.Z. slang*)

misfortune 1 *often plural* = <u>bad luck</u>, adversity, hard luck, ill luck, infelicity 2 = <u>mishap</u>, trouble, disaster, reverse, tragedy, setback, calamity, affliction ≠ good luck

misguided = <u>unwise</u>, mistaken, misplaced, deluded, ill-advised, imprudent, injudicious

mislead = <u>deceive</u>, fool, delude, take someone in (*informal*), misdirect, misinform, hoodwink, misguide

misleading = <u>confusing</u>, false, ambiguous, deceptive, evasive, disingenuous ≠ straightforward

miss VERB 1 = <u>fail to notice</u>, overlook, pass over 2 = <u>long for</u>, yearn for, pine for, long to see, ache for, feel the loss of, regret the absence of 3 = <u>not go to</u>, skip, cut, omit, be absent from, fail to attend, skive off (*informal*), play truant from, bludge (*Austral. & N.Z. informal*) 4 = <u>avoid</u>, beat, escape, skirt, duck, cheat, bypass, dodge
● NOUN = <u>mistake</u>, failure, error, blunder, omission, oversight

missile = <u>projectile</u>, weapon, shell, rocket

missing = <u>lost</u>, misplaced, not present, astray, unaccounted for, mislaid

mission = <u>task</u>, job, commission, duty, undertaking, quest, assignment, vocation

missionary = <u>evangelist</u>, preacher, apostle

mist = <u>fog</u>, cloud, steam, spray, film, haze, vapour, smog

mistake NOUN 1 = <u>error</u>, blunder, oversight, slip, gaffe (*informal*), miscalculation, faux pas 2 = <u>oversight</u>, error, slip, fault, howler (*informal*), erratum
● VERB 1 = <u>confuse with</u>, take for, mix up with 2 = <u>misunderstand</u>, misinterpret, misjudge, misread, misconstrue, misapprehend

mistaken 1 = <u>wrong</u>, incorrect, misguided, wide of the mark ≠ correct 2 = <u>inaccurate</u>, false, faulty, erroneous, unsound ≠ accurate

mistress = <u>lover</u>, girlfriend, concubine, kept woman, paramour

misunderstand 1 = <u>misinterpret</u>, misread, mistake, misjudge, misconstrue, misapprehend, be at cross-purposes with 2 = <u>miss the point</u>, get the wrong end of the stick

misunderstanding = <u>mistake</u>, error, mix-up, misconception, misinterpretation, misjudgment

misuse NOUN 1 = <u>waste</u>, squandering 2 = <u>abuse</u> 3 = <u>misapplication</u>, abuse, illegal use, wrong use 4 = <u>perversion</u>, desecration 5 = <u>misapplication</u>
● VERB 1 = <u>abuse</u>, misapply, prostitute 2 = <u>waste</u>, squander, embezzle, misappropriate

mix VERB 1 = <u>combine</u>, blend, merge, join, cross, fuse, mingle, jumble 2 = <u>socialize</u>, associate, hang out (*informal*), mingle, circulate, consort, hobnob, fraternize 3 *often with* **up** = <u>combine</u>, marry, blend, integrate, amalgamate, coalesce, meld
● NOUN = <u>mixture</u>, combination, blend, fusion, compound, assortment, alloy, medley
● PHRASES **mix something up** 1 = <u>confuse</u>, scramble, muddle, confound 2 = <u>blend</u>, beat, mix, stir, fold

mixed 1 = <u>varied</u>, diverse, different, differing, cosmopolitan, assorted, jumbled, disparate ≠ homogeneous 2 = <u>combined</u>, blended, united, compound, composite, mingled, amalgamated ≠ pure

mixed-up = <u>confused</u>, disturbed, puzzled, bewildered, at sea, upset, distraught, muddled

mixture 1 = <u>blend</u>, mix, variety, fusion, assortment, brew, jumble, medley 2 = <u>composite</u>, compound 3 = <u>cross</u>, combination, blend **4** = concoction, compound, blend, brew, amalgam

mix-up = confusion, mistake, misunderstanding, mess, tangle, muddle

moan VERB **1** = groan, sigh, sob, whine, lament **2** (*Informal*) = grumble, complain, groan, whine, carp, grouse, whinge (*informal*), bleat

● NOUN **1** = groan, sigh, sob, lament, wail, grunt, whine **2** (*Informal*) = complaint, protest, grumble, whine, grouse, gripe (*informal*), grouch (*informal*)

mob NOUN **1** = crowd, pack, mass, host, drove, flock, swarm, horde **2** (*Slang*) = gang, group, set, lot, crew (*informal*)

● VERB = surround, besiege, jostle, fall on, set upon, crowd around, swarm around

mobile = movable, moving, travelling, wandering, portable, itinerant, peripatetic

mobilize 1 = rally, organize, stimulate, excite, prompt, marshal, activate, awaken **2** = deploy, prepare, ready, rally, assemble, call up, marshal, muster

mock VERB = laugh at, tease, ridicule, taunt, scorn, sneer, scoff, deride ≠ respect

● ADJECTIVE = imitation, pretended, artificial, fake, false, dummy, sham, feigned ≠ genuine

mocking = scornful, scoffing, satirical, contemptuous, sarcastic, sardonic, disrespectful, disdainful

mode 1 = method, way, system, form, process, style, technique, manner **2** = fashion, style, trend, rage, vogue, look, craze

model NOUN **1** = representation, image, copy, miniature, dummy, replica, imitation, duplicate **2** = pattern, example, standard, original, ideal, prototype, paradigm, archetype **3** – sitter, subject, poser

● VERB **1** = show off (*informal*), wear, display, sport **2** = shape, form, design, fashion, carve, mould, sculpt

moderate ADJECTIVE **1** = mild, reasonable, controlled, limited, steady, modest, restrained, middle-of-the-road ≠ extreme **2** = average, middling, fair, ordinary, indifferent, mediocre, so-so (*informal*), passable, half-pie (*N.Z. informal*)

● VERB **1** = soften, control, temper, regulate, curb, restrain, subdue, lessen **2** = lessen, ease ≠ intensify

modern 1 = current, contemporary, recent, present-day, latter-day **2** = up-to-date, fresh, new, novel, newfangled ≠ old-fashioned

modest 1 = moderate, small, limited, fair, ordinary, middling, meagre, frugal **2** = unpretentious, reserved, retiring, shy, coy, reticent, self-effacing, demure

modesty = reserve, humility, shyness, reticence, timidity, diffidence, coyness, bashfulness ≠ conceit

modification = change, variation, qualification, adjustment, revision, alteration, refinement

modify 1 = change, reform, convert, alter, adjust, adapt, revise, remodel **2** = tone down, lower, qualify, ease, moderate, temper, soften, restrain

mogul = tycoon, baron, magnate, big shot (*informal*), big noise (*informal*), big hitter (*informal*), heavy hitter (*informal*), V.I.P.

moist = damp, wet, soggy, humid, clammy, dewy

moisture = damp, water, liquid, dew, wetness

molecule = particle, jot, speck

moment 1 = instant, second, flash, twinkling, split second, jiffy (*informal*), trice **2** = time, point, stage, juncture

momentous = significant, important, vital, critical, crucial, historic, pivotal, fateful ≠ unimportant

momentum = impetus, force, power, drive, push, energy, strength, thrust

monarch = ruler, king or queen, sovereign, tsar, potentate, emperor or empress, prince or princess

monarchy 1 = sovereignty, autocracy, kingship, royalism, monocracy **2** = kingdom, empire, realm, principality

monastery = abbey, convent, priory, cloister, nunnery, friary

monetary = financial, money, economic, capital, cash, fiscal, budgetary, pecuniary

money = cash, capital, currency, hard cash, readies (*informal*), riches, silver, coin

monitor VERB = check, follow, watch, survey, observe, keep an eye on, keep track of, keep tabs on

● NOUN **1** = guide, observer, supervisor, invigilator **2** = prefect (*Brit.*), head girl, head boy, senior boy, senior girl

monk (*Loosely*) = friar, brother

■ RELATED WORD
adjective: monastic

monkey 1 = simian, ape, primate

2 = rascal, horror, devil, rogue, imp, tyke, scallywag, scamp, nointer (*Austral. slang*)

■ RELATED WORD

adjective: simian

monster NOUN **1** = giant, mammoth, titan, colossus, monstrosity **2** = brute, devil, beast, demon, villain, fiend

● ADJECTIVE = huge, massive, enormous, tremendous, immense, gigantic, mammoth, colossal

monstrous **1** = outrageous, shocking, foul, intolerable, disgraceful, scandalous, inhuman, diabolical ≠ decent **2** = huge, massive, enormous, tremendous, immense, mammoth, colossal, prodigious ≠ tiny **3** = unnatural, horrible, hideous, grotesque, gruesome, frightful, freakish, fiendish ≠ normal

monument = memorial, cairn, marker, shrine, tombstone, mausoleum, commemoration, headstone

monumental **1** = important, significant, enormous, historic, memorable, awesome, majestic, unforgettable ≠ unimportant **2** (*Informal*) = immense, great, massive, staggering, colossal ≠ tiny

mood = state of mind, spirit, humour, temper, disposition, frame of mind

moody **1** = changeable, volatile, unpredictable, erratic, fickle, temperamental, impulsive, mercurial ≠ stable **2** = sulky, irritable, temperamental, touchy, ill-tempered, tooshie (*Austral. slang*) ≠ cheerful **3** = gloomy, sad, sullen, glum, morose ≠ cheerful **4** = sad, gloomy, melancholy, sombre

moon NOUN = satellite

● VERB = idle, drift, loaf, languish, waste time, daydream, mope

■ RELATED WORD

adjective: lunar

moor[1] = moorland, fell (*Brit.*), heath

moor[2] = tie up, secure, anchor, dock, lash, berth, make fast

mop NOUN **1** = squeegee, sponge, swab **2** = mane, shock, mass, tangle, mat, thatch

● VERB = clean, wash, wipe, sponge, swab

moral ADJECTIVE = good, just, right, principled, decent, noble, ethical, honourable ≠ immoral

● NOUN = lesson, meaning, point, message, teaching, import, significance, precept

● PLURAL NOUN = morality, standards,

conduct, principles, behaviour, manners, habits, ethics

morale = confidence, heart, spirit, self-esteem, team spirit, esprit de corps

morality **1** = virtue, justice, morals, honour, integrity, goodness, honesty, decency **2** = ethics, conduct, principles, morals, manners, philosophy, mores **3** = rights and wrongs, ethics

moratorium = postponement, freeze, halt, suspension, standstill

more ADJECTIVE = extra, additional, new, other, added, further, new-found, supplementary

● ADVERB **1** = to a greater extent, longer, better, further, some more **2** = moreover, also, in addition, besides, furthermore, what's more, on top of that, to boot

moreover = furthermore, also, further, in addition, too, as well, besides, additionally

morning **1** = before noon, forenoon, morn (*poetic*), a.m. **2** = dawn, sunrise, first light, daybreak, break of day

mortal ADJECTIVE **1** = human, worldly, passing, fleshly, temporal, transient, ephemeral, perishable **2** = fatal, killing, terminal, deadly, destructive, lethal, murderous, death-dealing

● NOUN = human being, being, man, woman, person, human, individual, earthling

mortality **1** = humanity, transience, impermanence, corporeality, impermanency **2** = death, dying, fatality

mostly **1** = mainly, largely, chiefly, principally, primarily, on the whole, predominantly **2** = generally, usually, on the whole, as a rule

mother NOUN = female parent, mum (*Brit. informal*), ma (*informal*), mater, dam, mummy (*Brit. informal*), foster mother, biological mother

● VERB = nurture, raise, protect, tend, nurse, rear, care for, cherish

● ADJECTIVE = native, natural, innate, inborn

■ RELATED WORD

adjective: maternal

motherly = maternal, loving, caring, comforting, sheltering, protective, affectionate

motif **1** = design, shape, decoration, ornament **2** = theme, idea, subject, concept, leitmotif

motion NOUN **1** = movement,

mobility, travel, progress, flow, locomotion **2** = <u>proposal</u>, suggestion, recommendation, proposition, submission
● **VERB** = <u>gesture</u>, direct, wave, signal, nod, beckon, gesticulate

motivate 1 = <u>inspire</u>, drive, stimulate, move, cause, prompt, stir, induce
2 = <u>stimulate</u>, drive, inspire, stir, arouse, galvanize, incentivize

motivation = <u>incentive</u>, inspiration, motive, stimulus, reason, spur, inducement, incitement

motive = <u>reason</u>, ground(s), purpose, object, incentive, inspiration, stimulus, rationale

motto = <u>saying</u>, slogan, maxim, rule, adage, proverb, dictum, precept

mould¹ NOUN **1** = <u>cast</u>, shape, pattern
2 = <u>design</u>, style, fashion, build, form, kind, shape, pattern **3** = <u>nature</u>, character, sort, kind, quality, type, stamp, calibre
● **VERB 1** = <u>shape</u>, make, work, form, create, model, fashion, construct **2** = <u>influence</u>, make, form, control, direct, affect, shape

mould² = <u>fungus</u>, blight, mildew

mound 1 = <u>heap</u>, pile, drift, stack, rick
2 = <u>hill</u>, bank, rise, dune, embankment, knoll, hillock, kopje or koppie (*S. African*)

mount VERB **1** = <u>increase</u>, build, grow, swell, intensify, escalate, multiply ≠ decrease
2 = <u>accumulate</u>, increase, collect, gather, build up, pile up, amass **3** = <u>ascend</u>, scale, climb (up), go up, clamber up ≠ descend
4 = <u>get (up) on</u>, jump on, straddle, climb onto, hop on to, bestride, get on the back of ≠ get off **5** = <u>display</u>, present, prepare, put on, organize, put on display
● NOUN **1** = <u>horse</u>, steed (*literary*)
2 = <u>backing</u>, setting, support, stand, base, frame

mountain 1 = <u>peak</u>, mount, horn, ridge, fell (*Brit.*), berg (*S. African*), alp, pinnacle
2 = <u>heap</u>, mass, masses, pile, a great deal, ton, stack, abundance

mourn 1 *often with* **for** = <u>grieve for</u>, lament, weep for, wail for **2** = <u>bemoan</u>, rue, deplore, bewail

mourning 1 = <u>grieving</u>, grief, bereavement, weeping, woe, lamentation
2 = <u>black</u>, sackcloth and ashes, widow's weeds

mouth 1 = <u>lips</u>, jaws, gob (*slang, esp. Brit.*), maw, cakehole (*Brit. slang*) **2** = <u>entrance</u>, opening, gateway, door, aperture, orifice

3 = <u>opening</u> **4** = <u>inlet</u>, outlet, estuary, firth, outfall, debouchment
■ **RELATED WORD**
adjective: oral

move VERB **1** = <u>transfer</u>, change, switch, shift, transpose **2** = <u>go</u>, advance, progress, shift, proceed, stir, budge, make a move **3** = <u>relocate</u>, leave, remove, quit, migrate, emigrate, decamp, up sticks (*Brit. informal*) **4** = <u>drive</u>, cause, influence, persuade, shift, inspire, prompt, induce ≠ discourage **5** = <u>touch</u>, affect, excite, impress, stir, disquiet **6** = <u>propose</u>, suggest, urge, recommend, request, advocate, submit, put forward
● NOUN **1** = <u>action</u>, step, manoeuvre
2 = <u>ploy</u>, action, measure, step, initiative, stroke, tactic, manoeuvre **3** = <u>transfer</u>, posting, shift, removal, relocation
4 = <u>turn</u>, go, play, chance, shot (*informal*), opportunity

movement 1 = <u>group</u>, party, organization, grouping, front, faction **2** = <u>campaign</u>, drive, push, crusade **3** = <u>move</u>, action, motion, manoeuvre **4** = <u>activity</u>, moving, stirring, bustle **5** = <u>advance</u>, progress, flow **6** = <u>transfer</u>, transportation, displacement **7** = <u>development</u>, change, variation, fluctuation **8** = <u>progression</u>, progress **9** (*Music*) = <u>section</u>, part, division, passage

movie = <u>film</u>, picture, feature, flick (*slang*)

moving 1 = <u>emotional</u>, touching, affecting, inspiring, stirring, poignant ≠ unemotional **2** = <u>mobile</u>, running, active, going, operational, in motion, driving, kinetic ≠ stationary

mow VERB = <u>cut</u>, crop, trim, shear, scythe
● PHRASES **mow something or someone down** = <u>massacre</u>, butcher, slaughter, cut down, shoot down, cut to pieces

much ADVERB **1** = <u>greatly</u>, a lot, considerably, decidedly, exceedingly, appreciably ≠ hardly **2** = <u>often</u>, a lot, routinely, a great deal, many times, habitually, on many occasions, customarily
● DETERMINER = <u>great</u>, a lot of, plenty of, considerable, substantial, piles of (*informal*), ample, abundant ≠ little
● PRONOUN = <u>a lot</u>, plenty, a great deal, lots (*informal*), masses (*informal*), loads (*informal*), tons (*informal*), heaps (*informal*) ≠ little

muck 1 = <u>dirt</u>, mud, filth, ooze, sludge, mire, slime, gunge (*informal*), kak (*S. African informal*) **2** = <u>manure</u>, dung, ordure

mud = <u>dirt</u>, clay, ooze, silt, sludge, mire, slime

muddle NOUN = <u>confusion</u>, mess, disorder, chaos, tangle, mix-up, disarray, predicament
● VERB **1** = <u>jumble</u>, disorder, scramble, tangle, mix up **2** = <u>confuse</u>, bewilder, daze, confound, perplex, disorient, stupefy, befuddle

muddy 1 = <u>boggy</u>, swampy, marshy, quaggy **2** = <u>dirty</u>, soiled, grimy, mucky, mud-caked, bespattered

mug¹ = <u>cup</u>, pot, beaker, tankard

mug² (*Informal*) **1** = <u>face</u>, features, countenance, visage **2** = <u>fool</u>, sucker (*slang*), chump (*informal*), simpleton, easy *or* soft touch (*slang*), dorba *or* dorb (*Austral. slang*), bogan (*Austral. slang*)

mug³ VERB = <u>attack</u>, assault, beat up, rob, set about *or* upon
● PHRASES **mug up (on) something** = <u>study</u>, cram (*informal*), bone up on (*informal*), swot up on (*Brit. informal*)

multiple = <u>many</u>, several, various, numerous, sundry, manifold, multitudinous

multiply 1 = <u>increase</u>, extend, expand, spread, build up, proliferate ≠ decrease **2** = <u>reproduce</u>, breed, propagate

multitude 1 = <u>great number</u>, host, army, mass, horde, myriad **2** = <u>crowd</u>, host, mass, mob, swarm, horde, throng

mundane 1 = <u>ordinary</u>, routine, commonplace, banal, everyday, day-to-day, prosaic, humdrum ≠ extraordinary **2** = <u>earthly</u>, worldly, secular, mortal, terrestrial, temporal ≠ spiritual

municipal = <u>civic</u>, public, local, council, district, urban, metropolitan

murder NOUN = <u>killing</u>, homicide, massacre, assassination, slaying, bloodshed, carnage, butchery
● VERB = <u>kill</u>, massacre, slaughter, assassinate, eliminate (*slang*), butcher, slay, bump off (*slang*)

murderer = <u>killer</u>, assassin, slayer, butcher, slaughterer, cut-throat, hit man (*slang*)

murderous = <u>deadly</u>, savage, brutal, cruel, lethal, ferocious, cut-throat, bloodthirsty

murky 1 = <u>dark</u>, gloomy, grey, dull, dim, cloudy, misty, overcast ≠ bright **2** = <u>dark</u>, cloudy

murmur VERB = <u>mumble</u>, whisper, mutter
● NOUN **1** = <u>whisper</u>, drone, purr

muscle NOUN **1** = <u>tendon</u>, sinew **2** = <u>strength</u>, might, power, weight, stamina, brawn
● PHRASES **muscle in** (*Informal*) = <u>impose yourself</u>, encroach, butt in, force your way in

muscular = <u>strong</u>, powerful, athletic, strapping, robust, vigorous, sturdy, sinewy

muse = <u>ponder</u>, consider, reflect, contemplate, deliberate, brood, meditate, mull over

musical = <u>melodious</u>, lyrical, harmonious, melodic, tuneful, dulcet, sweet-sounding, euphonious ≠ discordant

must = <u>necessity</u>, essential, requirement, fundamental, imperative, requisite, prerequisite, sine qua non (*Latin*)

muster VERB **1** = <u>summon up</u>, marshal **2** = <u>rally</u>, gather, assemble, marshal, mobilize, call together **3** = <u>assemble</u>, convene
● NOUN = <u>assembly</u>, meeting, collection, gathering, rally, convention, congregation, roundup, hui (*N.Z.*), runanga (*N.Z.*)

mutation 1 = <u>anomaly</u>, variation, deviant, freak of nature **2** = <u>change</u>, variation, evolution, transformation, modification, alteration, metamorphosis, transfiguration

mute 1 = <u>close-mouthed</u>, silent **2** = <u>silent</u>, dumb, unspoken, tacit, wordless, voiceless, unvoiced **3** = <u>dumb</u>, speechless, voiceless

mutter = <u>grumble</u>, complain, murmur, rumble, whine, mumble, grouse, bleat

mutual = <u>shared</u>, common, joint, returned, reciprocal, interchangeable, requited

myriad NOUN = <u>multitude</u>, host, army, swarm, horde
● ADJECTIVE = <u>innumerable</u>, countless, untold, incalculable, immeasurable, multitudinous

mysterious 1 = <u>strange</u>, puzzling, secret, weird, perplexing, uncanny, mystifying, arcane ≠ clear **2** = <u>secretive</u>, enigmatic, evasive, discreet, covert, reticent, furtive, inscrutable

mystery = <u>puzzle</u>, problem, question, secret, riddle, enigma, conundrum, teaser

mystic *or* **mystical** = <u>supernatural</u>, mysterious, transcendental, occult, metaphysical, paranormal, inscrutable, otherworldly

myth 1 = <u>legend</u>, story, fiction, saga, fable, allegory, fairy story, folk tale 2 = <u>illusion</u>, story, fancy, fantasy, imagination, invention, delusion, superstition

mythology = <u>legend</u>, folklore, tradition, lore

n

nab = <u>catch</u>, arrest, apprehend, seize, grab, capture, collar (*informal*), snatch

nag¹ VERB = <u>scold</u>, harass, badger, pester, worry, plague, hassle (*informal*), upbraid
● NOUN = <u>scold</u>, complainer, grumbler, virago, shrew, tartar, moaner, harpy

nag² = <u>horse</u> (*U.S.*), hack

nagging 1 = <u>continuous</u>, persistent, continual, niggling, repeated, constant, endless, perpetual 2 = <u>scolding</u>, shrewish

nail NOUN 1 = <u>tack</u>, spike, rivet, hobnail, brad (*technical*) 2 = <u>fingernail</u>, toenail, talon, thumbnail, claw
● VERB 1 = <u>fasten</u>, fix, secure, attach, pin, hammer, tack 2 (*informal*) = <u>catch</u>, arrest, capture, apprehend, trap, snare, ensnare, entrap

naive *or* **naïve** = <u>gullible</u>, trusting, credulous, unsuspicious, green, simple, innocent, callow ≠ worldly

naked = <u>nude</u>, stripped, exposed, bare, undressed, starkers (*informal*), stark-naked, unclothed ≠ dressed

name NOUN 1 = <u>title</u>, nickname, designation, term, handle (*slang*), epithet, sobriquet, moniker *or* monicker (*slang*)
● VERB 1 = <u>call</u>, christen, baptize, dub, term, style, label, entitle 2 = <u>nominate</u>, choose, select, appoint, specify, designate

namely = <u>specifically</u>, to wit, viz.

nap¹ NOUN = <u>sleep</u>, rest, kip (*Brit. slang*), siesta, catnap, forty winks (*informal*)
● VERB = <u>sleep</u>, rest, drop off (*informal*), doze, kip (*Brit. slang*), snooze (*informal*), nod off (*informal*), catnap

nap² = <u>pile</u>, down, fibre, weave, grain

napkin = <u>serviette</u>, cloth

narcotic NOUN = <u>drug</u>, anaesthetic, painkiller, sedative, opiate, tranquillizer, anodyne, analgesic
● ADJECTIVE = <u>sedative</u>, calming, hypnotic, analgesic, soporific, painkilling

narrative = <u>story</u>, report, history, account, statement, tale, chronicle

narrator = <u>storyteller</u>, writer, author, reporter, commentator, chronicler

narrow ADJECTIVE 1 = <u>thin</u>, fine, slim, slender, tapering, attenuated ≠ broad
2 = <u>limited</u>, restricted, confined, tight, close, meagre, constricted ≠ wide
3 = <u>insular</u>, prejudiced, partial, dogmatic, intolerant, narrow-minded, small-minded, illiberal ≠ broad-minded
● VERB 1 = <u>restrict</u>, limit, reduce, constrict
2 = <u>get narrower</u>, taper, shrink, tighten, constrict

narrowly = <u>just</u>, barely, only just, scarcely, by the skin of your teeth

nasty 1 = <u>unpleasant</u>, ugly, disagreeable ≠ pleasant 2 = <u>spiteful</u>, mean, offensive, vicious, unpleasant, vile, malicious, despicable ≠ pleasant 3 = <u>disgusting</u>, unpleasant, offensive, vile, distasteful, obnoxious, objectionable, disagreeable, festy (*Austral. slang*), yucko (*Austral. slang*) 4 = <u>serious</u>, bad, dangerous, critical, severe, painful

nation 1 = <u>country</u>, state, realm 2 = <u>public</u>, people, society

national ADJECTIVE = <u>nationwide</u>, public, widespread, countrywide
● NOUN = <u>citizen</u>, subject, resident, native, inhabitant

nationalism = <u>patriotism</u>, loyalty to your country, chauvinism, jingoism, allegiance

nationality 1 = <u>citizenship</u>, birth 2 = <u>race</u>, nation

nationwide = <u>national</u>, general, widespread, countrywide

native ADJECTIVE = <u>mother</u>, indigenous, vernacular
● NOUN = <u>inhabitant</u>, national, resident, citizen, countryman, aborigine (*often offensive*), dweller

natural 1 = <u>logical</u>, valid, legitimate
2 = <u>normal</u>, common, regular, usual, ordinary, typical, everyday ≠ abnormal
3 = <u>innate</u>, native, characteristic, inherent, instinctive, intuitive, inborn,

essential 4 = <u>unaffected</u>, open,
genuine, spontaneous, unpretentious,
unsophisticated, dinkum (*Austral. & N.Z.
informal*), ingenuous, real ≠ affected
5 = <u>pure</u>, plain, organic, whole, unrefined
≠ processed

naturally 1 = <u>of course</u>, certainly
2 = <u>typically</u>, simply, normally,
spontaneously

nature 1 = <u>creation</u>, world, earth,
environment, universe, cosmos, natural
world 2 = <u>quality</u>, character, make-up,
constitution, essence, complexion
3 = <u>temperament</u>, character, personality,
disposition, outlook, mood, humour,
temper 4 = <u>kind</u>, sort, style, type, variety,
species, category, description

naughty 1 = <u>disobedient</u>, bad,
mischievous, badly behaved, wayward,
wicked, impish, refractory ≠ good
2 = <u>obscene</u>, vulgar, improper, lewd,
risqué, smutty, ribald ≠ clean

nausea = <u>sickness</u>, vomiting, retching,
squeamishness, queasiness, biliousness

naval = <u>nautical</u>, marine, maritime

navigation = <u>sailing</u>, voyaging,
seamanship, helmsmanship

navy = <u>fleet</u>, flotilla, armada

near 1 = <u>close</u>, neighbouring, nearby,
adjacent, adjoining ≠ far 2 = <u>imminent</u>,
forthcoming, approaching, looming,
impending, upcoming, nigh, in the offing
≠ far-off

nearby = <u>neighbouring</u>, adjacent,
adjoining

nearly 1 = <u>practically</u>, almost, virtually, just
about, as good as, well-nigh 2 = <u>almost</u>,
approaching, roughly, just about,
approximately

neat 1 = <u>tidy</u>, trim, orderly, spruce,
shipshape, spick-and-span ≠ untidy
2 = <u>methodical</u>, tidy, systematic, fastidious
≠ disorganized 3 = <u>smart</u>, trim, tidy,
spruce, dapper, natty (*informal*), well-
groomed, well-turned out 4 = <u>graceful</u>,
elegant, adept, nimble, adroit, efficient
≠ clumsy 5 = <u>clever</u>, efficient, handy,
apt, well-judged ≠ inefficient 6 = <u>cool</u>,
great (*informal*), excellent, brilliant,
superb, fantastic (*informal*), tremendous,
fabulous (*informal*), booshit (*Austral.
slang*), exo (*Austral. slang*), sik (*Austral.
slang*) ≠ terrible 7 (*of alcoholic drinks*)
= <u>undiluted</u>, straight, pure, unmixed

neatly 1 = <u>tidily</u>, smartly, systematically,
methodically, fastidiously 2 = <u>smartly</u>,
elegantly, tidily, nattily 3 = <u>gracefully</u>,
expertly, efficiently, adeptly, skilfully,
nimbly, adroitly, dexterously 4 = <u>cleverly</u>,
efficiently

necessarily 1 = <u>automatically</u>, naturally,
definitely, undoubtedly, certainly
2 = <u>inevitably</u>, of necessity, unavoidably,
incontrovertibly, nolens volens (*Latin*)

necessary 1 = <u>needed</u>, required,
essential, vital, compulsory, mandatory,
imperative, indispensable ≠ unnecessary
2 = <u>inevitable</u>, certain, unavoidable,
inescapable ≠ avoidable

necessity NOUN 1 = <u>essential</u>, need,
requirement, fundamental, requisite,
prerequisite, sine qua non (*Latin*),
desideratum 2 = <u>inevitability</u>, certainty
● PLURAL NOUN = <u>essentials</u>, needs,
requirements, fundamentals

need VERB 1 = <u>want</u>, miss, require, lack,
have to have, demand 2 = <u>require</u>, want,
demand, call for, entail, necessitate
3 = <u>have to</u>, be obliged to
● NOUN 1 = <u>requirement</u>, demand,
essential, necessity, requisite, desideratum
2 = <u>necessity</u>, call, demand, obligation
3 = <u>emergency</u>, want, necessity, urgency,
exigency 4 = <u>poverty</u>, deprivation,
destitution, penury

needed = <u>necessary</u>, wanted, required,
lacked, called for, desired

needle = <u>irritate</u>, provoke, annoy, harass,
taunt, nag, goad, rile

needless = <u>unnecessary</u>, pointless,
gratuitous, useless, unwanted, redundant,
superfluous, groundless ≠ essential

needy = <u>poor</u>, deprived, disadvantaged,
impoverished, penniless, destitute,
poverty-stricken, underprivileged
≠ wealthy

negative ADJECTIVE 1 = <u>pessimistic</u>,
cynical, unwilling, gloomy, jaundiced,
uncooperative ≠ optimistic 2 = <u>dissenting</u>,
contradictory, refusing, denying, rejecting,
opposing, resisting, contrary ≠ assenting
● NOUN = <u>denial</u>, no, refusal, rejection,
contradiction

neglect VERB 1 = <u>disregard</u>, ignore, fail to
look after ≠ look after 2 = <u>shirk</u>, forget,
overlook, omit, evade, pass over, skimp, be
remiss in or about 3 = <u>fail</u>, forget, omit
● NOUN 1 = <u>negligence</u>, inattention

≠ care 2 = <u>shirking</u>, failure, oversight, carelessness, dereliction, slackness, laxity

neglected 1 = <u>uncared-for</u>, abandoned, underestimated, disregarded, undervalued, unappreciated 2 = <u>run down</u>, derelict, overgrown, uncared-for

negligence = <u>carelessness</u>, neglect, disregard, dereliction, slackness, inattention, laxity, thoughtlessness

negotiate 1 = <u>bargain</u>, deal, discuss, debate, mediate, hold talks, cut a deal, conciliate 2 = <u>arrange</u>, work out, bring about, transact 3 = <u>get round</u>, clear, pass, cross, get over, get past, surmount

negotiation 1 = <u>bargaining</u>, debate, discussion, transaction, dialogue, mediation, arbitration, wheeling and dealing (*informal*) 2 = <u>arrangement</u>, working out, transaction, bringing about

negotiator = <u>mediator</u>, ambassador, diplomat, delegate, intermediary, moderator, honest broker

neighbourhood 1 = <u>district</u>, community, quarter, region, locality, locale 2 = <u>vicinity</u>, environs

neighbouring = <u>nearby</u>, next, near, bordering, surrounding, connecting, adjacent, adjoining ≠ remote

neighbourly = <u>helpful</u>, kind, friendly, obliging, harmonious, considerate, sociable, hospitable

nerve NOUN 1 = <u>bravery</u>, courage, bottle (*Brit. slang*), resolution, daring, guts (*informal*), pluck, grit 2 (*Informal*) = <u>impudence</u>, cheek (*informal*), audacity, boldness, temerity, insolence, impertinence, brazenness

● PLURAL NOUN = <u>tension</u>, stress, strain, anxiety, butterflies (in your stomach) (*informal*), nervousness, cold feet (*informal*), worry

● PHRASES **nerve yourself** = <u>brace yourself</u>, prepare yourself, steel yourself, fortify yourself, gear yourself up, gee yourself up

nervous = <u>apprehensive</u>, anxious, uneasy, edgy, worried, tense, fearful, uptight (*informal*), toey (*Austral. slang*) ≠ calm

nest = <u>refuge</u>, retreat, haunt, den, hideaway

nestle = <u>snuggle</u>, cuddle, huddle, curl up, nuzzle

nestling = <u>chick</u>, fledgling, baby bird

net¹ NOUN = <u>mesh</u>, netting, network, web, lattice, openwork

● VERB = <u>catch</u>, bag, capture, trap, entangle, ensnare, enmesh

net² *or* **nett** ADJECTIVE = <u>after taxes</u>, final, clear, take-home

● VERB = <u>earn</u>, make, clear, gain, realize, bring in, accumulate, reap

network 1 = <u>web</u>, system, arrangement, grid, lattice 2 = <u>maze</u>, warren, labyrinth

neurotic = <u>unstable</u>, nervous, disturbed, abnormal, obsessive, compulsive, manic, unhealthy ≠ rational

neutral 1 = <u>unbiased</u>, impartial, disinterested, even-handed, uninvolved, nonpartisan, unprejudiced, nonaligned ≠ biased 2 = <u>expressionless</u>, dull 3 = <u>uncontroversial</u> *or* noncontroversial, inoffensive 4 = <u>colourless</u>

never 1 = <u>at no time</u>, not once, not ever ≠ always 2 = <u>under no circumstances</u>, not at all, on no account, not ever

nevertheless = <u>even so</u>, still, however, yet, regardless, nonetheless, notwithstanding, in spite of that

new 1 = <u>modern</u>, recent, contemporary, up-to-date, latest, current, original, fresh ≠ old-fashioned 2 = <u>brand new</u> 3 = <u>extra</u>, more, added, new-found, supplementary 4 = <u>unfamiliar</u>, strange 5 = <u>renewed</u>, changed, improved, restored, altered, revitalized

newcomer 1 = <u>new arrival</u>, stranger 2 = <u>beginner</u>, novice, new arrival, parvenu, Johnny-come-lately (*informal*)

news = <u>information</u>, latest (*informal*), report, story, exposé, intelligence, rumour, revelation

next ADJECTIVE 1 = <u>following</u>, later, succeeding, subsequent 2 = <u>adjacent</u>, closest, nearest, neighbouring, adjoining

● ADVERB = <u>afterwards</u>, then, later, following, subsequently, thereafter

nice 1 = <u>pleasant</u>, delightful, agreeable, good, attractive, charming, pleasurable, enjoyable ≠ unpleasant 2 = <u>kind</u>, helpful, obliging, considerate ≠ unkind 3 = <u>likable</u> *or* likeable, friendly, engaging, charming, pleasant, agreeable 4 = <u>polite</u>, courteous, well-mannered ≠ vulgar 5 = <u>precise</u>, fine, careful, strict, subtle, delicate, meticulous, fastidious ≠ vague

nicely 1 = <u>pleasantly</u>, well, delightfully, attractively, charmingly, agreeably, acceptably, pleasurably ≠ unpleasantly

2 = kindly, politely, thoughtfully, amiably, courteously

niche 1 = recess, opening, corner, hollow, nook, alcove **2** = position, calling, place, slot (*informal*), vocation, pigeonhole (*informal*)

nick VERB **1** (*Slang*) = steal, pinch (*informal*), swipe (*slang*), pilfer **2** = cut, mark, score, chip, scratch, scar, notch, dent
● NOUN = cut, mark, scratch, chip, scar, notch, dent

nickname = pet name, label, diminutive, epithet, sobriquet, moniker *or* monicker (*slang*)

night = darkness, dark, night-time
■ RELATED WORD
adjective: nocturnal

nightly ADJECTIVE = nocturnal, night-time
● ADVERB = every night, nights (*informal*), each night, night after night

nightmare 1 = bad dream, hallucination **2** = ordeal, trial, hell, horror, torture, torment, tribulation, purgatory

nil 1 = nothing, love, zero **2** = zero, nothing, none, naught

nip¹ VERB **1** = pop, go, run, rush, dash **2** = bite **3** = pinch, squeeze, tweak
● PHRASES **nip something in the bud** = thwart, check, frustrate

nip² = dram, shot (*informal*), drop, sip, draught, mouthful, snifter (*informal*)

nirvana = paradise, peace, joy, bliss, serenity, tranquillity

no INTERJECTION = not at all, certainly not, of course not, absolutely not, never, no way, nay ≠ yes
● NOUN = refusal, rejection, denial, negation ≠ consent

noble ADJECTIVE **1** = worthy, generous, upright, honourable, virtuous, magnanimous ≠ despicable **2** = dignified, great, imposing, impressive, distinguished, splendid, stately ≠ lowly **3** = aristocratic, lordly, titled, patrician, blue-blooded, highborn ≠ humble
● NOUN = lord, peer, aristocrat, nobleman ≠ commoner

nobody PRONOUN = no-one
● NOUN = nonentity, lightweight (*informal*), zero, cipher ≠ celebrity

nod VERB **1** = incline, bow **2** = signal, indicate, motion, gesture **3** = salute, acknowledge
● NOUN **1** = signal, sign, motion,

gesture, indication **2** = salute, greeting, acknowledgment

noise = sound, row, racket, clamour, din, uproar, commotion, hubbub ≠ silence, calm

noisy 1 = rowdy, strident, boisterous, vociferous, uproarious, clamorous ≠ quiet **2** = loud, piercing, deafening, tumultuous, ear-splitting, cacophonous, clamorous ≠ quiet

nominal 1 = titular, formal, purported, in name only, supposed, so-called, theoretical, professed **2** = token, small, symbolic, minimal, trivial, trifling, insignificant, inconsiderable

nominate 1 = propose, suggest, recommend, put forward **2** = appoint, name, choose, select, elect, assign, designate

nomination 1 = proposal, suggestion, recommendation **2** = appointment, election, selection, designation, choice

nominee = candidate, applicant, entrant, contestant, aspirant, runner

none 1 = not any, nothing, zero, not one, nil **2** = no-one, nobody, not one

nonetheless = nevertheless, however, yet, even so, despite that, in spite of that

non-existent *or* **nonexistent** = imaginary, fictional, mythical, unreal, hypothetical, illusory ≠ real

nonsense 1 = rubbish, hot air (*informal*), twaddle, drivel, tripe (*informal*), gibberish, claptrap (*informal*), double Dutch (*Brit. informal*), bizzo (*Austral. slang*), bull's wool (*Austral. & N.Z. slang*) ≠ sense **2** = idiocy, stupidity

non-stop *or* **nonstop** ADJECTIVE = continuous, constant, relentless, uninterrupted, endless, unbroken, interminable, incessant ≠ occasional
● ADVERB = continuously, constantly, endlessly, relentlessly, perpetually, incessantly, ceaselessly, interminably

noon NOUN = midday, high noon, noonday, twelve noon, noontide
● ADJECTIVE = midday, noonday, noontide

norm = standard, rule, pattern, average, par, criterion, benchmark, yardstick

normal 1 = usual, common, standard, average, natural, regular, ordinary, typical ≠ unusual **2** = sane, reasonable, rational, well-adjusted, compos mentis (*Latin*), in your right mind, mentally sound

normally 1 = usually, generally, commonly, regularly, typically, ordinarily, as a rule, habitually 2 = as usual, naturally, properly, conventionally, in the usual way

north ADJECTIVE = northern, polar, arctic, boreal, northerly

• ADVERB = northward(s), in a northerly direction

nose NOUN = snout, bill, beak, hooter (slang), proboscis

• VERB = ease forward, push, edge, shove, nudge

■ RELATED WORD
adjective: nasal

nostalgia = reminiscence, longing, pining, yearning, remembrance, homesickness, wistfulness

nostalgic = sentimental, longing, emotional, homesick, wistful, maudlin, regretful

notable ADJECTIVE 1 = remarkable, striking, unusual, extraordinary, outstanding, memorable, uncommon, conspicuous ≠ imperceptible 2 = prominent, famous ≠ unknown

• NOUN = celebrity, big name, dignitary, luminary, personage, V.I.P.

notably = remarkably, unusually, extraordinarily, noticeably, strikingly, singularly, outstandingly, uncommonly

notch NOUN 1 = level (Informal), step, degree, grade 2 = cut, nick, incision, indentation, mark, score, cleft

• VERB = cut, mark, score, nick, scratch, indent

note NOUN 1 = message, letter, communication, memo, memorandum, epistle 2 = record, reminder, memo, memorandum, jotting, minute 3 = annotation, comment, remark 4 = document, form, record, certificate 5 = symbol, mark, sign, indication, token 6 = tone, touch, trace, hint, sound

• VERB 1 = notice, see, observe, perceive 2 = bear in mind, be aware, take into account 3 = mention, record, mark, indicate, register, remark 4 = write down, record, scribble, set down, jot down

notebook = notepad, exercise book, journal, diary

noted = famous, celebrated, distinguished, well-known, prominent, acclaimed, notable, renowned ≠ unknown

nothing 1 = nought, zero, nil, not a thing,

zilch (slang) 2 = a trifle 3 = nobody, cipher, nonentity 4 = void, emptiness, nothingness, nullity

notice VERB = observe, see, note, spot, distinguish, perceive, detect, discern ≠ overlook

• NOUN 1 = notification, warning, advice, intimation, news, communication, announcement, instruction 2 = attention, interest, note, regard, consideration, observation, scrutiny, heed ≠ oversight 3 = the sack (informal), dismissal, the boot (slang), the push (slang), marching orders (informal)

noticeable = obvious, clear, striking, plain, evident, manifest, conspicuous, perceptible

notify = inform, tell, advise, alert to, announce, warn, make known to

notion 1 = idea, view, opinion, belief, concept, impression, sentiment, inkling 2 = whim, wish, desire, fancy, impulse, inclination, caprice

notorious = infamous, disreputable, opprobrious

notoriously = infamously, disreputably

notwithstanding = despite, in spite of, regardless of

nought or (Archaic or literary) **naught** = zero, nothing, nil

nourish 1 = feed, supply, sustain, nurture 2 = encourage, support, maintain, promote, sustain, foster

nourishing = nutritious, beneficial, wholesome, nutritive

novel[1] = story, tale, fiction, romance, narrative

novel[2] = new, different, original, fresh, unusual, innovative, uncommon ≠ ordinary

novelty 1 = newness, originality, freshness, innovation, surprise, uniqueness, strangeness, unfamiliarity 2 = curiosity, rarity, oddity, wonder 3 = trinket, souvenir, memento, bauble, trifle, knick-knack

novice = beginner, pupil, amateur, newcomer, trainee, apprentice, learner, probationer ≠ expert

now ADVERB 1 = nowadays, at the moment 2 = immediately, promptly, instantly, at once, straightaway

• PHRASES **now and then** or **again** = occasionally, sometimes, from time

to time, on and off, intermittently,
infrequently, sporadically

nowadays = now, today, at the moment,
in this day and age

nucleus = centre, heart, focus, basis, core,
pivot, kernel, nub

nude = naked, stripped, bare, undressed,
stark-naked, disrobed, unclothed, unclad
≠ dressed

nudge VERB 1 = push, touch, dig, jog, prod,
elbow, shove, poke 2 = prompt, influence,
persuade, spur, prod, coax
● NOUN 1 = push, touch, dig, elbow, bump,
shove, poke, jog 2 = prompting, push,
encouragement, prod

nuisance = trouble, problem, trial, drag
(*informal*), bother, pest, irritation, hassle
(*informal*) ≠ benefit

numb ADJECTIVE 1 = unfeeling, dead,
frozen, paralysed, insensitive, deadened,
immobilized, torpid ≠ sensitive
2 = stupefied, deadened, unfeeling
● VERB 1 = stun, knock out, paralyse,
daze 2 = deaden, freeze, dull, paralyse,
immobilize, benumb

number NOUN 1 = numeral, figure,
character, digit, integer 2 = amount,
quantity, collection, aggregate ≠ shortage
3 = crowd, horde, multitude, throng
4 = group, set, band, crowd, gang
5 = issue, copy, edition, imprint, printing
● VERB 1 = amount to, come to, total,
add up to 2 = calculate, account, reckon,
compute, enumerate ≠ guess 3 = include,
count

numerous = many, several, countless,
lots, abundant, plentiful, innumerable,
copious ≠ few

nurse 1 = look after, treat, tend, care for,
take care of, minister to 2 = harbour, have,
maintain, preserve, entertain, cherish
3 = breast-feed, feed, nurture, nourish,
suckle, wet-nurse

nursery = crèche, kindergarten,
playgroup

nurture VERB = bring up, raise, look after,
rear, care for, develop ≠ neglect
● NOUN = upbringing, training, education,
instruction, rearing, development

nut 1 (*Slang*) = madman, psycho (*slang*),
crank (*informal*), lunatic, maniac, nutcase
(*slang*) 2 (*Slang*) = head, skull

nutrition = food, nourishment,
sustenance, nutriment

oath 1 = promise, bond, pledge, vow, word,
affirmation, avowal 2 = swear word, curse,
obscenity, blasphemy, expletive, four-letter
word, profanity

obedience = compliance, respect,
reverence, observance, subservience,
submissiveness, docility ≠ disobedience

obey 1 = submit to, surrender (to), give
way to, bow to, give in to, yield to, do
what you are told by ≠ disobey 2 = carry
out, follow, implement, act upon, carry
through ≠ disregard 3 = abide by, keep,
follow, comply with, observe, heed,
conform to, keep to

object¹ 1 = thing, article, body, item,
entity 2 = purpose, aim, end, point, plan,
idea, goal, design 3 = target, victim, focus,
recipient

object² 1 *with to* = protest against,
oppose, argue against, draw the line
at, take exception to, cry out against,
complain against, expostulate against
≠ accept 2 = disagree, demur, remonstrate,
express disapproval ≠ agree

objection = protest, opposition,
complaint, doubt, dissent, outcry,
protestation, scruple ≠ agreement

objective NOUN = purpose, aim, goal, end,
plan, hope, idea, target
● ADJECTIVE 1 = factual, real 2 = unbiased,
detached, fair, open-minded, impartial,
impersonal, disinterested, even-handed
≠ subjective

objectively = impartially, neutrally, fairly,
justly, without prejudice, dispassionately,
with an open mind, equitably

obligation 1 = duty, compulsion 2 = task,
job, duty, work, charge, role, function,
mission 3 = responsibility, duty, liability,
accountability, answerability

oblige 1 = compel, make, force, require,
bind, constrain, necessitate, impel
2 = help, assist, benefit, please, humour,
accommodate, indulge, gratify ≠ bother

obliged 1 = forced, required, bound,

compelled, duty-bound 2 = <u>grateful</u>, in (someone's) debt, thankful, indebted, appreciative, beholden

obliging = <u>accommodating</u>, kind, helpful, willing, polite, cooperative, agreeable, considerate ≠ unhelpful

obscene 1 = <u>indecent</u>, dirty, offensive, filthy, improper, immoral, pornographic, lewd ≠ decent 2 = <u>offensive</u>, shocking, evil, disgusting, outrageous, revolting, sickening, vile

obscure ADJECTIVE 1 = <u>unknown</u>, little-known, humble, unfamiliar, out-of-the-way, lowly, unheard-of, undistinguished ≠ famous 2 = <u>abstruse</u>, complex, confusing, mysterious, vague, unclear, ambiguous, enigmatic ≠ straightforward 3 = <u>unclear</u>, uncertain, confused, mysterious, doubtful, indeterminate ≠ well-known 4 = <u>indistinct</u>, vague, blurred, dark, faint, dim, gloomy, murky ≠ clear
● VERB 1 = <u>obstruct</u>, hinder 2 = <u>hide</u>, screen, mask, disguise, conceal, veil, cloak, camouflage ≠ expose

observation 1 = <u>watching</u>, study, survey, review, investigation, monitoring, examination, inspection 2 = <u>comment</u>, thought, note, statement, opinion, remark, explanation, reflection 3 = <u>remark</u>, comment, statement, reflection, utterance 4 = <u>observance of</u>, compliance with, honouring of, fulfilment of, carrying out of

observe 1 = <u>watch</u>, study, view, look at, check, survey, monitor, keep an eye on (*informal*) 2 = <u>notice</u>, see, note, discover, spot, regard, witness, distinguish 3 = <u>remark</u>, say, comment, state, note, reflect, mention, opine 4 = <u>comply with</u>, keep, follow, respect, carry out, honour, discharge, obey ≠ disregard

observer 1 = <u>witness</u>, viewer, spectator, looker-on, watcher, onlooker, eyewitness, bystander 2 = <u>commentator</u>, reporter, special correspondent 3 = <u>monitor</u>, watchdog, supervisor, scrutineer

obsessed = <u>absorbed</u>, dominated, gripped, haunted, distracted, hung up (*slang*), preoccupied ≠ indifferent

obsession = <u>preoccupation</u>, thing (*informal*), complex, hang-up (*informal*), mania, phobia, fetish, fixation

obsessive = <u>compulsive</u>, gripping, consuming, haunting, irresistible, neurotic,

besetting, uncontrollable

obsolete = <u>outdated</u>, old, passé, old-fashioned, discarded, extinct, out of date, archaic ≠ up-to-date

obstacle 1 = <u>obstruction</u>, block, barrier, hurdle, snag, impediment, blockage, hindrance 2 = <u>hindrance</u>, bar, difficulty, barrier, handicap, hurdle, hitch, drawback, uphill (*S. African*) ≠ help

obstruct 1 = <u>block</u>, close, bar, plug, barricade, stop up, bung up (*informal*) 2 = <u>hold up</u>, stop, check, block, restrict, slow down, hamper, hinder 3 = <u>impede</u>, hamper, hold back, thwart, hinder ≠ help 4 = <u>obscure</u>, screen, cover

obtain 1 = <u>get</u>, gain, acquire, land, net, pick up, secure, procure ≠ lose 2 = <u>achieve</u>, get, gain, accomplish, attain 3 (*Formal*) = <u>prevail</u>, hold, exist, be the case, abound, predominate, be in force, be current

obvious = <u>clear</u>, plain, apparent, evident, distinct, manifest, noticeable, conspicuous ≠ unclear

obviously 1 = <u>clearly</u>, of course, without doubt, assuredly 2 = <u>plainly</u>, patently, undoubtedly, evidently, manifestly, markedly, without doubt, unquestionably

occasion NOUN 1 = <u>time</u>, moment, point, stage, instance, juncture 2 = <u>function</u>, event, affair, do (*informal*), happening, experience, gathering, celebration 3 = <u>opportunity</u>, chance, time, opening, window 4 = <u>reason</u>, cause, call, ground(s), excuse, incentive, motive, justification
● VERB (*Formal*) = <u>cause</u>, produce, lead to, inspire, result in, generate, prompt, provoke

occasional = <u>infrequent</u>, odd, rare, irregular, sporadic, intermittent, few and far between, periodic ≠ constant

occasionally = <u>sometimes</u>, at times, from time to time, now and then, irregularly, now and again, periodically, once in a while ≠ constantly

occult NOUN = <u>magic</u>, witchcraft, sorcery, wizardry, enchantment, black art, necromancy
● ADJECTIVE = <u>supernatural</u>, magical, mysterious, psychic, mystical, unearthly, esoteric, uncanny

occupant = <u>occupier</u>, resident, tenant, inmate, inhabitant, incumbent, dweller, lessee

occupation 1 = <u>job</u>, calling, business,

line (of work), trade, career, employment, profession **2** = <u>hobby</u>, pastime, diversion, relaxation, leisure pursuit, (leisure) activity **3** = <u>invasion</u>, seizure, conquest, incursion, subjugation **4** = <u>occupancy</u>, residence, holding, control, possession, tenure, tenancy

occupied 1 = <u>in use</u>, taken, full, engaged, unavailable **2** = <u>inhabited</u>, peopled, lived-in, settled, tenanted ≠ uninhabited **3** = <u>busy</u>, engaged, employed, working, active, hard at work, rushed off your feet

occupy 1 = <u>inhabit</u>, own, live in, dwell in, reside in, abide in ≠ vacate **2** = <u>invade</u>, take over, capture, seize, conquer, overrun, annex, colonize ≠ withdraw **3** = <u>hold</u>, control, dominate, possess **4** = <u>take up</u>, consume, tie up, use up, monopolize **5** *often passive* = <u>engage</u>, involve, employ, divert, preoccupy, engross **6** = <u>fill</u>, take up, cover, fill up, pervade, permeate, extend over

occur VERB 1 = <u>happen</u>, take place, come about, turn up (*informal*), crop up (*informal*), transpire (*informal*), befall **2** = <u>exist</u>, appear, be found, develop, turn up, be present, manifest itself, present itself

● PHRASES **occur to someone** = <u>come to mind</u>, strike someone, dawn on someone, spring to mind, cross someone's mind, enter someone's head, suggest itself to someone

occurrence 1 = <u>incident</u>, happening, event, fact, matter, affair, circumstance, episode **2** = <u>existence</u>, instance, appearance, manifestation, materialization

odd 1 = <u>peculiar</u>, strange, unusual, extraordinary, bizarre, offbeat, freakish **2** = <u>unusual</u>, strange, rare, extraordinary, remarkable, bizarre, peculiar, irregular ≠ normal **3** = <u>occasional</u>, various, random, casual, irregular, periodic, sundry, incidental ≠ regular **4** = <u>spare</u>, remaining, extra, surplus, solitary, leftover, unmatched, unpaired ≠ matched

odds PLURAL NOUN 1 = <u>probability</u>, chances, likelihood

● PHRASES **at odds 1** = <u>in conflict</u>, arguing, quarrelling, at loggerheads, at daggers drawn **2** = <u>at variance</u>, conflicting, contrary to, at odds, out of line, out of step, at sixes and sevens (*informal*)

◆ **odds and ends** = <u>scraps</u>, bits, remains, fragments, debris, remnants, bits and pieces, bric-a-brac

odour = <u>smell</u>, scent, perfume, fragrance, stink, bouquet, aroma, stench

odyssey = <u>journey</u>, tour, trip, quest, trek, expedition, voyage, crusade

off ADVERB = <u>away</u>, out, apart, elsewhere, aside, hence, from here

● ADJECTIVE **1** = <u>absent</u>, gone, unavailable **2** = <u>cancelled</u>, abandoned, postponed, shelved **3** = <u>bad</u>, rotten, rancid, mouldy, turned, spoiled, sour, decayed

offence 1 = <u>crime</u>, sin, fault, violation, wrongdoing, trespass, felony, misdemeanour **2** = <u>outrage</u>, shock, anger, trouble, bother, resentment, irritation, hassle (*informal*) **3** = <u>insult</u>, slight, hurt, outrage, injustice, snub, affront, indignity

offend 1 = <u>distress</u>, upset, outrage, wound, slight, insult, annoy, snub ≠ please **2** = <u>break the law</u>, sin, err, do wrong, fall, go astray

offended = <u>upset</u>, hurt, bothered, disturbed, distressed, outraged, stung, put out (*informal*), tooshie (*Austral. slang*)

offender = <u>criminal</u>, convict, crook, villain, culprit, sinner, delinquent, felon

offensive ADJECTIVE 1 = <u>insulting</u>, rude, abusive, degrading, contemptuous, disparaging, objectionable, disrespectful ≠ respectful **2** = <u>disgusting</u>, gross, foul, unpleasant, revolting, vile, repellent, obnoxious, festy (*Austral. slang*), yucko (*Austral. slang*) ≠ pleasant **3** = <u>attacking</u>, threatening, aggressive, striking, hostile, invading, combative ≠ defensive

● NOUN = <u>attack</u>, charge, campaign, strike, push (*informal*), assault, raid, drive

offer VERB 1 = <u>provide</u>, present, furnish, afford ≠ withhold **2** = <u>volunteer</u>, come forward, offer your services **3** = <u>propose</u>, suggest, advance, submit **4** = <u>give</u>, show, bring, provide, render, impart **5** = <u>put up for sale</u>, sell **6** = <u>bid</u>, submit, propose, tender, proffer

● NOUN **1** = <u>proposal</u>, suggestion, proposition, submission **2** = <u>bid</u>, tender, bidding price

offering 1 = <u>contribution</u>, gift, donation, present, subscription, hand-out **2** = <u>sacrifice</u>, tribute, libation, burnt offering

office 1 = <u>place of work</u>, workplace, base,

workroom, place of business **2** = <u>branch</u>, department, division, section, wing, subdivision, subsection **3** = <u>post</u>, place, role, situation, responsibility, function, occupation

officer 1 = <u>official</u>, executive, agent, representative, appointee, functionary, office-holder, office bearer **2** = <u>police officer</u>, detective, PC, police constable, police man, police woman

official ADJECTIVE **1** = <u>authorized</u>, formal, sanctioned, licensed, proper, legitimate, authentic, certified ≠ unofficial **2** = <u>formal</u>, bureaucratic, ceremonial, solemn, ritualistic

● NOUN = <u>officer</u>, executive, agent, representative, bureaucrat, appointee, functionary, office-holder

offset = <u>cancel out</u>, balance, set off, make up for, compensate for, counteract, neutralize, counterbalance

offspring 1 = <u>child</u>, baby, kid (*informal*), youngster, infant, successor, babe, toddler, littlie (*Austral. informal*), ankle-biter (*Austral. slang*), tacker (*Austral. slang*) ≠ parent **2** = <u>children</u>, young, family, issue, stock, heirs, descendants, brood

often = <u>frequently</u>, generally, commonly, repeatedly, time and again, habitually, not infrequently ≠ never

oil VERB = <u>lubricate</u>, grease

● NOUN **1** = <u>lubricant</u>, grease, lubrication, fuel oil **2** = <u>lotion</u>, cream, balm, salve, liniment, embrocation, solution

oily = <u>greasy</u>, slimy, fatty, slippery, oleaginous

OK *or* **okay** ADJECTIVE (*Informal*) **1** = <u>all right</u>, fine, fitting, in order, permitted, suitable, acceptable, allowable ≠ unacceptable **2** = <u>fine</u>, good, average, fair, all right, acceptable, adequate, satisfactory ≠ unsatisfactory **3** = <u>well</u>, all right, safe, sound, healthy, unharmed, uninjured

● INTERJECTION = <u>all right</u>, right, yes, agreed, very good, roger, very well, ya (*S. African*), righto (*Brit. informal*), yebo (*S. African informal*)

● VERB = <u>approve</u>, allow, agree to, permit, sanction, endorse, authorize, rubber-stamp (*informal*)

● NOUN = <u>authorization</u>, agreement, sanction, approval, go-ahead (*informal*), blessing, permission, consent

old 1 = <u>aged</u>, elderly, ancient, mature, venerable, antiquated, senile, decrepit ≠ young **2** = <u>former</u>, earlier, past, previous, prior, one-time, erstwhile **3** = <u>long-standing</u>, established, fixed, enduring, abiding, long-lasting, long-established, time-honoured **4** = <u>stale</u>, worn-out, banal, threadbare, trite, overused, timeworn

old-fashioned 1 = <u>out of date</u>, dated, outdated, unfashionable, outmoded, passé, old hat, behind the times ≠ up-to-date **2** = <u>oldfangled</u>, square (*informal*), outdated, unfashionable, obsolescent

ominous = <u>threatening</u>, sinister, grim, fateful, foreboding, unpromising, portentous, inauspicious ≠ promising

omission 1 = <u>exclusion</u>, removal, elimination, deletion, excision ≠ inclusion **2** = <u>gap</u>, space, exclusion, lacuna **3** = <u>failure</u>, neglect, negligence, oversight, carelessness, dereliction, slackness, laxity

omit 1 = <u>leave out</u>, drop, exclude, eliminate, skip ≠ include **2** = <u>forget</u>, overlook, neglect, pass over, lose sight of

once ADVERB **1** = <u>on one occasion</u>, one time, one single time **2** = <u>at one time</u>, previously, formerly, long ago, once upon a time

● CONJUNCTION = <u>as soon as</u>, when, after, the moment, immediately, the instant

● PHRASES **at once 1** = <u>immediately</u>, now, straight away, directly, promptly, instantly, right away, forthwith **2** = <u>simultaneously</u>, together, at the same time, concurrently

one-sided 1 = <u>unequal</u>, unfair, uneven, unjust, unbalanced, lopsided, ill-matched ≠ equal **2** = <u>biased</u>, prejudiced, weighted, unfair, partial, distorted, partisan, slanted ≠ unbiased

ongoing = <u>in progress</u>, developing, progressing, evolving, unfolding, unfinished

onlooker = <u>spectator</u>, witness, observer, viewer, looker-on, watcher, eyewitness, bystander

only ADJECTIVE = <u>sole</u>, one, single, individual, exclusive, unique, lone, solitary

● ADVERB **1** = <u>just</u>, simply, purely, merely **2** = <u>hardly</u>, just, barely, only just, scarcely, at a push

onset = <u>beginning</u>, start, birth, outbreak, inception, commencement ≠ end

onslaught = <u>attack</u>, charge, campaign, strike, assault, raid, invasion, offensive

≠ retreat

onward or **onwards** = <u>forward</u>, on, forwards, ahead, beyond, in front, forth

ooze[1] 1 = <u>seep</u>, well, escape, leak, drain, filter, drip, trickle 2 = <u>emit</u>, release, leak, drip, dribble, give off, pour forth 3 = <u>exude</u>, emit

ooze[2] = <u>mud</u>, clay, dirt, silt, sludge, mire, slime, alluvium

open VERB 1 = <u>unfasten</u>, unlock ≠ close 2 = <u>unwrap</u>, uncover, undo, unravel, untie ≠ wrap 3 = <u>uncork</u> 4 = <u>unfold</u>, spread (out), expand, unfurl, unroll ≠ fold 5 = <u>clear</u>, unblock ≠ block 6 = <u>undo</u>, unbutton, unfasten ≠ fasten 7 = <u>begin</u> business 8 = <u>start</u>, begin, launch, trigger, kick off (informal), initiate, commence, get going ≠ end 9 = <u>begin</u>, start, commence ≠ end

● ADJECTIVE 1 = <u>unclosed</u>, unlocked, ajar, unfastened, yawning ≠ closed 2 = <u>unsealed</u>, unstoppered ≠ unopened 3 = <u>extended</u>, unfolded, stretched out, unfurled, straightened out, unrolled ≠ shut 4 = <u>frank</u>, direct, straightforward, sincere, transparent, honest, candid, truthful ≠ sly 5 = <u>receptive</u>, sympathetic, responsive, amenable 6 = <u>unresolved</u>, unsettled, undecided, debatable, moot, arguable 7 = <u>clear</u>, passable, unhindered, unimpeded, navigable, unobstructed ≠ obstructed 8 = <u>available</u>, to hand, accessible, handy, at your disposal 9 = <u>general</u>, public, free, universal, blanket, across-the-board, unrestricted, overarching ≠ restricted 10 = <u>vacant</u>, free, available, empty, unoccupied, unfilled

open-air = <u>outdoor</u>, outside, out-of-door(s), alfresco

opening ADJECTIVE = <u>first</u>, earliest, beginning, premier, primary, initial, maiden, inaugural

● NOUN 1 = <u>beginning</u>, start, launch, dawn, outset, initiation, inception, commencement ≠ ending 2 = <u>hole</u>, space, tear, crack, gap, slot, puncture, aperture ≠ blockage 3 = <u>opportunity</u>, chance, time, moment, occasion, look-in (informal) 4 = <u>job</u>, position, post, situation, opportunity, vacancy

openly = <u>frankly</u>, plainly, honestly, overtly, candidly, unreservedly, unhesitatingly, forthrightly ≠ privately

open-minded = <u>unprejudiced</u>, liberal,

balanced, objective, reasonable, tolerant, impartial, receptive ≠ narrow-minded

operate 1 = <u>manage</u>, run, direct, handle, supervise, be in charge of 2 = <u>function</u>, work, act 3 = <u>run</u>, work, use, control, manoeuvre 4 = <u>work</u>, go, run, perform, function ≠ break down

operation = <u>performance</u>, action, movement, motion

operational = <u>working</u>, going, running, ready, functioning, operative, viable, functional ≠ inoperative

operative ADJECTIVE = <u>in force</u>, effective, functioning, active, in effect, operational, in operation ≠ inoperative

● NOUN 1 = <u>worker</u>, employee, labourer, workman, artisan 2 (U.S. & Canad.) = <u>spy</u>, undercover agent, mole, nark (Brit., Austral., & N.Z. slang)

operator = <u>worker</u>, driver, mechanic, operative, conductor, technician, handler

opinion 1 = <u>belief</u>, feeling, view, idea, theory, conviction, point of view, sentiment 2 = <u>estimation</u>, view, impression, assessment, judgment, appraisal, considered opinion

opponent 1 = <u>adversary</u>, rival, enemy, competitor, challenger, foe, contestant, antagonist ≠ ally 2 = <u>opposer</u>, dissident, objector ≠ supporter

opportunity = <u>chance</u>, opening, time, turn, moment, possibility, occasion, slot

oppose = <u>be against</u>, fight (against), block, take on, counter, contest, resist, combat ≠ support

opposed 1 with to = <u>against</u>, hostile, adverse, in opposition, averse, antagonistic, (dead) set against 2 = <u>contrary</u>, conflicting, clashing, counter, adverse, contradictory, dissentient

opposing 1 = <u>conflicting</u>, different, contrasting, opposite, differing, contrary, contradictory, incompatible 2 = <u>rival</u>, conflicting, competing, enemy, opposite, hostile

opposite PREPOSITION = <u>facing</u>, face to face with, across from, eyeball to eyeball (informal)

● ADJECTIVE 1 = <u>facing</u>, other, opposing 2 = <u>different</u>, conflicting, contrasted, contrasting, unlike, contrary, dissimilar, divergent ≠ alike 3 = <u>rival</u>, conflicting, opposing, competing

● NOUN = <u>reverse</u>, contrary, converse,

antithesis, contradiction, inverse, obverse

opposition 1 = <u>hostility</u>, resistance, resentment, disapproval, obstruction, animosity, antagonism, antipathy ≠ support 2 = <u>opponent(s)</u>, competition, rival(s), enemy, competitor(s), other side, challenger(s), foe

oppress 1 = <u>subjugate</u>, abuse, suppress, wrong, master, overcome, subdue, persecute ≠ liberate 2 = <u>depress</u>, burden, discourage, torment, harass, afflict, sadden, vex

oppression = <u>persecution</u>, control, abuse, injury, injustice, cruelty, domination, repression ≠ justice

oppressive 1 = <u>tyrannical</u>, severe, harsh, cruel, brutal, authoritarian, unjust, repressive ≠ merciful 2 = <u>stifling</u>, close, sticky, stuffy, humid, sultry, airless, muggy

opt VERB = <u>choose</u>, decide, prefer, select, elect ≠ reject

● PHRASES **opt for something** or **someone** = <u>choose</u>, pick, select, adopt, go for, designate, decide on, plump for

optimistic 1 = <u>hopeful</u>, positive, confident, encouraged, cheerful, rosy, buoyant, sanguine ≠ pessimistic 2 = <u>encouraging</u>, promising, bright, good, reassuring, rosy, heartening, auspicious ≠ discouraging

optimum or **optimal** = <u>ideal</u>, best, highest, finest, perfect, supreme, peak, outstanding ≠ worst

option = <u>choice</u>, alternative, selection, preference, freedom of choice, power to choose

optional = <u>voluntary</u>, open, discretionary, possible, extra, elective ≠ compulsory

opus = <u>work</u>, piece, production, creation, composition, work of art, brainchild, oeuvre (*French*)

oral = <u>spoken</u>, vocal, verbal, unwritten

orbit NOUN 1 = <u>path</u>, course, cycle, circle, revolution, rotation, trajectory, sweep 2 = <u>sphere of influence</u>, reach, range, influence, province, scope, domain, compass

● VERB = <u>circle</u>, ring, go round, revolve around, encircle, circumscribe, circumnavigate

orchestrate 1 = <u>organize</u>, plan, run, set up, arrange, put together, marshal, coordinate 2 = <u>score</u>, set, arrange, adapt

ordain 1 = <u>appoint</u>, name, commission, select, invest, nominate, anoint, consecrate 2 (*Formal*) = <u>order</u>, will, rule, demand, require, direct, command, dictate

ordeal = <u>hardship</u>, trial, difficulty, test, suffering, nightmare, torture, agony ≠ pleasure

order VERB 1 = <u>command</u>, instruct, direct, charge, demand, require, bid, compel ≠ forbid 2 = <u>decree</u>, rule, demand, prescribe, pronounce, ordain ≠ ban 3 = <u>request</u>, ask (for), book, seek, reserve, apply for, solicit, send away for 4 = <u>arrange</u>, group, sort, position, line up, organize, catalogue, sort out ≠ disarrange ● NOUN 1 = <u>instruction</u>, ruling, demand, direction, command, dictate, decree, mandate 2 = <u>request</u>, booking, demand, commission, application, reservation, requisition 3 = <u>sequence</u>, grouping, series, structure, chain, arrangement, line-up, array 4 = <u>organization</u>, system, method, pattern, symmetry, regularity, neatness, tidiness ≠ chaos 5 = <u>peace</u>, control, law, quiet, calm, discipline, law and order, tranquillity 6 = <u>society</u>, company, group, club, community, association, institute, organization 7 = <u>class</u>, set, rank, grade, caste 8 = <u>kind</u>, group, class, family, sort, type, variety, category

orderly 1 = <u>well-behaved</u>, controlled, disciplined, quiet, restrained, law-abiding, peaceable ≠ disorderly 2 = <u>well-organized</u>, regular, in order, organized, precise, neat, tidy, systematic ≠ disorganized

ordinary 1 = <u>usual</u>, standard, normal, common, regular, typical, conventional, routine 2 = <u>commonplace</u>, plain, modest, humble, mundane, banal, unremarkable, run-of-the-mill ≠ extraordinary

organ 1 = <u>body part</u>, part of the body, element, biological structure 2 = <u>newspaper</u>, medium, voice, vehicle, gazette, mouthpiece

organic 1 = <u>natural</u>, biological, living, live, animate 2 = <u>systematic</u>, ordered, structured, organized, integrated, orderly, methodical

organism = <u>creature</u>, being, thing, body, animal, structure, beast, entity

organization 1 = <u>group</u>, company, party, body, association, band, institution, corporation 2 = <u>management</u>, running, planning, control, operation, handling, structuring, administration 3 = <u>structure</u>, form, pattern, make-up, arrangement, construction, format, formation

organize 1 = <u>arrange</u>, run, plan, prepare, set up, devise, put together, take care of, jack up (*N.Z. informal*) ≠ disrupt **2** = <u>put in order</u>, arrange, group, list, file, index, classify, inventory ≠ muddle

orient *or* **orientate 1** = <u>adjust</u>, adapt, alter, accustom, align, familiarize, acclimatize **2** = <u>get your bearings</u>, establish your location

orientation 1 = <u>inclination</u>, tendency, disposition, predisposition, predilection, proclivity, partiality **2** = <u>induction</u>, introduction, adjustment, settling in, adaptation, assimilation, familiarization, acclimatization **3** = <u>position</u>, situation, location, bearings, direction, arrangement, whereabouts

origin 1 = <u>beginning</u>, start, birth, launch, foundation, creation, emergence, onset ≠ end **2** = <u>root</u>, source, basis, base, seed, foundation, nucleus, derivation

original ADJECTIVE **1** = <u>first</u>, earliest, initial **2** = <u>initial</u>, first, starting, opening, primary, introductory ≠ final **3** = <u>new</u>, fresh, novel, unusual, unprecedented, innovative, unfamiliar, seminal ≠ unoriginal **4** = <u>creative</u>, inspired, imaginative, artistic, fertile, ingenious, visionary, inventive
● NOUN = <u>prototype</u>, master, pattern ≠ copy

originally = <u>initially</u>, first, firstly, at first, primarily, to begin with, in the beginning

originate 1 = <u>begin</u>, start, emerge, come, happen, rise, appear, spring ≠ end **2** = <u>invent</u>, create, design, launch, introduce, institute, generate, pioneer

ornament NOUN **1** = <u>decoration</u>, trimming, accessory, festoon, trinket, bauble, knick-knack **2** = <u>embellishment</u>, decoration, embroidery, elaboration, adornment, ornamentation
● VERB = <u>decorate</u>, adorn, array, do up (*informal*), embellish, festoon, beautify, prettify

orthodox 1 = <u>established</u>, official, accepted, received, common, traditional, normal, usual ≠ unorthodox **2** = <u>conformist</u>, conservative, traditional, strict, devout, observant ≠ nonconformist

orthodoxy 1 = <u>doctrine</u>, teaching, opinion, principle, belief, convention, creed, dogma **2** = <u>conformity</u>, received

wisdom, traditionalism, conventionality ≠ nonconformity

other 1 = <u>additional</u>, more, further, new, added, extra, fresh, spare **2** = <u>different</u>, alternative, contrasting, distinct, diverse, dissimilar, separate, alternative

otherwise 1 = <u>or else</u>, or, if not, or then **2** = <u>apart from that</u>, in other ways, in (all) other respects **3** = <u>differently</u>, any other way, contrarily

ounce = <u>shred</u>, bit, drop, trace, scrap, grain, fragment, atom

oust = <u>expel</u>, turn out, dismiss, exclude, exile, throw out, displace, topple

out ADJECTIVE **1** = <u>not in</u>, away, elsewhere, outside, gone, abroad, from home, absent **2** = <u>extinguished</u>, ended, finished, dead, exhausted, expired, used up, at an end ≠ alight **3** = <u>in bloom</u>, opening, open, flowering, blooming, in flower, in full bloom **4** = <u>available</u>, on sale, in the shops, to be had, purchasable **5** = <u>revealed</u>, exposed, common knowledge, public knowledge, (out) in the open ≠ kept secret
● VERB = <u>expose</u>

outbreak 1 = <u>eruption</u>, burst, explosion, epidemic, rash, outburst, flare-up, upsurge **2** = <u>onset</u>, beginning, outset, opening, dawn, commencement

outburst = <u>explosion</u>, fit, surge, outbreak, flare-up, eruption, spasm, outpouring

outcome = <u>result</u>, end, consequence, conclusion, payoff (*informal*), upshot

outcry = <u>protest</u>, complaint, objection, dissent, outburst, clamour, uproar, commotion

outdated = <u>old-fashioned</u>, dated, obsolete, out of date, passé, archaic, unfashionable, antiquated ≠ modern

outdoor = <u>open-air</u>, outside, out-of-door(s), alfresco ≠ indoor

outer 1 = <u>external</u>, outside, outward, exterior, exposed, outermost ≠ inner **2** = <u>surface</u> **3** = <u>outlying</u>, distant, provincial, out-of-the-way, peripheral, far-flung ≠ central

outfit 1 = <u>costume</u>, dress, clothes, clothing, suit, get-up (*informal*), kit, ensemble **2** (*Informal*) = <u>group</u>, company, team, party, unit, crowd, squad, organization

outgoing 1 = <u>leaving</u>, former, previous, retiring, withdrawing, prior, departing, erstwhile ≠ incoming **2** = <u>sociable</u>, open, social, warm, friendly, expansive, affable, extrovert ≠ reserved

outgoings = expenses, costs, payments, expenditure, overheads, outlay

outing = journey, run, trip, tour, expedition, excursion, spin (*informal*), jaunt

outlaw VERB 1 = ban, bar, veto, forbid, exclude, prohibit, disallow, proscribe ≠ legalise 2 = banish, put a price on (someone's) head

● NOUN (*History*) = bandit, criminal, thief, robber, fugitive, outcast, felon, highwayman

outlet 1 = shop, store, supermarket, market, boutique, emporium, hypermarket 2 = channel, release, medium, avenue, vent, conduit 3 = pipe, opening, channel, exit, duct

outline VERB 1 = summarize, draft, plan, trace, sketch (in), sum up, encapsulate, delineate 2 = silhouette, etch

● NOUN 1 = summary, review, résumé, rundown, mood, synopsis, précis, thumbnail sketch, recapitulation 2 = shape, lines, form, figure, profile, silhouette, configuration, contour(s)

outlook 1 = attitude, opinion, position, approach, mood, perspective, point of view, stance 2 = prospect(s), future, expectations, forecast, prediction, probability, prognosis

out of date 1 = old-fashioned, dated, outdated, obsolete, démodé (*French*), antiquated, outmoded, passé ≠ modern 2 = invalid, expired, lapsed, void, null and void

output = production, manufacture, manufacturing, yield, productivity

outrage VERB = offend, shock, upset, wound, insult, infuriate, incense, madden

● NOUN = indignation, shock, anger, rage, fury, hurt, resentment, scorn

outrageous 1 = atrocious, shocking, terrible, offensive, appalling, cruel, savage, horrifying ≠ mild 2 = unreasonable, unfair, steep (*informal*), shocking, extravagant, scandalous, preposterous, unwarranted ≠ reasonable

outright ADJECTIVE 1 = absolute, complete, total, perfect, sheer, thorough, unconditional, unqualified 2 = definite, clear, certain, flat, absolute, black-and-white, straightforward, unequivocal

● ADVERB 1 = openly, frankly, plainly,

overtly, candidly, unreservedly, unhesitatingly, forthrightly 2 = absolutely, completely, totally, fully, entirely, thoroughly, wholly, utterly

outset = beginning, start, opening, onset, inauguration, inception, commencement, kickoff (*informal*) ≠ finish

outside NOUN = exterior, face, front, covering, skin, surface, shell, coating

● ADJECTIVE 1 = external, outer, exterior, outward, extraneous ≠ inner 2 = remote, small, unlikely, slight, slim, distant, faint, marginal

● ADVERB = outdoors, out of the house, out-of-doors

outsider = stranger, incomer, visitor, newcomer, intruder, interloper, odd one out

outskirts = edge, boundary, suburbs, fringe, perimeter, periphery, suburbia, environs

outspan (*S. African*) = relax, chill out (*slang, chiefly U.S.*), take it easy, loosen up, put your feet up

outspoken = forthright, open, frank, straightforward, blunt, explicit, upfront (*informal*), unequivocal ≠ reserved

outstanding 1 = excellent, good, great, important, special, fine, brilliant, impressive, booshit (*Austral. slang*), exo (*Austral. slang*), sik (*Austral. slang*) ≠ mediocre 2 = unpaid, remaining, due, pending, payable, unsettled, uncollected 3 = undone, left, omitted, unfinished, unfulfilled, unperformed

outward = apparent, seeming, surface, ostensible ≠ inward

outwardly = apparently, externally, seemingly, it seems that, on the surface, it appears that, ostensibly, on the face of it

outweigh = override, cancel (out), eclipse, offset, compensate for, supersede, neutralize, counterbalance

oval = elliptical, egg-shaped, ovoid

ovation = applause, hand, cheers, praise, tribute, acclaim, clapping, accolade ≠ derision

over PREPOSITION 1 = above, on top of 2 = on top of, on, across, upon 3 = across, (looking) onto 4 = more than, above, exceeding, in excess of, upwards of 5 = about, regarding, relating to, concerning, apropos of

● ADVERB 1 = above, overhead, in the sky, on high, aloft, up above 2 = extra, more, further, beyond, additional, in addition, surplus, in excess

● ADJECTIVE = finished, done (with), through, ended, closed, past, completed, complete

■■■■ RELATED WORDS

prefixes: hyper-, super-

overall ADJECTIVE = total, full, whole, general, complete, entire, global, comprehensive

● ADVERB = in general, generally, mostly, all things considered, on average, on the whole, predominantly, in the main

overcome VERB 1 = defeat, beat, conquer, master, overwhelm, subdue, rout, overpower 2 = conquer, beat, master, subdue, triumph over, vanquish

● ADJECTIVE = overwhelmed, moved, affected, emotional, choked, speechless, bowled over (*informal*), at a loss for words

overdue 1 = delayed, belated, late, behind schedule, tardy, unpunctual, behindhand ≠ early 2 = unpaid, owing

overflow VERB = spill over, well over, run over, pour over, bubble over, brim over

● NOUN 1 = flood, spilling over 2 = surplus, extra, excess, overspill, overabundance, additional people *or* things

overhaul VERB 1 = check, service, maintain, examine, restore, tune (up), repair, go over 2 = overtake, pass, leave behind, catch up with, get past, outstrip, get ahead of, outdistance

● NOUN = check, service, examination, going-over (*informal*), inspection, once-over (*informal*), checkup, reconditioning

overhead ADJECTIVE = raised, suspended, elevated, aerial, overhanging

● ADVERB = above, in the sky, on high, aloft, up above ≠ underneath

overheads = running costs, expenses, outgoings, operating costs

overlook 1 = look over *or* out on, have a view of 2 = miss, forget, neglect, omit, disregard, pass over ≠ notice 3 = ignore, excuse, forgive, pardon, disregard, condone, turn a blind eye to, wink at

overpower 1 = overcome, master, overwhelm, overthrow, subdue, quell, subjugate, prevail over 2 = defeat, crush, triumph over, vanquish 3 = overwhelm, overcome, bowl over (*informal*), stagger

override 1 = outweigh, eclipse, supersede, take precedence over, prevail

over 2 = overrule, cancel, overturn, repeal, rescind, annul, nullify, countermand 3 = ignore, reject, discount, overlook, disregard, pass over, take no notice of

overrun 1 = overwhelm, attack, assault, occupy, raid, invade, penetrate, rout 2 = spread over, overwhelm, choke, swamp, infest, inundate, permeate, swarm over 3 = exceed, go beyond, surpass, overshoot, run over *or* on

overshadow 1 = spoil, ruin, mar, wreck, blight, crool *or* cruel (*Austral. slang*), mess up, put a damper on 2 = outshine, eclipse, surpass, dwarf, tower above, leave *or* put in the shade

overt = open, obvious, plain, public, manifest, blatant, observable, undisguised ≠ hidden

overtake 1 = pass, leave behind, overhaul, catch up with, get past, outdistance, go by *or* past 2 = outdo, top, exceed, eclipse, surpass, outstrip, get the better of, outclass 3 = befall, hit, happen to, catch off guard, catch unawares 4 = engulf, overwhelm, hit, strike, swamp, envelop, swallow up

overthrow VERB = defeat, overcome, conquer, bring down, oust, topple, rout, overpower ≠ uphold

● NOUN = downfall, fall, defeat, collapse, destruction, ousting, undoing, unseating ≠ preservation

overturn 1 = tip over, topple, upturn, capsize, upend, keel over, overbalance 2 = knock over *or* down, upturn, tip over, upend 3 = reverse, change, cancel, abolish, overthrow, set aside, repeal, quash 4 = overthrow, defeat, destroy, overcome, bring down, oust, topple, depose

overweight = fat, heavy, stout, hefty, plump, bulky, chunky, chubby ≠ underweight

overwhelm 1 = overcome, devastate, stagger, bowl over (*informal*), knock (someone) for six (*informal*), sweep (someone) off his *or* her feet, take (someone's) breath away 2 = destroy, defeat, overcome, crush, massacre, conquer, wipe out, overthrow

overwhelming 1 = overpowering, strong, powerful, towering, stunning, crushing, devastating, shattering ≠ negligible 2 = vast, huge, massive, enormous, tremendous, immense, very large

≠ insignificant

owe = be in debt (to), be in arrears (to), be overdrawn (by), be obligated or indebted (to)

owing to = because of, thanks to, as a result of, on account of, by reason of

own ADJECTIVE = personal, special, private, individual, particular, exclusive
● VERB = possess, have, keep, hold, enjoy, retain, be in possession of, have to your name

owner = possessor, holder, proprietor, titleholder, landlord or landlady

ownership = possession, occupation, tenure, dominion

p

pace NOUN 1 = speed, rate, tempo, velocity 2 = step, walk, stride, tread, gait 3 = footstep, step, stride
● VERB = stride, walk, pound, patrol, march up and down

pack VERB 1 = package, load, store, bundle, stow 2 = cram, crowd, press, fill, stuff, jam, ram, compress
● NOUN 1 = packet, box, package, carton 2 = bundle, parcel, load, burden, rucksack, knapsack, back pack, kitbag 3 = group, crowd, company, band, troop, gang, bunch, mob
● PHRASES **pack someone off** = send away, dismiss, send packing (informal)
◆ **pack something in** 1 (Brit. informal) = resign from, leave, give up, quit (informal), chuck (informal), jack in (informal) 2 = stop, give up, kick (informal), cease, chuck (informal)

package NOUN 1 = parcel, box, container, packet, carton 2 = collection, lot, unit, combination, compilation
● VERB = pack, box, parcel (up)

packet 1 = container, box, package, carton 2 = package, parcel 3 (Slang) = a fortune, a bomb (Brit. slang), a pile (informal), a small fortune, a tidy sum (informal), a king's ransom (informal)

pact = agreement, alliance, treaty, deal, understanding, bargain, covenant

pad¹ NOUN 1 = wad, dressing, pack, padding, compress, wadding 2 = cushion, filling, stuffing, pillow, bolster, upholstery 3 = notepad, block, notebook, jotter, writing pad 4 (Slang) = home, flat, apartment, place 5 = paw, foot, sole
● VERB = pack, fill, protect, stuff, cushion

pad² = sneak, creep, steal, go barefoot

padding 1 = filling, stuffing, packing, wadding 2 = waffle (informal, chiefly Brit.), hot air (informal), verbiage, wordiness, verbosity

paddle¹ NOUN = oar, scull
● VERB = row, pull, scull

paddle² = wade, splash (about), slop

pagan ADJECTIVE = heathen, infidel, polytheistic, idolatrous
● NOUN = heathen, infidel, polytheist, idolater

page¹ = folio, side, leaf, sheet

page² VERB = call, summon, send for
● NOUN 1 = attendant, pageboy 2 = servant, attendant, squire, pageboy

pain NOUN 1 = suffering, discomfort, hurt, irritation, tenderness, soreness 2 = ache, stinging, aching, cramp, throb, throbbing, pang, twinge 3 = sorrow, suffering, torture, distress, despair, misery, agony, sadness
● PLURAL NOUN = trouble, effort, care, bother, diligence
● VERB 1 = distress, hurt, torture, grieve, torment, sadden, agonize, cut to the quick 2 = hurt

painful 1 = sore, smarting, aching, tender ≠ painless 2 = distressing, unpleasant, grievous, distasteful, agonizing, disagreeable ≠ pleasant 3 = difficult, arduous, trying, hard, troublesome, laborious ≠ easy

painfully = distressingly, clearly, sadly, unfortunately, dreadfully

paint NOUN = colouring, colour, stain, dye, tint, pigment, emulsion
● VERB 1 = colour, cover, coat, stain, whitewash, daub, distemper, apply paint to 2 = depict, draw, portray, picture, represent, sketch

pair NOUN 1 = set 2 = couple, brace, duo
● VERB = team, match (up), join, couple, twin, bracket

pal (Informal) = friend, companion, mate (informal), buddy (informal), comrade, chum (*informal*), crony, cobber (*Austral. & N.Z. old-fashioned informal*), E hoa (*N.Z.*)

pale ADJECTIVE 1 = <u>light</u>, soft, faded, subtle, muted, bleached, pastel, light-coloured 2 = <u>dim</u>, weak, faint, feeble, thin, wan, watery 3 = <u>white</u>, pasty, bleached, wan, colourless, pallid, ashen ≠ rosy-cheeked
● VERB = <u>become pale</u>, blanch, whiten, go white, lose colour

pamper = <u>spoil</u>, indulge, pet, cosset, coddle, mollycoddle

pamphlet = <u>booklet</u>, leaflet, brochure, circular, tract

pan¹ NOUN = <u>pot</u>, container, saucepan
● VERB 1 (*Informal*) = <u>criticize</u>, knock, slam (*slang*), censure, tear into (*informal*) 2 = <u>sift out</u>, look for, search for

pan² = <u>move along</u> or across, follow, track, sweep

panic NOUN = <u>fear</u>, alarm, terror, anxiety, hysteria, fright, trepidation, a flap (*informal*)
● VERB 1 = <u>go to pieces</u>, become hysterical, lose your nerve 2 = <u>alarm</u>, scare, unnerve

panorama 1 = <u>view</u>, prospect, vista 2 = <u>survey</u>, perspective, overview, overall picture

pant = <u>puff</u>, blow, breathe, gasp, wheeze, heave

pants 1 (*Brit.*) = <u>underpants</u>, briefs, drawers, knickers, panties, boxer shorts, broekies (*S. African*), underdaks (*Austral. slang*) 2 (*U.S.*) = <u>trousers</u>, slacks

paper NOUN 1 = <u>newspaper</u>, daily, journal, gazette 2 = <u>essay</u>, article, treatise, dissertation 3 = <u>examination</u>, test, exam 4 = <u>report</u>
● PLURAL NOUN 1 = <u>letters</u>, records, documents, file, diaries, archive, paperwork, dossier 2 = <u>documents</u>, records, certificates, identification, deeds, identity papers, I.D. (*informal*)
● VERB = <u>wallpaper</u>, hang

parade NOUN 1 = <u>procession</u>, march, pageant, cavalcade 2 = <u>show</u>, display, spectacle
● VERB 1 = <u>march</u>, process, promenade 2 = <u>flaunt</u>, display, exhibit, show off (*informal*) 3 = <u>strut</u>, show off (*informal*), swagger, swank

paradigm = <u>model</u>, example, pattern, ideal

paradise 1 = <u>heaven</u>, Promised Land, Happy Valley (*Islam*), Elysian fields 2 = <u>bliss</u>, delight, heaven, felicity, utopia

paradox = <u>contradiction</u>, puzzle, anomaly, enigma, oddity

paragraph = <u>section</u>, part, item, passage, clause, subdivision

parallel NOUN 1 = <u>equivalent</u>, counterpart, match, equal, twin, analogue ≠ opposite 2 = <u>similarity</u>, comparison, analogy, resemblance, likeness ≠ difference
● ADJECTIVE 1 = <u>matching</u>, corresponding, like, similar, resembling, analogous ≠ different 2 = <u>equidistant</u>, alongside, side by side ≠ divergent

paralyse 1 = <u>disable</u>, cripple, lame, incapacitate 2 = <u>freeze</u>, stun, numb, petrify, halt, immobilize 3 = <u>immobilize</u>, freeze, halt, disable, cripple, incapacitate, bring to a standstill

paralysis 1 = <u>immobility</u>, palsy 2 = <u>standstill</u>, breakdown, stoppage, halt

parameter (*Informal*) *usually plural* = <u>limit</u>, restriction, framework, limitation, specification

paramount = <u>principal</u>, prime, first, chief, main, primary, supreme, cardinal ≠ secondary

paranoid 1 (*Informal*) = <u>suspicious</u>, worried, nervous, fearful, antsy (*informal*) 2 = <u>obsessive</u>, disturbed, manic, neurotic, mentally ill, psychotic, deluded, paranoiac

parasite = <u>sponger</u> (*informal*), leech, hanger-on, scrounger (*informal*), bloodsucker (*informal*), quandong (*Austral. slang*)

parcel NOUN = <u>package</u>, case, box, pack, bundle
● VERB *often with* **up** = <u>wrap</u>, pack, package, tie up, do up, gift-wrap, box up, fasten together

pardon VERB 1 = <u>forgive</u>, excuse ≠ condemn 2 = <u>acquit</u>, let off (*informal*), exonerate, absolve ≠ punish
● NOUN 1 = <u>forgiveness</u>, absolution ≠ condemnation 2 = <u>acquittal</u>, amnesty, exoneration ≠ punishment

parent = <u>father</u> or mother, sire, progenitor, procreator, old (*Austral. & N.Z. informal*), patriarch

parish 1 = <u>district</u>, community 2 = <u>community</u>, flock, church, congregation

park 1 = <u>recreation ground</u>, garden, playground, pleasure garden, playpark, domain (*N.Z.*), forest park (*N.Z.*)

2 = parkland, grounds, estate, lawns, woodland, grassland **3** = field, pitch, playing field

parliament 1 = assembly, council, congress, senate, convention, legislature **2** = sitting

parliamentary = governmental, legislative, law-making

parlour or (U.S.) **parlor 1** (Old-fashioned) = sitting room, lounge, living room, drawing room, front room **2** = establishment, shop, store, salon

parody NOUN = takeoff (informal), satire, caricature, send-up (Brit. informal), spoof (informal), skit, burlesque

● VERB = take off (informal), caricature, send up (Brit. informal), burlesque, satirize, do a takeoff of (informal)

parrot = repeat, echo, imitate, copy, mimic

parry 1 = evade, avoid, dodge, sidestep **2** = ward off, block, deflect, repel, rebuff, repulse

parson = clergyman, minister, priest, vicar, preacher, pastor, cleric, churchman

part NOUN **1** = piece, share, proportion, percentage, bit, section, scrap, portion ≠ entirety **2** often plural = region, area, district, neighbourhood, quarter, vicinity **3** = component, bit, unit, constituent **4** = branch, division, office, section, wing, subdivision, subsection **5** = organ, member, limb **6** (Theatre) = role, representation, persona, portrayal, depiction, character part **7** (Theatre) = lines, words, script, dialogue **8** = side, behalf

● VERB **1** = divide, separate, break, tear, split, rend, detach, sever ≠ join **2** = part company, separate, split up ≠ meet

● PHRASES **in good part** = good-naturedly, well, cheerfully, without offence

partial 1 = incomplete, unfinished, imperfect, uncompleted ≠ complete **2** = biased, prejudiced, discriminatory, partisan, unfair, one-sided, unjust ≠ unbiased

partially = partly, somewhat, in part, not wholly, fractionally, incompletely

participant = participator, member, player, contributor, stakeholder

participate = take part, be involved, perform, join, partake ≠ refrain from

participation = taking part, contribution, involvement, sharing in, joining in, partaking

particle = bit, piece, scrap, grain, shred, mite, jot, speck

particular ADJECTIVE **1** = specific, special, exact, precise, distinct, peculiar ≠ general **2** = special, exceptional, notable, uncommon, marked, unusual, remarkable, singular **3** = fussy, demanding, fastidious, choosy (informal), picky (informal), finicky, pernickety (informal) ≠ indiscriminate

● NOUN usually plural = detail, fact, feature, item, circumstance, specification

particularly 1 = specifically, expressly, explicitly, especially, in particular, distinctly **2** = especially, notably, unusually, exceptionally, singularly, uncommonly

parting 1 = farewell, goodbye **2** = division, breaking, split, separation, rift, rupture

partisan ADJECTIVE = prejudiced, one-sided, biased, partial, sectarian ≠ unbiased

● NOUN **1** = supporter, devotee, adherent, upholder ≠ opponent **2** = underground fighter, guerrilla, freedom fighter, resistance fighter

partition NOUN **1** = screen, wall, barrier **2** = division, separation, segregation

● VERB = separate, screen, divide

partly = partially, somewhat, slightly ≠ completely

partner 1 = spouse, consort, significant other (U.S. informal), mate, husband or wife **2** = companion, ally, colleague, associate, mate, comrade **3** = associate, colleague, collaborator

partnership 1 = cooperation, alliance, sharing, union, connection, participation, copartnership **2** = company, firm, house, interest, society, cooperative

party 1 = faction, set, side, league, camp, clique, coterie **2** = get-together (informal), celebration, do (informal), gathering, function, reception, festivity, social gathering **3** = group, team, band, company, unit, squad, crew, gang

pass VERB **1** = go by or past, overtake, drive past, lap, leave behind, pull ahead of ≠ stop **2** = go, move, travel, progress, flow, proceed **3** = run, move, stroke **4** = give, hand, send, transfer, deliver, convey **5** = be left, come, be bequeathed, be inherited by **6** = kick, hit, loft, head, lob **7** = elapse, progress, go by, lapse, wear on, go past, tick by **8** = end, go, cease, blow over **9** = spend, fill, occupy, while away

10 = <u>exceed</u>, beat, overtake, go beyond, surpass, outstrip, outdo **11** = <u>be successful in</u>, qualify (in), succeed (in), graduate (in), get through, do, gain a pass in ≠ fail **12** = <u>approve</u>, accept, decree, enact, ratify, ordain, legislate (for) ≠ ban

● NOUN **1** = <u>licence</u>, ticket, permit, passport, warrant, authorization **2** = <u>gap</u>, route, canyon, gorge, ravine

● PHRASES **pass away** *or* **on** (*Euphemistic*) = die, pass on, expire, pass over, snuff it (*informal*), kick the bucket (*slang*), shuffle off this mortal coil, cark it (*Austral. & N.Z. informal*) ◆ **pass out** (*Informal*) = faint, black out (*informal*), lose consciousness, become unconscious ◆ **pass something over** = disregard, ignore, not dwell on ◆ **pass something up** (*Informal*) = miss, let slip, decline, neglect, forgo, abstain from, give (something) a miss (*informal*)

passage 1 = <u>corridor</u>, hall, lobby, vestibule **2** = <u>alley</u>, way, close (*Brit.*), course, road, channel, route, path **3** = <u>extract</u>, reading, piece, section, text, excerpt, quotation **4** = <u>journey</u>, crossing, trip, trek, voyage **5** = <u>safe-conduct</u>, right to travel, freedom to travel, permission to travel

passenger = <u>traveller</u>, rider, fare, commuter, fare payer

passer-by = <u>bystander</u>, witness, observer, viewer, spectator, looker-on, watcher, onlooker

passing 1 = <u>momentary</u>, fleeting, short-lived, transient, ephemeral, brief, temporary, transitory **2** = <u>superficial</u>, short, quick, glancing, casual, summary, cursory, perfunctory

passion 1 = <u>love</u>, desire, lust, infatuation, ardour **2** = <u>emotion</u>, feeling, fire, heat, excitement, intensity, warmth, zeal ≠ indifference **3** = <u>mania</u>, enthusiasm, obsession, bug (*informal*), craving, fascination, craze **4** = <u>rage</u>, fit, storm, anger, fury, outburst, frenzy, paroxysm

passionate 1 = <u>emotional</u>, eager, strong, intense, fierce, ardent, fervent, heartfelt ≠ unemotional **2** = <u>loving</u>, erotic, hot, ardent, amorous, lustful ≠ cold

passive 1 = <u>submissive</u>, compliant, receptive, docile, quiescent ≠ spirited **2** = <u>inactive</u>, uninvolved ≠ active

past NOUN **1** = <u>former times</u>, long ago, days gone by, the olden days ≠ future

2 = <u>background</u>, life, history, past life, story, career to date

● ADJECTIVE **1** = <u>former</u>, early, previous, ancient, bygone, olden ≠ future **2** = <u>previous</u>, former, one-time, ex- **3** = <u>last</u>, previous **4** = <u>over</u>, done, ended, finished, gone

● PREPOSITION **1** = <u>after</u>, beyond, later than **2** = <u>by</u>, across, in front of

● ADVERB = <u>on</u>, by, along

paste NOUN **1** = <u>adhesive</u>, glue, cement, gum **2** = <u>purée</u>, pâté, spread

● VERB = <u>stick</u>, glue, cement, gum

pastel = <u>pale</u>, light, soft, delicate, muted ≠ bright

pastime = <u>activity</u>, game, entertainment, hobby, recreation, amusement, diversion

pastor = <u>clergyman</u>, minister, priest, vicar, parson, rector, curate, churchman

pastoral 1 = <u>ecclesiastical</u>, priestly, ministerial, clerical **2** = <u>rustic</u>, country, rural, bucolic

pasture = <u>grassland</u>, grass, meadow, grazing

pat VERB = <u>stroke</u>, touch, tap, pet, caress, fondle

● NOUN = <u>tap</u>, stroke, clap

patch NOUN **1** = <u>spot</u>, bit, scrap, shred, small piece **2** = <u>plot</u>, area, ground, land, tract **3** = <u>reinforcement</u>, piece of fabric, piece of cloth, piece of material, piece sewn on

● VERB *often with* **up** = mend, cover, repair, reinforce, stitch (up), sew (up)

patent NOUN = <u>copyright</u>, licence, franchise, registered trademark

● ADJECTIVE = <u>obvious</u>, apparent, evident, clear, glaring, manifest

path 1 = <u>way</u>, road, walk, track, trail, avenue, footpath, berm (*N.Z.*) **2** = <u>route</u>, way, course, direction **3** = <u>course</u>, way, road, route

pathetic = <u>sad</u>, moving, touching, affecting, distressing, tender, poignant, plaintive ≠ funny

patience 1 = <u>forbearance</u>, tolerance, serenity, restraint, calmness, sufferance ≠ impatience **2** = <u>endurance</u>, resignation, submission, fortitude, long-suffering, perseverance, stoicism, constancy

patient NOUN = <u>sick person</u>, case, sufferer, invalid

● ADJECTIVE **1** = <u>forbearing</u>, understanding, forgiving, mild, tolerant, indulgent, lenient even-tempered ≠ impatient 2 = <u>long-suffering</u>, resigned, calm, enduring, philosophical, persevering, stoical, submissive

patriot = <u>nationalist</u>, loyalist, chauvinist

patriotic = <u>nationalistic</u>, loyal, chauvinistic, jingoistic

patriotism = <u>nationalism</u>, jingoism

patrol VERB = <u>police</u>, guard, keep watch (on), inspect, safeguard, keep guard (on)
● NOUN = <u>guard</u>, watch, watchman, sentinel, patrolman

patron 1 = <u>supporter</u>, friend, champion, sponsor, backer, helper, benefactor, philanthropist 2 = <u>customer</u>, client, buyer, frequenter, shopper, habitué

patronage = <u>support</u>, promotion, sponsorship, backing, help, aid, assistance

pattern 1 = <u>order</u>, plan, system, method, sequence 2 = <u>design</u>, arrangement, motif, figure, device, decoration 3 = <u>plan</u>, design, original, guide, diagram, stencil, template

pause VERB = <u>stop briefly</u>, delay, break, wait, rest, halt, cease, interrupt ≠ continue
● NOUN = <u>stop</u>, break, interval, rest, gap, halt, respite, lull ≠ continuance

pave = <u>cover</u>, floor, surface, concrete, tile

paw (*Informal*) = <u>manhandle</u>, grab, maul, molest, handle roughly

pay VERB 1 = <u>reward</u>, compensate, reimburse, recompense, requite, remunerate 2 = <u>spend</u>, give, fork out (*informal*), remit, shell out (*informal*) 3 = <u>settle</u> 4 = <u>bring in</u>, earn, return, net, yield 5 = <u>be profitable</u>, make money, make a return 6 = <u>benefit</u>, repay, be worthwhile 7 = <u>give</u>, extend, present with, grant, hand out, bestow
● NOUN = <u>wages</u>, income, payment, earnings, fee, reward, salary, allowance
● PHRASES **pay off** = <u>succeed</u>, work, be effective ♦ **pay something off** = <u>settle</u>, clear, square, discharge, pay in full

payable = <u>due</u>, outstanding, owed, owing

payment 1 = <u>remittance</u>, advance, deposit, premium, instalment 2 = <u>settlement</u>, paying, discharge, remittance 3 = <u>wages</u>, fee, reward, hire, remuneration

peace 1 = <u>truce</u>, ceasefire, treaty, armistice ≠ war 2 = <u>stillness</u>, rest, quiet, silence, calm, hush, tranquillity, seclusion 3 = <u>serenity</u>, calm, composure, contentment, repose, equanimity, peacefulness,

harmoniousness 4 = <u>harmony</u>, accord, agreement, concord

peaceful 1 = <u>at peace</u>, friendly, harmonious, amicable, nonviolent ≠ hostile 2 = <u>peace-loving</u>, conciliatory, peaceable, unwarlike ≠ belligerent 3 = <u>calm</u>, still, quiet, tranquil, restful ≠ agitated 4 = <u>serene</u>, placid, undisturbed

peak NOUN 1 = <u>high point</u>, crown, climax, culmination, zenith, acme 2 = <u>point</u>, top, tip, summit, brow, crest, pinnacle, apex
● VERB = <u>culminate</u>, climax, come to a head

peasant = <u>rustic</u>, countryman

peck VERB 1 = <u>pick</u>, hit, strike, tap, poke, jab, prick 2 = <u>kiss</u>, plant a kiss, give someone a smacker, give someone a peck *or* kiss
● NOUN = <u>kiss</u>, smacker, osculation (*rare*)

peculiar 1 = <u>odd</u>, strange, unusual, bizarre, funny, extraordinary, curious, weird ≠ ordinary 2 = <u>special</u>, particular, unique, characteristic ≠ common

peddle = <u>sell</u>, trade, push (*informal*), market, hawk, flog (*slang*)

pedestrian NOUN = <u>walker</u>, foot-traveller ≠ driver
● ADJECTIVE = <u>dull</u>, ordinary, boring, commonplace, mundane, mediocre, banal, prosaic, half-pie (*N.Z. informal*) ≠ exciting

pedigree ADJECTIVE = <u>purebred</u>, thoroughbred, full-blooded
● NOUN = <u>lineage</u>, family, line, race, stock, blood, breed, descent

peel NOUN = <u>rind</u>, skin, peeling
● VERB = <u>skin</u>, scale, strip, pare, shuck, flake off, take the skin *or* rind off

peep VERB = <u>peek</u>, look, eyeball (*slang*), sneak a look, steal a look
● NOUN = <u>look</u>, glimpse, peek, look-see (*slang*)

peer[1] = <u>squint</u>, look, spy, gaze, scan, inspect, peep, peek

peer[2] 1 = <u>noble</u>, lord, aristocrat, nobleman 2 = <u>equal</u>, like, fellow, contemporary, compeer

peg NOUN = <u>pin</u>, spike, rivet, skewer, dowel, spigot
● VERB = <u>fasten</u>, join, fix, secure, attach

pen[1] = <u>write (down)</u>, draft, compose, pencil, draw up, scribble, take down, inscribe

pen[2] NOUN = <u>enclosure</u>, pound, fold, cage, coop, hutch, sty
● VERB = <u>enclose</u>, confine, cage, fence in,

coop up, hedge in, shut up *or* in

penalty = <u>punishment</u>, price, fine, handicap, forfeit

pending ADJECTIVE 1 = <u>undecided</u>, unsettled, in the balance, undetermined 2 = <u>forthcoming</u>, imminent, prospective, impending, in the wind
● PREPOSITION = <u>awaiting</u>, until, waiting for, till

penetrate 1 = <u>pierce</u>, enter, go through, bore, stab, prick 2 = <u>grasp</u>, work out, figure out (*informal*), comprehend, fathom, decipher, suss (out) (*slang*), get to the bottom of

penetrating 1 = <u>sharp</u>, harsh, piercing, carrying, piping, loud, strident, shrill ≠ sweet 2 = <u>pungent</u> 3 = <u>piercing</u> 4 = <u>intelligent</u>, quick, sharp, keen, acute, shrewd, astute, perceptive ≠ dull 5 = <u>perceptive</u>, sharp, keen ≠ unperceptive

penetration 1 = <u>piercing</u>, entry, entrance, puncturing, incision 2 = <u>entry</u>, entrance

pension = <u>allowance</u>, benefit, welfare, annuity, superannuation

pensioner = <u>senior citizen</u>, retired person, retiree (*U.S.*), old-age pensioner, O.A.P.

people PLURAL NOUN 1 = <u>persons</u>, individuals, folk (*informal*), men and women, humanity, mankind, mortals, the human race 2 = <u>nation</u>, public, community, subjects, population, residents, citizens, folk 3 = <u>race</u>, tribe 4 = <u>family</u>, parents, relations, relatives, folk, folks (*informal*), clan, kin
● VERB = <u>inhabit</u>, occupy, settle, populate, colonize

pepper NOUN = <u>seasoning</u>, flavour, spice
● VERB 1 = <u>pelt</u>, hit, shower, blitz, rake, bombard, assail, strafe 2 = <u>sprinkle</u>, spot, scatter, dot, fleck, intersperse, speck, spatter

perceive 1 = <u>see</u>, notice, note, identify, discover, spot, observe, recognize 2 = <u>understand</u>, gather, see, learn, realize, grasp, comprehend, suss (out) (*slang*) 3 = <u>consider</u>, believe, judge, suppose, rate, deem, adjudge

perception 1 = <u>awareness</u>, understanding, sense, impression, feeling, idea, notion, consciousness 2 = <u>understanding</u>, intelligence, observation, discrimination, insight, sharpness, cleverness, keenness

perch VERB 1 = <u>sit</u>, rest, balance, settle 2 = <u>place</u>, put, rest, balance 3 = <u>land</u>, alight, roost
● NOUN = <u>resting place</u>, post, branch, pole

perennial = <u>continual</u>, lasting, constant, enduring, persistent, abiding, recurrent, incessant

perfect ADJECTIVE 1 = <u>faultless</u>, correct, pure, impeccable, exemplary, flawless, foolproof ≠ deficient 2 = <u>excellent</u>, ideal, supreme, superb, splendid, sublime, superlative 3 = <u>immaculate</u>, impeccable, flawless, spotless, unblemished ≠ flawed 4 = <u>complete</u>, absolute, sheer, utter, consummate, unmitigated ≠ partial 5 = <u>exact</u>, true, accurate, precise, correct, faithful, unerring
● VERB = <u>improve</u>, develop, polish, refine ≠ mar

perfection = <u>excellence</u>, integrity, superiority, purity, wholeness, sublimity, exquisiteness, faultlessness

perfectly 1 = <u>completely</u>, totally, absolutely, quite, fully, altogether, thoroughly, wholly ≠ partially 2 = <u>flawlessly</u>, ideally, wonderfully, superbly, supremely, impeccably, faultlessly ≠ badly

perform 1 = <u>do</u>, achieve, carry out, complete, fulfil, accomplish, execute, pull off 2 = <u>fulfil</u>, carry out, execute, discharge 3 = <u>present</u>, act (out), stage, play, produce, represent, put on, enact 4 = <u>appear on stage</u>, act 5 = <u>function</u>, go, work, run, operate, handle, respond, behave

performance 1 = <u>presentation</u>, playing, acting (out), staging, production, exhibition, rendering, portrayal 2 = <u>show</u>, appearance, concert, gig (*informal*), recital 3 = <u>work</u>, acts, conduct, exploits, feats 4 = <u>carrying out</u>, practice, achievement, execution, completion, accomplishment, fulfilment

performer = <u>artiste</u>, player, Thespian, trouper, actor *or* actress

perfume 1 = <u>fragrance</u>, scent 2 = <u>scent</u>, smell, fragrance, bouquet, aroma, odour

perhaps = <u>maybe</u>, possibly, it may be, it is possible (that), conceivably, perchance (*archaic*), feasibly, happen (*Northern English dialect*)

peril 1 = <u>danger</u>, risk, threat, hazard,

menace, jeopardy, perilousness **2** *often plural* = pitfall, problem, risk, hazard ≠ safety

perimeter = boundary, edge, border, bounds, limit, margin, confines, periphery ≠ centre

period = time, term, season, space, run, stretch, spell, phase

periodic = recurrent, regular, repeated, occasional, cyclical, sporadic, intermittent

peripheral 1 = secondary, minor, marginal, irrelevant, unimportant, incidental, inessential **2** = outermost, outside, external, outer, exterior

perish 1 = die, be killed, expire, pass away, lose your life, cark it (*Austral. & N.Z. slang*) **2** = be destroyed, fall, decline, collapse, disappear, vanish **3** = rot, waste away, decay, disintegrate, decompose, moulder

perk (*Brit. informal*) = bonus, benefit, extra, plus, fringe benefit, perquisite

permanent 1 = lasting, constant, enduring, persistent, eternal, abiding, perpetual, everlasting ≠ temporary **2** = long-term, established, secure, stable, steady ≠ temporary

permission = authorization, sanction, licence, approval, leave, go-ahead (*informal*), liberty, consent ≠ prohibition

permit VERB **1** = allow, grant, sanction, let, entitle, license, authorize, consent to ≠ forbid **2** = enable, let, allow, cause
● NOUN = licence, pass, document, certificate, passport, visa, warrant, authorization ≠ prohibition

perpetual 1 = everlasting, permanent, endless, eternal, lasting, perennial, infinite, never-ending ≠ temporary **2** = continual, repeated, constant, endless, continuous, persistent, recurrent, never-ending ≠ brief

perpetuate = maintain, preserve, keep going, immortalize ≠ end

persecute 1 = victimize, torture, torment, oppress, pick on, ill-treat, maltreat ≠ mollycoddle **2** = harass, bother, annoy, tease, hassle (*informal*), badger, pester ≠ leave alone

persist 1 = continue, last, remain, carry on, keep up, linger **2** = persevere, continue, go on, carry on, keep on, keep going, press on, not give up

persistence = determination, resolution, grit, endurance, tenacity, perseverance, doggedness, pertinacity

persistent 1 = continuous, constant, repeated, endless, perpetual, continual, never-ending, incessant ≠ occasional **2** = determined, dogged, steady, stubborn, persevering, tireless, tenacious, steadfast ≠ irresolute

person NOUN = individual, being, body, human, soul, creature, mortal, man *or* woman
● PHRASES **in person 1** = personally, yourself **2** = in the flesh, actually, physically, bodily

personal 1 = own, special, private, individual, particular, peculiar **2** = individual, special, particular, exclusive **3** = private **4** = offensive, nasty, insulting, disparaging, derogatory

personality 1 = nature, character, make-up, identity, temperament, disposition, individuality **2** = character, charm, attraction, charisma, magnetism **3** = celebrity, star, notable, household name, famous name, personage, megastar (*informal*)

personally 1 = in your opinion, in your book, for your part, from your own viewpoint, in your own view **2** = by yourself, alone, independently, solely, on your own **3** = individually, specially, subjectively, individualistically **4** = privately, in private, off the record

personnel = employees, people, staff, workers, workforce, human resources, helpers

perspective 1 = outlook, attitude, context, angle, frame of reference **2** = objectivity, proportion, relation, relativity, relative importance

persuade 1 = talk (someone) into, urge, influence, win (someone) over, induce, sway, entice, coax ≠ dissuade **2** = cause, lead, move, influence, motivate, induce, incline, dispose **3** = convince, satisfy, assure, cause to believe

persuasion 1 = urging, inducement, wheedling, enticement, cajolery **2** = belief, views, opinion, party, school, side, camp, faith

persuasive = convincing, telling, effective, sound, compelling, influential, valid, credible ≠ unconvincing

pervasive = widespread, general, common, extensive, universal, prevalent, ubiquitous, rife

perverse 1 = <u>stubborn</u>, contrary, dogged, troublesome, <u>rebellious</u>, wayward, intractable, wilful ≠ cooperative 2 = <u>ill-natured</u>, cross, surly, fractious, churlish, ill-tempered, stroppy (*Brit. slang*), peevish ≠ good-natured 3 = <u>abnormal</u>, unhealthy, improper, deviant

pervert VERB 1 = <u>distort</u>, abuse, twist, misuse, warp, misrepresent, falsify 2 = <u>corrupt</u>, degrade, deprave, debase, debauch, lead astray
● NOUN = <u>deviant</u>, degenerate, sicko (*informal*), weirdo or weirdie (*informal*)

pessimistic = <u>gloomy</u>, dark, despairing, bleak, depressed, cynical, hopeless, glum ≠ optimistic

pest 1 = <u>infection</u>, bug, insect, plague, epidemic, blight, scourge, pestilence, gogga (*S. African informal*) 2 = <u>nuisance</u>, trial, pain (*informal*), drag (*informal*), bother, irritation, annoyance, bane

pet ADJECTIVE = <u>favourite</u>, favoured, dearest, cherished, fave (*informal*), dear to your heart
● NOUN = <u>favourite</u>, treasure, darling, jewel, idol
● VERB 1 = <u>fondle</u>, pat, stroke, caress 2 = <u>pamper</u>, spoil, indulge, cosset, baby, dote on, coddle, mollycoddle 3 (*Informal*) = <u>cuddle</u>, kiss, snog (*Brit. slang*), smooch (*informal*), neck (*informal*), canoodle (*slang*)

petition NOUN 1 = <u>appeal</u>, round robin, list of signatures 2 = <u>entreaty</u>, appeal, suit, application, request, prayer, plea, solicitation
● VERB = <u>appeal</u>, plead, ask, pray, beg, solicit, beseech, entreat

petty 1 = <u>trivial</u>, insignificant, little, small, slight, trifling, negligible, unimportant ≠ important 2 = <u>small-minded</u>, mean, shabby, spiteful, ungenerous, mean-minded ≠ broad-minded

phantom = <u>spectre</u>, ghost, spirit, shade (*literary*), spook (*informal*), apparition, wraith, phantasm

phase NOUN = <u>stage</u>, time, point, position, step, development, period, chapter
● PHRASES **phase something in** = <u>introduce</u>, incorporate, ease in, start
◆ **phase something out** = <u>eliminate</u>, close, remove, withdraw, pull out, wind up, run down, terminate

phenomenal = <u>extraordinary</u>, outstanding, remarkable, fantastic, unusual, marvellous, exceptional, miraculous ≠ unremarkable

phenomenon 1 = <u>occurrence</u>, happening, fact, event, incident, circumstance, episode 2 = <u>wonder</u>, sensation, exception, miracle, marvel, prodigy, rarity

philosopher = <u>thinker</u>, theorist, sage, wise man, logician, metaphysician

philosophical or **philosophic** 1 = <u>theoretical</u>, abstract, wise, rational, logical, thoughtful, sagacious ≠ practical 2 = <u>stoical</u>, calm, composed, cool, collected, serene, tranquil, unruffled ≠ emotional

philosophy 1 = <u>thought</u>, knowledge, thinking, reasoning, wisdom, logic, metaphysics 2 = <u>outlook</u>, values, principles, convictions, thinking, beliefs, doctrine, ideology

phone NOUN 1 = <u>telephone</u>, blower (*informal*) 2 = <u>call</u>, ring (*informal, chiefly Brit.*), tinkle (*Brit. informal*)
● VERB = <u>call</u>, telephone, ring (up) (*informal, chiefly Brit.*), give someone a call, give someone a ring (*informal, chiefly Brit.*), make a call, give someone a tinkle (*Brit. informal*), get on the blower (*informal*)

photograph NOUN = <u>picture</u>, photo (*informal*), shot, print, snap (*informal*), snapshot, transparency
● VERB = <u>take a picture of</u>, record, film, shoot, snap (*informal*), take (someone's) picture

photographic 1 = <u>pictorial</u>, visual, graphic, cinematic, filmic 2 = <u>accurate</u>, exact, precise, faithful, retentive

phrase NOUN = <u>expression</u>, saying, remark, construction, quotation, maxim, idiom, adage
● VERB = <u>express</u>, say, word, put, voice, communicate, convey, put into words

physical 1 = <u>corporal</u>, fleshly, bodily, corporeal 2 = <u>earthly</u>, fleshly, mortal, incarnate 3 = <u>material</u>, real, substantial, natural, solid, tangible, palpable

physician = <u>doctor</u>, doc (*informal*), medic (*informal*), general practitioner, medical practitioner, doctor of medicine, G.P., M.D.

pick VERB 1 = <u>select</u>, choose, identify, elect, nominate, specify, opt for, single out ≠ reject 2 = <u>gather</u>, pull, collect, take in, harvest, pluck, garner **3** = <u>provoke</u>, start, cause, stir up, incite, instigate **4** = <u>open</u>, force, crack (*informal*), break into, break open

● NOUN **1** = <u>choice</u>, decision, option, selection, preference **2** = <u>best</u>, prime, finest, elect, elite, cream, jewel in the crown, crème de la crème (*French*)

● PHRASES **pick on someone**
1 = <u>torment</u>, bully, bait, tease, get at (*informal*), badger, persecute, hector
2 = <u>choose</u>, select, prefer, elect, single out, fix on, settle upon ◆ **pick something** *or* **someone out 1** = <u>identify</u>, recognize, distinguish, perceive, discriminate, make someone *or* something out, tell someone *or* something apart ◆ **pick something** *or* **someone up 1** = <u>lift</u>, raise, gather, take up, grasp, uplift **2** = <u>collect</u>, get, call for ◆ **pick something up 1** = <u>learn</u>, master, acquire, get the hang of (*informal*), become proficient in **2** = <u>obtain</u>, get, find, buy, discover, purchase, acquire, locate ◆ **pick up 1** = <u>improve</u>, recover, rally, get better, bounce back, make progress, perk up, turn the corner **2** = <u>recover</u>, improve, rally, get better, mend, turn the corner, be on the mend, take a turn for the better

picket VERB = <u>blockade</u>, boycott, demonstrate outside

● NOUN **1** = <u>demonstration</u>, strike, blockade **2** = <u>protester</u>, demonstrator, picketer **3** = <u>lookout</u>, watch, guard, patrol, sentry, sentinel **4** = <u>stake</u>, post, pale, paling, upright, stanchion

pickle VERB = <u>preserve</u>, marinade, steep

● NOUN **1** = <u>chutney</u>, relish, piccalilli **2** (*Informal*) = <u>predicament</u>, fix (*informal*), difficulty, bind (*informal*), jam (*informal*), dilemma, scrape (*informal*), hot water (*informal*), uphill (*S. African*)

pick-up = <u>improvement</u>, recovery, rise, rally, strengthening, revival, upturn, change for the better

picnic = <u>excursion</u>, barbecue, barbie (*informal*), cookout (*U.S. & Canad.*), alfresco meal, clambake (*U.S. & Canad.*), outdoor meal, outing

picture NOUN **1** = <u>representation</u>, drawing, painting, portrait, image, print, illustration, sketch **2** = <u>photograph</u>, photo, still, shot, image, print, frame, slide **3** = <u>film</u>, movie (*U.S. informal*), flick (*slang*), feature film, motion picture **4** = <u>idea</u>, vision, concept,

impression, notion, visualization, mental picture, mental image **5** = <u>description</u>, impression, explanation, report, account, image, sketch, depiction **6** = <u>personification</u>, embodiment, essence, epitome

● VERB **1** = <u>imagine</u>, see, envision, visualize, conceive of, fantasize about, conjure up an image of **2** = <u>represent</u>, show, draw, paint, illustrate, sketch, depict **3** = <u>show</u>, photograph, capture on film

picturesque 1 = <u>interesting</u>, pretty, beautiful, attractive, charming, scenic, quaint ≠ unattractive **2** = <u>vivid</u>, striking, graphic, colourful, memorable ≠ dull

piece 1 = <u>bit</u>, slice, part, block, quantity, segment, portion, fragment **2** = <u>component</u>, part, section, bit, unit, segment, constituent, module **3** = <u>item</u>, report, story, study, review, article **4** = <u>composition</u>, work, production, opus **5** = <u>work of art</u>, work, creation **6** = <u>share</u>, cut (*informal*), slice, percentage, quantity, portion, quota, fraction

pier 1 = <u>jetty</u>, wharf, quay, promenade, landing place **2** = <u>pillar</u>, support, post, column, pile, upright, buttress

pierce = <u>penetrate</u>, stab, spike, enter, bore, drill, puncture, prick

piercing 1 (*of sound*) = <u>penetrating</u>, sharp, loud, shrill, high-pitched, ear-splitting ≠ low **2** = <u>perceptive</u>, sharp, keen, alert, penetrating, shrewd, perspicacious, quick-witted ≠ unperceptive **3** = <u>sharp</u>, acute, severe, intense, painful, stabbing, excruciating, agonizing **4** (*of weather*) = <u>cold</u>, biting, freezing, bitter, arctic, wintry, nippy

pig 1 = <u>hog</u>, sow, boar, swine, porker **2** (*Informal*) = <u>slob</u>, glutton **3** (*Informal*) = <u>brute</u>, monster, scoundrel, rogue, swine, rotter, boor

pigment = <u>colour</u>, colouring, paint, stain, dye, tint, tincture

pile¹ NOUN **1** = <u>heap</u>, collection, mountain, mass, stack, mound, accumulation, hoard **2** (*Informal*) *often plural* = <u>lot(s)</u>, mountain(s), load(s) (*informal*), oceans, wealth, great deal, stack(s), abundance **3** = <u>mansion</u>, building, residence, manor, country house, seat, big house, stately home

● VERB **1** = <u>load</u>, stuff, pack, stack, charge, heap, cram, lade **2** = <u>crowd</u>, pack, rush,

climb, flood, stream, crush, squeeze
- PHRASES **pile up** = <u>accumulate</u>, collect, gather (up), build up, amass

pile² = <u>foundation</u>, support, post, column, beam, upright, pillar

pile³ = <u>nap</u>, fibre, down, hair, fur, plush

pile-up (*Informal*) = <u>collision</u>, crash, accident, smash, smash-up (*informal*), multiple collision

pilgrim = <u>traveller</u>, wanderer, devotee, wayfarer

pilgrimage = <u>journey</u>, tour, trip, mission, expedition, excursion

pill = <u>tablet</u>, capsule, pellet

pillar 1 = <u>support</u>, post, column, prop, shaft, upright, pier, stanchion 2 = <u>supporter</u>, leader, mainstay, leading light (*informal*), upholder

pilot NOUN 1 = <u>airman</u>, flyer, aviator, aeronaut 2 = <u>helmsman</u>, navigator, steersman
- VERB 1 = <u>fly</u>, operate, be at the controls of 2 = <u>navigate</u>, drive, direct, guide, handle, conduct, steer 3 = <u>direct</u>, conduct, steer
- ADJECTIVE = <u>trial</u>, test, model, sample, experimental

pin NOUN 1 = <u>tack</u>, nail, needle, safety pin 2 = <u>peg</u>, rod, brace, bolt
- VERB 1 = <u>fasten</u>, stick, attach, join, fix, secure, nail, clip 2 = <u>hold fast</u>, hold down, constrain, immobilize, pinion
- PHRASES **pin someone down** = <u>force</u>, pressure, compel, put pressure on, pressurize, nail someone down, make someone commit themselves ◆ **pin something down** = <u>determine</u>, identify, locate, name, specify, pinpoint

pinch VERB 1 = <u>nip</u>, press, squeeze, grasp, compress 2 = <u>hurt</u>, crush, squeeze, pain, cramp 3 (*Brit. informal*) = <u>steal</u>, lift (*informal*), nick (*slang, chiefly Brit.*), swipe (*slang*), knock off (*slang*), pilfer, purloin, filch
- NOUN 1 = <u>nip</u>, squeeze 2 = <u>dash</u>, bit, mite, jot, speck, soupçon (*French*) 3 = <u>emergency</u>, crisis, difficulty, plight, scrape (*informal*), strait, uphill (*S. African*), predicament

pine VERB = <u>waste</u>, decline, sicken, fade, languish
- PHRASES **pine for something or someone** 1 = <u>long</u>, ache, crave, yearn, eat your heart out over 2 = <u>hanker after</u>, crave, wish for, yearn for, thirst for, hunger for

pink NOUN or ADJECTIVE = <u>rosy</u>, rose, salmon, flushed, reddish, roseate

pinnacle 1 = <u>summit</u>, top, height, peak 2 = <u>height</u>, top, crown, crest, zenith, apex, vertex

pinpoint 1 = <u>identify</u>, discover, define, distinguish, put your finger on 2 = <u>locate</u>, find, identify, zero in on

pioneer NOUN 1 = <u>founder</u>, leader, developer, innovator, trailblazer 2 = <u>settler</u>, explorer, colonist
- VERB = <u>develop</u>, create, establish, start, discover, institute, invent, initiate

pipe NOUN = <u>tube</u>, drain, canal, pipeline, line, main, passage, cylinder
- VERB = <u>convey</u>, channel, conduct
- PHRASES **pipe down** (*Informal*) = <u>be quiet</u>, shut up (*informal*), hush, stop talking, quieten down, shush, shut your mouth, hold your tongue

pipeline = <u>tube</u>, passage, pipe, conduit, duct

pirate NOUN = <u>buccaneer</u>, raider, marauder, corsair, freebooter
- VERB = <u>copy</u>, steal, reproduce, bootleg, appropriate, poach, crib (*informal*), plagiarize

pit NOUN 1 = <u>coal mine</u>, mine, shaft, colliery, mine shaft 2 = <u>hole</u>, depression, hollow, crater, trough, cavity, abyss, chasm
- VERB = <u>scar</u>, mark, dent, indent, pockmark

pitch NOUN 1 = <u>sports field</u>, ground, stadium, arena, park, field of play 2 = <u>tone</u>, sound, key, frequency, timbre, modulation 3 = <u>level</u>, point, degree, summit, extent, height, intensity, high point 4 = <u>talk</u>, patter, spiel (*informal*)
- VERB 1 = <u>throw</u>, cast, toss, hurl, fling, chuck (*informal*), sling, lob (*informal*) 2 = <u>fall</u>, drop, plunge, dive, tumble, topple, plummet, fall headlong 3 = <u>set up</u>, raise, settle, put up, erect 4 = <u>toss (about)</u>, roll, plunge, lurch
- PHRASES **pitch in** = <u>help</u>, contribute, participate, join in, cooperate, chip in (*informal*), get stuck in (*Brit. informal*), lend a hand

pitfall *usually plural* = <u>danger</u>, difficulty, peril, catch, trap, hazard, drawback, snag, uphill (*S. African*)

pity NOUN 1 = <u>compassion</u>, charity, sympathy, kindness, fellow feeling ≠ mercilessness 2 = <u>shame</u>, sin (*informal*), misfortune, bummer (*slang*), crying

shame 3 = <u>mercy</u>, kindness, clemency, forbearance
● VERB = <u>feel sorry for</u>, feel for, sympathize with, grieve for, weep for, bleed for, have compassion for

pivotal = <u>crucial</u>, central, vital, critical, decisive

place NOUN 1 = <u>spot</u>, point, position, site, area, location, venue, whereabouts 2 = <u>region</u>, quarter, district, neighbourhood, vicinity, locality, locale, dorp (*S. African*) 3 = <u>position</u>, point, spot, location 4 = <u>space</u>, position, seat, chair 5 = <u>rank</u>, standing, position, footing, station, status, grade, niche 6 = <u>situation</u>, position, circumstances, shoes (*informal*) 7 = <u>job</u>, position, post, situation, office, employment, appointment 8 = <u>home</u>, house, room, property, accommodation, pad (*slang*), residence, dwelling 9 (In this context, the construction is always negative) = <u>duty</u>, right, job, charge, concern, role, affair, responsibility
● VERB 1 = <u>lay (down)</u>, put (down), set (down), stand, position, rest, station, stick (*informal*) 2 = <u>put</u>, lay, set, invest, pin 3 = <u>classify</u>, class, group, put, order, sort, rank, arrange 4 = <u>entrust to</u>, give to, assign to, appoint to, allocate to, find a home for 5 = <u>identify</u>, remember, recognize, pin someone down, put your finger on, put a name to
● PHRASES **take place** = <u>happen</u>, occur, go on, go down (*U.S. & Canad.*), arise, come about, crop up, transpire (*informal*)

plague NOUN 1 = <u>disease</u>, infection, epidemic, pestilence 2 = <u>infestation</u>, invasion, epidemic, influx, host, swarm, multitude
● VERB 1 = <u>torment</u>, trouble, torture 2 = <u>pester</u>, trouble, bother, annoy, tease, harry, harass, hassle

plain ADJECTIVE 1 = <u>unadorned</u>, simple, basic, severe, bare, stark, austere, spartan ≠ ornate 2 = <u>clear</u>, obvious, patent, evident, visible, distinct, understandable, manifest ≠ hidden 3 = <u>straightforward</u>, open, direct, frank, blunt, outspoken, honest, downright ≠ roundabout 4 = <u>ugly</u>, unattractive, homely (*U.S. & Canad.*), unlovely, unprepossessing, not beautiful, no oil painting (*informal*), ill-favoured ≠ attractive 5 = <u>ordinary</u>, common, simple, everyday, commonplace, unaffected,

unpretentious ≠ sophisticated
● NOUN = <u>flatland</u>, plateau, prairie, grassland, steppe, veld

plan NOUN 1 = <u>scheme</u>, system, design, programme, proposal, strategy, method, suggestion 2 = <u>diagram</u>, map, drawing, chart, representation, sketch, blueprint, layout
● VERB 1 = <u>devise</u>, arrange, scheme, plot, draft, organize, outline, formulate 2 = <u>intend</u>, aim, mean, propose, purpose 3 = <u>design</u>, outline, draw up a plan of

plane NOUN 1 = <u>aeroplane</u>, aircraft, jet, airliner, jumbo jet 2 = <u>flat surface</u>, the flat, horizontal, level surface 3 = <u>level</u>, position, stage, condition, standard, degree, rung, echelon
● ADJECTIVE = <u>level</u>, even, flat, regular, smooth, horizontal
● VERB = <u>skim</u>, sail, skate, glide

plant[1] NOUN 1 = <u>flower</u>, bush, vegetable, herb, weed, shrub
● VERB 1 = <u>sow</u>, scatter, transplant, implant, put in the ground 2 = <u>seed</u>, sow, implant 3 = <u>place</u>, put, set, fix 4 = <u>hide</u>, put, place, conceal 5 = <u>place</u>, put, establish, found, fix, insert

plant[2] 1 = <u>factory</u>, works, shop, yard, mill, foundry 2 = <u>machinery</u>, equipment, gear, apparatus

plaster NOUN 1 = <u>mortar</u>, stucco, gypsum, plaster of Paris 2 = <u>bandage</u>, dressing, sticking plaster, Elastoplast®, adhesive plaster
● VERB = <u>cover</u>, spread, coat, smear, overlay, daub

plastic = <u>pliant</u>, soft, flexible, supple, pliable, ductile, mouldable ≠ rigid

plate NOUN 1 = <u>platter</u>, dish, dinner plate, salver, trencher (*archaic*) 2 = <u>helping</u>, course, serving, dish, portion, platter, plateful 3 = <u>layer</u>, panel, sheet, slab 4 = illustration, picture, photograph, print, engraving, lithograph
● VERB = <u>coat</u>, gild, laminate, cover, overlay

plateau 1 = <u>upland</u>, table, highland, tableland 2 = <u>levelling off</u>, level, stage, stability

platform 1 = <u>stage</u>, stand, podium, rostrum, dais, soapbox 2 = <u>policy</u>, programme, principle, objective(s), manifesto, party line

plausible 1 = <u>believable</u>, possible, likely, reasonable, credible, probable, persuasive, conceivable ≠ unbelievable 2 = glib, smooth, specious, smooth-talking, smooth-tongued

play VERB 1 = amuse yourself, have fun, sport, fool, romp, revel, trifle, entertain yourself 2 = take part in, be involved in, engage in, participate in, compete in 3 = compete against, challenge, take on, oppose, contend against 4 = perform, carry out 5 = act, portray, represent, perform, act the part of 6 = perform on, strum, make music on

● NOUN 1 = amusement, pleasure, leisure, games, sport, fun, entertainment, relaxation 2 = drama, show, piece, comedy, tragedy, farce, soapie (*Austral. slang*), pantomime

● PHRASES **play on** or **upon something** = take advantage of, abuse, exploit, impose on, trade on, capitalize on ◆ **play something down** = minimize, make light of, gloss over, talk down, underrate, underplay, pooh-pooh (*informal*), soft-pedal (*informal*) ◆ **play something up** = emphasize, highlight, underline, stress, accentuate ◆ **play up** 1 (*Brit. informal*) = hurt, be painful, bother you, trouble you, be sore, pain you 2 (*Brit. informal*) = malfunction, not work properly, be on the blink (*slang*) 3 (*Brit. informal*) = be awkward, misbehave, give trouble, be disobedient, be stroppy (*Brit. slang*)

playboy = womanizer, philanderer, rake, lady-killer (*informal*), roué, ladies' man

player 1 = sportsman or sportswoman, competitor, participant, contestant 2 = musician, artist, performer, virtuoso, instrumentalist 3 = performer, entertainer, Thespian, trouper, actor or actress

plea 1 = appeal, request, suit, prayer, petition, entreaty, intercession, supplication 2 = excuse, defence, explanation, justification

plead = appeal, ask, request, beg, petition, implore, beseech, entreat

pleasant 1 = pleasing, nice, fine, lovely, amusing, delightful, enjoyable, agreeable, lekker (*S. African slang*) ≠ horrible 2 = friendly, nice, agreeable, likable or likeable, engaging, charming, amiable, genial ≠ disagreeable

please = delight, entertain, humour, amuse, suit, satisfy, indulge, gratify ≠ annoy

pleased = happy, delighted, contented, satisfied, thrilled, glad, gratified, over the moon (*informal*)

pleasing 1 = enjoyable, satisfying, charming, delightful, gratifying, agreeable, pleasurable ≠ unpleasant 2 = likable or likeable, engaging, charming, delightful, agreeable ≠ disagreeable

pleasure 1 = happiness, delight, satisfaction, enjoyment, bliss, gratification, gladness, delectation ≠ displeasure 2 = amusement, joy ≠ duty

pledge NOUN 1 = promise, vow, assurance, word, undertaking, warrant, oath, covenant 2 = guarantee, security, deposit, bail, collateral, pawn, surety

● VERB = promise, vow, swear, contract, engage, give your word, give your oath

plentiful = abundant, liberal, generous, lavish, ample, overflowing, copious, bountiful ≠ scarce

plenty 1 = abundance, wealth, prosperity, fertility, profusion, affluence, plenitude, fruitfulness 2 usually with **of** = lots of (*informal*), enough, a great deal of, masses of, piles of (*informal*), stacks of, heaps of (*informal*), an abundance of

plight = difficulty, condition, state, situation, trouble, predicament

plot¹ NOUN 1 = plan, scheme, intrigue, conspiracy, cabal, stratagem, machination 2 = story, action, subject, theme, outline, scenario, narrative, story line

● VERB 1 = plan, scheme, conspire, intrigue, manoeuvre, contrive, collude, machinate 2 = devise, design, lay, conceive, hatch, contrive, concoct, cook up (*informal*) 3 = chart, mark, map, locate, calculate, outline

plot² = patch, lot, area, ground, parcel, tract, allotment

plough VERB = turn over, dig, till, cultivate

● PHRASES **plough through something** = forge, cut, drive, press, push, plunge, wade

ploy = tactic, move, trick, device, scheme, manoeuvre, dodge, ruse

pluck VERB 1 = pull out or off, pick, draw, collect, gather, harvest 2 = tug, catch, snatch, clutch, jerk, yank, tweak, pull at 3 = strum, pick, finger, twang

● NOUN = courage, nerve, bottle (*Brit. slang*), guts (*informal*), grit, bravery, backbone, boldness

plug NOUN 1 = <u>stopper</u>, cork, bung, spigot
2 (*Informal*) = <u>mention</u>, advertisement,
advert (*Brit. informal*), push, publicity, hype
● VERB 1 = <u>seal</u>, close, stop, fill, block, stuff,
pack, cork 2 (*Informal*) = <u>mention</u>, push,
promote, publicize, advertise, build up,
hype
● PHRASES **plug away** (*Informal*) = <u>slog</u>
<u>away</u>, labour, toil away, grind away
(*informal*), peg away, plod away

plum = <u>choice</u>, prize, first-class

plumb VERB = <u>delve into</u>, explore, probe,
go into, penetrate, gauge, unravel, fathom
● ADVERB = <u>exactly</u>, precisely, bang, slap,
spot-on (*Brit. informal*)

plummet 1 = <u>drop</u>, fall, crash, nose-dive,
descend rapidly 2 = <u>plunge</u>, fall, drop,
crash, tumble, nose-dive, descend rapidly

plump = <u>chubby</u>, fat, stout, round, tubby,
dumpy, roly-poly, rotund ≠ scrawny

plunder VERB 1 = <u>loot</u>, strip, sack, rob,
raid, rifle, ransack, pillage 2 = <u>steal</u>, rob,
take, nick (*informal*), pinch (*informal*),
embezzle, pilfer, thieve
● NOUN 1 = <u>pillage</u> 2 = <u>loot</u>, spoils, booty,
swag (*slang*), ill-gotten gains

plunge VERB 1 = <u>descend</u>, fall, drop,
crash, pitch, sink, dive, tumble 2 = <u>hurtle</u>,
charge, career, jump, tear, rush, dive,
dash 3 = <u>submerge</u>, dip 4 = <u>throw</u>, cast,
pitch, propel 5 = <u>fall steeply</u>, drop, crash
(*informal*), slump, plummet, take a nosedive
(*informal*)
● NOUN 1 = <u>dive</u>, jump, duck, descent
2 = <u>fall</u>, crash (*informal*), slump, drop,
tumble

plus PREPOSITION = <u>and</u>, with, added to,
coupled with
● NOUN (*Informal*) = <u>advantage</u>, benefit,
asset, gain, extra, bonus, good point
● ADJECTIVE = <u>additional</u>, added, extra,
supplementary, add-on

plush = <u>luxurious</u>, luxury, lavish, rich,
sumptuous, opulent, de luxe

ply = <u>work at</u>, follow, exercise, pursue, carry
on, practise

pocket NOUN = <u>pouch</u>, bag, sack,
compartment, receptacle
● ADJECTIVE = <u>small</u>, compact, miniature,
portable, little
● VERB = <u>steal</u>, take, lift (*informal*),
appropriate, pilfer, purloin, filch

pod = <u>shell</u>, case, hull, husk, shuck

podium = <u>platform</u>, stand, stage, rostrum,
dais

poem = <u>verse</u>, song, lyric, rhyme, sonnet,
ode, verse composition

poet = <u>bard</u>, rhymer, lyricist, lyric poet,
versifier, elegist

poetic 1 = <u>figurative</u>, creative, lyric,
symbolic, lyrical 2 = <u>lyrical</u>, lyric, elegiac,
metrical

poetry = <u>verse</u>, poems, rhyme, rhyming,
verse composition

poignant = <u>moving</u>, touching, sad, bitter,
intense, painful, distressing, pathetic

point NOUN 1 = <u>essence</u>, meaning, subject,
question, heart, import, drift, thrust
2 = <u>purpose</u>, aim, object, end, reason, goal,
intention, objective 3 = <u>aspect</u>, detail,
feature, quality, particular, respect, item,
characteristic 4 = <u>place</u>, area, position, site,
spot, location, locality, locale 5 = <u>moment</u>,
time, stage, period, phase, instant,
juncture, moment in time 6 = <u>stage</u>,
level, position, condition, degree, pitch,
circumstance, extent 7 = <u>end</u>, tip, sharp
end, top, spur, spike, apex, prong 8 = <u>score</u>,
tally, mark 9 = <u>pinpoint</u>, mark, spot, dot,
fleck
● VERB 1 = <u>aim</u>, level, train, direct
2 = <u>indicate</u>, show, signal, point to, gesture
towards 3 = <u>face</u>, look, direct
● PHRASES **point at** *or* **to something** *or*
someone = <u>indicate</u>, point out, specify,
designate, gesture towards

pointed 1 = <u>sharp</u>, edged, acute, barbed
2 = <u>cutting</u>, telling, biting, sharp, keen,
acute, penetrating, pertinent

pointer 1 = <u>hint</u>, tip, suggestion,
recommendation, caution, piece of
information, piece of advice 2 = <u>indicator</u>,
hand, guide, needle, arrow

pointless = <u>senseless</u>, meaningless,
futile, fruitless, stupid, silly, useless, absurd
≠ worthwhile

poised 1 = <u>ready</u>, waiting, prepared,
standing by, all set 2 = <u>composed</u>, calm,
together (*informal*), collected, dignified,
self-confident, self-possessed ≠ agitated

poison NOUN = <u>toxin</u>, venom, bane
(*archaic*)
● VERB 1 = <u>murder</u>, kill, give someone
poison, administer poison to
2 = <u>contaminate</u>, foul, infect, spoil, pollute,
blight, taint, befoul 3 = <u>corrupt</u>, colour,
undermine, bias, sour, pervert, warp, taint

poisonous 1 = <u>toxic</u>, fatal, deadly, lethal,

mortal, virulent, noxious, venomous
2 = evil, malicious, corrupting, pernicious, baleful

poke VERB **1** = jab, push, stick, dig, stab, thrust, shove, nudge **2** = protrude, stick, thrust, jut

● NOUN = jab, dig, thrust, nudge, prod
pole = rod, post, support, staff, bar, stick, stake, paling
police NOUN = the law (*informal*), police force, constabulary, fuzz (*slang*), boys in blue (*informal*), the Old Bill (*slang*), rozzers (*slang*)

● VERB = control, patrol, guard, watch, protect, regulate
policy 1 = procedure, plan, action, practice, scheme, code, custom **2** = line, rules, approach
polish NOUN **1** = varnish, wax, glaze, lacquer, japan **2** = sheen, finish, glaze, gloss, brightness, lustre **3** = style, class (*informal*), finish, breeding, grace, elegance, refinement, finesse

● VERB **1** = shine, wax, smooth, rub, buff, brighten, burnish **2** *often with* **up** = perfect, improve, enhance, refine, finish, brush up, touch up
polished 1 = elegant, sophisticated, refined, polite, cultivated, suave, well-bred ≠ unsophisticated **2** = accomplished, professional, masterly, fine, expert, skilful, adept, superlative ≠ amateurish **3** = shining, bright, smooth, gleaming, glossy, burnished ≠ dull
polite 1 = mannerly, civil, courteous, gracious, respectful, well-behaved, complaisant, well-mannered ≠ rude **2** = refined, cultured, civilized, polished, sophisticated, elegant, genteel, well-bred ≠ uncultured
politic = wise, diplomatic, sensible, prudent, advisable, expedient, judicious
political = governmental, government, state, parliamentary, constitutional, administrative, legislative, ministerial
politician = statesman *or* stateswoman, representative, senator (*U.S.*), congressman (*U.S.*), Member of Parliament, legislator, public servant, congresswoman (*U.S.*)
politics 1 = affairs of state, government, public affairs, civics **2** = political beliefs, party politics, political allegiances, political leanings, political sympathies

3 = political science, statesmanship, civics, statecraft
poll NOUN **1** = survey, figures, count, sampling, returns, ballot, tally, census **2** = election, vote, voting, referendum, ballot, plebiscite

● VERB **1** = question, interview, survey, sample, ballot, canvass **2** = gain, return, record, register, tally
pollute 1 = contaminate, dirty, poison, soil, foul, infect, spoil, stain ≠ decontaminate **2** = defile, corrupt, sully, deprave, debase, profane, desecrate, dishonour ≠ honour
pollution 1 = contamination, dirtying, corruption, taint, foulness, defilement, uncleanness **2** = waste, poisons, dirt, impurities
pond = pool, tarn, small lake, fish pond, duck pond, millpond
ponder = think about, consider, reflect on, contemplate, deliberate about, muse on, brood on, meditate on
pool¹ 1 = swimming pool, lido, swimming bath(s) (*Brit.*), bathing pool (*archaic*) **2** = pond, lake, mere, tarn **3** = puddle, drop, patch
pool² NOUN 1 = supply, reserve, fall-back **2** = kitty, bank, fund, stock, store, pot, jackpot, stockpile

● VERB = combine, share, merge, put together, amalgamate, lump together, join forces on
poor 1 = impoverished, broke (*informal*), hard up (*informal*), short, needy, penniless, destitute, poverty-stricken ≠ rich
2 = unfortunate, unlucky, hapless, pitiful, luckless, wretched, ill-starred, pitiable ≠ fortunate **3** = inferior, unsatisfactory, mediocre, second-rate, rotten (*informal*), low-grade, below par, substandard, half-pie (*N.Z. informal*), bodger *or* bodgie (*Austral. slang*) ≠ excellent **4** = meagre, inadequate, insufficient, lacking, incomplete, scant, deficient, skimpy ≠ ample
poorly ADVERB = badly, incompetently, inadequately, unsuccessfully, insufficiently, unsatisfactorily, inexpertly ≠ well

● ADJECTIVE (*Informal*) = ill, sick, unwell, crook (*Austral. & N.Z. informal*), seedy (*informal*), below par, off colour, under the weather (*informal*), feeling rotten (*informal*) ≠ healthy

pop NOUN = bang, report, crack, noise, burst, explosion
● VERB 1 = burst, crack, snap, bang, explode, go off (with a bang) 2 = put, insert, push, stick, slip, thrust, tuck, shove
pope = Holy Father, pontiff, His Holiness, Bishop of Rome, Vicar of Christ
popular 1 = well-liked, liked, in, accepted, favourite, approved, in favour, fashionable ≠ unpopular 2 = common, general, prevailing, current, conventional, universal, prevalent ≠ rare
popularity 1 = favour, esteem, acclaim, regard, approval, vogue 2 = currency, acceptance, circulation, vogue, prevalence
populate 1 = inhabit, people, live in, occupy, reside in, dwell in (formal) 2 = settle, occupy, pioneer, colonize
population = inhabitants, people, community, society, residents, natives, folk, occupants
pore = opening, hole, outlet, orifice
pornography = obscenity, porn (informal), dirt, filth, indecency, smut
port = harbour, haven, anchorage, seaport
portable = light, compact, convenient, handy, manageable, movable, easily carried
porter¹ (Chiefly Brit.) = doorman, caretaker, janitor, concierge, gatekeeper
porter² = baggage attendant, carrier, bearer, baggage-carrier
portion 1 = part, bit, piece, section, scrap, segment, fragment, chunk 2 = helping, serving, piece, plateful 3 = share, allowance, lot, measure, quantity, quota, ration, allocation
portrait 1 = picture, painting, image, photograph, representation, likeness 2 = description, profile, portrayal, depiction, characterization, thumbnail sketch
portray 1 = play, take the role of, act the part of, represent, personate (rare) 2 = describe, present, depict, evoke, delineate, put in words 3 = represent, draw, paint, illustrate, sketch, figure, picture, depict 4 = characterize, represent, depict
portrayal 1 = performance, interpretation, characterization 2 = depiction, picture, representation, sketch, rendering 3 = description, account,

representation 4 = characterization, representation, depiction
pose VERB 1 = position yourself, sit, model, arrange yourself 2 = put on airs, posture, show off (informal)
● NOUN 1 = posture, position, bearing, attitude, stance 2 = act, façade, air, front, posturing, pretence, mannerism, affectation
● PHRASES **pose as something** or **someone** = impersonate, pretend to be, profess to be, masquerade as, pass yourself off as
posh (Informal, chiefly Brit.) 1 = smart, grand, stylish, luxurious, classy (slang), swish (informal, chiefly Brit.), up-market, swanky (informal) 2 = upper-class, high-class
position NOUN 1 = location, place, point, area, post, situation, station, spot 2 = posture, attitude, arrangement, pose, stance 3 = status, place, standing, footing, station, rank, reputation, importance 4 = job, place, post, opening, office, role, situation, duty 5 = place, standing, rank, status 6 = attitude, view, perspective, point of view, opinion, belief, stance, outlook
● VERB = place, put, set, stand, arrange, locate, lay out
positive 1 = beneficial, useful, practical, helpful, progressive, productive, worthwhile, constructive ≠ harmful 2 = certain, sure, convinced, confident, satisfied, assured, free from doubt ≠ uncertain 3 = definite, real, clear, firm, certain, express, absolute, decisive ≠ inconclusive 4 (Informal) = absolute, complete, perfect, right (Brit. informal), real, total, sheer, utter
positively 1 = definitely, surely, firmly, certainly, absolutely, emphatically, unquestionably, categorically 2 = really, completely, simply, plain (informal), absolutely, thoroughly, utterly, downright
possess 1 = own, have, hold, be in possession of, be the owner of, have in your possession 2 = be endowed with, have, enjoy, benefit from, be possessed of, be gifted with 3 = seize, hold, control, dominate, occupy, take someone over, have power over, have mastery over
possession NOUN = ownership, control, custody, hold, hands, tenure

● PLURAL NOUN = <u>property</u>, things, effects, estate, assets, belongings, chattels

possibility 1 = <u>feasibility</u>, likelihood, potentiality, practicability, workableness 2 = <u>likelihood</u>, chance, risk, odds, prospect, liability, probability 3 *often plural* = <u>potential</u>, promise, prospects, talent, capabilities, potentiality

possible 1 = <u>feasible</u>, viable, workable, achievable, practicable, attainable, doable, realizable ≠ unfeasible 2 = <u>likely</u>, potential, anticipated, probable, odds-on, on the cards ≠ improbable 3 = <u>conceivable</u>, likely, credible, plausible, hypothetical, imaginable, believable, thinkable ≠ inconceivable 4 = <u>aspiring</u>, would-be, promising, hopeful, prospective, wannabe (*informal*)

possibly = <u>perhaps</u>, maybe, perchance (*archaic*)

post[1] NOUN 1 = <u>mail</u>, collection, delivery, postal service, snail mail (*informal*) 2 = <u>correspondence</u>, letters, cards, mail
● VERB = <u>send (off)</u>, forward, mail, get off, transmit, dispatch, consign
● PHRASES **keep someone posted** = <u>notify</u>, brief, advise, inform, report to, keep someone informed, keep someone up to date, apprise

post[2] NOUN 1 = <u>job</u>, place, office, position, situation, employment, appointment, assignment 2 = <u>position</u>, place, base, beat, station
● VERB = <u>station</u>, assign, put, place, position, situate, put on duty

post[3] NOUN = <u>support</u>, stake, pole, column, shaft, upright, pillar, picket
● VERB = <u>put something up</u>, display, affix, pin something up

poster = <u>notice</u>, bill, announcement, advertisement, sticker, placard, public notice

postpone = <u>put off</u>, delay, suspend, adjourn, shelve, defer, put back, put on the back burner (*informal*) ≠ go ahead with

posture NOUN = <u>bearing</u>, set, attitude, stance, carriage, disposition
● VERB = <u>show off</u> (*informal*), pose, affect, put on airs

pot = <u>container</u>, bowl, pan, vessel, basin, cauldron, skillet

potent 1 = <u>powerful</u>, commanding,

dynamic, dominant, influential, authoritative 2 = <u>strong</u>, powerful, mighty, vigorous, forceful ≠ weak

potential ADJECTIVE 1 = <u>possible</u>, future, likely, promising, probable 2 = <u>hidden</u>, possible, inherent, dormant, latent
● NOUN = <u>ability</u>, possibilities, capacity, capability, aptitude, wherewithal, potentiality

potter *usually with **around** or **about*** = <u>mess about</u>, tinker, dabble, footle (*informal*)

pottery = <u>ceramics</u>, terracotta, crockery, earthenware, stoneware

pounce = <u>attack</u>, strike, jump, leap, swoop

pound[1] 1 = <u>enclosure</u>, yard, pen, compound, kennels

pound[2] 1 *sometimes with **on*** = <u>beat</u>, strike, hammer, batter, thrash, thump, clobber (*slang*), pummel 2 = <u>crush</u>, powder, pulverize 3 = <u>pulsate</u>, beat, pulse, throb, palpitate 4 = <u>stomp</u>, tramp, march, thunder (*informal*)

pour 1 = <u>let flow</u>, spill, splash, dribble, drizzle, slop (*informal*), slosh (*informal*), decant 2 = <u>flow</u>, stream, run, course, rush, emit, cascade, gush 3 = <u>rain</u>, pelt (down), teem, bucket down (*informal*) 4 = <u>stream</u>, crowd, flood, swarm, gush, throng, teem

pout VERB = <u>sulk</u>, glower, look petulant, pull a long face
● NOUN = <u>sullen look</u>, glower, long face

poverty 1 = <u>pennilessness</u>, want, need, hardship, insolvency, privation, penury, destitution ≠ wealth 2 = <u>scarcity</u>, lack, absence, want, deficit, shortage, deficiency, inadequacy ≠ abundance

powder NOUN = <u>dust</u>, talc, fine grains, loose particles
● VERB = <u>dust</u>, cover, scatter, sprinkle, strew, dredge

power 1 = <u>control</u>, authority, influence, command, dominance, domination, mastery, dominion, mana (*N.Z.*) 2 = <u>ability</u>, capacity, faculty, property, potential, capability, competence, competency ≠ inability 3 = <u>authority</u>, right, licence, privilege, warrant, prerogative, authorization 4 = <u>strength</u>, might, energy, muscle, vigour, potency, brawn ≠ weakness 5 = <u>forcefulness</u>, force, strength, punch (*informal*), intensity, potency, eloquence, persuasiveness

powerful 1 = <u>influential</u>, dominant,

controlling, commanding, prevailing, authoritative ≠ powerless 2 = strong, strapping, mighty, vigorous, potent, energetic, sturdy ≠ weak 3 = persuasive, convincing, telling, moving, striking, storming, dramatic, impressive

powerless 1 = defenceless, vulnerable, dependent, subject, tied, ineffective, unarmed 2 = weak, disabled, helpless, incapable, frail, feeble, debilitated, impotent ≠ strong

practical 1 = functional, realistic, pragmatic ≠ impractical 2 = empirical, real, applied, actual, hands-on, in the field, experimental, factual ≠ theoretical 3 = sensible, ordinary, realistic, down-to-earth, matter-of-fact, businesslike, hard-headed ≠ impractical 4 = feasible, possible, viable, workable, practicable, doable ≠ impractical 5 = useful, ordinary, appropriate, sensible, everyday, functional, utilitarian, serviceable 6 = skilled, experienced, efficient, accomplished, proficient ≠ inexperienced

practically 1 = almost, nearly, essentially, virtually, basically, fundamentally, all but, just about 2 = sensibly, reasonably, matter-of-factly, realistically, rationally, pragmatically

practice 1 = custom, way, system, rule, method, tradition, habit, routine, tikanga (*N.Z.*) 2 = training, study, exercise, preparation, drill, rehearsal, repetition 3 = profession, work, business, career, occupation, pursuit, vocation 4 = business, company, office, firm, enterprise, partnership, outfit (*informal*) 5 = use, experience, action, operation, application, enactment

practise 1 = rehearse, study, prepare, perfect, repeat, go through, go over, refine 2 = do, train, exercise, drill 3 = carry out, follow, apply, perform, observe, engage in 4 = work at, pursue, carry on

practised = skilled, trained, experienced, seasoned, able, expert, accomplished, proficient ≠ inexperienced

pragmatic = practical, sensible, realistic, down-to-earth, utilitarian, businesslike, hard-headed ≠ idealistic

praise VERB 1 = acclaim, approve of, honour, cheer, admire, applaud, compliment, congratulate ≠ criticize 2 = give thanks to, bless, worship, adore, glorify, exalt
● NOUN 1 = approval, acclaim, tribute, compliment, congratulations, eulogy, commendation, approbation ≠ criticism 2 = thanks, glory, worship, homage, adoration

pray 1 = say your prayers, offer a prayer, recite the rosary 2 = beg, ask, plead, petition, request, solicit, implore, beseech

prayer 1 = supplication, devotion 2 = orison, litany, invocation, intercession 3 = plea, appeal, request, petition, entreaty, supplication

preach 1 *often with to* = deliver a sermon, address, evangelize, preach a sermon 2 = urge, teach, champion, recommend, advise, counsel, advocate, exhort

preacher = clergyman, minister, parson, missionary, evangelist

precarious 1 = insecure, dangerous, tricky, risky, dodgy (*Brit., Austral., & N.Z. informal*), unsure, hazardous, shaky ≠ secure 2 = dangerous, shaky, insecure, unsafe, unreliable ≠ stable

precaution 1 = safeguard, insurance, protection, provision, safety measure 2 = forethought, care, caution, prudence, providence, wariness

precede 1 = go before, antedate 2 = go ahead of, lead, head, go before 3 = preface, introduce, go before

precedent = instance, example, standard, model, pattern, prototype, paradigm, antecedent

precinct = area, quarter, section, sector, district, zone

precious 1 = valuable, expensive, fine, prized, dear, costly, invaluable, priceless ≠ worthless 2 = loved, prized, dear, treasured, darling, beloved, adored, cherished 3 = affected, artificial, twee (*Brit. informal*), overrefined, overnice

precipitate VERB 1 = quicken, trigger, accelerate, advance, hurry, speed up, bring on, hasten 2 = throw, launch, cast, hurl, fling, let fly
● ADJECTIVE 1 = hasty, rash, reckless, impulsive, precipitous, impetuous, heedless 2 = sudden, quick, brief, rushing, rapid, unexpected, swift, abrupt

precise 1 = exact, specific, particular, express, correct, absolute, accurate, explicit ≠ vague 2 = strict, particular, exact, formal, careful, stiff, rigid, meticulous ≠ inexact

precisely 1 = exactly, squarely, correctly, absolutely, strictly, accurately, plumb (*informal*), square on **2** = just so, yes, absolutely, exactly, quite so, you bet (*informal*), without a doubt, indubitably **3** = just, entirely, absolutely, altogether, exactly, in all respects **4** = word for word, literally, exactly, to the letter

precision = exactness, care, accuracy, particularity, meticulousness, preciseness

predecessor 1 = previous job holder, precursor, forerunner, antecedent **2** = ancestor, forebear, antecedent, forefather, tupuna *or* tipuna (*N.Z.*)

predicament = fix (*informal*), situation, spot (*informal*), hole (*slang*), mess, jam (*informal*), dilemma, pinch

predict = foretell, forecast, divine, prophesy, augur, portend

predictable = likely, expected, sure, certain, anticipated, reliable, foreseeable ≠ unpredictable

prediction = prophecy, forecast, prognosis, divination, prognostication, augury

predominantly = mainly, largely, chiefly, mostly, generally, principally, primarily, for the most part

prefer 1 = like better, favour, go for, pick, fancy, opt for, incline towards, be partial to **2** = choose, opt for, pick, desire, would rather, would sooner, incline towards

preferable = better, best, chosen, preferred, recommended, favoured, superior, more suitable ≠ undesirable

preferably = ideally, if possible, rather, sooner, by choice, in *or* for preference

preference 1 = liking, wish, taste, desire, leaning, bent, bias, inclination **2** = first choice, choice, favourite, pick, option, selection **3** = priority, first place, precedence, favouritism, favoured treatment

pregnant 1 = expectant, expecting (*informal*), with child, in the club (*Brit. slang*), big *or* heavy with child **2** = meaningful, pointed, charged, significant, telling, loaded, expressive, eloquent

prejudice NOUN **1** = discrimination, injustice, intolerance, bigotry, unfairness, chauvinism, narrow-mindedness **2** = bias,

preconception, partiality, preconceived notion, prejudgment

● VERB **1** = bias, influence, colour, poison, distort, slant, predispose **2** = harm, damage, hurt, injure, mar, undermine, spoil, impair, crool *or* cruel (*Austral. slang*)

prejudiced = biased, influenced, unfair, one-sided, bigoted, intolerant, opinionated, narrow-minded ≠ unbiased

preliminary ADJECTIVE **1** = first, opening, trial, initial, test, pilot, prior, introductory **2** = qualifying, eliminating

● NOUN = introduction, opening, beginning, start, prelude, preface, overture, preamble

prelude 1 = introduction, beginning, start **2** = overture, opening, introduction, introductory movement

premature 1 = early, untimely, before time, unseasonable **2** = hasty, rash, too soon, untimely, ill-timed, overhasty

premier NOUN = head of government, prime minister, chancellor, chief minister, P.M.

● ADJECTIVE = chief, leading, first, highest, head, main, prime, primary

premiere = first night, opening, debut

premise = assumption, proposition, argument, hypothesis, assertion, supposition, presupposition, postulation

premises = building(s), place, office, property, site, establishment

premium NOUN **1** = fee, charge, payment, instalment **2** = surcharge, extra charge, additional fee *or* charge **3** = bonus, reward, prize, perk (*Brit. informal*), bounty, perquisite

● PHRASES **at a premium** = in great demand, rare, scarce, in short supply, hard to come by

preoccupation 1 = obsession, fixation, bee in your bonnet **2** = absorption, abstraction, daydreaming, immersion, reverie, absent-mindedness, engrossment, woolgathering

preoccupied 1 = absorbed, lost, wrapped up, immersed, engrossed, rapt **2** = lost in thought, distracted, oblivious, absent-minded

preparation 1 = groundwork, preparing, getting ready **2** *usually plural* = arrangement, plan, measure, provision **3** = mixture, medicine, compound, concoction

prepare 1 = make *or* get ready, arrange, jack up (*N.Z. informal*) 2 = train, guide, prime, direct, brief, discipline, put someone in the picture 3 = make, cook, put together, get, produce, assemble, muster, concoct 4 = get ready 5 = practise, get ready, train, exercise, warm up, get into shape

prepared 1 = willing, inclined, disposed 2 = ready, set 3 = fit, primed, in order, arranged, in readiness

prescribe 1 = specify, order, direct, stipulate, write a prescription for 2 = ordain, set, order, rule, recommend, dictate, lay down, decree

prescription 1 = instruction, direction, formula, script (*informal*), recipe 2 = medicine, drug, treatment, preparation, cure, mixture, dose, remedy

presence NOUN 1 = being, existence, residence, attendance, showing up, occupancy, inhabitance 2 = personality, bearing, appearance, aspect, air, carriage, aura, poise

● PHRASES **presence of mind** = level-headedness, assurance, composure, poise, cool (*slang*), wits, countenance, coolness

present¹ ADJECTIVE 1 = current, existing, immediate, contemporary, present-day, existent 2 = here, there, near, ready, nearby, at hand ≠ absent 3 = in existence, existing, existent, extant

● PHRASES **the present** = now, today, the time being, here and now, the present moment

present² NOUN = gift, offering, grant, donation, hand-out, endowment, boon, gratuity, bonsela (*S. African*), koha (*N.Z.*)

● VERB 1 = give, award, hand over, grant, hand out, confer, bestow 2 = put on, stage, perform, give, show, render 3 = launch, display, parade, exhibit, unveil 4 = introduce, make known, acquaint someone with

presentation 1 = giving, award, offering, donation, bestowal, conferral 2 = appearance, look, display, packaging, arrangement, layout 3 = performance, production, show

presently 1 = at present, currently, now, today, these days, nowadays, at the present time, in this day and age 2 = soon, shortly, directly, before long, momentarily (*U.S. & Canad.*), by and by, in a jiffy

(*informal*)

preservation 1 = upholding, support, maintenance 2 = protection, safety, maintenance, conservation, salvation, safeguarding, safekeeping

preserve VERB 1 = maintain, keep, continue, sustain, keep up, prolong, uphold, conserve ≠ end 2 = protect, keep, save, maintain, defend, shelter, shield, care for ≠ attack

● NOUN = area, department, field, territory, province, arena, sphere

preside = officiate, chair, moderate, be chairperson

press 1 = push (down), depress, lean on, press down, force down 2 = push, squeeze, jam, thrust, ram, wedge, shove 3 = hug, squeeze, embrace, clasp, crush, hold close, fold in your arms 4 = urge, beg, petition, exhort, implore, pressurize, entreat 5 = plead, present, lodge, submit, tender, advance insistently 6 = steam, iron, smooth, flatten 7 = compress, grind, reduce, mill, crush, pound, squeeze, tread 8 = crowd, push, gather, surge, flock, herd, swarm, seethe

pressing = urgent, serious, vital, crucial, imperative, important, high-priority, importunate ≠ unimportant

pressure 1 = force, crushing, squeezing, compressing, weight, compression 2 = power, influence, force, constraint, sway, compulsion, coercion 3 = stress, demands, strain, heat, load, burden, urgency, hassle (*informal*), uphill (*S. African*)

prestige = status, standing, credit, reputation, honour, importance, fame, distinction, mana (*N.Z.*)

prestigious = celebrated, respected, prominent, great, important, esteemed, notable, renowned ≠ unknown

presumably = it would seem, probably, apparently, seemingly, on the face of it, in all probability, in all likelihood

presume 1 = believe, think, suppose, assume, guess (*informal, chiefly U.S. & Canad.*), take for granted, infer, conjecture 2 = dare, venture, go so far as, take the liberty, make so bold as

pretend 1 = feign, affect, assume, allege, fake, simulate, profess, sham 2 = make believe, suppose, imagine, act, make up

pretty ADJECTIVE = attractive, beautiful,

lovely, charming, fair, good-looking, bonny, comely ≠ plain
● ADVERB (*Informal*) = <u>fairly</u>, rather, quite, kind of (*informal*), somewhat, moderately, reasonably

prevail 1 = <u>win</u>, succeed, triumph, overcome, overrule, be victorious 2 = <u>be widespread</u>, abound, predominate, be current, be prevalent, exist generally

prevailing 1 = <u>widespread</u>, general, established, popular, common, current, usual, ordinary 2 = <u>predominating</u>, ruling, main, existing, principal

prevalent = <u>common</u>, established, popular, general, current, usual, widespread, universal ≠ rare

prevent = <u>stop</u>, avoid, frustrate, hamper, foil, inhibit, avert, thwart ≠ help

prevention = <u>elimination</u>, safeguard, precaution, thwarting, avoidance, deterrence

preview = <u>sample</u>, sneak preview, trailer, taster, foretaste, advance showing

previous 1 = <u>earlier</u>, former, past, prior, preceding, erstwhile ≠ later 2 = <u>preceding</u>, past, prior, foregoing

previously = <u>before</u>, earlier, once, in the past, formerly, hitherto, beforehand

prey 1 = <u>quarry</u>, game, kill 2 = <u>victim</u>, target, mug (*Brit. slang*), dupe, fall guy (*informal*)

price NOUN 1 = <u>cost</u>, value, rate, charge, figure, worth, damage (*informal*), amount 2 = <u>consequences</u>, penalty, cost, result, toll, forfeit
● VERB = <u>evaluate</u>, value, estimate, rate, cost, assess

priceless = <u>valuable</u>, expensive, precious, invaluable, dear, costly ≠ worthless

prick VERB = <u>pierce</u>, stab, puncture, punch, lance, jab, perforate
● NOUN = <u>puncture</u>, hole, wound, perforation, pinhole

prickly 1 = <u>spiny</u>, barbed, thorny, bristly 2 = <u>itchy</u>, sharp, smarting, stinging, crawling, tingling, scratchy

pride 1 = <u>satisfaction</u>, achievement, fulfilment, delight, content, pleasure, joy, gratification 2 = <u>self-respect</u>, honour, ego, dignity, self-esteem, self-image, self-worth 3 = <u>conceit</u>, vanity, arrogance, pretension, hubris, self-importance, egotism, self-love ≠ humility

priest = <u>clergyman</u>, minister, father,

divine, vicar, pastor, cleric, curate

primarily 1 = <u>chiefly</u>, largely, generally, mainly, essentially, mostly, principally, fundamentally 2 = <u>at first</u>, originally, initially, in the first place, in the beginning, first and foremost, at or from the start

primary = <u>chief</u>, main, first, highest, greatest, prime, principal, cardinal ≠ subordinate

prime ADJECTIVE 1 = <u>main</u>, leading, chief, central, major, key, primary, supreme 2 = <u>best</u>, top, select, highest, quality, choice, excellent, first-class
● NOUN = <u>peak</u>, flower, bloom, height, heyday, zenith
● VERB 1 = <u>inform</u>, tell, train, coach, brief, fill in (*informal*), notify, clue in (*informal*) 2 = <u>prepare</u>, set up, load, equip, get ready, make ready

primitive 1 = <u>early</u>, first, earliest, original, primary, elementary, primordial, primeval ≠ modern 2 = <u>crude</u>, simple, rough, rudimentary, unrefined ≠ elaborate

prince = <u>ruler</u>, lord, monarch, sovereign, crown prince, liege, prince regent, crowned head

princely 1 = <u>substantial</u>, considerable, large, huge, massive, enormous, sizable or sizeable 2 = <u>regal</u>, royal, imperial, noble, sovereign, majestic

princess = <u>ruler</u>, lady, monarch, sovereign, liege, crowned head, crowned princess, dynast

principal ADJECTIVE = <u>main</u>, leading, chief, prime, first, key, essential, primary ≠ minor
● NOUN 1 = <u>headmaster</u> or <u>headmistress</u>, head (*informal*), dean, head teacher, rector, master or mistress 2 = <u>star</u>, lead, leader, prima ballerina, leading man or lady, coryphée 3 = <u>capital</u>, money, assets, working capital

principally = <u>mainly</u>, largely, chiefly, especially, mostly, primarily, above all, predominantly

principle NOUN 1 = <u>morals</u>, standards, ideals, honour, virtue, ethics, integrity, conscience, kaupapa (*N.Z.*) 2 = <u>rule</u>, law, truth, precept
● PHRASES **in principle** 1 = <u>in general</u> 2 = <u>in theory</u>, ideally, on paper, theoretically, in an ideal world, en principe (*French*)

print VERB 1 = <u>run off</u>, publish, copy, reproduce, issue, engrave 2 = <u>publish</u>,

release, circulate, issue, disseminate
3 = <u>mark</u>, impress, stamp, imprint
● NOUN **1** = <u>photograph</u>, photo, snap
2 = <u>picture</u>, plate, etching, engraving, lithograph, woodcut, linocut **3** = <u>copy</u>, photo (*informal*), picture, reproduction, replica

prior ADJECTIVE = <u>earlier</u>, previous, former, preceding, foregoing, pre-existing, pre-existent

● PHRASES **prior to** = <u>before</u>, preceding, earlier than, in advance of, previous to

priority 1 = <u>prime concern</u>
2 = <u>precedence</u>, preference, primacy, predominance **3** = <u>supremacy</u>, rank, precedence, seniority, right of way, pre-eminence

prison = <u>jail</u>, confinement, nick (*Brit. slang*), cooler (*slang*), jug (*slang*), dungeon, clink (*slang*), gaol, boob (*Austral. slang*)

prisoner 1 = <u>convict</u>, con (*slang*), lag (*slang*), jailbird **2** = <u>captive</u>, hostage, detainee, internee

privacy = <u>seclusion</u>, isolation, solitude, retirement, retreat

private 1 = <u>exclusive</u>, individual, privately owned, own, special, reserved ≠ public
2 = <u>secret</u>, confidential, covert, unofficial, clandestine, off the record, hush-hush (*informal*) ≠ public **3** = <u>personal</u>, individual, secret, intimate, undisclosed, unspoken, innermost, unvoiced
4 = <u>secluded</u>, secret, separate, isolated, sequestered ≠ busy **5** = <u>solitary</u>, reserved, retiring, withdrawn, discreet, secretive, self-contained, reclusive ≠ sociable

privilege = <u>right</u>, due, advantage, claim, freedom, liberty, concession, entitlement

privileged = <u>special</u>, advantaged, favoured, honoured, entitled, elite

prize¹ NOUN **1** = <u>reward</u>, cup, award, honour, medal, trophy, accolade
2 = <u>winnings</u>, haul, jackpot, stakes, purse
● ADJECTIVE = <u>champion</u>, best, winning, top, outstanding, award-winning, first-rate

prize² = <u>value</u>, treasure, esteem, cherish, hold dear

prize³ *or* **prise 1** = <u>force</u>, pull, lever
2 = <u>drag</u>, force, draw, wring, extort

probability 1 = <u>likelihood</u>, prospect, chance, odds, expectation, liability, likeliness **2** = <u>chance</u>, odds, possibility, likelihood

probable = <u>likely</u>, possible, apparent,

reasonable to think, credible, plausible, feasible, presumable ≠ unlikely

probably = <u>likely</u>, perhaps, maybe, possibly, presumably, most likely, doubtless, perchance (*archaic*)

probation = <u>trial period</u>, trial, apprenticeship

probe VERB **1** *often with* **into** = <u>examine</u>, go into, investigate, explore, search, look into, analyze, dissect **2** = <u>explore</u>, examine, poke, prod, feel around
● NOUN = <u>investigation</u>, study, inquiry, analysis, examination, exploration, scrutiny, scrutinization

problem 1 = <u>difficulty</u>, trouble, dispute, plight, obstacle, dilemma, headache (*informal*), complication **2** = <u>puzzle</u>, question, riddle, enigma, conundrum, poser

problematic = <u>tricky</u>, puzzling, doubtful, dubious, debatable, problematical ≠ clear

procedure = <u>method</u>, policy, process, course, system, action, practice, strategy

proceed 1 = <u>begin</u>, go ahead
2 = <u>continue</u>, go on, progress, carry on, go ahead, press on ≠ discontinue **3** = <u>go on</u>, continue, progress, carry on, go ahead, move on, move forward, press on ≠ stop
4 = <u>arise</u>, come, issue, result, spring, flow, stem, derive

proceeding = <u>action</u>, process, procedure, move, act, step, measure, deed

proceeds = <u>income</u>, profit, revenue, returns, products, gain, earnings, yield

process NOUN **1** = <u>procedure</u>, means, course, system, action, performance, operation, measure **2** = <u>development</u>, growth, progress, movement, advance, evolution, progression **3** = <u>method</u>, system, practice, technique, procedure
● VERB = <u>handle</u>, manage, action, deal with, fulfil

procession = <u>parade</u>, train, march, file, cavalcade, cortege

proclaim 1 = <u>announce</u>, declare, advertise, publish, indicate, herald, circulate, profess ≠ keep secret
2 = <u>pronounce</u>, announce, declare

prod VERB **1** = <u>poke</u>, push, dig, shove, nudge, jab **2** = <u>prompt</u>, move, urge, motivate, spur, stimulate, rouse, incite
● NOUN **1** = <u>poke</u>, push, dig, shove, nudge, jab **2** = <u>prompt</u>, signal, cue, reminder, stimulus

prodigy = genius, talent, wizard, mastermind, whizz (*informal*)

produce VERB 1 = cause, effect, generate, bring about, give rise to 2 = make, create, develop, manufacture, construct, invent, fabricate 3 = create, develop, write, turn out, compose, originate, churn out (*informal*) 4 = yield, provide, grow, bear, give, supply, afford, render 5 = bring forth, bear, deliver, breed, give birth to, beget, bring into the world 6 = show, provide, present, advance, demonstrate, offer, come up with, exhibit 7 = display, show, present, proffer 8 = present, stage, direct, put on, do, show, mount, exhibit
● NOUN = fruit and vegetables, goods, food, products, crops, yield, harvest, greengrocery (*Brit.*)

producer 1 = director, promoter, impresario 2 = maker, manufacturer, builder, creator, fabricator 3 = grower, farmer

product 1 = goods, produce, creation, commodity, invention, merchandise, artefact 2 = result, consequence, effect, outcome, upshot

production 1 = producing, making, manufacture, manufacturing, construction, formation, fabrication 2 = creation, development, fashioning, composition, origination 3 = management, administration, direction 4 = presentation, staging, mounting

productive 1 = fertile, rich, prolific, plentiful, fruitful, fecund ≠ barren 2 = creative, inventive 3 = useful, rewarding, valuable, profitable, effective, worthwhile, beneficial, constructive ≠ useless

productivity = output, production, capacity, yield, efficiency, work rate

profess 1 = claim, allege, pretend, fake, make out, purport, feign 2 = state, admit, announce, declare, confess, assert, proclaim, affirm

professed 1 = supposed, would-be, alleged, so-called, pretended, purported, self-styled, ostensible 2 = declared, confirmed, confessed, proclaimed, self-confessed, avowed, self-acknowledged

profession = occupation, calling, business, career, employment, office, position, sphere

professional ADJECTIVE 1 = qualified, trained, skilled, white-collar 2 = expert, experienced, skilled, masterly, efficient, competent, adept, proficient ≠ amateurish
● NOUN = expert, master, pro (*informal*), specialist, guru, adept, maestro, virtuoso, fundi (*S. African*)

professor = don (*Brit.*), fellow (*Brit.*), prof (*informal*)

profile 1 = outline, lines, form, figure, silhouette, contour, side view 2 = biography, sketch, vignette, characterization, thumbnail sketch

profit NOUN 1 *often plural* = earnings, return, revenue, gain, yield, proceeds, receipts, takings ≠ loss 2 = benefit, good, use, value, gain, advantage, advancement ≠ disadvantage
● VERB 1 = make money, gain, earn 2 = benefit, help, serve, gain, promote, be of advantage to

profitable 1 = money-making, lucrative, paying, commercial, worthwhile, cost-effective, fruitful, remunerative 2 = beneficial, useful, rewarding, valuable, productive, worthwhile, fruitful, advantageous ≠ useless

profound 1 = sincere, acute, intense, great, keen, extreme, heartfelt, deeply felt ≠ insincere 2 = wise, learned, deep, penetrating, philosophical, sage, abstruse, sagacious ≠ uninformed

programme 1 = schedule, plan, agenda, timetable, listing, list, line-up, calendar 2 = course, curriculum, syllabus 3 = show, performance, production, broadcast, episode, presentation, transmission, telecast

progress NOUN 1 = development, growth, advance, gain, improvement, breakthrough, headway ≠ regression 2 = movement forward, passage, advancement, course, advance, headway ≠ movement backward
● VERB 1 = move on, continue, travel, advance, proceed, go forward, make headway ≠ move back 2 = develop, improve, advance, grow, gain ≠ get behind
● PHRASES **in progress** = going on, happening, continuing, being done, occurring, taking place, proceeding, under way

progression 1 = progress, advance,

advancement, gain, headway, furtherance, movement forward **2** = <u>sequence</u>, course, series, chain, cycle, string, succession

progressive 1 = <u>enlightened</u>, liberal, modern, advanced, radical, revolutionary, avant-garde, reformist **2** = <u>growing</u>, continuing, increasing, developing, advancing, ongoing

prohibit 1 = <u>forbid</u>, ban, veto, outlaw, disallow, proscribe, debar ≠ permit **2** = <u>prevent</u>, restrict, stop, hamper, hinder, impede ≠ allow

prohibition = <u>ban</u>, boycott, embargo, bar, veto, prevention, exclusion, injunction

project NOUN **1** = <u>scheme</u>, plan, job, idea, campaign, operation, activity, venture **2** = <u>assignment</u>, task, homework, piece of research

● VERB **1** = <u>forecast</u>, expect, estimate, predict, reckon, calculate, gauge, extrapolate **2** = <u>stick out</u>, extend, stand out, bulge, protrude, overhang, jut

projection = <u>forecast</u>, estimate, reckoning, calculation, estimation, computation, extrapolation

proliferation = <u>multiplication</u>, increase, spread, expansion

prolific 1 = <u>productive</u>, creative, fertile, inventive, copious **2** = <u>fruitful</u>, fertile, abundant, luxuriant, profuse, fecund ≠ unproductive

prolong = <u>lengthen</u>, continue, perpetuate, draw out, extend, delay, stretch out, spin out ≠ shorten

prominence 1 = <u>fame</u>, name, reputation, importance, celebrity, distinction, prestige, eminence **2** = <u>conspicuousness</u>, markedness

prominent 1 = <u>famous</u>, leading, top, important, main, distinguished, well-known, notable ≠ unknown **2** = <u>noticeable</u>, obvious, outstanding, pronounced, conspicuous, eye-catching, obtrusive ≠ inconspicuous

promise VERB **1** = <u>guarantee</u>, pledge, vow, swear, contract, assure, undertake, warrant **2** = <u>seem likely</u>, look like, show signs of, augur, betoken

● NOUN **1** = <u>guarantee</u>, word, bond, vow, commitment, pledge, undertaking, assurance **2** = <u>potential</u>, ability, talent, capacity, capability, aptitude

promising 1 = <u>encouraging</u>, likely, bright, reassuring, hopeful, favourable, rosy,

auspicious ≠ unpromising **2** = <u>talented</u>, able, gifted, rising

promote 1 = <u>help</u>, back, support, aid, forward, encourage, advance, boost ≠ impede **2** = <u>advertise</u>, sell, hype, publicize, push, plug (*informal*) **3** = <u>raise</u>, upgrade, elevate, exalt ≠ demote

promotion 1 = <u>rise</u>, upgrading, move up, advancement, elevation, exaltation, preferment **2** = <u>publicity</u>, advertising, plugging (*informal*) **3** = <u>encouragement</u>, support, boosting, advancement, furtherance

prompt VERB **1** = <u>cause</u>, occasion, provoke, give rise to, elicit **2** = <u>remind</u>, assist, cue, help out

● ADJECTIVE = <u>immediate</u>, quick, rapid, instant, timely, early, swift, speedy ≠ slow

● ADVERB (*Informal*) = <u>exactly</u>, sharp, promptly, on the dot, punctually

promptly 1 = <u>immediately</u>, swiftly, directly, quickly, at once, speedily **2** = <u>punctually</u>, on time, spot on (*informal*), bang on (*informal*), on the dot, on the button (*U.S.*), on the nail

prone 1 = <u>liable</u>, given, subject, inclined, tending, bent, disposed, susceptible ≠ disinclined **2** = <u>face down</u>, flat, horizontal, prostrate, recumbent ≠ face up

pronounce 1 = <u>say</u>, speak, sound, articulate, enunciate **2** = <u>declare</u>, announce, deliver, proclaim, decree, affirm

pronounced = <u>noticeable</u>, decided, marked, strong, obvious, evident, distinct, definite ≠ imperceptible

proof NOUN = <u>evidence</u>, demonstration, testimony, confirmation, verification, corroboration, authentication, substantiation

● ADJECTIVE = <u>impervious</u>, strong, resistant, impenetrable, repellent

prop VERB **1** = <u>lean</u>, place, set, stand, position, rest, lay, balance **2** *often with **up*** = <u>support</u>, sustain, hold up, brace, uphold, bolster, buttress

● NOUN **1** = <u>support</u>, stay, brace, mainstay, buttress, stanchion **2** = <u>mainstay</u>, support, sustainer, anchor, backbone, cornerstone, upholder

propaganda = <u>information</u>, advertising, promotion, publicity, hype, disinformation

propel 1 = <u>drive</u>, launch, force, send, shoot, push, thrust, shove ≠ stop **2** = <u>impel</u>, drive, push, prompt, spur, motivate ≠ hold back

proper 1 = real, actual, genuine, true, bona fide, dinkum (*Austral. & N.Z. informal*) 2 = correct, accepted, established, appropriate, right, formal, conventional, precise ≠ improper 3 = polite, right, becoming, seemly, fitting, fit, mannerly, suitable ≠ unseemly

properly 1 = correctly, rightly, fittingly, appropriately, accurately, suitably, aptly ≠ incorrectly 2 = politely, decently, respectably ≠ badly

property 1 = possessions, goods, effects, holdings, capital, riches, estate, assets 2 = land, holding, estate, real estate, freehold 3 = quality, feature, characteristic, attribute, trait, hallmark

prophecy 1 = prediction, forecast, prognostication, augury 2 = second sight, divination, augury, telling the future, soothsaying

prophet *or* **prophetess** = soothsayer, forecaster, diviner, oracle, seer, sibyl, prophesier

proportion NOUN 1 = part, share, amount, division, percentage, segment, quota, fraction 2 = relative amount, relationship, ratio 3 = balance, harmony, correspondence, symmetry, concord, congruity

● PLURAL NOUN = dimensions, size, volume, capacity, extent, expanse

proportional *or* **proportionate** = correspondent, corresponding, even, balanced, consistent, compatible, equitable, in proportion ≠ disproportionate

proposal = suggestion, plan, programme, scheme, offer, project, bid, recommendation

propose 1 = put forward, present, suggest, advance, submit 2 = intend, mean, plan, aim, design, scheme, have in mind 3 = nominate, name, present, recommend 4 = offer marriage, pop the question (*informal*), ask for someone's hand (in marriage)

proposition NOUN 1 = task, problem, activity, job, affair, venture, undertaking 2 = theory, idea, argument, concept, thesis, hypothesis, theorem, premiss 3 = proposal, plan, suggestion, scheme, bid, recommendation 4 = advance, pass (*informal*), proposal, overture, improper suggestion, come-on (*informal*)

● VERB = make a pass at, solicit, accost, make an improper suggestion to

proprietor *or* **proprietress** = owner, titleholder, landlord *or* landlady

prosecute (*Law*) = take someone to court, try, sue, indict, arraign, put someone on trial, litigate, bring someone to trial

prospect NOUN 1 = likelihood, chance, possibility, hope, promise, odds, expectation, probability 2 = idea, outlook 3 = view, landscape, scene, sight, outlook, spectacle, vista

● PLURAL NOUN = possibilities, chances, future, potential, expectations, outlook, scope

● VERB = look, search, seek, dowse

prospective 1 = potential, possible 2 = expected, coming, future, likely, intended, anticipated, forthcoming, imminent

prospectus = catalogue, list, programme, outline, syllabus, synopsis

prosper = succeed, advance, progress, thrive, get on, do well, flourish

prosperity = success, riches, plenty, fortune, wealth, luxury, good fortune, affluence ≠ poverty

prosperous 1 = wealthy, rich, affluent, well-off, well-heeled (*informal*), well-to-do, moneyed ≠ poor 2 = successful, booming, thriving, flourishing, doing well ≠ unsuccessful

prostitute NOUN = whore, hooker (*U.S. slang*), pro (*slang*), tart (*informal*), call girl, harlot, streetwalker, loose woman

● VERB = cheapen, sell out, pervert, degrade, devalue, squander, demean, debase

protagonist 1 = supporter, champion, advocate, exponent 2 = leading character, principal, central character, hero *or* heroine

protect = keep someone safe, defend, support, save, guard, preserve, look after, shelter ≠ endanger

protection 1 = safety, care, defence, protecting, security, custody, safeguard, aegis 2 = safeguard, cover, guard, shelter, screen, barrier, shield, buffer 3 = armour, cover, screen, barrier, shelter, shield

protective 1 = protecting 2 = caring, defensive, motherly, fatherly, maternal, vigilant, watchful, paternal

protector 1 = defender, champion, guard,

guardian, patron, bodyguard **2** = <u>guard</u>, screen, protection, shield, pad, cushion, buffer

protest VERB **1** = <u>object</u>, demonstrate, oppose, complain, disagree, cry out, disapprove, demur **2** = <u>assert</u>, insist, maintain, declare, affirm, profess, attest, avow
● NOUN **1** = <u>demonstration</u>, march, rally, sit-in, demo (*informal*), hikoi (*N.Z.*)
2 = <u>objection</u>, complaint, dissent, outcry, protestation, remonstrance

protocol = <u>code of behaviour</u>, manners, conventions, customs, etiquette, propriety, decorum

prototype = <u>original</u>, model, first, example, standard

protracted = <u>extended</u>, prolonged, drawn-out, spun out, dragged out, long-drawn-out

proud 1 = <u>satisfied</u>, pleased, content, thrilled, glad, gratified, joyful, well-pleased ≠ dissatisfied **2** = <u>conceited</u>, arrogant, lordly, imperious, overbearing, haughty, snobbish, self-satisfied ≠ humble

prove 1 = <u>turn out</u>, come out, end up **2** = <u>verify</u>, establish, determine, show, confirm, demonstrate, justify, substantiate ≠ disprove

proven = <u>established</u>, proved, confirmed, tested, reliable, definite, verified, attested

provide VERB **1** = <u>supply</u>, give, distribute, outfit, equip, donate, furnish, dispense ≠ withhold **2** = <u>give</u>, bring, add, produce, present, serve, afford, yield
● PHRASES **provide for someone** = <u>support</u>, care for, keep, maintain, sustain, take care of, fend for ◆ **provide for something** = <u>take precautions against</u>, plan for, prepare for, anticipate, plan ahead for, forearm for

provided *often with* **that** = <u>if</u>, given, on condition, as long as

provider 1 = <u>supplier</u>, giver, source, donor **2** = <u>breadwinner</u>, supporter, earner, wage earner

providing *often with* **that** = <u>on condition that</u>, given that, as long as

province 1 = <u>region</u>, section, district, zone, patch, colony, domain **2** = <u>area</u>, business, concern, responsibility, line, role, department, field

provincial ADJECTIVE **1** = <u>regional</u>, state, local, county, district, territorial, parochial

2 = <u>rural</u>, country, local, rustic, homespun, hick (*informal*, *chiefly U.S. & Canad.*), backwoods ≠ urban **3** = <u>parochial</u>, insular, narrow-minded, unsophisticated, limited, narrow, small-town (*chiefly U.S.*), inward-looking ≠ cosmopolitan

provision NOUN **1** = <u>supplying</u>, giving, providing, supply, delivery, distribution, catering, presentation **2** = <u>condition</u>, term, requirement, demand, rider, restriction, qualification, clause
● PLURAL NOUN = <u>food</u>, supplies, stores, fare, rations, foodstuff, kai (*N.Z. informal*), victuals, edibles

provisional 1 = <u>temporary</u>, interim ≠ permanent **2** = <u>conditional</u>, limited, qualified, contingent, tentative ≠ definite

provocation 1 = <u>cause</u>, reason, grounds, motivation, stimulus, incitement
2 = <u>offence</u>, challenge, insult, taunt, injury, dare, grievance, annoyance

provocative = <u>offensive</u>, provoking, insulting, stimulating, annoying, galling, goading

provoke 1 = <u>anger</u>, annoy, irritate, infuriate, hassle (*informal*), aggravate (*informal*), incense, enrage ≠ pacify **2** = <u>rouse</u>, cause, produce, promote, occasion, prompt, stir, induce ≠ curb

prowess 1 = <u>skill</u>, ability, talent, expertise, genius, excellence, accomplishment, mastery ≠ inability **2** = <u>bravery</u>, daring, courage, heroism, mettle, valour, fearlessness, valiance ≠ cowardice

proximity = <u>nearness</u>, closeness

proxy = <u>representative</u>, agent, deputy, substitute, factor, delegate

prudent 1 = <u>cautious</u>, careful, wary, discreet, vigilant ≠ careless **2** = <u>wise</u>, politic, sensible, shrewd, discerning, judicious ≠ unwise **3** = <u>thrifty</u>, economical, sparing, careful, canny, provident, frugal, far-sighted ≠ extravagant

prune 1 = <u>cut</u>, trim, clip, dock, shape, shorten, snip **2** = <u>reduce</u>, cut, cut back, trim, cut down, pare down, make reductions in

psyche = <u>soul</u>, mind, self, spirit, personality, individuality, anima, wairua (*N.Z.*)

psychiatrist = <u>psychotherapist</u>, analyst, therapist, psychologist, shrink (*slang*), psychoanalyst, headshrinker (*slang*)

psychic ADJECTIVE **1** = <u>supernatural</u>,

mystic, occult 2 = <u>mystical</u>, spiritual, magical, other-worldly, paranormal, preternatural 3 = <u>psychological</u>, emotional, mental, spiritual, inner, psychiatric, cognitive
● NOUN = <u>clairvoyant</u>, fortune teller

psychological 1 = <u>mental</u>, emotional, intellectual, inner, cognitive, cerebral 2 = <u>imaginary</u>, psychosomatic, irrational, unreal, all in the mind

psychology 1 = <u>behaviourism</u>, study of personality, science of mind 2 (*Informal*) = <u>way of thinking</u>, attitude, behaviour, temperament, mentality, thought processes, mental processes, what makes you tick

pub or **public house** = <u>tavern</u>, bar, inn, saloon

public NOUN = <u>people</u>, society, community, nation, everyone, citizens, electorate, populace
● ADJECTIVE 1 = <u>civic</u>, government, state, national, local, official, community, social 2 = <u>general</u>, popular, national, shared, common, widespread, universal, collective 3 = <u>open</u>, accessible, communal, unrestricted ≠ private 4 = <u>well-known</u>, leading, important, respected, famous, celebrated, recognized, distinguished 5 = <u>known</u>, open, obvious, acknowledged, plain, patent, overt ≠ secret

publication 1 = <u>pamphlet</u>, newspaper, magazine, issue, title, leaflet, brochure, periodical 2 = <u>announcement</u>, publishing, broadcasting, reporting, declaration, disclosure, proclamation, notification

publicity 1 = <u>advertising</u>, press, promotion, hype, boost, plug (*informal*) 2 = <u>attention</u>, exposure, fame, celebrity, fuss, public interest, limelight, notoriety

publish 1 = <u>put out</u>, issue, produce, print 2 = <u>announce</u>, reveal, spread, advertise, broadcast, disclose, proclaim, circulate

pudding = <u>dessert</u>, afters (*Brit. informal*), sweet, pud (*informal*)

puff VERB 1 = <u>smoke</u>, draw, drag (*slang*), suck, inhale, pull at *or* on 2 = <u>breathe heavily</u>, pant, exhale, blow, gasp, gulp, wheeze, fight for breath
● NOUN 1 = <u>drag</u>, pull (*slang*), moke 2 = <u>blast</u>, breath, whiff, draught, gust

pull VERB 1 = <u>draw</u>, haul, drag, trail, tow, tug, jerk, yank ≠ push 2 = <u>extract</u>, pick, remove, gather, take out, pluck, uproot,

draw out ≠ insert 3 (*Informal*) = <u>attract</u>, draw, bring in, tempt, lure, interest, entice, pull in ≠ repel 4 = <u>strain</u>, tear, stretch, rip, wrench, dislocate, sprain
● NOUN 1 = <u>tug</u>, jerk, yank, twitch, heave ≠ shove 2 = <u>puff</u>, drag (*slang*), inhalation 3 (*Informal*) = <u>influence</u>, power, weight, muscle, clout (*informal*), kai (*N.Z. informal*)
● PHRASES **pull out (of)** 1 = <u>withdraw</u>, quit 2 = <u>leave</u>, abandon, get out, quit, retreat from, depart, evacuate ◆ **pull someone up** = <u>reprimand</u>, rebuke, admonish, read the riot act to, tell someone off (*informal*), reprove, bawl someone out (*informal*), tear someone off a strip (*Brit. informal*) ◆ **pull something off** (*Informal*) = <u>succeed in</u>, manage, carry out, accomplish ◆ **pull something out** = <u>produce</u>, draw, bring out, draw out ◆ **pull up** = <u>stop</u>, halt, brake

pulp NOUN 1 = <u>paste</u>, mash, mush 2 = <u>flesh</u>, meat, soft part
● ADJECTIVE = <u>cheap</u>, lurid, trashy, rubbishy
● VERB = <u>crush</u>, squash, mash, pulverize

pulse NOUN = <u>beat</u>, rhythm, vibration, beating, throb, throbbing, pulsation
● VERB = <u>beat</u>, throb, vibrate, pulsate

pump 1 = <u>supply</u>, send, pour, inject 2 = <u>interrogate</u>, probe, quiz, cross-examine

punch¹ VERB = <u>hit</u>, strike, box, smash, belt (*informal*), sock (*slang*), swipe (*informal*), bop (*informal*)
● NOUN 1 = <u>blow</u>, hit, sock (*slang*), jab, swipe (*informal*), bop (*informal*), wallop (*informal*) 2 (*Informal*) = <u>effectiveness</u>, bite, impact, drive, vigour, verve, forcefulness

punch² = <u>pierce</u>, cut, bore, drill, stamp, puncture, prick, perforate

punctuate = <u>interrupt</u>, break, pepper, sprinkle, intersperse

puncture NOUN 1 = <u>flat tyre</u>, flat, flattie (*N.Z.*) 2 = <u>hole</u>, opening, break, cut, nick, leak, slit
● VERB = <u>pierce</u>, cut, nick, penetrate, prick, rupture, perforate, bore a hole

punish = <u>discipline</u>, correct, castigate, chastise, sentence, chasten, penalize

punishing = <u>hard</u>, taxing, wearing, tiring, exhausting, gruelling, strenuous, arduous ≠ easy

punishment 1 = <u>penalizing</u>, discipline, correction, retribution, chastening,

chastisement 2 = <u>penalty</u>, penance
punitive = <u>retaliatory</u>, in reprisal, retaliative
punt VERB = <u>bet</u>, back, stake, gamble, lay, wager
• NOUN = <u>bet</u>, stake, gamble, wager
punter 1 = <u>gambler</u>, better, backer
2 (*Informal*) = <u>person</u>, man in the street
pupil 1 = <u>student</u>, schoolboy *or* schoolgirl, schoolchild ≠ teacher 2 = <u>learner</u>, novice, beginner, disciple ≠ instructor
puppet 1 = <u>marionette</u>, doll, glove puppet, finger puppet 2 = <u>pawn</u>, tool, instrument, mouthpiece, stooge, cat's-paw
purchase VERB = <u>buy</u>, pay for, obtain, get, score (*slang*), gain, pick up, acquire ≠ sell
• NOUN 1 = <u>acquisition</u>, buy, investment, property, gain, asset, possession 2 = <u>grip</u>, hold, support, leverage, foothold
pure 1 = <u>unmixed</u>, real, simple, natural, straight, genuine, neat, authentic ≠ adulterated 2 = <u>clean</u>, wholesome, sanitary, spotless, sterilized, squeaky-clean, untainted, uncontaminated ≠ contaminated 3 = <u>complete</u>, total, perfect, absolute, sheer, patent, utter, outright ≠ qualified 4 = <u>innocent</u>, modest, good, moral, impeccable, righteous, virtuous, squeaky-clean ≠ corrupt
purely = <u>absolutely</u>, just, only, completely, simply, entirely, exclusively, merely
purge VERB 1 = <u>rid</u>, clear, cleanse, strip, empty, void 2 = <u>get rid of</u>, remove, expel, wipe out, eradicate, do away with, exterminate
• NOUN = <u>removal</u>, elimination, expulsion, eradication, ejection
purity 1 = <u>cleanness</u>, cleanliness, wholesomeness, pureness, faultlessness, immaculateness ≠ impurity 2 = <u>innocence</u>, virtue, integrity, honesty, decency, virginity, chastity, chasteness ≠ immorality
purport = <u>claim</u>, allege, assert, profess
purpose NOUN 1 = <u>reason</u>, point, idea, aim, object, intention 2 = <u>aim</u>, end, plan, hope, goal, wish, desire, object 3 = <u>determination</u>, resolve, will, resolution, ambition, persistence, tenacity, firmness
• PHRASES **on purpose** = <u>deliberately</u>, purposely, intentionally, knowingly, designedly
purposely = <u>deliberately</u>, expressly, consciously, intentionally, knowingly, with intent, on purpose ≠ accidentally

purse NOUN 1 = <u>pouch</u>, wallet, money-bag 2 (*U.S.*) = <u>handbag</u>, bag, shoulder bag, pocket book, clutch bag 3 = <u>funds</u>, means, money, resources, treasury, wealth, exchequer
• VERB = <u>pucker</u>, contract, tighten, pout, press together
pursue 1 = <u>engage in</u>, perform, conduct, carry on, practise 2 = <u>try for</u>, seek, desire, search for, aim for, work towards, strive for 3 = <u>continue</u>, maintain, carry on, keep on, persist in, proceed in, persevere in 4 = <u>follow</u>, track, hunt, chase, dog, shadow, tail (*informal*), hound ≠ flee
pursuit 1 = <u>quest</u>, seeking, search, aim of, aspiration for, striving towards 2 = <u>pursuing</u>, seeking, search, hunt, chase, trailing 3 = <u>occupation</u>, activity, interest, line, pleasure, hobby, pastime
push VERB 1 = <u>shove</u>, force, press, thrust, drive, knock, sweep, plunge ≠ pull 2 = <u>press</u>, operate, depress, squeeze, activate, hold down 3 = <u>make</u> *or* <u>force your way</u>, move, shoulder, inch, squeeze, thrust, elbow, shove 4 = <u>urge</u>, encourage, persuade, spur, press, incite, impel ≠ discourage
• NOUN 1 = <u>shove</u>, thrust, butt, elbow, nudge ≠ pull 2 (*Informal*) = <u>drive</u>, go (*informal*), energy, initiative, enterprise, ambition, vitality, vigour
• PHRASES **the push** (*Informal, chiefly Brit.*) = <u>dismissal</u>, the sack (*informal*), discharge, the boot (*slang*), your cards (*informal*)
put VERB 1 = <u>place</u>, leave, set, position, rest, park (*informal*), plant, lay 2 = <u>express</u>, state, word, phrase, utter
• PHRASES **put someone off**
1 = <u>discourage</u>, intimidate, deter, daunt, dissuade, demoralize, scare off, dishearten 2 = <u>disconcert</u>, confuse, unsettle, throw (*informal*), dismay, perturb, faze, discomfit ♦ **put someone up** 1 = <u>accommodate</u>, house, board, lodge, quarter, take someone in, billet 2 = <u>nominate</u>, put forward, offer, present, propose, recommend, submit ♦ **put something across** *or* **over** = <u>communicate</u>, explain, convey, make clear, get across, make yourself understood ♦ **put something off** = <u>postpone</u>, delay, defer, adjourn, hold over, put on the back burner (*informal*),

take a rain check on (*U.S. & Canad. informal*) ◆ **put something up** 1 = <u>build</u>, raise, set up, construct, erect, fabricate 2 = <u>offer</u>, present, mount, put forward

puzzle VERB = <u>perplex</u>, confuse, baffle, stump, bewilder, confound, mystify, faze ● NOUN 1 = <u>problem</u>, riddle, question, conundrum, poser 2 = <u>mystery</u>, problem, paradox, enigma, conundrum

puzzling = <u>perplexing</u>, baffling, bewildering, involved, enigmatic, incomprehensible, mystifying, abstruse ≠ simple

q

quake = <u>shake</u>, tremble, quiver, move, rock, shiver, shudder, vibrate

qualification 1 = <u>eligibility</u>, quality, ability, skill, fitness, attribute, capability, aptitude 2 = <u>condition</u>, proviso, requirement, rider, reservation, limitation, modification, caveat

qualified 1 = <u>capable</u>, trained, experienced, seasoned, able, fit, expert, chartered ≠ untrained 2 = <u>restricted</u>, limited, provisional, conditional, reserved, bounded, adjusted, moderated ≠ unconditional

qualify 1 = <u>certify</u>, equip, empower, train, prepare, fit, ready, permit ≠ disqualify 2 = <u>restrict</u>, limit, reduce, ease, moderate, regulate, diminish, temper

quality 1 = <u>standard</u>, standing, class, condition, rank, grade, merit, classification 2 = <u>excellence</u>, status, merit, position, value, worth, distinction, virtue 3 = <u>characteristic</u>, feature, attribute, point, side, mark, property, aspect 4 = <u>nature</u>, character, make, sort, kind

quantity 1 = <u>amount</u>, lot, total, sum, part, number 2 = <u>size</u>, measure, mass, volume, length, capacity, extent, bulk

quarrel NOUN = <u>disagreement</u>, fight, row, argument, dispute, controversy, breach, contention, biffo (*Austral. slang*) ≠ accord

● VERB = <u>disagree</u>, fight, argue, row, clash, dispute, differ, fall out (*informal*) ≠ get on *or* along (with)

quarry = <u>prey</u>, victim, game, goal, aim, prize, objective

quarter NOUN 1 = <u>district</u>, region, neighbourhood, place, part, side, area, zone 2 = <u>mercy</u>, pity, compassion, charity, sympathy, tolerance, kindness, forgiveness ● PLURAL NOUN = <u>lodgings</u>, rooms, chambers, residence, dwelling, barracks, abode, habitation ● VERB = <u>accommodate</u>, house, lodge, place, board, post, station, billet

quash 1 = <u>annul</u>, overturn, reverse, cancel, overthrow, revoke, overrule, rescind 2 = <u>suppress</u>, crush, put down, beat, overthrow, squash, subdue, repress

queen 1 = <u>sovereign</u>, ruler, monarch, leader, Crown, princess, majesty, head of state 2 = <u>leading light</u>, star, favourite, celebrity, darling, mistress, big name

queer 1 = <u>strange</u>, odd, funny, unusual, extraordinary, curious, weird, peculiar ≠ normal 2 = <u>faint</u>, dizzy, giddy, queasy, light-headed

query NOUN 1 = <u>question</u>, inquiry, problem 2 = <u>doubt</u>, suspicion, objection ● VERB 1 = <u>question</u>, challenge, doubt, suspect, dispute, object to, distrust, mistrust 2 = <u>ask</u>, inquire *or* enquire, question

quest 1 = <u>search</u>, hunt, mission, enterprise, crusade 2 = <u>expedition</u>, journey, adventure

question NOUN 1 = <u>inquiry</u>, enquiry, query, investigation, examination, interrogation ≠ answer 2 = <u>difficulty</u>, problem, doubt, argument, dispute, controversy, query, contention 3 = <u>issue</u>, point, matter, subject, problem, debate, proposal, theme ● VERB 1 = <u>interrogate</u>, cross-examine, interview, examine, probe, quiz, ask questions 2 = <u>dispute</u>, challenge, doubt, suspect, oppose, query, mistrust, disbelieve ≠ accept ● PHRASES **out of the question** = <u>impossible</u>, unthinkable, inconceivable, not on (*informal*), hopeless, unimaginable, unworkable, unattainable

questionable = <u>dubious</u>, suspect, doubtful, controversial, suspicious, dodgy (*Brit., Austral., & N.Z. informal*), debatable, moot ≠ indisputable

queue = <u>line</u>, row, file, train, series, chain, string, column

quick 1 = fast, swift, speedy, express, cracking (*Brit. informal*), smart, rapid, fleet ≠ slow 2 = brief, passing, hurried, flying, fleeting, summary, lightning, short-lived ≠ long 3 = immediate, instant, prompt, sudden, abrupt, instantaneous 4 = excitable, passionate, irritable, touchy, irascible, testy ≠ calm 5 = intelligent, bright (*informal*), alert, sharp, acute, smart, clever, shrewd ≠ stupid

quicken 1 = speed up, hurry, accelerate, hasten, gee up (*informal*) 2 = stimulate, inspire, arouse, excite, revive, incite, energize, invigorate

quickly 1 = swiftly, rapidly, hurriedly, fast, hastily, briskly, apace ≠ slowly 2 = soon, speedily, as soon as possible, momentarily (*U.S.*), instantaneously, pronto (*informal*), a.s.a.p. (*informal*) 3 = immediately, at once, directly, promptly, abruptly, without delay

quiet ADJECTIVE 1 = soft, low, muted, lowered, whispered, faint, suppressed, stifled ≠ loud 2 = peaceful, silent, hushed, soundless, noiseless ≠ noisy 3 = calm, peaceful, tranquil, mild, serene, placid, restful ≠ exciting 4 = still, calm, peaceful, tranquil ≠ troubled 5 = undisturbed, isolated, secluded, private, sequestered, unfrequented ≠ crowded 6 = silent 7 = reserved, retiring, shy, gentle, mild, sedate, meek ≠ excitable • NOUN = peace, rest, tranquillity, ease, silence, solitude, serenity, stillness ≠ noise

quietly 1 = noiselessly, silently 2 = softly, inaudibly, in an undertone, under your breath 3 = calmly, serenely, placidly, patiently, mildly 4 = silently, mutely

quilt = bedspread, duvet, coverlet, eiderdown, counterpane, doona (*Austral.*), continental quilt

quip = joke, sally, jest, riposte, wisecrack (*informal*), retort, pleasantry, gibe

quirky = odd, unusual, eccentric, idiosyncratic, peculiar, offbeat

quit 1 = resign (from), leave, retire (from), pull out (of), step down (from) (*informal*), abdicate 2 = stop, give up, cease, end, drop, abandon, halt, discontinue ≠ continue 3 = leave, depart from, go out of, go away from, pull out from

quite 1 = somewhat, rather, fairly, reasonably, relatively, moderately 2 = absolutely, perfectly, completely, totally, fully, entirely, wholly

quiz NOUN = examination, questioning, interrogation, interview, investigation, grilling (*informal*), cross-examination, cross-questioning • VERB = question, ask, interrogate, examine, investigate

quota = share, allowance, ration, part, limit, slice, quantity, portion

quotation 1 = passage, quote (*informal*), excerpt, reference, extract, citation 2 (*Commerce*) = estimate, price, tender, rate, cost, charge, figure, quote (*informal*)

quote 1 = repeat, recite, recall 2 = refer to, cite, give, name, detail, relate, mention, instance

r

race¹ NOUN 1 = competition, contest, chase, dash, pursuit 2 = contest, competition, rivalry • VERB 1 = compete against, run against 2 = compete, run, contend, take part in a race 3 = run, fly, career, speed, tear, dash, hurry, dart

race² = people, nation, blood, stock, type, folk, tribe

racial = ethnic, ethnological, national, folk, genetic, tribal, genealogical

rack NOUN = frame, stand, structure, framework • VERB = torture, torment, afflict, oppress, harrow, crucify, agonize, pain

racket 1 = noise, row, fuss, disturbance, outcry, clamour, din, pandemonium 2 = fraud, scheme

radiate 1 = emit, spread, send out, pour, shed, scatter 2 = shine, be diffused 3 = show, display, demonstrate, exhibit, emanate, give off *or* out 4 = spread out, diverge, branch out

radical ADJECTIVE 1 = extreme, complete, entire, sweeping, severe, thorough, drastic 2 = revolutionary, extremist, fanatical 3 = fundamental, natural, basic, profound, innate, deep-seated ≠ superficial • NOUN = extremist, revolutionary, militant, fanatic ≠ conservative

rage NOUN 1 = <u>fury</u>, temper, frenzy, rampage, tantrum, foulie (*Austral. slang*) ≠ calmness 2 = <u>anger</u>, passion, madness, wrath, ire 3 = <u>craze</u>, fashion, enthusiasm, vogue, fad (*informal*), latest thing
● VERB = <u>be furious</u>, blow up (*informal*), fume, lose it (*informal*), seethe, lose the plot (*informal*), go ballistic (*slang, chiefly U.S.*), lose your temper ≠ stay calm

ragged 1 = <u>tatty</u>, worn, torn, run-down, shabby, seedy, scruffy, in tatters ≠ smart 2 = <u>rough</u>, rugged, unfinished, uneven, jagged, serrated

raid VERB 1 = <u>steal from</u>, plunder, pillage, sack 2 = <u>attack</u>, invade, assault 3 = <u>make a search of</u>, search, bust (*informal*), make a raid on, make a swoop on
● NOUN 1 = <u>attack</u>, invasion, foray, sortie, incursion, sally, inroad 2 = <u>bust</u> (*informal*), swoop 3 = <u>robbery</u>, sacking

raider = <u>attacker</u>, thief, robber, plunderer, invader, marauder

railing = <u>fence</u>, rails, barrier, paling, balustrade

rain NOUN 1 = <u>rainfall</u>, fall, showers, deluge, drizzle, downpour, raindrops, cloudburst
● VERB 1 = <u>pour</u>, pelt (down), teem, bucket down (*informal*), drizzle, come down in buckets (*informal*) 2 = <u>fall</u>, shower, be dropped, sprinkle, be deposited

rainy = <u>wet</u>, damp, drizzly, showery ≠ dry

raise 1 = <u>lift</u>, elevate, uplift, heave 2 = <u>set upright</u>, lift, elevate 3 = <u>increase</u>, intensify, heighten, advance, boost, strengthen, enhance, enlarge ≠ reduce 4 = <u>make louder</u>, heighten, amplify, louden 5 = <u>collect</u>, gather, obtain 6 = <u>cause</u>, start, produce, create, occasion, provoke, originate, engender 7 = <u>put forward</u>, suggest, introduce, advance, broach, moot 8 = <u>bring up</u>, develop, rear, nurture 9 = <u>build</u>, construct, put up, erect ≠ demolish

rake[1] 1 = <u>gather</u>, collect, remove 2 = <u>search</u>, comb, scour, scrutinize, fossick (*Austral. & N.Z.*)

rake[2] = <u>libertine</u>, playboy, swinger (*slang*), lecher, roué, debauchee ≠ puritan

rally NOUN 1 = <u>gathering</u>, convention, meeting, congress, assembly, hui (*N.Z.*) 2 = <u>recovery</u>, improvement, revival, recuperation ≠ relapse
● VERB 1 = <u>gather together</u>, unite, regroup,

reorganize, reassemble 2 = <u>recover</u>, improve, revive, get better, recuperate ≠ get worse

ram 1 = <u>hit</u>, force, drive into, crash, impact, smash, dash, butt 2 = <u>cram</u>, force, stuff, jam, thrust

ramble NOUN = <u>walk</u>, tour, stroll, hike, roaming, roving, saunter
● VERB 1 = <u>walk</u>, range, wander, stroll, stray, roam, rove, saunter, go walkabout (*Austral.*) 2 *often with* **on** = <u>babble</u>, rabbit (on) (*Brit. informal*), waffle (*informal, chiefly Brit.*), witter on (*informal*)

ramp = <u>slope</u>, incline, gradient, rise

rampage VERB = <u>go berserk</u>, storm, rage, run riot, run amok
● PHRASES **on the rampage** = <u>berserk</u>, wild, violent, raging, out of control, amok, riotous, berko (*Austral. slang*)

rampant 1 = <u>widespread</u>, prevalent, rife, uncontrolled, unchecked, unrestrained, profuse, spreading like wildfire 2 (*Heraldry*) = <u>upright</u>, standing, rearing, erect

random ADJECTIVE 1 = <u>chance</u>, casual, accidental, incidental, haphazard, fortuitous, hit or miss, adventitious ≠ planned 2 = <u>casual</u>
● PHRASES **at random** = <u>haphazardly</u>, randomly, arbitrarily, by chance, willy-nilly, unsystematically

randy (*Informal*) = <u>lustful</u>, hot, turned-on (*slang*), aroused, horny (*slang*), amorous, lascivious

range NOUN 1 = <u>series</u>, variety, selection, assortment, lot, collection, gamut 2 = <u>limits</u>, reach 3 = <u>scope</u>, area, bounds, province, orbit, radius
● VERB 1 = <u>vary</u>, run, reach, extend, stretch 2 = <u>roam</u>, wander, rove, ramble, traverse

rank[1] NOUN 1 = <u>status</u>, level, position, grade, order, sort, type, division 2 = <u>class</u>, caste 3 = <u>row</u>, line, file, column, group, range, series, tier
● VERB 1 = <u>order</u>, dispose 2 = <u>arrange</u>, sort, line up, array, align

rank[2] 1 = <u>absolute</u>, complete, total, gross, sheer, utter, thorough, blatant 2 = <u>foul</u>, bad, offensive, disgusting, revolting, stinking, noxious, rancid, festy (*Austral. slang*) 3 = <u>abundant</u>, lush, luxuriant, dense, profuse

ransom = <u>payment</u>, money, price, payoff

rant = <u>shout</u>, roar, yell, rave, cry, declaim

rap VERB = hit, strike, knock, crack, tap
- NOUN 1 = blow, knock, crack, tap, clout (*informal*) 2 (*Slang*) = rebuke, blame, responsibility, punishment

rape VERB = sexually assault, violate, abuse, ravish, force, outrage
- NOUN = sexual assault, violation, ravishment, outrage

rapid 1 = sudden, prompt, speedy, express, swift ≠ gradual 2 = quick, fast, hurried, swift, brisk, hasty ≠ slow

rapidly = quickly, fast, swiftly, briskly, promptly, hastily, hurriedly, speedily

rare 1 = uncommon, unusual, few, strange, scarce, singular, sparse, infrequent ≠ common 2 = superb, great, fine, excellent, superlative, choice, peerless

rarely = seldom, hardly, hardly ever, infrequently ≠ often

raring (in construction *raring to do something*) = eager, impatient, longing, ready, keen, desperate, enthusiastic

rarity 1 = curio, find, treasure, gem, collector's item 2 = uncommonness, scarcity, infrequency, unusualness, shortage, strangeness, sparseness

rash¹ = reckless, hasty, impulsive, imprudent, careless, ill-advised, foolhardy, impetuous ≠ cautious

rash² 1 = outbreak of spots, (skin) eruption 2 = spate, series, wave, flood, plague, outbreak

rate NOUN 1 = speed, pace, tempo, velocity, frequency 2 = degree, standard, scale, proportion, ratio 3 = charge, price, cost, fee, figure
- VERB 1 = evaluate, consider, rank, reckon, value, measure, estimate, count 2 = deserve, merit, be entitled to, be worthy of
- PHRASES **at any rate** = in any case, anyway, anyhow, at all events

rather 1 = preferably, sooner, more readily, more willingly 2 = to some extent, quite, a little, fairly, relatively, somewhat, moderately, to some degree

ratify = approve, establish, confirm, sanction, endorse, uphold, authorize, affirm ≠ annul

rating = position, placing, rate, order, class, degree, rank, status

ratio = proportion, rate, relation, percentage, fraction

ration NOUN = allowance, quota, allotment, helping, part, share, measure, portion
- VERB = limit, control, restrict, budget

rational = sensible, sound, wise, reasonable, intelligent, realistic, logical, sane ≠ insane

rationale = reason, grounds, theory, principle, philosophy, logic, motivation, raison d'être (*French*)

rattle 1 = clatter, bang, jangle 2 = shake, jolt, vibrate, bounce, jar 3 (*Informal*) = fluster, shake, upset, disturb, disconcert, perturb, faze

ravage VERB = destroy, ruin, devastate, spoil, demolish, ransack, lay waste, despoil
- PLURAL NOUN = damage, destruction, devastation, ruin, havoc, ruination, spoliation

rave 1 = rant, rage, roar, go mad (*informal*), babble, be delirious 2 (*Informal*) = enthuse, praise, gush, be mad about (*informal*), be wild about (*informal*)

raving = mad, wild, crazy, hysterical, insane, irrational, crazed, delirious, berko (*Austral. slang*), off the air (*Austral. slang*)

raw 1 = unrefined, natural, crude, unprocessed, basic, rough, coarse, unfinished ≠ refined 2 = uncooked, natural, fresh ≠ cooked 3 = inexperienced, new, green, immature, callow ≠ experienced 4 = chilly, biting, cold, freezing, bitter, piercing, parky (*Brit. informal*)

ray = beam, bar, flash, shaft, gleam

re = concerning, about, regarding, with regard to, with reference to, apropos

reach VERB 1 = arrive at, get to, make, attain 2 = attain, get to 3 = touch, grasp, extend to, stretch to, contact 4 = contact, get in touch with, get through to, communicate with, get hold of
- NOUN 1 = grasp, range, distance, stretch, capacity, extent, extension, scope 2 = jurisdiction, power, influence

react = respond, act, proceed, behave

reaction 1 = response, answer, reply 2 = counteraction, backlash, recoil 3 = conservatism, the right

reactionary ADJECTIVE = conservative,

right-wing
● NOUN = conservative, die-hard, right-winger ≠ radical

read 1 = scan, study, look at, pore over, peruse 2 = understand, interpret, comprehend, construe, decipher, see, discover 3 = register, show, record, display, indicate

readily 1 = willingly, freely, quickly, gladly, eagerly ≠ reluctantly 2 = promptly, quickly, easily, smoothly, effortlessly, speedily, unhesitatingly ≠ with difficulty

readiness 1 = willingness, eagerness, keenness 2 = promptness, facility, ease, dexterity, adroitness

reading 1 = perusal, study, examination, inspection, scrutiny 2 = learning, education, knowledge, scholarship, erudition 3 = recital, performance, lesson, sermon 4 = interpretation, version, impression, grasp

ready 1 = prepared, set, primed, organized ≠ unprepared 2 = completed, arranged 3 = mature, ripe, mellow, ripened, seasoned 4 = willing, happy, glad, disposed, keen, eager, inclined, prone ≠ reluctant 5 = prompt, smart, quick, bright, sharp, keen, alert, clever ≠ slow 6 = available, handy, present, near, accessible, convenient ≠ unavailable

real 1 = true, genuine, sincere, factual, dinkum (*Austral. & N.Z. informal*), unfeigned 2 = genuine, authentic, dinkum (*Austral. & N.Z. informal*) ≠ fake 3 = proper, true, valid 4 = true, actual 5 = typical, true, genuine, sincere, dinkum (*Austral. & N.Z. informal*), unfeigned 6 = complete, total, perfect, utter, thorough

realistic 1 = practical, real, sensible, common-sense, down-to-earth, matter-of-fact, level-headed ≠ impractical 2 = attainable, sensible 3 = lifelike, true to life, authentic, true, natural, genuine, faithful

reality 1 = fact, truth, realism, validity, verity, actuality 2 = truth, fact, actuality

realization 1 = awareness, understanding, recognition, perception, grasp, conception, comprehension, cognizance 2 = achievement, accomplishment, fulfilment

realize 1 = become aware of, understand, take in, grasp, comprehend, get the message 2 = fulfil, achieve, accomplish,

make real 3 = achieve, do, effect, complete, perform, fulfil, accomplish, carry out *or* through

really 1 = certainly, genuinely, positively, surely 2 = truly, actually, in fact, indeed, in actuality

realm 1 = field, world, area, province, sphere, department, branch, territory 2 = kingdom, country, empire, land, domain, dominion

reap 1 = get, gain, obtain, acquire, derive 2 = collect, gather, bring in, harvest, garner, cut

rear¹ NOUN 1 = back part, back ≠ front 2 = back, end, tail, rearguard, tail end
● ADJECTIVE = back, hind, last, following ≠ front

rear² 1 = bring up, raise, educate, train, foster, nurture 2 = breed, keep 3 = rise, tower, soar, loom

reason NOUN 1 = cause, grounds, purpose, motive, goal, aim, object, intention 2 = sense, mind, understanding, judgment, logic, intellect, sanity, rationality ≠ emotion
● VERB = deduce, conclude, work out, make out, infer, think
● PHRASES **reason with someone** = persuade, bring round, urge, win over, prevail upon (*informal*), talk into *or* out of

reasonable 1 = sensible, sound, practical, wise, logical, sober, plausible, sane ≠ irrational 2 = fair, just, right, moderate, equitable, tenable ≠ unfair 3 = within reason, fit, proper ≠ impossible 4 = low, cheap, competitive, moderate, modest, inexpensive 5 = average, fair, moderate, modest, O.K. *or* okay (*informal*)

reassure = encourage, comfort, hearten, gee up, restore confidence to, put *or* set your mind at rest

rebate = refund, discount, reduction, bonus, allowance, deduction

rebel NOUN 1 = revolutionary, insurgent, secessionist, revolutionist 2 = nonconformist, dissenter, heretic, apostate, schismatic
● VERB 1 = revolt, resist, rise up, mutiny 2 = defy, dissent, disobey
● ADJECTIVE = rebellious, revolutionary, insurgent, insurrectionary

rebellion 1 = resistance, rising, revolution, revolt, uprising, mutiny 2 = nonconformity, defiance, heresy, schism

rebellious 1 = <u>defiant</u>, difficult, resistant, unmanageable, refractory ≠ obedient 2 = <u>revolutionary</u>, rebel, disorderly, unruly, insurgent, disloyal, seditious, mutinous ≠ obedient

rebound 1 = <u>bounce</u>, ricochet, recoil 2 = <u>misfire</u>, backfire, recoil, boomerang

rebuff VERB = <u>reject</u>, refuse, turn down, cut, slight, snub, spurn, knock back (*slang*) ≠ encourage
● NOUN = <u>rejection</u>, snub, knock-back, slight, refusal, repulse, cold shoulder, slap in the face (*informal*) ≠ encouragement

rebuke VERB = <u>scold</u>, censure, reprimand, castigate, chide, dress down (*informal*), admonish, tell off (*informal*) ≠ praise
● NOUN = <u>scolding</u>, censure, reprimand, row, dressing down (*informal*), telling-off (*informal*), admonition ≠ praise

recall VERB 1 = <u>recollect</u>, remember, evoke, call to mind 2 = <u>call back</u> 3 = <u>annul</u>, withdraw, cancel, repeal, revoke, retract, countermand
● NOUN 1 = <u>recollection</u>, memory, remembrance 2 = <u>annulment</u>, withdrawal, repeal, cancellation, retraction, rescindment

recede = <u>fall back</u>, withdraw, retreat, return, retire, regress

receipt 1 = <u>sales slip</u>, proof of purchase, counterfoil 2 = <u>receiving</u>, delivery, reception, acceptance

receive 1 = <u>get</u>, accept, be given, pick up, collect, obtain, acquire, take 2 = <u>experience</u>, suffer, bear, encounter, sustain, undergo 3 = <u>greet</u>, meet, admit, welcome, entertain, accommodate

recent = <u>new</u>, modern, up-to-date, late, current, fresh, novel, present-day ≠ old

recently = <u>not long ago</u>, newly, lately, currently, freshly, of late, latterly

reception 1 = <u>party</u>, gathering, get-together, social gathering, function, celebration, festivity, soirée 2 = <u>response</u>, reaction, acknowledgment, treatment, welcome, greeting

recess 1 = <u>break</u>, rest, holiday, interval, vacation, respite, intermission 2 = <u>alcove</u>, corner, bay, hollow, niche, nook

recession = <u>depression</u>, drop, decline, slump ≠ boom

recipe = <u>directions</u>, instructions, ingredients

recital 1 = <u>performance</u>, rendering, rehearsal, reading 2 = <u>account</u>, telling, statement, relation, narrative 3 = <u>recitation</u>

recite = <u>perform</u>, deliver, repeat, declaim

reckless = <u>careless</u>, wild, rash, precipitate, hasty, mindless, headlong, thoughtless ≠ cautious

reckon 1 (*Informal*) = <u>think</u>, believe, suppose, imagine, assume, guess (*informal, chiefly U.S. & Canad.*) 2 = <u>consider</u>, rate, account, judge, regard, count, esteem, deem 3 = <u>count</u>, figure, total, calculate, compute, add up, tally, number

reckoning = <u>count</u>, estimate, calculation, addition

reclaim 1 = <u>retrieve</u>, regain 2 = <u>regain</u>, salvage, recapture

recognition 1 = <u>identification</u>, recollection, discovery, remembrance 2 = <u>acceptance</u>, admission, allowance, confession

recognize 1 = <u>identify</u>, know, place, remember, spot, notice, recall, recollect 2 = <u>acknowledge</u>, allow, accept, admit, grant, concede ≠ ignore 3 = <u>appreciate</u>, respect, notice

recollection = <u>memory</u>, recall, impression, remembrance, reminiscence

recommend 1 = <u>advocate</u>, suggest, propose, approve, endorse, commend ≠ disapprove of 2 = <u>put forward</u>, approve, endorse, commend, praise 3 = <u>advise</u>, suggest, advance, propose, counsel, advocate, prescribe, put forward

recommendation 1 = <u>advice</u>, proposal, suggestion, counsel 2 = <u>commendation</u>, reference, praise, sanction, approval, endorsement, advocacy, testimonial

reconcile 1 = <u>resolve</u>, settle, square, adjust, compose, rectify, put to rights 2 = <u>reunite</u>, bring back together, conciliate 3 = <u>make peace between</u>, reunite, propitiate

reconciliation = <u>reunion</u>, conciliation, pacification, reconcilement ≠ separation

reconsider = <u>rethink</u>, review, revise, think again, reassess

reconstruct 1 = <u>rebuild</u>, restore, recreate, remake, renovate, remodel, regenerate 2 = <u>build up a picture of</u>, build up, piece together, deduce

record NOUN 1 = <u>document</u>, file, register, log, report, account, entry, journal

2 = evidence, trace, documentation, testimony, witness **3** = disc, single, album, LP, vinyl **4** = background, history, performance, career
- VERB **1** = set down, minute, note, enter, document, register, log, chronicle **2** = make a recording of, video, tape, video-tape, tape-record **3** = register, show, indicate, give evidence of

recorder = chronicler, archivist, historian, clerk, scribe, diarist

recording = record, video, tape, disc

recount = tell, report, describe, relate, repeat, depict, recite, narrate

recover 1 = get better, improve, get well, recuperate, heal, revive, mend, convalesce ≠ relapse **2** = rally **3** = save, rescue, retrieve, salvage, reclaim ≠ abandon **4** = recoup, restore, get back, regain, retrieve, reclaim, redeem, recapture ≠ lose

recovery 1 = improvement, healing, revival, mending, recuperation, convalescence **2** = retrieval, repossession, reclamation, restoration

recreation = leisure, play, sport, fun, entertainment, relaxation, enjoyment, amusement

recruit VERB **1** = gather, obtain, engage, procure **2** = assemble, raise, levy, muster, mobilize **3** = enlist, draft, enrol ≠ dismiss
- NOUN = beginner, trainee, apprentice, novice, convert, initiate, helper, learner

recur = happen again, return, repeat, persist, revert, reappear, come again

recycle = reprocess, reuse, salvage, reclaim, save

red NOUN or ADJECTIVE **1** = crimson, scarlet, ruby, vermilion, cherry, coral, carmine **2** = flushed, embarrassed, blushing, florid, shamefaced **3** (of hair) = chestnut, reddish, flame-coloured, sandy, Titian, carroty
- PHRASES **in the red** (Informal) = in debt, insolvent, in arrears, overdrawn ◆ see red (Informal) = lose your temper, lose it (informal), go mad (informal), crack up (informal), lose the plot (informal), go ballistic (slang, chiefly U.S.), fly off the handle (informal), blow your top

redeem 1 = reinstate, absolve, restore to favour **2** = make up for, compensate for, atone for, make amends for **3** = buy back, recover, regain, retrieve, reclaim, repurchase **4** = save, free, deliver, liberate, ransom, emancipate

redemption 1 = compensation, amends, reparation, atonement **2** = salvation, release, rescue, liberation, emancipation, deliverance

redress VERB **1** = make amends for, make up for, compensate for **2** = put right, balance, correct, adjust, regulate, rectify, even up
- NOUN = amends, payment, compensation, reparation, atonement, recompense

reduce 1 = lessen, cut, lower, moderate, weaken, diminish, decrease, cut down ≠ increase **2** = degrade, downgrade, break, humble, bring low ≠ promote

redundancy 1 = layoff, sacking, dismissal **2** = unemployment, the sack (informal), the axe (informal), joblessness

redundant = superfluous, extra, surplus, unnecessary, unwanted, inessential, supernumerary ≠ essential

reel 1 = stagger, rock, roll, pitch, sway, lurch **2** = whirl, spin, revolve, swirl

refer VERB = direct, point, send, guide
- PHRASES **refer to something** or **someone 1** = allude to, mention, cite, speak of, bring up **2** = relate to, concern, apply to, pertain to, be relevant to **3** = consult, go, apply, turn to, look up

referee NOUN = umpire, judge, ref (informal), arbiter, arbitrator, adjudicator
- VERB = umpire, judge, mediate, adjudicate, arbitrate

reference 1 = allusion, note, mention, quotation **2** = citation **3** = testimonial, recommendation, credentials, endorsement, character reference

referendum = public vote, popular vote, plebiscite

refine 1 = purify, process, filter, cleanse, clarify, distil **2** = improve, perfect, polish, hone

refined 1 = purified, processed, pure, filtered, clean, clarified, distilled ≠ unrefined **2** = cultured, polished, elegant, polite, cultivated, civilized, well-bred ≠ coarse **3** = discerning, fine, sensitive, delicate, precise, discriminating, fastidious

reflect 1 = show, reveal, display, indicate, demonstrate, manifest **2** = throw back, return, mirror, echo, reproduce **3** = consider, think, muse, ponder, meditate, ruminate, cogitate, wonder

reflection 1 = <u>image</u>, echo, mirror image
2 = <u>consideration</u>, thinking, thought, idea, opinion, observation, musing, meditation

reflective = <u>thoughtful</u>, contemplative, meditative, pensive

reform NOUN = <u>improvement</u>, amendment, rehabilitation, betterment
● VERB 1 = <u>improve</u>, correct, restore, amend, mend, rectify 2 = <u>mend your ways</u>, go straight (*informal*), shape up (*informal*), turn over a new leaf, clean up your act (*informal*), pull your socks up (*Brit. informal*)

refrain[1] = <u>stop</u>, avoid, cease, renounce, abstain, leave off, desist, forbear

refrain[2] = <u>chorus</u>, tune, melody

refresh 1 = <u>revive</u>, freshen, revitalize, stimulate, brace, enliven, invigorate
2 = <u>stimulate</u>, prompt, renew, jog

refreshing 1 = <u>new</u>, original, novel
2 = <u>stimulating</u>, fresh, bracing, invigorating ≠ tiring

refreshment = <u>food and drink</u>, drinks, snacks, titbits, kai (*N.Z. informal*)

refuge 1 = <u>protection</u>, shelter, asylum
2 = <u>haven</u>, retreat, sanctuary, hide-out

refugee = <u>exile</u>, émigré, displaced person, escapee

refund NOUN = <u>repayment</u>, reimbursement, return
● VERB = <u>repay</u>, return, restore, pay back, reimburse

refurbish = <u>renovate</u>, restore, repair, clean up, overhaul, revamp, mend, do up (*informal*)

refusal = <u>rejection</u>, denial, rebuff, knock-back (*slang*)

refuse[1] 1 = <u>decline</u>, reject, turn down, say no to 2 = <u>deny</u>, decline, withhold ≠ allow

refuse[2] = <u>rubbish</u>, waste, junk (*informal*), litter, garbage, trash

regain 1 = <u>recover</u>, get back, retrieve, recapture, win back, take back, recoup
2 = <u>get back to</u>, return to, reach again

regal = <u>royal</u>, majestic, kingly *or* queenly, noble, princely, magnificent

regard VERB 1 = <u>consider</u>, see, rate, view, judge, think of, esteem, deem 2 = <u>look at</u>, view, eye, watch, observe, clock (*Brit. slang*), check out (*informal*), gaze at
● NOUN 1 = <u>respect</u>, esteem, thought, concern, care, consideration 2 = <u>look</u>, gaze, scrutiny, stare, glance

● PLURAL NOUN = <u>good wishes</u>, respects, greetings, compliments, best wishes
● PHRASES **as regards** = <u>concerning</u>, regarding, relating to, pertaining to

regarding = <u>concerning</u>, about, on the subject of, re, respecting, as regards, with reference to, in *or* with regard to

regardless 1 = <u>in spite of everything</u>, anyway, nevertheless, in any case 2 *with* **of** = <u>irrespective of</u>, heedless of, unmindful of

regime 1 = <u>government</u>, rule, management, leadership, reign 2 = <u>plan</u>, course, system, policy, programme, scheme, regimen

region = <u>area</u>, place, part, quarter, section, sector, district, territory

regional = <u>local</u>, district, provincial, parochial, zonal

register NOUN = <u>list</u>, record, roll, file, diary, catalogue, log, archives
● VERB 1 = <u>enrol</u>, enlist, list, note, enter 2 = <u>record</u>, catalogue, chronicle
3 = <u>indicate</u>, show 4 = <u>show</u>, mark, indicate, manifest 5 = <u>express</u>, show, reveal, display, exhibit

regret VERB 1 = <u>be</u> *or* feel sorry about, rue, deplore, bemoan, repent (of), bewail ≠ be satisfied with 2 = <u>mourn</u>, miss, grieve for *or* over
● NOUN 1 = <u>remorse</u>, compunction, bitterness, repentance, contrition, penitence 2 = <u>sorrow</u> ≠ satisfaction

regular 1 = <u>frequent</u> 2 = <u>normal</u>, common, usual, ordinary, typical, routine, customary, habitual ≠ infrequent
3 = <u>steady</u>, consistent 4 = <u>even</u>, level, balanced, straight, flat, fixed, smooth, uniform ≠ uneven

regulate 1 = <u>control</u>, run, rule, manage, direct, guide, handle, govern
2 = <u>moderate</u>, control, modulate, fit, tune, adjust

regulation 1 = <u>rule</u>, order, law, dictate, decree, statute, edict, precept 2 = <u>control</u>, government, management, direction, supervision

rehearsal = <u>practice</u>, rehearsing, run-through, preparation, drill

rehearse = <u>practise</u>, prepare, run through, go over, train, repeat, drill, recite

reign VERB 1 = <u>be supreme</u>, prevail, predominate, hold sway 2 = <u>rule</u>, govern, be in power, influence, command

● NOUN = rule, power, control, command, monarchy, dominion

rein = control, harness, bridle, hold, check, brake, curb, restraint

reincarnation = rebirth, transmigration of souls

reinforce 1 = support, strengthen, fortify, toughen, stress, prop, supplement, emphasize 2 = increase, extend, add to, strengthen, supplement

reinforcement NOUN 1 = strengthening, increase, fortification, augmentation 2 = support, stay, prop, brace, buttress ● PLURAL NOUN = reserves, support, auxiliaries, additional or fresh troops

reinstate = restore, recall, re-establish, return

reiterate (*Formal*) = repeat, restate, say again, do again

reject VERB 1 = rebuff, jilt, turn down, spurn, refuse, say no to, repulse ≠ accept 2 = deny, exclude, veto, relinquish, renounce, disallow, forsake, disown ≠ approve 3 = discard, decline, eliminate, scrap, jettison, throw away or out ≠ accept ● NOUN 1 = castoff, second, discard ≠ treasure 2 = failure, loser, flop

rejection 1 = denial, veto, dismissal, exclusion, disowning, thumbs down, renunciation, repudiation ≠ approval 2 = rebuff, refusal, knock-back (*slang*), kick in the teeth (*slang*), brushoff (*slang*) ≠ acceptance

rejoice = be glad, celebrate, be happy, glory, be overjoyed, exult ≠ lament

rejoin = reply, answer, respond, retort, riposte

relate VERB = tell, recount, report, detail, describe, recite, narrate
● PHRASES **relate to something** or **someone** = concern, refer to, apply to, have to do with, pertain to, be relevant to 2 = connect with, associate with, link with, couple with, join with, correlate to

related 1 = associated, linked, joint, connected, affiliated, akin, interconnected ≠ unconnected 2 = akin, kindred ≠ unrelated

relation NOUN 1 = similarity, link, bearing, bond, comparison, correlation, connection 2 = relative, kin, kinsman or kinswoman
● PLURAL NOUN 1 = dealings, relationship, affairs, contact, connections, interaction, intercourse 2 = family, relatives, tribe, clan,

kin, kindred, kinsmen, kinsfolk, ainga (*N.Z.*)

relationship 1 = association, bond, connection, affinity, rapport, kinship 2 = affair, romance, liaison, amour, intrigue 3 = connection, link, parallel, similarity, tie-up, correlation

relative NOUN = relation, kinsman or kinswoman, member of your or the family ● ADJECTIVE 1 = comparative 2 = corresponding 3 *with* *to* = in proportion to, proportionate to

relatively = comparatively, rather, somewhat

relax 1 = be or feel at ease, chill out (*slang, chiefly U.S.*), take it easy, lighten up (*slang*), outspan (*S. African*) ≠ be alarmed 2 = calm down, calm, unwind 3 = make less tense, rest 4 = lessen, reduce, ease, relieve, weaken, loosen, let up, slacken ≠ tighten 5 = moderate, ease, relieve, weaken, slacken ≠ tighten up

relaxation = leisure, rest, fun, pleasure, recreation, enjoyment

relay = broadcast, carry, spread, communicate, transmit, send out

release VERB 1 = set free, free, discharge, liberate, drop, loose, undo, extricate ≠ imprison 2 = acquit, let go, let off, exonerate, absolve 3 = issue, publish, make public, make known, launch, distribute, put out, circulate ≠ withhold ● NOUN 1 = liberation, freedom, liberty, discharge, emancipation, deliverance ≠ imprisonment 2 = acquittal, exemption, absolution, exoneration 3 = issue, publication, proclamation

relegate = demote, degrade, downgrade

relentless 1 = merciless, fierce, cruel, ruthless, unrelenting, implacable, remorseless, pitiless ≠ merciful 2 = unremitting, persistent, unrelenting, incessant, nonstop, unrelieved

relevant = significant, appropriate, related, fitting, to the point, apt, pertinent, apposite ≠ irrelevant

reliable 1 = dependable, trustworthy, sure, sound, true, faithful, staunch ≠ unreliable 2 = safe, dependable 3 = definitive, sound, dependable, trustworthy

reliance 1 = dependency, dependence 2 = trust, confidence, belief, faith

relic = remnant, vestige, memento, trace, fragment, souvenir, keepsake

relief 1 = <u>ease</u>, release, comfort, cure, remedy, solace, deliverance, mitigation 2 = <u>rest</u>, respite, relaxation, break, breather (*informal*) 3 = <u>aid</u>, help, support, assistance, succour

relieve 1 = <u>ease</u>, soothe, alleviate, relax, comfort, calm, cure, soften ≠ intensify 2 = <u>help</u>, support, aid, sustain, assist, succour

religion = <u>belief</u>, faith, theology, creed

religious 1 = <u>spiritual</u>, holy, sacred, devotional 2 = <u>conscientious</u>, faithful, rigid, meticulous, scrupulous, punctilious

relinquish (*Formal*) = <u>give up</u>, leave, drop, abandon, surrender, let go, renounce, forsake

relish VERB 1 = <u>enjoy</u>, like, savour, revel in ≠ dislike 2 = <u>look forward to</u>, fancy, delight in
● NOUN 1 = <u>enjoyment</u>, liking, love, taste, fancy, penchant, fondness, gusto ≠ distaste 2 = <u>condiment</u>, seasoning, sauce

reluctance = <u>unwillingness</u>, dislike, loathing, distaste, aversion, disinclination, repugnance

reluctant = <u>unwilling</u>, hesitant, loath, disinclined, unenthusiastic ≠ willing

rely on 1 = <u>depend on</u>, lean on 2 = <u>be confident of</u>, bank on, trust, count on, bet on

remain 1 = <u>stay</u>, continue, go on, stand, dwell 2 = <u>stay behind</u>, wait, delay ≠ go 3 = <u>continue</u>, be left, linger

remainder = <u>rest</u>, remains, balance, excess, surplus, remnant, residue, leavings

remains 1 = <u>remnants</u>, leftovers, rest, debris, residue, dregs, leavings 2 = <u>corpse</u>, body, carcass, cadaver 3 = <u>relics</u>

remark VERB 1 = <u>comment</u>, say, state, reflect, mention, declare, observe, pass comment 2 = <u>notice</u>, note, observe, perceive, see, mark, make out, espy
● NOUN = <u>comment</u>, observation, reflection, statement, utterance

remarkable = <u>extraordinary</u>, striking, outstanding, wonderful, rare, unusual, surprising, notable ≠ ordinary

remedy NOUN = <u>cure</u>, treatment, medicine, nostrum
● VERB = <u>put right</u>, rectify, fix, correct, set to rights

remember 1 = <u>recall</u>, think back to, recollect, reminisce about, call to mind ≠ forget 2 = <u>bear in mind</u>, keep in mind 3 = <u>look back (on)</u>, commemorate

remembrance 1 = <u>commemoration</u>, memorial 2 = <u>souvenir</u>, token, reminder, monument, memento, keepsake 3 = <u>memory</u>, recollection, thought, recall, reminiscence

remind = <u>jog your memory</u>, prompt, make you remember

reminiscent = <u>suggestive</u>, evocative, similar

remnant = <u>remainder</u>, remains, trace, fragment, end, rest, residue, leftovers

remorse = <u>regret</u>, shame, guilt, grief, sorrow, anguish, repentance, contrition

remote 1 = <u>distant</u>, far, isolated, out-of-the-way, secluded, inaccessible, in the middle of nowhere ≠ nearby 2 = <u>far</u>, distant 3 = <u>slight</u>, small, outside, unlikely, slim, faint, doubtful, dubious ≠ strong 4 = <u>aloof</u>, cold, reserved, withdrawn, distant, abstracted, detached, uncommunicative ≠ outgoing

removal 1 = <u>extraction</u>, withdrawal, uprooting, eradication, dislodgment, taking away or off or out 2 = <u>dismissal</u>, expulsion, elimination, ejection 3 = <u>move</u>, transfer, departure, relocation, flitting (*Scot. & Northern English dialect*)

remove 1 = <u>take out</u>, withdraw, extract ≠ insert 2 = <u>take off</u> ≠ put on 3 = <u>erase</u>, eliminate, take out 4 = <u>dismiss</u>, eliminate, get rid of, discharge, abolish, expel, throw out, oust ≠ appoint 5 = <u>get rid of</u>, erase, eradicate, expunge 6 = <u>take away</u>, detach, displace ≠ put back 7 = <u>delete</u>, get rid of, erase, excise 8 = <u>move</u>, depart, relocate, flit (*Scot. & Northern English dialect*)

renaissance or **renascence** = <u>rebirth</u>, revival, restoration, renewal, resurgence, reappearance, reawakening

rend (*Literary*) = <u>tear</u>, rip, separate, wrench, rupture

render 1 = <u>make</u>, cause to become, leave 2 = <u>provide</u>, give, pay, present, supply, submit, tender, hand out 3 = <u>represent</u>, portray, depict, do, give, play, act, perform

renew 1 = <u>recommence</u>, continue, extend, repeat, resume, reopen, recreate, reaffirm 2 = <u>reaffirm</u>, resume, recommence 3 = <u>replace</u>, refresh, replenish, restock 4 = <u>restore</u>, repair, overhaul, mend, refurbish, renovate, refit, modernize

renounce 1 = <u>disown</u>, quit, forsake,

recant, forswear, abjure 2 = <u>disclaim</u>, deny, give up, relinquish, waive, abjure ≠ assert

renovate = <u>restore</u>, repair, refurbish, do up (*informal*), renew, overhaul, refit, modernize

renowned = <u>famous</u>, noted, celebrated, well-known, distinguished, esteemed, notable, eminent ≠ unknown

rent¹ VERB 1 = <u>hire</u>, lease 2 = <u>let</u>, lease
● **NOUN** = <u>hire</u>, rental, lease, fee, payment

rent² 1 = <u>tear</u>, split, rip, slash, slit, gash, hole 2 = <u>opening</u>, hole

repair VERB 1 = <u>mend</u>, fix, restore, heal, patch, renovate, patch up ≠ damage 2 = <u>put right</u>, make up for, compensate for, rectify, redress
● **NOUN 1** = <u>mend</u>, restoration, overhaul 2 = <u>darn</u>, mend, patch 3 = <u>condition</u>, state, form, shape (*informal*)

repay = <u>pay back</u>, refund, settle up, return, square, compensate, reimburse, recompense

repeal VERB = <u>abolish</u>, reverse, revoke, annul, recall, cancel, invalidate, nullify ≠ pass
● **NOUN** = <u>abolition</u>, cancellation, annulment, invalidation, rescindment ≠ passing

repeat VERB 1 = <u>reiterate</u>, restate 2 = <u>retell</u>, echo, replay, reproduce, rerun, reshow
● **NOUN 1** = <u>repetition</u>, echo, reiteration 2 = <u>rerun</u>, replay, reshowing

repeatedly = <u>over and over</u>, often, frequently, many times

repel 1 = <u>drive off</u>, fight, resist, parry, hold off, rebuff, ward off, repulse ≠ submit to 2 = <u>disgust</u>, offend, revolt, sicken, nauseate, gross out (*U.S. slang*) ≠ delight

repertoire = <u>range</u>, list, stock, supply, store, collection, repertory

repetition 1 = <u>recurrence</u>, repeating, echo 2 = <u>repeating</u>, replication, restatement, reiteration, tautology

replace 1 = <u>take the place of</u>, follow, succeed, oust, take over from, supersede, supplant 2 = <u>substitute</u>, change, exchange, switch, swap 3 = <u>put back</u>, restore

replacement 1 = <u>replacing</u> 2 = <u>successor</u>, double, substitute, stand-in, proxy, surrogate, understudy

replica 1 = <u>reproduction</u>, model, copy, imitation, facsimile, carbon copy ≠ original 2 = <u>duplicate</u>, copy, carbon copy

replicate = <u>copy</u>, reproduce, recreate, mimic, duplicate, reduplicate

reply VERB = <u>answer</u>, respond, retort, counter, rejoin, retaliate, reciprocate
● **NOUN** = <u>answer</u>, response, reaction, counter, retort, retaliation, counterattack, rejoinder

report VERB 1 = <u>inform of</u>, communicate, recount 2 *often with* **on** = <u>communicate</u>, tell, state, detail, describe, relate, broadcast, pass on 3 = <u>present yourself</u>, come, appear, arrive, turn up
● **NOUN 1** = <u>article</u>, story, piece, write-up 2 = <u>account</u>, record, statement, communication, description, narrative 3 *often plural* = <u>news</u>, word 4 = <u>bang</u>, sound, crack, noise, blast, boom, explosion, discharge 5 = <u>rumour</u>, talk, buzz, gossip, hearsay

reporter = <u>journalist</u>, writer, correspondent, hack (*derogatory*), pressman, journo (*slang*)

represent 1 = <u>act for</u>, speak for 2 = <u>stand for</u>, serve as 3 = <u>express</u>, correspond to, symbolize, mean 4 = <u>exemplify</u>, embody, symbolize, typify, personify, epitomize 5 = <u>depict</u>, show, describe, picture, illustrate, outline, portray, denote

representation 1 = <u>picture</u>, model, image, portrait, illustration, likeness 2 = <u>portrayal</u>, depiction, account, description

representative NOUN 1 = <u>delegate</u>, member, agent, deputy, proxy, spokesman *or* spokeswoman 2 = <u>agent</u>, salesman, rep, commercial traveller
● **ADJECTIVE 1** = <u>typical</u>, characteristic, archetypal, exemplary ≠ uncharacteristic 2 = <u>symbolic</u>

repress 1 = <u>control</u>, suppress, hold back, bottle up, check, curb, restrain, inhibit ≠ release 2 = <u>hold back</u>, suppress, stifle 3 = <u>subdue</u>, abuse, wrong, persecute, quell, subjugate, maltreat ≠ liberate

repression 1 = <u>subjugation</u>, control, constraint, domination, tyranny, despotism 2 = <u>suppression</u>, crushing, quashing 3 = <u>inhibition</u>, control, restraint, bottling up

reprieve VERB = <u>grant a stay of execution to</u>, pardon, let off the hook (*slang*)
● **NOUN** = <u>stay of execution</u>, amnesty, pardon, remission, deferment, postponement of punishment

reproduce 1 = <u>copy</u>, recreate, replicate, duplicate, match, mirror, echo, imitate 2 = <u>print</u>, copy 3 (*Biology*) = <u>breed</u>, procreate, multiply, spawn, propagate

reproduction 1 = <u>copy</u>, picture, print, replica, imitation, duplicate, facsimile ≠ original 2 (*Biology*) = <u>breeding</u>, increase, generation, multiplication

Republican ADJECTIVE = <u>right-wing</u>, Conservative

● NOUN = <u>right-winger</u>, Conservative

reputation = <u>name</u>, standing, character, esteem, stature, renown, repute

request VERB 1 = <u>ask for</u>, appeal for, put in for, demand, desire 2 = <u>invite</u>, entreat 3 = <u>seek</u>, ask (for), solicit

● NOUN 1 = <u>appeal</u>, call, demand, plea, desire, entreaty, suit 2 = <u>asking</u>, plea

require 1 = <u>need</u>, crave, want, miss, lack, wish, desire 2 = <u>order</u>, demand, command, compel, exact, oblige, call upon, insist upon 3 = <u>ask</u>

requirement = <u>necessity</u>, demand, stipulation, want, need, must, essential, prerequisite

rescue VERB 1 = <u>save</u>, get out, release, deliver, recover, liberate ≠ desert 2 = <u>salvage</u>, deliver, redeem

● NOUN = <u>saving</u>, salvage, deliverance, release, recovery, liberation, salvation, redemption

research NOUN = <u>investigation</u>, study, analysis, examination, probe, exploration

● VERB = <u>investigate</u>, study, examine, explore, probe, analyse

resemblance = <u>similarity</u>, correspondence, parallel, likeness, kinship, sameness, similitude ≠ dissimilarity

resemble = <u>be like</u>, look like, mirror, parallel, be similar to, bear a resemblance to

resent = <u>be bitter about</u>, object to, grudge, begrudge, take exception to, take offence at ≠ be content with

resentment = <u>bitterness</u>, indignation, ill feeling, ill will, grudge, animosity, pique, rancour

reservation 1 *often plural* = <u>doubt</u>, scruples, hesitancy 2 = <u>reserve</u>, territory, preserve, sanctuary

reserve VERB 1 = <u>book</u>, prearrange, engage 2 = <u>put by</u>, secure 3 = <u>keep</u>, hold, save, store, retain, set aside, stockpile, hoard

● NOUN 1 = <u>store</u>, fund, savings, stock, supply, reservoir, hoard, cache 2 = <u>park</u>, reservation, preserve, sanctuary, tract, forest park (*N.Z.*) 3 = <u>shyness</u>, silence, restraint, constraint, reticence, secretiveness, taciturnity 4 = <u>reservation</u>, doubt, delay, uncertainty, indecision, hesitancy, vacillation, irresolution

● ADJECTIVE = <u>substitute</u>, extra, spare, secondary, fall-back, auxiliary

reserved 1 = <u>uncommunicative</u>, retiring, silent, shy, restrained, secretive, reticent, taciturn ≠ uninhibited 2 = <u>set aside</u>, taken, kept, held, booked, retained, engaged, restricted

reservoir 1 = <u>lake</u>, pond, basin 2 = <u>store</u>, stock, source, supply, reserves, pool

reside (*Formal*) = <u>live</u>, lodge, dwell, stay, abide ≠ visit

residence = <u>home</u>, house, dwelling, place, flat, lodging, abode, habitation

resident 1 = <u>inhabitant</u>, citizen, local ≠ nonresident 2 = <u>tenant</u>, occupant, lodger 3 = <u>guest</u>, lodger

residue = <u>remainder</u>, remains, remnant, leftovers, rest, extra, excess, surplus

resign VERB 1 = <u>quit</u>, leave, step down (*informal*), vacate, abdicate, give or hand in your notice 2 = <u>give up</u>, abandon, yield, surrender, relinquish, renounce, forsake, forgo

● PHRASES **resign yourself to something** = <u>accept</u>, succumb to, submit to, give in to, yield to, acquiesce to

resignation 1 = <u>leaving</u>, departure, abandonment, abdication 2 = <u>acceptance</u>, patience, submission, compliance, endurance, passivity, acquiescence, sufferance ≠ resistance

resigned = <u>stoical</u>, patient, subdued, long-suffering, compliant, unresisting

resist 1 = <u>oppose</u>, battle against, combat, defy, stand up to, hinder ≠ accept 2 = <u>refrain from</u>, avoid, keep from, forgo, abstain from, forbear ≠ indulge in 3 = <u>withstand</u>, be proof against

resistance 1 = <u>opposition</u>, hostility, aversion 2 = <u>fighting</u>, fight, battle, struggle, defiance, obstruction, impediment, hindrance

resistant 1 = <u>opposed</u>, hostile, unwilling, intractable, antagonistic, intransigent 2 = <u>impervious</u>, hard, strong, tough, unaffected

resolution 1 = declaration 2 = decision, resolve, intention, aim, purpose, determination, intent 3 = determination, purpose, resolve, tenacity, perseverance, willpower, firmness, steadfastness

resolve VERB 1 = work out, answer, clear up, crack, fathom 2 = decide, determine, agree, purpose, intend, fix, conclude
● NOUN 1 = determination, resolution, willpower, firmness, steadfastness, resoluteness ≠ indecision 2 = decision, resolution, objective, purpose, intention

resort 1 = holiday centre, spot, retreat, haunt, tourist centre 2 = recourse to, reference to

resound 1 = echo, resonate, reverberate, re-echo 2 = ring

resounding 1 = echoing, full, ringing, powerful, booming, reverberating, resonant, sonorous

resource NOUN 1 = facility 2 = means, course, resort, device, expedient
● PLURAL NOUN 1 = funds, holdings, money, capital, riches, assets, wealth 2 = reserves, supplies, stocks

respect VERB 1 = think highly of, value, honour, admire, esteem, look up to, defer to, have a good or high opinion of 2 = show consideration for, honour, observe, heed 3 = abide by, follow, observe, comply with, obey, heed, keep to, adhere to ≠ disregard
● NOUN 1 = regard, honour, recognition, esteem, admiration, estimation ≠ contempt 2 = consideration, kindness, deference, tact, thoughtfulness, considerateness 3 = particular, way, point, matter, sense, detail, feature, aspect

respectable 1 = honourable, good, decent, worthy, upright, honest, reputable, estimable ≠ disreputable 2 = decent, neat, spruce 3 = reasonable, considerable, substantial, fair, ample, appreciable, sizable or sizeable ≠ small

respective = specific, own, individual, particular, relevant

respite = pause, break, rest, relief, halt, interval, recess, lull

respond 1 = answer, return, reply, counter, retort, rejoin ≠ remain silent 2 often with **to** = reply to, answer 3 = react, retaliate, reciprocate

response = answer, return, reply, reaction, feedback, retort, counterattack, rejoinder

responsibility 1 = duty, business, job, role, task, accountability, answerability 2 = fault, blame, liability, guilt, culpability 3 = obligation, duty, liability, charge, care 4 = authority, power, importance, mana (N.Z.) 5 = job, task, function, role 6 = level-headedness, rationality, dependability, trustworthiness, conscientiousness, sensibleness

responsible 1 = to blame, guilty, at fault, culpable 2 = in charge, in control, in authority 3 = accountable, liable, answerable ≠ unaccountable 4 = sensible, reliable, rational, dependable, trustworthy, level-headed ≠ unreliable

responsive = sensitive, open, alive, susceptible, receptive, reactive, impressionable ≠ unresponsive

rest¹ VERB 1 = relax, take it easy, sit down, be at ease, put your feet up, outspan (S. African) ≠ work 2 = stop, have a break, break off, take a breather (informal), halt, cease ≠ keep going 3 = place, repose, sit, lean, prop 4 = be placed, sit, lie, be supported, recline
● NOUN 1 = relaxation, repose, leisure ≠ work 2 = pause, break, stop, halt, interval, respite, lull, interlude 3 = refreshment, release, relief, ease, comfort, cure, remedy, solace 4 = inactivity 5 = support, stand, base, holder, prop 6 = calm, tranquillity, stillness

rest² = remainder, remains, excess, remnants, others, balance, surplus, residue

restaurant = café, diner (chiefly U.S. & Canad.), bistro, cafeteria, tearoom, eatery or eaterie

restless 1 = unsettled, nervous, edgy, fidgeting, on edge, restive, jumpy, fidgety ≠ relaxed 2 = moving, wandering, unsettled, unstable, roving, transient, nomadic ≠ settled

restoration 1 = reinstatement, return, revival, restitution, re-establishment, replacement ≠ abolition 2 = repair, reconstruction, renewal, renovation, revitalization ≠ demolition

restore 1 = reinstate, re-establish, reintroduce ≠ abolish 2 = revive, build up, strengthen, refresh, revitalize ≠ make worse 3 = re-establish, replace, reinstate, give back 4 = repair, refurbish, renovate, reconstruct, fix (up), renew, rebuild, mend ≠ demolish 5 = return, replace, recover, bring back, send back, hand back

restrain 1 = <u>hold back</u>, control, check, contain, restrict, curb, hamper, hinder ≠ encourage 2 = <u>control</u>, inhibit

restrained 1 = <u>controlled</u>, moderate, self-controlled, calm, mild, undemonstrative ≠ hot-headed 2 = <u>unobtrusive</u>, discreet, subdued, tasteful, quiet ≠ garish

restraint 1 = <u>limitation</u>, limit, check, ban, embargo, curb, rein, interdict ≠ freedom 2 = <u>self-control</u>, self-discipline, self-restraint, self-possession ≠ self-indulgence 3 = <u>constraint</u>, limitation, inhibition, control, restriction

restrict 1 = <u>limit</u>, regulate, curb, ration ≠ widen 2 = <u>hamper</u>, handicap, restrain, inhibit

restriction 1 = <u>control</u>, rule, regulation, curb, restraint, confinement 2 = <u>limitation</u>, handicap, inhibition

result NOUN 1 = <u>consequence</u>, effect, outcome, end result, product, sequel, upshot ≠ cause 2 = <u>outcome</u>, end ● VERB = <u>arise</u>, follow, issue, happen, appear, develop, spring, derive

resume = <u>begin again</u>, continue, go on with, proceed with, carry on, reopen, restart ≠ discontinue

résumé = <u>summary</u>, synopsis, précis, rundown, recapitulation

resumption = <u>continuation</u>, carrying on, reopening, renewal, restart, resurgence, re-establishment

resurgence = <u>revival</u>, return, renaissance, resurrection, resumption, rebirth, re-emergence

resurrect 1 = <u>revive</u>, renew, bring back, reintroduce 2 = <u>restore to life</u>, raise from the dead

resurrection 1 = <u>revival</u>, restoration, renewal, resurgence, return, renaissance, rebirth, reappearance ≠ killing off 2 *usually caps* = <u>raising or rising from the dead</u>, return from the dead ≠ demise

retain 1 = <u>maintain</u>, reserve, preserve, keep up, continue to have 2 = <u>keep</u>, save ≠ let go

retaliate = <u>pay someone back</u>, hit back, strike back, reciprocate, take revenge, get even with (*informal*), get your own back (*informal*) ≠ turn the other cheek

retaliation = <u>revenge</u>, repayment, vengeance, reprisal, an eye for an eye, reciprocation, requital, counterblow

retard = <u>slow down</u>, check, arrest, delay, handicap, hinder, impede, set back ≠ speed up

retire 1 = <u>stop working</u>, give up work 2 = <u>withdraw</u>, leave, exit, go away, depart 3 = <u>go to bed</u>, turn in (*informal*), hit the sack (*slang*), hit the hay (*slang*)

retirement = <u>withdrawal</u>, retreat, privacy, solitude, seclusion

retiring = <u>shy</u>, reserved, quiet, timid, unassuming, self-effacing, bashful, unassertive ≠ outgoing

retort VERB = <u>reply</u>, return, answer, respond, counter, come back with, riposte ● NOUN = <u>reply</u>, answer, response, comeback, riposte, rejoinder

retreat VERB = <u>withdraw</u>, back off, draw back, leave, go back, depart, fall back, pull back ≠ advance ● NOUN 1 = <u>flight</u>, retirement, departure, withdrawal, evacuation ≠ advance 2 = <u>refuge</u>, haven, shelter, sanctuary, hideaway, seclusion

retrieve 1 = <u>get back</u>, regain, recover, restore, recapture 2 = <u>redeem</u>, save, win back, recoup

retrospect = <u>hindsight</u>, review, re-examination ≠ foresight

return VERB 1 = <u>come back</u>, go back, retreat, turn back, revert, reappear ≠ depart 2 = <u>put back</u>, replace, restore, reinstate ≠ keep 3 = <u>give back</u>, repay, refund, pay back, reimburse, recompense ≠ keep 4 = <u>recur</u>, repeat, persist, revert, happen again, reappear, come again 5 = <u>elect</u>, choose, vote in ● NOUN 1 = <u>reappearance</u> ≠ departure 2 = <u>restoration</u>, reinstatement, re-establishment ≠ removal 3 = <u>recurrence</u>, repetition, reappearance, reversion, persistence 4 = <u>profit</u>, interest, gain, income, revenue, yield, proceeds, takings 5 = <u>statement</u>, report, form, list, account, summary

revamp = <u>renovate</u>, restore, overhaul, refurbish, do up (*informal*), recondition

reveal 1 = <u>make known</u>, disclose, give away, make public, tell, announce, proclaim, let out ≠ keep secret 2 = <u>show</u>, display, exhibit, unveil, uncover, manifest, unearth, unmask ≠ hide

revel VERB = <u>celebrate</u>, carouse, live it up (*informal*), make merry ● NOUN *often plural* = <u>merrymaking</u>, party, celebration, spree, festivity, carousal

revelation 1 = <u>disclosure</u>, news, announcement, publication, leak, confession, divulgence 2 = <u>exhibition</u>, publication, exposure, unveiling, uncovering, unearthing, proclamation

revenge NOUN = <u>retaliation</u>, vengeance, reprisal, retribution, an eye for an eye
● VERB = <u>avenge</u>, repay, take revenge for, get your own back for (*informal*)

revenue = <u>income</u>, returns, profits, gain, yield, proceeds, receipts, takings ≠ expenditure

revere = <u>be in awe of</u>, respect, honour, worship, reverence, exalt, look up to, venerate ≠ despise

reverse VERB 1 (*Law*) = <u>change</u>, cancel, overturn, overthrow, undo, repeal, quash, revoke ≠ implement 2 = <u>turn round</u>, turn over, turn upside down, upend 3 – <u>transpose</u>, change, move, exchange, transfer, switch, shift, alter 4 = <u>go backwards</u>, retreat, back up, turn back, move backwards, back ≠ go forward
● NOUN 1 = <u>opposite</u>, contrary, converse, inverse 2 = <u>misfortune</u>, blow, failure, disappointment, setback, hardship, reversal, adversity 3 = <u>back</u>, rear, other side, wrong side, underside ≠ front
● ADJECTIVE = <u>opposite</u>, contrary, converse

revert 1 = <u>go back</u>, return, come back, resume 2 = return

review NOUN 1 = <u>survey</u>, study, analysis, examination, scrutiny 2 = <u>critique</u>, commentary, evaluation, notice, criticism, judgment 3 = <u>inspection</u>, parade, march past 4 = <u>magazine</u>, journal, periodical, zine (*informal*)
● VERB 1 = <u>reconsider</u>, revise, rethink, reassess, re-examine, re-evaluate, think over 2 = <u>assess</u>, study, judge, evaluate, criticize 3 = <u>inspect</u>, check, survey, examine, vet 4 = <u>look back on</u>, remember, recall, reflect on, recollect

reviewer = <u>critic</u>, judge, commentator

revise 1 = <u>change</u>, review 2 = <u>edit</u>, correct, alter, update, amend, rework, redo, emend 3 = <u>study</u>, go over, run through, cram (*Informal*), swot up on (*Brit. informal*)

revision 1 = <u>emendation</u>, updating, correction 2 = <u>change</u>, amendment 3 = <u>studying</u>, cramming (*informal*), swotting (*Brit. informal*), homework

revival 1 = <u>resurgence</u> ≠ decline

2 = <u>reawakening</u>, renaissance, renewal, resurrection, rebirth, revitalization

revive 1 = <u>revitalize</u>, restore, renew, rekindle, invigorate, reanimate 2 = <u>bring round</u>, awaken 3 = <u>come round</u>, recover 4 = <u>refresh</u> ≠ exhaust

revolt NOUN = <u>uprising</u>, rising, revolution, rebellion, mutiny, insurrection, insurgency
● VERB 1 = <u>rebel</u>, rise up, resist, mutiny 2 = <u>disgust</u>, sicken, repel, repulse, nauseate, gross out (*U.S. slang*), turn your stomach, make your flesh creep

revolting = <u>disgusting</u>, foul, horrible, sickening, horrid, repellent, repulsive, nauseating, yucko (*Austral. slang*) ≠ delightful

revolution 1 = <u>revolt</u>, rising, coup, rebellion, uprising, mutiny, insurgency 2 = <u>transformation</u>, shift, innovation, upheaval, reformation, sea change 3 = <u>rotation</u>, turn, cycle, circle, spin, lap, circuit, orbit

revolutionary ADJECTIVE 1 = <u>rebel</u>, radical, extremist, subversive, insurgent ≠ reactionary 2 = <u>innovative</u>, new, different, novel, radical, progressive, drastic, ground-breaking ≠ conventional
● NOUN = <u>rebel</u>, insurgent, revolutionist ≠ reactionary

revolve 1 = <u>go round</u>, circle, orbit 2 = <u>rotate</u>, turn, wheel, spin, twist, whirl

reward NOUN 1 = <u>punishment</u>, retribution, comeuppance (*slang*), just deserts 2 = <u>payment</u>, return, prize, wages, compensation, bonus, premium, repayment ≠ penalty
● VERB = <u>compensate</u>, pay, repay, recompense, remunerate ≠ penalize

rewarding = <u>satisfying</u>, fulfilling, valuable, profitable, productive, worthwhile, beneficial, enriching ≠ unrewarding

rhetoric 1 = <u>hyperbole</u>, bombast, wordiness, verbosity, grandiloquence, magniloquence 2 = <u>oratory</u>, eloquence, public speaking, speech-making, elocution, declamation, grandiloquence, whaikorero (*N.Z.*)

rhetorical = <u>high-flown</u>, bombastic, verbose, oratorical, grandiloquent, declamatory, arty-farty (*informal*), magniloquent

rhyme = <u>poem</u>, song, verse, ode

rhythm 1 = <u>beat</u>, swing, accent, pulse, tempo, cadence, lilt 2 = <u>metre</u>, time

rich 1 = <u>wealthy</u>, affluent, well-off, loaded (*slang*), prosperous, well-heeled (*informal*), well-to-do, moneyed ≠ poor 2 = <u>well-stocked</u>, full, productive, ample, abundant, plentiful, copious, well-supplied ≠ scarce 3 = <u>full-bodied</u>, sweet, fatty, tasty, creamy, luscious, succulent ≠ bland 4 = <u>fruitful</u>, productive, fertile, prolific ≠ barren 5 = <u>abounding</u>, luxurious, lush, abundant

riches 1 = <u>wealth</u>, assets, plenty, fortune, substance, treasure, affluence ≠ poverty 2 = <u>resources</u>, treasures

richly 1 = <u>elaborately</u>, lavishly, elegantly, splendidly, exquisitely, expensively, luxuriously, gorgeously 2 = <u>fully</u>, well, thoroughly, amply, appropriately, properly, suitably

rid VERB = <u>free</u>, clear, deliver, relieve, purge, unburden, make free, disencumber
● PHRASES **get rid of something** *or* **someone** = <u>dispose of</u>, throw away *or* out, dump, remove, eliminate, expel, eject

riddle[1] 1 = <u>puzzle</u>, problem, conundrum, poser 2 = <u>enigma</u>, question, secret, mystery, puzzle, conundrum, teaser, problem

riddle[2] 1 = <u>pierce</u>, pepper, puncture, perforate, honeycomb 2 = <u>pervade</u>, fill, spread through

riddled 1 = <u>filled</u>, spoilt, pervaded, infested, permeated

ride VERB 1 = <u>control</u>, handle, manage 2 = <u>travel</u>, be carried, go, move
● NOUN = <u>journey</u>, drive, trip, lift, outing, jaunt

ridicule VERB = <u>laugh at</u>, mock, make fun of, sneer at, jeer at, deride, poke fun at, chaff
● NOUN = <u>mockery</u>, scorn, derision, laughter, jeer, chaff, gibe, raillery

ridiculous = <u>laughable</u>, stupid, silly, absurd, ludicrous, farcical, comical, risible ≠ sensible

rife = <u>widespread</u>, rampant, general, common, universal, frequent, prevalent, ubiquitous

rifle = <u>ransack</u>, rob, burgle, loot, strip, sack, plunder, pillage

rift 1 = <u>breach</u>, division, split, separation, falling out (*informal*), disagreement, quarrel 2 = <u>split</u>, opening, crack, gap, break, fault, flaw, cleft

rig VERB 1 = <u>fix</u>, engineer (*informal*), arrange, manipulate, tamper with, gerrymander 2 (*Nautical*) = <u>equip</u>, fit out, kit out, outfit, supply, furnish
● PHRASES **rig something up** = <u>set up</u>, build, construct, put up, arrange, assemble, put together, erect

right ADJECTIVE 1 = <u>correct</u>, true, genuine, accurate, exact, precise, valid, factual, dinkum (*Austral. & N.Z. informal*) ≠ wrong 2 = <u>proper</u>, done, becoming, seemly, fitting, fit, appropriate, suitable ≠ inappropriate 3 = <u>just</u>, good, fair, moral, proper, ethical, honest, equitable ≠ unfair
● ADVERB 1 = <u>correctly</u>, truly, precisely, exactly, genuinely, accurately ≠ wrongly 2 = <u>suitably</u>, fittingly, appropriately, properly, aptly ≠ improperly 3 = <u>exactly</u>, squarely, precisely 4 = <u>directly</u>, straight, precisely, exactly, unswervingly, without deviation, by the shortest route, in a beeline 5 = <u>straight</u>, directly, quickly, promptly, straightaway ≠ indirectly
● NOUN 1 = <u>prerogative</u>, business, power, claim, authority, due, freedom, licence 2 = <u>justice</u>, truth, fairness, legality, righteousness, lawfulness ≠ injustice
● VERB = <u>rectify</u>, settle, fix, correct, sort out, straighten, redress, put right

right away = <u>immediately</u>, now, directly, instantly, at once, straightaway, forthwith, pronto (*informal*)

righteous = <u>virtuous</u>, good, just, fair, moral, pure, ethical, upright ≠ wicked

rigid 1 = <u>strict</u>, set, fixed, exact, rigorous, stringent ≠ flexible 2 = <u>inflexible</u>, uncompromising, unbending 3 = <u>stiff</u>, inflexible, inelastic ≠ pliable

rigorous = <u>strict</u>, hard, demanding, tough, severe, exacting, harsh, stern ≠ soft

rim 1 = <u>edge</u>, lip, brim 2 = <u>border</u>, edge, trim 3 = <u>margin</u>, border, verge, brink

ring[1] VERB 1 = <u>phone</u>, call, telephone, buzz (*informal, chiefly Brit.*) 2 = <u>chime</u>, sound, toll, reverberate, clang, peal 3 = <u>reverberate</u>
● NOUN 1 = <u>call</u>, phone call, buzz (*informal, chiefly Brit.*) 2 = <u>chime</u>, knell, peal

ring[2] NOUN 1 = <u>circle</u>, round, band, circuit, loop, hoop, halo 2 = <u>arena</u>, enclosure, circus, rink 3 = <u>gang</u>, group, association, band, circle, mob, syndicate, cartel
● VERB = <u>encircle</u>, surround, enclose, girdle, gird

rinse VERB = <u>wash</u>, clean, dip, splash, cleanse, bathe

● NOUN = <u>wash</u>, dip, splash, bath

riot NOUN 1 = <u>disturbance</u>, disorder, confusion, turmoil, upheaval, strife, turbulence, lawlessness 2 = <u>display</u>, show, splash, extravaganza, profusion 3 = <u>laugh</u>, joke, scream (*informal*), hoot (*informal*), lark

● VERB = <u>rampage</u>, run riot, go on the rampage

● PHRASES **run riot** 1 = <u>rampage</u>, go wild, be out of control 2 = <u>grow profusely</u>, spread like wildfire

rip VERB 1 = <u>tear</u>, cut, split, burst, rend, slash, claw, slit 2 = <u>be torn</u>, tear, split, burst

● NOUN = <u>tear</u>, cut, hole, split, rent, slash, slit, gash

● PHRASES **rip someone off** (*Slang*) = <u>cheat</u>, rob, con (*informal*), skin (*slang*), fleece, defraud, swindle

ripe 1 = <u>ripened</u>, seasoned, ready, mature, mellow ≠ unripe 2 = <u>right</u>, suitable 3 = <u>mature</u> 4 = <u>suitable</u>, timely, ideal, favourable, auspicious, opportune ≠ unsuitable

rip-off *or* **ripoff** (*Slang*) = <u>cheat</u>, con (*informal*), scam (*slang*), con trick (*informal*), fraud, theft, swindle

rise VERB 1 = <u>get up</u>, stand up, get to your feet 2 = <u>arise</u> 3 = <u>go up</u>, climb, ascend ≠ descend 4 = <u>loom</u>, tower 5 = <u>get steeper</u>, ascend, go uphill, slope upwards ≠ drop 6 = <u>increase</u>, mount ≠ decrease 7 = <u>grow</u>, go up, intensify 8 = <u>rebel</u>, revolt, mutiny 9 = <u>advance</u>, progress, get on, prosper

● NOUN 1 = <u>upward slope</u>, incline, elevation, ascent, kopje *or* koppie (*S. African*) 2 = <u>increase</u>, upturn, upswing, upsurge ≠ decrease 3 = <u>pay increase</u>, raise (*U.S.*), increment, promotion 4 = <u>advancement</u>, progress, climb, promotion

● PHRASES **give rise to something** = <u>cause</u>, produce, effect, result in, bring about

risk NOUN 1 = <u>danger</u>, chance, possibility, hazard 2 = <u>gamble</u>, chance, speculation, leap in the dark 3 = <u>peril</u>, jeopardy

● VERB 1 = <u>stand a chance of</u> 2 = <u>dare</u>, endanger, jeopardize, imperil, venture, gamble, hazard

risky = <u>dangerous</u>, hazardous, unsafe, perilous, uncertain, dodgy (*Brit., Austral., & N.Z. informal*), dicey (*informal, chiefly Brit.*), chancy (*informal*) ≠ safe

rite = <u>ceremony</u>, custom, ritual, practice, procedure, observance

ritual NOUN 1 = <u>ceremony</u>, rite, observance 2 = <u>custom</u>, tradition, routine, convention, practice, procedure, habit, protocol, tikanga (*N.Z.*)

● ADJECTIVE = <u>ceremonial</u>, conventional, routine, customary, habitual

rival NOUN = <u>opponent</u>, competitor, contender, contestant, adversary ≠ supporter

● VERB = <u>compete with</u>, match, equal, compare with, come up to, be a match for

● ADJECTIVE = <u>competing</u>, conflicting, opposing

rivalry = <u>competition</u>, opposition, conflict, contest, contention

river 1 = <u>stream</u>, brook, creek, waterway, tributary, burn (*Scot.*) 2 = <u>flow</u>, rush, flood, spate, torrent

riveting = <u>enthralling</u>, gripping, fascinating, absorbing, captivating, hypnotic, engrossing, spellbinding

road 1 = <u>roadway</u>, highway, motorway, track, route, path, lane, pathway 2 = <u>way</u>, path

roam = <u>wander</u>, walk, range, travel, stray, ramble, prowl, rove

roar VERB 1 = <u>thunder</u> 2 = <u>guffaw</u>, laugh heartily, hoot, split your sides (*informal*) 3 = <u>cry</u>, shout, yell, howl, bellow, bawl, bay

● NOUN 1 = <u>guffaw</u>, hoot 2 = <u>cry</u>, shout, yell, howl, outcry, bellow

rob 1 = <u>steal from</u>, hold up, mug (*informal*) 2 = <u>raid</u>, hold up, loot, plunder, burgle, pillage 3 = <u>dispossess</u>, con (*informal*), cheat, defraud 4 = <u>deprive</u>, do out of (*informal*)

robber = <u>thief</u>, raider, burglar, looter, fraud, cheat, bandit, plunderer

robbery 1 = <u>burglary</u>, raid, hold-up, rip-off (*slang*), stick-up (*slang, chiefly U.S.*) 2 = <u>theft</u>, stealing, mugging (*informal*), plunder, swindle, pillage, larceny

robe = <u>gown</u>, costume, habit

robot = <u>machine</u>, automaton, android, mechanical man

robust = <u>strong</u>, tough, powerful, fit, healthy, strapping, hardy, vigorous ≠ weak

rock¹ = <u>stone</u>, boulder

rock² 1 = <u>sway</u>, pitch, swing, reel, toss, lurch, roll 2 = <u>shock</u>, surprise, shake, stun, astonish, stagger, astound

rocky¹ = <u>rough</u>, rugged, stony, craggy

rocky² = <u>unstable</u>, shaky, wobbly, rickety, unsteady

rod 1 = <u>stick</u>, bar, pole, shaft, cane 2 = <u>staff</u>, baton, wand

rogue 1 = <u>scoundrel</u>, crook (*informal*), villain, fraud, blackguard, skelm (*S. African*), rorter (*Austral. slang*) 2 = <u>scamp</u>, rascal, scally (*Northwest English dialect*), nointer (*Austral. slang*)

role 1 = <u>job</u>, part, position, post, task, duty, function, capacity 2 = <u>part</u>, character, representation, portrayal

roll VERB 1 = <u>turn</u>, wheel, spin, go round, revolve, rotate, whirl, swivel 2 = <u>trundle</u>, go, move 3 = <u>flow</u>, run, course 4 *often with up* = <u>wind</u>, bind, wrap, swathe, envelop, furl, enfold 5 = <u>level</u>, even, press, smooth, flatten 6 = <u>toss</u>, rock, lurch, reel, tumble, sway
● NOUN 1 = <u>rumble</u>, boom, roar, thunder, reverberation 2 = <u>register</u>, record, list, index, census 3 = <u>turn</u>, spin, rotation, cycle, wheel, revolution, reel, whirl

romance 1 = <u>love affair</u>, relationship, affair, attachment, liaison, amour 2 = <u>excitement</u>, colour, charm, mystery, glamour, fascination 3 = <u>story</u>, tale, fantasy, legend, fairy tale, love story, melodrama

romantic ADJECTIVE 1 = <u>loving</u>, tender, passionate, fond, sentimental, amorous, icky (*informal*) ≠ unromantic 2 = <u>idealistic</u>, unrealistic, impractical, dreamy, starry-eyed ≠ realistic 3 = <u>exciting</u>, fascinating, mysterious, colourful, glamorous ≠ unexciting
● NOUN = <u>idealist</u>, dreamer, sentimentalist

romp VERB = <u>frolic</u>, sport, have fun, caper, cavort, frisk, gambol
● NOUN = <u>frolic</u>, lark (*informal*), caper

room 1 = <u>chamber</u>, office, apartment 2 = <u>space</u>, area, capacity, extent, expanse 3 = <u>opportunity</u>, scope, leeway, chance, range, occasion, margin

root¹ NOUN 1 = <u>stem</u>, tuber, rhizome 2 = <u>source</u>, cause, heart, bottom, base, seat, seed, foundation
● PLURAL NOUN = <u>sense of belonging</u>, origins, heritage, birthplace, home, family, cradle
● PHRASES **root something** *or* **someone out** = <u>get rid of</u>, remove, eliminate, abolish, eradicate, do away with, weed out, exterminate

root² = <u>dig</u>, burrow, ferret

rope NOUN = <u>cord</u>, line, cable, strand, hawser
● PHRASES **know the ropes** = <u>be experienced</u>, be knowledgeable, be an old hand ◆ **rope someone in** *or* **into something** (*Brit.*) = <u>persuade</u>, involve, engage, enlist, talk into, inveigle

rosy ADJECTIVE 1 = <u>glowing</u>, blooming, radiant, ruddy, healthy-looking ≠ pale 2 = <u>promising</u>, encouraging, bright, optimistic, hopeful, cheerful, favourable, auspicious ≠ gloomy
● NOUN = <u>pink</u>, red

rot VERB 1 = <u>decay</u>, spoil, deteriorate, perish, decompose, moulder, go bad, putrefy 2 = <u>crumble</u> 3 = <u>deteriorate</u>, decline, waste away
● NOUN 1 = <u>decay</u>, decomposition, corruption, mould, blight, canker, putrefaction 2 (*Informal*) = <u>nonsense</u>, rubbish, drivel, twaddle, garbage (*chiefly U.S.*), trash, tripe (*informal*), claptrap (*informal*), bizzo (*Austral. slang*), bull's wool (*Austral. & N.Z. slang*)
▇ RELATED WORD
adjective: putrid

rotate 1 = <u>revolve</u>, turn, wheel, spin, reel, go round, swivel, pivot 2 = <u>follow in sequence</u>, switch, alternate, take turns

rotation 1 = <u>revolution</u>, turning, turn, wheel, spin, spinning, reel, orbit 2 = <u>sequence</u>, switching, cycle, succession, alternation

rotten 1 = <u>decaying</u>, bad, rank, corrupt, sour, stinking, perished, festering, festy (*Austral. slang*) ≠ fresh 2 = <u>crumbling</u>, perished 3 (*Informal*) = <u>despicable</u>, mean, base, dirty, nasty, contemptible 4 (*Informal*) = <u>inferior</u>, poor, inadequate, duff (*Brit. informal*), unsatisfactory, lousy (*slang*), substandard, crummy (*slang*), bodger *or* bodgie (*Austral. slang*) 5 = <u>corrupt</u>, immoral, crooked (*informal*), dishonest, dishonourable, perfidious ≠ honourable

rough ADJECTIVE 1 = <u>uneven</u>, broken, rocky, irregular, jagged, bumpy, stony, craggy ≠ even 2 = <u>boisterous</u>, hard, tough, arduous 3 = <u>ungracious</u>, blunt, rude, coarse, brusque, uncouth, impolite, uncivil ≠ refined 4 = <u>unpleasant</u>, hard, difficult, tough, uncomfortable ≠ easy 5 = <u>approximate</u>, estimated ≠ exact 6 = <u>vague</u>, general, sketchy, imprecise, inexact **7** = basic, crude, unfinished, incomplete, imperfect, rudimentary, sketchy, unrefined ≠ complete **8** = stormy, wild, turbulent, choppy, squally ≠ calm **9** = harsh, tough, nasty, cruel, unfeeling ≠ gentle

● NOUN = outline, draft, mock-up, preliminary sketch

● PHRASES **rough and ready 1** = makeshift, crude, provisional, improvised, sketchy, stopgap **2** = unrefined, shabby, untidy, unkempt, unpolished, ill-groomed ◆ **rough something out** = outline, plan, draft, sketch

round NOUN **1** = series, session, cycle, sequence, succession **2** = stage, turn, level, period, division, session, lap **3** = sphere, ball, band, ring, circle, disc, globe, orb **4** = course, tour, circuit, beat, series, schedule, routine

● ADJECTIVE **1** = spherical, rounded, curved, circular, cylindrical, rotund, globular **2** = plump, full, ample, fleshy, rotund, full-fleshed

● VERB = go round, circle, skirt, flank, bypass, encircle, turn

● PHRASES **round something** *or* **someone up** = gather, muster, group, drive, collect, rally, herd, marshal

roundabout 1 = indirect, devious, tortuous, circuitous, evasive, discursive ≠ direct **2** = oblique, implied, indirect, circuitous

roundup = muster, collection, rally, assembly, herding

rouse 1 = wake up, call, wake, awaken **2** = excite, move, stir, provoke, anger, animate, agitate, inflame **3** = stimulate, provoke, incite

rousing = lively, moving, spirited, exciting, inspiring, stirring, stimulating ≠ dull

rout VERB = defeat, beat, overthrow, thrash, destroy, crush, conquer, wipe the floor with (*informal*)

● NOUN = defeat, beating, overthrow, thrashing, pasting (*slang*), debacle, drubbing

route 1 = way, course, road, direction, path, journey, itinerary **2** = beat, circuit

routine NOUN = procedure, programme, order, practice, method, pattern, custom

● ADJECTIVE **1** = usual, standard, normal, customary, ordinary, typical, everyday,

habitual ≠ unusual **2** = boring, dull, predictable, tedious, tiresome, humdrum

row[1] NOUN = line, bank, range, series, file, string, column

● PHRASES **in a row** = consecutively, running, in turn, one after the other, successively, in sequence

row[2] NOUN (*Informal*) **1** = quarrel, dispute, argument, squabble, tiff, trouble, brawl **2** = disturbance, noise, racket, uproar, commotion, rumpus, tumult

● VERB = quarrel, fight, argue, dispute, squabble, wrangle

royal 1 = regal, kingly, queenly, princely, imperial, sovereign **2** = splendid, grand, impressive, magnificent, majestic, stately

rub VERB **1** = stroke, massage, caress **2** = polish, clean, shine, wipe, scour **3** = chafe, scrape, grate, abrade

● NOUN **1** = massage, caress, kneading **2** = polish, stroke, shine, wipe

● PHRASES **rub something out** = erase, remove, cancel, wipe out, delete, obliterate, efface

rubbish 1 = waste, refuse, scrap, junk (*informal*), litter, garbage (*chiefly U.S.*), trash, lumber **2** = nonsense, garbage (*chiefly U.S.*), twaddle, rot, trash, hot air (*informal*), tripe (*informal*), claptrap (*informal*), bizzo (*Austral. slang*), bull's wool (*Austral. & N.Z. slang*)

rude 1 = impolite, insulting, cheeky, abusive, disrespectful, impertinent, insolent, impudent ≠ polite **2** = uncivilized, rough, coarse, brutish, boorish, uncouth, loutish, graceless **3** = vulgar ≠ refined **4** = unpleasant, sharp, sudden, harsh, startling, abrupt **5** = roughly-made, simple, rough, raw, crude, primitive, makeshift, artless ≠ well-made

rue (*Literary*) = regret, mourn, lament, repent, be sorry for, kick yourself for

ruffle 1 = disarrange, disorder, mess up, rumple, tousle, dishevel **2** = annoy, upset, irritate, agitate, nettle, fluster, peeve (*informal*) ≠ calm

rugged 1 = rocky, broken, rough, craggy, difficult, ragged, irregular, uneven ≠ even **2** = strong-featured, rough-hewn, weather-beaten ≠ delicate **3** = well-built, strong, tough, robust, sturdy **4** = tough, strong, robust, muscular, sturdy, burly, husky (*informal*), brawny ≠ delicate

ruin VERB 1 = <u>destroy</u>, devastate, wreck, defeat, smash, crush, demolish, lay waste ≠ create 2 = <u>bankrupt</u>, break, impoverish, beggar, pauperize 3 = <u>spoil</u>, damage, mess up, blow (*slang*), screw up (*informal*), botch, make a mess of, crool or cruel (*Austral. slang*) ≠ improve
● NOUN 1 = <u>bankruptcy</u>, insolvency, destitution 2 = <u>disrepair</u>, decay, disintegration, ruination, wreckage 3 = <u>destruction</u>, fall, breakdown, defeat, collapse, wreck, undoing, downfall ≠ preservation

rule NOUN 1 = <u>regulation</u>, law, direction, guideline, decree 2 = <u>precept</u>, principle, canon, maxim, tenet, axiom 3 = <u>custom</u>, procedure, practice, routine, tradition, habit, convention 4 = <u>government</u>, power, control, authority, command, regime, reign, jurisdiction, mana (*N.Z.*)
● VERB 1 = <u>govern</u>, control, direct, have power over, command over, have charge of 2 = <u>reign</u>, govern, be in power, be in authority 3 = <u>decree</u>, decide, judge, settle, pronounce 4 = <u>be prevalent</u>, prevail, predominate, be customary, preponderate
● PHRASES **as a rule** = <u>usually</u>, generally, mainly, normally, on the whole, ordinarily ◆ **rule someone out** = <u>exclude</u>, eliminate, disqualify, ban, reject, dismiss, prohibit, leave out ◆ **rule something out** = <u>reject</u>, exclude, eliminate

ruler 1 = <u>governor</u>, leader, lord, commander, controller, monarch, sovereign, head of state 2 = <u>measure</u>, rule, yardstick

ruling ADJECTIVE 1 = <u>governing</u>, reigning, controlling, commanding 2 = <u>predominant</u>, dominant, prevailing, preponderant, chief, main, principal, pre-eminent ≠ minor
● NOUN = <u>decision</u>, verdict, judgment, decree, adjudication, pronouncement

rumour = <u>story</u>, news, report, talk, word, whisper, buzz, gossip

run VERB 1 = <u>race</u>, rush, dash, hurry, sprint, bolt, gallop, hare (*Brit. informal*) ≠ dawdle 2 = <u>flee</u>, escape, take off (*informal*), bolt, beat it (*slang*), leg it (*informal*), take flight, do a runner (*slang*) ≠ stay 3 = <u>take part</u>, compete 4 = <u>continue</u>, go, stretch, reach, extend, proceed ≠ stop 5 (*Chiefly U.S. & Canad.*) = <u>compete</u>, stand, contend, be a candidate, put yourself up for,

take part 6 = <u>manage</u>, lead, direct, be in charge of, head, control, operate, handle 7 = <u>go</u>, work, operate, perform, function 8 = <u>perform</u>, carry out 9 = <u>work</u>, go, operate, function 10 = <u>pass</u>, go, move, roll, glide, skim 11 = <u>flow</u>, pour, stream, go, leak, spill, discharge, gush 12 = <u>publish</u>, feature, display, print 13 = <u>melt</u>, dissolve, liquefy, go soft 14 = <u>smuggle</u>, traffic in, bootleg
● NOUN 1 = <u>race</u>, rush, dash, sprint, gallop, jog, spurt 2 = <u>ride</u>, drive, trip, spin (*informal*), outing, excursion, jaunt 3 = <u>sequence</u>, period, stretch, spell, course, season, series, string 4 = <u>enclosure</u>, pen, coop
● PHRASES **run away** = <u>flee</u>, escape, bolt, abscond, do a runner (*slang*), make a run for it, scram (*informal*), fly the coop (*U.S. & Canad. informal*) ◆ **run into someone** = <u>meet</u>, encounter, bump into, run across, come across or upon ◆ **run into something** 1 = <u>be beset by</u>, encounter, come across or upon, face, experience 2 = <u>collide with</u>, hit, strike ◆ **run out** 1 = <u>be used up</u>, dry up, give out, fail, finish, be exhausted 2 = <u>expire</u>, end, terminate ◆ **run over something** 1 = <u>exceed</u>, overstep, go over the top of, go over the limit of 2 = <u>review</u>, check, go through, go over, run through, rehearse ◆ **run over something** or **someone** = <u>knock down</u>, hit, run down, knock over ◆ **run something** or **someone down** 1 = <u>criticize</u>, denigrate, belittle, knock (*informal*), rubbish (*informal*), slag (off) (*slang*), disparage, decry 2 = <u>downsize</u>, cut, reduce, trim, decrease, cut back, curtail 3 = <u>knock down</u>, hit, run into, run over, knock over

run-down or **rundown** 1 = <u>exhausted</u>, weak, drained, weary, unhealthy, worn-out, debilitated, below par ≠ fit 2 = <u>dilapidated</u>, broken-down, shabby, worn-out, seedy, ramshackle, decrepit

runner 1 = <u>athlete</u>, sprinter, jogger 2 = <u>messenger</u>, courier, errand boy, dispatch bearer

running NOUN 1 = <u>management</u>, control, administration, direction, leadership, organization, supervision 2 = <u>working</u>, performance, operation, functioning, maintenance
● ADJECTIVE 1 = <u>continuous</u>, constant, perpetual, uninterrupted, incessant 2 = <u>in succession</u>, unbroken 3 = <u>flowing</u>, moving,

streaming, coursing

rupture NOUN = <u>break</u>, tear, split, crack, rent, burst, breach, fissure

● VERB = <u>break</u>, separate, tear, split, crack, burst, sever

rural 1 = <u>agricultural</u>, country 2 = <u>rustic</u>, country, pastoral, sylvan ≠ urban

rush VERB 1 = <u>hurry</u>, run, race, shoot, fly, career, speed, tear ≠ dawdle 2 = <u>push</u>, hurry, press, hustle 3 = <u>attack</u>, storm, charge at

● NOUN 1 = <u>dash</u>, charge, race, scramble, stampede 2 = <u>hurry</u>, haste, hustle 3 = <u>surge</u>, flow, gush 4 = <u>attack</u>, charge, assault, onslaught

● ADJECTIVE = <u>hasty</u>, fast, quick, hurried, rapid, urgent, swift ≠ leisurely

rust NOUN 1 = <u>corrosion</u>, oxidation 2 = <u>mildew</u>, must, mould, rot, blight

● VERB = <u>corrode</u>, oxidize

rusty 1 = <u>corroded</u>, rusted, oxidized, rust-covered 2 = <u>out of practice</u>, weak, stale, unpractised 3 = <u>reddish-brown</u>, chestnut, reddish, russet, coppery, rust-coloured

ruthless = <u>merciless</u>, harsh, cruel, brutal, relentless, callous, heartless, remorseless ≠ merciful

S

sabotage VERB = <u>damage</u>, destroy, wreck, disable, disrupt, subvert, incapacitate, vandalize

● NOUN = <u>damage</u>, destruction, wrecking

sack¹ NOUN 1 = <u>bag</u>, pocket, sac, pouch, receptacle 2 = <u>dismissal</u>, discharge, the boot (*slang*), the axe (*informal*), the push (*slang*)

● VERB (*Informal*) = <u>dismiss</u>, fire (*informal*), axe (*informal*), discharge, kiss off (*slang, chiefly U.S. & Canad.*), give (someone) the push (*informal*)

sack² VERB = <u>plunder</u>, loot, pillage, strip, rob, raid, ruin

● NOUN = <u>plundering</u>, looting, pillage

sacred 1 = <u>holy</u>, hallowed, blessed, divine, revered, sanctified ≠ secular 2 = <u>religious</u>, holy, ecclesiastical, hallowed ≠ unconsecrated 3 = <u>inviolable</u>, protected, sacrosanct, hallowed, inalienable, unalterable

sacrifice VERB 1 = <u>offer</u>, offer up, immolate 2 = <u>give up</u>, abandon, relinquish, lose, surrender, let go, do without, renounce

● NOUN 1 = <u>offering</u>, oblation 2 = <u>surrender</u>, loss, giving up, rejection, abdication, renunciation, repudiation, forswearing

sad 1 = <u>unhappy</u>, down, low, blue, depressed, melancholy, mournful, dejected ≠ happy 2 = <u>tragic</u>, moving, upsetting, depressing, dismal, pathetic, poignant, harrowing 3 = <u>deplorable</u>, bad, sorry, terrible, unfortunate, regrettable, lamentable, wretched ≠ good

sadden = <u>upset</u>, depress, distress, grieve, make sad, deject

saddle = <u>burden</u>, load, lumber (*Brit. informal*), encumber

sadness = <u>unhappiness</u>, sorrow, grief, depression, the blues, misery, melancholy, poignancy ≠ happiness

safe ADJECTIVE 1 = <u>protected</u>, secure, impregnable, out of danger, safe and sound, in safe hands, out of harm's way ≠ endangered 2 = <u>all right</u>, intact, unscathed, unhurt, unharmed, undamaged, O.K. *or* okay (*informal*) 3 = <u>risk-free</u>, sound, secure, certain, impregnable

● NOUN = <u>strongbox</u>, vault, coffer, repository, deposit box, safe-deposit box

safeguard VERB = <u>protect</u>, guard, defend, save, preserve, look after, keep safe

● NOUN = <u>protection</u>, security, defence, guard

safely = <u>in safety</u>, with impunity, without risk, safe and sound

safety 1 = <u>security</u>, protection, safeguards, precautions, safety measures, impregnability ≠ risk 2 = <u>shelter</u>, haven, protection, cover, retreat, asylum, refuge, sanctuary

sag 1 = <u>sink</u>, bag, droop, fall, slump, dip, give way, hang loosely 2 = <u>drop</u>, sink, slump, flop, droop, loll 3 = <u>decline</u>, tire, flag, weaken, wilt, wane, droop

saga 1 = <u>carry-on</u> (*informal, chiefly Brit.*), performance (*informal*), pantomime (*informal*) 2 = <u>epic</u>, story, tale, narrative, yarn

sage NOUN = <u>wise man</u>, philosopher, guru, master, elder, tohunga (*N.Z.*)

● ADJECTIVE = <u>wise</u>, sensible, judicious, sagacious, sapient

sail NOUN = <u>sheet</u>, canvas

● VERB 1 = <u>go by water</u>, cruise, voyage, ride the waves, go by sea 2 = <u>set sail</u>, embark, get under way, put to sea, put off, leave port, hoist sail, cast *or* weigh anchor 3 = <u>pilot</u>, steer 4 = <u>glide</u>, sweep, float, fly, wing, soar, drift, skim

sailor = <u>mariner</u>, marine, seaman, sea dog, seafarer

sake NOUN = <u>purpose</u>, interest, reason, end, aim, objective, motive

● PHRASES **for someone's sake** = <u>in someone's interests</u>, to someone's advantage, on someone's account, for the benefit of, for the good of, for the welfare of, out of respect for, out of consideration for

salary = <u>pay</u>, income, wage, fee, payment, wages, earnings, allowance

sale 1 = <u>selling</u>, marketing, dealing, transaction, disposal 2 = <u>auction</u>, fair, mart, bazaar

salt NOUN = <u>seasoning</u>

● ADJECTIVE = <u>salty</u>, saline, brackish, briny

salute VERB 1 = <u>greet</u>, welcome, acknowledge, address, hail, mihi (*N.Z.*) 2 = <u>honour</u>, acknowledge, recognize, pay tribute *or* homage to

● NOUN = <u>greeting</u>, recognition, salutation, address

salvage = <u>save</u>, recover, rescue, get back, retrieve, redeem

salvation = <u>saving</u>, rescue, recovery, salvage, redemption, deliverance ≠ ruin

same 1 = <u>identical</u>, similar, alike, equal, twin, corresponding, duplicate ≠ different 2 = <u>the very same</u>, one and the same, selfsame 3 = <u>aforementioned</u>, aforesaid 4 = <u>unchanged</u>, consistent, constant, unaltered, invariable, unvarying, changeless ≠ altered

sample NOUN 1 = <u>specimen</u>, example, model, pattern, instance 2 = <u>cross section</u>

● VERB = <u>test</u>, try, experience, taste, inspect

● ADJECTIVE = <u>test</u>, trial, specimen, representative

sanction VERB = <u>permit</u>, allow, approve, endorse, authorize ≠ forbid

● NOUN 1 *often plural* = <u>ban</u>, boycott, embargo, exclusion, penalty, coercive measures ≠ permission 2 = <u>permission</u>, backing, authority, approval, authorization, O.K. *or* okay (*informal*), stamp *or* seal of approval ≠ ban

sanctuary 1 = <u>protection</u>, shelter, refuge, haven, retreat, asylum 2 = <u>reserve</u>, park, preserve, reservation, national park, tract, nature reserve, conservation area

sane 1 = <u>rational</u>, all there (*informal*), of sound mind, compos mentis (*Latin*), in your right mind, mentally sound ≠ insane 2 = <u>sensible</u>, sound, reasonable, balanced, judicious, level-headed ≠ foolish

sap¹ 1 = <u>juice</u>, essence, vital fluid, lifeblood 2 (*Slang*) = <u>fool</u>, jerk (*slang, chiefly U.S. & Canad.*), idiot, wally (*slang*), twit (*informal*), simpleton, ninny, dorba *or* dorb (*Austral. slang*), bogan (*Austral. slang*)

sap² = <u>weaken</u>, drain, undermine, exhaust, deplete

satanic = <u>evil</u>, demonic, hellish, black, wicked, devilish, infernal, fiendish ≠ godly

satire 1 = <u>mockery</u>, irony, ridicule 2 = <u>parody</u>, mockery, caricature, lampoon, burlesque

satisfaction 1 = <u>fulfilment</u>, pleasure, achievement, relish, gratification, pride ≠ dissatisfaction 2 = <u>contentment</u>, content, comfort, pleasure, happiness, enjoyment, satiety, repletion ≠ discontent

satisfactory = <u>adequate</u>, acceptable, good enough, average, fair, all right, sufficient, passable ≠ unsatisfactory

satisfy 1 = <u>content</u>, please, indulge, gratify, pander to, assuage, pacify, quench ≠ dissatisfy 2 = <u>convince</u>, persuade, assure, reassure ≠ dissuade 3 = <u>comply with</u>, meet, fulfil, answer, serve, fill, observe, obey ≠ fail to meet

saturate 1 = <u>flood</u>, overwhelm, swamp, overrun 2 = <u>soak</u>, steep, drench, imbue, suffuse, wet through, waterlog, souse

saturated = <u>soaked</u>, soaking (wet), drenched, sodden, dripping, waterlogged, sopping (wet), wet through

sauce = <u>dressing</u>, dip, relish, condiment

savage ADJECTIVE 1 = <u>cruel</u>, brutal, vicious, fierce, harsh, ruthless, ferocious, sadistic ≠ gentle 2 = <u>wild</u>, fierce, ferocious, unbroken, feral, untamed, undomesticated ≠ tame 3 = <u>primitive</u>, undeveloped, uncultivated, uncivilized 4 = <u>uncultivated</u>, rugged, unspoilt, uninhabited, rough, uncivilized

≠ cultivated

● NOUN = <u>lout</u>, yob (*Brit. slang*), barbarian, yahoo, hoon (*Austral. & N.Z.*), boor, cougan (*Austral. slang*), scozza (*Austral. slang*), bogan (*Austral. slang*)

● VERB = <u>maul</u>, tear, claw, attack, mangle, lacerate, mangulate (*Austral. slang*)

save 1 = <u>rescue</u>, free, release, deliver, recover, get out, liberate, salvage ≠ endanger 2 = <u>keep</u>, reserve, set aside, store, collect, gather, hold, hoard ≠ spend 3 = <u>protect</u>, keep, guard, preserve, look after, safeguard, salvage, conserve 4 = <u>put aside</u>, keep, reserve, collect, retain, set aside, put by

saving NOUN = <u>economy</u>, discount, reduction, bargain

● PLURAL NOUN = <u>nest egg</u>, fund, store, reserves, resources

saviour = <u>rescuer</u>, deliverer, defender, protector, liberator, redeemer, preserver

Saviour = <u>Christ</u>, Jesus, the Messiah, the Redeemer

savour VERB 1 = <u>relish</u>, delight in, revel in, luxuriate in 2 = <u>enjoy</u>, appreciate, relish, delight in, revel in, luxuriate in

● NOUN = <u>flavour</u>, taste, smell, relish, smack, tang, piquancy

say VERB 1 = <u>state</u>, declare, remark, announce, maintain, mention, assert, affirm 2 = <u>speak</u>, utter, voice, express, pronounce 3 = <u>suggest</u>, express, imply, communicate, disclose, give away, convey, divulge 4 = <u>suppose</u>, supposing, imagine, assume, presume 5 = <u>estimate</u>, suppose, guess, conjecture, surmise

● NOUN 1 = <u>influence</u>, power, control, authority, weight, clout (*informal*), mana (*N.Z.*) 2 = <u>chance to speak</u>, vote, voice

saying = <u>proverb</u>, maxim, adage, dictum, axiom, aphorism

scale¹ = <u>flake</u>, plate, layer, lamina

scale² NOUN 1 = <u>degree</u>, size, range, extent, dimensions, scope, magnitude, breadth 2 = <u>system of measurement</u>, measuring system 3 = <u>ranking</u>, ladder, hierarchy, series, sequence, progression 4 = <u>ratio</u>, proportion

● VERB = <u>climb up</u>, mount, ascend, surmount, clamber up, escalade

scan 1 = <u>glance over</u>, skim, look over, eye, check, examine, check out (*informal*), run over 2 = <u>survey</u>, search, investigate, sweep, scour, scrutinize

scandal 1 = <u>disgrace</u>, crime, offence, sin, embarrassment, wrongdoing, dishonourable behaviour, discreditable behaviour 2 = <u>gossip</u>, talk, rumours, dirt, slander, tattle, aspersion 3 = <u>shame</u>, disgrace, stigma, infamy, opprobrium 4 = <u>outrage</u>, shame, insult, disgrace, injustice, crying shame

scant = <u>inadequate</u>, meagre, sparse, little, minimal, barely sufficient ≠ adequate

scapegoat = <u>fall guy</u>, whipping boy

scar NOUN 1 = <u>mark</u>, injury, wound, blemish 2 = <u>trauma</u>, suffering, pain, torture, anguish

● VERB = <u>mark</u>, disfigure, damage, mar, mutilate, blemish, deface

scarce 1 = <u>in short supply</u>, insufficient ≠ plentiful 2 = <u>rare</u>, few, uncommon, few and far between, infrequent ≠ common

scarcely 1 = <u>hardly</u>, barely 2 (*Often used ironically*) = <u>by no means</u>, hardly, definitely not

scare VERB = <u>frighten</u>, alarm, terrify, panic, shock, startle, intimidate, dismay

● NOUN 1 = <u>fright</u>, shock, start 2 = <u>panic</u>, hysteria 3 = <u>alert</u>, warning, alarm

scared = <u>afraid</u>, alarmed, frightened, terrified, shaken, startled, fearful, petrified

scary (*Informal*) = <u>frightening</u>, alarming, terrifying, chilling, horrifying, spooky (*informal*), creepy (*informal*), spine-chilling

scatter 1 = <u>throw about</u>, spread, sprinkle, strew, shower, fling, diffuse, disseminate ≠ gather 2 = <u>disperse</u>, dispel, disband, dissipate ≠ assemble

scenario 1 = <u>situation</u> 2 = <u>story line</u>, résumé, outline, summary, synopsis

scene 1 = <u>act</u>, part, division, episode 2 = <u>setting</u>, set, background, location, backdrop 3 = <u>site</u>, place, setting, area, position, spot, locality 4 (*Informal*) = <u>world</u>, business, environment, arena 5 = <u>view</u>, prospect, panorama, vista, landscape, outlook 6 = <u>fuss</u>, to-do, row, performance, exhibition, carry-on (*informal, chiefly Brit.*), tantrum, commotion

scenery 1 = <u>landscape</u>, view, surroundings, terrain, vista 2 (*Theatre*) = <u>set</u>, setting, backdrop, flats, stage set

scenic = picturesque, beautiful, spectacular, striking, panoramic

scent NOUN **1** = fragrance, smell, perfume, bouquet, aroma, odour **2** = trail, track, spoor

● VERB = smell, sense, detect, sniff, discern, nose out

scented = fragrant, perfumed, aromatic, sweet-smelling, odoriferous

sceptic 1 = doubter, cynic, disbeliever **2** = agnostic, doubter, unbeliever, doubting Thomas

sceptical = doubtful, cynical, dubious, unconvinced, disbelieving, incredulous, mistrustful ≠ convinced

scepticism = doubt, suspicion, disbelief, cynicism, incredulity

schedule NOUN **1** = plan, programme, agenda, calendar, timetable

● VERB = plan, set up, book, programme, arrange, organize

scheme NOUN **1** = plan, programme, strategy, system, project, proposal, tactics **2** = plot, ploy, ruse, intrigue, conspiracy, manoeuvre, subterfuge, stratagem

● VERB = plot, plan, intrigue, manoeuvre, conspire, contrive, collude, machinate

scheming = calculating, cunning, sly, tricky, wily, artful, conniving, underhand ≠ straightforward

scholar 1 = intellectual, academic, savant, acca (*Austral. slang*) **2** = student, pupil, learner, schoolboy *or* schoolgirl

scholarly = learned, academic, intellectual, lettered, erudite, scholastic, bookish ≠ uneducated

scholarship 1 = grant, award, payment, endowment, fellowship, bursary **2** = learning, education, knowledge, erudition, book-learning

school NOUN **1** = academy, college, institution, institute, seminary **2** = group, set, circle, faction, followers, disciples, devotees, denomination

● VERB = train, coach, discipline, educate, drill, tutor, instruct

science = discipline, body of knowledge, branch of knowledge

scientific = systematic, accurate, exact, precise, controlled, mathematical

scientist = researcher, inventor, boffin (*informal*), technophile

scoff¹ = scorn, mock, laugh at, ridicule, knock (*informal*), despise, sneer, jeer

scoff² = gobble (up), wolf, devour, bolt, guzzle, gulp down, gorge yourself on

scoop VERB **1** = win, get, land, gain, achieve, earn, secure, obtain

● NOUN **1** = ladle, spoon, dipper **2** = exclusive, exposé, revelation, sensation

● PHRASES **scoop something** or **someone up** = gather up, lift, pick up, take up, sweep up *or* away ◆ **scoop something out 1** = take out, empty, spoon out, bail *or* bale out **2** = dig, shovel, excavate, gouge, hollow out

scope 1 = opportunity, room, freedom, space, liberty, latitude **2** = range, capacity, reach, area, outlook, orbit, span, sphere

scorch = burn, sear, roast, wither, shrivel, parch, singe

scorching = burning, boiling, baking, flaming, roasting, searing, fiery, red-hot

score VERB **1** = gain, win, achieve, make, get, attain, notch up (*informal*), chalk up (*informal*) **2** (*Music*) = arrange, set, orchestrate, adapt **3** = cut, scratch, mark, slash, scrape, graze, gouge, deface

● NOUN **1** = rating, mark, grade, percentage **2** = points, result, total, outcome **3** = composition, soundtrack, arrangement, orchestration **4** = grievance, wrong, injury, injustice, grudge

● PLURAL NOUN = lots, loads, many, millions, hundreds, masses, swarms, multitudes

● PHRASES **score something out** or **through** = cross out, delete, strike out, cancel, obliterate

scorn NOUN = contempt, disdain, mockery, derision, sarcasm, disparagement ≠ respect

● VERB = despise, reject, disdain, slight, be above, spurn, deride, flout ≠ respect

scour¹ = scrub, clean, polish, rub, buff, abrade

scour² = search, hunt, comb, ransack

scout NOUN = vanguard, lookout, precursor, outrider, reconnoitrer, advance guard

● VERB = reconnoitre, investigate, watch, survey, observe, spy, probe, recce (*slang*)

scramble VERB **1** = struggle, climb, crawl, swarm, scrabble **2** = strive, rush, contend, vie, run, push, jostle **3** = jumble, mix up, muddle, shuffle

● NOUN **1** = clamber, ascent **2** = race, competition, struggle, rush, confusion, commotion, melee *or* mêlée

scrap¹ NOUN 1 = <u>piece</u>, fragment, bit, grain, particle, portion, part, crumb 2 = <u>waste</u>, junk, off cuts
● PLURAL NOUN = <u>leftovers</u>, remains, bits, leavings
● VERB = <u>get rid of</u>, drop, abandon, ditch (*slang*), discard, write off, jettison, throw away *or* out ≠ bring back
scrap² (*Informal*) NOUN = <u>fight</u>, battle, row, argument, dispute, disagreement, quarrel, squabble, biffo (*Austral. slang*)
● VERB = <u>fight</u>, argue, row, squabble, wrangle
scrape VERB 1 = <u>rake</u>, sweep, drag, brush 2 = <u>grate</u>, grind, scratch, squeak, rasp 3 = <u>graze</u>, skin, scratch, bark, scuff, rub 4 = <u>clean</u>, remove, scour
● NOUN (*Informal*) = <u>predicament</u>, difficulty, fix (*informal*), mess, dilemma, plight, tight spot, awkward situation
scratch VERB 1 = <u>rub</u>, scrape, claw at 2 = <u>mark</u>, cut, score, damage, grate, graze, etch, lacerate
● NOUN = <u>mark</u>, scrape, graze, blemish, gash, laceration, claw mark
● PHRASES **up to scratch** (*Informal*) = <u>adequate</u>, acceptable, satisfactory, sufficient, up to standard
scream VERB = <u>cry</u>, yell, shriek, screech, bawl, howl
● NOUN = <u>cry</u>, yell, howl, shriek, screech, yelp
screen NOUN = <u>cover</u>, guard, shade, shelter, shield, partition, cloak, canopy
● VERB 1 = <u>broadcast</u>, show, put on, present, air, cable, beam, transmit 2 = <u>cover</u>, hide, conceal, shade, mask, veil, cloak 3 = <u>investigate</u>, test, check, examine, scan 4 = <u>process</u>, sort, examine, filter, scan, evaluate, gauge, sift 5 = <u>protect</u>, guard, shield, defend, shelter
screw NOUN = <u>nail</u>, pin, tack, rivet, fastener, spike
● VERB 1 = <u>fasten</u>, fix, attach, bolt, clamp, rivet 2 = <u>turn</u>, twist, tighten 3 (*Informal*) = <u>cheat</u>, do (*slang*), rip (someone) off (*slang*), skin (*slang*), trick, con, sting (*informal*), fleece 4 (*Informal*) *often with* **out of** = <u>squeeze</u>, wring, extract, wrest
● PHRASES **screw something up** 1 = <u>contort</u>, wrinkle, distort, pucker 2 (*Informal*) = <u>bungle</u>, botch, mess up, spoil, mishandle, make a mess of (*slang*), make a hash of (*informal*), crool *or* cruel

(*Austral. slang*)
scribble = <u>scrawl</u>, write, jot, dash off
script NOUN 1 = <u>text</u>, lines, words, book, copy, dialogue, libretto 2 = <u>handwriting</u>, writing, calligraphy, penmanship
● VERB = <u>write</u>, draft
scripture = <u>The Bible</u>, The Gospels, The Scriptures, The Good Book, Holy Scripture, Holy Writ, Holy Bible
scrub 1 = <u>scour</u>, clean, polish, rub, wash, cleanse, buff 2 (*Informal*) = <u>cancel</u>, drop, give up, abolish, forget about, call off, delete
scrutiny = <u>examination</u>, study, investigation, search, analysis, inspection, exploration, perusal
sculpture NOUN = <u>statue</u>, figure, model, bust, effigy, figurine, statuette
● VERB = <u>carve</u>, form, model, fashion, shape, mould, sculpt, chisel
sea NOUN 1 = <u>ocean</u>, the deep, the waves, main 2 = <u>mass</u>, army, host, crowd, mob, abundance, swarm, horde
● PHRASES **at sea** = <u>bewildered</u>, lost, confused, puzzled, baffled, perplexed, mystified, flummoxed
◼ RELATED WORDS
adjectives: marine, maritime
seal VERB = <u>settle</u>, clinch, conclude, consummate, finalize
● NOUN 1 = <u>sealant</u>, sealer, adhesive 2 = <u>authentication</u>, stamp, confirmation, ratification, insignia, imprimatur
seam 1 = <u>joint</u>, closure 2 = <u>layer</u>, vein, stratum, lode
sear = <u>wither</u>, burn, scorch, sizzle
search VERB = <u>examine</u>, investigate, explore, inspect, comb, scour, ransack, scrutinize, fossick (*Austral. & N.Z.*)
● NOUN = <u>hunt</u>, look, investigation, examination, pursuit, quest, inspection, exploration
● PHRASES **search for something** *or* **someone** = <u>look for</u>, hunt for, pursue
searching = <u>keen</u>, sharp, probing, close, intent, piercing, penetrating, quizzical ≠ superficial
searing 1 = <u>acute</u>, intense, shooting, severe, painful, stabbing, piercing, gut-wrenching 2 = <u>cutting</u>, biting, bitter, harsh, barbed, hurtful, caustic
season NOUN = <u>period</u>, time, term, spell
● VERB = <u>flavour</u>, salt, spice, enliven, pep up

seasoned = <u>experienced</u>, veteran, practised, hardened, time-served ≠ inexperienced

seasoning = <u>flavouring</u>, spice, salt and pepper, condiment

seat NOUN 1 = <u>chair</u>, bench, stall, stool, pew, settle 2 = <u>membership</u>, place, constituency, chair, incumbency 3 = <u>centre</u>, place, site, heart, capital, situation, source, hub 4 = <u>mansion</u>, house, residence, abode, ancestral hall

● VERB 1 = <u>sit</u>, place, settle, set, fix, locate, install 2 = <u>hold</u>, take, accommodate, sit, contain, cater for

second¹ ADJECTIVE 1 = <u>next</u>, following, succeeding, subsequent 2 = <u>additional</u>, other, further, extra, alternative 3 = <u>inferior</u>, secondary, subordinate, lower, lesser

● NOUN = <u>supporter</u>, assistant, aide, colleague, backer, helper, right-hand man

● VERB = <u>support</u>, back, endorse, approve, go along with

second² = <u>moment</u>, minute, instant, flash, sec (*informal*), jiffy (*informal*), trice

secondary 1 = <u>subordinate</u>, minor, lesser, lower, inferior, unimportant ≠ main 2 = <u>resultant</u>, contingent, derived, indirect ≠ original

second-hand = <u>used</u>, old, hand-me-down (*informal*), nearly new

secondly = <u>next</u>, second, moreover, furthermore, also, in the second place

secrecy 1 = <u>mystery</u>, stealth, concealment, furtiveness, secretiveness, clandestineness, covertness 2 = <u>confidentiality</u>, privacy 3 = <u>privacy</u>, silence, seclusion

secret ADJECTIVE 1 = <u>undisclosed</u>, unknown, confidential, underground, undercover, unrevealed 2 = <u>concealed</u>, hidden, disguised ≠ unconcealed 3 = <u>undercover</u>, furtive ≠ open 4 = <u>secretive</u>, reserved, close ≠ frank 5 = <u>mysterious</u>, cryptic, abstruse, occult, clandestine, arcane ≠ straightforward

● NOUN = <u>private affair</u>

● PHRASES **in secret** = <u>secretly</u>, surreptitiously, slyly

secretive = <u>reticent</u>, reserved, close, deep, uncommunicative, tight-lipped ≠ open

secretly = <u>in secret</u>, privately, surreptitiously, quietly, covertly, furtively, stealthily, clandestinely

sect = <u>group</u>, division, faction, party, camp, denomination, schism

section 1 = <u>part</u>, piece, portion, division, slice, passage, segment, fraction 2 = <u>district</u>, area, region, sector, zone

sector 1 = <u>part</u>, division 2 = <u>area</u>, part, region, district, zone, quarter

secular = <u>worldly</u>, lay, earthly, civil, temporal, nonspiritual ≠ religious

secure VERB 1 = <u>obtain</u>, get, acquire, score (*slang*), gain, procure ≠ lose 2 = <u>attach</u>, stick, fix, bind, fasten ≠ detach

● ADJECTIVE 1 = <u>safe</u>, protected, immune, unassailable ≠ unprotected 2 = <u>fast</u>, firm, fixed, stable, steady, fastened, immovable ≠ insecure 3 = <u>confident</u>, sure, easy, certain, assured, reassured ≠ uneasy

security 1 = <u>precautions</u>, defence, safeguards, protection, safety measures 2 = <u>assurance</u>, confidence, conviction, certainty, reliance, sureness, positiveness ≠ insecurity 3 = <u>pledge</u>, insurance, guarantee, hostage, collateral, pawn, gage, surety 4 = <u>protection</u>, safety, custody, refuge, sanctuary, safekeeping ≠ vulnerability

sediment = <u>dregs</u>, grounds, residue, lees, deposit

seduce 1 = <u>tempt</u>, lure, entice, mislead, deceive, beguile, lead astray, inveigle 2 = <u>corrupt</u>, deprave, dishonour, debauch, deflower

seductive = <u>tempting</u>, inviting, attractive, enticing, provocative, alluring, bewitching

see VERB 1 = <u>perceive</u>, spot, notice, sight, witness, observe, distinguish, glimpse 2 = <u>understand</u>, get, follow, realize, appreciate, grasp, comprehend, fathom 3 = <u>find out</u>, learn, discover, determine, verify, ascertain 4 = <u>consider</u>, decide, reflect, deliberate, think over 5 = <u>make sure</u>, ensure, guarantee, make certain, see to it 6 = <u>accompany</u>, show, escort, lead, walk, usher 7 = <u>speak to</u>, receive, interview, consult, confer with 8 = <u>meet</u>, come across, happen on, bump into, run across, chance on 9 = <u>go out with</u>, court, date (*informal*, *chiefly U.S.*), go steady with (*informal*)

● PHRASES **seeing as** = <u>since</u>, as, in view of the fact that, inasmuch as

seed NOUN 1 = <u>grain</u>, pip, germ, kernel, egg, embryo, spore, ovum 2 = <u>beginning</u>, start, germ 3 = <u>origin</u>, source, nucleus 4 (*Chiefly Bible*) = <u>offspring</u>, children, descendants, issue, progeny

● PHRASES **go** or **run to seed** = <u>decline</u>, deteriorate, degenerate, decay, go downhill (*informal*), let yourself go, go to pot

seek 1 = <u>look for</u>, pursue, search for, be after, hunt 2 = <u>try</u>, attempt, aim, strive, endeavour, essay, aspire to

seem = <u>appear</u>, give the impression of being, look

seep = <u>ooze</u>, well, leak, soak, trickle, exude, permeate

seethe 1 = <u>be furious</u>, rage, fume, simmer, see red (*informal*), be livid, go ballistic (*slang, chiefly U.S.*) 2 = <u>boil</u>, bubble, foam, fizz, froth

segment = <u>section</u>, part, piece, division, slice, portion, wedge

segregate = <u>set apart</u>, divide, separate, isolate, discriminate against, dissociate ≠ unite

segregation = <u>separation</u>, discrimination, apartheid, isolation

seize 1 = <u>grab</u>, grip, grasp, take, snatch, clutch, snap up, pluck ≠ let go 2 = <u>take by storm</u>, take over, acquire, occupy, conquer 3 = <u>capture</u>, catch, arrest, apprehend, take captive ≠ release

seizure 1 = <u>attack</u>, fit, spasm, convulsion, paroxysm 2 = <u>taking</u>, grabbing, annexation, confiscation, commandeering 3 = <u>capture</u>, arrest, apprehension

seldom = <u>rarely</u>, not often, infrequently, hardly ever ≠ often

select VERB 1 = <u>choose</u>, take, pick, opt for, decide on, single out, adopt, settle upon ≠ reject

● ADJECTIVE 1 = <u>choice</u>, special, excellent, superior, first-class, hand-picked, top-notch (*informal*) ≠ ordinary 2 = <u>exclusive</u>, elite, privileged, cliquish ≠ indiscriminate

selection 1 = <u>choice</u>, choosing, pick, option, preference 2 = <u>anthology</u>, collection, medley, choice

selective = <u>particular</u>, discriminating, careful, discerning, tasteful, fastidious ≠ indiscriminate

selfish = <u>self-centred</u>, self-interested, greedy, ungenerous, egoistic or egoistical, egotistic or egoistical ≠ unselfish

sell VERB 1 = <u>trade</u>, exchange, barter ≠ buy 2 = <u>deal in</u>, market, trade in, stock, handle, retail, peddle, traffic in ≠ buy

● PHRASES **sell out of something** = <u>run</u> out of, be out of stock of

seller = <u>dealer</u>, merchant, vendor, agent, retailer, supplier, purveyor, salesman or saleswoman

send VERB 1 = <u>dispatch</u>, forward, direct, convey, remit 2 = <u>propel</u>, hurl, fling, shoot, fire, cast, let fly

● PHRASES **send something** or **someone up** (*Brit. informal*) = <u>mock</u>, mimic, parody, spoof (*informal*), imitate, take off (*informal*), make fun of, lampoon

send-off = <u>farewell</u>, departure, leave-taking, valediction

senior 1 = <u>higher ranking</u>, superior ≠ subordinate 2 = <u>the elder</u>, major (*Brit.*) ≠ junior

sensation 1 = <u>feeling</u>, sense, impression, perception, awareness, consciousness 2 = <u>excitement</u>, thrill, stir, furore, commotion

sensational 1 = <u>amazing</u>, dramatic, thrilling, astounding ≠ dull 2 = <u>shocking</u>, exciting, melodramatic, shock-horror (*facetious*) ≠ unexciting 3 (*Informal*) = <u>excellent</u>, superb, mean (*slang*), impressive, smashing (*informal*), fabulous (*informal*), marvellous, out of this world (*informal*), booshit (*Austral. slang*), exo (*Austral. slang*), sik (*Austral. slang*) ≠ ordinary

sense NOUN 1 = <u>faculty</u> 2 = <u>feeling</u>, impression, perception, awareness, consciousness, atmosphere, aura 3 = <u>understanding</u>, awareness 4 *sometimes plural* = <u>intelligence</u>, reason, understanding, brains (*informal*), judgment, wisdom, wit(s), common sense ≠ foolishness 5 = <u>meaning</u>, significance, import, implication, drift, gist

● VERB = <u>perceive</u>, feel, understand, pick up, realize, be aware of, discern, get the impression ≠ be unaware of

sensibility *often plural* = <u>feelings</u>, emotions, sentiments, susceptibilities, moral sense

sensible 1 = <u>wise</u>, practical, prudent, shrewd, judicious ≠ foolish 2 = <u>intelligent</u>, practical, rational, sound, realistic, sage, shrewd, down-to-earth ≠ senseless

sensitive 1 = <u>thoughtful</u>, kindly, concerned, patient, attentive, tactful, unselfish 2 = <u>delicate</u>, tender 3 = <u>susceptible to</u>, responsive to, easily affected by 4 = <u>touchy</u>, oversensitive,

easily upset, easily offended, easily hurt
≠ insensitive 5 = <u>precise</u>, fine, acute, keen,
responsive ≠ imprecise

sensitivity 1 = <u>susceptibility</u>,
responsiveness, receptiveness,
sensitiveness 2 = <u>consideration</u>,
patience, thoughtfulness 3 = <u>touchiness</u>,
oversensitivity 4 = <u>responsiveness</u>,
precision, keenness, acuteness

sensual 1 = <u>sexual</u>, erotic, raunchy
(*slang*), lewd, lascivious, lustful, lecherous
2 = <u>physical</u>, bodily, voluptuous, animal,
luxurious, fleshly, carnal

sentence NOUN 1 = <u>punishment</u>,
condemnation 2 = <u>verdict</u>, order, ruling,
decision, judgment, decree
● VERB 1 = <u>condemn</u>, doom 2 = <u>convict</u>,
condemn, penalize

sentiment 1 = <u>feeling</u>, idea, view,
opinion, attitude, belief, judgment
2 = <u>sentimentality</u>, emotion, tenderness,
romanticism, sensibility, emotionalism,
mawkishness

sentimental = <u>romantic</u>, touching,
emotional, nostalgic, maudlin, weepy
(*informal*), slushy (*informal*), schmaltzy
(*slang*) ≠ unsentimental

separate ADJECTIVE 1 = <u>unconnected</u>,
individual, particular, divided, divorced,
isolated, detached, disconnected
≠ connected 2 = <u>individual</u>, independent,
apart, distinct ≠ joined
● VERB 1 = <u>divide</u>, detach, disconnect,
disjoin ≠ combine 2 = <u>come apart</u>, split,
come away ≠ connect 3 = <u>sever</u>, break
apart, split in two, divide in two ≠ join
4 = <u>split up</u>, part, divorce, break up, part
company, get divorced, be estranged
5 = <u>distinguish</u>, mark, single out, set apart
≠ link

separated 1 = <u>estranged</u>,
parted, separate, apart, disunited
2 = <u>disconnected</u>, parted, divided,
separate, disassociated, disunited,
sundered

separately 1 = <u>alone</u>, apart, not together,
severally ≠ together 2 = <u>individually</u>,
singly

separation 1 = <u>division</u>, break,
dissociation, disconnection, disunion
2 = <u>split-up</u>, parting, split, divorce, break-
up, rift

sequel 1 = <u>follow-up</u>, continuation,
development 2 = <u>consequence</u>, result,

outcome, conclusion, end, upshot

sequence = <u>succession</u>, course,
series, order, chain, cycle, arrangement,
progression

series 1 = <u>sequence</u>, course, chain,
succession, run, set, order, train 2 = <u>drama</u>,
serial, soap (*informal*), sitcom (*informal*),
soap opera, soapie (*Austral. slang*),
situation comedy

serious 1 = <u>grave</u>, bad, critical, dangerous,
acute, severe 2 = <u>important</u>, crucial,
urgent, pressing, worrying, significant,
grim, momentous ≠ unimportant
3 = <u>thoughtful</u>, detailed, careful,
deep, profound, in-depth 4 = <u>deep</u>,
sophisticated 5 = <u>solemn</u>, earnest, grave,
sober, staid, humourless, unsmiling
≠ light-hearted 6 = <u>sincere</u>, earnest,
genuine, honest, in earnest ≠ insincere

seriously 1 = <u>truly</u>, in earnest, all joking
aside 2 = <u>badly</u>, severely, gravely, critically,
acutely, dangerously

seriousness 1 = <u>importance</u>, gravity,
urgency, significance 2 = <u>solemnity</u>,
gravity, earnestness, gravitas

sermon = <u>homily</u>, address

servant = <u>attendant</u>, domestic, slave,
maid, help, retainer, skivvy (*chiefly Brit.*)

serve 1 = <u>work for</u>, help, aid, assist, be in
the service of 2 = <u>perform</u>, do, complete,
fulfil, discharge 3 = <u>be adequate</u>, do,
suffice, suit, satisfy, be acceptable, answer
the purpose 4 = <u>present</u>, provide, supply,
deliver, set out, dish up

service NOUN 1 = <u>facility</u>, system, resource,
utility, amenity 2 = <u>ceremony</u>, worship,
rite, observance 3 = <u>work</u>, labour,
employment, business, office, duty
4 = <u>check</u>, maintenance check
● VERB = <u>overhaul</u>, check, maintain, tune
(up), go over, fine tune

session = <u>meeting</u>, hearing, sitting,
period, conference, congress, discussion,
assembly

set¹ VERB 1 = <u>put</u>, place, lay, position, rest,
plant, station, stick 2 = <u>arrange</u>, decide
(upon), settle, establish, determine, fix,
schedule, appoint 3 = <u>assign</u>, give, allot,
prescribe 4 = <u>harden</u>, stiffen, solidify,
cake, thicken, crystallize, congeal 5 = <u>go
down</u>, sink, dip, decline, disappear, vanish,
subside 6 = <u>prepare</u>, lay, spread, arrange,
make ready
● ADJECTIVE 1 = <u>established</u>, planned,

decided, agreed, arranged, rigid, definite, inflexible **2** = <u>strict</u>, rigid, stubborn, inflexible ≠ flexible **3** = <u>conventional</u>, traditional, stereotyped, unspontaneous
● NOUN **1** = <u>scenery</u>, setting, scene, stage set **2** = <u>position</u>, bearing, attitude, carriage, posture
● PHRASES **be set on** or **upon something** = <u>be determined to</u>, be intent on, be bent on, be resolute about ◆ **set something up 1** = <u>arrange</u>, organize, prepare, prearrange **2** = <u>establish</u>, begin, found, institute, initiate **3** = <u>build</u>, raise, construct, put up, assemble, put together, erect **4** = <u>assemble</u>, put up

set² 1 = <u>series</u>, collection, assortment, batch, compendium, ensemble **2** = <u>group</u>, company, crowd, circle, band, gang, faction, clique

setback = <u>hold-up</u>, check, defeat, blow, reverse, disappointment, hitch, misfortune

setting = <u>surroundings</u>, site, location, set, scene, background, context, backdrop

settle 1 = <u>resolve</u>, work out, put an end to, straighten out **2** = <u>pay</u>, clear, square (up), discharge **3** = <u>move to</u>, take up residence in, live in, dwell in, inhabit, reside in, set up home in, put down roots in **4** = <u>colonize</u>, populate, people, pioneer **5** = <u>land</u>, alight, descend, light, come to rest **6** = <u>calm</u>, quiet, relax, relieve, reassure, soothe, lull, quell ≠ disturb

settlement 1 = <u>agreement</u>, arrangement, working out, conclusion, establishment, confirmation **2** = <u>payment</u>, clearing, discharge **3** = <u>colony</u>, community, outpost, encampment, kainga or kaika (N.Z.)

settler = <u>colonist</u>, immigrant, pioneer, frontiersman

set-up (Informal) = <u>arrangement</u>, system, structure, organization, conditions, regime

sever 1 = <u>cut</u>, separate, split, part, divide, detach, disconnect, cut in two ≠ join **2** = <u>discontinue</u>, terminate, break off, put an end to, dissociate ≠ continue

several ADJECTIVE = <u>some</u>, a few, a number of, a handful of
● PRONOUN = <u>various</u>, different, diverse, sundry

severe 1 = <u>serious</u>, critical, terrible, desperate, extreme, awful, drastic, catastrophic **2** = <u>acute</u>, intense, violent, piercing, harrowing, unbearable, agonizing, insufferable **3** = <u>strict</u>, hard,

harsh, cruel, rigid, drastic, oppressive, austere ≠ lenient **4** = <u>grim</u>, serious, grave, forbidding, stern, unsmiling, tight-lipped ≠ genial **5** = <u>plain</u>, simple, austere, classic, restrained, Spartan, unadorned, unfussy ≠ fancy

severely 1 = <u>seriously</u>, badly, extremely, gravely, acutely **2** = <u>strictly</u>, harshly, sternly, sharply

severity = <u>strictness</u>, harshness, toughness, hardness, sternness, severeness

sew = <u>stitch</u>, tack, seam, hem

sex 1 = <u>gender</u> **2** (Informal) = <u>lovemaking</u>, sexual relations, copulation, fornication, coitus, coition

sexual 1 = <u>carnal</u>, erotic, intimate **2** = <u>sexy</u>, erotic, sensual, arousing, naughty, provocative, seductive, sensuous

sexuality = <u>desire</u>, lust, eroticism, sensuality, sexiness (informal), carnality

sexy = <u>erotic</u>, sensual, seductive, arousing, naughty, provocative, sensuous, suggestive

shabby 1 = <u>tatty</u>, worn, ragged, scruffy, tattered, threadbare ≠ smart **2** = <u>run-down</u>, seedy, mean, dilapidated **3** = <u>mean</u>, low, rotten (informal), cheap, dirty, despicable, contemptible, scurvy ≠ fair

shack = <u>hut</u>, cabin, shanty, whare (N.Z.)

shade NOUN **1** = <u>hue</u>, tone, colour, tint **2** = <u>shadow</u> **3** = <u>dash</u>, trace, hint, suggestion **4** = <u>nuance</u>, difference, degree **5** = <u>screen</u>, covering, cover, blind, curtain, shield, veil, canopy **6** (Literary) = <u>ghost</u>, spirit, phantom, spectre, apparition, kehua (N.Z.)
● VERB **1** = <u>darken</u>, shadow, cloud, dim **2** = <u>cover</u>, protect, screen, hide, shield, conceal, obscure, veil

shadow NOUN **1** = <u>silhouette</u>, shape, outline, profile **2** = <u>shade</u>, dimness, darkness, gloom, cover, dusk
● VERB **1** = shade, screen, shield, darken, overhang **2** = <u>follow</u>, tail (informal), trail, stalk

shady 1 = <u>shaded</u>, cool, dim ≠ sunny **2** (Informal) = <u>crooked</u>, dodgy (Brit., Austral., & N.Z. informal), unethical, suspect, suspicious, dubious, questionable, shifty ≠ honest

shaft 1 = <u>tunnel</u>, hole, passage, burrow, passageway, channel **2** = <u>handle</u>, staff, pole, rod, stem, baton, shank **3** = <u>ray</u>, beam, gleam

shake VERB 1 = <u>jiggle</u>, agitate 2 = <u>tremble</u>, shiver, quake, quiver 3 = <u>rock</u>, totter 4 = <u>wave</u>, wield, flourish, brandish 5 = <u>upset</u>, shock, frighten, disturb, distress, rattle (*informal*), unnerve, traumatize
● NOUN = <u>vibration</u>, trembling, quaking, jerk, shiver, shudder, jolt, tremor

shaky 1 = <u>unstable</u>, weak, precarious, rickety ≠ stable 2 = <u>unsteady</u>, faint, trembling, faltering, quivery 3 = <u>uncertain</u>, suspect, dubious, questionable, iffy (*informal*) ≠ reliable

shallow = <u>superficial</u>, surface, empty, slight, foolish, trivial, meaningless, frivolous ≠ deep

sham NOUN = <u>fraud</u>, imitation, hoax, pretence, forgery, counterfeit, humbug, impostor ≠ the real thing
● ADJECTIVE = <u>false</u>, artificial, bogus, pretended, mock, imitation, simulated, counterfeit ≠ real

shambles 1 = <u>chaos</u>, mess, disorder, confusion, muddle, havoc, disarray, madhouse 2 = <u>mess</u>, jumble, untidiness

shame NOUN 1 = <u>embarrassment</u>, humiliation, ignominy, mortification, abashment ≠ shamelessness 2 = <u>disgrace</u>, scandal, discredit, smear, disrepute, reproach, dishonour, infamy ≠ honour
● VERB 1 = <u>embarrass</u>, disgrace, humiliate, humble, mortify, abash ≠ make proud 2 = <u>dishonour</u>, degrade, stain, smear, blot, debase, defile ≠ honour

shameful = <u>disgraceful</u>, outrageous, scandalous, mean, low, base, wicked, dishonourable ≠ admirable

shape NOUN 1 = <u>appearance</u>, form, aspect, guise, likeness, semblance 2 = <u>form</u>, profile, outline, lines, build, figure, silhouette, configuration 3 = <u>pattern</u>, model, frame, mould 4 = <u>condition</u>, state, health, trim, fettle
● VERB 1 = <u>form</u>, make, produce, create, model, fashion, mould 2 = <u>mould</u>, form, make, fashion, model, frame

share NOUN = <u>part</u>, portion, quota, ration, lot, due, contribution, allowance
● VERB 1 = <u>divide</u>, split, distribute, assign 2 = <u>go halves on</u>, go fifty-fifty on (*informal*)

sharp ADJECTIVE 1 = <u>keen</u>, jagged, serrated ≠ blunt 2 = <u>quick-witted</u>, clever, astute, knowing, quick, bright, alert,

penetrating ≠ dim 3 = <u>cutting</u>, biting, bitter, harsh, barbed, hurtful, caustic ≠ gentle 4 = <u>sudden</u>, marked, abrupt, extreme, distinct ≠ gradual 5 = <u>clear</u>, distinct, well-defined, crisp ≠ indistinct 6 = <u>sour</u>, tart, pungent, hot, acid, acrid, piquant ≠ bland 7 = <u>acute</u>, severe, intense, painful, shooting, stabbing, piercing, gut-wrenching
● ADVERB = <u>promptly</u>, precisely, exactly, on time, on the dot, punctually ≠ approximately

sharpen = <u>make sharp</u>, hone, whet, grind, edge

shatter 1 = <u>smash</u>, break, burst, crack, crush, pulverize 2 = <u>destroy</u>, ruin, wreck, demolish, torpedo

shattered 1 = <u>devastated</u>, crushed, gutted (*slang*) 2 (*informal*) = <u>exhausted</u>, drained, worn out, done in (*informal*), all in (*slang*), knackered (*slang*), tired out, ready to drop

shave 1 = <u>trim</u>, crop 2 = <u>scrape</u>, trim, shear, pare

shed[1] = <u>hut</u>, shack, outhouse, whare (*N.Z.*)

shed[2] 1 = <u>drop</u>, spill, scatter 2 = <u>cast off</u>, discard, moult, slough off 3 = <u>give out</u>, cast, emit, give, radiate

sheen = <u>shine</u>, gleam, gloss, polish, brightness, lustre

sheer 1 = <u>total</u>, complete, absolute, utter, pure, downright, out-and-out, unmitigated ≠ moderate 2 = <u>steep</u>, abrupt, precipitous ≠ gradual 3 = <u>fine</u>, thin, transparent, see-through, gossamer, diaphanous, gauzy ≠ thick

sheet 1 = <u>page</u>, leaf, folio, piece of paper 2 = <u>plate</u>, piece, panel, slab 3 = <u>coat</u>, film, layer, surface, stratum, veneer, overlay, lamina 4 = <u>expanse</u>, area, stretch, sweep, covering, blanket

shell NOUN 1 = <u>husk</u>, case, pod 2 = <u>carapace</u> 3 = <u>frame</u>, structure, hull, framework, chassis
● VERB = <u>bomb</u>, bombard, attack, blitz, strafe
● PHRASES **shell something out** (with money or a specified sum of money as object) = <u>pay out</u>, fork out (*slang*), give, hand over

shelter NOUN 1 = <u>cover</u>, screen 2 = <u>protection</u>, safety, refuge, cover 3 = <u>refuge</u>, haven, sanctuary, retreat, asylum

- **VERB** 1 = <u>take shelter</u>, hide, seek refuge, take cover 2 = <u>protect</u>, shield, harbour, safeguard, cover, hide, guard, defend ≠ endanger

sheltered 1 = <u>screened</u>, covered, protected, shielded, secluded ≠ exposed 2 = <u>protected</u>, screened, shielded, quiet, isolated, secluded, cloistered

shelve = <u>postpone</u>, defer, freeze, suspend, put aside, put on ice, put on the back burner (*informal*), take a rain check on (*U.S. & Canad. informal*)

shepherd NOUN = <u>drover</u>, stockman, herdsman, grazier

- **VERB** = <u>guide</u>, conduct, steer, herd, usher

▬▬ RELATED WORD

adjective: pastoral

shield NOUN = <u>protection</u>, cover, defence, screen, guard, shelter, safeguard

- **VERB** = <u>protect</u>, cover, screen, guard, defend, shelter, safeguard

shift VERB 1 = <u>move</u>, move around, budge 2 = <u>remove</u>, move, displace, relocate, rearrange, reposition

- **NOUN** 1 = <u>change</u>, shifting, displacement 2 = <u>move</u>, rearrangement

shimmer VERB = <u>gleam</u>, twinkle, glisten, scintillate

- **NOUN** = <u>gleam</u>, iridescence

shine VERB 1 = <u>gleam</u>, flash, beam, glow, sparkle, glitter, glare, radiate 2 = <u>polish</u>, buff, burnish, brush 3 = <u>be outstanding</u>, stand out, excel, be conspicuous

- **NOUN** 1 = <u>polish</u>, gloss, sheen, lustre 2 = <u>brightness</u>, light, sparkle, radiance

shining = <u>bright</u>, brilliant, gleaming, beaming, sparkling, shimmering, radiant, luminous

shiny = <u>bright</u>, gleaming, glossy, glistening, polished, lustrous

ship = <u>vessel</u>, boat, craft

shiver VERB = <u>shudder</u>, shake, tremble, quake, quiver

- **NOUN** = <u>tremble</u>, shudder, quiver, trembling, flutter, tremor

shock NOUN 1 = <u>upset</u>, blow, trauma, bombshell, turn (*informal*), distress, disturbance 2 = <u>impact</u>, blow, clash, collision 3 = <u>start</u>, scare, fright, turn, jolt

- **VERB** 1 = <u>shake</u>, stun, stagger, jolt, stupefy 2 = <u>horrify</u>, appal, disgust, revolt, sicken, nauseate, scandalize

shocking 1 (*Informal*) = <u>terrible</u>, appalling, dreadful, bad, horrendous,

ghastly, deplorable, abysmal 2 = <u>appalling</u>, outrageous, disgraceful, disgusting, dreadful, horrifying, revolting, sickening ≠ wonderful

shoot VERB 1 = <u>open fire on</u>, blast (*slang*), hit, kill, plug (*slang*), bring down 2 = <u>fire</u>, launch, discharge, project, hurl, fling, propel, emit 3 = <u>speed</u>, race, rush, charge, fly, tear, dash, barrel (along) (*informal, chiefly U.S. & Canad.*)

- **NOUN** = <u>sprout</u>, branch, bud, sprig, offshoot

shop = <u>store</u>, supermarket, boutique, emporium, hypermarket, dairy (*N.Z.*)

shore = <u>beach</u>, coast, sands, strand (*poetic*), seashore

short ADJECTIVE 1 = <u>brief</u>, fleeting, momentary ≠ long 2 = <u>concise</u>, brief, succinct, summary, compressed, terse, laconic, pithy ≠ lengthy 3 = <u>small</u>, little, squat, diminutive, petite, dumpy ≠ tall 4 = <u>abrupt</u>, sharp, terse, curt, brusque, impolite, discourteous, uncivil ≠ polite 5 = <u>scarce</u>, wanting, low, limited, lacking, scant, deficient ≠ plentiful

- **ADVERB** = <u>abruptly</u>, suddenly, without warning ≠ gradually

shortage = <u>deficiency</u>, want, lack, scarcity, dearth, paucity, insufficiency ≠ abundance

shortcoming = <u>failing</u>, fault, weakness, defect, flaw, imperfection

shorten 1 = <u>cut</u>, reduce, decrease, diminish, lessen, curtail, abbreviate, abridge ≠ increase 2 = <u>turn up</u>

shortly = <u>soon</u>, presently, before long, in a little while

shot 1 = <u>discharge</u>, gunfire, crack, blast, explosion, bang 2 = <u>ammunition</u>, bullet, slug, pellet, projectile, lead, ball 3 = <u>marksman</u>, shooter, markswoman 4 (*Informal*) = <u>strike</u>, throw, lob 5 = <u>attempt</u>, go (*informal*), try, turn, effort, stab (*informal*), endeavour

shoulder 1 = <u>bear</u>, carry, take on, accept, assume, be responsible for 2 = <u>push</u>, elbow, shove, jostle, press

shout VERB = <u>cry (out)</u>, call (out), yell, scream, roar, bellow, bawl, holler (*informal*)

- **NOUN** = <u>cry</u>, call, yell, scream, roar, bellow

- **PHRASES** **shout someone down** = <u>drown out</u>, overwhelm, drown, silence

shove VERB = <u>push</u>, thrust, elbow, drive, press, propel, jostle, impel

● NOUN = push, knock, thrust, elbow, bump, nudge, jostle

● PHRASES **shove off** (*Informal*) = go away, leave, clear off (*informal*), depart, push off (*informal*), scram (*informal*)

shovel 1 = move, scoop, dredge, load, heap 2 = stuff, ladle

show VERB 1 = indicate, demonstrate, prove, reveal, display, point out, manifest, testify to ≠ disprove 2 = display, exhibit 3 = guide, lead, conduct, accompany, direct, escort 4 = demonstrate, describe, explain, teach, illustrate, instruct 5 = be visible ≠ be invisible 6 = express, display, reveal, indicate, register, demonstrate, manifest ≠ hide 7 = turn up, appear, attend 8 = broadcast, transmit, air, beam, relay, televise, put on the air

● NOUN 1 = display, sight, spectacle, array 2 = exhibition, fair, display, parade, pageant 3 = appearance, display, pose, parade 4 = pretence, appearance, illusion, affectation 5 = programme, broadcast, presentation, production 6 = entertainment, production, presentation

● PHRASES **show off** (*Informal*) = boast, brag, blow your own trumpet, swagger ◆ **show someone up** (*Informal*) = embarrass, let down, mortify, put to shame ◆ **show something off** = exhibit, display, parade, demonstrate, flaunt ◆ **show something up** = reveal, expose, highlight, lay bare

showdown (*Informal*) = confrontation, clash, face-off (*slang*)

shower NOUN = deluge

● VERB 1 = cover, dust, spray, sprinkle 2 = inundate, heap, lavish, pour, deluge

show-off (*Informal*) = exhibitionist, boaster, poseur, braggart

shred 1 = strip, bit, piece, scrap, fragment, sliver, tatter 2 = particle, trace, scrap, grain, atom, jot, iota

shrewd = astute, clever, sharp, keen, smart, calculating, intelligent, cunning ≠ naive

shriek VERB = scream, cry, yell, screech, squeal

● NOUN = scream, cry, yell, screech, squeal

shrink = decrease, dwindle, lessen, grow or get smaller, contract, narrow, diminish, shorten ≠ grow

shroud NOUN 1 = winding sheet, grave

clothes 2 = covering, veil, mantle, screen, pall

● VERB = conceal, cover, screen, hide, blanket, veil, cloak, envelop

shudder VERB = shiver, shake, tremble, quake, quiver, convulse

● NOUN = shiver, tremor, quiver, spasm

shuffle 1 = shamble, stagger, stumble, dodder 2 = scuffle, drag, scrape 3 = rearrange, jumble, mix, disorder, disarrange

shun = avoid, steer clear of, keep away from

shut VERB = close, secure, fasten, seal, slam ≠ open

● ADJECTIVE = closed, fastened, sealed, locked ≠ open

● PHRASES **shut down** = stop work, halt work, close down

shuttle = go back and forth, commute, go to and fro, alternate

shy ADJECTIVE 1 = timid, self-conscious, bashful, retiring, shrinking, coy, self-effacing, diffident ≠ confident 2 = cautious, wary, hesitant, suspicious, distrustful, chary ≠ reckless

● VERB *sometimes with* **off** *or* **away** = recoil, flinch, draw back, start, balk

sick 1 = unwell, ill, poorly (*informal*), diseased, crook (*Austral. & N.Z. informal*), ailing, under the weather, indisposed ≠ well 2 = nauseous, ill, queasy, nauseated 3 = tired, bored, fed up, weary, jaded 4 (*Informal*) = morbid, sadistic, black, macabre, ghoulish

sicken 1 = disgust, revolt, nauseate, repel, gross out (*U.S. slang*), turn your stomach 2 = fall ill, take sick, ail

sickening = disgusting, revolting, offensive, foul, distasteful, repulsive, nauseating, loathsome, yucko (*Austral. slang*) ≠ delightful

sickness 1 = illness, disorder, ailment, disease, complaint, bug (*informal*), affliction, malady 2 = nausea, queasiness 3 = vomiting

side NOUN 1 = border, margin, boundary, verge, flank, rim, perimeter, edge ≠ middle 2 = face, surface, facet 3 = party, camp, faction, cause 4 = point of view, viewpoint, position, opinion, angle, slant, standpoint 5 = team, squad, line-up 6 = aspect, feature, angle, facet

● ADJECTIVE = subordinate, minor,

secondary, subsidiary, lesser, marginal, incidental, ancillary ≠ main

● PHRASES **side with someone** = support, agree with, stand up for, favour, go along with, take the part of, ally yourself with

sidewalk (*U.S. & Canad.*) = pavement, footpath (*Austral. & N.Z.*)

sideways ADVERB 1 = indirectly, obliquely 2 = to the side, laterally

● ADJECTIVE = sidelong, oblique

sift 1 = part, filter, strain, separate, sieve 2 = examine, investigate, go through, research, analyse, work over, scrutinize

sight NOUN 1 = vision, eyes, eyesight, seeing, eye 2 = spectacle, show, scene, display, exhibition, vista, pageant 3 = view, range of vision, visibility 4 (*Informal*) = eyesore, mess, monstrosity

● VERB = spot, see, observe, distinguish, perceive, make out, discern, behold

RELATED WORDS
adjectives: optical, visual

sign NOUN 1 = symbol, mark, device, logo, badge, emblem 2 = figure 3 = notice, board, warning, placard 4 = indication, evidence, mark, signal, symptom, hint, proof, gesture 5 = omen, warning, portent, foreboding, augury, auspice

● VERB 1 = gesture, indicate, signal, beckon, gesticulate 2 = autograph, initial, inscribe

signal NOUN 1 = flare, beam, beacon 2 = cue, sign, prompting, reminder 3 = sign, gesture, indication, mark, note, expression, token

● VERB = gesture, sign, wave, indicate, motion, beckon, gesticulate

significance = importance, consequence, moment, weight

significant 1 = important, serious, material, vital, critical, momentous, weighty, noteworthy ≠ insignificant 2 = meaningful, expressive, eloquent, indicative, suggestive ≠ meaningless

signify = indicate, mean, suggest, imply, intimate, be a sign of, denote, connote

silence NOUN 1 = quiet, peace, calm, hush, lull, stillness ≠ noise 2 = reticence, dumbness, taciturnity, muteness ≠ speech

● VERB = quieten, still, quiet, cut off, stifle, cut short, muffle, deaden ≠ make louder

silent 1 = mute, dumb, speechless, wordless, voiceless ≠ noisy 2 = uncommunicative, quiet, taciturn

3 = quiet, still, hushed, soundless, noiseless, muted ≠ loud

silently 1 = quietly, in silence, soundlessly, noiselessly, inaudibly, without a sound 2 = mutely, in silence, wordlessly

silhouette NOUN = outline, form, shape, profile

● VERB = outline, etch

silly 1 = stupid, ridiculous, absurd, daft, inane, senseless, idiotic, fatuous ≠ clever 2 = foolish, stupid, unwise, rash, irresponsible, thoughtless, imprudent ≠ sensible

similar 1 = alike, resembling, comparable ≠ different 2 *with* **to** = like, comparable to, analogous to, close to

similarity = resemblance, likeness, sameness, agreement, correspondence, analogy, affinity, closeness ≠ difference

simmer VERB 1 = bubble, boil gently, seethe 2 = fume, seethe, smoulder, rage, be angry

● PHRASES **simmer down** (*Informal*) = calm down, control yourself, cool off *or* down

simple 1 = uncomplicated, clear, plain, understandable, lucid, recognizable, comprehensible, intelligible ≠ complicated 2 = easy, straightforward, not difficult, effortless, painless, uncomplicated, undemanding 3 = plain, natural, classic, unfussy, unembellished ≠ elaborate 4 = pure, mere, sheer, unalloyed 5 = artless, innocent, naive, natural, sincere, unaffected, childlike, unsophisticated ≠ sophisticated 6 = unpretentious, modest, humble, homely, unfussy, unembellished ≠ fancy

simplicity 1 = straightforwardness, ease, clarity, clearness ≠ complexity 2 = plainness, restraint, purity, lack of adornment ≠ elaborateness

simplify = make simpler, streamline, disentangle, dumb down, reduce to essentials

simply 1 = just, only, merely, purely, solely 2 = totally, really, completely, absolutely, wholly, utterly 3 = clearly, straightforwardly, directly, plainly, intelligibly 4 = plainly, naturally, modestly, unpretentiously 5 = without doubt, surely, certainly, definitely, beyond question

simulate = pretend, act, feign, affect, put

on, sham

simultaneous = coinciding, concurrent, contemporaneous, coincident, synchronous, happening at the same time

simultaneously = at the same time, together, concurrently

sin NOUN 1 = wickedness, evil, crime, error, transgression, iniquity 2 = crime, offence, error, wrongdoing, misdeed, transgression, act of evil, guilt

● VERB = transgress, offend, lapse, err, go astray, do wrong

sincere = honest, genuine, real, true, serious, earnest, frank, candid, dinkum (*Austral. & N.Z. informal*) ≠ false

sincerely = honestly, truly, genuinely, seriously, earnestly, wholeheartedly, in earnest

sincerity = honesty, truth, candour, frankness, seriousness, genuineness

sing 1 = croon, carol, chant, warble, yodel, pipe 2 = trill, chirp, warble

singer = vocalist, crooner, minstrel, soloist, chorister, balladeer

single ADJECTIVE 1 = one, sole, lone, solitary, only, only one 2 = individual, separate, distinct 3 = unmarried, free, unattached, unwed 4 = separate, individual, exclusive, undivided, unshared 5 = simple, unmixed, unblended

● PHRASES **single something** or **someone out** = pick, choose, select, separate, distinguish, fix on, set apart, pick on or out

singly = one by one, individually, one at a time, separately

singular 1 = single, individual 2 = remarkable, outstanding, exceptional, notable, eminent, noteworthy ≠ ordinary 3 = unusual, odd, strange, extraordinary, curious, peculiar, eccentric, queer ≠ conventional

sinister = threatening, evil, menacing, dire, ominous, malign, disquieting ≠ reassuring

sink 1 = go down, founder, go under, submerge, capsize 2 = slump, drop 3 = fall, drop, slip, plunge, subside, abate 4 = drop, fall 5 = stoop, be reduced to, lower yourself 6 = decline, fade, fail, flag, weaken, diminish, decrease, deteriorate ≠ improve 7 = dig, bore, drill, drive, excavate

sip VERB = drink, taste, sample, sup

● NOUN = swallow, drop, taste, thimbleful

sit 1 = take a seat, perch, settle down 2 = place, set, put, position, rest, lay, settle, deposit 3 = be a member of, serve on, have a seat on, preside on 4 = convene, meet, assemble, officiate

site NOUN 1 = area, plot 2 = location, place, setting, point, position, situation, spot

● VERB = locate, put, place, set, position, establish, install, situate

situation 1 = position, state, case, condition, circumstances, equation, plight, state of affairs 2 = scenario, state of affairs 3 = location, place, setting, position, site, spot

size NOUN = dimensions, extent, range, amount, mass, volume, proportions, bulk

● PHRASES **size something** or **someone up** (*Informal*) = assess, evaluate, appraise, take stock of

sizeable or **sizable** = large, considerable, substantial, goodly, decent, respectable, largish

sizzle = hiss, spit, crackle, fry, frizzle

skeleton = bones, bare bones

sketch NOUN = drawing, design, draft, delineation

● VERB = draw, outline, represent, draft, depict, delineate, rough out

skilful = expert, skilled, masterly, able, professional, clever, practised, competent ≠ clumsy

skill = expertise, ability, proficiency, art, technique, facility, talent, craft ≠ clumsiness

skilled = expert, professional, able, masterly, skilful, proficient ≠ unskilled

skim 1 = remove, separate, cream 2 = glide, fly, coast, sail, float 3 *usually with* **over** or **through** = scan, glance, run your eye over

skin NOUN 1 = hide, pelt, fell 2 = peel, rind, husk, casing, outside, crust 3 = film, coating

● VERB 1 = peel 2 = scrape, flay

skinny = thin, lean, scrawny, emaciated, undernourished ≠ fat

skip 1 = hop, dance, bob, trip, bounce, caper, prance, frisk 2 = miss out, omit, leave out, overlook, pass over, eschew, give (something) a miss

skirt 1 = border, edge, flank 2 *often with* **around** or **round** = go round, circumvent

3 *often with **around** or **round*** = <u>avoid</u>, evade, steer clear of, circumvent

sky = <u>heavens</u>, firmament, rangi (*N.Z.*)

▬ RELATED WORD
adjective: celestial

slab = <u>piece</u>, slice, lump, chunk, wedge, portion

slack ADJECTIVE **1** = <u>limp</u>, relaxed, loose, lax **2** = <u>loose</u>, baggy ≠ taut **3** = <u>slow</u>, quiet, inactive, dull, sluggish, slow-moving ≠ busy **4** = <u>negligent</u>, lazy, lax, idle, inactive, slapdash, neglectful, slipshod ≠ strict

● VERB = <u>shirk</u>, idle, dodge, skive (*Brit. slang*), bludge (*Austral. & N.Z. informal*)

● NOUN **1** = <u>surplus</u>, excess, glut, surfeit, superabundance, superfluity **2** = <u>room</u>, excess, leeway, give (*informal*)

slam 1 = <u>bang</u>, crash, smash **2** = <u>throw</u>, dash, hurl, fling

slant VERB **1** = <u>slope</u>, incline, tilt, list, bend, lean, heel, cant **2** = <u>bias</u>, colour, twist, angle, distort

● NOUN **1** = <u>slope</u>, incline, tilt, gradient, camber **2** = <u>bias</u>, emphasis, prejudice, angle, point of view, one-sidedness

slanting = <u>sloping</u>, angled, inclined, tilted, tilting, bent, diagonal, oblique

slap VERB = <u>smack</u>, beat, clap, cuff, swipe, spank, clobber (*slang*), wallop (*informal*)

● NOUN = <u>smack</u>, blow, cuff, swipe, spank

slash VERB **1** = <u>cut</u>, slit, gash, lacerate, score, rend, rip, hack **2** = <u>reduce</u>, cut, decrease, drop, lower, moderate, diminish, cut down

● NOUN = <u>cut</u>, slit, gash, rent, rip, incision, laceration

slate (*Informal, chiefly Brit.*) = <u>criticize</u>, censure, rebuke, scold, tear into (*informal*)

slaughter VERB **1** = <u>kill</u>, murder, massacre, destroy, execute, assassinate **2** = <u>butcher</u>, kill, slay, massacre

● NOUN = <u>slaying</u>, killing, murder, massacre, bloodshed, carnage, butchery

slave NOUN **1** = <u>servant</u>, serf, vassal **2** = <u>drudge</u>, skivvy (*chiefly Brit.*)

● VERB = <u>toil</u>, drudge, slog

slavery = <u>enslavement</u>, servitude, subjugation, captivity, bondage ≠ freedom

slay 1 (*Archaic or literary*) = <u>kill</u>, slaughter, massacre, butcher **2** = <u>murder</u>, kill, massacre, slaughter, mow down

sleaze (*Informal*) = <u>corruption</u>, fraud,

dishonesty, bribery, extortion, venality, unscrupulousness

sleek = <u>glossy</u>, shiny, lustrous, smooth ≠ shaggy

sleep NOUN = <u>slumber(s)</u>, nap, doze, snooze (*informal*), hibernation, siesta, forty winks (*informal*), zizz (*Brit. informal*)

● VERB = <u>slumber</u>, doze, snooze (*informal*), hibernate, take a nap, catnap, drowse

sleepy = <u>drowsy</u>, sluggish, lethargic, heavy, dull, inactive ≠ wide-awake

slender 1 = <u>slim</u>, narrow, slight, lean, willowy ≠ chubby **2** = <u>faint</u>, slight, remote, slim, thin, tenuous ≠ strong **3** = <u>meagre</u>, little, small, scant, scanty ≠ large

slice NOUN = <u>piece</u>, segment, portion, wedge, sliver, helping, share, cut

● VERB = <u>cut</u>, divide, carve, sever, dissect, bisect

slick ADJECTIVE **1** = <u>skilful</u>, deft, adroit, dexterous, professional, polished ≠ clumsy **2** = <u>glib</u>, smooth, plausible, polished, specious

● VERB = <u>smooth</u>, sleek, plaster down

slide = <u>slip</u>, slither, glide, skim, coast

slight ADJECTIVE **1** = <u>small</u>, minor, insignificant, trivial, feeble, trifling, meagre, unimportant ≠ large **2** = <u>slim</u>, small, delicate, spare, fragile, lightly-built ≠ sturdy

● VERB = <u>snub</u>, insult, ignore, affront, scorn, disdain ≠ compliment

● NOUN = <u>insult</u>, snub, affront, rebuff, slap in the face (*informal*), (the) cold shoulder ≠ compliment

slightly = <u>a little</u>, a bit, somewhat

slim ADJECTIVE **1** = <u>slender</u>, slight, trim, thin, narrow, lean, svelte, willowy ≠ chubby **2** = <u>slight</u>, remote, faint, slender ≠ strong

● VERB = <u>lose weight</u>, diet ≠ put on weight

sling 1 (*Informal*) = <u>throw</u>, cast, toss, hurl, fling, chuck (*informal*), lob (*informal*), heave **2** = <u>hang</u>, suspend

slip VERB **1** = <u>fall</u>, skid **2** = <u>slide</u>, slither **3** = <u>sneak</u>, creep, steal

● NOUN = <u>mistake</u>, failure, error, blunder, lapse, omission, oversight

● PHRASES **give someone the slip** = <u>escape from</u>, get away from, evade, elude, lose (someone), flee, dodge

◆ **slip up** = <u>make a mistake</u>, blunder, err, miscalculate

slippery 1 = <u>smooth</u>, icy, greasy, glassy, slippy (*informal, dialect*), unsafe

2 = <u>untrustworthy</u>, tricky, cunning, dishonest, devious, crafty, evasive, shifty

slit VERB **1** = <u>cut (open)</u>, rip, slash, knife, pierce, lance, gash

● NOUN **1** = <u>cut</u>, gash, incision, tear, rent **2** = <u>opening</u>, split

slogan = <u>catch phrase</u>, motto, tag-line, catchword

slope NOUN = <u>inclination</u>, rise, incline, tilt, slant, ramp, gradient

● VERB = <u>slant</u>, incline, drop away, fall, rise, lean, tilt

● PHRASES **slope off** (*Informal*) = <u>slink away</u>, slip away, creep away

sloping = <u>slanting</u>, leaning, inclined, oblique

sloppy 1 (*Informal*) = <u>careless</u>, slovenly, slipshod, messy, untidy **2** (*Informal*) = <u>sentimental</u>, soppy (*Brit. informal*), slushy (*informal*), gushing, mawkish, icky (*informal*)

slot NOUN **1** = <u>opening</u>, hole, groove, vent, slit, aperture **2** (*Informal*) = <u>place</u>, time, space, opening, position, vacancy

● VERB = <u>fit</u>, insert

slow ADJECTIVE **1** = <u>unhurried</u>, sluggish, leisurely, lazy, ponderous, dawdling, laggard, lackadaisical ≠ quick **2** = <u>prolonged</u>, protracted, long-drawn-out, lingering, gradual **3** = <u>late</u>, behind, tardy **4** = <u>stupid</u>, dim, dense, thick, retarded, dozy (*Brit. informal*), obtuse, braindead (*informal*) ≠ bright

● VERB **1** often with **down** = <u>decelerate</u>, brake **2** often with **down** = <u>delay</u>, hold up, handicap, retard ≠ speed up

slowly = <u>gradually</u>, unhurriedly ≠ quickly

sluggish = <u>inactive</u>, slow, lethargic, heavy, dull, inert, indolent, torpid ≠ energetic

slum = <u>hovel</u>, ghetto, shanty

slump VERB **1** = <u>fall</u>, sink, plunge, crash, collapse, slip ≠ increase **2** = <u>sag</u>, hunch, droop, slouch, loll

● NOUN **1** = <u>fall</u>, drop, decline, crash, collapse, reverse, downturn, trough ≠ increase **2** = <u>recession</u>, depression, stagnation, inactivity, hard *or* bad times

slur = <u>insult</u>, stain, smear, affront, innuendo, calumny, insinuation, aspersion

sly ADJECTIVE **1** = <u>roguish</u>, knowing, arch, mischievous, impish **2** = <u>cunning</u>, scheming, devious, secret, clever, subtle, wily, crafty ≠ open

● PHRASES **on the sly** = <u>secretly</u>, privately,

covertly, surreptitiously, on the quiet

smack VERB **1** = <u>slap</u>, hit, strike, clap, cuff, swipe, spank **2** = <u>drive</u>, hit, strike

● NOUN = <u>slap</u>, blow, cuff, swipe, spank

● ADVERB (*Informal*) = <u>directly</u>, right, straight, squarely, precisely, exactly, slap (*informal*)

small 1 = <u>little</u>, minute, tiny, mini, miniature, minuscule, diminutive, petite ≠ big **2** = <u>young</u>, little, junior, wee, juvenile, youthful, immature **3** = <u>unimportant</u>, minor, trivial, insignificant, little, petty, trifling, negligible ≠ important **4** = <u>modest</u>, humble, unpretentious ≠ grand

smart ADJECTIVE **1** = <u>chic</u>, trim, neat, stylish, elegant, spruce, snappy, natty (*informal*) ≠ scruffy **2** = <u>clever</u>, bright, intelligent, quick, sharp, keen, acute, shrewd ≠ stupid **3** = <u>brisk</u>, quick, lively, vigorous

● VERB = <u>sting</u>, burn, hurt

smash VERB **1** = <u>break</u>, crush, shatter, crack, demolish, pulverize **2** = <u>shatter</u>, break, disintegrate, crack, splinter **3** = <u>collide</u>, crash, meet head-on, clash, come into collision **4** = <u>destroy</u>, ruin, wreck, trash (*slang*), lay waste

● NOUN = <u>collision</u>, crash, accident

smashing (*Informal, chiefly Brit.*) = <u>excellent</u>, mean (*slang*), great (*informal*), wonderful, brilliant (*informal*), cracking (*Brit. informal*), superb, fantastic (*informal*), booshit (*Austral. slang*), exo (*Austral. slang*), sik (*Austral. slang*) ≠ awful

smear VERB **1** = <u>spread over</u>, daub, rub on, cover, coat, bedaub **2** = <u>slander</u>, malign, blacken, besmirch **3** = <u>smudge</u>, soil, dirty, stain, sully

● NOUN **1** = <u>smudge</u>, daub, streak, blot, blotch, splotch **2** = <u>slander</u>, libel, defamation, calumny

smell NOUN **1** = <u>odour</u>, scent, fragrance, perfume, bouquet, aroma **2** = <u>stink</u>, stench, pong (*Brit. informal*), fetor

● VERB **1** = <u>stink</u>, reek, pong (*Brit. informal*) **2** = <u>sniff</u>, scent

smile VERB = <u>grin</u>, beam, smirk, twinkle, grin from ear to ear

● NOUN = <u>grin</u>, beam, smirk

smooth ADJECTIVE **1** = <u>even</u>, level, flat, plane, flush, horizontal ≠ uneven **2** = <u>sleek</u>, polished, shiny, glossy, silky, velvety ≠ rough **3** = <u>mellow</u>, pleasant, mild, agreeable **4** = <u>flowing</u>, steady, regular,

uniform, rhythmic **5** = <u>easy</u>, effortless,
well-ordered **6** = <u>suave</u>, slick, persuasive,
urbane, glib, facile, unctuous, smarmy
(*Brit. informal*)

● VERB **1** = <u>flatten</u>, level, press, plane, iron
2 = <u>ease</u>, facilitate ≠ hinder

smother 1 = <u>extinguish</u>, put out, stifle,
snuff **2** = <u>suffocate</u>, choke, strangle, stifle
3 = <u>suppress</u>, stifle, repress, hide, conceal,
muffle

smug = <u>self-satisfied</u>, superior,
complacent, conceited

snack = <u>light meal</u>, bite, refreshment(s)

snag NOUN = <u>difficulty</u>, hitch, problem,
obstacle, catch, disadvantage,
complication, drawback

● VERB = <u>catch</u>, tear, rip

snake = <u>serpent</u>

   ◼ RELATED WORD

adjective: serpentine

snap VERB **1** = <u>break</u>, crack, separate
2 = <u>pop</u>, click, crackle **3** = <u>speak sharply</u>,
bark, lash out at, jump down (someone's)
throat (*informal*) **4** = <u>bite at</u>, bite, nip

● ADJECTIVE = <u>instant</u>, immediate, sudden,
spur-of-the-moment

● PHRASES **snap something up** = <u>grab</u>,
seize, take advantage of, pounce upon

snare NOUN = <u>trap</u>, net, wire, gin, noose

● VERB = <u>trap</u>, catch, net, wire, seize, entrap

snatch VERB **1** = <u>grab</u>, grip, grasp, clutch
2 = <u>steal</u>, take, nick (*slang, chiefly Brit.*),
pinch (*informal*), lift (*informal*), pilfer, filch,
thieve **3** = <u>win</u> **4** = <u>save</u>, recover, get out,
salvage

● NOUN = <u>bit</u>, part, fragment, piece, snippet

sneak VERB **1** = <u>slink</u>, slip, steal, pad, skulk
2 = <u>slip</u>, smuggle, spirit

● NOUN = <u>informer</u>, betrayer, telltale, Judas,
accuser, stool pigeon, nark (*Brit., Austral., &*
N.Z. slang), fizgig (*Austral. slang*)

sneaking 1 = <u>nagging</u>, worrying,
persistent, uncomfortable **2** = <u>secret</u>,
private, hidden, unexpressed, unvoiced,
undivulged

sneer VERB **1** = <u>scorn</u>, mock, ridicule,
laugh, jeer, disdain, deride **2** = <u>say</u>
<u>contemptuously</u>, snigger

● NOUN = <u>scorn</u>, ridicule, mockery, derision,
jeer, gibe

sniff 1 = <u>breathe in</u>, inhale **2** = <u>smell</u>, scent
3 = <u>inhale</u>, breathe in, suck in, draw in

snub VERB = <u>insult</u>, slight, put down,
humiliate, cut (*informal*), rebuff, cold-

shoulder

● NOUN = <u>insult</u>, put-down, affront, slap in
the face

so = <u>therefore</u>, thus, hence, consequently,
then, as a result, accordingly, thence

soak VERB **1** = <u>steep</u> **2** = <u>wet</u>, damp,
saturate, drench, moisten, suffuse,
wet through, waterlog **3** = <u>penetrate</u>,
permeate, seep

● PHRASES **soak something up** = <u>absorb</u>,
suck up, assimilate

soaking = <u>soaked</u>, dripping, saturated,
drenched, sodden, streaming, sopping,
wet through

soar 1 = <u>rise</u>, increase, grow, mount, climb,
go up, rocket, escalate **2** = <u>fly</u>, wing, climb,
ascend ≠ plunge **3** = <u>tower</u>, climb, go up

sob VERB = <u>cry</u>, weep, howl, shed tears

● NOUN = <u>cry</u>, whimper, howl

sober 1 = <u>abstinent</u>, temperate,
abstemious, moderate ≠ drunk
2 = <u>serious</u>, cool, grave, reasonable, steady,
composed, rational, solemn ≠ frivolous
3 = <u>plain</u>, dark, sombre, quiet, subdued,
drab ≠ bright

so-called = <u>alleged</u>, supposed, professed,
pretended, self-styled

social ADJECTIVE **1** = <u>communal</u>,
community, collective, group, public,
general, common **2** = <u>organized</u>,
gregarious

● NOUN = <u>get-together</u> (*informal*), party,
gathering, function, reception, social
gathering

society 1 = <u>the community</u>, people, the
public, humanity, civilization, mankind
2 = <u>culture</u>, community, population
3 = <u>organization</u>, group, club, union,
league, association, institute, circle
4 = <u>upper classes</u>, gentry, elite, high
society, beau monde **5** (*Old-fashioned*)
= <u>companionship</u>, company, fellowship,
friendship

sofa = <u>couch</u>, settee, divan, chaise longue

soft 1 = <u>velvety</u>, smooth, silky, feathery,
downy, fleecy ≠ rough **2** = <u>yielding</u>,
elastic ≠ hard **3** = <u>soggy</u>, swampy,
marshy, boggy **4** = <u>squashy</u>, sloppy,
mushy, spongy, gelatinous, pulpy
5 = <u>pliable</u>, flexible, supple, malleable,
plastic, elastic, bendable, mouldable
6 = <u>quiet</u>, gentle, murmured, muted,
dulcet, soft-toned ≠ loud **7** = <u>lenient</u>,
easy-going, lax, indulgent, permissive,

spineless, overindulgent ≠ harsh **8** = kind, tender, sentimental, compassionate, sensitive, gentle, tenderhearted, touchy-feely (*informal*) **9** (*Informal*) = easy, comfortable, undemanding, cushy (*informal*) **10** = pale, light, subdued, pastel, bland, mellow ≠ bright **11** = dim, faint, dimmed ≠ bright **12** = mild, temperate, balmy

soften 1 = melt, tenderize **2** = lessen, moderate, temper, ease, cushion, subdue, allay, mitigate

soil¹ 1 = earth, ground, clay, dust, dirt **2** = territory, country, land

soil² = dirty, foul, stain, pollute, tarnish, sully, defile, besmirch ≠ clean

soldier = fighter, serviceman, trooper, warrior, man-at-arms, squaddie or squaddy (*Brit. slang*)

sole = only, one, single, individual, alone, exclusive, solitary

solely = only, completely, entirely, exclusively, alone, merely

solemn 1 = serious, earnest, grave, sober, sedate, staid ≠ cheerful **2** = formal, grand, grave, dignified, ceremonial, stately, momentous ≠ informal

solid 1 = firm, hard, compact, dense, concrete ≠ unsubstantial **2** = strong, stable, sturdy, substantial, unshakable ≠ unstable **3** = reliable, dependable, upstanding, worthy, upright, trusty ≠ unreliable **4** = sound, real, reliable, good, genuine, dinkum (*Austral. & N.Z. informal*) ≠ unsound

solidarity = unity, unification, accord, cohesion, team spirit, unanimity, concordance, like-mindedness, kotahitanga (*N.Z.*)

solitary 1 = unsociable, reclusive, unsocial, isolated, lonely, cloistered, lonesome, friendless ≠ sociable **2** = lone, alone **3** = isolated, remote, out-of-the-way, hidden, unfrequented ≠ busy

solution 1 = answer, key, result, explanation **2** (*Chemistry*) = mixture, mix, compound, blend, solvent

solve = answer, work out, resolve, crack, clear up, unravel, decipher, suss (out) (*slang*)

sombre 1 = gloomy, sad, sober, grave, dismal, mournful, lugubrious, joyless ≠ cheerful **2** = dark, dull, gloomy, sober, drab ≠ bright

somebody = celebrity, name, star, notable, household name, dignitary, luminary, personage ≠ nobody

somehow = one way or another, come what may, come hell or high water (*informal*), by fair means or foul, by hook or (by) crook, by some means or other

sometimes = occasionally, at times, now and then ≠ always

song = ballad, air, tune, carol, chant, chorus, anthem, number, waiata (*N.Z.*)

soon = before long, shortly, in the near future

soothe 1 = calm, still, quiet, hush, appease, lull, pacify, mollify ≠ upset **2** = relieve, ease, alleviate, assuage ≠ irritate**

soothing 1 = calming, relaxing, peaceful, quiet, calm, restful **2** = emollient, palliative**

sophisticated 1 = complex, advanced, complicated, subtle, delicate, elaborate, refined, intricate ≠ simple **2** = cultured, refined, cultivated, worldly, cosmopolitan, urbane ≠ unsophisticated**

sophistication = poise, worldliness, savoir-faire, urbanity, finesse, worldly wisdom

sore 1 = painful, smarting, raw, tender, burning, angry, sensitive, irritated **2** = annoyed, cross, angry, pained, hurt, upset, stung, irritated, tooshie (*Austral. slang*), hoha (*N.Z.*) **3** = annoying, troublesome **4** (*Literary*) = urgent, desperate, extreme, dire, pressing, critical, acute**

sorrow NOUN 1 = grief, sadness, woe, regret, distress, misery, mourning, anguish ≠ joy **2** = hardship, trial, tribulation, affliction, trouble, woe, misfortune ≠ good fortune

● **VERB = grieve, mourn, lament, be sad, bemoan, agonize, bewail ≠ rejoice**

sorry 1 = regretful, apologetic, contrite, repentant, remorseful, penitent, shamefaced, conscience-stricken ≠ unapologetic **2** = sympathetic, moved, full of pity, compassionate, commiserative ≠ unsympathetic **3** = wretched, miserable, pathetic, mean, poor, sad, pitiful, deplorable**

**sort NOUN = kind, type, class, make, order, style, quality, nature

● VERB = arrange, group, order, rank, divide, grade, classify, categorize**

soul 1 = spirit, essence, life, vital force,**

wairua (*N.Z.*) **2** = embodiment, essence, epitome, personification, quintessence, type **3** = person, being, individual, body, creature, man *or* woman

sound¹ NOUN **1** = noise, din, report, tone, reverberation **2** = idea, impression, drift **3** = cry, noise, peep, squeak **4** = tone, music, note

● VERB **1** = toll, set off **2** = resound, echo, go off, toll, set off, chime, reverberate, clang **3** = seem, seem to be, appear to be

▓▓▓ RELATED WORDS
adjectives: sonic, acoustic

sound² **1** = fit, healthy, perfect, intact, unhurt, uninjured, unimpaired ≠ frail **2** = sturdy, strong, solid, stable **3** = sensible, wise, reasonable, right, correct, proper, valid, rational ≠ irresponsible **4** = deep, unbroken, undisturbed, untroubled ≠ troubled

sour **1** = sharp, acid, tart, bitter, pungent, acetic ≠ sweet **2** = rancid, turned, gone off, curdled, gone bad, off ≠ fresh **3** = bitter, tart, acrimonious, embittered, disagreeable, ill-tempered, waspish, ungenerous ≠ good-natured

source **1** = cause, origin, derivation, beginning, author **2** = informant, authority **3** = origin, fount

souvenir = keepsake, reminder, memento

sovereign ADJECTIVE **1** = supreme, ruling, absolute, royal, principal, imperial, kingly *or* queenly **2** = excellent, efficient, effectual

● NOUN = monarch, ruler, king *or* queen, chief, potentate, emperor *or* empress, prince *or* princess

sovereignty = supreme power, domination, supremacy, primacy, kingship, rangatiratanga (*N.Z.*)

sow = scatter, plant, seed, implant

space **1** = room, capacity, extent, margin, scope, play, expanse, leeway **2** = period, interval, time, while, span, duration **3** = outer space, the universe, the galaxy, the solar system, the cosmos **4** = blank, gap, interval

spacious = roomy, large, huge, broad, extensive, ample, expansive, capacious ≠ limited

span NOUN **1** = period, term, duration, spell **2** = extent, reach, spread, length, distance, stretch

● VERB = extend across, cross, bridge, cover,

link, traverse

spar = argue, row, squabble, scrap (*informal*), wrangle, bicker

spare ADJECTIVE **1** = back-up, reserve, second, extra, additional, auxiliary **2** = extra, surplus, leftover, over, free, odd, unwanted, unused ≠ necessary **3** = free, leisure, unoccupied **4** = thin, lean, meagre, gaunt, wiry ≠ plump

● VERB **1** = afford, give, grant, do without, part with, manage without, let someone have **2** = have mercy on, pardon, leave, let off (*informal*), go easy on (*informal*), save (from harm) ≠ show no mercy to

sparing = economical, frugal, thrifty, saving, careful, prudent ≠ lavish

spark NOUN **1** = flicker, flash, gleam, glint, flare **2** = trace, hint, scrap, atom, jot, vestige

● VERB *often with* **off** = start, stimulate, provoke, inspire, trigger (off), set off, precipitate

sparkle VERB = glitter, flash, shine, gleam, shimmer, twinkle, dance, glint

● NOUN **1** = glitter, flash, gleam, flicker, brilliance, twinkle, glint **2** = vivacity, life, spirit, dash, vitality, élan, liveliness

spate = flood, flow, torrent, rush, deluge, outpouring

speak **1** = talk, say something **2** = articulate, say, pronounce, utter, tell, state, talk, express **3** = converse, talk, chat, discourse, confer, commune, exchange views, korero (*N.Z.*) **4** = lecture, address an audience

speaker = orator, public speaker, lecturer, spokesperson, spokesman *or* spokeswoman

spearhead = lead, head, pioneer, launch, set off, initiate, set in motion

special **1** = exceptional, important, significant, particular, unique, unusual, extraordinary, memorable ≠ ordinary **2** = specific, particular, distinctive, individual, appropriate, precise ≠ general

specialist = expert, authority, professional, master, consultant, guru, buff (*informal*), connoisseur, fundi (*S. African*)

speciality = forte, métier, specialty, bag (*slang*), pièce de résistance (*French*)

species = kind, sort, type, group, class, variety, breed, category

specific **1** = particular, special, characteristic, distinguishing ≠ general

2 = precise, exact, explicit, definite, express, clear-cut, unequivocal ≠ vague
3 = peculiar, appropriate, individual, particular, unique

specification = requirement, detail, particular, stipulation, condition, qualification

specify = state, designate, stipulate, name, detail, mention, indicate, define

specimen 1 = sample, example, model, type, pattern, instance, representative, exemplification **2** = example, model, type

spectacle 1 = show, display, exhibition, event, performance, extravaganza, pageant **2** = sight, wonder, scene, phenomenon, curiosity, marvel

spectacular ADJECTIVE = impressive, striking, dramatic, stunning (*informal*), grand, magnificent, splendid, dazzling ≠ unimpressive
● NOUN = show, display, spectacle

spectator = onlooker, observer, viewer, looker-on, watcher, bystander ≠ participant

spectre = ghost, spirit, phantom, vision, apparition, wraith, kehua (*N.Z.*)

speculate 1 = conjecture, consider, wonder, guess, surmise, theorize, hypothesize **2** = gamble, risk, venture, hazard

speculation 1 = theory, opinion, hypothesis, conjecture, guess, surmise, guesswork, supposition **2** = gamble, risk, hazard

speculative = hypothetical, academic, theoretical, notional, conjectural, suppositional

speech 1 = communication, talk, conversation, discussion, dialogue **2** = diction, pronunciation, articulation, delivery, fluency, inflection, intonation, elocution **3** = language, tongue, jargon, dialect, idiom, parlance, articulation, diction **4** = talk, address, lecture, discourse, homily, oration, spiel (*informal*), whaikorero (*N.Z.*)

speed NOUN **1** = rate, pace **2** = swiftness, rush, hurry, haste, rapidity, quickness ≠ slowness
● VERB **1** = race, rush, hurry, zoom, career, tear, barrel (along) (*informal, chiefly U.S. & Canad.*), gallop ≠ crawl **2** = help, advance, aid, boost, assist, facilitate, expedite ≠ hinder

speedy = quick, fast, rapid, swift, express, immediate, prompt, hurried ≠ slow

spell[1] = indicate, mean, signify, point to, imply, augur, portend

spell[2] **1** = incantation, charm, makutu (*N.Z.*) **2** = enchantment, magic, fascination, glamour, allure, bewitchment

spell[3] = period, time, term, stretch, course, season, interval, bout

spend 1 = pay out, fork out (*slang*), expend, disburse ≠ save **2** = pass, fill, occupy, while away **3** = use up, waste, squander, empty, drain, exhaust, consume, run through ≠ save

sphere 1 = ball, globe, orb, globule, circle **2** = field, department, function, territory, capacity, province, patch, scope

spice 1 = seasoning **2** = excitement, zest, colour, pep, zing (*informal*), piquancy

spicy 1 = hot, seasoned, aromatic, savoury, piquant **2** (*Informal*) = risqué, racy, ribald, hot (*informal*), suggestive, titillating, indelicate

▇ RELATED WORD
fear of: arachnophobia

spike NOUN = point, stake, spine, barb, prong
● VERB = impale, spit, spear, stick

spill 1 = tip over, overturn, capsize, knock over **2** = shed, discharge, disgorge **3** = slop, flow, pour, run, overflow

spin VERB **1** = revolve, turn, rotate, reel, whirl, twirl, gyrate, pirouette **2** = reel, swim, whirl
● NOUN **1** (*Informal*) = drive, ride, joy ride (*informal*) **2** = revolution, roll, whirl, gyration
● PHRASES **spin something out** = prolong, extend, lengthen, draw out, drag out, delay, amplify

spine 1 = backbone, vertebrae, spinal column, vertebral column **2** = barb, spur, needle, spike, ray, quill

spiral ADJECTIVE = coiled, winding, whorled, helical
● NOUN = coil, helix, corkscrew, whorl

spirit NOUN **1** = soul, life **2** = life force, vital spark, mauri (*N.Z.*) **3** = ghost, phantom, spectre, apparition, atua (*N.Z.*), kehua (*N.Z.*) **4** = courage, guts (*informal*), grit, backbone, spunk (*informal*), gameness **5** = liveliness, energy, vigour, life, force, fire, enthusiasm, animation **6** = attitude, character, temper, outlook, temperament, disposition 7 = <u>heart</u>, sense, nature, soul, core, substance, essence, quintessence 8 = <u>intention</u>, meaning, purpose, purport, gist 9 = <u>feeling</u>, atmosphere, character, tone, mood, tenor, ambience

● **PLURAL NOUN** = <u>mood</u>, feelings, morale, temper, disposition, state of mind, frame of mind

spirited = <u>lively</u>, energetic, animated, active, feisty (*informal, chiefly U.S. & Canad.*), vivacious, mettlesome ≠ lifeless

spiritual 1 = <u>nonmaterial</u>, immaterial, incorporeal ≠ material **2** = <u>sacred</u>, religious, holy, divine, devotional

spit VERB 1 = <u>expectorate</u> **2** = <u>eject</u>, throw out

● **NOUN** = <u>saliva</u>, dribble, spittle, drool, slaver

spite NOUN = <u>malice</u>, malevolence, ill will, hatred, animosity, venom, spleen, spitefulness ≠ kindness

● **VERB** = <u>annoy</u>, hurt, injure, harm, vex ≠ benefit

● **PHRASES in spite of** = <u>despite</u>, regardless of, notwithstanding, (even) though

splash VERB 1 = <u>paddle</u>, plunge, bathe, dabble, wade, wallow **2** = <u>scatter</u>, shower, spray, sprinkle, wet, spatter, slop **3** = <u>spatter</u>, mark, stain, speck, speckle

● **NOUN 1** = <u>dash</u>, touch, spattering **2** = <u>spot</u>, burst, patch, spurt **3** = <u>blob</u>, spot, smudge, stain, smear, fleck, speck

splendid 1 = <u>excellent</u>, wonderful, marvellous, great (*informal*), cracking (*Brit. informal*), fantastic (*informal*), first-class, glorious, booshit (*Austral. slang*), exo (*Austral. slang*), sik (*Austral. slang*) ≠ poor **2** = <u>magnificent</u>, grand, impressive, rich, superb, costly, gorgeous, lavish ≠ squalid

splendour = <u>magnificence</u>, grandeur, show, display, spectacle, richness, nobility, pomp ≠ squalor

splinter NOUN = <u>sliver</u>, fragment, chip, flake

● **VERB** = <u>shatter</u>, split, fracture, disintegrate

split VERB 1 = <u>break</u>, crack, burst, open, give way, come apart, come undone **2** = <u>cut</u>, break, crack, snap, chop **3** = <u>divide</u>, separate, disunite, disband, cleave **4** = <u>diverge</u>, separate, branch, fork, part **5** = <u>tear</u>, rend, rip **6** = <u>share out</u>, divide, distribute, halve, allocate, partition, allot, apportion

● **NOUN 1** = <u>division</u>, breach, rift, rupture, discord, schism, estrangement, dissension **2** = <u>separation</u>, break-up, split-up **3** = <u>crack</u>, tear, rip, gap, rent, breach, slit, fissure

● **ADJECTIVE 1** = <u>divided</u> **2** = <u>broken</u>, cracked, fractured, ruptured, cleft

spoil VERB 1 = <u>ruin</u>, destroy, wreck, damage, injure, harm, mar, trash (*slang*), crool or cruel (*Austral. slang*) ≠ improve **2** = <u>overindulge</u>, indulge, pamper, cosset, coddle, mollycoddle ≠ deprive **3** = <u>indulge</u>, pamper, satisfy, gratify, pander to **4** = <u>go bad</u>, turn, go off (*Brit. informal*), rot, decay, decompose, curdle, addle

● **PLURAL NOUN** = <u>booty</u>, loot, plunder, prey, swag (*slang*)

spoken = <u>verbal</u>, voiced, expressed, uttered, oral, said, told, unwritten

spokesperson = <u>speaker</u>, official, spokesman *or* spokeswoman, voice, spin doctor (*informal*), mouthpiece

sponsor VERB = <u>back</u>, fund, finance, promote, subsidize, patronize

● **NOUN** = <u>backer</u>, patron, promoter

spontaneous = <u>unplanned</u>, impromptu, unprompted, willing, natural, voluntary, instinctive, impulsive ≠ planned

sport NOUN 1 = <u>game</u>, exercise, recreation, play, amusement, diversion, pastime **2** = <u>fun</u>, joking, teasing, banter, jest, badinage

● **VERB** (*Informal*) = <u>wear</u>, display, flaunt, exhibit, flourish, show off, vaunt

sporting = <u>fair</u>, sportsmanlike, game (*informal*) ≠ unfair

sporty = <u>athletic</u>, outdoor, energetic

spot NOUN 1 = <u>mark</u>, stain, speck, scar, blot, smudge, blemish, speckle **2** = <u>pimple</u>, pustule, zit (*slang*) **3** = <u>place</u>, site, point, position, scene, location **4** (*Informal*) = <u>predicament</u>, trouble, difficulty, mess, plight, hot water (*informal*), quandary, tight spot

● **VERB 1** = <u>see</u>, observe, catch sight of, sight, recognize, detect, make out, discern **2** = <u>mark</u>, stain, soil, dirty, fleck, spatter, speckle, splodge

spotlight NOUN = <u>attention</u>, limelight, public eye, fame

● **VERB** = <u>highlight</u>, draw attention to, accentuate

spotted = <u>speckled</u>, dotted, flecked,

mottled, dappled

spouse = <u>partner</u>, mate, husband *or* wife, consort, significant other (*U.S. informal*)

sprawl = <u>loll</u>, slump, lounge, flop, slouch

spray[1] NOUN 1 = <u>droplets</u>, fine mist, drizzle 2 = <u>aerosol</u>, sprinkler, atomizer
● VERB = <u>scatter</u>, shower, sprinkle, diffuse

spray[2] = <u>sprig</u>, floral arrangement, branch, corsage

spread VERB 1 = <u>open (out)</u>, extend, stretch, unfold, sprawl, unroll 2 = <u>extend</u>, open, stretch 3 = <u>grow</u>, increase, expand, widen, escalate, proliferate, multiply, broaden 4 = <u>circulate</u>, broadcast, propagate, disseminate, make known ≠ suppress 5 = <u>diffuse</u>, cast, shed, radiate
● NOUN 1 = <u>increase</u>, development, advance, expansion, proliferation, dissemination, dispersal 2 = <u>extent</u>, span, stretch, sweep

spree = <u>fling</u>, binge (*informal*), orgy

spring NOUN = <u>flexibility</u>, bounce, resilience, elasticity, buoyancy
● VERB 1 = <u>jump</u>, bound, leap, bounce, vault 2 *often with* **from** = <u>originate</u>, come, derive, start, issue, proceed, arise, stem
■ RELATED WORD
adjective: vernal

sprinkle = <u>scatter</u>, dust, strew, pepper, shower, spray, powder, dredge

sprinkling = <u>scattering</u>, dusting, few, dash, handful, sprinkle

sprint = <u>run</u>, race, shoot, tear, dash, dart, hare (*Brit. informal*)

sprout 1 = <u>germinate</u>, bud, shoot, spring 2 = <u>grow</u>, develop, ripen

spur VERB = <u>incite</u>, drive, prompt, urge, stimulate, animate, prod, prick
● NOUN = <u>stimulus</u>, incentive, impetus, motive, impulse, inducement, incitement
● PHRASES **on the spur of the moment** = <u>on impulse</u>, impulsively, on the spot, impromptu, without planning

spurn = <u>reject</u>, slight, scorn, rebuff, snub, despise, disdain, repulse ≠ accept

spy NOUN = <u>undercover agent</u>, mole, nark (*Brit., Austral., & N.Z. slang*)
● VERB = <u>catch sight of</u>, spot, notice, observe, glimpse, espy

squabble VERB = <u>quarrel</u>, fight, argue, row, dispute, wrangle, bicker
● NOUN = <u>quarrel</u>, fight, row, argument, dispute, disagreement, tiff

squad = <u>team</u>, group, band, company, force, troop, crew, gang

squander = <u>waste</u>, spend, fritter away, blow (*slang*), misuse, expend, misspend ≠ save

square ADJECTIVE = <u>fair</u>, straight, genuine, ethical, honest, on the level (*informal*), kosher (*informal*), dinkum (*Austral. & N.Z. informal*), above board
● VERB *often with* **with** = <u>agree</u>, match, fit, correspond, tally, reconcile

squash 1 = <u>crush</u>, press, flatten, mash, smash, distort, pulp, compress 2 = <u>suppress</u>, quell, silence, crush, annihilate 3 = <u>embarrass</u>, put down, shame, degrade, mortify

squeeze VERB 1 = <u>press</u>, crush, squash, pinch 2 = <u>clutch</u>, press, grip, crush, pinch, squash, compress, wring 3 = <u>cram</u>, press, crowd, force, stuff, pack, jam, ram 4 = <u>hug</u>, embrace, cuddle, clasp, enfold
● NOUN 1 = <u>press</u>, grip, clasp, crush, pinch, squash, wring 2 = <u>crush</u>, jam, squash, press, crowd, congestion 3 = <u>hug</u>, embrace, clasp

stab VERB = <u>pierce</u>, stick, wound, knife, thrust, spear, jab, transfix
● NOUN 1 (*Informal*) = <u>attempt</u>, go, try, endeavour 2 = <u>twinge</u>, prick, pang, ache

stability = <u>firmness</u>, strength, soundness, solidity, steadiness ≠ instability

stable 1 = <u>secure</u>, lasting, strong, sound, fast, sure, established, permanent ≠ insecure 2 = <u>well-balanced</u>, balanced, sensible, reasonable, rational 3 = <u>solid</u>, firm, fixed, substantial, durable, well-made, well-built, immovable ≠ unstable

stack NOUN 1 = <u>pile</u>, heap, mountain, mass, load, mound 2 = <u>lot</u>, mass, load (*informal*), ton (*informal*), heap (*informal*), great amount
● VERB = <u>pile</u>, heap up, load, assemble, accumulate, amass

staff 1 = <u>workers</u>, employees, personnel, workforce, team 2 = <u>stick</u>, pole, rod, crook, cane, stave, wand, sceptre

stage = <u>step</u>, leg, phase, point, level, period, division, lap

stagger 1 = <u>totter</u>, reel, sway, lurch, wobble 2 = <u>astound</u>, amaze, stun, shock, shake, overwhelm, astonish, confound

stain NOUN 1 = <u>mark</u>, spot, blot, blemish, discoloration, smirch 2 = <u>stigma</u>, shame, disgrace, slur, dishonour 3 = <u>dye</u>, colour, tint

● **VERB 1** = <u>mark</u>, soil, discolour, dirty, tinge, spot, blot, blemish **2** = <u>dye</u>, colour, tint

stake[1] NOUN = <u>pole</u>, post, stick, pale, paling, picket, palisade

stake[2] NOUN = <u>bet</u>, ante, wager

● **VERB 1** = <u>bet</u>, gamble, wager, chance, risk, venture, hazard **2** = <u>interest</u>, share, involvement, concern, investment

stale 1 = <u>old</u>, hard, dry, decayed ≠ fresh **2** = <u>musty</u>, fusty **3** = <u>tasteless</u>, flat, sour **4** = <u>unoriginal</u>, banal, trite, stereotyped, worn-out, threadbare, hackneyed, overused ≠ original

stalk = <u>pursue</u>, follow, track, hunt, shadow, haunt

stall VERB **1** = <u>play for time</u>, delay, hedge, temporize **2** = <u>stop dead</u>, jam, seize up, catch, stick, stop short

● NOUN = <u>stand</u>, table, counter, booth, kiosk

stalwart 1 = <u>loyal</u>, faithful, firm, true, dependable, steadfast **2** = <u>strong</u>, strapping, sturdy, stout ≠ puny

stamina = <u>staying power</u>, endurance, resilience, force, power, energy, strength

stammer = <u>stutter</u>, falter, pause, hesitate, stumble over your words

stamp NOUN = <u>imprint</u>, mark, brand, signature, earmark, hallmark

● **VERB 1** = <u>print</u>, mark, impress **2** = <u>trample</u>, step, tread, crush **3** = <u>identify</u>, mark, brand, label, reveal, show to be, categorize

● PHRASES **stamp something out** = <u>eliminate</u>, destroy, eradicate, crush, suppress, put down, scotch, quell

stance 1 = <u>attitude</u>, stand, position, viewpoint, standpoint **2** = <u>posture</u>, carriage, bearing, deportment

stand VERB **1** = <u>be upright</u>, be erect, be vertical **2** = <u>get to your feet</u>, rise, stand up, straighten up **3** = <u>be located</u>, be, sit, be positioned, be situated or located **4** = <u>be valid</u>, continue, exist, prevail, remain valid **5** = <u>put</u>, place, position, set, mount **6** = <u>sit</u>, mellow **7** = <u>resist</u>, endure, tolerate, stand up to **8** = <u>tolerate</u>, bear, abide, stomach, endure, brook **9** = <u>take</u>, bear, handle, endure, put up with (*informal*), countenance

● NOUN **1** = <u>position</u>, attitude, stance, opinion, determination **2** = <u>stall</u>, booth, kiosk, table

● PHRASES **stand by** = <u>be prepared</u>, wait

◆ **stand for something 1** = <u>represent</u>,

mean, signify, denote, indicate, symbolize, betoken **2** (*Informal*) = <u>tolerate</u>, bear, endure, put up with, brook ◆ **stand in for someone** = <u>be a substitute for</u>, represent, cover for, take the place of, deputize for ◆ **stand up for something** or **someone** = <u>support</u>, champion, defend, uphold, stick up for (*informal*)

standard NOUN **1** = <u>level</u>, grade **2** = <u>criterion</u>, measure, guideline, example, model, average, norm, gauge **3** *often plural* = <u>principles</u>, ideals, morals, ethics **4** = <u>flag</u>, banner, ensign

● **ADJECTIVE 1** = <u>usual</u>, normal, customary, average, basic, regular, typical, orthodox ≠ unusual **2** = <u>accepted</u>, official, established, approved, recognized, definitive, authoritative ≠ unofficial

stand-in = <u>substitute</u>, deputy, replacement, reserve, surrogate, understudy, locum, stopgap

standing NOUN **1** = <u>status</u>, position, footing, rank, reputation, eminence, repute **2** = <u>duration</u>, existence, continuance

● **ADJECTIVE 1** = <u>permanent</u>, lasting, fixed, regular **2** = <u>upright</u>, erect, vertical

staple = <u>principal</u>, chief, main, key, basic, fundamental, predominant

star NOUN **1** = <u>heavenly body</u>, celestial body **2** = <u>celebrity</u>, big name, megastar (*informal*), name, luminary **3** = <u>leading man</u> or <u>lady</u>, hero or heroine, principal, main attraction

● **VERB** = <u>play the lead</u>, appear, feature, perform

● **ADJECTIVE** = <u>leading</u>, major, celebrated, brilliant, well-known, prominent

▓▓▓ RELATED WORDS

adjectives: astral, stellar

stare = <u>gaze</u>, look, goggle, watch, gape, eyeball (*slang*), gawp (*Brit. slang*), gawk

stark ADJECTIVE **1** = <u>plain</u>, harsh, basic, grim, straightforward, blunt **2** = <u>sharp</u>, clear, striking, distinct, clear-cut **3** = <u>austere</u>, severe, plain, bare, harsh **4** = <u>bleak</u>, grim, barren, hard **5** = <u>absolute</u>, pure, sheer, utter, downright, out-and-out, unmitigated

● **ADVERB** = <u>absolutely</u>, quite, completely, entirely, altogether, wholly, utterly

start VERB **1** = <u>set about</u>, begin, proceed, embark upon, take the first step, make

a beginning ≠ stop **2** = begin, arise, originate, issue, appear, commence ≠ end **3** = set in motion, initiate, instigate, open, trigger, originate, get going, kick-start ≠ stop **4** = establish, begin, found, create, launch, set up, institute, pioneer ≠ terminate **5** = start up, activate, get something going ≠ turn off **6** = jump, shy, jerk, flinch, recoil
● NOUN **1** = beginning, outset, opening, birth, foundation, dawn, onset, initiation ≠ end **2** = jump, spasm, convulsion

startle = surprise, shock, frighten, scare, make (someone) jump

starving = hungry, starved, ravenous, famished

state NOUN **1** = country, nation, land, republic, territory, federation, commonwealth, kingdom **2** = government, ministry, administration, executive, regime, powers-that-be **3** = condition, shape **4** = frame of mind, condition, spirits, attitude, mood, humour **5** = ceremony, glory, grandeur, splendour, majesty, pomp **6** = circumstances, situation, position, predicament
● VERB = say, declare, specify, present, voice, express, assert, utter

stately = grand, majestic, dignified, royal, august, noble, regal, lofty ≠ lowly

statement 1 = announcement, declaration, communication, communiqué, proclamation **2** = account, report

station NOUN **1** = railway station, stop, stage, halt, terminal, train station, terminus **2** = headquarters, base, depot **3** = position, rank, status, standing, post, situation **4** = post, place, location, position, situation
● VERB = assign, post, locate, set, establish, install

stature 1 = height, build, size **2** = importance, standing, prestige, rank, prominence, eminence

status 1 = position, rank, grade **2** = prestige, standing, authority, influence, weight, honour, importance, fame, mana (N.Z.) **3** = state of play, development, progress, condition, evolution

staunch = loyal, faithful, stalwart, firm, sound, true, trusty, steadfast

stay VERB **1** = remain, continue to be, linger, stop, wait, halt, pause, abide ≠ go **2** often with **at** = lodge, visit, sojourn, put up at, be accommodated at **3** = continue, remain, go on, survive, endure
● NOUN **1** = visit, stop, holiday, stopover, sojourn **2** = postponement, delay, suspension, stopping, halt, deferment

steady 1 = continuous, regular, constant, consistent, persistent, unbroken, uninterrupted, incessant ≠ irregular **2** = stable, fixed, secure, firm, safe ≠ unstable **3** = regular, established **4** = dependable, sensible, reliable, secure, calm, supportive, sober, level-headed ≠ undependable

steal 1 = take, nick (slang, chiefly Brit.), pinch (informal), lift (informal), embezzle, pilfer, misappropriate, purloin **2** = copy, take, appropriate, pinch (informal) **3** = sneak, slip, creep, tiptoe, slink

stealth = secrecy, furtiveness, slyness, sneakiness, unobtrusiveness, stealthiness, surreptitiousness

steep[1] 1 = sheer, precipitous, abrupt, vertical ≠ gradual **2** = sharp, sudden, abrupt, marked, extreme, distinct **3** (Informal) = high, exorbitant, extreme, unreasonable, overpriced, extortionate ≠ reasonable

steep[2] = soak, immerse, marinate (Cookery), submerge, drench, moisten, souse

steeped = saturated, pervaded, permeated, filled, infused, imbued, suffused

steer 1 = drive, control, direct, handle, pilot **2** = direct, lead, guide, conduct, escort

stem[1] NOUN = stalk, branch, trunk, shoot, axis
● PHRASES **stem from something** = originate from, be caused by, derive from, arise from

stem[2] = stop, hold back, staunch, check, dam, curb

step NOUN **1** = pace, stride, footstep **2** = footfall **3** = move, measure, action, means, act, deed, expedient **4** = stage, point, phase **5** = level, rank, degree
● VERB = walk, pace, tread, move
● PHRASES **step in** (Informal) = intervene, take action, become involved ◆ **step something up** = increase, intensify, raise

stereotype NOUN = formula, pattern
● VERB = categorize, typecast, pigeonhole,

standardize

sterile 1 = <u>germ-free</u>, sterilized, disinfected, aseptic ≠ unhygienic 2 = <u>barren</u>, infertile, unproductive, childless ≠ fertile

sterling = <u>excellent</u>, sound, fine, superlative

stern 1 = <u>strict</u>, harsh, hard, grim, rigid, austere, inflexible ≠ lenient 2 = <u>severe</u>, serious, forbidding ≠ friendly

stick¹ 1 = <u>twig</u>, branch 2 = <u>cane</u>, staff, pole, rod, crook, baton 3 (*Slang*) = <u>abuse</u>, criticism, flak (*informal*), fault-finding

stick² VERB 1 (*Informal*) = <u>put</u>, place, set, lay, deposit 2 = <u>poke</u>, dig, stab, thrust, pierce, penetrate, spear, prod 3 = <u>fasten</u>, fix, bind, hold, bond, attach, glue, paste 4 = <u>adhere</u>, cling, become joined, become welded 5 = <u>stay</u>, remain, linger, persist 6 (*Slang*) = <u>tolerate</u>, take, stand, stomach, abide

● PHRASES **stick out** = <u>protrude</u>, stand out, jut out, show, project, bulge, obtrude

◆ **stick up for someone** (*Informal*) = <u>defend</u>, support, champion, stand up for

sticky 1 = <u>adhesive</u>, gummed, adherent 2 = <u>gooey</u>, tacky (*informal*), viscous, glutinous, gummy, icky (*informal*), gluey, clinging 3 (*Informal*) = <u>difficult</u>, awkward, tricky, embarrassing, nasty, delicate, unpleasant, barro (*Austral. slang*) 4 = <u>humid</u>, close, sultry, oppressive, sweltering, clammy, muggy

stiff 1 = <u>inflexible</u>, rigid, unyielding, hard, firm, tight, solid, tense ≠ flexible 2 = <u>formal</u>, constrained, forced, unnatural, stilted, unrelaxed ≠ informal 3 = <u>vigorous</u>, great, strong 4 = <u>severe</u>, strict, harsh, hard, heavy, extreme, drastic 5 = <u>difficult</u>, hard, tough, exacting, arduous

stifle 1 = <u>suppress</u>, repress, stop, check, silence, restrain, hush, smother 2 = <u>restrain</u>, suppress, repress, smother

stigma = <u>disgrace</u>, shame, dishonour, stain, slur, smirch

still ADJECTIVE 1 = <u>motionless</u>, stationary, calm, peaceful, serene, tranquil, undisturbed, restful ≠ moving 2 = <u>silent</u>, quiet, hushed ≠ noisy

● VERB = <u>quieten</u>, calm, settle, quiet, silence, soothe, hush, lull ≠ get louder

● ADVERB = <u>however</u>, but, yet, nevertheless, notwithstanding

stimulate = <u>encourage</u>, inspire, prompt,

fire, spur, provoke, arouse, rouse

stimulating = <u>exciting</u>, inspiring, stirring, rousing, provocative, exhilarating ≠ boring

stimulus = <u>incentive</u>, spur, encouragement, impetus, inducement, goad, incitement, fillip

sting 1 = <u>hurt</u>, burn, wound 2 = <u>smart</u>, burn, pain, hurt, tingle

stink VERB = <u>reek</u>, pong (*Brit. informal*)

● NOUN = <u>stench</u>, pong (*Brit. informal*), foul smell, fetor

stint NOUN = <u>term</u>, time, turn, period, share, shift, stretch, spell

● VERB = <u>be mean</u>, hold back, be sparing, skimp on, be frugal

stipulate = <u>specify</u>, agree, require, contract, settle, covenant, insist upon

stir VERB 1 = <u>mix</u>, beat, agitate 2 = <u>stimulate</u>, move, excite, spur, provoke, arouse, awaken, rouse ≠ inhibit 3 = <u>spur</u>, drive, prompt, stimulate, prod, urge, animate, prick

● NOUN = <u>commotion</u>, excitement, activity, disorder, fuss, disturbance, bustle, flurry

stock NOUN 1 = <u>shares</u>, holdings, securities, investments, bonds, equities 2 = <u>property</u>, capital, assets, funds 3 = <u>goods</u>, merchandise, wares, range, choice, variety, selection, commodities 4 = <u>supply</u>, store, reserve, fund, stockpile, hoard 5 = <u>livestock</u>, cattle, beasts, domestic animals

● VERB 1 = <u>sell</u>, supply, handle, keep, trade in, deal in 2 = <u>fill</u>, supply, provide with, equip, furnish, fit out

● ADJECTIVE 1 = <u>hackneyed</u>, routine, banal, trite, overused 2 = <u>regular</u>, usual, ordinary, conventional, customary

stomach NOUN 1 = <u>belly</u>, gut (*informal*), abdomen, tummy (*informal*), puku (*N.Z.*) 2 = <u>tummy</u>, pot 3 = <u>inclination</u>, taste, desire, appetite, relish

● VERB = <u>bear</u>, take, tolerate, endure, swallow, abide

▨ RELATED WORD
adjective: gastric

stone 1 = <u>masonry</u>, rock 2 = <u>rock</u>, pebble 3 = <u>pip</u>, seed, pit, kernel

stoop VERB 1 = <u>hunch</u> 2 = <u>bend</u>, lean, bow, duck, crouch

● NOUN = <u>slouch</u>, bad posture, round-shoulderedness

stop VERB 1 = <u>quit</u>, cease, refrain, put an end to, discontinue, desist ≠ start

2 = <u>prevent</u>, cut short, arrest, restrain, hold back, hinder, repress, impede ≠ facilitate 3 = <u>end</u>, conclude, finish, terminate ≠ continue 4 = <u>cease</u>, shut down, discontinue, desist ≠ continue 5 = <u>halt</u>, pause ≠ keep going 6 = <u>pause</u>, wait, rest, take a break, have a breather (*informal*), stop briefly 7 = <u>stay</u>, rest, lodge
● NOUN 1 = <u>halt</u>, standstill 2 = <u>station</u>, stage, depot, terminus 3 = <u>stay</u>, break, rest

store NOUN 1 = <u>shop</u>, outlet, market, mart 2 = <u>supply</u>, stock, reserve, fund, quantity, accumulation, stockpile, hoard 3 = <u>repository</u>, warehouse, depository, storeroom
● VERB 1 *often with **away** or **up*** = <u>put by</u>, save, hoard, keep, reserve, deposit, garner, stockpile 2 = <u>put away</u>, put in storage, put in store 3 = <u>keep</u>, hold, preserve, maintain, retain, conserve

storm NOUN 1 = <u>tempest</u>, hurricane, gale, blizzard, squall 2 = <u>outburst</u>, row, outcry, furore, outbreak, turmoil, disturbance, strife
● VERB 1 = <u>rush</u>, stamp, flounce, fly 2 = <u>rage</u>, rant, thunder, rave, bluster 3 = <u>attack</u>, charge, rush, assault, assail

stormy 1 = <u>wild</u>, rough, raging, turbulent, windy, blustery, inclement, squally 2 = <u>rough</u>, wild, turbulent, raging 3 = <u>angry</u>, heated, fierce, passionate, fiery, impassioned

story 1 = <u>tale</u>, romance, narrative, history, legend, yarn 2 = <u>anecdote</u>, account, tale, report 3 = <u>report</u>, news, article, feature, scoop, news item

stout 1 = <u>fat</u>, big, heavy, overweight, plump, bulky, burly, fleshy ≠ slim 2 = <u>strong</u>, strapping, muscular, robust, sturdy, stalwart, brawny, able-bodied ≠ puny 3 = <u>brave</u>, bold, courageous, fearless, resolute, gallant, intrepid, valiant ≠ timid

straight ADJECTIVE 1 = <u>direct</u> ≠ indirect 2 = <u>level</u>, even, right, square, true, smooth, aligned, horizontal ≠ crooked 3 = <u>frank</u>, plain, straightforward, blunt, outright, honest, candid, forthright ≠ evasive 4 = <u>successive</u>, consecutive, continuous, running, solid, nonstop ≠ discontinuous 5 (*Slang*) = <u>conventional</u>, conservative, bourgeois ≠ fashionable 6 = <u>honest</u>, just, fair, reliable, respectable, upright, honourable, law-abiding ≠ dishonest

7 = <u>undiluted</u>, pure, neat, unadulterated, unmixed 8 = <u>in order</u>, organized, arranged, neat, tidy, orderly, shipshape ≠ untidy
● ADVERB 1 = <u>directly</u>, precisely, exactly, unswervingly, by the shortest route, in a beeline 2 = <u>immediately</u>, directly, promptly, instantly, at once, straight away, without delay, forthwith

straight away = <u>immediately</u>, now, at once, directly, instantly, right away

straighten = <u>neaten</u>, arrange, tidy (up), order, put in order

straightforward 1 (*Chiefly Brit.*) = <u>simple</u>, easy, uncomplicated, routine, elementary, easy-peasy (*slang*) ≠ complicated 2 = <u>honest</u>, open, direct, genuine, sincere, candid, truthful, forthright, dinkum (*Austral. & N.Z. informal*) ≠ devious

strain¹ NOUN 1 = <u>pressure</u>, stress, demands, burden 2 = <u>stress</u>, anxiety 3 = <u>worry</u>, effort, struggle ≠ ease 4 = <u>burden</u>, tension 5 = <u>injury</u>, wrench, sprain, pull
● VERB 1 = <u>stretch</u>, tax, overtax 2 = <u>strive</u>, struggle, endeavour, labour, go for it (*informal*), bend over backwards (*informal*), give it your best shot (*informal*), knock yourself out (*informal*) ≠ relax 3 = <u>sieve</u>, filter, sift, purify

strain² 1 = <u>trace</u>, suggestion, tendency, streak 2 = <u>breed</u>, family, race, blood, descent, extraction, ancestry, lineage

strained 1 = <u>tense</u>, difficult, awkward, embarrassed, stiff, uneasy ≠ relaxed 2 = <u>forced</u>, put on, false, artificial, unnatural ≠ natural

strait NOUN *often plural* = <u>channel</u>, sound, narrows
● PLURAL NOUN = <u>difficulty</u>, dilemma, plight, hardship, uphill (*S. African*), predicament, extremity

strand = <u>filament</u>, fibre, thread, string

stranded 1 = <u>beached</u>, grounded, marooned, ashore, shipwrecked, aground 2 = <u>helpless</u>, abandoned, high and dry

strange 1 = <u>odd</u>, curious, weird, wonderful, extraordinary, bizarre, peculiar, abnormal ≠ ordinary 2 = <u>unfamiliar</u>, new, unknown, foreign, novel, alien, exotic, untried ≠ familiar

stranger 1 = <u>unknown person</u> 2 = <u>newcomer</u>, incomer, foreigner, guest, visitor, alien, outlander

strangle 1 = <u>throttle</u>, choke, asphyxiate, strangulate 2 = <u>suppress</u>, inhibit, subdue, stifle, repress, overpower, quash, quell

strap NOUN 1 = <u>tie</u>, thong, belt
● VERB = <u>fasten</u>, tie, secure, bind, lash, buckle

strapping = <u>well-built</u>, big, powerful, robust, sturdy, husky (*informal*), brawny

strategic 1 = <u>tactical</u>, calculated, deliberate, planned, politic, diplomatic 2 = <u>crucial</u>, important, key, vital, critical, decisive, cardinal

strategy 1 = <u>policy</u>, procedure, approach, scheme 2 = <u>plan</u>, approach, scheme

stray VERB 1 = <u>wander</u>, go astray, drift 2 = <u>drift</u>, wander, roam, meander, rove 3 = <u>digress</u>, diverge, deviate, get off the point
● ADJECTIVE 1 = <u>lost</u>, abandoned, homeless, roaming, vagrant 2 = <u>random</u>, chance, accidental

streak NOUN 1 = <u>band</u>, line, strip, stroke, layer, slash, vein, stripe 2 = <u>trace</u>, touch, element, strain, dash, vein
● VERB = <u>speed</u>, fly, tear, flash, sprint, dart, zoom, whizz (*informal*)

stream NOUN 1 = <u>river</u>, brook, burn (*Scot.*), beck, tributary, bayou, rivulet 2 = <u>flow</u>, current, rush, run, course, drift, surge, tide
● VERB 1 = <u>flow</u>, run, pour, issue, flood, spill, cascade, gush 2 = <u>rush</u>, fly, speed, tear, flood, pour

streamlined = <u>efficient</u>, organized, rationalized, slick, smooth-running

street = <u>road</u>, lane, avenue, terrace, row, roadway

strength 1 = <u>might</u>, muscle, brawn ≠ weakness 2 = <u>will</u>, resolution, courage, character, nerve, determination, pluck, stamina 3 = <u>health</u>, fitness, vigour 4 = <u>mainstay</u> 5 = <u>toughness</u>, soundness, robustness, sturdiness 6 = <u>force</u>, power, intensity ≠ weakness 7 = <u>potency</u>, effectiveness, efficacy 8 = <u>strong point</u>, skill, asset, advantage, talent, forte, speciality ≠ failing

strengthen 1 = <u>fortify</u>, harden, toughen, consolidate, stiffen, gee up, brace up ≠ weaken 2 = <u>reinforce</u>, support, intensify, bolster, buttress 3 = <u>bolster</u>, harden, reinforce 4 = <u>heighten</u>, intensify 5 = <u>make stronger</u>, build up, invigorate, restore, give strength to 6 = <u>support</u>, brace, reinforce, consolidate, harden, bolster, augment, buttress 7 = <u>become stronger</u>, intensify, gain strength

stress VERB 1 = <u>emphasize</u>, underline, dwell on 2 = <u>place the emphasis on</u>, emphasize, give emphasis to, lay emphasis upon
● NOUN 1 = <u>emphasis</u>, significance, force, weight 2 = <u>strain</u>, pressure, worry, tension, burden, anxiety, trauma 3 = <u>accent</u>, beat, emphasis, accentuation

stretch VERB 1 = <u>extend</u>, cover, spread, reach, put forth, unroll 2 = <u>last</u>, continue, go on, carry on, reach 3 = <u>expand</u> 4 = <u>pull</u>, distend, strain, tighten, draw out, elongate
● NOUN 1 = <u>expanse</u>, area, tract, spread, distance, extent 2 = <u>period</u>, time, spell, stint, term, space

strict 1 = <u>severe</u>, harsh, stern, firm, stringent ≠ easy-going 2 = <u>stern</u>, firm, severe, harsh, authoritarian 3 = <u>exact</u>, accurate, precise, close, true, faithful, meticulous, scrupulous 4 = <u>absolute</u>, total, utter

strife = <u>conflict</u>, battle, clash, quarrel, friction, discord, dissension

strike NOUN 1 = <u>walkout</u>, industrial action, mutiny, revolt
● VERB 1 = <u>walk out</u>, down tools, revolt, mutiny 2 = <u>hit</u>, smack, thump, beat, knock, punch, hammer, slap 3 = <u>drive</u>, hit, smack, wallop (*informal*) 4 = <u>collide with</u>, hit, run into, bump into 5 = <u>knock</u>, smack, thump, beat 6 = <u>affect</u>, touch, devastate, overwhelm, leave a mark on 7 = <u>attack</u>, assault someone, set upon someone, lay into someone (*informal*) 8 = <u>occur to</u>, hit, come to, register (*informal*), dawn on *or* upon 9 = <u>seem to</u>, appear to, look to, give the impression to 10 = <u>move</u>, touch, hit, affect, overcome, stir, disturb, perturb

striking = <u>impressive</u>, dramatic, outstanding, noticeable, conspicuous, jaw-dropping ≠ unimpressive

string 1 = <u>cord</u>, twine, fibre 2 = <u>series</u>, line, row, file, sequence, succession, procession 3 = <u>sequence</u>, run, series, chain, succession

stringent = <u>strict</u>, tough, rigorous, tight, severe, rigid, inflexible ≠ lax

strip[1] 1 = <u>undress</u>, disrobe, unclothe 2 = <u>plunder</u>, rob, loot, empty, sack, ransack, pillage, divest

strip[2] 1 = <u>piece</u>, shred, band, belt 2 = <u>stretch</u>, area, tract, expanse, extent

strive = <u>try</u>, labour, struggle, attempt, toil, go all out (*informal*), bend over backwards (*informal*), do your best

stroke VERB = <u>caress</u>, rub, fondle, pet
● NOUN 1 = <u>apoplexy</u>, fit, seizure, attack, collapse 2 = <u>blow</u>, hit, knock, pat, rap, thump, swipe

stroll VERB = <u>walk</u>, ramble, amble, promenade, saunter
● NOUN = <u>walk</u>, promenade, constitutional, ramble, breath of air

strong 1 = <u>powerful</u>, muscular, tough, athletic, strapping, hardy, sturdy, burly ≠ weak 2 = <u>fit</u>, robust, lusty 3 = <u>durable</u>, substantial, sturdy, heavy-duty, well-built, hard-wearing ≠ flimsy 4 = <u>extreme</u>, radical, drastic, strict, harsh, rigid, forceful, uncompromising 5 = <u>decisive</u>, firm, forceful, decided, determined, resolute, incisive 6 = <u>persuasive</u>, convincing, compelling, telling, sound, effective, potent, weighty 7 = <u>keen</u>, deep, acute, fervent, zealous, vehement 8 = <u>intense</u>, deep, passionate, ardent, fierce, fervent, vehement, fervid 9 = <u>staunch</u>, firm, fierce, ardent, enthusiastic, passionate, fervent 10 = <u>distinct</u>, marked, clear, unmistakable ≠ slight 11 = <u>bright</u>, brilliant, dazzling, bold ≠ dull

stronghold 1 = <u>bastion</u>, fortress, bulwark 2 = <u>refuge</u>, haven, retreat, sanctuary, hide-out

structure NOUN 1 = <u>arrangement</u>, form, make-up, design, organization, construction, formation, configuration 2 = <u>building</u>, construction, erection, edifice
● VERB = <u>arrange</u>, organize, design, shape, build up, assemble

struggle VERB 1 = <u>strive</u>, labour, toil, work, strain, go all out (*informal*), give it your best shot (*informal*), exert yourself 2 = <u>fight</u>, battle, wrestle, grapple, compete, contend
● NOUN 1 = <u>effort</u>, labour, toil, work, pains, scramble, exertion 2 = <u>fight</u>, battle, conflict, clash, contest, brush, combat, tussle, biffo (*Austral. slang*)

strut = <u>swagger</u>, parade, peacock, prance

stubborn = <u>obstinate</u>, dogged, inflexible, persistent, intractable, tenacious, recalcitrant, unyielding ≠ compliant

stuck 1 = <u>fastened</u>, fast, fixed, joined, glued, cemented 2 (*Informal*) = <u>baffled</u>, stumped, beaten

student 1 = <u>undergraduate</u>, scholar 2 = <u>pupil</u>, scholar, schoolchild, schoolboy

or schoolgirl 3 = <u>learner</u>, trainee, apprentice, disciple

studied = <u>planned</u>, deliberate, conscious, intentional, premeditated ≠ unplanned

studio = <u>workshop</u>, workroom, atelier

study VERB 1 = <u>learn</u>, cram (*informal*), swot (up) (*Brit. informal*), read up, mug up (*Brit. slang*) 2 = <u>examine</u>, survey, look at, scrutinize 3 = <u>contemplate</u>, read, examine, consider, go into, pore over
● NOUN 1 = <u>examination</u>, investigation, analysis, consideration, inspection, scrutiny, contemplation 2 = <u>piece of research</u>, survey, report, review, inquiry, investigation 3 = <u>learning</u>, lessons, school work, reading, research, swotting (*Brit. informal*)

stuff NOUN 1 = <u>things</u>, gear, possessions, effects, equipment, objects, tackle, kit 2 = <u>substance</u>, material, essence, matter
● VERB 1 = <u>shove</u>, force, push, squeeze, jam, ram 2 = <u>cram</u>, fill, pack, crowd

stuffing = <u>wadding</u>, filling, packing

stumble VERB 1 = <u>trip</u>, fall, slip, reel, stagger, falter, lurch 2 = <u>totter</u>, reel, lurch, wobble
● PHRASES **stumble across** *or* **on** *or* **upon something** *or* **someone** = <u>discover</u>, find, come across, chance upon

stump NOUN = <u>tail end</u>, end, remnant, remainder
● VERB = <u>baffle</u>, confuse, puzzle, bewilder, perplex, mystify, flummox, nonplus

stun 1 = <u>overcome</u>, shock, confuse, astonish, stagger, bewilder, astound, overpower 2 = <u>daze</u>, knock out, stupefy, numb, benumb

stunning (*Informal*) = <u>wonderful</u>, beautiful, impressive, striking, lovely, spectacular, marvellous, splendid ≠ unimpressive

stunt = <u>feat</u>, act, trick, exploit, deed

stunted = <u>undersized</u>, little, small, tiny, diminutive

stupid 1 = <u>unintelligent</u>, thick, simple, slow, dim, dense, simple-minded, moronic ≠ intelligent 2 = <u>silly</u>, foolish, daft (*informal*), rash, pointless, senseless, idiotic, fatuous ≠ sensible 3 = <u>senseless</u>, dazed, groggy, insensate, semiconscious

sturdy 1 = <u>robust</u>, hardy, powerful, athletic, muscular, lusty, brawny ≠ puny 2 = <u>substantial</u>, solid, durable, well-made, well-built ≠ flimsy

style NOUN 1 = manner, way, method, approach, technique, mode 2 = elegance, taste, chic, flair, polish, sophistication, panache, élan 3 = design, form, cut 4 = type, sort, kind, variety, category, genre 5 = fashion, trend, mode, vogue, rage 6 = luxury, ease, comfort, elegance, grandeur, affluence
● VERB 1 = design, cut, tailor, fashion, shape, arrange, adapt 2 = call, name, term, label, entitle, dub, designate

stylish = smart, chic, fashionable, trendy (*Brit. informal*), modish, dressy (*informal*), voguish ≠ scruffy

subdue 1 = overcome, defeat, master, break, control, crush, conquer, tame 2 = moderate, suppress, soften, mellow, tone down, quieten down ≠ arouse

subdued 1 = quiet, serious, sad, chastened, dejected, downcast, crestfallen, down in the mouth ≠ lively 2 = hushed, soft, quiet, muted ≠ loud

subject NOUN 1 = topic, question, issue, matter, point, business, affair, object 2 = citizen, resident, native, inhabitant, national 3 = dependant, subordinate
● ADJECTIVE = subordinate, dependent, satellite, inferior, obedient
● VERB = put through, expose, submit, lay open
● PHRASES **subject to** 1 = liable to, open to, exposed to, vulnerable to, prone to, susceptible to 2 = bound by 3 = dependent on, contingent on, controlled by, conditional on

subjective = personal, prejudiced, biased, nonobjective ≠ objective

sublime = noble, glorious, high, great, grand, elevated, lofty, exalted ≠ lowly

submerge 1 = flood, swamp, engulf, overflow, inundate, deluge 2 = immerse, plunge, duck 3 = sink, plunge, go under water 4 = overwhelm, swamp, engulf, deluge

submission 1 = surrender, yielding, giving in, cave-in (*informal*), capitulation 2 = presentation, handing in, entry, tendering 3 = compliance, obedience, meekness, resignation, deference, passivity, docility

submit 1 = surrender, yield, give in, agree, endure, tolerate, comply, succumb 2 = present, hand in, tender, put forward, table, proffer

subordinate NOUN = inferior, junior, assistant, aide, second, attendant ≠ superior
● ADJECTIVE = inferior, lesser, lower, junior, subject, minor, secondary, dependent ≠ superior

subscribe 1 = support, advocate, endorse 2 = contribute, give, donate

subscription (*Chiefly Brit.*) = membership fee, dues, annual payment

subsequent = following, later, succeeding, after, successive, ensuing ≠ previous

subsequently = later, afterwards

subside 1 = decrease, diminish, lessen, ease, wane, ebb, abate, slacken ≠ increase 2 = collapse, sink, cave in, drop, lower, settle

subsidiary NOUN = branch, division, section, office, department, wing, subdivision, subsection
● ADJECTIVE = secondary, lesser, subordinate, minor, supplementary, auxiliary, ancillary ≠ main

subsidy = aid, help, support, grant, assistance, allowance

substance 1 = material, body, stuff, fabric 2 = importance, significance, concreteness 3 = meaning, main point, gist, import, significance, essence 4 = wealth, means, property, assets, resources, estate

substantial = big, significant, considerable, large, important, ample, sizable *or* sizeable ≠ small

substitute VERB = replace, exchange, swap, change, switch, interchange
● NOUN = replacement, reserve, surrogate, deputy, sub, proxy, locum
● ADJECTIVE = replacement, reserve, surrogate, second, alternative, fall-back, proxy

subtle 1 = faint, slight, implied, delicate, understated ≠ obvious 2 = crafty, cunning, sly, shrewd, ingenious, devious, wily, artful ≠ straightforward 3 = muted, soft, subdued, low-key, toned down 4 = fine, minute, narrow, tenuous, hair-splitting

subtlety 1 = fine point, refinement, sophistication, delicacy 2 = skill, ingenuity, cleverness, deviousness, craftiness, artfulness, slyness, wiliness

subversive ADJECTIVE = seditious, riotous, treasonous
● NOUN = dissident, terrorist, saboteur, fifth

columnist

succeed 1 = <u>triumph</u>, win, prevail
2 = <u>work out</u>, work, be successful
3 = <u>make it</u> (*informal*), do well, be
successful, triumph, thrive, flourish, make
good, prosper ≠ fail 4 = <u>take over from</u>,
assume the office of 5 *with to* = <u>take over</u>,
assume, attain, come into, inherit, accede
to, come into possession of 6 = <u>follow</u>,
come after, follow after ≠ precede

success 1 = <u>victory</u>, triumph ≠ failure
2 = <u>prosperity</u>, fortune, luck, fame 3 = <u>hit</u>
(*informal*), winner, smash (*informal*),
triumph, sensation ≠ flop (*informal*)
4 = <u>big name</u>, star, hit (*informal*), celebrity,
sensation, megastar (*informal*) ≠ nobody

successful 1 = <u>triumphant</u>, victorious,
lucky, fortunate 2 = <u>thriving</u>, profitable,
rewarding, booming, flourishing, fruitful
≠ unprofitable 3 = <u>top</u>, prosperous,
wealthy

successfully = <u>well</u>, favourably, with
flying colours, victoriously

succession 1 = <u>series</u>, run, sequence,
course, order, train, chain, cycle 2 = <u>taking
over</u>, assumption, inheritance, accession

successive = <u>consecutive</u>, following, in
succession

succumb 1 *often with to* = <u>surrender</u>,
yield, submit, give in, cave in (*informal*),
capitulate ≠ beat 2 *with to* (with an illness
as object) = <u>catch</u>, fall ill with

suck 1 = <u>drink</u>, sip, draw 2 = <u>take</u>, draw,
pull, extract

sudden = <u>quick</u>, rapid, unexpected, swift,
hurried, abrupt, hasty ≠ gradual

suddenly = <u>abruptly</u>, all of a sudden,
unexpectedly

sue (*Law*) = <u>take (someone) to court</u>,
prosecute, charge, summon, indict

suffer 1 = <u>be in pain</u>, hurt, ache 2 = <u>be
affected</u>, have trouble with, be afflicted,
be troubled with 3 = <u>undergo</u>, experience,
sustain, bear, go through, endure
4 = <u>tolerate</u>, stand, put up with (*informal*),
bear, endure

suffering = <u>pain</u>, distress, agony, misery,
ordeal, discomfort, torment, hardship

suffice = <u>be enough</u>, do, be sufficient, be
adequate, serve, meet requirements

sufficient = <u>adequate</u>, enough, ample,
satisfactory ≠ insufficient

suggest 1 = <u>recommend</u>, propose, advise,
advocate, prescribe 2 = <u>indicate</u> 3 = <u>hint</u>

at, imply, intimate 4 = <u>bring to mind</u>,
evoke

suggestion 1 = <u>recommendation</u>,
proposal, proposition, plan, motion
2 = <u>hint</u>, insinuation, intimation 3 = <u>trace</u>,
touch, hint, breath, indication, whisper,
intimation

suit NOUN 1 = <u>outfit</u>, costume, ensemble,
dress, clothing, habit 2 = <u>lawsuit</u>, case, trial,
proceeding, cause, action, prosecution
● VERB 1 = <u>be acceptable to</u>, please, satisfy,
do, gratify 2 = <u>agree with</u>, become, match,
go with, harmonize with

suitable 1 = <u>appropriate</u>, right, fitting,
fit, becoming, satisfactory, apt, befitting
≠ inappropriate 2 = <u>seemly</u>, fitting,
becoming, proper, correct ≠ unseemly
3 = <u>suited</u>, appropriate, in keeping with
≠ out of keeping 4 = <u>pertinent</u>, relevant,
applicable, fitting, appropriate, to the
point, apt ≠ irrelevant 5 = <u>convenient</u>,
timely, appropriate, well-timed, opportune
≠ inopportune

suite = <u>rooms</u>, apartment

sum 1 = <u>amount</u>, quantity, volume
2 = <u>calculation</u>, figures, arithmetic,
mathematics, maths (*Brit. informal*), tally,
math (*U.S. informal*), arithmetical problem
3 = <u>total</u>, aggregate 4 = <u>totality</u>, whole

summarize = <u>sum up</u>, condense,
encapsulate, epitomize, abridge, précis

summary = <u>synopsis</u>, résumé, précis,
review, outline, rundown, abridgment

summit 1 = <u>peak</u>, top, tip, pinnacle, apex,
head ≠ base 2 = <u>height</u>, pinnacle, peak,
zenith, acme ≠ depths

summon 1 = <u>send for</u>, call, bid, invite
2 *often with up* = <u>gather</u>, muster, draw on

sumptuous = <u>luxurious</u>, grand, superb,
splendid, gorgeous, lavish, opulent ≠ plain

sunny 1 = <u>bright</u>, clear, fine, radiant, sunlit,
summery, unclouded ≠ dull 2 = <u>cheerful</u>,
happy, cheery, buoyant, joyful, light-
hearted ≠ gloomy

sunset = <u>nightfall</u>, dusk, eventide, close
of (the) day

superb 1 = <u>splendid</u>, excellent,
magnificent, fine, grand, superior,
marvellous, world-class, booshit (*Austral.
slang*), exo (*Austral. slang*), sik (*Austral.
slang*) ≠ inferior 2 = <u>magnificent</u>, superior,
marvellous, exquisite, superlative
≠ terrible

superficial 1 = <u>shallow</u>, frivolous, empty-

headed, silly, trivial ≠ serious 2 = hasty,
cursory, perfunctory, hurried, casual,
sketchy, desultory, slapdash ≠ thorough
3 = slight, surface, external, on the surface,
exterior ≠ profound
superintendent = supervisor, director,
manager, chief, governor, inspector,
controller, overseer
superior ADJECTIVE 1 = better, higher,
greater, grander, surpassing, unrivalled
≠ inferior 2 = first-class, excellent, first-
rate, choice, exclusive, exceptional,
de luxe, booshit (*Austral. slang*), exo
(*Austral. slang*), sik (*Austral. slang*)
≠ average 3 = supercilious, patronizing,
condescending, haughty, disdainful, lordly,
lofty, pretentious
● NOUN = boss, senior, director, manager,
chief (*informal*), principal, supervisor, baas
(*S. African*) ≠ subordinate
superiority = supremacy, lead,
advantage, excellence, ascendancy,
predominance
supernatural = paranormal, unearthly,
uncanny, ghostly, psychic, mystic,
miraculous, occult
supervise 1 = observe, guide, monitor,
oversee, keep an eye on 2 = oversee, run,
manage, control, direct, handle, look after,
superintend
supervision = superintendence,
direction, control, charge, care,
management, guidance
supervisor = boss (*informal*), manager,
chief, inspector, administrator, foreman,
overseer, baas (*S. African*)
supplement VERB = add to, reinforce,
augment, extend
● NOUN 1 = pull-out, insert 2 = appendix,
add-on, postscript 3 = addition, extra
supply VERB 1 = provide, give, furnish,
produce, stock, grant, contribute, yield
2 = furnish, provide, equip, endow
● NOUN = store, fund, stock, source, reserve,
quantity, hoard, cache
● PLURAL NOUN = provisions, necessities,
stores, food, materials, equipment, rations
support VERB 1 = help, back, champion,
second, aid, defend, assist, side with
≠ oppose 2 = provide for, maintain, look
after, keep, fund, finance, sustain ≠ live off
3 = bear out, confirm, verify, substantiate,
corroborate ≠ refute 4 = bear, carry,
sustain, prop (up), reinforce, hold, brace,

buttress
● NOUN 1 = furtherance, backing,
promotion, assistance, encouragement
2 = help, loyalty ≠ opposition 3 = aid, help,
benefits, relief, assistance 4 = prop, post,
foundation, brace, pillar 5 = supporter,
prop, mainstay, tower of strength,
second, backer ≠ antagonist 6 = upkeep,
maintenance, keep, subsistence,
sustenance
supporter = follower, fan, advocate,
friend, champion, sponsor, patron, helper
≠ opponent
supportive = helpful, encouraging,
understanding, sympathetic
suppose 1 = imagine, consider,
conjecture, postulate, hypothesize
2 = think, imagine, expect, assume, guess
(*informal*, *chiefly U.S. & Canad.*), presume,
conjecture
supposed 1 *usually with* to = meant,
expected, required, obliged 2 = presumed,
alleged, professed, accepted, assumed
supposedly = presumably, allegedly,
ostensibly, theoretically, hypothetically
≠ actually
suppress 1 = stamp out, stop, check,
crush, conquer, subdue, put an end to,
overpower ≠ encourage 2 = check, inhibit,
subdue, stop, quell 3 = restrain, stifle,
contain, silence, conceal, curb, repress,
smother
suppression 1 = elimination, crushing,
check, quashing 2 = inhibition, blocking,
restraint, smothering
supremacy = domination, sovereignty,
sway, mastery, primacy, predominance,
supreme power
supreme 1 = paramount ≠ least 2 = chief,
leading, principal, highest, head, top,
prime, foremost ≠ lowest 3 = ultimate,
highest, greatest
supremo (*Brit. informal*) = head, leader,
boss (*informal*), director, master, governor,
commander, principal, baas (*S. African*)
sure 1 = certain, positive, decided,
convinced, confident, assured, definite
≠ uncertain 2 = inevitable, guaranteed,
bound, assured, inescapable ≠ unsure
3 = reliable, accurate, dependable,
undoubted, undeniable, foolproof,
infallible, unerring ≠ unreliable
surely 1 = it must be the case that
2 = undoubtedly, certainly, definitely,

without doubt, unquestionably, indubitably, doubtlessly

surface NOUN 1 = <u>covering</u>, face, exterior, side, top, veneer 2 = <u>façade</u>
● VERB 1 = <u>emerge</u>, come up, come to the surface 2 = <u>appear</u>, emerge, arise, come to light, crop up (informal), transpire, materialize

surge NOUN 1 = <u>rush</u>, flood 2 = <u>flow</u>, wave, rush, roller, gush, outpouring 3 = <u>tide</u>, swell, billowing 4 = <u>rush</u>, wave, storm, torrent, eruption
● VERB 1 = <u>rush</u>, pour, rise, gush 2 = <u>roll</u>, rush, heave 3 = <u>sweep</u>, rush, storm

surpass = <u>outdo</u>, beat, exceed, eclipse, excel, transcend, outstrip, outshine

surpassing = <u>supreme</u>, extraordinary, outstanding, exceptional, unrivalled, incomparable, matchless

surplus NOUN = <u>excess</u>, surfeit ≠ shortage
● ADJECTIVE = <u>extra</u>, spare, excess, remaining, odd, superfluous ≠ insufficient

surprise NOUN 1 = <u>shock</u>, revelation, jolt, bombshell, eye-opener (informal) 2 = <u>amazement</u>, astonishment, wonder, incredulity
● VERB 1 = <u>amaze</u>, astonish, stun, startle, stagger, take aback 2 = <u>catch unawares</u> or off-guard, spring upon

surprised = <u>amazed</u>, astonished, speechless, thunderstruck

surprising = <u>amazing</u>, remarkable, incredible, astonishing, unusual, extraordinary, unexpected, staggering

surrender VERB 1 = <u>give in</u>, yield, submit, give way, succumb, cave in (informal), capitulate ≠ resist 2 = <u>give up</u>, abandon, relinquish, yield, concede, part with, renounce, waive
● NOUN = <u>submission</u>, cave-in (informal), capitulation, resignation, renunciation, relinquishment

surround = <u>enclose</u>, ring, encircle, encompass, envelop, hem in

surrounding ADJECTIVE = <u>nearby</u>, neighbouring
● PLURAL NOUN = <u>environment</u>, setting, background, location, milieu

surveillance = <u>observation</u>, watch, scrutiny, supervision, inspection

survey NOUN 1 = <u>poll</u>, study, research, review, inquiry, investigation
2 = <u>examination</u>, inspection, scrutiny
3 = <u>valuation</u>, estimate, assessment,
appraisal
● VERB 1 = <u>interview</u>, question, poll, research, investigate 2 = <u>look over</u>, view, examine, observe, contemplate, inspect, eyeball (slang), scrutinize 3 = <u>measure</u>, estimate, assess, appraise

survive 1 = <u>remain alive</u>, last, live on, endure 2 = <u>continue</u>, last, live on 3 = <u>live longer than</u>, outlive, outlast

susceptible 1 = <u>responsive</u>, sensitive, receptive, impressionable, suggestible ≠ unresponsive 2 usually with **to** = <u>liable</u>, inclined, prone, given, subject, vulnerable, disposed ≠ resistant

suspect VERB 1 = <u>believe</u>, feel, guess, consider, suppose, speculate ≠ know 2 = <u>distrust</u>, doubt, mistrust ≠ trust
● ADJECTIVE = <u>dubious</u>, doubtful, questionable, iffy (informal) ≠ innocent

suspend 1 = <u>postpone</u>, put off, cease, interrupt, shelve, defer, cut short, discontinue ≠ continue 2 = <u>hang</u>, attach, dangle

suspension = <u>postponement</u>, break, breaking off, interruption, abeyance, deferment, discontinuation

suspicion 1 = <u>distrust</u>, scepticism, mistrust, doubt, misgiving, qualm, wariness, dubiety 2 = <u>idea</u>, notion, hunch, guess, impression 3 = <u>trace</u>, touch, hint, suggestion, shade, streak, tinge, soupçon (French)

suspicious 1 = <u>distrustful</u>, sceptical, doubtful, unbelieving, wary ≠ trusting 2 = <u>suspect</u>, dubious, questionable, doubtful, dodgy (Brit., Austral., & N.Z. informal), fishy (informal) ≠ beyond suspicion

sustain 1 = <u>maintain</u>, continue, keep up, prolong, protract 2 = <u>suffer</u>, experience, undergo, feel, bear, endure, withstand 3 = <u>help</u>, aid, assist 4 = <u>keep alive</u>, nourish, provide for 5 = <u>support</u>, bear, uphold

sustained = <u>continuous</u>, constant, steady, prolonged, perpetual, unremitting, nonstop ≠ periodic

swallow 1 = <u>eat</u>, consume, devour, swig (informal) 2 = <u>gulp</u>, drink

swamp NOUN = <u>bog</u>, marsh, quagmire, slough, fen, mire, morass, pakihi (N.Z.)
● VERB 1 = <u>flood</u>, engulf, submerge, inundate 2 = <u>overload</u>, overwhelm, inundate

swap or **swop** = <u>exchange</u>, trade, switch,

interchange, barter

swarm NOUN 1 = <u>multitude</u>, crowd, mass, army, host, flock, herd, horde
● VERB 1 = <u>crowd</u>, flock, throng, mass, stream 2 = <u>teem</u>, crawl, abound, bristle

swathe NOUN = <u>area</u>, section, tract
● VERB = <u>wrap</u>, drape, envelop, cloak, shroud, bundle up

sway VERB 1 = <u>move from side to side</u>, rock, roll, swing, bend, lean 2 = <u>influence</u>, affect, guide, persuade, induce
● NOUN = <u>power</u>, control, influence, authority, clout (*informal*)

swear 1 = <u>curse</u>, blaspheme, be foul-mouthed 2 = <u>vow</u>, promise, testify, attest 3 = <u>declare</u>, assert, affirm

swearing = <u>bad language</u>, cursing, profanity, blasphemy, foul language

sweat NOUN 1 = <u>perspiration</u> 2 (*Informal*) = <u>panic</u>, anxiety, worry, distress, agitation
● VERB 1 = <u>perspire</u>, glow 2 (*Informal*) = <u>worry</u>, fret, agonize, torture yourself

sweep VERB 1 = <u>brush</u>, clean 2 = <u>clear</u>, remove, brush, clean 3 = <u>sail</u>, pass, fly, tear, zoom, glide, skim
● NOUN 1 = <u>movement</u>, move, swing, stroke 2 = <u>extent</u>, range, stretch, scope

sweeping 1 = <u>indiscriminate</u>, blanket, wholesale, exaggerated, overstated, unqualified 2 = <u>wide-ranging</u>, global, comprehensive, wide, broad, extensive, all-inclusive, all-embracing ≠ limited

sweet ADJECTIVE 1 = <u>sugary</u>, cloying, saccharine, icky (*informal*) ≠ sour 2 = <u>fragrant</u>, aromatic ≠ stinking 3 = <u>fresh</u>, clean, pure 4 = <u>melodious</u>, musical, harmonious, mellow, dulcet ≠ harsh 5 = <u>charming</u>, kind, agreeable ≠ nasty 6 = <u>delightful</u>, appealing, cute, winning, engaging, lovable, likable *or* likeable ≠ unpleasant
● NOUN 1 *usually plural* = <u>confectionery</u>, candy (*U.S.*), lolly (*Austral. & N.Z.*), bonbon 2 (*Brit.*) = <u>dessert</u>, pudding

sweetheart 1 = <u>dearest</u>, beloved, sweet, angel, treasure, honey, dear, sweetie (*informal*) 2 = <u>love</u>, boyfriend *or* girlfriend, beloved, lover, darling

swell VERB 1 = <u>increase</u>, rise, grow, mount, expand, accelerate, escalate, multiply ≠ decrease 2 = <u>expand</u>, increase, grow, rise, balloon, enlarge, bulge, dilate ≠ shrink
● NOUN = <u>wave</u>, surge, billow

swelling = <u>enlargement</u>, lump, bump, bulge, inflammation, protuberance, distension

swift 1 = <u>quick</u>, prompt, rapid 2 = <u>fast</u>, quick, rapid, hurried, speedy ≠ slow

swiftly 1 = <u>quickly</u>, rapidly, speedily 2 = <u>fast</u>, promptly, hurriedly

swing VERB 1 = <u>brandish</u>, wave, shake, flourish, wield, dangle 2 = <u>sway</u>, rock, wave, veer, oscillate 3 *usually with round* = <u>turn</u>, swivel, curve, rotate, pivot 4 = <u>hit out</u>, strike, swipe, lash out at, slap 5 = <u>hang</u>, dangle, suspend
● NOUN 1 = <u>swaying</u>, sway 2 = <u>fluctuation</u>, change, shift, switch, variation

swirl = <u>whirl</u>, churn, spin, twist, eddy

switch NOUN 1 = <u>control</u>, button, lever, on/off device 2 = <u>change</u>, shift, reversal
● VERB 1 = <u>change</u>, shift, divert, deviate 2 = <u>exchange</u>, swap, substitute

swollen = <u>enlarged</u>, bloated, inflamed, puffed up, distended

swoop 1 = <u>pounce</u>, attack, charge, rush, descend 2 = <u>drop</u>, plunge, dive, sweep, descend, pounce, stoop

symbol 1 = <u>metaphor</u>, image, sign, representation, token = <u>representation</u>, sign, figure, mark, image, token, logo, badge

symbolic 1 = <u>representative</u>, emblematic, allegorical 2 = <u>representative</u>, figurative

sympathetic 1 = <u>caring</u>, kind, understanding, concerned, interested, warm, pitying, supportive ≠ uncaring 2 = <u>like-minded</u>, compatible, agreeable, friendly, congenial, companionable ≠ uncongenial

sympathy 1 = <u>compassion</u>, understanding, pity, commiseration, aroha (*N.Z.*) ≠ indifference 2 = <u>affinity</u>, agreement, rapport, fellow feeling ≠ opposition

symptom 1 = <u>sign</u>, mark, indication, warning 2 = <u>manifestation</u>, sign, indication, mark, evidence, expression, proof, token

synthetic = <u>artificial</u>, fake, man-made ≠ real

system 1 = <u>arrangement</u>, structure, organization, scheme, classification 2 = <u>method</u>, practice, technique, procedure, routine

systematic = <u>methodical</u>, organized, efficient, orderly ≠ unmethodical

t

table NOUN 1 = <u>counter</u>, bench, stand, board, surface, work surface 2 = <u>list</u>, chart, tabulation, record, roll, register, diagram, itemization
  ● VERB (*Brit.*) = <u>submit</u>, propose, put forward, move, suggest, enter, file, lodge
taboo NOUN = <u>prohibition</u>, ban, restriction, anathema, interdict, proscription, tapu (*N.Z.*)
  ● ADJECTIVE = <u>forbidden</u>, banned, prohibited, unacceptable, outlawed, anathema, proscribed, unmentionable ≠ permitted
tack NOUN = <u>nail</u>, pin, drawing pin
  ● VERB 1 = <u>fasten</u>, fix, attach, pin, nail, affix 2 (*Brit.*) = <u>stitch</u>, sew, hem, bind, baste
  ● PHRASES **tack something on to something** = <u>append</u>, add, attach, tag
tackle VERB 1 = <u>deal with</u>, set about, get stuck into (*informal*), come or get to grips with 2 = <u>undertake</u>, attempt, embark upon, get stuck into (*informal*), have a go or stab at (*informal*) 3 = <u>intercept</u>, stop, challenge
  ● NOUN 1 = <u>block</u>, challenge 2 = <u>rig</u>, apparatus
tactic NOUN = <u>policy</u>, approach, move, scheme, plans, method, manoeuvre, ploy
  ● PLURAL NOUN = <u>strategy</u>, campaigning, manoeuvres, generalship
tactical = <u>strategic</u>, shrewd, smart, diplomatic, cunning ≠ impolitic
tag NOUN = <u>label</u>, tab, note, ticket, slip, identification, marker, flap
  ● VERB = <u>label</u>, mark
tail NOUN 1 = <u>extremity</u>, appendage, brush, rear end, hindquarters, hind part 2 = <u>train</u>, end, trail, tailpiece
  ● VERB (*Informal*) = <u>follow</u>, track, shadow, trail, stalk
  ● PHRASES **turn tail** = <u>run away</u>, flee, run off, retreat, cut and run, take to your heels
tailor NOUN = <u>outfitter</u>, couturier, dressmaker, seamstress, clothier, costumier

  ● VERB = <u>adapt</u>, adjust, modify, style, fashion, shape, alter, mould
taint = <u>spoil</u>, ruin, contaminate, damage, stain, corrupt, pollute, tarnish ≠ purify
take VERB 1 = <u>grip</u>, grab, seize, catch, grasp, clasp, take hold of 2 = <u>carry</u>, bring, bear, transport, ferry, haul, convey, fetch ≠ send 3 = <u>accompany</u>, lead, bring, guide, conduct, escort, convoy, usher 4 = <u>remove</u>, draw, pull, fish, withdraw, extract 5 = <u>steal</u>, appropriate, pocket, pinch (*informal*), misappropriate, purloin ≠ return 6 = <u>capture</u>, seize, take into custody, lay hold of ≠ release 7 = <u>tolerate</u>, stand, bear, stomach, endure, abide, put up with (*informal*), withstand ≠ avoid 8 = <u>require</u>, need, involve, demand, call for, entail, necessitate 9 = <u>understand</u>, follow, comprehend, get, see, grasp, apprehend 10 = <u>regard as</u>, believe to be, consider to be, perceive to be, presume to be 11 = <u>have room for</u>, hold, contain, accommodate, accept
  ● PHRASES **take off** 1 = <u>lift off</u>, take to the air 2 (*Informal*) = <u>depart</u>, go, leave, disappear, abscond, decamp, slope off
  ◆ **take someone in** = <u>deceive</u>, fool, con (*informal*), trick, cheat, mislead, dupe, swindle ◆ **take someone off** (*Informal*) = <u>parody</u>, imitate, mimic, mock, caricature, send up (*Brit. informal*), lampoon, satirize
  ◆ **take something in** = <u>understand</u>, absorb, grasp, digest, comprehend, assimilate, get the hang of (*informal*)
  ◆ **take something up** 1 = <u>start</u>, begin, engage in, adopt, become involved in 2 = <u>occupy</u>, absorb, consume, use up, cover, fill, waste, squander
takeover = <u>merger</u>, coup, incorporation
tale = <u>story</u>, narrative, anecdote, account, legend, saga, yarn (*informal*), fable
talent = <u>ability</u>, gift, aptitude, capacity, genius, flair, knack
talented = <u>gifted</u>, able, expert, master, masterly, brilliant, ace (*informal*), consummate
talk VERB 1 = <u>speak</u>, chat, chatter, converse, communicate, natter 2 = <u>discuss</u>, confer, negotiate, parley, confabulate, korero (*N.Z.*) 3 = <u>inform</u>, grass (*Brit. slang*), tell all, give the game away, blab, let the cat out of the bag
  ● NOUN = <u>speech</u>, lecture, presentation, report, address, discourse, sermon,

symposium, whaikorero (*N.Z.*)

talking-to (*Informal*) = reprimand, lecture, rebuke, scolding, criticism, reproach, ticking-off (*informal*), dressing-down (*informal*) ≠ praise

tall 1 = lofty, big, giant, long-legged, lanky, leggy 2 = high, towering, soaring, steep, elevated, lofty ≠ short 3 (*Informal*) = implausible, incredible, far-fetched, exaggerated, absurd, unbelievable, preposterous, cock-and-bull (*informal*) ≠ plausible 4 = difficult, hard, demanding, unreasonable, well-nigh impossible

tally NOUN = record, score, total, count, reckoning, running total
• VERB = agree, match, accord, fit, square, coincide, correspond, conform ≠ disagree

tame ADJECTIVE 1 = domesticated, docile, broken, gentle, obedient, amenable, tractable ≠ wild 2 = submissive, meek, compliant, subdued, manageable, obedient, docile, unresisting ≠ stubborn 3 = unexciting, boring, dull, bland, uninspiring, humdrum, uninteresting, insipid ≠ exciting
• VERB 1 = domesticate, train, break in, house-train ≠ make fiercer 2 = subdue, suppress, master, discipline, humble, conquer, subjugate ≠ arouse

tangible = definite, real, positive, material, actual, concrete, palpable, perceptible ≠ intangible

tangle NOUN 1 = knot, twist, web, jungle, coil, entanglement 2 = mess, jam, fix (*informal*), confusion, complication, mix-up, shambles, entanglement
• VERB = twist, knot, mat, coil, mesh, entangle, interweave, ravel ≠ disentangle
• PHRASES **tangle with someone** = come into conflict with, come up against, cross swords with, dispute with, contend with, contest with, lock horns with

tantrum = outburst, temper, hysterics, fit, flare-up, foulie (*Austral. slang*)

tap[1] VERB = knock, strike, pat, rap, beat, touch, drum
• NOUN = knock, pat, rap, touch, drumming

tap[2] NOUN = valve, stopcock
• VERB = listen in on, monitor, bug (*informal*), spy on, eavesdrop on, wiretap
• PHRASES **on tap** 1 (*Informal*) = available, ready, standing by, to hand, on hand, at hand, in reserve 2 = on draught, cask-conditioned, from barrels, not bottled *or* canned

tape NOUN = binding, strip, band, string, ribbon
• VERB 1 = record, video, tape-record, make a recording of 2 sometimes with **up** = bind, secure, stick, seal, wrap

target 1 = mark, goal 2 = goal, aim, objective, end, mark, object, intention, ambition 3 = victim, butt, prey, scapegoat

tariff 1 = tax, duty, toll, levy, excise 2 = price list, schedule

tarnish VERB 1 = damage, taint, blacken, sully, smirch ≠ enhance 2 = stain, discolour, darken, blot, blemish ≠ brighten
• NOUN = stain, taint, discoloration, spot, blot, blemish

tart[1] = pie, pastry, pasty, tartlet, patty

tart[2] = sharp, acid, sour, bitter, pungent, tangy, piquant, vinegary ≠ sweet

tart[3] (*Informal*) = slut, prostitute, whore, call girl, trollop, floozy (*slang*)

task NOUN = job, duty, assignment, exercise, mission, enterprise, undertaking, chore
• PHRASES **take someone to task** = criticize, blame, censure, rebuke, reprimand, reproach, scold, tell off (*informal*)

taste NOUN 1 = flavour, savour, relish, smack, tang ≠ blandness 2 = bit, bite, mouthful, sample, dash, spoonful, morsel, titbit 3 = liking, preference, penchant, fondness, partiality, fancy, appetite, inclination ≠ dislike 4 = refinement, style, judgment, discrimination, appreciation, elegance, sophistication, discernment ≠ lack of judgment
• VERB 1 = have a flavour of, smack of, savour of 2 = sample, try, test, sip, savour 3 = distinguish, perceive, discern, differentiate 4 = experience, know, undergo, partake of, encounter, meet with ≠ miss

tasty = delicious, luscious, palatable, delectable, savoury, full-flavoured, scrumptious (*informal*), appetizing, lekker (*S. African slang*), yummo (*Austral. slang*) ≠ bland

taunt VERB = jeer, mock, tease, ridicule, provoke, insult, torment, deride
• NOUN = jeer, dig, insult, ridicule, teasing, provocation, derision, sarcasm

tavern = inn, bar, pub (*informal, chiefly*

Brit.), public house, hostelry, alehouse (*archaic*)

tax NOUN = <u>charge</u>, duty, toll, levy, tariff, excise, tithe

● VERB 1 = <u>charge</u>, rate, assess 2 = <u>strain</u>, stretch, try, test, load, burden, exhaust, weaken

teach VERB = <u>instruct</u>, train, coach, inform, educate, drill, tutor, enlighten

● VERB = <u>show</u>, train

teacher = <u>instructor</u>, coach, tutor, guide, trainer, lecturer, mentor, educator

team NOUN 1 = <u>side</u>, squad 2 = <u>group</u>, company, set, body, band, gang, line-up, bunch

● PHRASES **team up** = <u>join</u>, unite, work together, cooperate, couple, link up, get together, band together

tear VERB 1 = <u>rip</u>, split, rend, shred, rupture 2 = <u>run</u> 3 = <u>scratch</u>, cut (open), gash, lacerate, injure, mangle, cut to pieces, cut to ribbons, mangulate (*Austral. slang*) 4 = <u>pull apart</u>, claw, lacerate, mutilate, mangle, mangulate (*Austral. slang*) 5 = <u>rush</u>, run, charge, race, fly, speed, dash, hurry

● NOUN = <u>hole</u>, split, rip, rent, snag, rupture

tears PLURAL NOUN = <u>crying</u>, weeping, sobbing, wailing, blubbering

● PHRASES **in tears** = <u>weeping</u>, crying, sobbing, blubbering

tease 1 = <u>mock</u>, provoke, torment, taunt, goad, pull someone's leg (*informal*), make fun of 2 = <u>tantalize</u>, lead on, flirt with, titillate

technical = <u>scientific</u>, technological, skilled, specialist, specialized, hi-tech *or* high-tech

technique 1 = <u>method</u>, way, system, approach, manner, style, manner, procedure 2 = <u>skill</u>, performance, craft, touch, execution, artistry, craftsmanship, proficiency

tedious = <u>boring</u>, dull, dreary, monotonous, drab, tiresome, laborious, humdrum ≠ exciting

teenager = <u>youth</u>, minor, adolescent, juvenile, girl, boy

telephone NOUN = <u>phone</u>, mobile (phone), handset, dog and bone (*slang*)

● VERB = <u>call</u>, phone, ring (*chiefly Brit.*), dial

telescope NOUN = <u>glass</u>, scope (*informal*), spyglass

● VERB = <u>shorten</u>, contract, compress,

shrink, condense, abbreviate, abridge ≠ lengthen

television = <u>TV</u>, telly (*Brit. informal*), small screen (*informal*), the box (*Brit. informal*), the tube (*slang*)

tell VERB 1 = <u>inform</u>, notify, state to, reveal to, express to, disclose to, proclaim to, divulge 2 = <u>describe</u>, relate, recount, report, portray, depict, chronicle, narrate 3 = <u>instruct</u>, order, command, direct, bid 4 = <u>distinguish</u>, discriminate, discern, differentiate, identify 5 = <u>have or take effect</u>, register, weigh, count, take its toll, carry weight, make its presence felt

● PHRASES **tell someone off** = <u>reprimand</u>, rebuke, scold, lecture, censure, reproach, berate, chide

telling = <u>effective</u>, significant, considerable, marked, striking, powerful, impressive, influential ≠ unimportant

temper NOUN 1 = <u>irritability</u>, irascibility, passion, resentment, petulance, surliness, hot-headedness ≠ good humour 2 = <u>frame of mind</u>, nature, mind, mood, constitution, humour, temperament, disposition 3 = <u>rage</u>, fury, bad mood, passion, tantrum, foulie (*Austral. slang*) 4 = <u>self-control</u>, composure, cool (*slang*), calmness, equanimity ≠ anger

● VERB 1 = <u>moderate</u>, restrain, tone down, soften, soothe, lessen, mitigate, assuage ≠ intensify 2 = <u>strengthen</u>, harden, toughen, anneal ≠ soften

temperament 1 = <u>nature</u>, character, personality, make-up, constitution, bent, humour, temper 2 = <u>moods</u>, anger, volatility, petulance, excitability, moodiness, hot-headedness

temple = <u>shrine</u>, church, sanctuary, house of God

temporarily = <u>briefly</u>, for the time being, momentarily, fleetingly, pro tem

temporary 1 = <u>impermanent</u>, transitory, brief, fleeting, interim, short-lived, momentary, ephemeral ≠ permanent 2 = <u>short-term</u>, acting, interim, supply, stand-in, fill-in, caretaker, provisional

tempt 1 = <u>attract</u>, allure 2 = <u>entice</u>, lure, lead on, invite, seduce, coax ≠ discourage

temptation 1 = <u>enticement</u>, lure, inducement, pull, seduction, allurement, tantalization 2 = <u>appeal</u>, attraction

tempting = <u>inviting</u>, enticing, seductive, alluring, attractive, mouthwatering, appetizing ≠ uninviting

tenant = leaseholder, resident, renter, occupant, inhabitant, occupier, lodger, boarder

tend[1] = be inclined, be liable, have a tendency, be apt, be prone, lean, incline, gravitate

tend[2] 1 = take care of, look after, keep, attend, nurture, watch over ≠ neglect 2 = maintain, take care of, nurture, cultivate, manage ≠ neglect

tendency = inclination, leaning, liability, disposition, propensity, susceptibility, proclivity, proneness

tender[1] 1 = gentle, loving, kind, caring, sympathetic, affectionate, compassionate, considerate ≠ harsh 2 = vulnerable, young, sensitive, raw, youthful, inexperienced, immature, impressionable ≠ experienced 3 = sensitive, painful, sore, raw, bruised, inflamed

tender[2] NOUN = offer, bid, estimate, proposal, submission
● VERB = offer, present, submit, give, propose, volunteer, hand in, put forward

tense ADJECTIVE 1 = strained, uneasy, stressful, fraught, charged, difficult, worrying, exciting 2 = nervous, edgy, strained, anxious, apprehensive, uptight (*informal*), on edge, jumpy ≠ calm 3 = rigid, strained, taut, stretched, tight ≠ relaxed
● VERB = tighten, strain, brace, stretch, flex, stiffen ≠ relax

tension 1 = strain, stress, nervousness, pressure, anxiety, unease, apprehension, suspense ≠ calmness 2 = friction, hostility, unease, antagonism, antipathy, enmity 3 = rigidity, tightness, stiffness, pressure, stress, stretching, tautness

tentative 1 = unconfirmed, provisional, indefinite, test, trial, pilot, preliminary, experimental ≠ confirmed 2 = hesitant, cautious, uncertain, doubtful, faltering, unsure, timid, undecided ≠ confident

term NOUN 1 = word, name, expression, title, label, phrase 2 = period, time, spell, while, season, interval, span, duration
● PLURAL NOUN 1 = conditions, particulars, provisions, provisos, stipulations, qualifications, specifications 2 = relationship, standing, footing, relations, status
● VERB = call, name, label, style, entitle, tag,

dub, designate

terminal ADJECTIVE 1 = fatal, deadly, lethal, killing, mortal, incurable, inoperable, untreatable 2 = final, last, closing, finishing, concluding, ultimate, terminating ≠ initial
● NOUN = terminus, station, depot, end of the line

terminate 1 = end, stop, conclude, finish, complete, discontinue ≠ begin 2 = cease, end, close, finish 3 = abort, end

terrain = ground, country, land, landscape, topography, going

terrestrial = earthly, worldly, global

terrible 1 = awful, shocking, terrifying, horrible, dreadful, horrifying, fearful, horrendous 2 (*Informal*) = bad, awful, dreadful, dire, abysmal, poor, rotten (*informal*) ≠ wonderful 3 = serious, desperate, severe, extreme, dangerous, insufferable ≠ mild

terribly 1 = very much, very, dreadfully, seriously, extremely, desperately, thoroughly, decidedly 2 = extremely, very, dreadfully, seriously, desperately, thoroughly, decidedly, awfully (*informal*)

terrific 1 (*Informal*) = excellent, wonderful, brilliant, amazing, outstanding, superb, fantastic (*informal*), magnificent, booshit (*Austral. slang*), exo (*Austral. slang*), sik (*Austral. slang*), ka pai (*N.Z.*) ≠ awful 2 = intense, great, huge, enormous, tremendous, fearful, gigantic

terrified = frightened, scared, petrified, alarmed, panic-stricken, horror-struck

terrify = frighten, scare, alarm, terrorize

territory = district, area, land, region, country, zone, province, patch

terror 1 = fear, alarm, dread, fright, panic, anxiety 2 = nightmare, monster, bogeyman, devil, fiend, bugbear

test VERB 1 = check, investigate, assess, research, analyse, experiment with, try out, put something to the test 2 = examine, put someone to the test
● NOUN 1 = trial, research, check, investigation, analysis, assessment, examination, evaluation 2 = examination, paper, assessment, evaluation

testament 1 = proof, evidence, testimony, witness, demonstration, tribute 2 = will, last wishes

testify = bear witness, state, swear, certify, assert, affirm, attest, corroborate

≠ disprove

testimony 1 = <u>evidence</u>, statement, submission, affidavit, deposition 2 = <u>proof</u>, evidence, demonstration, indication, support, manifestation, verification, corroboration

testing = <u>difficult</u>, demanding, taxing, challenging, searching, tough, exacting, rigorous ≠ undemanding

text 1 = <u>contents</u>, words, content, wording, body, subject matter 2 = <u>words</u>, wording 3 = <u>transcript</u>, script

texture = <u>feel</u>, consistency, structure, surface, tissue, grain

thank = <u>say thank you to</u>, show your appreciation to

thanks PLURAL NOUN = <u>gratitude</u>, appreciation, credit, recognition, acknowledgment, gratefulness

● PHRASES **thanks to** = <u>because of</u>, through, due to, as a result of, owing to

thaw = <u>melt</u>, dissolve, soften, defrost, warm, liquefy, unfreeze ≠ freeze

theatrical 1 = <u>dramatic</u>, stage, Thespian 2 = <u>exaggerated</u>, dramatic, melodramatic, histrionic, affected, mannered, showy, ostentatious ≠ natural

theft = <u>stealing</u>, robbery, thieving, fraud, embezzlement, pilfering, larceny, purloining

theme 1 = <u>motif</u>, leitmotif 2 = <u>subject</u>, idea, topic, essence, subject matter, keynote, gist

theological = <u>religious</u>, ecclesiastical, doctrinal

theoretical 1 = <u>abstract</u>, speculative ≠ practical 2 = <u>hypothetical</u>, academic, notional, unproven, conjectural, postulatory

theory = <u>belief</u>, feeling, speculation, assumption, hunch, presumption, conjecture, surmise

therapeutic = <u>beneficial</u>, healing, restorative, good, corrective, remedial, salutary, curative ≠ harmful

therapist = <u>psychologist</u>, analyst, psychiatrist, shrink (*informal*), counsellor, healer, psychotherapist, psychoanalyst

therapy = <u>remedy</u>, treatment, cure, healing, method of healing

therefore = <u>consequently</u>, so, thus, as a result, hence, accordingly, thence, ergo

thesis 1 = <u>proposition</u>, theory, hypothesis, idea, view, opinion, proposal, contention

2 = <u>dissertation</u>, paper, treatise, essay, monograph

thick 1 = <u>bulky</u>, broad, big, large, fat, solid, substantial, hefty ≠ thin 2 = <u>wide</u>, across, deep, broad, in extent *or* diameter 3 = <u>dense</u>, close, heavy, compact, impenetrable, lush 4 = <u>heavy</u>, heavyweight, dense, chunky, bulky, woolly 5 = <u>opaque</u>, heavy, dense, impenetrable 6 = <u>viscous</u>, concentrated, stiff, condensed, gelatinous, semi-solid, viscid ≠ runny 7 = <u>crowded</u>, full, covered, bursting, bristling, brimming ≠ empty 8 (*Informal*) = <u>stupid</u>, slow, dense, dopey (*informal*), moronic, obtuse, brainless, dumb-ass (*informal*) ≠ clever 9 (*Informal*) = <u>friendly</u>, close, intimate, familiar, pally (*informal*), devoted, inseparable ≠ unfriendly

thicken = <u>set</u>, condense, congeal, clot, jell, coagulate ≠ thin

thief = <u>robber</u>, burglar, stealer, plunderer, shoplifter, embezzler, pickpocket, pilferer

thin 1 = <u>narrow</u>, fine, attenuated ≠ thick 2 = <u>slim</u>, spare, lean, slight, slender, skinny, skeletal, bony ≠ fat 3 = <u>meagre</u>, sparse, scanty, poor, scattered, inadequate, insufficient, deficient ≠ plentiful 4 = <u>fine</u>, delicate, flimsy, sheer, skimpy, gossamer, diaphanous, filmy ≠ thick 5 = <u>unconvincing</u>, inadequate, feeble, poor, weak, superficial, lame, flimsy ≠ convincing 6 = <u>wispy</u>, thinning, sparse, scarce, scanty

thing NOUN 1 = <u>substance</u>, stuff, being, body, material, fabric, entity 2 (*Informal*) = <u>phobia</u>, fear, complex, horror, terror, hang-up (*informal*), aversion, neurosis 3 (*Informal*) = <u>obsession</u>, liking, preoccupation, mania, fetish, fixation, soft spot, predilection

● PLURAL NOUN 1 = <u>possessions</u>, stuff, gear, belongings, effects, luggage, clobber (*Brit. slang*), chattels 2 = <u>equipment</u>, gear, tools, stuff, tackle, implements, kit, apparatus 3 = <u>circumstances</u>, the situation, the state of affairs, matters, life, affairs

think VERB 1 = <u>believe</u>, be of the opinion, be of the view 2 = <u>judge</u>, consider, estimate, reckon, deem, regard as 3 = <u>ponder</u>, reflect, contemplate, deliberate, meditate, ruminate, cogitate, be lost in thought

● PHRASES **think something up** = <u>devise</u>, create, come up with, invent, contrive, visualize, concoct, dream something up

thinker = philosopher, intellect (*informal*), wise man, sage, brain (*informal*), theorist, mastermind

thinking NOUN = reasoning, idea, view, position, theory, opinion, judgment, conjecture

● ADJECTIVE = thoughtful, intelligent, reasoning, rational, philosophical, reflective, contemplative, meditative

thirst 1 = dryness, thirstiness, drought 2 = craving, appetite, longing, desire, passion, yearning, hankering, keenness ≠ aversion

thorn = prickle, spike, spine, barb

thorough 1 = comprehensive, full, complete, sweeping, intensive, in-depth, exhaustive ≠ cursory 2 = careful, conscientious, painstaking, efficient, meticulous, exhaustive, assiduous ≠ careless 3 = complete, total, absolute, utter, perfect, outright, unqualified, out-and-out ≠ partial

thoroughly 1 = carefully, fully, efficiently, meticulously, painstakingly, scrupulously, assiduously, intensively ≠ carelessly 2 = fully 3 = completely, quite, totally, perfectly, absolutely, utterly, downright, to the hilt ≠ partly

though CONJUNCTION = although, while, even if, even though, notwithstanding

● ADVERB = nevertheless, still, however, yet, nonetheless, for all that, notwithstanding

thought 1 = thinking, consideration, reflection, deliberation, musing, meditation, rumination, cogitation 2 = opinion, view, idea, concept, notion, judgment 3 = consideration, study, attention, care, regard, scrutiny, heed 4 = intention, plan, idea, design, aim, purpose, object, notion 5 = hope, expectation, prospect, aspiration, anticipation

thoughtful 1 = reflective, pensive, contemplative, meditative, serious, studious, deliberative, ruminative ≠ shallow 2 = considerate, kind, caring, kindly, helpful, attentive, unselfish, solicitous ≠ inconsiderate

thrash VERB 1 = defeat, beat, crush, slaughter (*informal*), rout, trounce, run rings around (*informal*), wipe the floor with (*informal*) 2 = beat, wallop, whip, belt (*informal*), cane, flog, scourge, spank 3 = thresh, flail, jerk, writhe, toss and turn

● PHRASES **thrash something out** = settle, resolve, discuss, debate, solve, argue out, have something out, talk something over

thrashing 1 = defeat, beating, hammering (*informal*), hiding (*informal*), rout, trouncing, drubbing 2 = beating, hiding (*informal*), belting (*informal*), whipping, flogging

thread NOUN 1 = strand, fibre, yarn, filament, line, string, twine 2 = theme, train of thought, direction, plot, drift, story line

● VERB = move, pass, ease, thrust, squeeze through, pick your way

threat 1 = danger, risk, hazard, menace, peril 2 = threatening remark, menace 3 = warning, foreshadowing, foreboding

threaten 1 = intimidate, bully, menace, terrorize, lean on (*slang*), pressurize, browbeat ≠ defend 2 = endanger, jeopardize, put at risk, imperil, put in jeopardy, put on the line ≠ protect 3 = be imminent, impend

threshold 1 = entrance, doorway, door, doorstep 2 = start, beginning, opening, dawn, verge, brink, outset, inception ≠ end 3 = limit, margin, starting point, minimum

thrift = economy, prudence, frugality, saving, parsimony, carefulness, thriftiness ≠ extravagance

thrill NOUN = pleasure, kick (*informal*), buzz (*slang*), high, stimulation, tingle, titillation ≠ tedium

● VERB = excite, stimulate, arouse, move, stir, electrify, titillate, give someone a kick

thrilling = exciting, gripping, stimulating, stirring, sensational, rousing, riveting, electrifying ≠ boring

thrive = prosper, do well, flourish, increase, grow, develop, succeed, get on ≠ decline

thriving = successful, flourishing, healthy, booming, blooming, prosperous, burgeoning ≠ unsuccessful

throb VERB 1 = pulsate, pound, beat, pulse, thump, palpitate 2 = vibrate, pulsate, reverberate, shake, judder (*informal*)

● NOUN 1 = pulse, pounding, beat, thump, thumping, pulsating, palpitation 2 = vibration, throbbing, reverberation, judder (*informal*), pulsation

throng NOUN = <u>crowd</u>, mob, horde, host, pack, mass, crush, swarm
● VERB 1 = <u>crowd</u>, flock, congregate, converge, mill around, swarm around ≠ disperse 2 = <u>pack</u>, crowd

throttle = <u>strangle</u>, choke, garrotte, strangulate

through PREPOSITION 1 = <u>via</u>, by way of, by, between, past, from one side to the other of 2 = <u>because of</u>, by way of, by means of 3 = <u>using</u>, via, by way of, by means of, by virtue of, with the assistance of 4 = <u>during</u>, throughout, for the duration of, in
● ADJECTIVE = <u>completed</u>, done, finished, ended
● PHRASES **through and through** = <u>completely</u>, totally, fully, thoroughly, entirely, altogether, wholly, utterly

throughout PREPOSITION 1 = <u>right through</u>, everywhere in, during the whole of, through the whole of 2 = <u>all over</u>, everywhere in, through the whole of
● ADVERB 1 = <u>from start to finish</u>, right through 2 = <u>all through</u>, right through

throw VERB 1 = <u>hurl</u>, toss, fling, send, launch, cast, pitch, chuck (*informal*) 2 = <u>toss</u>, fling, chuck (*informal*), cast, hurl, sling 3 (*Informal*) = <u>confuse</u>, baffle, faze, astonish, confound, disconcert, dumbfound
● NOUN 1 = <u>toss</u>, pitch, fling, sling, lob (*informal*), heave

thrust VERB = <u>push</u>, force, shove, drive, plunge, jam, ram, propel
● NOUN 1 = <u>stab</u>, pierce, lunge 2 = <u>push</u>, shove, poke, prod 3 = <u>momentum</u>, impetus, drive

thug = <u>ruffian</u>, hooligan, tough, heavy (*slang*), gangster, bully boy, bruiser (*informal*), tsotsi (*S. African*)

thump VERB = <u>strike</u>, hit, punch, pound, beat, knock, smack, clout (*informal*)
● NOUN 1 = <u>blow</u>, knock, punch, rap, smack, clout (*informal*), whack, swipe 2 = <u>thud</u>, crash, bang, clunk, thwack

thunder NOUN = <u>rumble</u>, crash, boom, explosion
● VERB 1 = <u>rumble</u>, crash, boom, roar, resound, reverberate, peal 2 = <u>shout</u>, roar, yell, bark, bellow

thus 1 = <u>therefore</u>, so, hence, consequently, accordingly, for this reason, ergo, on that account 2 = <u>in this way</u>, so, like this, as follows

thwart = <u>frustrate</u>, foil, prevent, snooker, hinder, obstruct, outwit, stymie ≠ assist

tick NOUN 1 = <u>check mark</u>, mark, line, stroke, dash 2 = <u>click</u>, tapping, clicking, ticktock 3 (*Brit. informal*) = <u>moment</u>, second, minute, flash, instant, twinkling, split second, trice
● VERB 1 = <u>mark</u>, indicate, check off 2 = <u>click</u>, tap, ticktock

ticket 1 = <u>voucher</u>, pass, coupon, card, slip, certificate, token, chit 2 = <u>label</u>, tag, marker, sticker, card, slip, tab, docket

tide 1 = <u>current</u>, flow, stream, ebb, undertow, tideway 2 = <u>course</u>, direction, trend, movement, tendency, drift

tidy ADJECTIVE 1 = <u>neat</u>, orderly, clean, spruce, well-kept, well-ordered, shipshape ≠ untidy 2 = <u>organized</u>, neat, methodical 3 (*Informal*) = <u>considerable</u>, large, substantial, goodly, healthy, generous, handsome, ample ≠ small
● VERB = <u>neaten</u>, straighten, order, clean, groom, spruce up ≠ disorder

tie VERB 1 = <u>fasten</u>, bind, join, link, connect, attach, knot ≠ unfasten 2 = <u>tether</u>, secure 3 = <u>restrict</u>, limit, confine, bind, restrain, hamper, hinder ≠ free 4 = <u>draw</u>, be level, match, equal
● NOUN 1 = <u>fastening</u>, binding, link, bond, knot, cord, fetter, ligature 2 = <u>bond</u>, relationship, connection, commitment, liaison, allegiance, affiliation 3 = <u>draw</u>, dead heat, deadlock, stalemate

tier = <u>row</u>, bank, layer, line, level, rank, storey, stratum

tight 1 = <u>close-fitting</u>, narrow, cramped, snug, constricted, close ≠ loose 2 = <u>secure</u>, firm, fast, fixed 3 = <u>taut</u>, stretched, rigid ≠ slack 4 = <u>close</u>, even, well-matched, hard-fought, evenly-balanced ≠ uneven 5 (*Informal*) = <u>miserly</u>, mean, stingy, grasping, parsimonious, niggardly, tightfisted ≠ generous 6 (*Informal*) = <u>drunk</u>, intoxicated, plastered (*slang*), under the influence (*informal*), tipsy, paralytic (*informal*), inebriated, out to it (*Austral. & N.Z. slang*) ≠ sober

tighten = <u>close</u>, narrow, strengthen, squeeze, harden, constrict ≠ slacken

till[1] = <u>cultivate</u>, dig, plough, work

till[2] = <u>cash register</u>, cash box

tilt VERB = <u>slant</u>, tip, slope, list, lean, heel, incline
● NOUN 1 = <u>slope</u>, angle, inclination, list,

pitch, incline, slant, camber **2** (*Medieval history*) = joust, fight, tournament, lists, combat, duel

timber 1 = beams, boards, planks
2 = wood, logs

time NOUN **1** = period, term, space, stretch, spell, span **2** = occasion, point, moment, stage, instance, point in time, juncture **3** = age, duration **4** = tempo, beat, rhythm, measure
● VERB = schedule, set, plan, book, programme, set up, fix, arrange

timeless = eternal, lasting, permanent, enduring, immortal, everlasting, ageless, changeless ≠ temporary

timely = opportune, appropriate, well-timed, suitable, convenient, judicious, propitious, seasonable ≠ untimely

timetable 1 = schedule, programme, agenda, list, diary, calendar **2** = syllabus, course, curriculum, programme, teaching programme

tinge NOUN **1** = tint, colour, shade **2** = trace, bit, drop, touch, suggestion, dash, sprinkling, smattering
● VERB = tint, colour

tinker = meddle, play, potter, fiddle (*informal*), dabble, mess about

tint NOUN **1** = shade, colour, tone, hue
2 = dye, wash, rinse, tinge, tincture
● VERB = dye, colour

tiny = small, little, minute, slight, miniature, negligible, microscopic, diminutive ≠ huge

tip¹ NOUN **1** = end, point, head, extremity, sharp end, nib, prong **2** = peak, top, summit, pinnacle, zenith, spire, acme, vertex
● VERB = cap, top, crown, surmount, finish

tip² VERB **1** = reward, remunerate, give a tip to, sweeten (*informal*) **2** = predict, back, recommend, think of
● NOUN **1** = gratuity, gift, reward, present, sweetener (*informal*) **2** = hint, suggestion, piece of advice, pointer

tip³ VERB **1** = pour, drop, empty, dump, drain, discharge, unload, jettison **2** (*Brit.*) = dump, empty, unload, pour out
● NOUN (*Brit.*) = dump, midden, rubbish heap, refuse heap

tire 1 = exhaust, drain, fatigue, weary, wear out ≠ refresh **2** = flag, become tired, fail **3** = bore, weary, exasperate, irritate, irk

tired 1 = exhausted, fatigued, weary,

flagging, drained, sleepy, worn out, drowsy, tuckered out (*Austral. & N.Z. informal*) ≠ energetic **2** = bored, fed up, weary, sick, hoha (*N.Z.*) ≠ enthusiastic about **3** = hackneyed, stale, well-worn, old, corny (*slang*), threadbare, trite, clichéd ≠ original

tiring = exhausting, demanding, wearing, tough, exacting, strenuous, arduous, laborious

title 1 = name, designation, term, handle (*slang*), moniker *or* monicker (*slang*) **2** (*Sport*) = championship, trophy, bays, crown, honour **3** (*Law*) = ownership, right, claim, privilege, entitlement, tenure, prerogative, freehold

toast¹ 1 = brown, grill, crisp, roast
2 = warm (up), heat (up), thaw, bring back to life

toast² NOUN **1** = tribute, compliment, salute, health, pledge, salutation
2 = favourite, celebrity, darling, talk, pet, focus of attention, hero *or* heroine, blue-eyed boy *or* girl (*Brit. informal*)
● VERB = drink to, honour, salute, drink (to) the health of

together ADVERB **1** = collectively, jointly, as one, with each other, in conjunction, side by side, mutually, in partnership ≠ separately **2** = at the same time, simultaneously, concurrently, contemporaneously, at one fell swoop
● ADJECTIVE (*Informal*) = self-possessed, composed, well-balanced, well-adjusted

toil VERB **1** = labour, work, struggle, strive, sweat (*informal*), slave, graft (*informal*), slog **2** = struggle, trek, slog, trudge, fight your way, footslog
● NOUN = hard work, effort, application, sweat, graft (*informal*), slog, exertion, drudgery ≠ idleness

toilet 1 = lavatory, bathroom, loo (*Brit. informal*), privy, cloakroom (*Brit.*), urinal, latrine, washroom, dunny (*Austral. & N.Z. old-fashioned informal*), bogger (*Austral. slang*), brasco (*Austral. slang*) **2** = bathroom, gents *or* ladies (*Brit. informal*), privy, latrine, water closet, ladies' room, W.C.

token NOUN = symbol, mark, sign, note, expression, indication, representation, badge
● ADJECTIVE = nominal, symbolic, minimal, hollow, superficial, perfunctory

tolerance 1 = <u>broad-mindedness</u>, indulgence, forbearance, permissiveness, open-mindedness ≠ intolerance 2 = <u>endurance</u>, resistance, stamina, fortitude, resilience, toughness, staying power, hardiness 3 = <u>resistance</u>, immunity, resilience, non-susceptibility

tolerant = <u>broad-minded</u>, understanding, open-minded, catholic, long-suffering, permissive, forbearing, unprejudiced ≠ intolerant

tolerate 1 = <u>endure</u>, stand, take, stomach, put up with (*informal*) 2 = <u>allow</u>, accept, permit, take, brook, put up with (*informal*), condone ≠ forbid

toll¹ VERB = <u>ring</u>, sound, strike, chime, knell, clang, peal
● NOUN = <u>ringing</u>, chime, knell, clang, peal

toll² 1 = <u>charge</u>, tax, fee, duty, payment, levy, tariff 2 = <u>damage</u>, cost, loss, roll, penalty, sum, number, roster 3 = <u>adverse effects</u>, price, cost, suffering, damage, penalty, harm

tomb = <u>grave</u>, vault, crypt, mausoleum, sarcophagus, catacomb, sepulchre

tone NOUN 1 = <u>pitch</u>, inflection, intonation, timbre, modulation 2 = <u>volume</u>, timbre 3 = <u>character</u>, style, feel, air, spirit, attitude, manner, mood 4 = <u>colour</u>, shade, tint, tinge, hue
● VERB = <u>harmonize</u>, match, blend, suit, go well with
● PHRASES **tone something down** = <u>moderate</u>, temper, soften, restrain, subdue, play down = <u>reduce</u>, moderate

tongue = <u>language</u>, speech, dialect, parlance

tonic = <u>stimulant</u>, boost, pick-me-up (*informal*), fillip, shot in the arm (*informal*), restorative

too 1 = <u>also</u>, as well, further, in addition, moreover, besides, likewise, to boot 2 = <u>excessively</u>, very, extremely, overly, unduly, unreasonably, inordinately, immoderately

tool 1 = <u>implement</u>, device, appliance, machine, instrument, gadget, utensil, contraption 2 = <u>puppet</u>, creature, pawn, stooge (*slang*), minion, lackey, flunkey, hireling

top NOUN 1 = <u>peak</u>, summit, head, crown, height, ridge, brow, crest ≠ bottom 2 = <u>lid</u>, cover, cap, plug, stopper, bung 3 = <u>first place</u>, head, peak, lead, high point
● ADJECTIVE 1 = <u>highest</u>, loftiest, furthest up, uppermost 2 = <u>leading</u>, best, first, highest, head, finest, elite, foremost ≠ lowest 3 = <u>chief</u>, most important, principal, most powerful, highest, head, leading, main 4 = <u>prime</u>, best, select, first-class, quality, choice, excellent, premier
● VERB 1 = <u>lead</u>, head, be at the top of, be first in 2 = <u>cover</u>, garnish, finish, crown, cap 3 = <u>surpass</u>, better, beat, improve on, cap, exceed, eclipse, excel ≠ not be as good as

topic = <u>subject</u>, point, question, issue, matter, theme, subject matter

topical = <u>current</u>, popular, contemporary, up-to-date, up-to-the-minute, newsworthy

topple 1 = <u>fall over</u>, fall, collapse, tumble, overturn, totter, keel over, overbalance 2 = <u>knock over</u> 3 = <u>overthrow</u>, overturn, bring down, oust, unseat, bring low

torment NOUN = <u>suffering</u>, distress, misery, pain, hell, torture, agony, anguish ≠ bliss
● VERB 1 = <u>torture</u>, distress, rack, crucify ≠ comfort 2 = <u>tease</u>, annoy, bother, irritate, harass, hassle (*informal*), pester, vex

torn 1 = <u>cut</u>, split, rent, ripped, ragged, slit, lacerated 2 = <u>undecided</u>, uncertain, unsure, wavering, vacillating, in two minds (*informal*), irresolute

tornado = <u>whirlwind</u>, storm, hurricane, gale, cyclone, typhoon, tempest, squall

torture VERB 1 = <u>torment</u>, abuse, persecute, afflict, scourge, molest, crucify, mistreat ≠ comfort 2 = <u>distress</u>, torment, worry, trouble, rack, afflict, harrow, inflict anguish on
● NOUN 1 = <u>ill-treatment</u>, abuse, torment, persecution, maltreatment, harsh treatment 2 = <u>agony</u>, suffering, anguish, distress, torment, heartbreak ≠ bliss

toss VERB 1 = <u>throw</u>, pitch, hurl, fling, launch, cast, flip, sling 2 = <u>shake</u> 3 = <u>thrash (about)</u>, twitch, wriggle, squirm, writhe
● NOUN = <u>throw</u>, pitch, lob (*informal*)

tot NOUN 1 = <u>infant</u>, child, baby, toddler, mite, littlie (*Austral. informal*), ankle-biter (*Austral. slang*), tacker (*Austral. slang*) 2 = <u>measure</u>, shot (*informal*), finger, nip, slug, dram, snifter (*informal*)
● PHRASES **tot something up** = <u>add up</u>, calculate, total, reckon, compute, tally, enumerate, count up

total NOUN = <u>sum</u>, entirety, grand total, whole, aggregate, totality, full amount,

sum total ≠ part
● ADJECTIVE = complete, absolute, utter, whole, entire, undivided, overarching, thoroughgoing ≠ partial
● VERB 1 = amount to, make, come to, reach, equal, run to, number, add up to 2 = add up, work out, compute, reckon, tot up ≠ subtract

totally = completely, entirely, absolutely, fully, comprehensively, thoroughly, wholly, utterly ≠ partly

touch VERB 1 = feel, handle, finger, stroke, brush, make contact with, caress, fondle 2 = come into contact, meet, contact, border, graze, adjoin, be in contact, abut 3 = tap 4 = affect, influence, inspire, impress 5 = consume, take, drink, eat, partake of 6 = move, stir, disturb 7 = match, rival, equal, compare with, parallel, hold a candle to (informal)
● NOUN 1 = contact, push, stroke, brush, press, tap, poke, nudge 2 = feeling, handling, physical contact 3 = bit, spot, trace, drop, dash, small amount, jot, smattering 4 = style, method, technique, way, manner, trademark
● PHRASES **touch and go** = risky, close, near, critical, precarious, nerve-racking
◆ **touch on** or **upon something** = refer to, cover, raise, deal with, mention, bring in, speak of, hint at

touching = moving, affecting, sad, stirring, pathetic, poignant, emotive, pitiable

tough ADJECTIVE 1 = strong ≠ weak 2 = hardy, strong, seasoned, strapping, vigorous, sturdy, stout 3 = violent, rough, ruthless, pugnacious, hard-bitten 4 = strict, severe, stern, hard, firm, resolute, merciless, unbending ≠ lenient 5 = hard, difficult, troublesome, uphill, strenuous, arduous, laborious 6 = resilient, hard, resistant, durable, strong, solid, rugged, sturdy ≠ fragile
● NOUN = ruffian, bully, thug, hooligan, bruiser (informal), roughneck (slang), tsotsi (S. African)

tour NOUN = journey, expedition, excursion, trip, outing, jaunt, junket
● VERB 1 = travel round, travel through, journey round, trek round, go on a trip through 2 = visit, explore, go round, inspect, walk round, drive round, sightsee

tourist = traveller, voyager, tripper, globetrotter, holiday-maker, sightseer, excursionist

tournament = competition, meeting, event, series, contest

tow = drag, draw, pull, haul, tug, yank, lug

towards 1 = in the direction of, to, for, on the way to, en route for 2 = regarding, about, concerning, respecting, in relation to, with regard to, with respect to, apropos

tower = column, pillar, turret, belfry, steeple, obelisk

toxic = poisonous, deadly, lethal, harmful, pernicious, noxious, septic, pestilential ≠ harmless

toy NOUN = plaything, game, doll
● PHRASES **toy with something** = play with, consider, trifle with, dally with, entertain the possibility of, amuse yourself with, think idly of

trace VERB 1 = search for, track, unearth, hunt down 2 = find, track (down), discover, detect, unearth, hunt down, ferret out, locate 3 = outline, sketch, draw 4 = copy, map, draft, outline, sketch, reproduce, draw over
● NOUN 1 = bit, drop, touch, shadow, suggestion, hint, suspicion, tinge 2 = remnant, sign, record, mark, evidence, indication, vestige 3 = track, trail, footstep, path, footprint, spoor, footmark

track NOUN 1 = path, way, road, route, trail, pathway, footpath 2 = course, line, path, orbit, trajectory 3 = line, tramline
● VERB = follow, pursue, chase, trace, tail (informal), shadow, trail, stalk
● PHRASES **track something** or **someone down** = find, discover, trace, unearth, dig up, hunt down, sniff out, run to earth or ground

tract[1] = area, region, district, stretch, territory, extent, plot, expanse

tract[2] = treatise, essay, booklet, pamphlet, dissertation, monograph, homily

trade NOUN 1 = commerce, business, transactions, dealing, exchange, traffic, truck, barter 2 = job, employment, business, craft, profession, occupation, line of work, métier
● VERB 1 = deal, do business, traffic, truck, bargain, peddle, transact, cut a deal 2 = exchange, switch, swap, barter 3 = operate, run, deal, do business

trader = dealer, supplier, merchant, seller, purveyor

tradition 1 = customs, institution, ritual,

folklore, lore, tikanga (*N.Z.*) **2** = established practice, custom, convention, habit, ritual

traditional 1 = old-fashioned, old, established, conventional, usual, accustomed, customary, time-honoured ≠ revolutionary **2** = folk, old

traffic NOUN **1** = transport, vehicles, transportation, freight **2** = trade, commerce, business, exchange, truck, dealings, peddling
● VERB = trade, deal, exchange, bargain, do business, peddle, cut a deal, have dealings

tragedy = disaster, catastrophe, misfortune, adversity, calamity ≠ fortune

tragic 1 = distressing, sad, appalling, deadly, unfortunate, disastrous, dreadful, dire ≠ fortunate **2** = sad, miserable, pathetic, mournful ≠ happy

trail NOUN **1** = path, track, route, way, course, road, pathway, footpath **2** = tracks, path, marks, wake, trace, scent, footprints, spoor **3** = wake, stream, tail
● VERB **1** = follow, track, chase, pursue, dog, hunt, shadow, trace **2** = drag, draw, pull, sweep, haul, tow, dangle, droop **3** = lag, follow, drift, wander, linger, trudge, plod, meander

train VERB **1** = instruct, school, prepare, coach, teach, guide, educate, drill **2** = exercise, prepare, work out, practise, do exercise, get into shape **3** = aim, point, level, position, direct, focus, sight, zero in
● NOUN = sequence, series, chain, string, set, cycle, trail, succession

trainer = coach, manager, guide, adviser, tutor, instructor, counsellor, guru

trait = characteristic, feature, quality, attribute, quirk, peculiarity, mannerism, idiosyncrasy

traitor = betrayer, deserter, turncoat, renegade, defector, Judas, quisling, apostate, fizgig (*Austral. slang*) ≠ loyalist

tramp VERB **1** = trudge, stump, toil, plod, traipse (*informal*) **2** = hike, walk, trek, roam, march, ramble, slog, rove
● NOUN **1** = vagrant, derelict, drifter, down-and-out, derro (*Austral. slang*) **2** = tread, stamp, footstep, footfall **3** = hike, march, trek, ramble, slog

trample *often with* **on** = stamp, crush, squash, tread, flatten, run over, walk over

trance = daze, dream, abstraction, rapture, reverie, stupor, unconsciousness

transaction = deal, negotiation, business, enterprise, bargain, undertaking

transcend = surpass, exceed, go beyond, rise above, eclipse, excel, outstrip, outdo

transcript = copy, record, manuscript, reproduction, duplicate, transcription

transfer VERB = move, transport, shift, relocate, transpose, change
● NOUN = transference, move, handover, change, shift, transmission, translation, relocation

transform 1 = change, convert, alter, transmute **2** = make over, remodel, revolutionize

transformation 1 = change, conversion, alteration, metamorphosis, transmutation **2** = revolution, sea change

transit = movement, transfer, transport, passage, crossing, transportation, carriage, conveyance

transition = change, passing, development, shift, conversion, alteration, progression, metamorphosis

transitional 1 = changing, passing, fluid, intermediate, unsettled, developmental **2** = temporary, working, acting, short-term, interim, fill-in, caretaker, provisional

translate = render, put, change, convert, interpret, decode, construe, paraphrase

translation = interpretation, version, rendering, rendition, decoding, paraphrase

transmission 1 = transfer, spread, spreading, passing on, circulation, dispatch, relaying, mediation **2** = broadcasting, showing, putting out, relaying, sending **3** = programme, broadcast, show, production, telecast

transmit 1 = broadcast, televise, relay, air, radio, send out, disseminate, beam out **2** = pass on, carry, spread, send, bear, transfer, hand on, convey

transparent 1 = clear, sheer, see-through, lucid, translucent, crystalline, limpid, diaphanous ≠ opaque **2** = obvious, plain, patent, evident, explicit, manifest, recognizable, unambiguous ≠ uncertain

transplant 1 = implant, transfer, graft **2** = transfer, take, bring, carry, remove, transport, shift, convey

transport NOUN **1** = vehicle, transportation, conveyance **2** = transference, carrying, delivery, distribution, transportation, shipment, freight, haulage **3** *often plural* = ecstasy,

delight, heaven, bliss, euphoria, rapture, enchantment, ravishment ≠ despondency
● VERB 1 = convey, take, move, bring, send, carry, bear, transfer 2 = enrapture, move, delight, entrance, enchant, captivate, ravish 3 (*History*) = exile, banish, deport

trap NOUN 1 = snare, net, gin, pitfall, noose 2 = ambush, set-up (*informal*) 3 = trick, set-up (*informal*), deception, ploy, ruse, trickery, subterfuge, stratagem
● VERB 1 = catch, snare, ensnare, entrap, take, corner, bag, lay hold of 2 = trick, fool, cheat, lure, seduce, deceive, dupe, beguile 3 = capture, catch, arrest, seize, take, secure, collar (*informal*), apprehend

trash 1 = nonsense, rubbish, rot, drivel, twaddle, tripe (*informal*), moonshine, hogwash, kak (*S. African taboo slang*), bizzo (*Austral. slang*), bull's wool (*Austral. & N.Z. slang*) ≠ sense 2 (*Chiefly U.S. & Canad.*) = litter, refuse, waste, rubbish, junk (*informal*), garbage, dross

trauma 1 = shock, suffering, pain, torture, ordeal, anguish 2 = injury, damage, hurt, wound, agony

traumatic = shocking, upsetting, alarming, awful, disturbing, devastating, painful, distressing ≠ calming

travel VERB = go, journey, move, tour, progress, wander, trek, voyage
● NOUN *usually plural* = journey, wandering, expedition, globetrotting, tour, trip, voyage, excursion

traveller or (*U.S.*) **traveler** = voyager, tourist, explorer, globetrotter, holiday-maker, wayfarer

tread VERB = step, walk, march, pace, stamp, stride, hike
● NOUN = step, walk, pace, stride, footstep, gait, footfall

treason = disloyalty, mutiny, treachery, duplicity, sedition, perfidy, lese-majesty, traitorousness ≠ loyalty

treasure NOUN 1 = riches, money, gold, fortune, wealth, valuables, jewels, cash 2 (*Informal*) = angel, darling, jewel, gem, paragon, nonpareil
● VERB = prize, value, esteem, adore, cherish, revere, hold dear, love

treasury = storehouse, bank, store, vault, hoard, cache, repository

treat VERB 1 = behave towards, deal with, handle, act towards, use, consider, serve, manage 2 = take care of, minister

to, attend to, give medical treatment to, doctor (*informal*), nurse, care for, prescribe medicine for 3 = provide, stand (*informal*), entertain, lay on, regale
● NOUN 1 = entertainment, party, surprise, gift, celebration, feast, outing, excursion 2 = pleasure, delight, joy, thrill, satisfaction, enjoyment, source of pleasure, fun

treatment 1 = care, medical care, nursing, medicine, surgery, therapy, healing, medication 2 = cure, remedy, medication, medicine 3 *often with of* = handling, dealings with, behaviour towards, conduct towards, management, manipulation, action towards

treaty = agreement, pact, contract, alliance, convention, compact, covenant, entente

trek VERB 1 = journey, march, hike, tramp, rove, go walkabout (*Austral.*) 2 = trudge, traipse (*informal*), footslog, slog
● NOUN 1 = slog, tramp 2 = journey, hike, expedition, safari, march, odyssey

tremble VERB 1 = shake, shiver, quake, shudder, quiver, totter 2 = vibrate, shake, quake, wobble
● NOUN = shake, shiver, quake, shudder, wobble, tremor, quiver, vibration

tremendous 1 = huge, great, enormous, terrific, formidable, immense, gigantic, colossal ≠ tiny 2 = excellent, great, wonderful, brilliant, amazing, extraordinary, fantastic (*informal*), marvellous, booshit (*Austral. slang*), exo (*Austral. slang*), sik (*Austral. slang*) ≠ terrible

trench = ditch, channel, drain, gutter, trough, furrow, excavation

trend 1 = tendency, swing, drift, inclination, current, direction, flow, leaning 2 = fashion, craze, fad (*informal*), mode, thing, style, rage, vogue

trendy (*Brit. informal*) = fashionable, with it (*informal*), stylish, in fashion, in vogue, modish, voguish

trial 1 (*Law*) = hearing, case, court case, inquiry, tribunal, lawsuit, appeal, litigation 2 = test, experiment, evaluation, audition, dry run (*informal*), assessment, probation, appraisal 3 = hardship, suffering, trouble, distress, ordeal, adversity, affliction, tribulation

tribe = race, people, family, clan, hapu (*N.Z.*), iwi (*N.Z.*)

tribunal = <u>hearing</u>, court, trial

tribute = <u>accolade</u>, testimonial, eulogy, recognition, compliment, commendation, panegyric ≠ criticism

trick NOUN 1 = <u>joke</u>, stunt, spoof (*informal*), prank, practical joke, antic, jape, leg-pull (*Brit. informal*) 2 = <u>deception</u>, trap, fraud, manoeuvre, ploy, hoax, swindle, ruse 3 = <u>sleight of hand</u>, stunt, legerdemain 4 = <u>secret</u>, skill, knack, hang (*informal*), technique, know-how (*informal*) 5 = <u>mannerism</u>, habit, characteristic, trait, quirk, peculiarity, foible, idiosyncrasy
● VERB = <u>deceive</u>, trap, take someone in (*informal*), fool, cheat, con (*informal*), kid (*informal*), mislead

trickle VERB = <u>dribble</u>, run, drop, stream, drip, ooze, seep, exude
● NOUN = <u>dribble</u>, drip, seepage, thin stream

tricky 1 = <u>difficult</u>, sensitive, complicated, delicate, risky, hairy (*informal*), problematic, thorny ≠ simple 2 = <u>crafty</u>, scheming, cunning, slippery, sly, devious, wily, artful ≠ open

trifle = <u>knick-knack</u>, toy, plaything, bauble, bagatelle

trifling = <u>insignificant</u>, trivial, worthless, negligible, unimportant, paltry, measly ≠ significant

trigger = <u>bring about</u>, start, cause, produce, generate, prompt, provoke, set off ≠ prevent

trim ADJECTIVE 1 = <u>neat</u>, smart, tidy, spruce, dapper, natty (*informal*), well-groomed, shipshape ≠ untidy 2 = <u>slender</u>, fit, slim, sleek, streamlined, shapely, svelte, willowy
● VERB 1 = <u>cut</u>, crop, clip, shave, tidy, prune, pare, even up 2 = <u>decorate</u>, dress, array, adorn, ornament, embellish, deck out, beautify
● NOUN 1 = <u>decoration</u>, edging, border, piping, trimming, frill, embellishment, adornment 2 = <u>condition</u>, health, shape (*informal*), fitness, wellness, fettle 3 = <u>cut</u>, crop, clipping, shave, pruning, shearing, tidying up

trimming NOUN = <u>decoration</u>, edging, border, piping, frill, embellishment, adornment, ornamentation
● PLURAL NOUN = <u>extras</u>, accessories, ornaments, accompaniments, frills, trappings, paraphernalia

trinity = <u>threesome</u>, trio, triad, triumvirate

trio = <u>threesome</u>, trinity, trilogy, triad, triumvirate

trip NOUN 1 = <u>journey</u>, outing, excursion, day out, run, drive, tour, spin (*informal*) 2 = <u>stumble</u>, fall, slip, misstep
● VERB 1 = <u>stumble</u>, fall, fall over, slip, tumble, topple, stagger, misstep 2 = <u>skip</u>, dance, hop, gambol
● PHRASES **trip someone up** = <u>catch out</u>, trap, wrongfoot

triple ADJECTIVE 1 = <u>treble</u>, three times 2 = <u>three-way</u>, threefold, tripartite
● VERB = <u>treble</u>, increase threefold

triumph NOUN 1 = <u>success</u>, victory, accomplishment, achievement, coup, feat, conquest, attainment ≠ failure 2 = <u>joy</u>, pride, happiness, rejoicing, elation, jubilation, exultation
● VERB 1 *often with* **over** = <u>succeed</u>, win, overcome, prevail, prosper, vanquish ≠ fail 2 = <u>rejoice</u>, celebrate, glory, revel, gloat, exult, crow

triumphant 1 = <u>victorious</u>, winning, successful, conquering ≠ defeated 2 = <u>celebratory</u>, jubilant, proud, elated, exultant, cock-a-hoop

trivial = <u>unimportant</u>, small, minor, petty, meaningless, worthless, trifling, insignificant ≠ important

troop NOUN = <u>group</u>, company, team, body, unit, band, crowd, squad
● PLURAL NOUN = <u>soldiers</u>, men, armed forces, servicemen, army, soldiery
● VERB = <u>flock</u>, march, stream, swarm, throng, traipse (*informal*)

trophy 1 = <u>prize</u>, cup, award, laurels 2 = <u>souvenir</u>, spoils, relic, memento, booty, keepsake

tropical = <u>hot</u>, stifling, steamy, torrid, sultry, sweltering ≠ cold

trot VERB = <u>run</u>, jog, scamper, lope, canter
● NOUN = <u>run</u>, jog, lope, canter

trouble NOUN 1 = <u>bother</u>, problems, concern, worry, stress, difficulty (*informal*), anxiety, distress 2 *usually plural* = <u>distress</u>, problem, worry, pain, anxiety, grief, torment, sorrow ≠ pleasure 3 = <u>ailment</u>, disease, failure, complaint, illness, disorder, defect, malfunction 4 = <u>disorder</u>, fighting, conflict, bother, unrest, disturbance, to-do (*informal*), furore, biffo (*Austral. slang*) ≠ peace 5 = <u>effort</u>, work, thought, care, labour, pains, hassle (*informal*), inconvenience ≠ convenience

● **VERB 1** = <u>bother</u>, worry, upset, disturb, distress, plague, pain, sadden ≠ please **2** = <u>afflict</u>, hurt, bother, cause discomfort to, pain, grieve **3** = <u>inconvenience</u>, disturb, burden, put out, impose upon, incommode ≠ relieve **4** = <u>take pains</u>, take the time, make an effort, exert yourself ≠ avoid

troublesome 1 = <u>bothersome</u>, trying, taxing, demanding, difficult, worrying, annoying, tricky ≠ simple **2** = <u>disorderly</u>, violent, turbulent, rebellious, unruly, rowdy, undisciplined, uncooperative ≠ well-behaved

trough = <u>manger</u>, water trough

truce = <u>ceasefire</u>, peace, moratorium, respite, lull, cessation, let-up (*informal*), armistice

true 1 = <u>correct</u>, right, accurate, precise, factual, truthful, veracious ≠ false **2** = <u>actual</u>, real, genuine, proper, authentic, dinkum (*Austral. & N.Z. informal*) **3** = <u>faithful</u>, loyal, devoted, dedicated, steady, reliable, staunch, trustworthy ≠ unfaithful **4** = <u>exact</u>, perfect, accurate, precise, spot-on (*Brit. informal*), on target, unerring ≠ inaccurate

truly 1 = <u>genuinely</u>, correctly, truthfully, rightly, precisely, exactly, legitimately, authentically ≠ falsely **2** = <u>really</u>, very, greatly, indeed, extremely **3** = <u>faithfully</u>, steadily, sincerely, staunchly, dutifully, loyally, devotedly

trumpet NOUN = <u>horn</u>, clarion, bugle ● **VERB** = <u>proclaim</u>, advertise, tout (*informal*), announce, broadcast, shout from the rooftops ≠ keep secret

trunk 1 = <u>stem</u>, stalk, bole **2** = <u>chest</u>, case, box, crate, coffer, casket **3** = <u>body</u>, torso **4** = <u>snout</u>, nose, proboscis

trust VERB **1** = <u>believe in</u>, have faith in, depend on, count on, bank on, rely upon ≠ distrust **2** = <u>entrust</u>, commit, assign, confide, consign, put into the hands of, allow to look after, hand over **3** = <u>expect</u>, hope, suppose, assume, presume, surmise ● NOUN = <u>confidence</u>, credit, belief, faith, expectation, conviction, assurance, certainty ≠ distrust

trusting *or* **trustful** = <u>unsuspecting</u>, naive, gullible, unwary, credulous, unsuspicious ≠ suspicious

truth 1 = <u>reality</u>, fact(s), real life **2** = <u>truthfulness</u>, fact, accuracy, precision, validity, legitimacy, veracity, genuineness ≠ inaccuracy

try VERB **1** = <u>attempt</u>, seek, aim, strive, struggle, endeavour, have a go, make an effort **2** = <u>experiment with</u>, try out, put to the test, test, taste, examine, investigate, sample ● NOUN = <u>attempt</u>, go (*informal*), shot (*informal*), effort, crack (*informal*), stab (*informal*), bash (*informal*), whack (*informal*)

trying = <u>annoying</u>, hard, taxing, difficult, tough, stressful, exasperating, tiresome ≠ straightforward

tuck VERB = <u>push</u>, stick, stuff, slip, ease, insert, pop (*informal*) ● NOUN **1** (*Brit. informal*) = <u>food</u>, grub (*slang*), kai (*N.Z. informal*), nosh (*slang*) **2** = <u>fold</u>, gather, pleat, pinch

tug VERB **1** = <u>pull</u>, pluck, jerk, yank, wrench **2** = <u>drag</u>, pull, haul, tow, lug, heave, draw ● NOUN = <u>pull</u>, jerk, yank

tuition = <u>training</u>, schooling, education, teaching, lessons, instruction, tutoring, tutelage

tumble VERB = <u>fall</u>, drop, topple, plummet, stumble, flop ● NOUN = <u>fall</u>, drop, trip, plunge, spill, stumble

tumour = <u>growth</u>, cancer, swelling, lump, carcinoma (*Pathology*), sarcoma (*Medical*)

tune NOUN **1** = <u>melody</u>, air, song, theme, strain(s), jingle, ditty **2** = <u>harmony</u>, pitch, euphony ● VERB **1** = <u>tune up</u>, adjust **2** = <u>regulate</u>, adapt, modulate, harmonize, attune, pitch

tunnel NOUN = <u>passage</u>, underpass, passageway, subway, channel, hole, shaft ● VERB = <u>dig</u>, burrow, mine, bore, drill, excavate

turbulent = <u>stormy</u>, rough, raging, tempestuous, furious, foaming, agitated, tumultuous ≠ calm

turf NOUN **1** = <u>grass</u>, sward **2** = <u>sod</u> ● PHRASES **the turf** = <u>horse-racing</u>, the flat, racing

turmoil = <u>confusion</u>, disorder, chaos, upheaval, disarray, uproar, agitation, commotion ≠ peace

turn VERB **1** = <u>change course</u>, swing round, wheel round, veer, move, switch, shift, swerve **2** = <u>rotate</u>, spin, go round (and round), revolve, roll, circle, twist, spiral **3** = <u>change</u>, transform, shape, convert, alter, mould, remodel, mutate **4 = shape**, form, fashion, cast, frame, mould, make **5 = go bad**, go off (*Brit. informal*), curdle **6 = make rancid**, spoil, sour, taint

● NOUN **1 = rotation**, cycle, circle, revolution, spin, twist, whirl, swivel **2 = change of direction**, shift, departure, deviation **3 = direction**, course, tack, tendency, drift **4 = opportunity**, go, time, try, chance, crack (*informal*), stint **5 = deed**, service, act, action, favour, gesture

● PHRASES **turn on someone = attack**, assault, fall on, round on, lash out at, assail, lay into (*informal*), let fly at ◆ **turn someone on** (*Informal*) = **arouse**, attract, excite, thrill, stimulate, please, titillate ◆ **turn something down 1 = refuse**, decline, reject, spurn, rebuff, repudiate **2 = lower**, soften, mute, lessen, muffle, quieten ◆ **turn something in = hand in**, return, deliver, give up, hand over, submit, surrender, tender ◆ **turn something off = switch off**, turn out, put out, stop, cut out, shut down, unplug, flick off ◆ **turn something on = switch on**, activate, start, start up, ignite, kick-start ◆ **turn something up 1 = find**, reveal, discover, expose, disclose, unearth, dig up **2 = increase**, raise, boost, enhance, intensify, amplify ◆ **turn up 1 = arrive**, come, appear, show up (*informal*), attend, put in an appearance, show your face **2 = come to light**, show up, pop up, materialize

turning = turn-off, turn, bend, curve, junction, crossroads, side road, exit

turning point = crossroads, change, crisis, crux, moment of truth

turnout = attendance, crowd, audience, gate, assembly, congregation, number, throng

turnover 1 = output, business, productivity **2 = movement**, coming and going, change

tutor NOUN **= teacher**, coach, instructor, educator, guide, guardian, lecturer, guru

● VERB **= teach**, educate, school, train, coach, guide, drill, instruct

twig = branch, stick, sprig, shoot, spray

twilight 1 = dusk, evening, sunset, early evening, nightfall, sundown, gloaming (*Scot. poetic*), close of day, evo (*Austral. slang*) ≠ dawn **2 = half-light**, gloom, dimness, semi-darkness

twin NOUN **= double**, counterpart, mate, match, fellow, clone, duplicate, lookalike

● VERB **= pair**, match, join, couple, link, yoke

twinkle VERB **= sparkle**, flash, shine, glitter, gleam, blink, flicker, shimmer

● NOUN **= sparkle**, flash, spark, gleam, flicker, shimmer, glimmer

twist VERB **1 = coil**, curl, wind, wrap, screw, twirl **2 = intertwine 3 = distort**, screw up, contort, mangle, mangulate (*Austral. slang*) ≠ straighten

● NOUN **1 = surprise**, change, turn, development, revelation **2 = development**, emphasis, variation, slant **3 = wind**, turn, spin, swivel, twirl **4 = curve**, turn, bend, loop, arc, kink, zigzag, dog-leg

twitch VERB **1 = jerk**, flutter, jump, squirm **2 = pull (at)**, tug (at), pluck (at), yank (at)

● NOUN **= jerk**, tic, spasm, jump, flutter

tycoon = magnate, capitalist, baron, industrialist, financier, fat cat (*slang, chiefly U.S.*), mogul, plutocrat

type = kind, sort, class, variety, group, order, style, species

typical 1 = archetypal, standard, model, normal, stock, representative, usual, regular ≠ unusual **2 = characteristic 3 = average**, normal, usual, routine, regular, orthodox, predictable, run-of-the-mill

tyranny = oppression, cruelty, dictatorship, authoritarianism, despotism, autocracy, absolutism, high-handedness ≠ liberality

u

ubiquitous = ever-present, pervasive, omnipresent, everywhere, universal

ugly 1 = unattractive, homely (*chiefly U.S.*), plain, unsightly, unlovely, unprepossessing, ill-favoured ≠ beautiful **2 = unpleasant**, shocking, terrible, nasty, distasteful, horrid, objectionable, disagreeable ≠ pleasant **3 = bad-**

tempered, dangerous, menacing, sinister, baleful

ulcer = sore, abscess, peptic ulcer, gumboil

ultimate 1 = final, last, end 2 = supreme, highest, greatest, paramount, superlative 3 = worst, greatest, utmost, extreme 4 = best, greatest, supreme, optimum, quintessential

ultimately 1 = finally, eventually, in the end, after all, at last, sooner or later, in due time 2 = fundamentally, essentially, basically, primarily, at heart, deep down

umpire NOUN = referee, judge, arbiter, arbitrator

● VERB = referee, judge, adjudicate, arbitrate

unable = incapable, powerless, unfit, impotent, unqualified, ineffectual ≠ able

unanimous 1 = agreed, united, in agreement, harmonious, like-minded, of the same mind ≠ divided 2 = united, common, concerted, solid, consistent, harmonious, undivided, congruent ≠ split

unarmed = defenceless, helpless, unprotected ≠ armed

unaware = ignorant, unconscious, oblivious, uninformed, unknowing, not in the loop (informal) ≠ aware

unbearable = intolerable, insufferable, too much (informal), unacceptable ≠ tolerable

unborn = expected, awaited, embryonic

uncertain = unsure, undecided, vague, unclear, dubious, hazy, irresolute ≠ sure

uncertainty 1 = unpredictability, precariousness, ambiguity, unreliability, fickleness, chanciness, changeableness ≠ predictability 2 = doubt, confusion ≠ confidence 3 = hesitancy, indecision

uncomfortable 1 = uneasy, troubled, disturbed, embarrassed, awkward, discomfited ≠ comfortable 2 = painful, awkward, rough

uncommon 1 = rare, unusual, odd, novel, strange, peculiar, scarce, queer ≠ common 2 = extraordinary, remarkable, special, outstanding, distinctive, exceptional, notable ≠ ordinary

uncompromising = inflexible, strict, rigid, firm, tough, inexorable, intransigent, unbending

unconditional = absolute, full, complete, total, positive, entire, outright, unlimited

≠ qualified

unconscious 1 = senseless, knocked out, out cold (informal), out, stunned, dazed, in a coma, stupefied ≠ awake 2 = unaware, ignorant, oblivious, unknowing ≠ aware 3 = unintentional, unwitting, inadvertent, accidental ≠ intentional

uncover 1 = reveal, expose, disclose, divulge, make known ≠ conceal 2 = open, unveil, unwrap, show, strip, expose, bare, lay bare

under PREPOSITION 1 = below, beneath, underneath ≠ over 2 = subordinate to, subject to, governed by, secondary to ● ADVERB = below, down, beneath ≠ up

undercover = secret, covert, private, hidden, concealed ≠ open

underdog = weaker party, little fellow (informal), outsider

underestimate 1 = undervalue, understate, diminish, play down, minimize, downgrade, miscalculate, trivialize ≠ overestimate 2 = underrate, undervalue, belittle ≠ overrate

undergo = experience, go through, stand, suffer, bear, sustain, endure

underground ADJECTIVE 1 = subterranean, basement, lower-level, sunken, covered, buried, subterrestrial 2 = secret, covert, hidden, guerrilla, revolutionary, confidential, dissident, closet ● PHRASES **the underground** 1 = the tube (Brit.), the subway, the metro 2 = the Resistance, partisans, freedom fighters

underline 1 = emphasize, stress, highlight, accentuate ≠ minimize 2 = underscore, mark

underlying = fundamental, basic, prime, primary, elementary, intrinsic

undermine = weaken, sabotage, subvert, compromise, disable ≠ reinforce

understand 1 = comprehend, get, take in, perceive, grasp, see, follow, realize 2 = believe, gather, think, see, suppose, notice, assume, fancy

understandable = reasonable, natural, justified, expected, inevitable, legitimate, predictable, accountable

understanding NOUN 1 = perception, knowledge, grasp, sense, know-how (informal), judgment, awareness, appreciation ≠ ignorance 2 = agreement, deal, promise, arrangement, accord, contract, bond, pledge ≠ disagreement

3 = <u>belief</u>, view, opinion, impression, interpretation, feeling, idea, notion
● ADJECTIVE = <u>sympathetic</u>, kind, compassionate, considerate, patient, sensitive, tolerant ≠ unsympathetic

undertake = <u>agree</u>, promise, contract, guarantee, engage, pledge

undertaking 1 = <u>task</u>, business, operation, project, attempt, effort, affair, venture **2** = <u>promise</u>, commitment, pledge, word, vow, assurance

underwear = <u>underclothes</u>, lingerie, undies (*informal*), undergarments, underthings, brookies (*S. African informal*), underdaks (*Austral. slang*)

underworld 1 = <u>criminals</u>, gangsters, organized crime, gangland (*informal*) **2** = <u>nether world</u>, Hades, nether regions

underwrite = <u>finance</u>, back, fund, guarantee, sponsor, insure, ratify, subsidize

undesirable = <u>unwanted</u>, unwelcome, disagreeable, objectionable, unacceptable, unsuitable, unattractive, distasteful ≠ desirable

undo 1 = <u>open</u>, unfasten, loose, untie, unbutton, disentangle **2** = <u>reverse</u>, cancel, offset, neutralize, invalidate, annul **3** = <u>ruin</u>, defeat, destroy, wreck, shatter, upset, undermine, overturn

undone 1 = <u>unfinished</u>, left, neglected, omitted, unfulfilled, unperformed ≠ finished

undoubtedly = <u>certainly</u>, definitely, surely, doubtless, without doubt, assuredly

unearth 1 = <u>discover</u>, find, reveal, expose, uncover **2** = <u>dig up</u>, excavate, exhume, dredge up

unearthly = <u>eerie</u>, strange, supernatural, ghostly, weird, phantom, uncanny, spooky (*informal*)

uneasy 1 = <u>anxious</u>, worried, troubled, nervous, disturbed, uncomfortable, edgy, perturbed ≠ relaxed **2** = <u>precarious</u>, strained, uncomfortable, tense, awkward, shaky, insecure

unemployed = <u>out of work</u>, redundant, laid off, jobless, idle ≠ working

unfair 1 = <u>biased</u>, prejudiced, unjust, one-sided, partial, partisan, bigoted **2** = <u>unscrupulous</u>, dishonest, unethical, wrongful, unsporting ≠ ethical

unfit 1 = <u>out of shape</u>, feeble, unhealthy, flabby, in poor condition ≠ healthy

2 = <u>incapable</u>, inadequate, incompetent, no good, useless, unqualified ≠ capable **3** = <u>unsuitable</u>, inadequate, useless, unsuited ≠ suitable

unfold 1 = <u>reveal</u>, tell, present, show, disclose, uncover, divulge, make known **2** = <u>open</u>, spread out, undo, expand, unfurl, unwrap, unroll

unfortunate 1 = <u>disastrous</u>, calamitous, adverse, ill-fated ≠ opportune **2** = <u>regrettable</u>, deplorable, lamentable, unsuitable, unbecoming ≠ becoming **3** = <u>unlucky</u>, unhappy, doomed, cursed, unsuccessful, hapless, wretched ≠ fortunate

unhappy 1 = <u>sad</u>, depressed, miserable, blue, melancholy, mournful, dejected, despondent ≠ happy **2** = <u>unlucky</u>, unfortunate, hapless, cursed, wretched, ill-fated ≠ fortunate

unhealthy 1 = <u>harmful</u>, detrimental, unwholesome, insanitary, insalubrious ≠ beneficial **2** = <u>sick</u>, sickly, unwell, delicate, crook (*Austral. & N.Z. informal*), ailing, frail, feeble, invalid ≠ well **3** = <u>weak</u>, ailing ≠ strong

unification = <u>union</u>, uniting, alliance, coalition, federation, confederation, amalgamation, coalescence

uniform NOUN **1** = <u>regalia</u>, suit, livery, colours, habit **2** = <u>outfit</u>, dress, costume, attire, gear (*informal*), get-up (*informal*), ensemble, garb
● ADJECTIVE **1** = <u>consistent</u>, unvarying, similar, even, same, matching, regular, constant ≠ varying **2** = <u>alike</u>, similar, like, same, equal

unify = <u>unite</u>, join, combine, merge, consolidate, confederate, amalgamate ≠ divide

union 1 = <u>joining</u>, uniting, unification, combination, coalition, merger, mixture, blend **2** = <u>alliance</u>, league, association, coalition, federation, confederacy

unique 1 = <u>distinct</u>, special, exclusive, peculiar, only, single, lone, solitary **2** = <u>unparalleled</u>, unmatched, unequalled, matchless, without equal

unit 1 = <u>entity</u>, whole, item, feature **2** = <u>section</u>, company, group, force, detail, division, cell, squad **3** = <u>measure</u>, quantity, measurement **4** = <u>part</u>, section, segment, class, element, component, constituent, tutorial

unite 1 = join, link, combine, couple, blend, merge, unify, fuse ≠ separate 2 = cooperate, ally, join forces, band, pool, collaborate ≠ split

unity 1 = union, unification, coalition, federation, integration, confederation, amalgamation 2 = wholeness, integrity, oneness, union, entity, singleness ≠ disunity 3 = agreement, accord, consensus, harmony, solidarity, unison, assent, concord ≠ disagreement

universal 1 = widespread, general, common, whole, total, unlimited, overarching 2 = global, worldwide, international, pandemic

universally = without exception, everywhere, always, invariably

universe = cosmos, space, creation, nature, heavens, macrocosm, all existence

unknown 1 = strange, new, undiscovered, uncharted, unexplored, virgin, remote, alien 2 = unidentified, mysterious, anonymous, unnamed, nameless, incognito 3 = obscure, humble, unfamiliar ≠ famous

unlike 1 = different from, dissimilar to, distinct from, unequal to ≠ slmilar to 2 = contrasted with, not like, in contradiction to, in contrast with or to, as opposed to, differently from, opposite to

unlikely 1 = improbable, doubtful, remote, slight, faint ≠ probable 2 = unbelievable, incredible, implausible, questionable ≠ believable

unload 1 = empty, clear, unpack, dump, discharge 2 = unburden

unnatural 1 = abnormal, odd, strange, unusual, extraordinary, perverted, queer, irregular ≠ normal 2 = false, forced, artificial, affected, stiff, feigned, stilted, insincere ≠ genuine

unpleasant 1 = nasty, bad, horrid, distasteful, displeasing, objectionable, disagreeable ≠ nice 2 = obnoxious, rude ≠ likable or likeable

unravel 1 = solve, explain, work out, resolve, figure out (informal) 2 = undo, separate, disentangle, free, unwind, untangle

unrest = discontent, rebellion, protest, strife, agitation, discord, sedition, dissension ≠ peace

unsettled 1 = unstable, shaky, insecure, disorderly, unsteady 2 = restless, tense, shaken, confused, disturbed, anxious, agitated, flustered 3 = inconstant, changing, variable, uncertain

unstable 1 = changeable, volatile, unpredictable, variable, fluctuating, fitful, inconstant ≠ constant 2 = insecure, shaky, precarious, unsettled, wobbly, tottering, unsteady 3 = unpredictable, irrational, erratic, inconsistent, temperamental, capricious, changeable ≠ level-headed

unthinkable 1 = impossible, out of the question, inconceivable, absurd, unreasonable 2 = inconceivable, incredible, unimaginable

untold 1 = indescribable, unthinkable, unimaginable, undreamed of, unutterable, inexpressible 2 = countless, incalculable, innumerable, myriad, numberless, uncountable

untrue 1 = false, lying, wrong, mistaken, incorrect, inaccurate, dishonest, deceptive ≠ true 2 = unfaithful, disloyal, deceitful, treacherous, faithless, false, untrustworthy, inconstant ≠ faithful

unusual 1 = rare, odd, strange, extraordinary, different, curious, queer, uncommon ≠ common 2 = extraordinary, unique, remarkable, exceptional, uncommon, singular, unconventional ≠ average

upbeat (Informal) = cheerful, positive, optimistic, encouraging, hopeful, cheery

upbringing = education, training, breeding, rearing, raising

update = bring up to date, improve, correct, renew, revise, upgrade, amend, overhaul

upgrade 1 = improve, better, update, reform, add to, enhance, refurbish, renovate 2 = promote, raise, advance, boost, move up, elevate, kick upstairs (informal), give promotion to ≠ demote

upheaval = disturbance, revolution, disorder, turmoil, disruption

uphill 1 = ascending, rising, upward, mounting, climbing ≠ descending 2 = arduous, hard, taxing, difficult, tough, exhausting, gruelling, strenuous

uphold 1 = support, back, defend, aid, champion, maintain, promote, sustain 2 = confirm, endorse

uplift VERB = improve, better, raise, advance, inspire, refine, edify

 • NOUN = improvement, enlightenment,

advancement, refinement, enhancement, enrichment, edification

upper 1 = topmost, top ≠ bottom
2 = higher, high ≠ lower **3** = superior, senior, higher-level, greater, top, important, chief, most important ≠ inferior

upper class = aristocratic, upper-class, noble, high-class, patrician, blue-blooded, highborn

upright 1 = vertical, straight, standing up, erect, perpendicular, bolt upright ≠ horizontal **2** = honest, good, principled, just, ethical, honourable, righteous, conscientious ≠ dishonourable

uprising = rebellion, rising, revolution, revolt, disturbance, mutiny, insurrection, insurgence

uproar 1 = commotion, noise, racket, riot, turmoil, mayhem, din, pandemonium **2** = protest, outrage, complaint, objection, fuss, stink (*informal*), outcry, furore

upset ADJECTIVE **1** = distressed, shaken, disturbed, worried, troubled, hurt, bothered, unhappy **2** = sick, queasy, bad, ill **3** = overturned, upside down, capsized, spilled
● VERB **1** = distress, trouble, disturb, worry, alarm, bother, grieve, agitate **2** = tip over, overturn, capsize, knock over, spill **3** = mess up, spoil, disturb, change, confuse, disorder, unsettle, disorganize
● NOUN **1** = distress, worry, trouble, shock, bother, disturbance, agitation **2** = reversal, shake-up (*informal*), defeat **3** = illness, complaint, disorder, bug (*informal*), sickness, malady

upside down *or* **upside-down** ADVERB = wrong side up
● ADJECTIVE **1** = inverted, overturned, upturned **2** (*Informal*) = confused, disordered, chaotic, muddled, topsy-turvy, higgledy-piggledy (*informal*)

up-to-date = modern, fashionable, trendy (*Brit. informal*), current, stylish, in vogue, up-to-the-minute ≠ out of date

urban = civic, city, town, metropolitan, municipal, dorp (*S. African*)

urge VERB **1** = beg, exhort, plead, implore, beseech, entreat **2** = advocate, recommend, advise, support, counsel ≠ discourage
● NOUN = impulse, longing, wish, desire, drive, yearning, itch (*informal*), thirst ≠ reluctance

urgency = importance, need, necessity, gravity, pressure, hurry, seriousness, extremity

urgent = crucial, desperate, pressing, great, important, crying, critical, immediate ≠ unimportant

usage 1 = use, operation, employment, running, control, management, handling **2** = practice, method, procedure, habit, regime, custom, routine, convention

use VERB **1** = employ, utilize, work, apply, operate, exercise, practise, resort to **2** *sometimes with up* = consume, exhaust, spend, run through, expend **3** = take advantage of, exploit, manipulate
● NOUN **1** = usage, employment, operation, application **2** = purpose, end, reason, object **3** = good, point, help, service, value, benefit, profit, advantage

used = second-hand, cast-off, nearly new, shopsoiled ≠ new

used to = accustomed to, familiar with

useful = helpful, effective, valuable, practical, profitable, worthwhile, beneficial, fruitful ≠ useless

useless 1 = worthless, valueless, impractical, fruitless, unproductive, ineffectual, unsuitable ≠ useful **2** = pointless, futile, vain ≠ worthwhile **3** (*Informal*) = inept, no good, hopeless, incompetent, ineffectual

usher VERB = escort, lead, direct, guide, conduct
● NOUN = attendant, guide, doorman, escort, doorkeeper

usual = normal, customary, regular, general, common, standard, ordinary, typical ≠ unusual

usually = normally, generally, mainly, commonly, mostly, on the whole, as a rule, habitually

utility = usefulness, benefit, convenience, practicality, efficacy, serviceableness

utilize = use, employ, deploy, take advantage of, make use of, put to use, bring into play, avail yourself of

utmost ADJECTIVE **1** = greatest, highest, maximum, supreme, paramount, pre-eminent **2** = farthest, extreme, last, final
● NOUN = best, greatest, maximum, highest, hardest

utter¹ = say, state, speak, voice, express, deliver, declare, mouth

utter² = absolute, complete, total,

sheer, outright, thorough, downright, unmitigated

utterly = <u>totally</u>, completely, absolutely, perfectly, fully, entirely, extremely, thoroughly

V

vacancy 1 = <u>opening</u>, job, post, place, position, role, situation, opportunity 2 = <u>room</u>, space, available accommodation, unoccupied room

vacant 1 = <u>empty</u>, free, available, abandoned, deserted, for sale, on the market, void ≠ occupied 2 = <u>unfilled</u>, unoccupied ≠ taken 3 = <u>blank</u>, vague, dreamy, empty, abstracted, idle, vacuous, inane ≠ thoughtful

vacuum 1 = <u>gap</u>, lack, absence, space, deficiency, void 2 = <u>emptiness</u>, space, void, gap, nothingness, vacuity

vague 1 = <u>unclear</u>, indefinite, hazy, confused, loose, uncertain, unsure, superficial ≠ clear 2 = <u>imprecise</u>, unspecified, generalized, rough, loose, ambiguous, hazy, equivocal 3 = <u>absent-minded</u>, distracted, vacant, preoccupied, oblivious, inattentive 4 = <u>indistinct</u>, unclear, faint, hazy, indeterminate, nebulous, ill-defined ≠ distinct

vain ADJECTIVE 1 = <u>futile</u>, useless, pointless, unsuccessful, idle, worthless, senseless, fruitless ≠ successful 2 = <u>conceited</u>, narcissistic, proud, arrogant, swaggering, egotistical, self-important ≠ modest

● PHRASES **in vain** 1 = <u>useless</u>, to no avail, unsuccessful, fruitless, vain 2 = <u>uselessly</u>, to no avail, unsuccessfully, fruitlessly, vainly, ineffectually

valid 1 = <u>sound</u>, good, reasonable, telling, convincing, rational, logical, viable ≠ unfounded 2 = <u>legal</u>, official, legitimate, genuine, authentic, lawful, bona fide ≠ invalid

validity 1 = <u>soundness</u>, force, power,

weight, strength, cogency 2 = <u>legality</u>, authority, legitimacy, right, lawfulness

valley = <u>hollow</u>, dale, glen, vale, depression, dell

valuable ADJECTIVE 1 = <u>useful</u>, important, profitable, worthwhile, beneficial, helpful ≠ useless 2 = <u>treasured</u>, prized, precious 3 = <u>precious</u>, expensive, costly, dear, high-priced, priceless, irreplaceable ≠ worthless

● PLURAL NOUN = <u>treasures</u>, prized possessions, precious items, heirlooms, personal effects, costly article

value NOUN 1 = <u>importance</u>, benefit, worth, merit, point, service, sense, profit ≠ worthlessness 2 = <u>cost</u>, price, worth, rate, market price, face value, asking price, selling price

● PLURAL NOUN = <u>principles</u>, morals, ethics, mores, standards of behaviour, (moral) standards

● VERB 1 = <u>appreciate</u>, rate, prize, regard highly, respect, admire, treasure, esteem ≠ undervalue 2 = <u>evaluate</u>, price, estimate, rate, cost, assess, set at, appraise

vanish 1 = <u>disappear</u>, dissolve, evaporate, fade away, melt away, evanesce ≠ appear 2 = <u>die out</u>, disappear, pass away, end, fade, dwindle, cease to exist, become extinct

vanity = <u>pride</u>, arrogance, conceit, narcissism, egotism, conceitedness ≠ modesty

variable = <u>changeable</u>, unstable, fluctuating, shifting, flexible, uneven, temperamental, unsteady ≠ constant

variant NOUN = <u>variation</u>, form, version, development, alternative, adaptation, revision, modification

● ADJECTIVE = <u>different</u>, alternative, modified, divergent

variation 1 = <u>alternative</u>, variety, modification, departure, innovation, variant 2 = <u>variety</u>, change, deviation, difference, diversity, diversion, novelty ≠ uniformity

varied = <u>different</u>, mixed, various, diverse, assorted, miscellaneous, sundry, motley ≠ unvarying

variety 1 = <u>diversity</u>, change, variation, difference, diversification, heterogeneity, multifariousness ≠ uniformity 2 = <u>range</u>, selection, assortment, mix, collection, line-up, mixture, array 3 = <u>type</u>, sort, kind, class, brand, species, breed, strain

various 1 = different, assorted, miscellaneous, varied, distinct, diverse, disparate, sundry ≠ similar 2 = many, numerous, countless, several, abundant, innumerable, sundry, profuse

varnish NOUN = lacquer, polish, glaze, gloss
● VERB = lacquer, polish, glaze, gloss

vary 1 = differ, be different, be dissimilar, disagree, diverge 2 = change, shift, swing, alter, fluctuate, oscillate, see-saw 3 = alternate

vast = huge, massive, enormous, great, wide, immense, gigantic, monumental ≠ tiny

vault¹ 1 = strongroom, repository, depository 2 = crypt, tomb, catacomb, cellar, mausoleum, charnel house, undercroft

vault² = jump, spring, leap, clear, bound, hurdle

veer = change direction, turn, swerve, shift, sheer, change course

vehicle 1 = conveyance, machine, motor vehicle 2 = medium, means, channel, mechanism, organ, apparatus

veil NOUN 1 = mask, cover, shroud, film, curtain, cloak 2 = screen, mask, disguise, blind 3 = film, cover, curtain, cloak, shroud
● VERB = cover, screen, hide, mask, shield, disguise, conceal, obscure ≠ reveal

veiled = disguised, implied, hinted at, covert, masked, concealed, suppressed

vein 1 = blood vessel 2 = mood, style, note, tone, mode, temper, tenor 3 = seam, layer, stratum, course, current, bed, deposit, streak

velocity = speed, pace, rapidity, quickness, swiftness

vengeance = revenge, retaliation, reprisal, retribution, requital ≠ forgiveness

vent NOUN = outlet, opening, aperture, duct, orifice
● VERB = express, release, voice, air, discharge, utter, emit, pour out ≠ hold back

venture NOUN = undertaking, project, enterprise, campaign, risk, operation, activity, scheme
● VERB 1 = go, travel, journey, set out, wander, stray, plunge into, rove 2 = dare, presume, have the courage to, be brave enough, hazard, go out on a limb (*informal*), take the liberty, go so far as

3 = put forward, volunteer

verbal = spoken, oral, word-of-mouth, unwritten

verdict = decision, finding, judgment, opinion, sentence, conclusion, conviction, adjudication

verge NOUN 1 = brink, point, edge, threshold 2 = border, edge, margin, limit, boundary, threshold, brim
● PHRASES **verge on something** = come near to, approach, border on, resemble, incline to, be similar to, touch on, be more or less

verify 1 = check, make sure, examine, monitor, inspect 2 = confirm, prove, substantiate, support, validate, bear out, corroborate, authenticate ≠ disprove

versatile 1 = adaptable, flexible, all-round, resourceful, multifaceted ≠ unadaptable 2 = all-purpose, variable, adjustable ≠ limited

versed = knowledgeable, experienced, seasoned, familiar, practised, acquainted, well-informed, proficient ≠ ignorant

version 1 = form, variety, variant, sort, class, design, style, model 2 = adaptation, edition, interpretation, form, copy, rendering, reproduction, portrayal 3 = account, report, description, record, reading, story, view, understanding

vertical = upright, sheer, perpendicular, straight (up and down), erect, plumb, on end, precipitous, vertiginous ≠ horizontal

very ADVERB = extremely, highly, greatly, really, deeply, unusually, profoundly, decidedly
● ADJECTIVE 1 = exact, precise, selfsame 2 = ideal

vessel 1 = ship, boat, craft 2 = container, receptacle, can, bowl, tank, pot, drum, barrel

vest VERB
● PHRASES **vest in something** or **someone** *usually passive* = place, invest, entrust, settle, confer, endow, bestow, consign ♦ **vest with something** *usually passive* = endow with, entrust with

vet = check, examine, investigate, review, appraise, scrutinize

veteran NOUN = old hand, past master, warhorse (*informal*), old stager ≠ novice
● ADJECTIVE = long-serving, seasoned, experienced, old, established, qualified, mature, practised

veto VERB 1 = <u>ban</u>, block, reject, rule out, turn down, forbid, boycott, prohibit ≠ pass
● NOUN = <u>ban</u>, dismissal, rejection, vetoing, boycott, embargo, prohibiting, prohibition ≠ ratification

viable = <u>workable</u>, practical, feasible, suitable, realistic, operational, applicable, usable ≠ unworkable

vibrant 1 = <u>energetic</u>, dynamic, sparkling, vivid, spirited, storming, alive, vigorous 2 = <u>vivid</u>, bright, brilliant, intense, clear, rich, glowing

vice 1 = <u>fault</u>, failing, weakness, limitation, defect, deficiency, flaw, shortcoming ≠ good point 2 = <u>wickedness</u>, evil, corruption, sin, depravity, immorality, iniquity, turpitude ≠ virtue

vice versa = <u>the other way round</u>, conversely, in reverse, contrariwise

vicious 1 = <u>savage</u>, brutal, violent, cruel, ferocious, barbarous ≠ gentle 2 = <u>malicious</u>, vindictive, spiteful, mean, cruel, venomous

victim 1 = <u>casualty</u>, sufferer, fatality ≠ survivor 2 = <u>scapegoat</u>, sacrifice, martyr

victor = <u>winner</u>, champion, conqueror, vanquisher, prizewinner ≠ loser

victorious = <u>winning</u>, successful, triumphant, first, champion, conquering, vanquishing, prizewinning ≠ losing

victory = <u>win</u>, success, triumph, conquest, walkover (*informal*) ≠ defeat

vie = <u>compete</u>, struggle, contend, strive

view NOUN 1 *sometimes plural* = <u>opinion</u>, belief, feeling, attitude, impression, conviction, point of view, sentiment 2 = <u>scene</u>, picture, sight, prospect, perspective, landscape, outlook, spectacle 3 = <u>vision</u>, sight, visibility, perspective, eyeshot
● VERB = <u>regard</u>, see, consider, perceive, treat, estimate, reckon, deem

viewer = <u>watcher</u>, observer, spectator, onlooker

vigorous 1 = <u>strenuous</u>, energetic, arduous, hard, taxing, active, rigorous 2 = <u>spirited</u>, lively, energetic, active, dynamic, animated, forceful, feisty (*informal*) ≠ lethargic 3 = <u>strong</u>, powerful, lively, lusty ≠ weak

vigorously 1 = <u>energetically</u>, hard, forcefully, strongly, strenuously, lustily 2 = <u>forcefully</u>, strongly, vehemently, strenuously

vigour *or (U.S.)* **vigor** = <u>energy</u>, vitality, power, spirit, strength, animation, verve, gusto ≠ weakness

vile 1 = <u>wicked</u>, evil, corrupt, perverted, degenerate, depraved, nefarious ≠ honourable 2 = <u>disgusting</u>, foul, revolting, offensive, nasty, sickening, horrid, repulsive, yucko (*Austral. slang*) ≠ pleasant

villain 1 = <u>evildoer</u>, criminal, rogue, scoundrel, wretch, reprobate, miscreant, blackguard 2 = <u>baddy</u> (*informal*), antihero ≠ hero

vindicate 1 = <u>clear</u>, acquit, exonerate, absolve, let off the hook, exculpate ≠ condemn 2 = <u>support</u>, defend, excuse, justify

vintage NOUN (always used of wines) = <u>harvest</u>
● ADJECTIVE 1 (always used of wines) = <u>high-quality</u>, best, prime, quality, choice, select, superior 2 = <u>classic</u>, old, veteran, historic, heritage, enduring, antique, timeless

violate 1 = <u>break</u>, infringe, disobey, transgress, ignore, defy, disregard, flout ≠ obey 2 = <u>invade</u>, infringe on, disturb, upset, shatter, disrupt, impinge on, encroach on 3 = <u>desecrate</u>, profane, defile, abuse, pollute, deface, dishonour, vandalize ≠ honour 4 = <u>rape</u>, molest, sexually assault, ravish, abuse, assault, interfere with, sexually abuse

violation 1 = <u>breach</u>, abuse, infringement, contravention, abuse, trespass, transgression, infraction 2 = <u>invasion</u>, intrusion, trespass, breach, disturbance, disruption, interruption, encroachment 3 = <u>desecration</u>, sacrilege, defilement, profanation, spoliation 4 = <u>rape</u>, sexual assault, molesting, ravishing (*old-fashioned*), abuse, sexual abuse, indecent assault, molestation

violence 1 = <u>brutality</u>, bloodshed, savagery, fighting, terrorism 2 = <u>force</u>, power, strength, might, ferocity, forcefulness, powerfulness 3 = <u>intensity</u>, force, cruelty, severity, fervour, vehemence

violent 1 = <u>brutal</u>, aggressive, savage, wild, fierce, bullying, cruel, vicious ≠ gentle 2 = <u>sharp</u> 3 = <u>passionate</u>, uncontrollable, unrestrained 4 = <u>fiery</u>, fierce, passionate

VIP = <u>celebrity</u>, big name, star, somebody, luminary, big hitter (*informal*), heavy hitter (*informal*)

virgin NOUN = maiden, girl (*archaic*)
- ADJECTIVE = pure, chaste, immaculate, virginal, vestal, uncorrupted, undefiled ≠ corrupted

virtual = practical, essential, in all but name

virtually = practically, almost, nearly, in effect, in essence, as good as, in all but name

virtue 1 = goodness, integrity, worth, morality, righteousness, probity, rectitude, incorruptibility ≠ vice 2 = merit, strength, asset, plus (*informal*), attribute, good point, strong point ≠ failing 3 = advantage, benefit, merit, credit, usefulness, efficacy

visible = perceptible, observable, clear, apparent, evident, manifest, in view, discernible ≠ invisible

vision 1 = image, idea, dream, plans, hopes, prospect, ideal, concept 2 = hallucination, illusion, apparition, revelation, delusion, mirage, chimera 3 = sight, seeing, eyesight, view, perception 4 = foresight, imagination, perception, insight, awareness, inspiration, innovation, creativity

visionary NOUN 1 = idealist, romantic, dreamer, daydreamer ≠ realist 2 = prophet, diviner, mystic, seer, soothsayer, sibyl, scryer, spaewife (*Scot.*)
- ADJECTIVE 1 = idealistic, romantic, unrealistic, utopian, speculative, impractical, unworkable, quixotic ≠ realistic 2 = prophetic, mystical, predictive, oracular, sibylline

visit VERB 1 = call on, drop in on (*informal*), stay at, stay with, stop by, spend time with, look someone up, go see (*U.S.*) 2 = stay in, stop by
- NOUN 1 = call, social call 2 = trip, stop, stay, break, tour, holiday, vacation (*informal*), stopover

visitor = guest, caller, company, manu(w)hiri (*N.Z.*)

vista = view, scene, prospect, landscape, panorama, perspective

visual 1 = optical, optic, ocular 2 = observable, visible, perceptible, discernible ≠ imperceptible

vital 1 = essential, important, necessary, key, basic, significant, critical, crucial ≠ unnecessary 2 = lively, vigorous,

energetic, spirited, dynamic, animated, vibrant, vivacious ≠ lethargic

vitality = energy, vivacity, life, strength, animation, vigour, exuberance, liveliness ≠ lethargy

vivid 1 = clear, detailed, realistic, telling, moving, affecting, arresting, powerful ≠ vague 2 = bright, brilliant, intense, clear, rich, glowing, colourful ≠ dull

vocabulary 1 = language, words, lexicon 2 = wordbook, dictionary, glossary, lexicon

vocal 1 = outspoken, frank, forthright, strident, vociferous, articulate, expressive, eloquent ≠ quiet 2 = spoken, voiced, uttered, oral, said

vocation = profession, calling, job, trade, career, mission, pursuit

vogue = fashion, trend, craze, style, mode, passing fancy, dernier cri (*French*)

voice NOUN 1 = tone, sound, articulation 2 = utterance 3 = opinion, will, feeling, wish, desire 4 = say, view, vote, comment, input
- VERB = express, declare, air, raise, reveal, mention, mouth, pronounce

RELATED WORD
adjective: vocal

void NOUN 1 = gap, space, lack, hole, emptiness 2 = emptiness, space, vacuum, oblivion, blankness, nullity, vacuity
- ADJECTIVE = invalid, null and void, inoperative, useless, ineffective, worthless
- VERB = invalidate, nullify, cancel, withdraw, reverse, undo, repeal, quash

volatile 1 = changeable, shifting, variable, unsettled, unstable, explosive, unreliable, unsteady ≠ stable 2 = temperamental, erratic, mercurial, up and down (*informal*), fickle, over-emotional ≠ calm

volley = barrage, blast, burst, shower, hail, bombardment, salvo, fusillade

volume 1 = amount, quantity, level, body, total, measure, degree, mass 2 = capacity, size, mass, extent, proportions, dimensions, bulk, measurements 3 = book, work, title, opus, publication, manual, tome, treatise 4 = loudness, sound, amplification

voluntarily = willingly, freely, by choice, off your own bat, of your own accord, of your own volition

voluntary 1 = intentional, deliberate, planned, calculated, wilful ≠ unintentional 2 = optional, discretionary, up to the individual, open, unforced, at your discretion, open to choice ≠ obligatory **3** = unpaid, free, willing, pro bono (*Law*)

volunteer = offer, step forward ≠ refuse

vomit 1 = be sick, throw up (*informal*), spew, chuck (*Austral. & N.Z. informal*), heave (*slang*), retch **2** *often with* **up** = bring up, throw up, regurgitate, emit (*informal*), disgorge, spew out *or* up

vote NOUN = poll, election, ballot, referendum, popular vote, plebiscite, straw poll, show of hands

● VERB = cast your vote

voucher = ticket, token, coupon, pass, slip, chit, chitty (*Brit. informal*), docket

vow VERB = promise, pledge, swear, commit, engage, affirm, avow, bind yourself

● NOUN = promise, commitment, pledge, oath, profession, avowal

voyage NOUN = journey, trip, passage, expedition, crossing, sail, cruise, excursion

● VERB = travel, journey, tour, cruise, steam, take a trip, go on an expedition

vulgar 1 = tasteless, common ≠ tasteful **2** = crude, rude, coarse, indecent, tasteless, risqué, ribald **3** = uncouth, unrefined, impolite, ill-bred ≠ refined

vulnerable 1 = susceptible, helpless, unprotected, defenceless, exposed, weak, sensitive, tender ≠ immune **2** = exposed, open, unprotected, defenceless, accessible, wide open, assailable ≠ well-protected

W

waddle = shuffle, totter, toddle, sway, wobble

wade 1 = paddle, splash, splash about, slop **2** = walk through, cross, ford, travel across

wag VERB **1** = wave, shake, waggle, stir, quiver, vibrate, wiggle **2** = waggle, wave, shake, flourish, brandish, wobble, wiggle

3 = shake, bob, nod

● NOUN **1** = wave, shake, quiver, vibration, wiggle, waggle **2** = nod, bob, shake

wage NOUN *often plural* = payment, pay, remuneration, fee, reward, income, allowance, recompense

● VERB = engage in, conduct, pursue, carry on, undertake, practise, prosecute, proceed with

wail VERB = cry, weep, grieve, lament, howl, bawl, yowl

● NOUN = cry, moan, howl, lament, yowl

wait VERB **1** = stay, remain, stop, pause, rest, linger, loiter, tarry **2** = stand by, hold back, hang fire **3** = be postponed, be suspended, be delayed, be put off, be put back, be deferred, be put on hold (*informal*), be shelved

● NOUN = delay, gap, pause, interval, stay, rest, halt, hold-up

waiter *or* **waitress** = attendant, server, flunkey, steward *or* stewardess, servant

waive 1 = give up, relinquish, renounce, forsake, drop, abandon, set aside, dispense with ≠ claim **2** = disregard, ignore, discount, overlook, set aside, pass over, dispense with, brush aside

wake¹ VERB **1** = awake, stir, awaken, come to, arise, get up, rouse, get out of bed ≠ fall asleep **2** = awaken, arouse, rouse, waken **3** = evoke, recall, renew, stimulate, revive, induce, arouse, call up

● NOUN = vigil, watch, funeral, deathwatch, tangi (*N.Z.*)

wake² NOUN = slipstream, wash, trail, backwash, train, track, waves, path

● PHRASES **in the wake of** = in the aftermath of, following, because of, as a result of, on account of, as a consequence of

walk VERB **1** = stride, stroll, go, move, step, march, pace, hike **2** = travel on foot **3** = escort, take, see, show, partner, guide, conduct, accompany

● NOUN **1** = stroll, hike, ramble, march, trek, trudge, promenade, saunter **2** = gait, step, bearing, carriage, tread **3** = path, footpath, track, way, road, lane, trail, avenue, berm (*N.Z.*)

● PHRASES **walk of life** = area, calling, business, line, trade, class, field, career

walker = hiker, rambler, wayfarer, pedestrian

wall 1 = partition, screen, barrier,

enclosure 2 = <u>barrier</u>, obstacle, barricade, obstruction, check, bar, fence, impediment

wallet = <u>purse</u>, pocketbook, pouch, case, holder, money-bag

wander VERB 1 = <u>roam</u>, walk, drift, stroll, range, stray, ramble, prowl

● NOUN = <u>excursion</u>, walk, stroll, cruise, ramble, meander, promenade, mosey (*informal*)

wanderer = <u>traveller</u>, rover, nomad, drifter, gypsy, explorer, rambler, voyager

wane 1 = <u>decline</u>, weaken, diminish, fail, fade, decrease, dwindle, lessen ≠ grow 2 = <u>diminish</u>, decrease, dwindle ≠ wax

want VERB 1 = <u>wish for</u>, desire, long for, crave, covet, hope for, yearn for, thirst for ≠ have 2 = <u>need</u>, demand, require, call for 3 = <u>should</u>, need, must, ought 4 = <u>desire</u>, long for, crave, wish for, yearn for, thirst for, hanker after, burn for 5 = <u>lack</u>, need, require, miss

● NOUN 1 = <u>lack</u>, need, absence, shortage, deficiency, famine, scarcity, dearth ≠ abundance 2 = <u>poverty</u>, hardship, privation, penury, destitution, neediness, pennilessness ≠ wealth 3 = <u>wish</u>, will, need, desire, requirement, longing, appetite, craving

wanting 1 = <u>deficient</u>, poor, inadequate, insufficient, faulty, defective, imperfect, unsound, badger *or* bodgie (*Austral. slang*) ≠ adequate 2 = <u>lacking</u>, missing, absent, incomplete, short, shy ≠ complete

war NOUN 1 = <u>conflict</u>, drive, attack, fighting, fight, operation, battle, movement ≠ peace 2 = <u>campaign</u>, drive, attack, operation, movement, push, mission, offensive

● VERB = <u>fight</u>, battle, clash, wage war, campaign, combat, do battle, take up arms ≠ make peace

ward NOUN 1 = <u>room</u>, department, unit, quarter, division, section, apartment, cubicle 2 = <u>district</u>, constituency, area, division, zone, parish, precinct 3 = <u>dependant</u>, charge, pupil, minor, protégé

● PHRASES **ward someone off** = <u>drive off</u>, resist, fight off, hold off, repel, fend off ◆ **ward something off** 1 = <u>avert</u>, fend off, stave off, avoid, frustrate, deflect, repel 2 = <u>parry</u>, avert, deflect, avoid, repel, turn aside

warden 1 = <u>steward</u>, guardian, administrator, superintendent, caretaker, curator, custodian 2 = <u>jailer</u>, prison officer, guard, screw (*slang*) 3 = <u>governor</u>, head, leader, director, manager, chief, executive, commander, baas (*S. African*) 4 = <u>ranger</u>, keeper, guardian, protector, custodian, official

wardrobe 1 = <u>clothes cupboard</u>, cupboard, closet (*U.S.*), cabinet 2 = <u>clothes</u>, apparel, attire

warehouse = <u>store</u>, depot, storehouse, repository, depository, stockroom

wares = <u>goods</u>, produce, stock, products, stuff, commodities, merchandise

warfare = <u>war</u>, fighting, battle, conflict, combat, hostilities, enmity ≠ peace

warm ADJECTIVE 1 = <u>balmy</u>, mild, temperate, pleasant, fine, bright, sunny, agreeable ≠ cool 2 = <u>cosy</u>, snug, toasty (*informal*), comfortable, homely, comfy (*informal*) 3 = <u>moderately hot</u>, heated ≠ cool 4 = <u>thermal</u>, winter, thick, chunky, woolly ≠ cool 5 = <u>mellow</u>, relaxing, pleasant, agreeable, restful 6 = <u>affable</u>, kindly, friendly, affectionate, loving, tender, amicable, cordial ≠ unfriendly 7 = <u>near</u>, close, hot, near to the truth

● VERB = <u>warm up</u>, heat, thaw (out), heat up ≠ cool down

● PHRASES **warm something** *or* **someone up** = <u>heat</u>, thaw, heat up

warmth 1 = <u>heat</u>, snugness, warmness, comfort, homeliness, hotness ≠ coolness 2 = <u>affection</u>, feeling, love, goodwill, kindness, tenderness, cordiality, kindliness ≠ hostility

warn 1 = <u>notify</u>, tell, remind, inform, alert, tip off, give notice, make someone aware 2 = <u>advise</u>, urge, recommend, counsel, caution, commend, exhort, admonish

warning 1 = <u>caution</u>, information, advice, injunction, notification 2 = <u>notice</u>, notification, sign, alarm, announcement, alert, tip-off (*informal*) 3 = <u>omen</u>, sign, forecast, indication, prediction, prophecy, foreboding, portent, rahui (*N.Z.*) 4 = <u>reprimand</u>, admonition

warp VERB 1 = <u>distort</u>, bend, twist, buckle, deform, disfigure, contort, malform 2 = <u>become distorted</u>, bend, twist, contort, become deformed, become misshapen 3 = <u>pervert</u>, twist, corrupt, degrade, deprave, debase, debauch, lead astray

● NOUN = <u>twist</u>, bend, defect, flaw,

distortion, imperfection, kink, contortion

warrant VERB 1 = <u>call for</u>, demand, require, merit, rate, earn, deserve, permit 2 = <u>guarantee</u>, declare, pledge, promise, ensure, affirm, certify, attest
● NOUN 1 = <u>authorization</u>, permit, licence, permission, authority, sanction 2 = <u>justification</u>, reason, grounds, basis, licence, rationale, vindication, authority

warranty = <u>guarantee</u>, promise, contract, bond, pledge, certificate, assurance, covenant

warrior = <u>soldier</u>, combatant, fighter, gladiator, trooper, man-at-arms

wary 1 = <u>suspicious</u>, sceptical, guarded, distrustful, chary 2 = <u>watchful</u>, careful, alert, cautious, vigilant, circumspect, heedful ≠ careless

wash VERB 1 = <u>clean</u>, scrub, sponge, rinse, scour, cleanse 2 = <u>launder</u>, clean, rinse, dry-clean 3 = <u>rinse</u>, clean, scrub, lather 4 = <u>bathe</u>, bath, clean yourself, soak, douse, scrub yourself down 5 = <u>move</u>, overcome, touch, upset, stir, disturb, perturb, surge through 6 (*Informal*) (always used in negative constructions) = <u>be plausible</u>, stand up, hold up, pass muster, hold water, stick, carry weight, be convincing
● NOUN 1 = <u>laundering</u>, cleaning, clean, cleansing 2 = <u>bathe</u>, dip, soak, scrub, rinse 3 = <u>backwash</u>, slipstream, path, trail, train, track, waves, aftermath 4 = <u>splash</u>, surge, swell, rise and fall, undulation 5 = <u>coat</u>, film, covering, layer, coating, overlay
● PHRASES **wash something** or **someone away** = <u>sweep away</u>, carry off, bear away ◆ **wash something away** = <u>erode</u>, wear something away

waste VERB 1 = <u>squander</u>, throw away, blow (*slang*), lavish, misuse, dissipate, fritter away ≠ save 2 = <u>wear out</u>, wither
● NOUN 1 = <u>squandering</u>, misuse, extravagance, frittering away, dissipation, wastefulness, prodigality ≠ saving 2 = <u>rubbish</u>, refuse, debris, scrap, litter, garbage, trash, leftovers
● PLURAL NOUN = <u>desert</u>, wilderness, wasteland
● ADJECTIVE 1 = <u>unwanted</u>, useless, worthless, unused, leftover, superfluous, unusable, supernumerary ≠ necessary 2 = <u>uncultivated</u>, wild, bare, barren, empty, desolate, unproductive, uninhabited ≠ cultivated
● PHRASES **waste away** = <u>decline</u>, dwindle, wither, fade, crumble, decay, wane, wear out

watch VERB 1 = <u>look at</u>, observe, regard, eye, see, view, contemplate, eyeball (*slang*) 2 = <u>spy on</u>, follow, track, monitor, keep an eye on, stake out, keep tabs on (*informal*), keep watch on 3 = <u>guard</u>, keep, mind, protect, tend, look after, shelter, take care of
● NOUN 1 = <u>wristwatch</u>, timepiece, chronometer 2 = <u>guard</u>, surveillance, observation, vigil, lookout

watchdog 1 = <u>guardian</u>, monitor, protector, custodian, scrutineer 2 = <u>guard dog</u>

water NOUN = <u>liquid</u>, H_2O, wai (*N.Z.*)
● PLURAL NOUN = <u>sea</u>, main, waves, ocean, depths, briny
● VERB 1 = <u>sprinkle</u>, spray, soak, irrigate, hose, dampen, drench, douse 2 = <u>get wet</u>, cry, weep, become wet, exude water
● PHRASES **water something down** = <u>dilute</u>, weaken, water, doctor, thin

▬ RELATED WORD
adjective: aquatic

waterfall = <u>cascade</u>, fall, cataract

wave VERB 1 = <u>signal</u>, sign, gesture, gesticulate 2 = <u>guide</u>, point, direct, indicate, signal, motion, gesture, nod 3 = <u>brandish</u>, swing, flourish, wag, shake 4 = <u>flutter</u>, flap, stir, shake, swing, wag, oscillate
● NOUN 1 = <u>gesture</u>, sign, signal, indication, gesticulation 2 = <u>ripple</u>, breaker, swell, ridge, roller, billow 3 = <u>outbreak</u>, rash, upsurge, flood, surge, ground swell 4 = <u>stream</u>, flood, surge, spate, current, flow, rush, tide

waver 1 = <u>hesitate</u>, dither (*chiefly Brit.*), vacillate, falter, fluctuate, seesaw, hum and haw ≠ be decisive 2 = <u>flicker</u>, shake, tremble, wobble, quiver, totter

wax 1 = <u>increase</u>, grow, develop, expand, swell, enlarge, magnify ≠ wane 2 = <u>become fuller</u>, enlarge

way 1 = <u>method</u>, means, system, process, technique, manner, procedure, mode 2 = <u>manner</u>, style, fashion, mode 3 *often plural* = <u>custom</u>, manner, habit, style, practice, nature, personality, wont, tikanga (*N.Z.*) 4 = <u>route</u>, direction, course, road, path 5 = <u>access</u>, road, track, channel, route, path, trail, pathway **6** = <u>journey</u>, approach, passage **7** = <u>distance</u>, length, stretch

wayward = <u>erratic</u>, unruly, unmanageable, unpredictable, capricious, ungovernable, inconstant ≠ obedient

weak 1 = <u>feeble</u>, frail, debilitated, fragile, sickly, puny, unsteady, infirm ≠ strong **2** = <u>slight</u>, faint, feeble, pathetic, hollow **3** = <u>fragile</u>, brittle, flimsy, fine, delicate, frail, dainty, breakable **4** = <u>unsafe</u>, exposed, vulnerable, helpless, unprotected, defenceless, unguarded ≠ secure **5** = <u>unconvincing</u>, unsatisfactory, lame, flimsy, pathetic ≠ convincing **6** = <u>tasteless</u>, thin, diluted, watery, runny, insipid ≠ strong

weaken 1 = <u>reduce</u>, undermine, moderate, diminish, lessen, sap ≠ boost **2** = <u>wane</u>, diminish, dwindle, lower, flag, fade, lessen ≠ grow **3** = <u>sap the strength of</u> ≠ strengthen

weakness 1 = <u>frailty</u>, fatigue, exhaustion, fragility, infirmity, feebleness, decrepitude ≠ strength **2** = <u>liking</u>, appetite, penchant, soft spot, passion, inclination, fondness, partiality ≠ aversion **3** = <u>powerlessness</u>, vulnerability, meekness, spinelessness, timorousness, cravenness, cowardliness **4** = <u>inadequacy</u>, deficiency, transparency, lameness, hollowness, implausibility, flimsiness, unsoundness **5** = <u>failing</u>, fault, defect, deficiency, flaw, shortcoming, blemish, imperfection ≠ strong point

wealth 1 = <u>riches</u>, fortune, prosperity, affluence, money, opulence ≠ poverty **2** = <u>property</u>, capital, fortune **3** = <u>abundance</u>, plenty, richness, profusion, fullness, cornucopia, copiousness ≠ lack

wealthy = <u>rich</u>, prosperous, affluent, well-off, flush (*informal*), opulent, well-heeled (*informal*), well-to-do ≠ poor

wear VERB **1** = <u>be dressed in</u>, have on, sport (*informal*), put on **2** = <u>show</u>, present, bear, display, assume, put on, exhibit **3** = <u>deteriorate</u>, fray, wear thin
● NOUN **1** = <u>clothes</u>, things, dress, gear (*informal*), attire, costume, garments, apparel **2** = <u>damage</u>, wear and tear, erosion, deterioration, attrition, corrosion, abrasion ≠ repair
● PHRASES **wear off** = <u>subside</u>, disappear, fade, diminish, decrease, dwindle, wane, peter out

wearing = <u>tiresome</u>, trying, fatiguing,

oppressive, exasperating, irksome, wearisome ≠ refreshing

weary ADJECTIVE **1** = <u>tired</u>, exhausted, drained, worn out, done in (*informal*), flagging, fatigued, sleepy, clapped out (*Austral. & N.Z. informal*) ≠ energetic **2** = <u>tiring</u>, arduous, tiresome, laborious, wearisome ≠ refreshing
● VERB = <u>grow tired</u>, tire, become bored ≠ invigorate

weather NOUN = <u>climate</u>, conditions, temperature, forecast, outlook, meteorological conditions, elements
● VERB = <u>withstand</u>, stand, survive, overcome, resist, brave, endure, come through ≠ surrender to

weave 1 = <u>knit</u>, intertwine, plait, braid, entwine, interlace **2** = <u>zigzag</u>, wind, crisscross **3** = <u>create</u>, tell, recount, narrate, build, relate, make up, spin

web 1 = <u>cobweb</u>, spider's web **2** = <u>mesh</u>, lattice **3** = <u>tangle</u>, network

wed 1 = <u>get married to</u>, be united to ≠ divorce **2** = <u>get married</u>, marry, be united, tie the knot (*informal*), take the plunge (*informal*) ≠ divorce **3** = <u>unite</u>, combine, join, link, ally, blend, merge, interweave ≠ divide

wedding = <u>marriage</u>, nuptials, wedding ceremony, marriage service, wedding service

wedge VERB = <u>squeeze</u>, force, lodge, jam, crowd, stuff, pack, thrust
● NOUN = <u>block</u>, lump, chunk

weep = <u>cry</u>, shed tears, sob, whimper, mourn, lament, blubber, snivel ≠ rejoice

weigh 1 = <u>have a weight of</u>, tip the scales at (*informal*) **2** *often with **up*** = <u>consider</u>, examine, contemplate, evaluate, ponder, think over, reflect upon, meditate upon **3** = <u>compare</u>, balance, contrast, juxtapose, place side by side **4** = <u>matter</u>, carry weight, count

weight NOUN **1** = <u>heaviness</u>, mass, poundage, load, tonnage **2** = <u>importance</u>, force, power, value, authority, influence, impact, import, mana (*N.Z.*)
● VERB **1** *often with **down*** = <u>load</u> **2** = <u>bias</u>, load, slant, unbalance

weird 1 = <u>strange</u>, odd, unusual, bizarre, mysterious, queer, eerie, unnatural ≠ normal **2** = <u>bizarre</u>, odd, strange, unusual, queer, unnatural, creepy (*informal*), freakish ≠ ordinary

welcome VERB 1 = greet, meet, receive, embrace, hail, karanga (*N.Z.*), mihi (*N.Z.*) ≠ reject 2 = accept gladly, appreciate, embrace, approve of, be pleased by, give the thumbs up to (*informal*), be glad about, express pleasure *or* satisfaction at
● NOUN = greeting, welcoming, reception, acceptance, hail, hospitality, salutation ≠ rejection
● ADJECTIVE 1 = pleasing, appreciated, acceptable, pleasant, desirable, refreshing, delightful, gratifying ≠ unpleasant 2 = wanted ≠ unwanted 3 = free

weld 1 = join, link, bond, bind, connect, fuse, solder 2 = unite, combine, blend, unify, fuse

welfare 1 = wellbeing, good, interest, health, security, benefit, safety, protection 2 = state benefit, support, benefits, pensions, dole (*slang*), social security, unemployment benefit, state benefits

well¹ ADVERB 1 = skilfully, expertly, adeptly, professionally, correctly, properly, efficiently, adequately ≠ badly 2 = satisfactorily, nicely, smoothly, successfully, pleasantly, splendidly, agreeably ≠ badly 3 = thoroughly, completely, fully, carefully, effectively, efficiently, rigorously 4 = intimately, deeply, fully, profoundly ≠ slightly 5 = favourably, highly, kindly, warmly, enthusiastically, approvingly, admiringly, with admiration ≠ unfavourably 6 = considerably, easily, very much, significantly, substantially, markedly 7 = fully, highly, greatly, amply, very much, thoroughly, considerably, substantially 8 = possibly, probably, certainly, reasonably, conceivably, justifiably 9 = decently, right, kindly, fittingly, fairly, properly, politely, suitably ≠ unfairly 10 = prosperously, comfortably, splendidly, in comfort, in (the lap of) luxury, without hardship
● ADJECTIVE 1 = healthy, sound, fit, blooming, in fine fettle, in good condition ≠ ill 2 = satisfactory, right, fine, pleasing, proper, thriving ≠ unsatisfactory 3 = advisable, proper, agreeable ≠ inadvisable

well² NOUN = hole, bore, pit, shaft
● VERB 1 = flow, spring, pour, jet, surge, gush, spurt, spout 2 = rise, increase, grow, mount, surge, intensify

wet ADJECTIVE 1 = damp, soaking, saturated, moist, watery, soggy, sodden, waterlogged ≠ dry 2 = rainy, damp, drizzly, showery, raining, pouring, drizzling, teeming ≠ sunny 3 (*informal*) = feeble, soft, weak, ineffectual, weedy (*informal*), spineless, effete, timorous
● VERB = moisten, spray, dampen, water, soak, saturate, douse, irrigate ≠ dry
● NOUN 1 = rain, drizzle ≠ fine weather 2 = moisture, water, liquid, damp, humidity, condensation, dampness, wetness ≠ dryness

whack (*Informal*) VERB = strike, hit, belt (*informal*), bang, smack, thrash, thump, swipe
● NOUN 1 = blow, hit, stroke, belt (*informal*), bang, smack, thump, swipe 2 (*Informal*) = share, part, cut (*informal*), bit, portion, quota 3 (*Informal*) = attempt, go (*informal*), try, turn, shot (*informal*), crack (*informal*), stab (*informal*), bash (*informal*)

wharf = dock, pier, berth, quay, jetty, landing stage

wheel NOUN = disc, ring, hoop
● VERB 1 = push, trundle, roll 2 = turn, swing, spin, revolve, rotate, whirl, swivel 3 = circle, go round, twirl, gyrate

whereabouts = position, situation, site, location

whiff = smell, hint, scent, sniff, aroma, odour

whim = impulse, caprice, fancy, urge, notion

whine VERB 1 = cry, sob, wail, whimper, sniffle, snivel, moan 2 = complain, grumble, gripe (*informal*), whinge (*informal*), moan, grouse, grizzle (*informal*, *chiefly Brit.*), grouch (*informal*)
● NOUN 1 = cry, moan, sob, wail, whimper 2 = drone, note, hum 3 = complaint, moan, grumble, grouse, gripe (*informal*), whinge (*informal*), grouch (*informal*)

whip NOUN = lash, cane, birch, crop, scourge, cat-o'-nine-tails
● VERB 1 = lash, cane, flog, beat, strap, thrash, birch, scourge 2 (*Informal*) = dash, shoot, fly, tear, rush, dive, dart, whisk 3 = whisk, beat, mix vigorously, stir vigorously 4 = incite, drive, stir, spur, work up, get going, agitate, inflame

whirl VERB 1 = spin, turn, twist, rotate, twirl 2 = rotate, roll, twist, revolve, swirl, twirl, pirouette 3 = feel dizzy, swim, spin, reel, go round

● NOUN 1 = <u>revolution</u>, turn, roll, spin, twist, swirl, rotation, twirl 2 = <u>bustle</u>, round, series, succession, flurry, merry-go-round 3 = <u>confusion</u>, daze, dither (*chiefly Brit.*), giddiness 4 = <u>tumult</u>, spin

whisk VERB 1 = <u>flick</u>, whip, sweep, brush 2 = <u>beat</u>, mix vigorously, stir vigorously, whip, fluff up

● NOUN 1 = <u>flick</u>, sweep, brush, whip 2 = <u>beater</u>, mixer, blender

whisper VERB 1 = <u>murmur</u>, breathe ≠ shout 2 = <u>rustle</u>, sigh, hiss, swish

● NOUN 1 = <u>murmur</u>, mutter, mumble, undertone 2 (*Informal*) = <u>rumour</u>, report, gossip, innuendo, insinuation 3 = <u>rustle</u>, sigh, hiss, swish

white = <u>pale</u>, wan, pasty, pallid, ashen

white-collar = <u>clerical</u>, professional, salaried, nonmanual

whittle VERB = <u>carve</u>, cut, hew, shape, trim, shave, pare

● PHRASES **whittle something** or **someone down** = <u>reduce</u>, cut down, cut, decrease, prune, scale down ◆ **whittle something away** = <u>undermine</u>, reduce, consume, erode, eat away, wear away

whole NOUN = <u>unit</u>, ensemble, entirety, totality ≠ part

● ADJECTIVE 1 = <u>complete</u>, full, total, entire, uncut, undivided, unabridged ≠ partial 2 = <u>undamaged</u>, intact, unscathed, unbroken, untouched, unharmed, in one piece ≠ damaged

● PHRASES **on the whole** 1 = <u>all in all</u>, altogether, all things considered, by and large 2 = <u>generally</u>, in general, as a rule, chiefly, mainly, mostly, principally, on average

wholesale ADJECTIVE = <u>extensive</u>, total, mass, sweeping, broad, comprehensive, wide-ranging, blanket ≠ limited

● ADVERB = <u>extensively</u>, comprehensively, across the board, indiscriminately

wholly = <u>completely</u>, totally, perfectly, fully, entirely, altogether, thoroughly, utterly ≠ partly

whore = <u>prostitute</u>, tart (*informal*), streetwalker, call girl

wide ADJECTIVE 1 = <u>spacious</u>, broad, extensive, roomy, commodious ≠ confined 2 = <u>baggy</u>, full, loose, ample, billowing, roomy, voluminous, capacious 3 = <u>expanded</u>, dilated, distended ≠ shut

4 = <u>broad</u>, extensive, wide-ranging, large, sweeping, vast, immense, expansive ≠ restricted 5 = <u>extensive</u>, general, far-reaching, overarching 6 = <u>large</u>, broad, vast, immense 7 = <u>distant</u>, remote, off course, off target

● ADVERB 1 = <u>fully</u>, completely ≠ partly 2 = <u>off target</u>, astray, off course, off the mark

widen 1 = <u>broaden</u>, expand, enlarge, dilate, spread, extend, stretch ≠ narrow 2 = <u>get wider</u>, spread, extend, expand, broaden ≠ narrow

widespread = <u>common</u>, general, popular, broad, extensive, universal, far-reaching, pervasive ≠ limited

width = <u>breadth</u>, extent, span, scope, diameter, compass, thickness, girth

wield 1 = <u>brandish</u>, flourish, manipulate, swing, use, manage, handle, employ 2 = <u>exert</u>, maintain, exercise, have, possess

wife = <u>spouse</u>, partner, mate, bride, better half (*humorous*), vrou (*S. African*), wahine (*N.Z.*)

wild ADJECTIVE 1 = <u>untamed</u>, fierce, savage, ferocious, unbroken, feral, undomesticated, free, warrigal (*Austral. literary*) ≠ tame 2 = <u>uncultivated</u>, natural ≠ cultivated 3 = <u>stormy</u>, violent, rough, raging, choppy, tempestuous, blustery 4 = <u>excited</u>, crazy (*informal*), enthusiastic, raving, hysterical ≠ unenthusiastic 5 = <u>uncontrolled</u>, disorderly, turbulent, wayward, unruly, rowdy, unfettered, riotous ≠ calm 6 = <u>mad</u> (*informal*), furious, fuming, infuriated, incensed, enraged, very angry, irate, tooshie (*Austral. slang*), off the air (*Austral. slang*) 7 = <u>uncivilized</u>, fierce, savage, primitive, ferocious, barbaric, brutish, barbarous ≠ civilized

● PLURAL NOUN = <u>wilderness</u>, desert, wasteland, middle of nowhere (*informal*), backwoods, back of beyond (*informal*)

wilderness = <u>wilds</u>, desert, wasteland, uncultivated region

will NOUN 1 = <u>determination</u>, drive, purpose, commitment, resolution, resolve, spine, backbone 2 = <u>wish</u>, mind, desire, intention, fancy, preference, inclination 3 = <u>choice</u>, prerogative, volition 4 = <u>decree</u>, wish, desire, command, dictate, ordinance 5 = <u>testament</u>, bequest(s), last wishes, last will and testament

● VERB 1 = <u>wish</u>, want, prefer, desire, see

fit 2 = <u>bequeath</u>, give, leave, transfer, gift, hand on, pass on, confer

willing 1 = <u>inclined</u>, prepared, consenting, agreeable, compliant, amenable ≠ unwilling 2 = <u>ready</u>, game (*informal*) ≠ reluctant

willingly = <u>readily</u>, freely, gladly, happily, eagerly, voluntarily, cheerfully, by choice ≠ unwillingly

willingness = <u>inclination</u>, will, agreement, wish, consent, volition ≠ reluctance

wilt 1 = <u>droop</u>, wither, sag, shrivel 2 = <u>weaken</u>, languish, droop 3 = <u>wane</u>, flag, fade

win VERB 1 = <u>be victorious in</u>, succeed in, prevail in, come first in, be the victor in ≠ lose 2 = <u>be victorious</u>, succeed, triumph, overcome, prevail, conquer, come first, sweep the board ≠ lose 3 = <u>gain</u>, get, land, achieve, earn, secure, obtain, acquire ≠ forfeit

● NOUN = <u>victory</u>, success, triumph, conquest ≠ defeat

● PHRASES **win someone over** or **round** = <u>convince</u>, influence, persuade, convert, sway, prevail upon, bring or talk round

wince VERB = <u>flinch</u>, start, shrink, cringe, quail, recoil, cower, draw back

● NOUN = <u>flinch</u>, start, cringe

wind¹ NOUN 1 = <u>air</u>, blast, hurricane, breeze, draught, gust, zephyr 2 = <u>flatulence</u>, gas 3 = <u>breath</u>, puff, respiration 4 = <u>nonsense</u>, talk, boasting, hot air, babble, bluster, humbug, twaddle (*informal*), bizzo (*Austral. slang*), bull's wool (*Austral. & N.Z. slang*)

● PHRASES **get wind of something** = <u>hear about</u>, learn of, find out about, become aware of, be told about, be informed of, be made aware of, hear tell of

wind² VERB 1 = <u>meander</u>, turn, bend, twist, curve, snake, ramble, twist and turn 2 = <u>wrap</u>, twist, reel, curl, loop, coil 3 = <u>coil</u>, curl, spiral, encircle

● PHRASES **wind someone up** (*Informal*) 1 = <u>irritate</u>, excite, anger, annoy, exasperate, nettle, work someone up, pique 2 = <u>tease</u>, kid (*informal*), have someone on (*informal*), annoy, rag (*informal*), rib (*informal*), josh (*informal*), vex ◆ **wind something up** 1 = <u>end</u>, finish, settle, conclude, tie up, wrap up, finalize 2 = <u>close down</u>, close, dissolve,

terminate, put something into liquidation

◆ **wind up** = <u>end up</u>, be left, finish up, fetch up (*informal*), land up

windfall = <u>godsend</u>, find, jackpot, bonanza, manna from heaven ≠ misfortune

windy = <u>breezy</u>, wild, stormy, windswept, blustery, gusty, squally, blowy ≠ calm

wing NOUN = <u>faction</u>, group, arm, section, branch

● VERB 1 = <u>fly</u>, soar, glide, take wing 2 = <u>wound</u>, hit, clip

wink VERB 1 = <u>blink</u>, bat, flutter 2 = <u>twinkle</u>, flash, shine, sparkle, gleam, shimmer, glimmer

● NOUN = <u>blink</u>, flutter

winner = <u>victor</u>, champion, master, champ (*informal*), conqueror, prizewinner ≠ loser

winning ADJECTIVE 1 = <u>victorious</u>, first, top, successful, unbeaten, conquering, triumphant, undefeated 2 = <u>charming</u>, pleasing, attractive, engaging, cute, disarming, enchanting, endearing ≠ unpleasant

● PLURAL NOUN = <u>spoils</u>, profits, gains, prize, proceeds, takings

wipe VERB 1 = <u>clean</u>, polish, brush, rub, sponge, mop, swab 2 = <u>erase</u>, remove

● NOUN = <u>rub</u>, brush

● PHRASES **wipe something** or **someone out** = <u>destroy</u>, massacre, erase, eradicate, obliterate, annihilate, exterminate, expunge

wisdom = <u>understanding</u>, learning, knowledge, intelligence, judgment, insight, enlightenment, erudition ≠ foolishness

wise 1 = <u>sage</u>, clever, intelligent, sensible, enlightened, discerning, perceptive, erudite ≠ foolish 2 = <u>sensible</u>, clever, intelligent, prudent, judicious ≠ unwise

wish NOUN = <u>desire</u>, want, hope, urge, intention, fancy (*informal*), ambition, yen (*informal*) ≠ aversion

● VERB = <u>want</u>, feel, choose, please, desire, think fit

● PHRASES **wish for something** = <u>desire</u>, want, hope for, long for, crave, aspire to, yearn for, hanker for

wit 1 = <u>humour</u>, quips, banter, puns, repartee, wordplay, witticisms, badinage ≠ seriousness 2 = <u>humorist</u>, card (*informal*), comedian, wag, joker, dag (*N.Z. informal*) 3 *often plural* = <u>cleverness</u>, sense, brains, wisdom, common sense, intellect, ingenuity, acumen ≠ stupidity

witch = <u>enchantress</u>, magician, hag, crone, sorceress, Wiccan

witchcraft = <u>magic</u>, voodoo, wizardry, black magic, enchantment, occultism, sorcery, Wicca, makutu (*N.Z.*)

withdraw 1 = <u>remove</u>, take off, pull out, extract, take away, pull back, draw out, draw back **2** = <u>take out</u>, extract, draw out

withdrawal = <u>removal</u>, ending, stopping, taking away, abolition, elimination, cancellation, termination

withdrawn = <u>uncommunicative</u>, reserved, retiring, distant, shy, taciturn, introverted, unforthcoming ≠ outgoing

wither 1 = <u>wilt</u>, decline, decay, disintegrate, perish, shrivel ≠ flourish **2** = <u>waste</u>, decline, shrivel **3** = <u>fade</u>, decline, perish ≠ increase

withering = <u>scornful</u>, devastating, humiliating, snubbing, hurtful, mortifying

withhold 1 = <u>keep secret</u>, refuse, hide, reserve, retain, conceal, suppress, hold back ≠ reveal **2** = <u>hold back</u>, suppress, keep back ≠ release

withstand = <u>resist</u>, suffer, bear, oppose, cope with, endure, tolerate, stand up to ≠ give in to

witness NOUN **1** = <u>observer</u>, viewer, spectator, looker-on, watcher, onlooker, eyewitness, bystander **2** = <u>testifier</u>
● VERB **1** = <u>see</u>, view, watch, note, notice, observe, perceive **2** = <u>countersign</u>, sign, endorse, validate

witty = <u>humorous</u>, funny, clever, amusing, sparkling, whimsical, droll, piquant ≠ dull

wizard = <u>magician</u>, witch, shaman, sorcerer, occultist, magus, conjuror, warlock, tohunga (*N.Z.*)

wobble VERB **1** = <u>shake</u>, rock, sway, tremble, teeter, totter **2** = <u>tremble</u>, shake
● NOUN **1** = <u>unsteadiness</u>, shake, tremble **2** = <u>unsteadiness</u>, shake, tremor

woe 1 = <u>misery</u>, distress, grief, agony, gloom, sadness, sorrow, anguish ≠ happiness **2** = <u>problem</u>, grief, misery, sorrow

woman 1 = <u>lady</u>, girl, female, sheila (*Austral. & N.Z. informal*), vrou (*S. African*), adult female, charlie (*Austral. slang*), chook (*Austral. slang*), wahine (*N.Z.*) ≠ man

womanly 1 = <u>feminine</u>, motherly, female, warm, tender, matronly, ladylike

2 = <u>curvaceous</u>, ample, voluptuous, shapely, curvy (*informal*), busty (*informal*), buxom, full-figured

wonder VERB **1** = <u>think</u>, question, puzzle, speculate, query, ponder, meditate, conjecture **2** = <u>be amazed</u>, stare, marvel, be astonished, gape
● NOUN **1** = <u>amazement</u>, surprise, admiration, awe, fascination, astonishment, bewilderment, wonderment
2 = <u>phenomenon</u>, sight, miracle, spectacle, curiosity, marvel, prodigy, rarity

wonderful 1 = <u>excellent</u>, great (*informal*), brilliant, outstanding, superb, fantastic (*informal*), tremendous, magnificent, booshit (*Austral. slang*), exo (*Austral. slang*), sik (*Austral. slang*) ≠ terrible **2** = <u>remarkable</u>, amazing, extraordinary, incredible, astonishing, staggering, startling, phenomenal ≠ ordinary

woo 1 = <u>seek</u>, cultivate **2** = <u>court</u>, pursue

wood 1 = <u>timber</u>, planks, planking, lumber (*U.S.*) **2** or **woods** = <u>woodland</u>, forest, grove, thicket, copse, coppice **3** = <u>firewood</u>, fuel, logs, kindling

wooded = <u>tree-covered</u>, forested, timbered, sylvan (*poetic*), tree-clad

wooden 1 = <u>made of wood</u>, timber, woody, ligneous **2** = <u>expressionless</u>, lifeless, deadpan, unresponsive

wool 1 = <u>fleece</u>, hair, coat **2** = <u>yarn</u>

word NOUN **1** = <u>term</u>, name, expression **2** = <u>chat</u>, tête-à-tête, talk, discussion, consultation, confab (*informal*), heart-to-heart, powwow (*informal*) **3** = <u>comment</u>, remark, utterance **4** = <u>message</u>, news, report, information, notice, intelligence, dispatch, communiqué **5** = <u>promise</u>, guarantee, pledge, vow, assurance, oath **6** = <u>command</u>, order, decree, bidding, mandate
● VERB = <u>express</u>, say, state, put, phrase, utter, couch, formulate

▎▎▎ RELATED WORDS
adjectives: lexical, verbal

wording = <u>phraseology</u>, words, language, phrasing, terminology

work VERB **1** = <u>be employed</u>, be in work **2** = <u>labour</u>, sweat, slave, toil, slog (away), drudge, peg away, exert yourself ≠ relax **3** = <u>function</u>, go, run, operate, be in working order ≠ be out of order **4** = <u>succeed</u>, work out, pay off (*informal*), be successful, be effective, do the trick (*informal*), do the business (*informal*), get results **5** = <u>cultivate</u>, farm, dig, till, plough **6** = <u>operate</u>, use, move, control, drive, manage, handle, manipulate **7** = <u>manipulate</u>, form, fashion, shape, mould, knead

● NOUN **1** = <u>employment</u>, business, job, trade, duty, profession, occupation, livelihood ≠ play **2** = <u>effort</u>, industry, labour, sweat, toil, exertion, drudgery, elbow grease (*facetious*) ≠ leisure **3** = <u>task</u>, jobs, projects, commissions, duties, assignments, chores, yakka (*Austral. & N.Z. informal*) **4** = <u>handiwork</u>, doing, act, feat, deed **5** = <u>creation</u>, piece, production, opus, achievement, composition, handiwork

● PLURAL NOUN **1** = <u>factory</u>, plant, mill, workshop **2** = <u>writings</u>, output, canon, oeuvre (*French*) **3** = <u>mechanism</u>, workings, parts, action, movement, machinery

● PHRASES **work something out** = solve, find out, calculate, figure out

worker = <u>employee</u>, hand, labourer, workman, craftsman, artisan, tradesman

workman = <u>labourer</u>, hand, worker, employee, mechanic, operative, craftsman, artisan

workshop 1 = <u>factory</u>, plant, mill **2** = <u>workroom</u>, studio

world 1 = <u>earth</u>, planet, globe **2** = <u>mankind</u>, man, everyone, the public, everybody, humanity, humankind **3** = <u>sphere</u>, area, field, environment, realm, domain **4** (usually used in phrase *a world of difference*) = <u>huge amount</u>, mountain, wealth, great deal, good deal, abundance, enormous amount, vast amount

worldly 1 = <u>earthly</u>, physical, secular, terrestrial, temporal, profane ≠ spiritual **2** = <u>materialistic</u>, grasping, selfish, greedy ≠ nonmaterialistic **3** = <u>worldly-wise</u>, knowing, experienced, sophisticated, cosmopolitan, urbane, blasé ≠ naive

worn = <u>ragged</u>, frayed, shabby, tattered, tatty, threadbare, the worse for wear

worried = <u>anxious</u>, concerned, troubled, afraid, frightened, nervous, tense, uneasy ≠ unworried

worry VERB **1** = <u>be anxious</u>, be concerned, be worried, obsess, brood, fret, agonize, get in a lather (*informal*) ≠ be unconcerned **2** = <u>trouble</u>, upset, bother, disturb, annoy, unsettle, pester, vex ≠ soothe

● NOUN **1** = <u>anxiety</u>, concern, fear, trouble, unease, apprehension, misgiving, trepidation ≠ peace of mind **2** = <u>problem</u>, care, trouble, bother, hassle (*informal*)

worsen 1 = <u>deteriorate</u>, decline, sink, decay, get worse, degenerate, go downhill (*informal*) ≠ improve **2** = <u>aggravate</u>, damage, exacerbate, make worse ≠ improve

worship VERB **1** = <u>revere</u>, praise, honour, adore, glorify, exalt, pray to, venerate ≠ dishonour **2** = <u>love</u>, adore, idolize, put on a pedestal ≠ despise

● NOUN = <u>reverence</u>, praise, regard, respect, honour, glory, devotion, adulation

worth 1 = <u>value</u>, price, rate, cost, estimate, valuation ≠ worthlessness **2** = <u>merit</u>, value, quality, importance, excellence, goodness, worthiness ≠ unworthiness **3** = <u>usefulness</u>, value, quality, importance, excellence, goodness ≠ uselessness

worthless 1 = <u>valueless</u>, rubbishy, negligible ≠ valuable **2** = <u>useless</u>, unimportant, ineffectual, negligible ≠ useful **3** = <u>good-for-nothing</u>, vile, despicable, contemptible ≠ honourable

worthwhile = <u>useful</u>, valuable, helpful, profitable, productive, beneficial, meaningful, constructive ≠ useless

worthy = <u>praiseworthy</u>, deserving, valuable, worthwhile, admirable, virtuous, creditable, laudable ≠ disreputable

would-be = <u>budding</u>, self-styled, wannabe (*informal*), unfulfilled, self-appointed

wound NOUN **1** = <u>injury</u>, cut, hurt, trauma (*Pathology*), gash, lesion, laceration **2** *often plural* = <u>trauma</u>, offence, slight, insult

● VERB **1** = <u>injure</u>, cut, wing, hurt, pierce, gash, lacerate **2** = <u>offend</u>, hurt, annoy, sting, mortify, cut to the quick

wrangle VERB = <u>argue</u>, fight, row, dispute, disagree, contend, quarrel, squabble

● NOUN = <u>argument</u>, row, dispute, quarrel, squabble, bickering, tiff, altercation

wrap VERB **1** = <u>cover</u>, enclose, shroud, swathe, encase, enfold, bundle up **2** = <u>pack</u>, package, parcel (up), tie up, gift-wrap ≠ unpack **3** = <u>bind</u>, swathe ≠ unwind

● NOUN = <u>cloak</u>, cape, stole, mantle, shawl

● PHRASES **wrap something up 1** = <u>giftwrap</u>, pack, package, bundle up **2** (*Informal*) = <u>end</u>, conclude, wind up, terminate, finish off, round off, polish off

wrath = <u>anger</u>, rage, temper, fury, resentment, indignation, ire, displeasure ≠ satisfaction

wreck VERB 1 = <u>destroy</u>, break, smash, ruin, devastate, shatter, spoil, demolish ≠ build 2 = <u>spoil</u>, ruin, devastate, shatter, crool or cruel (Austral. slang) ≠ save
● NOUN = <u>shipwreck</u>, hulk

wreckage = <u>remains</u>, pieces, ruin, fragments, debris, rubble

wrench VERB 1 = <u>twist</u>, force, pull, tear, rip, tug, jerk, yank 2 = <u>sprain</u>, strain, rick
● NOUN 1 = <u>twist</u>, pull, rip, tug, jerk, yank 2 = <u>sprain</u>, strain, twist 3 = <u>blow</u>, shock, upheaval, pang 4 = <u>spanner</u>, adjustable spanner

wrestle = <u>fight</u>, battle, struggle, combat, grapple, tussle, scuffle

wrinkle NOUN 1 = <u>line</u>, fold, crease, furrow, crow's-foot, corrugation 2 = <u>crease</u>, fold, crumple, furrow, crinkle, corrugation
● VERB = <u>crease</u>, gather, fold, crumple, furrow, rumple, pucker, corrugate ≠ smooth

writ = <u>summons</u>, document, decree, indictment, court order, subpoena, arraignment

write 1 = <u>record</u>, scribble, inscribe, set down, jot down 2 = <u>compose</u>, draft, pen, draw up 3 = <u>correspond</u>, get in touch, keep in touch, write a letter, drop a line, drop a note

writer = <u>author</u>, novelist, hack, scribbler, scribe, wordsmith, penpusher

writing = <u>script</u>, hand, printing, fist (informal), scribble, handwriting, scrawl, calligraphy

wrong ADJECTIVE 1 = <u>amiss</u>, faulty, unsatisfactory, not right, defective, awry 2 = <u>incorrect</u>, mistaken, false, inaccurate, untrue, erroneous, wide of the mark, fallacious 3 = <u>inappropriate</u>, incorrect, unsuitable, unacceptable, undesirable, incongruous, unseemly, unbecoming ≠ correct 4 = <u>bad</u>, criminal, illegal, evil, unlawful, immoral, unjust, dishonest ≠ moral 5 = <u>defective</u>, faulty, awry, askew
● ADVERB 1 = <u>incorrectly</u>, badly, wrongly, mistakenly, erroneously, inaccurately ≠ correctly 2 = <u>amiss</u>, astray, awry, askew
● NOUN = <u>offence</u>, injury, crime, error, sin, injustice, misdeed, transgression ≠ good deed
● VERB = <u>mistreat</u>, abuse, hurt, harm, cheat, take advantage of, oppress, malign ≠ treat well

X

X-ray = <u>radiograph</u>, x-ray image

y

yank VERB = <u>pull</u>, tug, jerk, seize, snatch, pluck, hitch, wrench
● NOUN = <u>pull</u>, tug, jerk, snatch, hitch, wrench, tweak

yarn 1 = <u>thread</u>, fibre, cotton, wool 2 (Informal) = <u>story</u>, tale, anecdote, account, narrative, fable, reminiscence, urban myth

yawning = <u>gaping</u>, wide, huge, vast, cavernous

yearly ADJECTIVE = <u>annual</u>, each year, every year, once a year
● ADVERB = <u>annually</u>, every year, by the year, once a year, per annum

yearn often with for = <u>long</u>, desire, hunger, ache, crave, covet, itch, hanker after

yell VERB = <u>scream</u>, shout, cry out, howl, call out, wail, shriek, screech ≠ whisper
● NOUN = <u>scream</u>, cry, shout, roar, howl, shriek, whoop, screech ≠ whisper

yen = <u>longing</u>, desire, craving, yearning, passion, hunger, ache, itch

yet ADVERB 1 = <u>so far</u>, until now, up to now, still, as yet, even now, thus far, up till now 2 = <u>now</u>, right now, just now, so soon 3 = <u>still</u>, in addition, besides, to boot, into the bargain
● CONJUNCTION = <u>nevertheless</u>, still, however, for all that, notwithstanding, just the same, be that as it may

yield VERB 1 = <u>bow</u>, submit, give in, surrender, succumb, cave in (informal), capitulate 2 = <u>relinquish</u>, resign, hand

over, surrender, turn over, make over, give over, bequeath ≠ retain ≠ resist
3 = produce, give, provide, return, supply, bear, net, earn ≠ use up
● NOUN **1** = produce, crop, harvest, output
2 = profit, return, income, revenue, earnings, takings ≠ loss
yielding 1 = soft, pliable, springy, elastic, supple, spongy, unresisting
2 = submissive, obedient, compliant, docile, flexible, accommodating, pliant, acquiescent ≠ obstinate
yob *or* **yobbo** = thug, hooligan, lout, hoon (*Austral. & N.Z. slang*), ruffian, roughneck (*slang*), tsotsi (*S. African*), cougan (*Austral. slang*), scozza (*Austral. slang*), bogan (*Austral. slang*)
young ADJECTIVE **1** = immature, juvenile, youthful, little, green, junior, infant, adolescent ≠ old **2** = early, new, undeveloped, fledgling ≠ advanced
● PLURAL NOUN = offspring, babies, litter, family, issue, brood, progeny ≠ parents
youngster = youth, girl, boy, kid (*informal*), lad, teenager, juvenile, lass
youth 1 = immaturity, adolescence, boyhood *or* girlhood, salad days ≠ old age **2** = boy, lad, youngster, kid (*informal*), teenager, young man, adolescent, teen (*informal*) ≠ adult
youthful = young, juvenile, childish, immature, boyish, girlish ≠ elderly

district, territory, belt, sphere
zoom = speed, shoot, fly, rush, flash, dash, whizz (*informal*), hurtle

Z

zeal = enthusiasm, passion, zest, spirit, verve, fervour, eagerness, gusto ≠ apathy
zero 1 = nought, nothing, nil **2** = rock bottom, the bottom, an all-time low, a nadir, as low as you can get
zip VERB = speed, shoot, fly, flash, zoom, whizz (*informal*)
● NOUN (*Informal*) = energy, drive, vigour, verve, zest, gusto, liveliness ≠ lethargy
zone = area, region, section, sector,